1997

ACCOUNTING IN THE
ASIA-PACIFIC REGION

Accounting in the Asia-Pacific Region

Nabil Baydoun, Northern Territory University, Australia
Akira Nishimura, Kyushu University, Japan
Roger Willett, University of Otago, New Zealand

John Wiley & Sons (Asia) Pte Ltd
Singapore   New York   Chichester   Brisbane   Toronto   Weinheim

To Sandra, Junko and Maha

Other Wiley Editorial Offices

John Wiley & Sons, Inc. 605 Third Avenue,
New York, NY 10158-0012, USA

Jacaranda Wiley Ltd, G.P.O. Box 859, Brisbane,
Queensland 401, Australia

John Wiley & Sons (Canada) Ltd, 22 Worcester Road
Rexdale, Ontario M9W1L1, Canada

John Wiley & Sons Ltd, Baffins Lane, Chichester,
West Sussex PO19 1UD, England

Library of Congress Cataloging-in-Publication Data:

Accounting in the Asia-Pacific Region/ [editors], Nabil Baydoun,
Akira Nishimura, Roger Willett.
p. cm.
Includes bibliographical references
ISBN: 0-471-24866-5
1. Accounting - Asia,   2. Accounting - Pacific Area.   I. Baydoun, Nabil.
II. Nishimura, Akira, 1938-   .   III. Willett, Roger.
HF5616.A78A27   1997
657'.095-dc21
                                          97-15854
                                             CIP

Printed in the Republic of Singapore

10 9 8 7 6 5 4 3 2 1

CONTENTS

CHAPTER

LIST OF CONTRIBUTORS

Mike Adams, Glasgow University, United Kingdom

Laurent Aleonard, Associate Professor, Groupe ESC Reims, France

Professor Nabil Baydoun, Faculty of Business, Northern Territory University, Australia

Professor Frank Clarke, Dean, Faculty of Commerce, The University of Newcastle, Australia

Associate Professor Graeme Dean, Department of Accounting, The University of Sydney, Australia

Joselito Diga, Department of Commerce, The Australian National University

Liu Feng, Xiamen University, China

Mahmud Hossain, Massey University, New Zealand

Professor Ge Jiashu, Xiamen University, China

Associate Professor Jungpao Kang, Department of Accounting, National Chengchi University, Taipei, Taiwan

Song-Horng Lin, Department of Accounting, National Cheng Kung University, Tainan, Taiwan

Associate Professor Z. Jun Lin, University of Lethbridge, Canada

Kin Cheung Liu, Division of Commerce, College of Higher Vocational Studies, City University of Hong Kong

John Lowry, Department of Commerce, The University of Newcastle, Australia

Professor A. MacGregor, Department of Accountancy, University of Otago, New Zealand

Associate Professor Anthony Moung Yin Chan, Department of Accountancy, City University of Hong Kong, Hong Kong

Dr A.J.M. Humayun Murshed, Universiti Brunei Darussalam, Brunei

Patrick Po Hing Ng, Department of Business Administration, Hong Kong Technical College, Chai Wan, Hong Kong

Akira Nishimura, Professor of Management Accounting, Kyushu University, Japan

Associate Professor Jungpao Kang, Department of Accounting, National Chengchi University, Taipei, Taiwan

Professor M.H.B. Perera, Accountancy Department, Massey University, New Zealand

Fabian Pok, Commerce Department, University of Papua New Guinea

Associate Professor A.R. Rahman, Accountancy Department, Massey University, New Zealand

Dyna Seng, Department of Accountancy, University of Otago, New Zealand

Professor Sang-Moon Choi, College of Business, Pusan National University, Pusan, Korea

Taesik Ahn, Ajou University, Republic of Korea

Professor Murray Wells, Graduate School of Business, The University of Sydney, Australia

Professor Roger Willett, Department of Accountancy, University of Otago, New Zealand

Anita Wong, Macau University, Macau

Professor Frederick H. Wu, Department of Accounting, University of North Texas, Denton, Texas, USA

Dr K. Yap, The Malaysian Institute of Accountants, Kuala Lumpur, Malaysia

Professor Chih-Chung Yeh, Department of Accounting, National Cheng Kung University, Tainan, Taiwan

Desmond Yuen, Macau University, Macau

Dr Hadori Yunus, Department of Accounting, Gadjah Mada University, Indonesia

PREFACE

This book was originally conceived several years ago while the editors were working in the Department of Accountancy at the University of Otago, New Zealand. To begin with, it had the limited objective of recording accounting practices in a small number of countries around the Asia-Pacific Rim, but grew in the making and took much longer to complete than originally intended. By the time of its publication, the book contained a brief but comprehensive treatment of not only financial, but also in those cases where the information was available, of management accounting practices of all countries of the Asian (excluding Russia) and Australasian continent with a coastline on the Pacific Ocean. The motivation for letting the project expand in this way was the gradual realisation that little is known about financial accounting practices in *some* of the countries of the region, and even less about management accounting practices in *most* of the countries. At least on a comparative level, this is true. Consequently it is to be hoped that the material marshalled in this volume of contributions will bring together in one place a convenient catalogue of information for those readers who wish to study the way accounting is carried out in this economically important and dynamic region.

The contributions contained in the book were written and edited in such a way that they should be of equal interest to professionals who wish to become acquainted with some basic facts about accounting practices in the Asia-Pacific region, to academics as a starting point for research into deeper issues, and to teachers who wish to mount specialised courses in the field of international accounting. In the latter instance, it is envisaged that the content of the book would be useful as a basic or supplementary text for a third-year undergraduate course in comparative accounting studies and possibly, in some instances, for master's courses in accounting.

There is quite a lot of descriptive information contained in the book about both financial and management accounting practices in the region, but this is accompanied in many places by analyses of a variety of issues (e.g. historical developments, political processes and global influences). The contributions are therefore eclectic, but it has been attempted to draw these together by focusing on the nature of the accounting environment in the introductory and concluding chapters and, more particularly, on the question of whether cultural differences in countries of the region have any significance in relation to accounting practices. All bets are hedged with regard to answering this question. At the risk of mixing our metaphors, 'the jury is still out'. It will probably take a lot more research and the careful distillation of evidence before this matter can begin to be settled. This book, however, may at least provide a conceptual framework within which to explore the relationships between culture and accounting in an efficient and effective manner without prejudging the outcome.

R.J.W. December 1995

ACKNOWLEDGEMENTS

This book has many contributors from around the Asia-Pacific region and each of these contributors has no doubt become indebted to many colleagues and helpers in many different languages. We gratefully thank those unnamed colleagues and helpers with the acknowledgement that the content of this book is very much a collaborative effort by many people, including them. Apart from finally thanking our contributors for their forebearance in the editing process, we would also particularly like to thank Jenny Bromell, Leanne Bell and Glenda Ashton of the Department of Accountancy, University of Otago, for the enormous amount of secretarial and other assistance they have provided over the previous two years, as well as their efforts in bringing the book to its timely completion. Last but not least, our thanks go to Shalin Chanchani for the stamina he showed in collecting and tabulating data and to Shee Boon Law and John Hillier for their help in proofreading.

The Editors

ENVIRONMENTAL CONSIDERATIONS IN STUDYING ACCOUNTING IN THE ASIA-PACIFIC REGION

Roger Willett, Nabil Baydoun and Akira Nishimura[*]

THE ASIA-PACIFIC REGION AND THE IMPACT OF ENVIRONMENT ON ACCOUNTING PRACTICE

The chapters of this book consist of a series of essays describing in broad outline a variety of issues relating to the financial and management accounting systems of the countries of the Asia-Pacific region. This region is defined for present purposes as all the countries of the Asian continent, excluding Russia, which have a coastline on the Pacific Ocean, together with the islands of Japan, Taiwan, the Philippines, Indonesia, Brunei, Papua New Guinea, Australia and New Zealand. There is a considerable amount of physical, cultural, political and economic diversity in this region, and this makes it a natural choice as a field within which to reflect upon the 'environmental hypothesis' in accounting, i.e. the belief that the environment has a systematic and discernable influence on national accounting practices. Individual chapters deal with issues which tend to be specific to the countries with which they are concerned, and concentrate mainly on relatively factual matters. It seems appropriate, therefore, in this introductory chapter to review some of the opinions concerning the impact of

[*]Respectively Professor of Accounting, University of Otago, New Zealand; Professor of Accounting, Northern Territory University, Darwin, Australia; and Professor of Managerment Accounting, Kyushu University, Japan.

environmental factors on accounting practices, and to provide some summary background as well as environmental details on a regional basis. Taken in conjunction with the material contained in each chapter about each country, this should enable an assessment of the environmental hypothesis to be made. In the concluding chapter, this matter will be revisited and the question of cultural effects and consequences will be more specifically discussed.

Apart from the mere fact of the diversity just mentioned, the countries dealt with in this book possess more than a modicum of topical interest. Hong Kong, Japan, Singapore and South Korea are four of the 'Tiger' economies of Asia. The People's Republic of China (PRC) is a cultural giant undergoing massive restructuring of its socialist economy. Taiwan, the fifth 'Tiger' economy and the 'other' China, is a small island state as ideologically far removed as it could be from mainland China[1]. North Korea is a communist state, while socialist Vietnam is now a member of ASEAN and promises to be an example of rapid economic and social change in the near future. The Philippines is a part of South-east Asia on the edge of the mainstream cultural influences of that region, and with a long history of Spanish and latterly United States colonial history. Malaysia and Indonesia are both Islamic nations and the latter is the most populous Muslim country in the world. Brunei is an oil rich Sultanate and Papua New Guinea is a traditional society adjusting to the demands of modern commerce. Macau is a Portuguese dependency, the oldest European colony in the Far East, with an income level comparable to Hong Kong and also soon to revert to China. Cambodia is a country suffering from the effects of a long civil war. Modern Australian and New Zealand societies, both developed economies and members of the OECD, are still predominantly European in culture. Finally, Thailand is a culturally sophisticated society with a relatively advanced developing economy which has never been colonised by any European power.

Given the issue under discussion, the question should be posed as to whether one would, in fact, expect environment to affect accounting practice. There is a growing literature which argues that this is the case. Such theories are based upon observed differences in accounting practices at various levels. For example, studies have shown that the Japanese tend to be relatively 'conservative' in reporting income compared to countries like the UK, the US and France (Radebaugh and Gray, 1993). Certain countries (e.g. the PRC) tend to rely upon the government or government agencies to enforce accounting standards rather than allow standards to be set voluntarily (as would be the case in the UK). Some countries, such as Germany, are more rigid in the format allowed for the disclosure of financial information than others (e.g. Hong Kong) and much less information is disclosed in countries like Japan than in the US.

Having identified and classified a number of differences of the kind just mentioned, several theories of their more immediate causes have been proposed,

---

[1]Taiwan is considered by the mainland government to be a province of the People's Republic of China.

particularly in the international accounting literature (Nobes, 1983; Perera, 1989; Weetman and Gray, 1990; Nobes and Parker, 1995). It has been noted, for instance, that the inclination to use 'reserve accounting' to deflate profits is less likely to be discouraged in a system in which income is reported to closely-knit, powerful groups of suppliers of capital with access to detailed financial data (as is the case in Japan) than it would be in a system relying on widespread sources of finance from owners of capital, many of whom must rely upon the income figure being 'true and fair' (as is the case in the UK). Similarly, the trait of strong governmental interference has been variously explained in terms of weak professionalism, e.g. France (Nobes, 1990), type of political system, e.g. China (Chan, 1995), and patterns of funding enterprises (creditors versus investors), e.g. Japan (Radebaugh and Gray, 1993). Rigidity of format and the level of secrecy were also related to characteristics such as the ownership structure of industry (Choi and Mueller, 1992; Nobes and Parker, 1991).

This is a natural approach to analysing and explaining differences in international accounting practices. The connections advanced seem plausible enough. Cooke and Parker (1994) recently adopted this approach in describing and classifying financial reporting practices in some of the West Asia Pacific Rim countries, and many of the essays in this book are founded on the same kind of analysis. The relationships drawn are fairly direct, usually based upon the perceived effects of quite narrow economic factors. In some recent literature, however, there has been an inclination to look beyond the more immediate economic explanations of differences in accounting practices, to see if there are deeper environmental and cultural factors involved. For example, it might be asked if 'conservative' Japanese accounting practices reflect an underlying conservative trait in Japanese culture, or if uniformity in the presentation of data mirrors a more general cultural tendency to prefer an ordered life.

Probably the most well known exponent of this cultural approach to understanding the nature of accounting practices is Gray (1988). Gray attempted to relate a number of accounting values — preferences for conservatism, uniformity, secrecy and professional judgement — to Hofstede's (1980) dimensions of culture: power distance, uncertainty avoidance, individualism and masculinity. The Hofstede-Gray theory has been used by a number of writers as the basis of a framework for trying to understand why national accounting practices take the form they do (e.g. Perera, 1989; Gerhardy, 1990) and in some cases to try to determine normatively whether accounting techniques are appropriate to particular societies (e.g. Baydoun and Willett, 1995). Hofstede's approach, which is discussed in more detail below, is, however, just one of a number of ways of studying culture. The question of what culture is and whether Hofstede's or some other method of examining it is most suitable in an accounting context will be returned to in the concluding chapter.

The next section reviews in a little more detail the existing literature on the effects of the environment on accounting practices and the variety of approaches which have been taken to investigate this issue. Sections three and four give a regional overview of background factors which may be helpful in attempting to appreciate the impact of environmental factors on accounting practices. Section three deals with physical, cultural and political factors while section four summarises recent economic developments. The last section describes the presentation of the material in the following chapters of the book.

THE LITERATURE

Broadly speaking, the existing literature on the effects of the environment on accounting practices referred to above may be divided into three categories: (i) the common sense analysis of the links between immediate economic and political causes and their perceived effects on accounting practices; (ii) 'culturally based' theories using the Hofstede-Gray framework to explain differences or deficiencies in accounting practices and (iii) a 'catch-all' category often using a combination of both approaches under which the remaining work may be placed. Categories (i) and (ii) make up by far the majority of published work. Most, but not all, of this literature falls into the domain of international acounting.

With respect to category (i), examples have already been mentioned but Cooke and Parker (1994) contains a collection of some of the more oft-quoted perceived connections in the context of the financial reporting practices of some Asia-Pacific Rim countries. Among the several factors discussed are: Colonial history, the state of economic development[2], the financing structure of the economy and the involvement of government. Recent colonisation is usually by far the most obvious single factor determining the specific characteristics of financial reporting. Studies by Mueller (1967, 1968), Nair and Frank (1980), and Seidler (1967) are examples of studies using this approach. In the Asia-Pacific region, the influence of Anglo-American accounting in countries such as Malaysia, Hong Kong, the Philippines, Australia and New Zealand is obvious. The influence of government is also clear. Studies typically distinguish between countries like Sweden, where macro-economic planning is an important objective of reporting; Germany, where taxation plays an important part in determining accounting rules; and the UK approach where, typically, taxation influences are marginal. Nobes (1990) is a good example of this kind of paradigm.

In the Asia-Pacific region this approach is also useful. As will be seen, the most obvious characteristics of accounting practices often seem to be primarily determined by colonial history (the Philippines' use of a North American approach, for instance). Furthermore, there is the additional dimension of the presence of centrally planned economies in a period of transition to market economies, which is particularly important in this region. Both the effects of colonialism on accounting techniques

---

[2]Including structural details such as exports, imports, and the importance of primary products to the economy, etc.

and the results of modifying Soviet systems of accounting to the needs of market economies are interesting, important and, at the present time, under-researched areas of our discipline. In regard to the financing structure of industry, Cooke and Parker (1994) follow Zysman (1983) in distinguishing economies which are capital market-based; government credit-based; and private credit-based. According to this theory, in credit-based systems typified by the continental European model, government-driven and following taxation regulations, investors are more likely to attempt to influence the actions of management. Also, they are more likely to permit a rapid investment response to changing circumstances (possibly under central government guidance) and are more likely to avoid short-termism than are capital market-based systems. Japan, Korea and Taiwan are classified under this system as credit-based systems (similar, for instance, to Germany), although there is some evidence that Japan may now be moving toward a capital market system (Cooke and Parker, 1994). In capital market-based systems, the emphasis is on the public disclosure of information, an external audit and the existence of professional accounting bodies. Hong Kong, Singapore, Australia and New Zealand, all with strong UK connections, fall into this category[3].

The descriptive analysis just referred to is consistent with the approach found in the category (i) literature. With regard to the literature in category (ii), it can be seen how this evolves quite naturally from (i). Gray's theory (1988) takes as its subject matter the preferences of account's users and preparers. These preferences, it is supposed, will be formed under the influence of broader cultural values and will in turn affect the regulatory environment in which accounting takes place, the patterns of disclosure of accounting information and even, possibly, the characteristics of the accounting numbers chosen for decision making purposes. Gray's accounting values and the broad structure of this theory are shown in Figure 1.

The accounting values in Figure 1 and their relationships to accounting practices do not require a great deal of explanation — they have their natural intuitive meaning: A preference for professionalism, for example, leads to a tendency to prefer voluntary self-regulation to externally imposed government control and conservatism to a cautious, pessimistic approach in choosing between alternative courses of action. The motivation for such a theory can be understood in the category (i) literature discussed above. The preferences referred to surface in a number of different contexts. The European continental approach to the disclosure of data is more 'uniform' than the Anglo-American approach (Nobes and Parker, 1995; Nobes 1983, 1990; Baydoun and Willett, 1995), and the Japanese calculation of profit is measurably more 'conservative' than US standards would seem to be (Aron, 1990). Gray's theory can thus be seen as an attempt to summarise a number of apparently key

---

[3]See Nobes (1995) for a recent application of this approach in a European context.

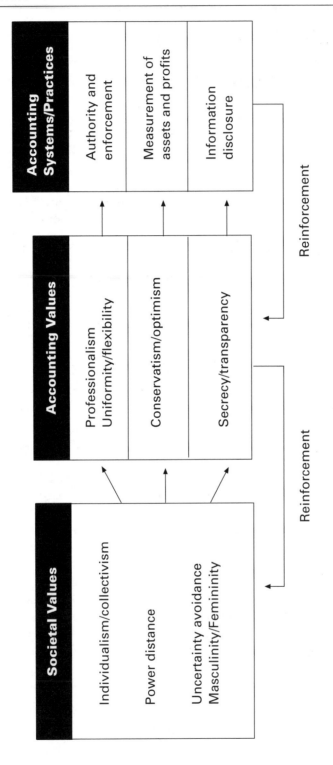

Source: Radebaugh and Gray (1993)

Figure 1

ingredients identified in the international accounting literature, affecting accounting practices across a number of countries. The suspicion (which of course may already be biased by the preconceptions of the contributors to the earlier literature) is then generated that cultural predispositions in different societies may be ultimately responsible for apparent differences in accounting practices. The link of Gray's accounting values to culture is where Hofstede's theory of the consequences of culture has become influential in the literature in recent years.[4]

Over the period 1968–73, Hofstede surveyed tens of thousands of employees of the IBM company in 50 countries to ascertain their attitudes toward work related values. Culture was defined by Hofstede as 'the collective programming of the mind which distinguishes one category of people from another.' Having collected data, Hofstede used factor analysis in an attempt to isolate any distinct factors which appeared to explain variations in responses. Four dimensions were identified by this process, which Hofstede referred to as *Power Distance, Individualism, Uncertainty Avoidance* and *Masculinity*. These dimensions were related by Hofstede to a number of theoretical concepts in the sociological and anthropological literature, thus reinforcing their external validity (Hofstede, 1980). Power Distance was related to the concept of *relationship to authority*; Individualism to *the concept of the self*; Masculinity to *gender differentiation* and Uncertainty Avoidance to *ways of dealing with conflict, the control of aggression and the expression of feelings* (Inkeles and Levinson, 1969). Hofstede believed that he had identified certain traits of national culture. The dimensions for each country were measured on a series of complex ordinal scales and analysed graphically in a series of pair-wise comparisons. Countries of the Asia-Pacific region tended to cluster together in some instances as is shown in the case of Individualism plotted against Power Distance in Figure 2[5].

In a recent study, Hofstede and Bond (1988) identified a fifth dimension which supposedly characterises the extent to which people in society take a long-term versus a short-term view of life. This was thought to be particularly relevant to Asian societies. The 1988 study was carried out because of concern about the relevance of Hofstede's (1980) questionnaire, which was prepared by Western researchers but used to measure the responses of non-Western people. This led to the development of the Chinese Value Survey (CVS) by Michael Bond and a group of Chinese social scientists. A 40-item Chinese questionnaire was prepared and administered to 100 students in 22 countries. The questionnaire was designed to elicit information about basic values of the Chinese, including items referring to the Confucian ideal of 'filial piety'. The statistical analysis on the CVS yielded three dimensions similar to those

---

[4]Hofstede's discipline is cross-cultural psychology rather than anthropology, and his conceptual and methodological approach to the investigation of culture both reflect this fact.

[5]Similar plots of the relationships between the other dimensions can be found in Hofstede (1991). Not all reveal such strong patterns as those shown in Figure 2.

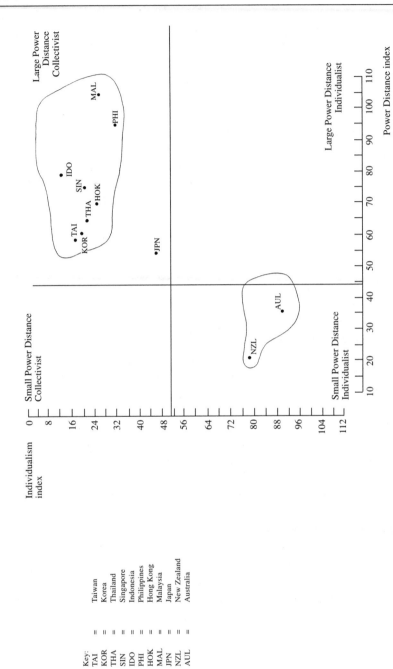

Source: Hofstede (1991)

Figure 2 Relationship between Power Distance and Individualism for countries of Asia-Pacific region

Table 1
ASIA-PACIFIC CULTURAL VALUES

Country	PDI Score	PDI Rank	IDV Score	IDV Rank	MAS Score	MAS Rank	UAI Score	UAI Rank	LTD Score	LTD Rank
Malaysia	104	1	26	36	50	25/26	36	46	NA	NA
Philippines	94	4	32	31	64	11/12	44	44	19	21
Indonesia	78	8/9	14	47/48	46	30/31	48	41/42	NA	NA
Singapore	74	13	20	39/41	48	28	8	53	48	9
Hong Kong	68	15/16	25	37	57	18/19	29	49/50	96	2
Thailand	64	21/23	20	39/41	34	44	64	30	56	8
South Korea	60	27/28	18	43	39	41	85	16/17	75	5
Taiwan	58	29/30	17	44	45	32/33	69	26	87	3
Japan	54	33	46	23/23	95	1	92	7	80	4
Australia	36	41	90	2	61	16	51	37	31	15
New Zealand	50	22	79	6	58	17	49	39/40	30	16
Vietnam	NA	NA	NA	NA	NA	NA	NA	NA	NA	NA
Cambodia	NA	NA	NA	NA	NA	NA	NA	NA	NA	NA
Brunei	NA	NA	NA	NA	NA	NA	NA	NA	NA	NA
Papa New Guinea	NA	NA	NA	NA	NA	NA	NA	NA	NA	NA
China	NA	NA	NA	NA	NA	NA	NA	NA	118	1

Source: Hofstede (1991)

NA: Not available.

found in Hofstede's (1980) study: Power Distance, Individualism and Masculinity. However, Uncertainty Avoidance was not identified in the CVS, a fact which Hofstede and Bond (1988) regarded as being due to the Chinese tendency to believe that man's search for truth is not an essential issue. Instead, a new dimension, uncorrelated with either of the other dimensions, was identified and related to economic growth. This new dimension was called 'Confucian Dynamism' and was explained as being based upon Confucius' ideas and teaching. Table 1 shows the Confucian Dynamism scores along with scores for the other cultural dimensions for some of the countries included in this book.

As might be expected, the table shows that Hong Kong, Taiwan, Japan and South Korea scored highest on Confucian Dynamism, following China. Thailand and Singapore's scores were also high. In contrast, Australia and New Zealand's scores were on the low side. It was claimed that some of the items in the CVS survey, underlying the new dimension, have the potential to encourage economic growth. For instance, the adoption of the long-term view associated with Confucian Dynamism might be expected to result in higher savings and capital accumulation. The five 'Tiger' countries have all exhibited high savings ratios in recent years. Also 'persistence' or 'perseverance' are said to lead to the more single-minded pursuit of personal goals, including economic growth (Hofstede and Bond, 1988, see also Chow et al, 1994).

How might one expect Hofstede's cultural values to affect accounting practices? Gray hypothesised some directional relationships between cultural and accounting values, assuming that it is possible to measure accounting values on at least a dichotomous scale. Gray's hypotheses relating to Hofstede's original four cultural values, together with our additional hypothesis on the potential effect of Confucian Dynamism on Gray's accounting values are summarised in Table 2[6]. The relationships relating to the first four cultural dimensions shown in Table 2 have been utilised (e.g. Gerhardy, 1990) or adapted (e.g. Perera, 1989; Perera and Mathews, 1991) in a number of theoretical and empirical studies of accounting systems in different countries. However, they have not been systematically tested. Radebaugh and Gray (1993) used a judgemental approach to classify accounting systems for categories of the countries of Hofstede's survey (e.g. Anglo-Saxon, Asian Colonial, less-developed Asian) on a two-way plot using pair-wise comparisons of Gray's accounting values. The plots of Professionalism *versus* Uniformity and Secrecy *versus* Conservation are shown in Figure 3. The possible connections between Hofstede's cultural values and Gray's accounting values will be further addressed in the concluding chapter.

---

[6]Hofstede's fifth dimension postdates Gray (1988) and has not yet been the subject of detailed analysis in accounting literature. Assuming 'long-term' is treated as 'high' Confucianism and 'short-term' as 'low', it seems plausible to hypothesise, as with Uncertainty Avoidance, an inverse relationship of Confucian Dynamism with Professionalism and a direct relationship with Gray's other three accounting value dimensions.

Table 2

HYOTHESISED RELATIONSHIPS BETWEEN GRAY'S ACCOUNTING VALUES
AND HOFSTEDE'S CULTURAL VALUES

Hofstede's cultural values	Gray's accounting values			
	Professionalism	Uniformity	Conservatism	Secrecy
Power Distance	−	+	?	+
Uncertainty Avoidance	−	+	+	+
Individualism	+	−	−	−
Masculinity	?	?	−	−
Confucian Dynamism	−	+	+	+

Note '+' indicates a direct relationship between the relevant variables, '−' indicates an inverse relationship. Question marks indicate that the nature of the relationship is indeterminate.
Source: Baydoun and Willett (1995)

Although by far the most popular approach adopted to date in the literature, Hofstede's approach is by no means the only one available to investigate the impact of the accounting environment on accounting practices. The third catch-all category (iii) of this literature review contains a number of alternative approaches which have as yet only been used on a piecemeal basis. Qualitative-, longitudinal-, anthropological-type studies of the detailed social environment in which particular changes in accounting practice take place, are probably essential complements to frameworks of the type offered by Hofstede, if our understanding of the forces which drive the adaptation of accounting technology is to progress beyond vague generalisations. Several studies (Laabs, 1992; Wilmott *et al.*, 1992; Johnson, 1991; Cole, 1990; Lie, 1990; Blake, 1990; Gambling, 1987) fall into this category. The textual analysis of financial and management reports is another possible approach which may be useful in revealing cultural predispositions, subtleties of meaning and important belief structures underlying the preparation and interpretation of financial data (Courtis, 1992). The analysis of accounting practices through the sociological constructs of role and social systems and the anthropological concepts of function and structure may also provide useful insight into the nature of accounting practice. The roles of leaders and the nature of power in social systems in relation to the function of accounting information have been addressed by a number of writers (e.g. Hoskins and Macve, 1985). The distribution of power within society is clearly significant in determining the forms which accounting practices take in the Asia-Pacific region. (For example, compare the People's Republic of China with New Zealand). Also, there is the need for a critical analysis of the effect of power structures in countries of the region. These are matters which seem to repeatedly call for attention in much of the comment contained in the chapters of this book. Following on from the earlier

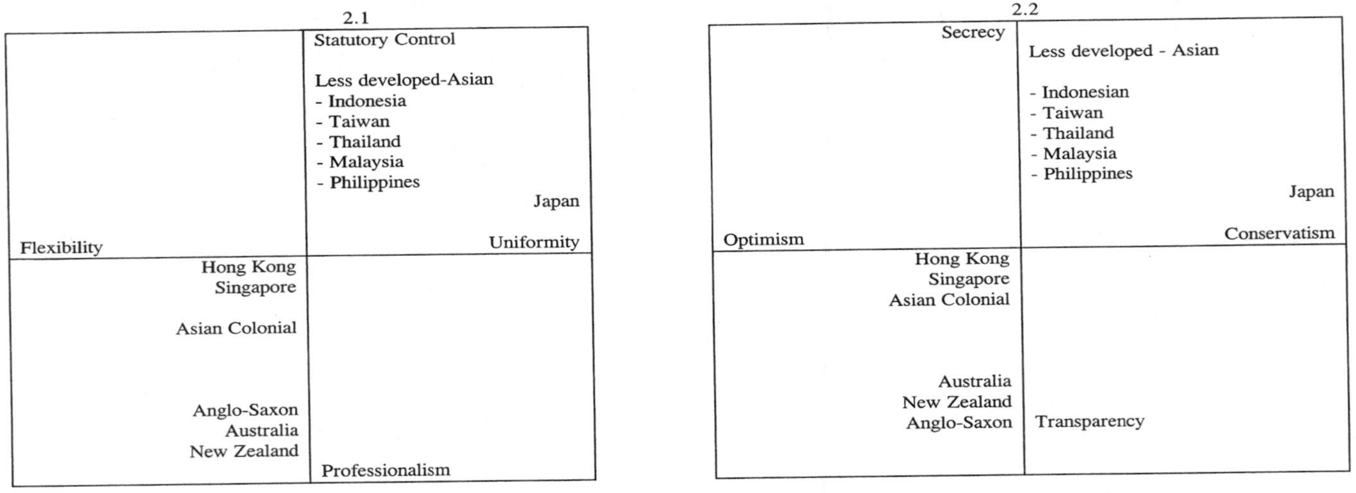

2.1

	Statutory Control	
	Less developed-Asian	
	- Indonesia	
	- Taiwan	
	- Thailand	
	- Malaysia	
	- Philippines	
		Japan
Hong Kong Singapore	Uniformity	
Asian Colonial		
Anglo-Saxon Australia New Zealand		
Flexibility	Professionalism	

2.2

	Secrecy	
	Less developed - Asian	
	- Indonesian	
	- Taiwan	
	- Thailand	
	- Malaysia	
	- Philippines	
		Japan
Hong Kong Singapore Asian Colonial	Conservatism	
Australia New Zealand Anglo-Saxon		
Optimism	Transparency	

Source: Radebaugh and Gray (1993), pp 75–6; and Hofstede (1980), p 336.

Figure 3   Accounting systems of a selected number of Asia-Pacific Countries

comment made concerning the use of Hofstede's framework in an Asia-Pacific context, it may turn out to be more appropriate (at least initially and in the case of the issues discussed in this book) to advance our knowledge through a careful and detailed critical analysis of instances of changing accounting practices rather than through a general framework of the Hofstede-Gray type. It is more likely that both approaches will contribute, through continuous refinement and dialectic development, to provide for progress[7].

There is insufficient space to fully recount all the many environmental elements which have been felt to be influential in determining the forms which accounting practices take in different countries. Some facts about these are contained in the background details given at the beginning of each chapter. The principles which governed the selection of this information may be summarised as follows. First, one must understand the physical environment in which a culture is set. In particular, physical geography, type of climate, availability of natural resources and size of population all seem to be of significance in establishing constraints and pressures relating to the form of organisation, economic development and attitudes towards other cultures. Second, one must appreciate the broad cultural context in which accounting is set. Basic facts about ethnic and linguistic matters, history and the current constitutional and legal system are helpful, for example, in understanding the forms which accounting systems and the regulatory framework take. Third, one must consider recent economic developments. Economic factors such as the inflation rate, unemployment levels, exchange rate trends, statistics on imports and exports, trading partners and government economic policies are often important to understanding why some countries jump toward one accounting policy direction rather than another. These are intuitive principles which correspond, to some extent, to theories about such matters found in the social anthropology literature (e.g. Johnson, 1978). Certainly, it seems that without this knowledge, insights into some aspects of accounting practices are lost — the obvious example being colonial history. In the next two sections, a review of the most central of these background elements is pursued in a regional context.

THE PHYSICAL, CULTURAL AND POLITICAL BACKGROUND OF THE ASIA-PACIFIC REGION

Physical geography

Excluding southern Australia and New Zealand, the dominant physical, environmental feature of the Asia-Pacific region is the size of the Asian land mass and the part it plays

---

[7]The anthropological-sociological approaches which typify the literature in category (iii) appear to be particularly suited to the study of the issue of acculturation (as opposed to the issue of cultural evolution). This and other related matters will be discussed in the concluding chapter.

in creating the monsoonal climate. The monsoon effect — the reversal of the prevailing wind system in winter and summer and the consequent wet and dry seasons — together with the physical pattern of mountain ranges, upland, plateaus, east and south-easterly delta areas on mainland Asia and the distribution of insular South-east Asia explains the main settlement patterns and methods of economic and political development in those areas. The climate mechanism is that during the northern hemisphere winter, a stable high pressure system forms over the cold northern Asian land mass, resulting in a south-eastward flow of cool air over east and South-east Asia. Some moisture is picked up over the Sea of Japan and deposited as snow in western Japan and insular South-east Asia receives winter rain from the South China Sea, but otherwise the winds are dry and winter is the dry season. In contrast, in the northern hemisphere summer the Asian land mass heats up, producing a depression and sucking in moist air from the southern and eastern oceans. Much of the moisture is deposited as the air flows over the mountain ranges that stretch out, finger-like, over the Himalayas and throughout the region. The monsoon effect also gives northern Australia dry southern hemisphere winters and wet summers. However, in central and southern parts, the flatness and expanse of Australia produces a dry arid climate everywhere other than in coastal regions which fall under the influence of prevailing westerlies. New Zealand's climate is temperate, oceanic and too far south to be influenced directly by the monsoon effect.

The river valleys and alluvial plains formed by the joint processes of geological uplifting and erosion have historically provided the main locations for the development of Asian wet rice agriculture, population and culture.[8] Today, the same agricultural areas are the most densely populated parts of a densely populated region and also tend to possess the greatest centres of urban development. Almost 60 percent of the world's population lives in Asia (excluding former Soviet Asia) and some areas are particularly densely populated (e.g. in eastern China and northern Vietnam). The potential for new markets in areas of dense populations and relatively unexploited natural resources has attracted the interest of Western capital in recent years.

Cultural history

Turning to cultural matters, the general direction of migration over the Asia-Pacific region has been from North to South, mostly under the influence of the expansion of agriculture. The peoples of the Asian region are predominately of Mongoloid-type,

---

[8]The development of the irrigation projects needed to expand into secondary areas not naturally suited to wet rice agriculture has been held to explain the prevalence and continuity of large scale oriental organisations, particularly in mainland China. This may be of significance for the development of an accounting 'mind set'.

the most important indigenous language families represented being Ural-Altaic, Sino-Tibetan, Austro-Asiatic, Tai-Kadai and Austronesian. Given that language is closely associated with cultural groups, it is helpful to use the linguistic record to map out what appear to be the main cultural areas in the region today. One theory about the main groups of languages is that their 'proto' forms originated in areas where agriculture originally developed. On this basis, it is argued that the middle to upper parts of the Yangtse region was in Neolithic times the centre of an outward expansion of the Austric languages[9], which were overlaid and largely replaced there by Chinese as that language was brought down by settlers from the Huang Ho region (Bellwood, 1992). A distinctive Chinese culture had been established within the boundaries of modern eastern China by the Han dynasty (206 BC–221 AD) and reinforced with little interruption thereafter. The Austro-Asiatic and Austronesian languages (including Malay) appear to have spread over the southern parts of South-east Asia in a pincer movement, first on the mainland, then through the island fringes by a process of colonisation.[10] With the later exception of Thai and Vietnamese military expansion (in modern Thailand and southern Vietnam respectively), the present day indigenous language boundaries were, roughly speaking, in place by 500 BC.

In contrast to this broadly established general picture is the great diversity in languages within the family groups. More than 200 distinct languages of the western Austronesian group, 150 of the Austro-Asiatic group and as many as 300 of the Sino-Tibetan group are spoken in the region covered by this book. This suggests considerable cultural diversity even within modern national boundaries. Nevertheless, despite considerable differences of detail, certain broad cultural influences can be identified with the region as a whole. East Asia and Vietnam constitute what we might refer to as 'Confucian countries'. The rest of South-east Asia may be referred to as Hinduised[11] because of the importance of cultural links with India. Both of these influences occurred after the main settlements of indigenous cultures, referred to in the previous paragraph, had taken place. Although China has been politically more dominant than India in South-east Asia, for a number of reasons Indian beliefs have had a more important influence on religion and concepts of government. One of the most significant reasons for this is probably the relative flexibility of Hindu ideas (including, for instance, those represented in Therevada Buddhism as well as the Hindu religion itself) in adapting to the loose and changing boundaries of the political institutions of the Thais, Javanese and Khmers. The more secular theories of Confucius were transmitted to the Koreans and Vietnamese through periods of Chinese overlordship and

---

[9]'Austric' is the covering term for the proto language of both Austro-Asiatic and Austronesian language families.

[10]Korean and Japanese may possibly be variants of the Altaic family of languages.

[11]'Hinduised' in this context refers to the general culture and attitudes of people of the Indian subcontinent and should not be confused with the more specific Hindu religion which is described below.

to the Japanese through Japan's involvement in Korea. Finally, to these layers of in-digenous and 'higher' cultural influences were added elements of the systems of European beliefs during the colonial period: British in Brunei, Singapore, Papua New Guinea, Malaya, Hong Kong, Australia and New Zealand; French in Cambodia and Vietnam; Dutch in Indonesia; Spanish and North American in the Philippines[12]; and Portuguese in Macau. Even Thailand, while never having been colonised as such, had its modern day boundaries determined by the Europeans and Japan (and indi-rectly the Koreas). It also consciously imported elements of German constitutional theory, practice and some accounting principles. China and the other socialist states of North Korea, Vietnam, and for a time Cambodia, were also heavily influenced by Russian Soviet accounting concepts and practices.

Regarding religious and philosophical viewpoints in the Asia-Pacific region, the Hindu religion dates from the second millennium BC and is a flexible system of beliefs based upon multiple gods, a priesthood (The Brahmans), the principle of reincarnation and, contingent upon good works, the possibility of salvation. The caste system is also a key part of its philosophy. Buddhism, which originated in Northern India about 500 BC, shares many of the beliefs of Hinduism (e.g. reincarnation and *karma*), but rejects the notion of gods and the caste system. Buddhism spread to Sri Lanka (about 100 AD) and later to mainland South-east Asia and China. Hinduism (i.e. the religion) was, like Buddhism, carried by traders and merchants and similarly influenced belief systems in the South-east Asian states. However, Buddhism flour-ished outside its homeland but virtually disappeared within it. This occurred particu-larly after the establishment of Muslim states in the 12th century. Hinduism, on the other hand, while retaining its adherents in India, became secondary in mainland South-east Asia and was ultimately replaced by Islam in most of island South-east Asia. The Hindu elements in South-east Asian culture today are therefore manifested most clearly through Buddhist beliefs. The form of Buddhism most common in South-east Asia is the personalised form associated with Sri Lanka and referred to as Therevada Buddhism. The form taken in China, Korea and Japan, referred to as Mahayana Buddhism, is a more formal and organised, but simplified, form assimi-lated with Daoism (the personal spiritual native religion of China) and Confucianism.

Confucius (551 – 479 BC) lived in the Chou dynasty period in a time of disruption and civil war. He taught an ethical code based on precepts which have become associated with Chinese attitudes towards life — harmony in society, respect for properly constituted authority and, in particular, filial piety within the family.

---

[12]It should be noted, incidentally, that the indigenous culture of the Philippines was relatively uninfluenced by either Hindu or Confucian beliefs prior to the era of Western colonisation (Hall, 1981).

Confucianism developed into a philosophical system of good government consistent with the Imperial Chinese political system and was exported to Korea, Japan and North Vietnam. Daoism, which dates from about 300 BC and developed into a spiritual counterpart of Confucianism, stressing harmony with nature and the universe, is associated with beliefs in supernatural forces. Although an important ingredient with Confucianism and Mahayana Buddhism, Daoism is a less significant element in the culture of the East Asian countries than either of the other two belief systems. Daoism, for instance, is less influential in Japan where Shintoism, the native folk religion based upon ancestor worship, fulfils similar spiritual functions. It seems that the East Asian forms of ancestor worship, more abstract concepts of heaven and systems of bureaucracy, governance and statecraft were not well enough suited to the circumstances of the early rulers of the South-east Asian *Mandalis*[13] to be adopted by them. Instead they preferred the Hinduised cults of the charismatic leader, legitimised by powerful gods. It was the system of beliefs, associated with that approach, that has since become most evident in the culture of South-east Asia outside of Vietnam (Mackerras, 1992).

The universalist West Asian religions of Islam and Christianity came to the Asia-Pacific area with their systems of beliefs in more recent times. One emphasising the teachings of Jesus of Nazareth (around whose birth Western calenders are dated), the other emphasising the teachings of the Prophet Muhammad[14]. Islam was brought to South-east Asia first by traders and later in the 13th Century through the establishment of kingdoms in Sumatra, the Malay Peninsula and a small area of the Southern Philippines. West China also has a significant population of Muslims who are culturally distinct from the Han Chinese. Christianity was imported by European and North American colonisation from the 16th Century onwards. Both religions, particularly Roman Catholicism in the Philippines, and Islam generally, have pervasive belief systems which govern ethical behaviour in everyday life. The influence of Protestant Christianity (with belief systems mostly derived from Northern European churches, which originally broke away from the Church of Rome in the Middle Ages) lie in those parts of the region colonised by the British and the Dutch. This influence is possibly less important in its overtly religious impact and more important in its direct effect on economic relationships and attitudes towards the accumulation of capital (Weber, 1958). The area of the region where these latter traits are most clearly reflected are Australia and New Zealand.

---

[13]The Mandalis was a form of early state or kingdom typical in the early history of South-east Asia, but with more flexible boundaries than the usual conception of the European state.
[14]The Islamic calendar begins with Prophet Mohammad's entry into Medina in 622 AD, (i.e. 622 years after the year of the birth of Jesus).

Legal systems

Throughout this book, references are made to the concepts 'civil law' and 'common law', or their equivalents. Since these terms are of general significance and because legal systems may have an impact on the regulatory environment of accounting, it is worth reflecting on what they mean in the context of the countries of the Asia-Pacific region.

The main types of modern legal systems in use throughout the world may be classified as civil, common, socialist and, possibly, given recent developments, Islamic. In addition to these systems of law which cross national boundaries, there are sources of customary law which are, by definition, specific to countries whose customs they describe. The first three types of legal systems are, at the present time, by far the most important sources of law in the field of commerce in the Asia-Pacific region, although it is conceivable this may change in the future. Islamic and local customary law tend to be more important in the fields of family law and succession. Otherwise, the main source of differences in the region in commercial areas arise from differences in economic philosophy, i.e. the effect of socialist law. However, the socialist system is sometimes seen as an offshoot of the civil law system. Therefore it seems appropriate to first consider the origins of, and differences between, civil and common law systems[15].

The civil law system took its modern form in a series of European national codifications beginning in the late 17th Century in Scandinavia and ending with the Swiss code of 1912. The process of codification emphasises the importance of statute law over judge-made case law. Different types of codes are usually held to be exemplified by the French (the *Code Napoleon* of 1804) and the German, which was implemented in stages in the latter half of the 19th Century and is more precise and orderly than the French. Of the systems influential in the Asia-Pacific region, the Dutch, Portuguese and Spanish codes followed the French pattern while the Swiss code followed the German model. Consequently, the French code has directly influenced the legal systems of Cambodia and Vietnam, and has indirectly influenced Indonesia (through the Dutch system), the Philippines (through Spain) and Macau (through the Portuguese). In each case, these influences were transmitted through colonial forces. In contrast, the German legal approach was adopted more voluntarily — directly in Japan, the Koreas and Thailand and directly and indirectly (e.g. through the adoption of Swiss code elements) in China and Taiwan.

The common law systems of England and the USA originated in England and, compared to civil code law, place more importance on the development of legal

---

[15]See David and Brierly (1985); and Zweigert and Kotz (1977) for further details.

principles decided through court cases ('judge-made' law)[16]. Common law has developed in significantly different ways in the US and England over several centuries, with the American version tending more toward legislation and codification, balanced by a more free interpretation of statutes by the courts. In the Asia-Pacific region, the legal systems of Australia, Hong Kong, Malaysia, New Zealand and Singapore have followed the English model, while the US legal system has influenced the originally predominantly civil code orientations of the Philippines and, in more recent times, Japan and South Korea.

Apart from these differences between common law and civil code law, the other main points of distinction between the two systems are that, firstly, the substantive elements of code law tend to be more systematic and abstract, based upon academic theorising, whereas common law is more *ad hoc* and piecemeal, based upon individual judicial opinion. Secondly significant procedural differences exist between the two systems. While both systems are adversarial, the role of the judge as an investigator is much more important in civil code countries. In common law countries, the responsibility for presenting evidence and examining witnesses in civil cases lies with the parties and their legal representatives. Juries are generally not used in civil cases in code countries. The degree of proof required of the plaintiff is generally higher, and the evidential role of experts and parties to a suit are different. Such procedural differences in law between countries in the Asia-Pacific region may indirectly influence the form taken by their regulatory frameworks as well as more directly affecting commercial dealings in the countries concerned (Cappelletti and Garth, 1987).

Socialist law originated in the Russian revolution of 1917 and adapted to the pre-existing legal traditions of other countries that were at some time in their past, one-party communist states. In the Asia-Pacific region, China, North Korea, Vietnam and Cambodia fall under this heading. As Soviet law itself was heavily dependent upon code law, especially in matters of procedure, it is evident that their legal procedures are, in many ways, more similar to code than to common law traditions. Despite the fact that the countries just named are, to differing degrees, undergoing a transition to market-based economies, it is likely that socialist legal principles will continue to play an important part in affecting commercial transactions and the practice of regulation.

Socialist law is generally characterised by the importance of the role it attaches to the interests of the State. This has a number of relevant ramifications here. Even more than in code countries, legislation is held to be the sole source of law in theory

---

[16]The distinction between the civil law and common law systems as statute-based and judge-made respectively is not clear cut. Much modern law in England and the USA is codified and judicial interpretations form the basis of many laws in code countries.

(which tends to allow political considerations to impinge upon economic transactions)[17] and the inquisitorial powers given to judges to examine witnesses and other evidence is greater. Furthermore, the domain of public law is considerably extended at the expense of private law. The State tends to be involved in formal contracting arrangements (e.g. with plant managers and collectives) in implementing economic plans which fix quantities and prices in a manner entirely different to the way these matters are arranged in free economies. It also has greater power to appeal decisions which would be taken as being final under both code and common law systems (Hazard *et al.*, 1977).

As stated above, Islamic law, as laid down in the *Shariah*, has tended to be more important in personal and family aspects of law in modern times, with Western systems of law forming the basis of the commercial law in most Islamic countries. Nevertheless, there are some distinct principles of Islamic law which affect commerce. There is also growing interest in widening the scope of Islamic law in countries like Brunei, Indonesia and Malaysia. The main differences between Islamic and the Western systems of law described above, are that the scope of the former is wider, governing the relationship of the individual to God as well as to other individuals and the State. It has an ethical, as well as a purely legal dimension. The Islamic law of transactions concerning selling, hiring, loaning and gifting property are laid down in the *Sharia* . The basic principles are *riba*, i.e. the effective disallowing of receipt of interest on loans and the prohibition of gambling. The latter is usually interpreted as disallowing speculation on any matter which is uncertain. Just how these Islamic legal principles may affect matters relating to accounting practices in the future remains to be seen (Mallat, 1993; Schact, 1964).

Finally, it may be noted that certain aspects of Indian and Chinese attitudes to law could be significant in some commercial contexts through their effect on local customary laws. Indian legal traditions were assimilated in Thailand, Java (in Indonesia) and Cambodia, and Chinese legal traditions are evident in some of the East Asian countries. Indian law (*Dharma*) originated in a set of rules written in Sanskrit governing Hindus. Its character is believed to be of divine and absolute inspiration, governing religious and ethical matters, as well as the more precise matters usually dealt with under Western laws. *Obligations* rather than *rights* are of central concern and this attitude, as well as the residual effects of more particular rulings on interest payments and the like could, as in the case of Islamic law, quite possibly influence aspects of economic behaviour (Rama Jois, 1984). Likewise, the Confucian tradition is against the use of law in solving disputes in a manner similar to that adopted by the West. Mediation is considered to be superior (Chiu *et al.*, 1991). This is also the case

---

[17]In practice, as in code countries, judicial processes contribute to law-making through interpretation and precedent to a greater degree than theory would usually allow.

in Japan. Japan having borrowed legal principles primarily from the German legal code, combined with ingredients of US constitutional and public law as well, presently takes a significantly different attitude from either of these countries towards settling commercial disputes. These are much more likely to be dealt with through a process of conciliation, often based upon much broader considerations than narrow legal definitions of rights and responsibilities (e.g. the wider social relationships between the parties in dispute may be taken into account). In attempting to understand the nature of commercial transactions, how to properly report these and the significance of regulatory forms in the Asia-Pacific region, there is evidently a need to be aware of quite subtle differences in attitude towards legal processes among the various countries concerned.

Constitutional forms

As in the case of legal systems, the background sections of each chapter contain some basic details of constitutional arrangements in each country for the reason that they may provide insights into the political institutions of the country covered and, more particularly, into such matters as the form and nature of the accounting regulatory framework adopted[18]. The modern view of a constitution is that it is a social contract containing details of the procedures and, often, certain basic substantive laws which describe the relationships existing between the people of a nation-state and their government. As such, these embody rules inherited under complex historical circumstances (including colonial influences) and sometimes also express cultural and political aspirations. Apart from containing any substantive provisions on basic human rights, the main function of a constitution is to define procedural arrangements for government. Usually these concern the form and division of powers between the three main branches of government, (the legislature, the executive and the judiciary) and the arrangements made for representation.

Nearly all nations which were formed or have undergone significant political changes in modern times have formal, written constitutions and this is the case for most of the countries dealt with in this book[19]. Written constitutions vary in their rigidity. Some, like Australia's and the PRC's, are relatively inflexible in that the legislative conditions for change are stricter than those required for the passing of ordinary statutes. In the PRC's case, for example, Article 64 of the 1982 constitution requires a two-thirds majority of deputies of the National People's Congress for change to take place. Some countries, such as Japan, allow for a judicial review of

---

[18]See Strong (1966); Cappelletti and Cohen (1973); Blaustein (1995).
[19]New Zealand's constitution is not written down in a single document.

legislation, (i.e. the process by which the judiciary, either in the form of the ordinary court system, or in the form of a special constitutional court, passes judgement on whether a particular piece of legislation is consistent with the constitution), and this may permit change through judicial interpretation. South Korea is an example of a country having special constitutional courts. New Zealand's constitution, on the other hand is an example of one which has no provision for judicial review and the provisions of which can be changed by ordinary majority vote of Parliament. Singapore also has a 'flexible', though written, constitution.[20]

As regards *form*, the main types of system of government lie on a continuum between unitary states such as New Zealand and Japan at one extreme, and federal states such as Australia and Malaysia at the other. Unitary states are typically small in geographical area, culturally homogenous and have a two-tier form of local and national government in contrast to a three-tier form of local, state and federal government under the federal system.[21] The possible effect of these differences in accounting, related matters is well illustrated in Clarke *et al's* analysis of the Australian accounting profession later in this book. Unitary states tend to be associated with unicameral legislative systems, i.e. those possessing a single legislative assembly whereas federal systems usually have a two-tier bicameral structure with an 'upper house' providing representation of individual state's interests. Both Australia and Malaysia are examples of the latter form. New Zealand has a unicameral structure, but Japan, also a unitary state, has a bicameral legislature. The government of the PRC is in most respects essentially unitary, but geography dictates the need for a regional form of government intermediate between national and local levels.

The main *styles* of executive government are Monarchy, Presidential and Parliamentary. Monarchies with real executive powers are rare in the modern world. Brunei is one of the exceptions and Malaysia also has an unusual form of a partly elected, partly hereditary monarchical system. The constitutional monarchy of Malaysia runs in conjunction with a Parliamentary system of government inherited from the UK (despite its federal characteristics). Australia and New Zealand are nominally constitutional monarchies at the present time. In the Parliamentary system, the distinction between the executive arm of government and the legislative arm is not as clear cut as in the Presidential system (the form of which often follows the US pattern). The Prime Minister in the Parliamentary system usually has most executive power, and is chosen from among members of the elected or appointed legislature. If the Parliamentary system is also Republican, a separate Presidential office often assumes the

---

[20]Another characteristic of constitutions is whether they are 'nominal' or 'actual'. Constitutions are 'nominal' when their written form fails to faithfully reflect the procedural and substantive law they embody and 'actual' when they do so. The possibility and extent of 'nominalism' should always be kept in mind when interpreting the significance of constitutional provisions.

[21]The example of Indonesia, however, warns against generalisation. It is a geographically large and culturally diverse state, but with a highly centralised government.

position of head of state though it usually has relatively nominal executive power. On the other hand, in the pure Presidential system of the US type, the main reigns of executive power are in the hands of the President whose office, along with its bureaucracy, are quite separate from the legislative arm of government (there is no prime ministerial office in the US system).

Presidential and Parliamentary styles, however, vary considerably in practice in the Asia-Pacific region and are usually hybrids of some sort. New Zealand is probably the most clear cut example of an English Westminster style, Parliamentary democracy. The Japanese constitution, on the other hand, has characteristics of both the Parliamentary and Presidential systems. The system of Indonesia gives considerable executive power to the President and, to a lesser extent, so do the systems of Taiwan and South Korea. The constitutions of the socialist countries of the PRC, North Korea and Vietnam are nominally one-party, Parliamentary systems (whether the chief executives are called 'presidents', 'premiers' or 'prime ministers'), but in actuality policy and executive power are both under the control of the Communist Party. Finally, Macau and Hong Kong until recently were effectively governed as colonies with limited local representation and executive power. Both will shortly revert back to being provinces of mainland China and the constitutional forms of their future governments remain unclear at the present time.

REGIONAL ECONOMIC BACKGROUND

As was stated earlier, economic factors are sometimes significant in understanding why accounting policies differ between countries. For example, in South Korea and the Philippines, where inflation rates have been relatively high historically, accounting standards are more flexible with respect to the revaluation of assets than they are in Japan, where inflation rates have not been of comparable concern. In a different way, the stage of economic and social development may be significant in determining the type of accounting system which is adopted. For instance, there might not be a sufficiently highly educated workforce to permit the adoption of professionally-based accounting practices.

Of course economic facts are also of some interest in themselves in the Asia-Pacific region. In 1990, with almost 40 percent of the world's population, the region's share of total world gross national product (GNP) was about 20 percent; its share of world exports and imports was approximately 26 percent and 22 percent respectively (Edwards, 1994; IMF, 1994). This compares to equivalent figures in 1962 of approximately 10 percent, 8 percent and 10 percent respectively (Forbes, 1994). Growth rates of GNP and exports in the region have been more than double the rest of the world in that period. Table 3 summarises some of the main national income statistics for the countries of the region for a number of years up to and including 1992 insofar as they are available. This type of data is the foundation for most of the

Table 3(a)
NATIONAL INCOME STATISTICS FOR COUNTRIES OF THE ASIA-PACIFIC REGION

All figures are in US$ M	Japan	Australia	New Zealand	Singapore	Hong Kong	Taiwan	South Korea	Brunei
	1992	1992	1992	1992	1992	1992	1992	1992
National Income at Current Prices								
Consumption: Private	2,090,628	186,731	25,442	19,821	58,055	115,234	158,517	NA
Government	341,524	54,665	6,697	4,503	8,291	36,216	33,689	NA
Investment	1,141,674	57,950	8,072	18,770	28,631	50,012	106,485	NA
Domestic expenditure	3,573,826	299,347	40,211	43,094	94,977	201,462	298,691	NA
Exports	374,331	55,058	12,781	80,862	138,031	91,933	88,866	NA
Imports	(285,701)	(56,673)	(11,859)	(78,023)	(136,302)	(86,810)	(91,941)	NA
Statistical adjustment	0	697	336	92	0	0	1,223	NA
Gross Domestic Product	3,662,456	298,429	41,469	46,025	96,706	206,585	296,839	NA
Net income from abroad	33,699	(10,367)	(1,499)	735	NA	4,103	(2,291)	NA
Gross National Product	3,696,155	288,062	39,970	46,760	NA	210,688	294,548	NA
Depreciation	(572,949)	(46,008)	(3,869)	(6,579)	NA	(18,035)	(28,399)	NA
National Income	3,123,206	242,054	36,101	40,181	NA	192,653	266,149	NA
Wages and salaries	2,067,446	150,425	17,987	NA	NA	111,128	140,906	NA
Government Spending 6		9				1		
Receipts	570,217	98,279	14,322	NA	17,482	33,151	54,770	NA
Expenditure	(570,217)	(109,681)	(15,388)	NA	(15,955)	(40,976)	(51,706)	NA
Surplus/(Deficit)	0	(11,402)	(1,066)	NA	1,527	(7,825)	3,064	NA
GDP by Economic Activity								
Agriculture 10	80,529	9,463	NA	96	190	5,524	22,650	118
Industry 10	1,506,159	87,750	NA	17,306	19,448	81,447	133,385	1,860
Services	2,233,841	208,541	NA	30,837	77,814	129,364	146,342	2,030
Adjustments 2	(158,073)	(7,325)	NA	(2,214)	(746)	(9,750)	(5,538)	(96)
GDP	3,662,456	298,429	NA	46,025	96,706	206,585	296,839	3,912

Table 3(a) (continued)
NATIONAL INCOME STATISTICS FOR COUNTRIES OF THE ASIA-PACIFIC REGION

All figures are in US$ M	Malaysia	Thailand	Philippines	Indonesia	China	Vietnam	Cambodia	Papua New Guinea
	1992	1992	1992	1992	1992	1991	1992	1992
National Income at Current Prices			7			4, 5	3	
Consumption: Private	29,852	60,641	39,864	67,693	NA	7,045	2,987	2,484
Government	7,578	11,131	5,087	12,183	NA	1,303	341	964
Investment	19,583	44,484	11,106	45,763	NA	1,019	351	1,020
Domestic expenditure	57,013	116,256	56,057	125,640	NA	9,367	3,679	4,468
Exports	45,235	40,488	15,451	37,330	78,757	2,087	562	1,939
Imports	(44,234)	(45,198)	(17,592)	(34,497)	(73,799)	(2,579)	(657)	(2,115)
Statistical adjustment	0	0	(1,293)	0	0	(107)	(1)	0
Gross Domestic Product	58,014	111,546	52,623	128,473	441,791	8,768	3,583	4,292
Net income from abroad	(2,951)	(2,017)	1,078	(6,017)	290	NA	NA	NA
Gross National Product	55,063	109,529	53,701	122,456	442,081	NA	NA	NA
Depreciation	NA	(11,219)	(4,250)	(6,426)	(45,443)	NA	NA	NA
National Income	NA	98,310	49,451	116,030	396,638	NA	NA	NA
Wages and salaries	NA	29,344	18,582	NA	NA	NA	NA	NA
Government Spending 6						(1992)		
Receipts	15,408	20,146	9,514	NA	75,309	1,801	156	965
Expenditure	(17,944)	(16,752)	(10,412)	NA	(79,601)	(2,243)	(246)	(1,387)
Surplus/(Deficit)	(2,536)	3,394	(898)	NA	(4,292)	(442)	(90)	(422)
GDP by Economic Activity	8					(1991)		
Agriculture 10	11,353	13,393	11,381	24,648	105,085	3,578	1,712	NA
Industry: 10	23,791	40,349	17,507	52,068	204,548	2,072	471	NA
Services	23,606	57,804	23,735	51,757	132,158	3,035	1,400	NA
Adjustments 2	(736)	0	0		0	83		NA
GDP	58,014	111,546	52,623	128,473	441,791	8,768	3,583	NA

Table 3(b)

COMPONENTS AND ANALYSIS OF NATIONAL INCOME AGGREGATES AS A PERCENTAGE OF GDP

	Japan	Australia	New Zealand	Singapore	Hong Kong	Taiwan	South Korea	Brunei
	1987–91	1987–91	1987–91	1987–91	1987–91	1991–92	1987–91	1987–91
National Income at Current Prices						1		
Consumption: Private	58	60	61	45	59	55	53	NA
Government	9	17	17	11	7	18	10	NA
Investment	31	23	21	38	28	24	35	NA
Domestic expenditure	98	100	99	94	94	97	98	NA
Exports	10	17	27	180	133	46	34	NA
Imports	–9	–18	–26	–174	–127	–43	–32	NA
Statistical adjustment	1	1	0	0	0	0	0	NA
Gross Domestic Product	100	100	100	100	100	100	100	NA
Net income from abroad	1	–4	–5	1	NA	2	–1	NA
Gross National Product	101	96	95	101	NA	102	99	NA
Depreciation	–15	–15	–9	–15	NA	–9	–10	NA
National Income	86	81	86	86	NA	93	89	NA
Wages and salaries	55	50	46	NA	NA	54	44	NA
Government Spending		9 (1990–92)		(1991–93)	(1992)		(1990–91)	(1990–91)
Receipts	14	35	37	25	18	16	18	44
Expenditure	16	34	38	20	17	20	16	45
Surplus/(Deficit)	–2	1	–1	5	1	–4	2	–1
GDP by Economic Activity			(1987–91)		(1987–91)			(1987–91)
Agriculture	3	4	8	0	0	3	9	2
Industry	42	31	27	37	25	41	45	54
Services	61	67	63	67	75	61	47	45
Adjustments	–6	–2	2	–4	0	–5	–1	–1
GDP	100	100	100	100	100	100	100	100

Table 3(b) (continued)
COMPONENTS AND ANALYSIS OF NATIONAL INCOME AGGREGATES AS A PERCENTAGE OF GDP

	Malaysia	Thailand	Philippines	Indonesia	China	Vietnam	Cambodia	Papua New Guinea
	1987–91	1987–91	1987–91	1987–91	1987–91	1987–89	1991–92	1987–91
National Income at Current Prices	[8]		[7]		[11]	[4, 5]	[3]	
Consumption: Private	52	57	71	56	52	83	85	61
Government	14	10	10	9	9	17	7	23
Investment	30	37	20	34	36	12	9	25
Domestic expenditure	96	104	101	99	97	112	101	109
Exports	74	34	29	26	20	19	12	42
Imports	–70	–38	–30	–25	17	–31	–13	–51
Statistical adjustment	0	0	0	0	0	0	0	0
Gross Domestic Product	100	100	100	100	100	100	100	100
Net income from abroad	–5	–1	1	–5	NA	NA	NA	NA
Gross National Product	95	99	101	95	NA	NA	NA	NA
Depreciation	NA	–9	–8	–5	NA	NA	NA	–10
National Income	NA	90	93	90	NA	NA	NA	NA
Wages and salaries	NA	24	34	NA	NA	NA	NA	39
Government Spending [6]	(1987–91)		[9]		(1987–91)	(1989)	(1991)	(1991)
Receipts	27	18	16	22	19	16	4	31
Expenditure	33	15	18	18	20	23	8	32
Surplus/(Deficit)	–6	3	–2	4	–1	–7	–4	–1
GDP by Economic Activity	(1987–91)				(1990–91)	(1987–91)	(1991–92)	(1987–91)
Agriculture [10]	20	14	22	22	27	40	50	28
Industry [10]	41	36	35	38	43	24	12	32
Services	41	49	43	39	30	35	38	37
Adjustments	–2	1	0	1	0	1	0	3
GDP	100	100	100	100	100	100	100	100

See next page for notes to Table 3(b)

The primary sources for this data are the *National Accounts Statistics: Mean Aggregates and Detailed Tables 1992*, supplemented where necessary by *The Far East and Australasia 1995 Europa World Yearbook 1995* and *International Financial Statistics Yearbook 1994, IMF.*

1.   For Taiwan, the components of GDP are based on 1991 figures only.

2.   Adjustments include items such as import duties, imputed bank service changes and VAT.

3.   Conversion is based on an exchange rate of 700 riels per US$. The US dollar figures could be misleading due to volatility in the exchange rate.

4.   The 1987 and 1988 figures for Vietnam are based upon an estimated split of private and government consumption expenditure of 5 to 1.

5.   Some estimates are based upon the *The Europa World Yearbook 1995*.

6.   Data for government revenues and expenditures are mostly from the IMF yearbook.

7.   Export and import percentages are based on 1991 and 1992 figures.

8.   For Malaysia, the allocation of GDP by economic activity in 1992 is based upon percentages using current prices for 1987–91.

9.   Figures for the government spending of Australia are from National Account Statistics. State government expenditure is not included.

10. 'Agriculture' includes agriculture, fishing and forestry while 'Industry' includes mining, manufacturing, energy, electricity, gas and water and construction. 'Services' include wholesale and retail trade, transport, storage and communication, finance, insurance, real estate and business, community, social and personal services.

11. Figures for structure of demand are from the *Far East Economic Review 1994 Yearbook*.

NA = Not available.

judgements on which relative national economic performance is based. Furthermore, it is accounting data ultimately based upon the same principles of measurement that one finds in financial and management accounting practice. It is therefore worth discussing, from an accountant's perspective and prior to summarising the state of economic affairs of the region at the present time, the national income statistics of the countries of the region in an accounting context, their sometimes severe limitations and their relationship to the micro-level accounting with which this book is mainly concerned.

As can be seen from the Table, GNP differs from gross domestic product (GDP) by the amount of net 'property' income received from, and remitted abroad. GDP, shown at market prices[22], may be thought of as being equivalent to the value added (i.e. sales less bought in goods and services) which would result from consolidating, in the usual accounting fashion, the value added statements of all the 'producers' of goods and services in a country. Roughly speaking, one can therefore think of GDP at market prices as being the profit before tax for the year of the production sector of a country after adding back wages, salaries and interest payments, regardless of whether some of the GDP may be due to foreigners. It thus corresponds quite closely to what an accountant would ordinarily think of as an economic performance measure regardless of the identity of particular shareholders. GNP is what the residents of a country gain from their own GDP and that of other countries. After making a deduction for depreciation ('capital consumption'), this gives the 'net national product' or more familiarly the 'National Income', which is the concept most commonly associated with 'well-offness'. In fact, great care should be taken in interpreting such data in this context. Even when expressed at constant prices in 'real' terms, international comparisons can be very sensitive to exchange rate fluctuations. Also, there are so many quantitative and qualitative items which affect perceptions of standards of living and which are left out of national income calculations that a straightforward comparison of GNP between two countries can be a highly unrealistic indicator of relative prosperity. GDP calculations adjusted for purchasing power are sometimes used to rectify this problem, as are the 'Human Development Indices' published by the United Nations Development Programme. The former are shown later in Table 4 for countries of the region where these are available. It can be seen that these sometimes differ significantly from nominal figures.

As with micro-accounting practices, international standardisation in national income accounting is an important issue. There are many differences in national income accounting practices (e.g. regarding the valuation of imputed services), but the

---

[22]When measured at market prices, GDP includes indirect taxes. GDP at factor cost excludes the value of indirect taxes. Oversimplifying somewhat, the latter is found by adding together incomes while the former is found by adding together expenditures.

two main categories of systems are those developed by the western European countries and the 'Material Product' system preferred by socialist countries. The main difference between the two systems lies in the definition of the production boundary, since the Material Product system follows the Marxist theory of value in excluding the value of most services from GDP, while many types of services (in particular government and financial services) are recognised as adding value under the Western capitalist system. The conventions of the standardised System of National Accounts (SNA) developed by the United Nations (UN, 1968) which are followed by most countries in reporting data to UN agencies, adapts to both kinds of system. It should be noted that data from the socialist countries is often not as readily available as it is for some of the other countries.

Both micro and macro-accounting systems are transactions-based and use essentially the same concepts, although Western national income systems differ somewhat from micro-accounting systems in basing the valuation of assets *in theory* on current cost, rather than historic cost principles. Also, it is important to appreciate that the macro-economic concept of 'gross domestic investment' corresponds to the micro-economic concept of *changes* in fixed assets and inventories, not to the level of accumulated investment at a point in time. Furthermore, unlike the situation in micro-accounting, usually no attempt is made to value intangible assets such as copyright and patents. Except under special circumstances, few attempts have been made anywhere in the world to estimate balances of expenditures and reserves brought and carried forward. The important aggregates of undistributed profits and household savings are flow concepts (i.e. changes due to transactions in the period) rather than levels or 'stock' variables as, for instance, are 'retained reserves carried forward' in the balance sheets of individual companies. In fact, there is currently no real equivalent in national income accounts to the information contained in the micro-level financial balance sheet, other than estimates of outstanding debt and monetary balances (e.g. the level of external debt). It should also be remembered that, unlike much financial accounting data at firm level, macro-economic data is the aggregate result of transactions which are indirectly estimated in many different ways from income and expenditure sources rather than the result of directly measured individual transactions which are then aggregated. This gives rise to the so-called 'statistical discrepancy', an error of measurement which can sometimes take on quite large values when compared to individual items.

Nevertheless, with these provisos, macro-economic accounting can be interpreted, in many ways, in a manner analogous to its micro-economic counterpart. The expenditure estimates of final demand or sales to the personal sector form the basis of the assessment of the value-added to the economy. This value-added is distributed in the form of taxes to the government, wages to the personal sector, interest and dividends to both of these sectors and the balance remains in the production sector as undistributed profits (including depreciation charges). Thus from an accounting point of view, the important variable of investment, upon which prospects for growth depend, must be funded either from personal savings, undistributed profits of the production sector, government receipts and expenditure surpluses, foreign trade surpluses or foreign borrowing. The first four sources of investment funds are analogous to retained reserves for the period, issues and retirements of share capital in the individual firm context, while the last is analogous to the loan finance of a company. Many of the same considerations of financial management apply to the national economy, just as they do to the individual firm. Too low a level of national income for a given consumption or investment expenditure pattern by the private and public sectors, leads to increased borrowing, which is risky to the financial profile, the economy and eventually to the currency. Inappropriate policy responses, such as a lack of control over the money supply in such circumstances, can create symptomatic indicators of weakness such as high interest rates, high general price inflation and possibly high rates of unemployment. These are the key factors which keep recurring in assessments of the economic well-being of the countries dealt with in this book.

In examining the structure of the economy in terms of the proportionate share of the primary, secondary and tertiary sectors in the provision of employment and their respective productivities, it is important to understand the underlying reasons behind the performance indicators and the relative stage of economic development achieved. Since the law of development is inexorably in the direction of the transfer of labour and share of GDP from the primary to the secondary and from there to the tertiary sector, data on sector shares is particularly important in an Asia-Pacific context. Furthermore, given the rather different influences exerted by the different sectors on both the measurement and disclosure of financial information at micro-level, some of the theories reviewed earlier state that it may be significant for financial and management accounting practices.

Data on each of the variables just mentioned is given where possible, though not always for the same year and not always in a form which it is safe to use for the comparison of economic performance between different countries. For purposes of comparison, some summary statistics are provided in Table 4.

Economically, the countries of the Asia-Pacific region may be characterised as one of six main types. Table 4 shows the countries by type and in order of *per capita* GDP or GNP if GDP is not available (where appropriate).

Japan is the wealthiest country and the economic power of region in the late 20th Century. The 'settler' economies of Australia and New Zealand, both long time members of the OECD, with developed economies and standards of living comparable with those of Western Europe, form an interdependent pair of economies with similar structures. The so-called 'Newly Industrialised Economies' (NIEs) of Hong Kong, Singapore, Taiwan and South Korea have all experienced rapid economic growth since the 1960s, so much so that the *per capita* income of both Hong Kong and Singapore

Table 4

SUMMARY ECONOMIC INDICATORS FOR COUNTRIES OF THE ASIA-PACIFIC REGION

	Notes	Japan	Australia	New Zealand	Singapore	Hong Kong	Macau	Taiwan	South Korea
Nominal GDP per capita ($) 1994	1, 11	36,803	18,000	16,640	22,139	21,442	NA	11,315	8,540
GNP per capita at PPP ($) 1994	1, 11, 12	21,090	18,490	16,588	20,470	21,670	NA	11,953	9,810
Average annual GDP growth rate for 1980–91 %	8	4.2	3.1	1.5	6.6	6.9	NA	7.6	9.6
Average annual growth in GDP for 1980–91 by Sector:	7								
Agriculture %	8	1.2	2.9	3.8	-6.6	NA	NA	4.7	2.1
Industry %	8	4.9	3.0	1.3	5.8	NA	NA	11.7	12.1
Services %	8	3.7	3.6	1.6	7.3	NA	NA	13.7	9.3
GNP real growth rate %	3	5.65	1.6	0.7	8.3	2.5	NA	5.2	9.0
Inflation rate % (1980–1991)	2, 8	1.5	7.0	10.3	1.9	7.5	NA	4.5	5.7
Unemployment %	5, 6, 9	2.1	9.1	7.4	1.7	1.8	NA	1.7	2.5
External debt as % GNP/GDP	8	neg	46	43	neg	NA	NA	neg	14
Industrial production growth rate %	4, 9	4.6	1.8	1.9	9.0	1.7	NA	4.7	8.6
Current account balance index	15	2.2	-4.5	-2.5	5	NA	NA	4	-2.2
Currency index %	10, 13	46	-23	-23	19	NA	NA	NA	NA
Employment by sector:									
Agriculture %	14	6	5	11	0	1	0	12	17
Industry %		35	24	23	35	30	38	39	35
Services %		59	71	66	65	69	62	49	48

Table 4 (continued)

SUMMARY ECONOMIC INDICATORS FOR COUNTRIES OF THE ASIA-PACIFIC REGION

	Brunei	Malaysia	Thailand	Philippines	Indonesia	North Korea	China	Vietnam	Cambodia	Papua New Guinea
Nominal GDP per capita ($) 1994	NA	3,547	2,403	953	840	NA	418	195	NA	1,230
GNP per capita at PPP ($) 1994	15,171	8,630	6,390	2,660	3,140	NA	2,120	1,040	NA	2,190
Average annual GDP growth rate for 1980–91 %	NA	5.7	7.9	1.1	5.6	NA	9.4	NA	NA	2.0
Average annual growth in GDP for 1980–91 by Sector:										
Agriculture %	NA	3.7	3.8	1.1	3.1	NA	5.7	NA	NA	1.6
Industry %	NA	7.7	9.6	0.05	5.9	NA	11.0	NA	NA	2.4
Services %	NA	4.7	8.0	2.8	6.8	NA	11.2	NA	NA	1.8
GNP real growth rate %	2.7	10.0	10.0	2.5	6.0	2.0	5.0	2.4	0	−30
Inflation rate % (1980–1991)	NA	1.7	3.7	14.6	8.5	NA	5.8	NA	NA	5.2
Unemployment %	2.5	6.0	4.9	9.3	3.0	NA	2.6	33.0	NA	5.0
External debt as % GNP/GDP	neg	35	34	63	62	NA	16	110	NA	85
Industrial production growth rate %	12.9	15.8	14.0	1.9	11.6	NA	7.6	10.0	NA	NA
Current account balance index	NA	0	−5.4	−3.5	−2.7	NA	NA	NA	NA	−8.6
Currency index %	NA	−18	−11	−221.8	−195	NA	NA	NA	NA	−22.5
Employment by sector:										
Agriculture %	2	23	61	45	54	43	60	73	74	77
Industry %	24	30	15	16	14	30	23	13	7	6
Services %	74	47	24	39	32	27	17	14	19	17

See next page for Notes to Table 4.

Notes to Table 4

1. Figures are from the *Asian Wall Street Journal* unless otherwise stated.

2. Average inflation for period 1980–91

3. Figures for Cambodia, Brunei and South Korea are for 1989, all other figures are for 1990.

4. Figures for Hong Kong, Indonesia and Vietnam are for 1989, Brunei's are for 1987 and the rest are for 1990.

5. Figures for Australia are for 1990, others are for 1991.

6. Indonesia reports underemployment of 44% and unemployment of 3%, North Korea has no official unemployment. Brunei has a shortage of skilled labor.

7. Agriculture includes agriculture, fishing and forestry while Industry includes mining, manufacturing, energy, electricity, gas and water and construction. Services include wholesale and retail trade, transport, storage and communication, finance, insurance, real estate and business, community, social and personal services.

8. Figures are from *The Far Easten Economic Review 1994 Yearbook* and *PC Globe*.

9. Figures are from *World Development Report* and *PC Globe*.

10. Figures are from *International Financial Statistics Yearbook 1994*, IMF and *The Far East and Australasia 1994 Yearbook*.

11. Figures for New Zealand, Papua New Guinea and Brunei are 1994 estimates of GDP per capita at purchasing power parity (PPP) (CIA database). Nominal GDP per capita for Papua New Guinea is estimated from 1992 data.

12. Taiwan's GNP at PPP is estimated on 1994 figures.

13. The currency index is the percentage change in exchange rate against the US dollar for the ten year period 1982–91. Exchange rate for Cambodia is for 30 April 1994, for Taiwan, Vietnam, Hong Kong, China and Brunei for the period 1991–93. Exchange rates for all other countries are averaged for the period 1982–91.

14. Figures for Australia, Taiwan, Malaysia, New Zealand, Philippines, Singapore and Vietnam are averaged for 1991–93. Figures for China and South Korea are averaged for the period 1990–92. Figures for Brunei are for 1991; Cambodia and North Korea's for mid-80s, Hong Kong's for 1993, Indonesia's for 1992, Japan's for 1991–92, Macau's for 1992, Papua New Guinea's for 1980 and Thailand's for 1992. Figures are from *The Far East and Australasia 1995 Yearbook*.

15. Current account balance index is the current account balance as a percentage of GDP averaged over the period 1987–91. South Korea: average for 1990–91 only; Papua New Guinea: 1987–89 only.

neg = negligible

is now approximately equal to that of Australia and New Zealand. Macau, a possible new NIE, has a relatively high level of GNP and, like Singapore and Hong Kong , has benefited from being an enclave in, and a route to and from, much larger Asian national markets.

Another group is formed from a fourth type of economy, namely those countries, other than Singapore and Vietnam, which belong to ASEAN: Brunei, Indonesia, Malaysia, the Philippines and Thailand. These countries form a middle group in terms of GDP *per capita* with high, and sometimes volatile, growth rates since the mid-1980s.

A fifth group consists of the socialist economies in transition: Cambodia, China, North Korea and Vietnam. All of these countries have lower levels of *per capita* GDP measured by SNA methods, but also have exceptional potential for future economic development.

Finally, Papua New Guinea represents another type of economy in transition, very recently 'decolonised' with an economy depending almost totally on its ability to export mineral resources — an economy, in fact, at the very first stage of economic development. The presumption seems to be that the NIEs will catch up in time with Japan and they will in their turn eventually be joined by the ASEAN countries. It is also generally assumed that the economies in transition will begin to embark on the same stages of development as those exhibited by the richer countries.

Average GDP *per capita* drops with each group, and the characteristics of each group appear to become more variable as one moves down the national income ladder. Japan and the economies in the second group have the characteristics of late stage economic development, i.e. high GDP with low growth rates, a high proportion of GDP contributed by the tertiary sector, a minor role for agriculture in terms of percentage of value-added, but with relatively high productivity and low growth rates of industrial production. Both Australia and New Zealand have quite high levels of external debt and, relative to Japan and the NIEs, a history of high inflation and high unemployment (comparable, in fact, to some of the less economically successful countries of the region). Close to the settler economies come the NIEs in terms of *per capita* GDP with higher GDP growth rates. The agricultural sectors of this group of economies can still be significant in terms of employment (as in the case of Taiwan and South Korea), but they have higher levels of growth of industrial production and lower levels of external debt, inflation and unemployment. Typically, exports play a greater role in these economies (as a proportion of GDP) than they do in the case of Australia and New Zealand.

The ASEAN countries exhibit a middle stage pattern of economic development with lower GDP *per capita,* but with sometimes quite volatile high growth rates of GDP. Agriculture is a more important, but less productive, sector of the economy than it is in the case of the other previously mentioned groups, and often there is a higher rate of growth of industrial production. Compared to the NIEs, these countries generally display a higher level of external debt, higher inflation, unemployment and, currently, less significance for exports as a proportion of GDP. In the transitional economies, GDP per capita is low. Cambodia, for example, has one of the lowest per capita GDP levels in the world. Agriculture is still important both as a contributor to GDP and as an employer. GDP and industrial growth are often high in individual years, and the tertiary sector is relatively unimportant compared to the more developed economies. Finally in PNG, the primary sector is the single most important part of the economy in employment terms, and is also significant as a value-added contributor. Its growth rate of GDP is less than in the NIE and ASEAN groups, and more like those of Australia and New Zealand.

Each chapter provides background of currently pursued economic policies. Sometimes it is easier to understand the reasons underlying economic performance with this information. It also enables a more informed decision as to whether present trends are likely to continue. Broadly speaking, two main schools of thought manifest themselves in the region with respect to economic policy after World War II. On the one hand, there were 'protectionist' policies designed to protect domestic markets, increase the importance of public expenditure and pursue growth by a process of import substitution. On the other hand, there were 'free market' policies of open access to the foreign supply of domestic markets, tight control of public expenditure and export-led growth. These policies were combined in different ways, but the experience of the post-war years has tended to favour the latter group of policies at the expense of the former.

Japan was the first country in the region to benefit from the effects of strong economic growth in a liberalised international trading regime. Australia and New Zealand continued into the 1980s to follow protectionist policies, whereas countries from the NIE group, not having the comfort of a rich resource base or secure, traditional OECD markets, were prompted much earlier to adopt policies of the free market kind. Taiwan and Hong Kong were the first of the NIE countries to follow export-led growth policies in the 1950s. South Korea adopted similar policies in the early 1960s in response to stagnating domestic conditions, while Singapore followed suit in the late 1960s due to changes in British foreign policy in the Far East. It should be understood, however, that the economic policies pursued by the NIE group are 'free market' only in a loose manner of speaking, and that there are considerable differences between NIE countries. For example, five year plans have been important in South Korea's economic development; government expenditure on the infrastructure has been instrumental in Hong Kong's continuing prosperity; and the public ownership of firms has played a significant role in Taiwan's economic success. Nevertheless, the success of export-led growth and, in particular, the example of the emphatic success of the open market approach adopted by Singapore and Hong Kong, led to other countries in the region seeking to copy and emulate the policies of the NIEs.

Since 1980, the ASEAN countries have moved toward free market policies to differing degrees. Indonesia, the Philippines and Thailand had experimented without much success in the policies of import substitution in the 1950s and 1960s. Since the early 1980s, ASEAN countries have attempted to focus on the adoption of export-oriented policies and these have evidently had a positive effect on economic performance in Thailand, Malaysia and Indonesia. The theories of state capitalism behind the some of the earlier policies now appear to have been ineffective, although in special circumstances (e.g. in the Bruneian context), they may be appropriate. The socialist economies in transition seem set to copy the export-led approach of the more successful economies of the region (as indeed does Australia and New Zealand, based upon recent policy changes). However, the extent to which the socialist states will embrace the full quota of private and open market policies remains to be seen. If one considers the overall patterns disclosed by Table 4 in the context of policy, it seems that the three components of the free market approach — export-led growth in a privately owned economy with open markets — have been more effective in promoting economic performance than have the protectionist alternatives[23]. Some countries may have benefited from protectionist elements in their economic strategies in the past, but with the increasing pressures to compete in the global economy it may not be possible to take advantage of such a position in the future.

There are a number of regional organisations of economic significance at the present time, which because of their institutional status may have significance for accounting practices. Probably the most important are ASEAN, already mentioned, and the much larger but more informal and less focused Asia-Pacific Economic Co-operation (APEC) grouping. ASEAN was formed by its five original founding members: Indonesia, Malaysia, Singapore, the Philippines and Thailand in 1967, and was joined by Brunei in 1984 and Vietnam in 1994. In 1992, an agreement to form an ASEAN Free Trade Area (AFTA) was signed. By 2010, the intention is to have established a common five percent tariff on an agreed set of industrial and agricultural products traded between member countries. AFTA is partly a defensive response to development of the trading blocks of the North American Free Trade Association (NAFTA) and the European Union (EU). The members of ASEAN are also members of the APEC group of countries, first proposed in 1989, which now additionally includes the United States, Canada, China, Taiwan, Hong Kong, Australia, New Zealand, Japan and the Republic of Korea. This is not yet (and may never become) a regional trading group, and has, to date, been limited to periodic meetings of heads of government and the issuing of statements of intent on policy matters of regional interest rather than resulting in formal, binding agreements of the type associated

---

[23]For a discussion of the sometimes overlooked role of the state in the successful economic performance of Japan, the NIEs and some of the ASEAN countries, see Dixon and Drakakis-Smith (1993).

with ASEAN, NAFTA and the EU. Other institutions of note in the region include the Economic and Social Commission for Asia and the South Pacific (ESCAP), an organi-sation whose head offices are in Bangkok, which co-ordinates UN development pro-grammes and information services; the Asian Development Bank (ADB), an organisation based in the Philippines which channels aid from the developed coun-tries to developing countries within Asia; and the Columbo Plan, among whose mem-bers are ten of the countries covered in this book. The latter, like the ADB, acts as a conduit for aid to its less economically developed members. The Asia-Pacific region does not yet have the regional institutional arrangements which would justify classi-fying them as constituting a trading block. Nevertheless, the ASEAN grouping was the impetus behind the formation of the ASEAN Federation of Accountants out of the more nebulous Confederation of Asia-Pacific Accountants, which encompasses American countries as well as countries of the Asia-Pacific region. However, the recently concluded Uruguay Round of GATT talks may reduce the need for defensive trading alliances and, given the importance of world trade to the economies of the region, this may turn out to be in their best economic interests.

ACCOUNTING PRACTICES IN THE ASIA-PACIFIC REGION

It can be gathered from the foregoing that the researcher interested in the influence of the environment on accounting practice in the Asia-Pacific region may need to be aware of patterns even more complex than usual. The problem of tracing these effects, either positively or normatively, even in those areas of accounting practice more susceptible to environmental analysis, is an intricate and delicate affair. The back-ground information on physical geography, cultural matters, political and legal systems and recent economic trends in each chapter, is accompanied by a description of financial accounting practices and, where possible, a discussion of aspects of management accounting practices in the country concerned. In some countries (e.g. Papua New Guinea), only some part of this task can be achieved at the present time. In others (e.g. Cambodia), the lack of information is so acute that analysis has to be mostly based upon personal communication and even then, material is usually too sensitive to be attributed. However, in most of the countries it has proved possible to describe practices or discuss issues more expansively. In several chapters, manage-ment accounting practices and research are extensively reviewed (Thailand, Taiwan, South Korea, the PRC, Hong Kong, Australia, New Zealand, Macau, Malaysia and Singapore). In Vietnam, the interplay and tension between the socialist, French and US forms of accounting in the transition of that country's economy is analysed. North Korea's system is an interesting example of a socialist system as yet relatively untainted by capitalist influences. The accounting systems of the Philippines, Indonesia and Brunei are discussed in an historical context and, in the case of the latter, more attention is focused on the role and needs of government in the supply of financial information. Finally, in Japan, the special characteristics of Japanese management accounting practices are discussed.

The foregoing review of environmental factors in the Asia-Pacific region suggests a number of alternative ways of structuring the individual chapters, i.e. by physical proximity, cultural proximity and political or economic similarities. The most obvious, single environmental factor affecting overt accounting practices apparent from the content of this book is a political one, which is closely associated with past or present colonial or neo-colonial influences. For instance, the seven countries of the old British empire (Australia, Brunei, Hong Kong, Malaysia, New Zealand, Papua New Guinea and Singapore) show very marked similarities in the structures of their regulatory frameworks, the form of their corporate reports and the general attitude towards professionalism in accounting. Similarly, the French influence is most evident in Cambodia; the Dutch in Indonesia; the Portuguese in Macau and the US in the Philippines. The socialist countries of China, Vietnam and North Korea are still predominantly guided by the old Soviet form of accounting, and in those other non-socialist countries which have been influenced less directly by non-regional colonial forces — Japan, South Korea, Taiwan and Thailand — the dominant outside influence on accounting practices at the present time comes from the US. The countries of the region classified by these dominant 'political' influences are shown in Table 5.

Table 5
CLASSIFICATION OF ACCOUNTING SYSTEM BY DOMINANT INFLUENCE

British	USA	European	Socialist
Australia	Japan	Cambodia	China
Brunei	Philippines	Indonesia	North Korea
Hong Kong	South Korea	Macau	Vietnam
Malaysia and Singapore	Taiwan		
New Zealand	Thailand		
Papua New Guinea			

Clearly, these categories are not mutually exclusive and only show dominant effects. For example, Japan and Thailand are still affected by European influences imported in past eras. The effects of socialist accounting techniques in Cambodia is likely to persist, and forms heavily influenced by US practices are currently being adopted in China and Indonesia. Similarly, Vietnam is a hybrid of socialist, US and French influences. However, as will be seen, colonial and neo-colonial history is, from the information contained in the chapters which follow, the most evident and obvious single influence on accounting practices. Consequently, we have chosen to use the classification of countries shown in Table 5 to determine the order of appearance of the relevant accounting practices of each in this book. The question of the importance of the other forces which may be at work in shaping accounting practices, and in particular the effect of culture, will be left open for the present. This is a variable which, as the literature review explained, is taken by some to be a more underlying cause of the form that accounting practices take. This issue will be returned to in the concluding chapter.

REFERENCES

Aron, P.H. (1990), 'Japanese P/E multiples in an era of increasing uncertainty', *Report No. 41, Daiwa Securities America*, New York, August.

Baydoun, N. and R. Willett (1995), 'Cultural relevance of western accounting systems to developing countries', *Abacus*, March, pp. 67–91.

Bellwood (1992), *Cambridge history of South-east Asia*, Cambridge University Press.

Blake, J. (1990), 'Problems in international accounting harmonisation', *Management accounting-London*, Vol. 68.

Blaustein, A.P. (1995), *Constitutions of dependencies and special sovereignties*, (ed), Oceana Publications.

Cappelletti, M. and W. Cohen (1973), 'Comparative constitutional law', *Civil Procedure, International encyclopedia of comparative law*, Vol. 16, Cappelletti, M. (ed), Martinus Nyhoff.

Cappelletti, M. and B.G. Garth (1987), 'Policies, trends and ideas in court procedure', *International encyclopedia of comparative law*, Cappelletti, M. and B.G. Garth (eds), Martinus Nyhoff.

Chan, M.Y.A. (1995), 'Structuration and accounting standard setting in China', Canadian Academic Accounting Association Annual Conference 1995, June 8–10, Montreal, Canada.

Chiu, C.W., I. Dobinson and M. Findley (1991), *Legal systems of PRC*, Longman.

Choi, F. and G. Muller (1992), *International accounting*, Prentice-Hall.

Chow, C.W., Y. Kato and M.D. Shields (1994), 'National culture and the preference for management controls: An explanatory study of the firm-labor market interface', *Accounting, organisations and society*, Vol. 19, May–July, pp. 381–400.

Cole, S. (1990), 'Cultural diversity and sustainable futures', *Futures*, Vol. 22, December, pp. 1044–58.

Cooke, T. and R . Parker (1994), *Financial reporting in the West Asia Pacific Rim*, Routledge.

Courtis, J. (1992), 'The reliability of presentation-based annual report disclosure studies', *Accounting and business research*, Winter, pp. 31–43.

David, R. and J.E.C. Brierly (1985), *Major legal systems in the world today: An introduction to the comparative study of law*, (3rd edition), Stevens and Sons, London.

Dixon, C. and D. Drakakis-Smith (1993), 'The Pacific Asia region', *Economic and social development in Pacific Asia*, Dixon, C. and D. Drakakis-Smith, Routledge.

Edwards, C. (1994), 'Current economic trends in Asia and the Pacific', *The Far East and Australasia*, (25th edition), Europa, pp. 15–21.

Forbes, D. (1994), 'Towards the "Pacific Century": Integration and disintegration in the Pacific Basin', *The Far East and Australasia*, (25th edition), Europa, pp. 22–4.

Gambling, T. (1987), 'Accounting for rituals', *Accounting, organisations and society*, Vol. 12, pp. 319–29.

Gerhardy, P. (1990), 'An evaluation of the role of culture in the development of accounting principles in West Germany', *Accounting and finance research paper 90/2*, Flinders University.

Gray, S. (1988), 'Towards a theory of cultural influence on the development of accounting systems internationally', *Abacus*, March, pp. 1–15.

Hall, D. (1981), *A history of South-east Asia*, (4th Edition), MacMillan.

Hazard, J.H., W.E. Butler and P.B. Maggs (1977), '*The Soviet legal system*', (3rd edition), Oceana Publications.

Hofstede, G. (1980), *Cultures consequences*, McGraw-Hill.

Hofstede, G. (1991), *Cultures and organisations: Software of the mind*, McGraw-Hill.

Hofstede, G. and M.H. Bond, (1988), 'The Confucius connection: From cultural roots to economic growth', *Organisational dynamics*, Vol. 16, Spring, pp. 4–21.

Hoskins, K. and R. Macve (1985), 'Accounting and the examination: A genealogy of disciplinary power', *Accounting, organisations and society*.

IMF (1994), *International Financial Statistics Yearbook 1994*.

Inkeles, A. and D. Levinson (1969), 'National character: The study of modal personality and sociocultural systems', in *Handbook of social psychology*, Vol. 4, (2nd edition), G. Lindsay and E. Aroason (eds), Addison-Wesley.

Jeffries, I. '*Socialist economics and the transition to the market: A guide*', Routledge.

Johnson, A.W. (1978), '*Research methods in social anthropology*', Edward Arnold.

Johnson (1991), 'Role making for accounting while the state is watching', *Accounting, organisations and society*, Vol. 16, Iss. 5, 6, pp. 521–46.

Laabs, J. (1992), 'Corporate Anthropologists', *Personal journal*, Vol. 71, January, pp. 81–91.

Lie, J. (1990), 'Is Korean management just like Japanese management?' *Management international review*, Vol. 30, Second Quarter, pp. 113–18.

Mackerras, C. (1992), *Eastern Asia: An introductory history*, (eds), Longmans.

Mallat, C. (1993), *The renewal of Islamic law*, Cambridge University Press.

Mueller, G.G. (1967), *International accounting*, Macmillan, New York.

Mueller, G.G. (1968), 'Accounting principles generally accepted in the United States versus those generally accepted elsewhere', *The international journal of accounting*, Spring, pp. 91–103.

Nair, R.D. and W.G. Frank (1980), 'The impact of disclosure and measurement practices on international accounting classifications', *The accounting review*, July, pp. 426–50.

Nobes, C. (1983), 'A judgemental classification of financial reporting practices', *Journal of business finance and accounting*, Spring, pp. 1–18.

Nobes, C. (1990), *Accounting comparisons: UK/Europe*, Coopers and Lybrand Deloitte, UK, January.

Nobes, C. (1995), 'Corporate financing and its effects on European accounting differences', Unpublished working paper, University of Reading.

Nobes, C. and R. Parker (1995), *Comparative international accounting*, Prentice-Hall.

Perera, H. (1989), 'Towards a framework to analyse the impact of culture on accounting', *International journal of accounting*, Vol. 24, pp. 42–56.

Perera, M.H.B. and M.R. Mathews (1990), 'The cultural relativity of accounting and international patterns of social accounting', *Advances in international accounting*, Vol. 3, pp. 215–51.

Radebaugh, L. and S. Gray (1993), *International accounting and multinational enterprises*, Wiley.

Rama Jois, M. (1984), *Constitutional history of India*, Vol. 1, Sweet & Maxwell.

Schact, J. (1964) *An introduction to Islamic law*, Oxford University Press.

Seidler, L.J. (1967), *The function of accounting in economic development: Turkey as a case study*, Praeger, New York.

Strong, C.F. (1966), *Modern political constitution,* (7th edition).

UN Department of economic and social affairs (1968), *A system of national accounts*, Studies in Methods Series F, No. 2, Rev. 5.

Weber, M. (1958) *The protestant ethic and the spirit of capitalism*, Allen & Unwin, 1968.

Weetman, P. and Gray, S.J. (1990), 'International financial analysis and comparative corporate performance: the Impact of U.K. versus U.S. accounting principles on earnings', *Journal of international financial management and accounting*, Summer/Autumn, Vol. 2:2 and 3.

Wilmott *et al* (1992), 'Regulation of accountancy and accountants: A comparative analysis of accounting for research and development in four advanced capitalist countries', *Accounting auditing and accountability journal*, Vol. 5, pp. 32–56.

Zweigert, K. and H. Kotz (1977), *An introduction to comparative law, Vol 1: The Framework*, North Holland.

Zysman, J. (1983), *Government, markets and growth: Financial systems and the politics of industrial change*, Cornell University Press.

FINANCIAL AND MANAGEMENT ACCOUNTING IN AUSTRALIA

Frank Clarke, Graeme Dean, John Lowry
*and Murray Wells**

BACKGROUND

Australia is a geologically stable, low-lying island continent with associated islands of approximately 8 m sq. km lying between 10° 41' and 43° 39'S and extending almost 4000 km from the Indian Ocean in the west and to the Pacific Ocean in the east. There are three main physical areas: a western plateau, a middle area of lowlands and the Great Dividing Range with a narrow band of low-lying land between it and the eastern coast-line. The flatness of the continent means that climate is determined mostly by latitudinal factors. The north has a tropical monsoon climate with dry winters and wet summers. The south is in a westerly air stream in the winter, which brings rainfall to the western coast. The east coast also receives precipitation from south easterlies to easterlies, but much of the centre is arid, creating large desert areas. Soil quality is generally low, particularly over 70 percent of the land area on the western side of the continent. Australia is rich in many resources including iron ore, nickel, lead, zinc, bauxite, gold, silver, diamonds, coal, oil and natural gas. In 1992, the population of Australia was about 17.5 m, just more than two persons per sq. km, one of the least densely populated countries in the world. However, more than 85 percent of the population live in the state capitals and their immediate hinterlands. Modern Australia is thus a highly urbanised society.

---

*Professor Frank Clarke is Dean, Faculty of Commerce, The University of Newcastle. Associate Professor Graeme Dean is in the Department of Accounting, The University of Sydney. John Lowry is lecturer in the Department of Commerce, The University of Newcastle and Professor Murray Wells is Director of the Graduate School of Business, The University of Sydney.

Aborigines have inhabited mainland Australia for at least 40 000 years, and numbered between 300 000 and one million when the first European settlements arrived. At that time, the Aborigines practised a hunting and gathering culture. Apart from minor contacts with European explorers and possibly even earlier contacts with Indonesian and Chinese traders, non-Aboriginal involvement in Australia first took place on a significant scale in 1788 when the British established a penal colony in Port Jackson (Sydney) with the intention of using convict labour on government farms. Other penal colonies and free settlements appeared in Hobart (1804), Brisbane (1825), Perth (1829), Melbourne (1835) and Adelaide (1836), prompted by a variety of strategic, economic and social motives. The formation of the states reflected Australia's physical geography. The original colony of New South Wales (NSW) covered the eastern lowlands and the Great Dividing Range, breaking up into its present state and Victoria, Tasmania and Queensland in the 1850s. South Australia was established in 1836 as a social experiment in colonisation at the southern end of the low lying lands west of the Great Dividing Range. It acquired the Northern Territory of the central lowlands up to the Gulf of Carpentaria from the British Government in 1863. Western Australia, first settled in 1827, is based on Perth and extends over the greater part of the Western Plateau. By 1900, each of these states had their own democratic constitutions headed by a governor acting on behalf of the British Crown, a bicameral, elected legislature (except for Queensland) from which a Westminster-style executive was formed and a separate judiciary. This political machinery was carried forward into the political federation of the Commonwealth of Australia in 1901. The present constitution is a federalist system having some North American characteristics. The Commonwealth of Australia, which exercises control over foreign policy, defence, trade and taxation, is formally headed by a Governor General (nominally on behalf of the British Crown) and legislative power is in the hands of the Federal Parliament. This consists of a lower House of Representatives of 147 single member constituencies and an upper Senate representing the rights of the States (12 from each State and 2 from each Territory). The government is formed from members of the legislature on political party lines by choice of Prime Minister and a Cabinet. The Northern Territory came under Commonwealth control in 1911 and received powers similar to the States in 1978. The Australian Capital Territory was created as the seat of the Federal Parliament in 1910. Its positioning between the capital cities of Sydney and Melbourne was a compromise between the representatives of NSW and Victoria, who were at that time the most powerful states. Both of the Territories have their own unicameral legislature (the ACT since 1989). The State and Territories have responsibility for matters residual to those dealt with by the Federal government, including matters of justice not dealt with by the Federal Supreme Court (e.g. education, health and state transport). The political history of both the State and Federal levels of government may be characterised as a battle between a labour party representing the interests of a strongly organised, mainly urbanised union movement and a more conservative party representing rural interests and the views of non-socialists. English is the official language and is used by the overwhelming majority of people. The main religion is Christianity, accounting for about 75 percent of the population. Immigration continues to be an important element in population growth in recent years and immigrants from Asia have begun to represent a significant portion of the settlers in Australia.

In 1993, Australian's GNP was US$299 323 m or US$17 070 per capita. Real growth in the economy is low (typically between zero and 3 percent in recent years). The economy, like that of New Zealand's, is quite dependent upon foreign trade (export and import expenditure are about 20 percent of GDP) and public sector expenditure constitutes about one-third of GDP. Agriculture, which employs approximately 5 percent of the work force and produces only 3 percent of GDP, accounts for about one-third of total exports by value, the most important commodities being wheat, sugar, fruit, beef cattle and sheep products. Similar statistics hold for mining, except that it is more capital intensive, employing only just over 1 percent of the workforce. Manufacturing, which depends predominantly on raw material processing, has declined in recent years to its present contribution to GDP of around 15 percent, and it employs about the same percentage of the workforce. The service sector, as in other developed countries, is the largest contributor to GDP (about two-thirds in 1992). In recent years, Australia has typically recorded a trade surplus, but a current account deficit (US$10 677 in 1992), due mainly to income paid abroad and the purchase of invisibles. Australia has balanced its foreign account by importing capital and increasing the level of foreign debt to US$147 b in 1994, representing about 40 percent of GDP. Inflation, which was moderately high during the 1980s, averaging over 7 percent, is currently among the lowest of the OECD countries (between 2 and 3 percent from 1992–95). This lower inflation rate was achieved at the expense of high interest rates (18 percent in 1989), although these have now fallen to much lower levels. The budget is currently running an anti-recession record deficit of about US$8 b. Reflecting this indifferent performance, the Australian dollar has depreciated significantly since the early 1980's. Australia's chief trading partners are currently Japan, the US and the EU. The need to address the problems of a weak currency, current account deficits and a large level of overseas debt are among the most important economic policy considerations for the present Australian government and it may be that a restructuring of its industries will be necessary to achieve the desired ends. With current high levels of unemployment, this process may be difficult and painful.

R.J.W.

INTRODUCTION

During the last two decades the major professional accounting bodies have unsuccessfully tried to merge their operations and present a unified public face. At the latest attempt there was more than the required support from the members of the Australian Society of Certified Practising Accountants (ASCPA), but the members of The Institute of Chartered Accountants in Australia (ICAA) failed to provide their required level of support. At present, this means there are three major bodies representing accountants, ASCPA, ICAA and another less influential body, the National Institute of Accountants (NIA) which has had a turbulent relationship with the ASCPA in recent years. Difficulties in achieving a unified professional front in Australia have a long history, and possibly reflect something deeper about the nature of vested interest groups in Australia. The next section summarises the history of that conflict and provides the backdrop for a description of the development of financial and management accounting in Australia. Section 3 describes the present regulatory environment, section 4 describes the structure of business financing and section 5 examines the characteristics of Australian financial accounting practices. Section 6 contains an analysis of Australian management accounting practices.

PROFESSIONAL BEGINNINGS

A need for representation coupled to rivalry between the colonies in the 1880s and 1890s, and then interstate tensions throughout the 20th century, were major determinants in the emergence of the numerous associations comprising the Australian accounting profession. Public accountants in South Australia joined forces to establish Australia's earliest professional accounting body, the Adelaide Society of Accountants, comprising 15 accountants in practice who incorporated in 1886 (Graham, 1978). Other accounting groups quickly followed the South Australian initiative. Later that year, the decision was taken to form the Incorporated Institute of Accountants of Victoria (Graham, 1978), followed by the formation of the Queensland Institute of Accountants in 1891, and the Sydney Institute of Public Accountants in May of 1894.

Presaging developments in the 20th century, the decision by the Sydney group of accountants to limit their membership to 'public' accountants provoked a reaction from commercial practice accountants and resulted in the formation of the Corporation of Accountants of Australia in 1899 in Sydney (Gavens, 1985; Graham, 1978). Resentment and a feeling of exclusion led to similar responses Australia-wide, so that by 1910 there were 13 accounting bodies in existence, including the Federal Institute of Accountants which had been incorporated in July of 1894. From 1901–3, a movement emerged to form the Australian Institute of Accountants (AIA). This movement faltered as Poullaos (1993) notes: 'over the rights of accountants not-in-practice and the location of the head office of the proposed institute.' The proliferation of professional bodies at this early stage provided a foreboding for later attempts to unify the accounting profession in the later decades of the 20th century.

Two threads lead from these events to the present day stand-off between the ASCPA and ICAA. The origins of the latter organisation may be traced to a conference in June 1907 which led to the incorporation in 1908 of the Australian Corporation of Public Accountants (ACPA) — a national association of accountants and their clerks. It enabled the integration of a number of existing bodies, including the Sydney Institute of Public Accountants, the Tasmanian Institute of Accountants and the Corporation of Accountants in Australia. The ACPA immediately petitioned for a royal charter in order to incorporate The Institute of Chartered Accountants in Australia. However, the Victorian Institute objected on the grounds that a royal charter should not be awarded to a group made up solely of public accountants and the request was denied. Poullaos (1993) describes how several factors produced a stalemate on this initial ACPA application for a royal charter, and it was not until 1928 that The Institute of Chartered Accountants in Australia was given approval by the respective authorities. The nature and identity of the ICAA has remained intact and relatively stable down to the present time and it is probably now perceived as the more conservative of the two major bodies, with its membership perceived as predominantly reflecting the interests of accountants in practice.

The present day ASCPA has its origins, perhaps significantly, in a Victorian rather than NSW institution. In October 1918, in order to emphasise its national character with activities in every state of Australia, the Victorian Institute changed its name to the Commonwealth Institute of Accountants. Over the next decade, it absorbed many of the smaller state-based bodies, including the South Australian Society of Accountants, Queensland Institute of Accountants, Institute of Accountants and Auditors of Western Australia, Institute of Public Accountants of Australasia, and the Institute of Incorporated Accountants in NSW. Further amalgamations took place with the Federal Institute of Accountants and the Commonwealth Institute of Accountants eventually agreeing in 1952 to form the Australian Society of Accountants. In 1955, the ASA absorbed the Victorian Society of Public Accountants, the International Institute of Accountants and the Corporation of Consulting Accountants. Details of these early accounting bodies appears in Zeff (1973).

The present NIA arose from developments in the education and training requirements of what is now the ASCPA. Prior to the adoption of a graduate entry requirement by the ASA in 1966, most members of its disparate professional bodies had received their training through the technical college system producing 'certificates' and 'diplomas'. The major difference between the two awards arose primarily from the school entry requirements — the New South Wales Intermediate Certificate (or its equivalent in other states) for the former and the NSW Leaving Certificate (or its equivalent) for the latter. The technical college curricula differed only marginally. Prior to this point, its members were unashamedly 'accounting technicians'. Many had taken out a 'diploma' to become qualified for full membership. However, the complete adoption by the ASA of the 1966 graduate entry requirement proposal would have abandoned those studying through the technical colleges, and left the way open for yet another accounting body to be established. Avoiding that outcome, the ASA assisted in the transition of the National Institute of Accountants into the Institute of Affiliate Accountants (IAA). This body catered for a 'second tier' of accounting technicians — which operated under the auspices of the ASA. The IAA was to become an active body in the next two decades. Zeff (1973) provides detailed accounts of these early accounting associations. Tensions, however, emerged between the IAA and the ASA. During the early 1980s the ASA threatened to withdraw all services to the IAA. A bitter struggle ensued, with the IAA eventually winning an injunction against the ASA preventing it or its officers from denigrating the IAA or referring to it or its members as 'technicians', 'technical', 'para-professional' or using related terms. The IAA completed the break from the ASA by reverting to its former name of the National Institute of Accountants. It continued to attract members, and in January 1994, with more than 12 000 members, it is the fastest growing accounting body in Australia. Furthermore, because it now takes in the graduates of the Technical and Further Education division (the former technical colleges) of the education sector and operates Australia-wide, it has considerable support within both state and federal government circles. The sometimes strained relationships between the professional accounting bodies reflects the effect of current political perceptions of the need to balance restrictive practices against the quality of professional training, as well as deeper rivalries and aspects of the Australian psyche. In fact, changes in policy regarding regulatory agencies in Australia over recent years has been such as to overshadow other factors. These affect other changes discussed in the next section.

THE REGULATORY ENVIRONMENT

Corporate financial reporting in Australia is controlled by the federal corporations law under the administration of the Australian Securities Commission. The corporations law sets out minimum reporting requirements and also incorporates Australian Accounting Standards (AAS) when approved by the Australian Accounting Standards Board (AASB). Pierson (1990) and Zeff (1973) describe in detail the various stages antecedent to the current regulatory position. Some brief discussion of those antecedents follows.

Since the formal adoption of federation in Australia in 1901, the corporate regulatory framework has been through a number of phases resulting from various attempts to establish a national regime. Under the Australian constitution, the administration of trade and commerce is a right of individual States. The consolidation of laws governing corporations thus required the agreement of all States and the delegation of their authority to the Federal Government. Given the sensitivity of States' rights in Australia, this was not easy to achieve. The first body to have national responsibility — the National Companies and Securities Commission — was formed in November 1978, with the responsibility of overall policy formulation and administration of the co-operative scheme between the Commonwealth and the States. It relied on the cooperation of States, and its operations proved cumbersome. In January 1991 it was replaced by the Australian Securities Commission, a genuinely national body responsible for the administration of companies in all Australian States and Territories.

Clarke and Dean's (1992) chronology of changes to the corporate regulatory framework in Australia since the 1950s indicates that the regulation of corporations, including Accounting and Auditing Standards, has in large part been a response to corporate failures or other corporate dilemmas. In particular, Table 1 discloses the extent to which the accounting profession has been under attack in recent years because of the perceived failure of company reports to inform investors of the true state of the affairs of companies, especially those that failed without any early warning signals in their accounts, and a perceived failure of the auditing of those companies' accounts.

The current framework for the regulation of accounting in Australia reflects a mix of public and private sector interests. Typically, private sector accounting standards have been prepared since 1966 by the Australian Accounting Research Foundation (AARF), which is supported by the ASCPA and ICAA.[1]

In the early 1980s, the Accounting Standards Review Board (ASRB) was formed in response to the difficulties in ensuring compliance with accounting standards, especially from directors who were not members of either the ICAA or the ASCPA. By 1984, three standards-setting bodies existed — the private sector Accounting Standards Board (AcSB), the Public Sector Accounting Standards Board (PSASB) and the Accounting Standards Review Board (ASRB). This remained so until the merger of the AcSB and the Accounting Standards Review Board in 1991, which produced the Australian Accounting Standards Board (AASB). The AASB now has responsibility for reviewing draft accounting standards and, upon approval, submitting them to Parliament for adoption. Standards now recommended by the AASB for adoption lie on the table of the House of Representatives (the lower House of Federal Parliament) for 14 sitting days. If no objection to the draft standard is raised within that time, it becomes incorporated into the corporations law.

Thus, approved Australian accounting standards have something of the force of law. In principle, the standard setting process is also participatory. However, whereas any individual or body can submit an accounting standard to the AASB, nearly all are prepared by AARF and released for comment before being submitted for formal approval by AASB. Some industry and other bodies with a particular interest in accounting standards have submitted draft standards for consideration — examples include the Australian Shareholders' Association proposed standard on consolidated statement presentation in the mid-1980s (Walker, 1987) and the early 1990s attempt by the representative body for the insurance industry. In the latter case, the insurance industry saw a gap in the reporting requirements of life insurance companies and prepared its own draft standard as the AARF had stated that this matter was not a high priority.

The standard setting process has led some (for example, Walker, 1987; 1993) to claim that the accounting profession has successfully 'captured' the process. Walker (1993) has claimed that the ICAA and ASCPA were particularly active in promoting a structure that would give accounting standards the force of law similar to the position

---

[1]In 1966, AARF was formed in response to recommendations contained in the ASA's report 'Accounting Principles and Practices Discussed in Reports on Company Failures' (General Council, ASA).

Table 1
ATTACKS ON THE ACCOUNTING PROFESSION

Date	Issue	Journal/Paper
29/4/89	'Auditors are being called to account'	*The Sydney Morning Herald (SMH)*
29/5/89	'The accounts are a joke'	*SMH*
2/6/89	'Creative accounting, ten legal ways to cook your books'	*Business Review Weekly (BRW)*
24/1/90	'Closing accounting loopholes would create a level playing field'	*Australian Business*
2/3/90	'Liquidator sues Ernst & Young for $175 million'	*The Australian Financial Review (AFR)*
5/7/90	'A much-needed warning for auditors'	*AFR*
7/9/90	'Profession faces its toughest test'	*BRW*
12/9/90	'Audit served no useful purpose'	*Australian Business*
23/9/90	'Accountants come under fire'	*The Sun-Herald*
11/1/91	'What makes an audit true and fair?'	*BRW*
18/1/91	'Why so many audits have been failing'	*BRW*
12/4/91	'Auditors saw 80s almost as an unqualified success'	*AFR*
11/6/91	'Auditors must share some of the blame – Bosch'	*AFR*
19/9/91	'Call for creation of board to "audit company audits"'	*AFR*
9/10/91	'Crashes lead to question on precision of auditing'	*SMH*
9/10/91	'Death to historic value accounting'	*Australian Business*
10/10/91	'Auditors need teeth'	*AFR*
10/1/92	'Auditors find themselves in hottest hot seat of all'	*AFR*
18/2/92	'Auditors slam critics, reject blame for 80s'	*AFR*
27/5/92	'Auditors v 1980s' excesses'	*AFR*

Source: Clarke and Dean (1992), 'Chaos in the Counting – House: Accounting Under Scrutiny', *Australian Journal of Corporate Law*, Vol. 2, No. 2, 1992, pp. 177–201.

that had existed in Canada since the early 1970s. Prior to obtaining the force of law, Australian accounting standards were only enforceable against members of the professional bodies. This meant that company directors could have the annual accounts depart from the accounting standards if they believed that doing so would result in the accounts providing 'a true and fair view'. This led to some curious anomalies, as directors could approve an annual report but auditors would subsequently have to qualify their report because the accounts did not conform with the profession's accounting standard. Furthermore, some directors who were members of one of the professional accounting bodies were placed in an impossible position of having either to vote against the adoption of a set of accounts because they did not conform

with the profession's standards or vote with their fellow directors and risk disciplinary action from their professional body.

A fundamental shift in policy in relation to corporate financial reporting occurred
in 1991. As noted, in common with the British law which Australia inherited, there
was until then an overriding first order imperative that accounts present a 'true and
fair view' of the state of affairs and results of the entity to which they referred. Following the corporate collapses of the late 1980s, and a perception that the true and fair
view override had been abused, there was considerable agitation to have the law
changed. In December 1991 a new requirement was introduced to the corporations
law. Accounts included in the annual report of companies from that date must conform with approved accounting standards and if directors believe that doing so will
lead to the accounts *not* presenting 'a true and fair view', they must state why in the
notes to the accounts. The 'true and fair view' override has been demoted to a second order imperative. Clarke and Dean (1992) canvass the arguments related to that
change.

As of 1 April 1994 there were 30 accounting standards in operation in Australia
(see Table 2). There also are 'Statements of accounting concepts' purporting to provide a 'conceptual framework' for the Standards. However, some of those concept
statements have been controversial, so much so that one (SAC 4, *Definition and
Recognition of the Elements of Financial Statements*) was withdrawn in late 1993. It
was reintroduced in 1995, this time on a *voluntary* basis. In 1994 the accounting
profession decided to codify the concept statements and standards into a set of generally accepted accounting principles (GAAP).

The introduction of fixed formats for the profit and loss account and the balance
sheet in the mid-1980s represented another important change to the system of corporate financial reporting. These formats are part of the prescribed account requirements contained in the regulations. These developments were accompanied by the
differential reporting requirements for categories of companies based on size and
public involvement — i.e. whether a company is an exempt proprietary, non-exempt
proprietary, public company, borrowing company or listed company.

Australian Accounting Standards generally conform with International Accounting Standards, with any minor discrepancies being noted in the Australian Standards.
This policy reflects the Australian accounting profession's strong support of the International Accounting Standards Committee (IASC).

Litigation, liability cap and incorporation

In common with their colleagues in other countries, Australian accountants in public
practice have been subject to large claims for damages following a spate of corporate
failures and related dilemmas — see Table 3 for a list of major claims extant September
1992. Australia is now *second* in the world in the-litigation-against-auditors' stakes,

Table 2
AUSTRALIAN ACCOUNTING STANDARDS

		Page Nos.
AAS1 - *DS1.2/301*	Profit and Loss or other Operating Statements	1003–8.10
AAS2 - *DS2/307*	Measurement and Presentation of Inventories in the Context of the Historical Cost System	1009–20.2
AAS3 - *DS4/306*	Accounting for Income Tax (Tax-effect Accounting)	1021–32.4
AAS4 - *DS5/302*	Depreciation of Non-Current Assets	1033–44.2
AAS5 - *DS7/305*	Materiality in Financial Statements	1045–48.2
AAS6 - *DS11/304*	Accounting Policies: Determination, Application and Disclosure	1049–54.2
AAS7 - *DS12/308*	Accounting for the Extractive Industries	1055–68.2
AAS8 - *DS13/310*	Events Occurring After Balance Date	1069–72.2
AAS9 - *DS10/303*	Expenditure Carried Forward to Subsequent Accounting Periods	1073–78
AAS10 -	Accounting for the Revaluation of Non-Current Assets	1079–88.12
AAS11 -	Accounting for Construction Contracts	1089–100.2
AAS12 - *(Withdrawn)*	Statement of Sources and Applications of Funds	1101–02
AAS13 -	Accounting for Research and Development Costs	1111–20
AAS14 -	Equity method of Accounting	1121–38
AAS15 -	Disclosure of Operating Revenue	1139–42
AAS16 -	Financial Reporting by Segments	1143–54.2
AAS17 -	Accounting for Leases	1155–90.4
AAS18 -	Accounting for Goodwill	1191–202
AAS19 -	Accounting for Interests in Joint Ventures	1203–210
AAS20 -	Foreign Currency Translation (Part A)	1211–48
AAS20 - *(Withdrawn)*	Foreign Currency Translation (Part B)	1248.1–.2
AAS21 -	Accounting for the Acquisition of Assets (including Business Entities)	1249–56
AAS22 -	Related Party Disclosures	1257–70.18
AAS23 -	Set-off and Extinguishment of Debt	1271–84
AAS24 -	Consolidated Financial Reports	1285–326
AAS25 -	Financial Reporting by Superannuation Plans	1331–88
AAS26 -	Financial Reporting of General Insurance Activities	1391–432
AAS27 -	Financial Reporting by Local Governments	1433–80.6
AAS28 -	Statement of Cash Flows	1481–504
AAS29 -	Financial Reporting by Government Departments	1505–83
AAS30 -	Accounting for Employee Entitlements	1585–613

Source: ASCPA Handbook Vol. 1, 1994

after the United States. Interestingly, the largest of those claims relating to the Tricontinental failure — against KPMG Peat Marwick for A$1.094 billion, was settled out-of-court in January 1994 for $136 million.[2] Settlements appear to be determined by the extent of practitioners' indemnity cover. Not surprisingly, professional indemnity insurance has become prohibitive (reportedly at $70,000 per partner), and public accountants, like their colleagues in other countries, are seeking ways of protecting themselves from the spiralling number and value of claims against them. These options include having a limit placed on the maximum damages to be paid out, allowing accounting firms to be incorporated, and allowing accounting firms to operate as limited liability partnerships.

One problem complicating the indemnity issue and the regulation of the profession is that the designation 'accountant' is not protected in Australia. At various times, other related terms have been protected — 'public accountant', 'chartered accountant', 'registered public accountant', 'tax agent', 'liquidator and receiver'. But the government has stated on a number of occasions that the designation 'accountant' is generic, not indicative of any particular professional status. It is a major reason cited

Table 3
CLAIMS AGAINST AUSTRALIAN ACCOUNTING FIRMS

Plaintiffs	Defendants	Damages $m
Duke Group	Ernst & Young, KPMG Peat Marwick & Ors	175
Farrow Group	Coopers and Lybrand/Ken Russell	na
Rothwells	KPMG Peat Marwick	40
National Safety Council	Horwath and Horwath	263
Estate Mortgage unit holders	Priestley and Morris & Ors	550
Battery Group	Deloitte Ross Tohmatsu	132
AWA	Deloitte Ross Tohmatsu	50
Titan Hills	Coopers and Lybrand & Ors	17
State Bank of Victoria	Day Neilson Jenkins & John & Ors	900
Spedley Securities	Priestley and Morris & Ors	750
Tricontinental	KPMG Peat Marwick	1094
Independent Resources	Deloitte Ross Tohmatsu	na
White Constructions	Coopers and Lybrand	na
Westmex	Thomson Douglas	na

Source: 'Clients — and liquidators of clients — sue firms for damages totalling $2 billion plus' *Chartac,* September 1991; and miscellaneous newspaper articles (as appeared in Clarke and Dean, 1992)

---

[2]In July 1994, the amount of the Tricontinental claim was surpassed by the $3.1 billion negligence claim lodged by the South Australian State Government in the Supreme Court. It alleges that KPMG failed in its statutory duties as auditor of the State Bank of South Australia.

for various governments' refusal, on many occasions, to place a cap on the liability of 'accountants' or to allow them limited liability in the exercise of their professional duties.

Such proposals have an approximately 70-odd year history.[3] The matter remains under parliamentary review — perhaps even given new life by the change of Federal Government in early 1996. A separate document (*Professional Liability in Relation to Corporations Law Matters*), prepared in June 1993 (updated in March 1996) by the Working Party of the Ministerial Council for Corporations, canvassed the professional bodies' alternative mechanisms to statutory capping, *inter alia*: combining self-regulation and auditor rotation, placing a limit on the useful life of financial accounts, permitting accountants to incorporate with consequential limited liability and, permitting companies to pay directors' indemnity premiums so as to split the claims on auditors by having directors well insured too.[4] Whilst 1990s NSW and WA legislation supposedly restricts liability, accounting firms are not satisfied as the Federal Trade Practices Legislation is perceived still — due to several claims against auditors during the mid-1990s — to provide users of accounts with the opportunity to seek damages of an unlimited amount.

Table 4
AUSTRALIAN COMPANIES REGISTERED AS OF 30 JUNE 1995

	Number	Percentage
Limited by Shares		
Public	7712	0.826
Proprietary	915437	98.049
Sub Total	923149	98.875
Limited by Guarantee	8557	0.917
Limited by Shares and Guarantee	401	0.043
No Liability	939	0.100
Unlimited	606	0.065
Total	933652	100

Source: Australian Securities Commission, Annual Report, 1995 and ASC officers.

---

[3]C. Napier "The antecedents of unlimited liability in the United Kingdom: a study of corporate governance", paper 19th EAA Congress, Berger May 1996.

[4]These and other proposals are listed in Working Party of the Ministerial Council for Corporations, *Professional Liability in Relation to Corporations Law Matters*, June 1993, especially pp. 10–35.

FINANCING STRUCTURE

Companies operating in Australia are relatively small. Table 4 shows that the majority of companies are private companies. The majority of those proprietary companies employ fewer than 50 employees.

Comparable with many Western developed countries, Australian companies rely extensively on internal sources of finance. Table 5 highlights the trend in the ratio of shareholders' funds to total funds since 1984; it indicates that on 'average', across all manufacturing industries there has been a nearly equal proportion of companies'

Table 5
DEBT TO EQUITY RATIOS 1984, 1987, 1989–92

	1992 (%)	1991 (%)	1990 (%)	1989 (%)	1987 (%)	1984 (%)
Gold	57.10	49.31	41.22	49.42	20.78	18.42
Other Metals	43.05	37.53	35.64	38.42	85.28	78.78
Solid Fuels	54.87	48.65	34.75	54.43	66.14	58.76
Oil & Gas	77.01	71.84	83.39	94.27	144.00	147.97
Diversified Resources	112.20	123.71	104.44	115.98	65.21	29.42
Developers & Contractors	67.88	59.49	59.66	68.67	80.41	84.03
Building Materials	56.19	65.98	83.54	58.25	59.20	47.97
Alcohol & Tobacco	301.90	106.55	118.03	74.53	57.34	33.84
Food & Household	79.57	76.35	91.82	91.48	59.47	30.39
Chemicals	35.21	42.33	60.15	52.63	43.72	50.83
Engineering	63.31	67.49	61.04	54.94	42.81	42.54
Paper & Packaging	178.78	180.89	145.04	131.29	59.56	61.71
Retail	202.78	104.87	67.60	69.82	44.03	37.22
Transport	92.42	143.20	122.93	134.10	105.27	100.55
Media	116.06	153.05	149.31	165.08	139.13	53.12
Banks & Finance	1183.41	1070.03	1230.77	1097.78	1141.98	1237.78
Insurance	65.58	69.15	86.30	106.80	260.93	62.78
Entrepreneurial Investors	318.33	151.89	84.95	85.23	139.22	145.21
Investment & Financial Serv.	52.88	53.44	47.09	33.20	102.46	62.26
Property Trusts	9.73	6.84	5.70	6.09	11.65	6.68
Miscellaneous Services	56.62	60.28	57.12	68.37	35.50	51.92
Miscellaneous Industrials	48.08	47.01	38.16	32.62	58.55	48.81
Diversified Industrials	87.80	77.86	86.13	89.20	66.01	51.00
Resources Average	68.30	65.08	61.20	68.19		
Resources Median	17.68	9.94	7.71	6.89		
Industrials Average*	109.09	100.18	92.50	86.05		
Industrials Median*	37.59	38.40	47.67	46.84		
All Company Sample – Average*	94.49	87.66	81.58	80.14	81.35	55.3
All Company Sample – Median*	29.33	29.82	30.28	30.19	43.08	32.81

*Banks & finance, Insurance and Property Trusts have been excluded.
Source: Stock Exchange and Financial Profitability Study, 1988, 1990 and 1993.

operations financed by debt and shareholders' funds. Table 5 also shows substantial variation across industries and over time. For example, finance companies have as their primary function the borrowing of funds in order to lend, resulting traditionally in a debt-to-equity ratio between 7-to-8:1. Evidence suggests that firms in wholesale, retailing, service industries and conglomerates generally do have higher leverage than mining and manufacturing firms (see Lowe and Shuetrim, 1992; Shuetrim, Lowe and Morling, 1993). Companies in the capital goods industries whose fortunes are closely tied to movements in the trade cycle are more likely to be conservatively financed.

Evidence suggests that size and the increase in real asset prices in the 1980s were the two major explanatory variables related to the increase in corporate leverage in the 1980s (see Lowe and Shuetrim, 1992). This was especially so around post-1983/4 deregulation of the financial sector, when the conjunction of unrestrained credit and real asset price increases stimulated recourse to debt financing across all industries, as well as increases in the size of entities' asset portfolios. Other significant variables were increased competition following the 1983–4 deregulation of the finance sector; increased corporate profitability; a tendency for bankers to move away from cautious lending practices and, some claim, a belief on the part of many investors that asset prices would never turn down. However, following the stock market crash in October 1987, corporate leverage has returned to its pre-1980 levels. This is not immediately visible in the data in Table 5 as the equity component of the debt/ equity ratio has been reduced by the major asset write downs of companies in the 1990s.

Debt financing of Australian companies relied almost exclusively on bank sources prior to the 1960s. In the late 1950s and throughout the 1960s and 1970s, there was a switch to non-bank, primarily debenture, finance. The upsurge in debt financing in the 1980s presaged a return to the banking sector as the major finance source. Since October 1987, there has been a switch back to equity capital raising as firms attempt to pare their debt levels. As the cycle changes in the mid-to-late 1990s one would expect to see debt levels rise again.

With the concomitant reckless actions of many market participants, the 1980s highlighted the inextricable link between accounting, finance and management. It demonstrated the important role of accounting in providing verifiable information, thereby acting as a check on the ability of the directors of companies to raise funds recklessly.

STRUCTURE AND CHARACTERISTICS OF AUSTRALIAN FINANCIAL ACCOUNTING

Under the corporations law, Australian companies are required to prepare accounts which entail a profit and loss account and balance sheet, notes to the accounts and a directors' statement. Also AASB 1026 requires companies to prepare a statement of cash flows.

Drawing upon Anglo-American practices, Australian accounting is predominantly historical-cost based. Yet, increasingly there are requirements in accounting standards to include market price information in the accounts. As in the UK, periodic revaluation of long-life physical assets is permitted (AAS 1010, *Accounting for the Revaluation of Non-Current Assets*) within the general rubric that recoverable amount is the upper limit of valuations, increments are transferred to reserves and further depreciation is charged to the income account.

In effect, the non-current asset valuation rule is perceived to be a back-door mechanism for implementing replacement price valuations — replacement price being a surrogate for the net present value of the anticipated income streams recoverable from using the asset. That creates a dilemma for reporting the present state of the financial position of an entity. Conventional price theory suggests that the prevailing purchase (replacement) price for a fixed asset would ordinarily be less than the price for which one of a similar kind and in a similar condition currently held by the would-be purchaser could be sold. Vehement opposition exists in the Australian accounting profession to the marking-to-market of non-current assets. Overstatement of the money's worth of assets is the avowed fear. Yet the AAS 1010 rule almost ensures that the non-current assets possessed by Australian companies are stated in balance sheets at higher amounts than would result if approximate selling prices were used.

The introduction of AAS 1010 led to some major fixed assets write-downs and some curious anomalies.[5] It requires all upward revaluations to be taken to reserves, while write-downs are taken to retained profits. In the case of at least one company, the Colonial Sugar Refining Ltd (CSR), this led to 'book-keeping gymnastics' as the write-downs led to negative retained profits making it impossible for the directors to declare a dividend. Shareholders subsequently approved a transfer from Share Premium Reserve to Retained Profits to allow a dividend to be paid, thereby defeating the apparent intent of AAS 1010 (Clarke and Dean, 1992).

Mark-to-market accounting

In contrast, marking-to-market — revaluation to approximate selling prices — is required when the net realisable value of short-term inventories is less than the price

---

[5]Other limitations were noted by the authors of the surveys — sample size, non-response bias — whilst the problem of to whom had the questionnaire been addressed was raised by R.C. Skinner, 'Cost and Management Accounting Practices', Australian Accounting Review, November 1993, pp. 31–33.

for which they were purchased. Interestingly, the original 'lower of cost, net realisable value and replacement price' inventory rule was modified by the dropping of the recourse to replacement price on the grounds that the latter was irrelevant. This is a strange case of a method being deemed relevant for one class of asset (non-current) and irrelevant for another (inventory).

Whereas no explicit prescription requires non-current assets to be stated at their current market prices, there is a move in the Australian standards to require financial assets be reported at their current selling prices. Prescriptions, however, are not consistent. AASB 23 (*Financial Reporting by General Insurance Companies*), for example, requires investments that are integral to general insurance activities to be '. . . measured at net market values as at balance date.' The definitions of AASB 23 (para. 7) are quite explicit that net market value means net selling price '. . . the amount . . . expected to be received from the disposal of an asset in an orderly market after deducting costs'. Investments are stated to include 'Land and Buildings' (Para. 24). In contrast, 'assets other than investments' integral to the general insurance business '. . . shall be measured at the lower of cost and recoverable amount' pursuant to the prescription for asset valuation contained in AASB 1010. Moreover, acquisition costs relating thereto, may be capitalised and amortised '. . . over the financial years expected to benefit from the acquisition costs'.

AAS 25 (*Accounting for Superannuation Plans*) pursues a similar accounting method. The net market values of the assets, the changes therein, and the methods used to determine the net market values of each class of assets are to be reported in a statement of financial position relating to a 'defined contribution plan' (paras. 42–62). ED 59 (*Financial Instruments*) also presents Australian accountants with a clear direction to mark-to-market. In this case, it applies to 'Financial assets and financial liabilities arising from investment or financing instruments'. It requires such assets and liabilities to be marked to 'net market value' and the variations between reporting periods therein to be reported as 'revenues and expenses as they occur' (Preface — Measurement). What is apparent from the Australian experience in the 1980s and early 1990s is the willingness to mark-to-market assets for which market prices appear comparatively easy to obtain. For a long time, disclosure of the market price of listed securities has been required under company law disclosure prescriptions. Nonetheless, progress in moving towards a complete market-based system is slow and the anomalies would seem to compel change. Yet some of the Big Six accounting firms are concerned that even this slow progress to mark-to-market is too rapid.

Consolidation accounting

Particular attention has been given in Australian accounting to consolidation practices. Unlike practices in many countries, in Australia the income statement and balance sheets of every entity (incorporated and unincorporated) over which a company (the parent) has significant 'control', are to be consolidated. The generally employed practices of consolidation are employed on the basis of the conventional assumptions: that the parent and the entities it controls comprise an economic group; that the financial effect of the intra-group transactions entered into subsequent to control being achieved 'cancel' each other; that the profits and losses resulting from intra-group transactions are to be eliminated to determine consolidated profits and losses and to record physical asset values at the 'cost to the group'; that intra-group payments of interest and dividends are to be eliminated in determining group results and the financial position of the group; that the consolidated financial statements be prepared employing the Australian accounting standards.

Within the consolidation framework, results achieved by companies, over which a corporation has a significant influence (by virtue of a shareholding expected to be between 20 percent and 50 percent of the voting shares, or by virtue of the level of its representative membership being able to influence the Board of Directors), are to be equity accounted for in a supplementary statement to the consolidated statements. Most companies applying equity accounting do so by including (adding or subtracting) their share of the associated companies' results in a supplementary column to the profit and loss account and balance sheet. The confusing outcomes of the product of consolidation accounting are discussed in Clarke and Dean (1993).

Accounting for goodwill

Accounting for '. . . the future benefits from unidentifiable assets' (AASB 1013, para. 10), varies in Australia according to the origin of the item. Under AASB 1013 'Internally generated goodwill' cannot be raised in the accounts. In contrast, 'purchased goodwill' — the excess of the fair value of assets acquired over their cost — may be brought to account and amortised over the expected period of the perceived benefit, but not exceeding 20 years. 'Fair value' is defined to mean the '. . . amount for which an asset could be exchanged between a knowledgeable, willing buyer and a knowledgable, willing seller in an arm's length transaction', (AASB 1013, para. 10). Accordingly, profit smoothing (profit increasing and profit decreasing) policies can be implemented by manipulating the amortisation period. Most Australian companies capitalise purchased goodwill in compliance with the Standard and extend the amortisation over the prescribed maximum period (Ryan, *et al.*, 1993).

Accounting for extraordinary and abnormal items

Profit and loss arising from transactions perceived to be unusual are to be reported separately, by way of note or otherwise, in the profit and loss account. No explicit disclosure is required of the amounts of items which relate to previous years, but the mechanism prescribed under AASB 1018 imposes implicit recognition through the accounting for 'abnormal items' and for 'extraordinary items'. AASB 1018 prescribes disclosure of the nature and amounts, before and after tax of abnormal items ' . . . items of revenue and expense included in the operating profit and loss after tax for the financial year, which are considered abnormal by reason of their size and effect on the operating profit' (AASB 1018, para. 9), and of extraordinary items '. . . items of revenue and expense which are attributable to transactions or other events of a type outside the ordinary operations of the company . . .' (AASB 1018, para. 9). In respect of each, where the items relate to other financial years than the one being reported on, those years must be identified. But no explicit requirement exists for the related amounts to be disclosed, though it might be presumed the intention is that it should be. How the disclosures are to be made is unspecified. Accordingly, wide variations exist in disclosure methods (Ryan *et al.*, 1993).

MANAGEMENT ACCOUNTING IN AUSTRALIA

There are no mandatory or advisory standards on management accounting in Australia. The primary influence of the professional bodies on the practice of management accounting is through accreditation requirements. These requirements influence what is taught by academic accounting departments and specify subjects students must study to gain admission to the relevant professional accounting bodies.

As management accounting is not regulated, we are forced to rely for the present task of describing management accounting upon descriptions of diverse, discretionary practices. Unfortunately, there is a paucity of large-sample, empirical research in this field in Australia. Accordingly, the commentary that follows is based upon the only two published, post-1979 studies of this *genre*: Joye and Blayney (1990 — *Survey 1*) and Dean, Joye, and Blayney (1991 — *Survey 2*).

Scope of surveys

Data gathered in the two surveys give some insight into management accounting practices in Australia. The surveys had the same sample population: all manufacturing firms in Australia with 1989 sales of A$7 million or more. Sample representativeness is affected by the exclusion of 'non-manufacturing' enterprises and manufacturing firms with less than A$7 m sales. Around half the management accountants in industry and commerce work in non-manufacturing industries and many management

Table 6
SUMMARY CHARACTERISTICS OF AUSTRALIAN MANUFACTURING FIRMS:
FROM TWO COMPREHENSIVE AUSTRALIAN MANAGEMENT ACCOUNTING
SURVEYS

Attribute	Key Findings
1. Firm Size – No. of employees	1.1 40% of the 2000 largest Australian manufacturers have fewer than 100 employees (72% fewer than 250 employees — Survey 2).
2. Diversification, Market Conditions, and Ownership	2.1 Most firms have a single product or product line which is the sole or dominant activity (Survey 1: 78%, Survey 2: 67%). 2.2 Most firms have a market that is **not** characterised by small firms and absence of market leaders (Survey 2). 2.3 54% of responding firms are price makers for **some** lines (21% for **most** lines (Survey 2)). 2.4 The number of products is stable for 74% of firms (Survey 1). 2.5 More firms are in mature industries (58%) than in growth industries (28% — Survey 2). 2.6 76% of firms are wholly-owned or controlled by one shareholder (Survey 2). 2.7 Most firms are unlisted (91% — Survey 1).
3. Organisational Sturcture	3.1 Many firms predominantly or exclusively use cost centres (57% — Survey 2) . Fewer firms predominantly or exclusively use profit centres or investment centres (23% — Survey 2). Few firms use investment centres (4% — Survey 1). 3.2 Most firms (80%) are exclusively or 'essentially' organised on a functional basis. By comparison, 23% exclusively or 'essentially' use the geographic or product related organisational forms (Survey 2).
4. Cost Structure	4.1 The average reported proportions of total manufacturing costs are materials 60%, overhead 23%, direct labour 17% (Survey 1 — similar results for Survey 2). 4.2 Few firms are expecting substantial future increases in the ratio of overhead to total manufacturing costs (Survey 1: 7% — similar results for Survey 2).

Source: Joye, M.P. and Blayney, P.J., *Cost and Management Accounting Practices in Australian Manufacturing Companies: Survey Results*, Monograph 7, Sydney: The Accounting and Finance Foundation within The University of Sydney, 1990; and Dean, G.W., Joye, M.P. and Blayney, P.J., *Strategic Management Accounting Survey: Overhead Cost Allocation and Performance Evaluation Practices of Australian Manufacturers*, Monograph 8, Sydney: The Accounting and Finance Foundation within The University of Sydney, 1991.
Note: all data relate to *responding* firms only unless otherwise specified; source specified in text.

accountants work in 'small' firms.[6] A difference between size of firms sampled in the two surveys and the overall employer size-distribution of Australian management accounting employment arises by virtue of the under-representation of firms with fewer than 50 employees. Twenty-five percent of management accountants in industry and commerce work in such firms, but only around 10 percent of responses to either survey were from firms of this size.[7]

Characteristics of respondents

Characteristics of firms surveyed in the two studies are set out in Table 6. For the most part, the firms surveyed are small, non-diversified, sell into highly concentrated product markets and have highly concentrated ownership. They make negligible use of the investment centre organisational structure. Generally, material costs constitute more than 50 percent of manufacturing costs.

Implications from firm characteristics

The majority of accountants assisting in the financial control of enterprises do so in comparatively small, simply-structured firms. Implications can be drawn from the data on market conditions. First, the role of costs in price setting is important as market concentration is high and price setting activity is prevalent. This role may be accentuated by the number of firms in mature industries, as these firms perhaps have less incentive for short-term sub-optimisation in pricing than firms in growth industries. Second, product proliferation is 'not' an 'increasing' problem. It is also apparent that researchers should control for the effect of ownership type on accounting system design choice. Given high levels of ownership concentration, the effects of endogenous factors may be confounded by 'group' specification of accounting practices (viewing ownership as an exogenous factor for these purposes).

In respect of costs, the importance of the control of materials costs is apparent as is the lesser incidence of direct labour than overhead. Most firms are expecting propor-

---

[6]Of the 55 497 ASCPA members for whom records of primary job function (PJF) and field of employment are held, 14 045 (25 percent) cite Management Accounting as their PJF. Of these, 10 282 (73 percent) work in Industry and Commerce. Fifty-three percent of their (the 10 282's) industry involvements were in non-manufacturing industries. (Source: all data on accounting employment in this paragraph are derived from the ASCPA's unpublished membership database, *circa* September, 1993).

[7]Other limitations were noted by the authors of the surveys — sample size, non-response bias — whilst the problem of to whom had the questionnaire been addressed was raised by R.C. Skinner, 'Cost and Management Accounting Practices', *Australian Accounting Review*, November 1993, pp. 31–3.

tionate spending on overheads to remain steady or to decrease. It might be argued that this non-proliferation cautions against overemphasising the importance of directing research and educational efforts upon overhead control. Alternatively, the data might reflect the scope for rationalising overheads and, therefore, the need to prepare accountants for this task.

Management accounting practices

Responses to survey questions on accounting practices are set out in Table 7.

Budgets: In a number of respects, budgetary accounting practices may not accord with the conventional wisdom of management accounting. Flexible budgets are used by only a minority of firms. Some cross-sectional differences in the use of flexible budgets (see *Survey 1,* Table 8) might indicate alternative forms of accountability for performance and/or conditions under which flexible budgeting is less valuable. The rate of flexible budgets use (overall, 29 percent) was noticeably less among de-centralised firms using profit centres (16 percent), firms structured by product or area (21 percent) and firms with diversified business lines (22 percent); decentralisation (profit centres, product-geographic divisionalisation) might contribute to use of 'global' rather than of 'micro-level' performance measures.

This rate of use of flexible budgets is less than that found by overseas researchers. Often, however, those researchers were sceptical whether 'true' flexible budget variances are calculated using sufficiently accurate estimates of fixed and variable cost components (for instance, Imhoff, 1978; Coates *et al.,* 1983; Cress and Pettijohn, 1985).

It is also notable that most firms here (69 percent) use budget variances in performance evaluation. It seems, despite text book disapproval, that *master* budget variances are often employed in performance assessment. This is rational behaviour if, due to the unreliability of fixed-variable cost estimates, subjective assessments of what costs *should have been* produce fairer evaluations of managerial performance. Moreover, it appears that budget variances of any kind are regarded as unimportant elements of reward systems: most respondents assess budgets as having little role in managerial compensation.

It is evident that, in Australia, budgets have only a minor role in decision decentralisation: departures from budgeted by-line-item expenditures and capital expenditure decisions are controlled centrally.

Goal Setting and Performance Evaluation: Other than in respect of budgets, there are few surprises in the results pertaining to goal setting and performance evaluation. But it is questionable whether inferences can be drawn from these descriptive statistics about what *should* be practised or *should* be taught: usage rates are usually neither sufficiently high nor sufficiently low to be conclusive on such issues.

Table 7

ACCOUNTING PRACTICES: FROM TWO COMPREHENSIVE
AUSTRALIAN MANAGEMENT ACCOUNTING SURVEYS

Attribute	Key Findings
1. Budgets	1.1 29% of firms use flexible budgets (Survey 1).
	1.2 In 18% of firms, line managers have discretion to substitute one budgetary item for another (Survey 1).
	1.3 In 80% of firms, capital expenditure proposals are decided by the CEO (Survey 1).
	1.4 Most firms (52%) do not give bonuses to line managers. 19% of firms have bonuses exceeding 10% of annual salary (Survey 1).
	1.5 Two-thirds of firms see budgets as not having an essential or important role in either managerial compensation or decision decentralisation. More than 80% see budgets as important in each of cost containment, objective setting, and forecasting (Survey 1).
2. Goal Setting and Performance Evaluation	2.1 Three performance indicators (PIs) are 'always used' by 50% or more of firms: sales (76%), budget variances (70%), and quality (defect rates, etc — 50%). (Survey 1).
	2.2 In assessing divisional managers, financial PIs are preferred to non-financial PIs. Most accounting PIs (except sales) are not assessed weekly or daily. (Survey 2).
	2.3 48% of firms do not use pre-defined measures for managerial performance evaluation (Survey 2).
	2.4 Non-comparative performance measures are 'exclusively' or 'predominantly' used by more firms (65%) than are relative measures (10%). (Survey 2).
	2.5 65% of firms are very or reasonably satisfied with their performance evaluation practices (Survey 2).
	2.6 Three factors were frequently cited as obstacles to desired changes: implementation cost (60%), tradition (54%), and management's emphasis on short-term results (46%). (Survey 2).
	2.7 The three most favoured changes to evaluation methods emphasise productivity measures (60%), link measurement and rewards (57%), and emphasise responsibility accounting (55%). The three most widely cited obstacles to change are implementation costs (60%), tradition (54%), and emphasis upon short-term results (46%). 27% of firms rate conceptual difficulty of identifying controllable factors as an obstacle to change.
3. Overhead Allocation	3.1 60% of firms use plant-wide overhead allocation rates or rates for **groups** of work centres. Direct labour is the most common allocation base (54%). Non-volume drivers are little used (Survey 1).
	3.2 Many firms cite pricing (80%) and cost control (73%) as 'major' reasons for cost allocation (Survey 1).

Table 7 (continued)
ACCOUNTING PRACTICES: FROM TWO COMPREHENSIVE
AUSTRALIAN MANAGEMENT ACCOUNTING SURVEYS

	3.3 Product addition/deletion (24%) and managerial evaluations (12%) are rarely cited as 'major' reasons for cost allocation (Survey 1).
	3.4 For over 70% of firms service department cost allocations are important (i) for cost awareness and (ii) because such costs would still be incurred if not centrally provided (Survey 2).
	3.5 Normal (30%) and standard costing (59%) are widely used (Survey 1).
	3.6 Both surveys found that around 12% of firms thought their cost allocation systems needed 'major improvements'.
	3.7 In both surveys, implementation costs (More than 70%) and difficulties in determining causal factors (approximately 50%) were cited as impediments to improving costs allocation.
	3.8 ABC is widely seen (51%) as likely to improve management information. More firms believe 'Strategic Cost Accounting' and 'Product Life Cycle Costing' would **not improve** management information (approximately 42%) than believe they would improve it (23% and 30%, respectively). (Survey 2).
4. Cost Behaviour and Transfer Pricing	4.1 70% of firms classify production labour as variable (Survey 1).
	4.2 Transfer pricing is used by 47% of firms and cost-based methods predominate; market prices and negotiated prices are used by 18% and 15%, respectively, of firms (Survey 1).

Unsurprisingly, sales, budget variances, and measures of quality are widely used and cash flow indices were used more in 'small' than in 'large' firms — presumably a consequence of under-capitalisation in small enterprises. Also, financial rather than non-financial indicators are preferred in assessing *divisional* managers; this might be due to advantages for large firms of aggregated, divisional performance indicators (such as return on investment). More emphasis on various *non*-financial performance indicators is, however, the most widely desired change in performance practices; such a change is likely to apply mainly at the *plant* level (see *Survey 2*, Qs 28 & 29 results).

One result which might surprise some, is the minimal use of pre-specified measures of managerial performance. This is further evidence of practitioners' tolerance for subjective approaches to performance assessment — as is the finding that most respondents were very or reasonably satisfied with their evaluation practices. Conversely, more objective performance assessment systems are desired by about half the firms surveyed, and only a minority rate the separation of controllable and non-controllable factors as an obstacle to change. Note too that answers to such questions can be affected by the work role of the staff member answering the questionnaire (divisional managers may have different attitudes to accountants — see Skinner, 1993). Nevertheless, there are mixed signals on desirable performance assessment practices, and this issue remains contentious.

Cost Allocation: With few exceptions, responses on cost allocation do not provide insight into the merits of elements of the classical debate over their value. Highly aggregated cost allocations are the norm, as are traditional volume-related allocation bases. Encouragingly, 8 percent of firms are using Activity Based Costing (see *Survey 2*, Q. 21 results). Judging by the reluctance to use allocated costs for product line decisions and performance assessment, firms seem to be aware of the limitations of allocated costs. What is interesting, therefore, is that most respondents are satisfied with their costing systems. Perhaps this is a case of accepting the possible, given considerable theoretical and practical obstacles to improvement.

As usual, pricing and cost control were prominent stated reasons for cost allocation; presumably because for many decisions there is *some* correspondence between avoidable costs and costs allocated to cost objects. Also, it would appear that non-manufacturing costs are factored into pricing decisions. But allocations do not solely determine prices: for over 50 percent of respondents in *Survey 2*, consumers and competitors are 'primary' factors in pricing deliberations. Often cost allocations are perceived as irrelevant for product addition/deletion (39 percent) and management evaluation (56 percent). Perhaps this is linked to the large number of respondents citing difficulties in determining causality as an obstacle to system improvement.

When examining job and process costing, actual, normal, and standard costing are widely used. This may provide comfort to some, given the time devoted to these topics in educational programs. Similarly, the widespread confidence in the potential value of ABC may be used to justify devoting resources to teaching and to continued research in this field.

Cost Behaviour and Transfer Pricing: Generally, little coincidence of classification of the behaviour of manufacturing costs (fixed, variable, mixed) was evident. Notably, many firms classify production labour as either a mixed or fixed cost. This indicates the substantial 'bridgehead' of opinion that, in many circumstances and for many purposes, production labour is not a variable expense. Ostensibly, many of the selected expenses should be classified as semi-variable in most firms: for instance, set-up labour, material handling costs, and repairs and maintenance. Yet, in each of these cases, only a minority of respondents classified them as semi-variable (*Survey 1*). This is consistent with overseas evidence that cost classification is highly judgmental (and thus imprecise), especially with respect to overheads where frequently costs are summarily classified as (mostly) fixed or (mostly) variable (for instance: Rayburn, 1981; Coates, *et al.*, 1983; Cress and Pettijohn, 1985; Mowen, 1986).

Impact of multinationals (including Japanese firms)

DuPont and other multinationals played a notable role in the development of management accounting practices in the United States and, thereby, in establishing international (including Australian) practices (Johnson and Kaplan, 1987). It appears that multinationals operating in this country have had little impact upon local practices. This omission is consistent with the comparative absence in Australia of truly large-scale, mass production operations. Accounting and other bureaucratic controls are more cost-effective in large firms, as large-scale operations would provide a favourable environment in which international best practice could be implemented and through which practices might be disseminated.

It is readily apparent that Just-In-Time (JIT), Target Costing, KANBAN, and other terms deriving from Japanese management practices have entered the lexicon of Australian managers. But there is only limited evidence that those practices are used. This is to be expected, given the small size of Australian firms: a high degree of market power is needed to command JIT deliveries and supplier adherence to target pricing regimes. It is likely that some firms have implemented JIT to the extent to which their production processes and relations with suppliers permit. This is especially so in respect of efforts to minimise work-in-process.

Impact of management accounting education

Most of the management accounting competencies taught at Australian universities parallel the content of US-origin introductory and intermediate (second-year) level texts. Accreditation requirements of the ICAA and the ASCPA and anecdotal evidence of subject offerings at different universities support this view. A casual review in 1990 of texts sold by the bookshop chain operating on campuses showed that US texts predominated among management accounting titles. It appears that this position has not changed. There is, furthermore, great uniformity in the content of these texts (Scapens, 1985, made the same observation on texts then available in the UK). Typically, accounting majors can study accreditation- and degree- optional units in management accounting in the final year of their pass degree. There is likely to be greater diversity between universities in the content of these units. It is believed that many of these subjects comprise studies of advanced quantitative techniques (for example: linear programming, cost separation using multiple regression, and various applications of matrix algebra) or of the research literature.

CONCLUSION

Traditionally, financial accounting practices in Australia have been influenced by developments in English law and accounting. With the globalisation of corporate activity, finance and securities regulation, that influence has been lessening. Increasingly, the influence of international accounting bodies such as the IASC and International Federation of Accountants, is evident in Australia. This brief summary of accounting in Australia illustrates the activities of a profession that have both followed and led its overseas counterparts. In respect of inflation accounting in the 1960s and 1970s, Australia's professional bodies led the world, with academics like Raymond Chambers and Reg Gynther promoting alternative market price systems of accounting. The international reputation gained is also evident in three Australians being honoured as the AICPA's International Distinguished Lecturer. Also, Ray Chambers is the only non-North American to be included in the USA's Ohio State University Accounting Hall of Fame. In the 1980s and 1990s there have been many instances where Australia has actively pursued improvements in the quality of financial accounting by strengthening the profession's influence on regulatory mechanisms. The influences on management accounting practices are problematic. In general, practices are similar to those found in the UK and the USA; allocated cost is used almost exclusively, pricing is influenced by 'what the market will bear', overheads account for approximately 25 percent of total manufacturing cost and more than 50 percent of respondents were reasonably happy with existing methods of cost allocation.

REFERENCES

Australian Society of Accountants General Council (1966), 'Accounting principles and practices discussed in reports on company failures', ASA.

Clarke, F.L. and G.W. Dean (1992), 'Chaos in the counting house: Accounting under scrutiny', *Australian journal of corporate law*, Vol. 2, No. 2, pp. 177–201.

Clarke, F.L. and G.W. Dean (1993), 'Law and accounting — The separate legal entity principle and consolidation accounting', *Australian business law review*, Vol. 21, No. 4, pp. 246–69.

Coates, J.B., Smith, J.E., and R.J. Stacy (1983), 'Results of a preliminary survey into the structure of divisionalised companies, divisionalised performance appraisal and the associated role of management accounting', *Management accounting research and practice*, D.J. Cooper, R.W. Scapens, and J.A. Arnold (eds), Institute of Cost and Management Accountants, London, pp. 265–82.

Cress, W.P. and J.B. Pettijohn (1985), 'A survey of budget-related planning and control policies and procedures', *Journal of accounting education*, Vol. 3, No. 2, pp. 61–78.

Dean, G.W., Joye, M.P., and P.J. Blayney (1991), *Strategic management accounting survey: Overhead cost allocation and performance evaluation practices of Australian manufacturers*, Monograph 8, Sydney: The Accounting and Finance Foundation within The University of Sydney.

J.B. Ryan, B.H. Andrew, M.J. Gaffikin & C.T. Heazlewood (1993), *Australian company financial reporting*, AARF.

Gavens, J.J. (1978), 'A historical perspective of integration of the Australian accounting profession', Accounting History Group, Accounting Association of Australia and New Zealand.

Graham, A.W. (1978), *Without fear or favour*, Butterworths, Sydney.

Imhoff, E.A. (1978), 'Management accounting techniques: A survey', *Management accounting (US)*, November, pp. 41–5.

Johnson, H.T. and R.S. Kaplan (1987), *Relevance lost: The rise and fall of management accounting*, Harvard Business School Press, Harvard.

Joye, M.P. and P.J. Blayney (1990), *Cost and management accounting practices in Australian manufacturing companies: Survey results*, Monograph 7, Sydney: The Accounting and Finance Foundation within The University of Sydney.

Lowe, P. and G. Shuetrim (1992), 'The evolution of corporate financial structure', *Research Discussion Paper*, Reserve Bank of Australia.

Shuetrim, G., Lowe, P. and S. Morling (1993), 'The determinants of corporate leverage: A panel data analysis', *Research Discussion Paper*, Reserve Bank of Australia.

Mowen, M.M. (1986), *Accounting for costs as fixed and variable*, NAA, Montvale.

Pierson, G. (1990), *A report on institutional arrangements for accounting standard setting in Australia*, AARF, Melbourne.

Poullaos, C. (1993), 'Making profession and state, 1907–14: The ACPA's first charter attempt', *Abacus*, September, pp. 196–229.

Rayburn, L.G. (1981), 'Marketing costs — Accountants to the rescue', *Management Accounting (US)*, January, pp. 32–41.

Scapens, R.W. (1985), *Management accounting: A review of contemporary developments*, Macmillan, London.

Skinner, R.C. (1993), 'Cost and management accounting practices', *Australian accounting review*, Vol. 3, No. 2, pp. 31–3.

Walker, R.G. (1987), 'Australia's ASRB: A case study of political activity and regulatory capture', *Accounting and business research*, Summer, pp. 269–86.

Walker, R.G. (1993), 'A feeling of déjà vu: Controversies in accounting and auditing regulation in Australia', *Critical perspectives on accounting*, Vol. 4, pp. 97–109.

Zeff, S.A. (1973), *Forging accounting principles in Australia*, Australian Society of Accountants.

ACCOUNTING IN BRUNEI DARUSSALAM

A.J.M. Humayun Murshed[*]

BACKGROUND

Brunei Darussalam, a Malay Muslim Sultanate, is situated on the north-west coast of the island of Borneo, between latitudes 4° and 5°5', looking onto the South China Sea. It is divided into two parts by the Malaysian territory of Sarawak, which forms its southern border. It covers an area of 5675 sq. km of mostly low coastal plains of which approximately three-quarters is dense equatorial forest. The climate is tropical, hot and humid. Annual rainfall is heavy in many parts of the interior, particularly during the monsoon period from November to March. The main resources are crude oil, natural gas and timber.

Brunei has been settled by Malays for several thousand years, and its position on the north-western corner of Borneo on the main trade route between India and China have made it a prosperous sea trading point since the 6th Century. Brunei was known to 6th Century Chinese historians as 'Puni' or 'Poli'. During the 1360s, Brunei was known to the Majapahit Empire as 'Buruneng'. A Javanese script of 1365 listed Brunei as paying symbolic tribute to Majapahit; but the tribute stopped during the reign of the first sultan, Muhammad Shah. Muslims first came to the region for trading reasons in the first century following the establishment of Islam in 622 AD. Ming historical records suggest Brunei was an established Malay Islamic monarchy by 1371 AD. The Portuguese established a trading post in Brunei in 1526, from when trade expanded along with the size of the Chinese population in the sultanate. During the period from the 14th to 16th centuries, Brunei's sovereignty extended throughout the Borneo and nearby islands in the Philippines. During that period, the sultanate reached its height in commerce and

*Universiti Brunei Darussalam, Brunei Darussalam.

prosperity. During the 1600s and 1700s, the territorial extent of the Brunei Sultanate was gradually reduced. With the growth of European influence throughout the region, the year 1888 saw the beginning of an association with Britain. From there, Brunei became a British protectorate. In 1890, Brunei had shrunk to its present small geographical area. In 1906, Brunei accepted a British resident who advised the sultan on all matters except the Islamic faith and Malay custom. In 1984, Brunei Darussalam became independent with responsibility for its own defence and foreign affairs. Brunei Darussalam has a written constitution which dates back to 1959. The constitution was amended with effect from 1st January 1984. The Sultan and Yang Di-Pertuan is both the supreme executive authority in Brunei Darussalam and has also occupied the position of prime minister since the resumption of independence. In addition to the Council of Cabinet Ministers, the Sultan is assisted and advised by the Privy Council, The Council of Succession and The Religious Council. The official religion of Brunei is Islam. Brunei's judicial power is vested in the Supreme Court and the Subordinate Courts, similar to English Common Law (as modified by Statute to meet local requirements). Matters relating to the Islamic faith are dealt with by Islamic (Shariah) Courts. The official language is Malay, but English is widely used. The population estimate in 1993 was 276 300 with a growth rate of 3.5 percent per annum. About two-thirds of the population are Malays, and the remainder includes Chinese as well as other indigenous people.

The GDP of Brunei was almost US$4 billion per annum in 1992, giving an average per capita GDP of in excess of US$15 000. GDP is growing at between 2–3 percent per annum, slightly behind the rate of population growth. The economy is dominated by crude oil and natural gas production, which directly accounts for approximately 40 percent of GDP (indirectly for a great deal more) and 95 percent of export earnings. The construction sector is an important employer. Agriculture (mainly vegetables and poultry) and manufacturing only contribute between 2 and 3 percent of GDP, respectively. Forestry, despite the extensive natural resources of timber, is not an important contributor to GDP. The deforestation rate is currently just under 4 percent per annum, and exports of timber have been banned. Most food and manufactured goods are imported, and government policy, implemented through development plans, aims to reduce this dependency. Considerable amounts of government money have been invested in the infrastructure (schools, hospitals, transport systems etc) over the past two decades, and education and health are both free to Bruneian citizens. The public sector employs about half of the working population. The private sector depends heavily on non-Malays, but there has been a recent trend toward increasing Malay participation. Government expenditure is financed by a corporate tax of 30 percent. There is no personal income tax. Substantial current account surpluses of more than US$1 billion are realised each year and foreign currency reserves are now above the US$15 billion mark. The main trading partners are Japan and Thailand for exports, and Singapore and the UK for imports. The financial regime is open with no restrictions on the movement of capital, but there is no stock exchange. The main problems facing the economy are its dependence on imports and a shortage of skilled labour. Although there is no stock exchange, there are currently eight commercial banks operating in Brunei including some international banks. The financial *sector also includes a number of locally incorporated finance and insurance companies. The unit of currency is the Bruneian dollar.*

A.J.M.H.M/R.J.W.

INTRODUCTION

A considerable body of research has been built up in recent decades describing the diversity of accounting systems in various parts of the world (Jaggi, 1973; Briston, 1978; Briston and El-Ashker, 1984; Enthoven, 1979, 1981; Samuels and Piper, 1985; Wallace, 1987, 1990; Bai, 1988; Solas and Ibrahim, 1992; Murshed, 1994). This acknowledges the belief that accounting systems operate within a socio-economic framework, and are influenced by traditions and cultural values of their respective countries. More attention is now being given to country-specific studies in order to broaden our understanding of the operation of accounting systems. However, there exists an academic void. In the fastest growing regions of the world, researchers have given little attention to the preparation of country case studies focusing on accounting systems. Little is known about Brunei Darussalam in particular. The only piece of research available on accounting and its cognate disciplines in Brunei Darussalam is an outline of the nature of its auditing profession and practice by Foo (1993). This chapter is thus a modest attempt to provide some initial insights into accounting practices in Brunei Darussalam.

Accounting, as a financial information system, covers both micro and macro economic activities, and is related to economic events and decision making process. In order to sustain economic development, an efficient accounting system is necessary. In recent years, Brunei Darussalam's government has made considerable efforts to accelerate its pace of economic development by spending billions of dollars to attain the avowed objective of socio-economic transformation. Due to the importance of the government sector in the Bruneian economy, while accounting is influenced by the measurement and reporting of the financial status of individual organisations, it is also affected by the demands of macro-economic decision making. Furthermore, the experience of several developed and developing countries suggest that socio-economic development and the development of the accounting system go hand-in-hand. The main influence in Bruneian accounting is British (SGV, 1984). All the professional accountants currently practising in Brunei qualified in the UK. Moreover, the accounting training and degree programmes are also linked up with UK universities and professional bodies.

The next section discusses the accounting traditions and training environment of Brunei. Section three describes financial accounting practices and its environment. Section four gives a brief analysis of management accounting practices, and Section five describes some of the special aspects of governmental accounting. Section six contains concluding observations.

ACCOUNTING TRADITIONS AND EDUCATION

Apart from the visible role of accounting in economic development, business and accounting are intertwined in more subtle ways. Early history outlines the Bruneians as being made rich from the production of gold and camphor crystals and the pursuit of trade. Cloth was imported in exchange for natural products (Nicholl, 1980; Brown, 1970). Brunei, called 'Java the Great' by Marco Polo, had extensive trade relations with many countries in the world, and merchants of the region reaped the benefit (Bellwood, 1978). According to the writings of Wang Ta-yuan, in the 14th Century, accounting was evidently an admired skill in this trading empire:

> "Wang Ta-yuan may have visited Brunei in the 1330s. In this *Tai I chih lio,* which he completed in 1349, he gives a brief description of Brunei. He merely comments that the people are lavish in their habits, but he notes that they are excellent accountants. Coming from a hard-headed Chinese businessman, this is praise indeed. It emphasises what is so often forgotten, namely that the Bruneians' were traders, and that their thalassocracies were basically trading empires." (Nicholl, 1980; p. 229).

This awareness of the importance of accounting among the people of Brunei, even if not reflected in the present numbers of professionally qualified accountants, continues today. A recent survey by the author focusing on secondary school children, shows that about 80 percent of students studying the principles of accounts have a plan to take up the profession of accounting. Similar trends can also be observed at the tertiary level of education in the country. Recently, the country's only university — *Universiti Brunei Darussalam* — reorganised its undergraduate programme in business by introducing, among others, a major in accounting and finance, and established a link programme leading to an accounting degree with a major UK university. In many countries, there exists a strong market demand for professional accountants and in many cases, this demand is met by the presence of a well organised professional accountancy body. Such demand is apparent in Brunei with a growing awareness of the need for a strong local profession. However, matters are at an early stage of development in this regard. The Brunei Darussalam Institute of Certified Public Accountants (BICPA), formed in 1987 is, as yet, the only accounting professional society in the country. If it is to fulfil the role expected of a national accounting body, a way needs to be found of attracting to its membership as many existing qualified accountants as possible. There are, however, relatively few professionally qualified accountants in Brunei at the present time. This fact is attributable to Brunei's small population and the nature of its economy, which is characterised by a relatively small private sector and the absence of a local capital market (Foo, 1993).

As of 1st September 1993, 27 of BICPA's 59 members were public accountants, 24 were from commerce and industry, five were in government employment and three were from academia.[1] Two-thirds of Brunei's practising accountants are expatriate accountants. There is no legislative requirement that states practising accountants should be the members of BICPA, although many have become members voluntarily. All of the 'big six' accounting firms (KPMG Peat Marwick, Coopers & Lybrand, Ernst & Young, Price Waterhouse, Arthur Andersen & Co., and Deloitte Touche Tohmatsu International) are operating in Brunei along with one local firm, one firm from Singapore and one from Malaysia. Brunei's accounting system is strongly influenced by the needs of government and has a legislative basis. Budgetary issues like the preparation of annual estimates, the allocation of funds and monitoring the uses of funds are particularly important. The reason for this is that most economic activity is centred around the machinery of government. *The Constitution (Financial Procedure) Order* illustrates the framework of government accounting (BML, 1984). Almost all of the small and medium sized firms in the private sector do not fall under the scope of the public companies' legislation, and they are not under any statutory obligation to submit financial statements to the Registrar of Companies. However, all companies are required to submit their audited accounts to the Collector of Income Tax.[2] There is a distinction between public and private companies. The latter prepare accounts mainly for their own use and do not publish financial statements. As private companies are owned by individual families, accounting in these enterprises takes the shape of what may be termed 'family based reporting'. Until recently, Brunei has been following accounting standards and policies of various other countries (Foo, 1993). However, BICPA is actively considering the development of its own accounting standards and procedures relating to the presentation of financial statements. More details about these matters are contained in the next section.

FINANCIAL ACCOUNTING

Financial accounting and reporting in Brunei Darussalam are generally regulated by legislation. Brunei's *Companies Act (Cap 39 Companies)* illustrates the requirements, and outlines the nature of accounts and audit functions to be carried out in companies. As a requirement of the law, each company has to keep books of accounts in respect of receipts of payments, purchases and sales, and assets and liabilities. In compliance with this, all companies in Brunei maintain a cash book, journals and ledgers. Companies also prepare income statements and a balance sheets. The Companies Act specifically defines the contents of the balance sheet. At present, there are no prescribed Bruneian accounting standards. Local companies prepare their accounting

---

[1]Source: *Report of BICPA Council*, 6th Annual General Meeting, 1993.
[2]The income of sole traders and partnerships is not subject to income tax and they are not required to submit their accounts to the tax authorities.

reports based on UK standards, while international firms operating in Brunei either follow the accounting standards of their parent companies or international accounting standards. International firms operating in Brunei do not publish their financial statements in Brunei; rather they prepare their accounts in order to provide information required by their parent company and their internal needs.[3]

Under the Companies Act, each public company is required to prepare an income statement and a balance sheet together with a director's report. All accounts of public companies must be audited by auditors registered in Brunei Darussalam. Private companies are not required to file their accounts with the Registrar of Companies. However, most business organisations are required to submit their accounting data annually to the Economic Planning Unit under the Ministry of Finance for statistical purposes. Private companies, sole tradership and partnership firms prepare accounts for their own purposes, and tend to be secretive about their accounting records. Their accounting systems appear to be mostly of the manual variety although some now use microcomputer systems. Of course big firms, mostly public companies, have computerised accounting systems.

Relatively strict financial accounting controls are imposed on banks or branches of foreign banks operating in Brunei Darussalam. Their accounts are regulated by the Banking Act (*Cap 95, Banking*). According to Section 10, every licensed bank or branch must produce and publish its balance sheet on or before 13th of April every year. In addition to this, each must submit returns to the Minister of Finance of their assets and liabilities at the close of business on the 13th day of June and 31st day of December. They must also submit comparative figures for the previous month and an analysis of advances and bills discounted as at the above dates.

An examination of significant accounting policies of Brunei's public companies reveals the following basic facts:

(i)   accounts are prepared on the basis of historical cost.
(ii)   income is recognised on the basis of both cash and accrual basis.
(iii) depreciation is calculated on a straight line basis.
(iv)   assets and liabilities expressed in foreign currencies are translated into Brunei dollars at the rates of exchange ruling at the balance sheet date. Transactions during the year are translated into Brunei dollars at the rates of exchange ruling on the transaction dates. All exchange differences are treated in the income statements.
(v)   investments are stated at cost.
(vi)   bad debts are written off and provisions are made for those debts which are considered to be doubtful.

---

[3]Two public companies operating in the financial service sector in Brunei Darussalam do publish their annual accounts, however.

There is no uniform format for the presentation of financial statements. Usually private companies restrict their financial reports to contain just an income statement and balance sheet. In addition to those two statements, public companies prepare a statement of changes in funds. A review of the formats used for income statements and balance sheets by private companies shows them to be typically of the forms described in Table 1.

Table 1
Typical format for Financial Statements

Typical format for Income Statement

Turnover	xxx
Less, Cost of goods sold	xxx
Gross profit	xxx
Less, Administrative and operating expenses (e.g. wages, depreciation etc.)	xxx
Add, Other operating incomes	xxx
Profit/(Loss)	xxx

Typical format for Balance Sheet

Assets		
Fixed Assets		xxx
Tangible assets	xxx	
Intangible assets	xxx	
Investments	xxx	
Net Current Assets		xxx
Current assets	xxx	
Current liabilities	xxx	
Total Assets		xxx
Liabilities		
Capital		xxx
Reserves		xxx
Total		xxx

Financial statements are of standard Western design.

MANAGEMENT ACCOUNTING

Management accounting is not widely practised as a distinct discipline in Brunei's accounting environment. Small and medium sized firms sometimes prepare a cash budget, but in most cases they use figures taken from financial accounts for management decision making purposes. Specific management information reports are not usually prepared. The major reason for this state of affairs is that most of the firms in Brunei are small in size, and therefore do not face the complicated intricacies of managing businesses. It is also not cost-effective to develop and set up user-designed management accounting information systems.

In addition, as most activities centre around government departments, in terms of ensuring proper control it is very common to follow legislation, rather than base systems on management accounting objectives. Management accounting is, of course, practised as a specialist discipline within large and international firms. International firms generally follow the management accounting system of their parent companies and produce their management reports on a quarterly basis. Consequently, the management accounting practices of international firms conform in the main with the requirements of their parent companies rather than with the decision making needs of their Brunei operations (insofar as these may be different).

To the extent that the management accounting practices of firms in Brunei reveal any evident pattern to the outsider, the following appear to be the most significant:

(i) *Budgeting*

This is an area which seems to attract most attention. Most large firms prepare annual budgets. These include a production budget, a cost budget and a cash budget. Most effort is expended on the cash budget, as the major focus of firms' planning seems to be in the area of working capital management. In many cases, cash budgets are prepared on a monthly basis. In addition, capital budgeting exercises are carried out in case of new investment or an expansion of existing businesses or capacity. The techniques used in capital budgeting appear to be simple, like payback period or accounting rate of return. Some firms, mainly in the construction and engineering sectors, use the net present value method, however.

(ii) *Cost Control*

This is another area where much accounting effort is focused. Firms identify controllable and uncontrollable costs and try to reduce their controllable costs. It would appear however that standard costing and variance analyses are not widely used, except by the international firms. The cost control issue in many firms is mechanical and based on previous trends and experiences, using historic data.

GOVERNMENT ACCOUNTING

As mentioned earlier, the *Constitutional Order* sets the framework of government accounting in Brunei Darussalam. It defines the duties of government accounting officers, preparation of annual estimates and the procedures for making payments and the preparation of financial statements. Government accounts are kept on a cash basis. The distribution of accounting functions and records among the various ministries, departments within ministries and the Treasury may obscure the double entry effect in the accounting system (Campbell, 1989). A characteristic of Brunei's government accounting is the 'consolidated fund' where all receipts are pooled and government payments are made by charging this fund. The main significance of the 'consolidated fund' is the part it plays in the strict internal control system for ensuring accountability to the government in respect of fund management. This fund is related to the UK system of national income accounting. The consolidated fund was established in the UK in 1787, and in terms of operation, the funds in the two countries are similar. For a discussion on the UK consolidated fund see, Jones and Pendlebury (1988). The Ministry of Finance has the overall responsibility for supervising and controlling the financial affairs of Brunei Darussalam.[4]

The accounting year, the fiscal year of Brunei Darussalam, runs from 1st January to 31st December. Before the beginning of the financial year, a statement of estimated receipts and expenditures is prepared for that year. This estimate principally highlights the total sum required to meet expenditures charged to the consolidated fund. The heads of various departments and controlling officers prepare the estimates of revenues and expenditures for their respective departments, in accordance to the instructions of the Treasury. These estimates are examined by the Treasury to ensure that the purpose of the proposed expenditure is in conformity with the government policy and that the amounts of proposed expenditures are within reasonable limits.

After this examination, the estimates may have to be revised, following which final estimates for all departments are consolidated by the Treasury in a form required by the constitution. Although the detailed contents of the estimates vary from ministry to ministry, each estimate must show salaries and wages; regular annual charges, including travelling and transportation, maintenance, equipment etc; and miscellaneous charges and special expenditures which do not recur every year.

Very tight controls, including daily bankings and detailed documentation, are kept over receipts. Furthermore, a substantial portion of government accounting in Brunei is devoted to the control of expenditures by way of a Treasury authorization, the recording of transactions, budgeting and reconciliation. At the end of the financial year, financial statements are prepared by the Ministry of Finance and forwarded to the Auditor General for audit. The Auditor General submits his report to HM the Sultan. The report contains a statement of the consolidated revenue account showing the amounts estimated, actually received and spent and a statement of receipts and payments accounted for in the consolidated trust account. Certain trust accounts are created by the government, and amounts paid into these accounts are paid out of the revenue accounts as part of the expenditures authorised by the government. Examples of the government trust funds include the housing loans fund, personal loan funds etc.

---

[4]The Treasury is responsible for managing the consolidated fund; overseeing the accounting systems in the ministries and departments to ensure that proper procedures are followed in recording the transactions; proper authorization of expenditures; operation of government bank accounts; and preparation of annual financial statements.

CONCLUDING OBSERVATIONS

Brunei's accounting has been, and still is, largely concerned with the needs of government. Traditionally, it has been more geared to taxation, revenue control and the accountability of receipts and payments, than to the modern Western ideas of decision usefulness. This is mostly due to the large size of the government sector in Brunei Darussalam. This has the consequence that the accounting needs of the government sector are at least as imperative as those of the business sector.

Many enterprise accounting techniques and procedures are used by the government sector. However, it is clear from the above discussion that, currently, the scope of detailed company accounting seems to be limited to only a relatively few enterprises. Only two public companies publish audited accounts, while other firms produce accounts mainly for their internal consumption. In the absence of Bruneian accounting standards, the accounting system is largely conditioned by legislative provisions and foreign standards.

The scope of enterprise management accounting also appears to be limited by the large government and small private sectors. In addition, the accounting profession in Brunei has a relatively short history. There is only one professional accounting body and it has no legislative backup to prescribe or enforce any accounting standards it might issue. Nevertheless, with the growing efforts to diversify the economy, Brunei has bright prospects for developing a strong indigenous company accounting system. It can be expected that in the coming years, the size of the private sector will grow in line with the economic diversification programme. With this growth, Brunei's company accounting will adapt, to ensure greater efficiency. This may be accompanied by the development of a more rigorous enterprise accounting, and possibly the adoption of International Accounting Standards. In order to respond to these potential challenges however, Brunei must develop a strong accounting body, perhaps with legislative backup. In the emerging economic scenario in Brunei, accounting is likely to become more visible.

REFERENCES

BML (Brunei Darussalam Ministry of Law), (1984), *The Laws of Brunei Darussalam* (Revised edition), Vol. 1, Constitutional Matters III, pp. 1–18.

Bai, Z. (1988), 'Accounting in the Peoples Republic of China — Contemporary situations and issues' in *Recent accounting and economic developments in the Far East*, V.K. Zimmerman (ed), Centre for International Education and Research in Accounting, University of Illinois at Urbana-Champaign, Illinois, pp. 27–50.

Bellwood, P. (1978), 'Trade patterns and political developments in Brunei and adjacent areas AD 700–1500' 10th International Congress of Anthropological and Ethnological Sciences, New Delhi, India.

Briston, R. (1978), 'The evolution of accounting in developing countries', *International journal of accounting education and research,* Vol. 14, pp. 105–20.

Briston, R. and A.A. El-Ashker (1984), 'The Egyptian accounting system: A case study in western influence', *International journal of accounting education and research,* Vol. 19, pp. 129–55.

Brown, D. (1970), *Brunei: The structure and history of a Bornean Malay sultanate,* Monograph of the Brunei Museum, No. 2.

Campbell, P. (1989), *Public sector financial administration in Negara Brunei Darussalam,* Universiti Brunei Darussalam, Bandar Seri Begawan.

EIU (1994), *Country profile- Malaysia and Brunei,* The Economist Intelligence Unit, London.

Enthoven, A. (1979), *Accounting systems in the Third World economies,* North Holland Amsterdam.

Enthoven, A. (1981), 'Accounting in developing countries', *Comparative international accounting,* Nobes, C.W. and R.H. Parker (eds), Philip Allan, Oxford.

Foo, S. (1993), 'The auditing profession in Brunei', *Research in Third World accounting,* Vol. 2, pp. 303–11.

Jaggi, B. (1973), 'Accounting systems in developing countries: An assessment', *The international journal of accounting education and research,* Vol. 9, pp. 159–70.

Jones, R. and M. Pendlebury (1988), 'Governmental accounting, auditing and financial reporting in the United Kingdom', *Governmental accounting and auditing: International comparisons,* Chan J. and R. Jones (eds), Routledge, London.

Murshed, A. (1994), 'Decision making in public enterprises in developing countries: Accounting vs politics', *Proceedings of joint conference sixth Asian-Pacific on international accounting issues and accounting theory and practice conference,* Peyvandi, A.A. and B.Y. Tai (eds), California State University, California, pp. 99–102.

Nicholl, R. (1980), 'Brunei rediscovered: A survey of early times', *Brunei Museum Journal,* Vol. 4, pp. 219–37.

Samuels, J. and A. Piper (1985), *International accounting: A survey,* Croom Helm, London.

SGV (1984), *Comparative accounting practices in ASEAN:* Ozey Longman, as cited in Tan Teck Meng (undated), *The auditing framework in ASEAN,* Nanyang Technological University, Singapore.

Solas, C. and M. Ibrahim (1992), 'Usefulness of disclosure items in financial reports: A comparison between Jordan and Kuwait', *Asian review of accounting,* Vol. 1, pp. 1–11.

Wallace, R. (1987), *Disclosure of accounting information in developing countries,* Ph.D. Thesis, University of Exeter.

Wallace, R. (1990), 'Accounting in developing countries- A review of literature', *Research in Third World accounting,* Vol. 1, pp. 3–54.

ACCOUNTING IN HONG KONG

Anthony Moung Yin CHAN, Kin Cheung LIU, and
*Patrick Po Hing NG**

BACKGROUND

Hong Kong consists of the island of Hong Kong, the Kowloon peninsular and the New Territories of mainland China. Together these constitute an area of just 1072 sq. km of very hilly, volcanic land of relatively poor quality lying between latitudes 22° 9' and 22° 37' N, and formed around a spectacular and deep, natural harbour east of the Pearl river delta near Guangzou. Otherwise, natural resources are poor, there being no significant mineral deposits or usable commercial timber. Only 7 percent of the land area is in agricultural use and even water has to be imported from China. The climate is subtropical monsoon with hot (29°C in July) wet summers and drier, cooler winters (16°C in January). Typhoons are sometimes a problem in the later summer months.

Hong Kong island, an integral part of China, was ceded to the British in 1842, Kowloon was annexed in 1860, and the New Territories were leased (for 99 years) in 1898 — all under conditions of duress. The system of government then instituted was based upon the British colonial model of a Governor representing the English Crown and advisory Executive and Legislative councils of 15 and 60 members respectively. This is still the basis of the constitution today. The Executive Council is entirely non-elected. The Legislative has developed into a partially elected body, 18 being directly elected by universal suffrage and 21 through functional constituencies representing various occupational groups. The remainder are appointees of the Governor. The Legislature Council passes Ordinances

*Respectively Associate Professor, Department of Accountancy, City University of Hong Kong; Senior Lecturer, Division of Commerce, College of Higher Vocational Studies, City University of Hong Kong; Lecturer, Department of Business Administration, Hong Kong Technical College.

which are the basis of the local laws. The British Parliament currently holds ultimate legislative sovereignty, but nowadays does not interfere with Hong Kong's domestic affairs and, in practice, the Governor always follows the advice of the Council. The judicial system is based upon District Courts and a Court of Appeal. Further appeals can presently be made to the UK's Privy Council. The 1985 Joint Declaration between the UK and China provides for the return of Hong Kong to China in 1997. It allows Hong Kong to become a Special Administrative Region with autonomy in matters of government, its legal system, taxation, monetary system and other matters including freedom of speech and religion. Since 1985, a committee in Beijing has been developing the form of a new constitution for Hong Kong after 1997 (the Basic Law). The Chinese population of Hong Kong is mostly Buddhist with some Confucian and Doaist influences. There are about half a million Christians and a much smaller number of representatives of the other faiths (e.g. Islam). Mandarin and Cantonese are the main languages spoken, apart from English. The population in 1992 was more than 5.5 m, giving an average density of over 5000 people per sq. km. Kowloon has some of the most densely populated areas in the world. The source of population growth is mainly from immigration, which has been a recurring political issue since 1945. The population is overwhelmingly Chinese, mostly of Cantonese origin.

Hong Kong has had very high recent economic growth rates, GDP per head increasing by a multiple of four over the last 25 years. The level of GDP per capita is now comparable to Australia and the UK. Economic growth has been encouraged by political stability, significant government expenditure on infrastructure, a liberal and supportive world trade environment and a currency fixed since 1983 against the US$. Inflation, running at about 10 percent in 1993, has been quite high historically. About three-quarters of output is accounted for by the services sector, with manufacturing contributing most of the remainder. About two-thirds of domestic demand for foodstuffs is met by imports. The major manufactures are textiles, electronic equipment, clocks, watches and toys. Most of this produce (which does not have a high-tech component) is exported. Re-exports are, however, three times as important as exports in terms of value and are an essential ingredient of Hong Kong's success. The current account balance is usually in deficit and is covered by a surplus on invisibles from air transport, shipping, banking and tourism. Hong Kong's main trading partners are China, Japan, Taiwan and the USA. It is a major financial centre with a stock exchange, a commodities exchange and a rapidly growing capital and banking sector. The government has recently increased expenditure on higher education and research and development to address the problem of shortages of skills and advanced technology. The unit of currency is the Hong Kong dollar.

R.J.W.

INTRODUCTION

Modern forms of accounting have been practised in Hong Kong for more than 100 years (Kelly, 1983). As a British colony, the development of accounting practice in

Hong Kong has been heavily influenced by British traditions. However, Hong Kong's future involvement in the international business community will determine the direction of the accounting information requirements of its corporations. International financial statement users will stimulate demand for accounting information, and this will determine the direction of accounting development in Hong Kong. The agreement between the Chinese and the British governments (to come into effect in 1997) is expected to shift Hong Kong's business practices from a UK to a China-oriented style. Hong Kong's business practices (including accounting principles) will then be more open to wider international influences (Chan, 1988).

THE REGULATORY FRAMEWORK

Three spheres of regulation

Since the establishment of the Hong Kong Society of Accountants (HKSA) in 1973, the regulation of accounting in Hong Kong has been pursued through three channels: the legal system, the stock exchange, and the HKSA. Through the legal system, regulation for accounting relies on the Companies Ordinance; through the stock exchange, regulation relies on the listing rules; and through the HKSA, regulation relies on accounting, auditing, and ethical standards (Piper, 1986).

Companies Ordinance[1]: The Hong Kong Companies Ordinance was first issued by the Hong Kong Legislative Council in 1932, based on the United Kingdom's Companies Act of 1929. Major amendments to the Ordinance were made in 1974 and 1980, which resulted respectively in the 1975 and 1984 versions of the Ordinance incorporating the provisions of the United Kingdom 1948 Companies Act (Wallace, 1987). The current Ordinance has also adopted some specific provisions of the 1967, 1980, and 1981 Companies Acts of the United Kingdom (Wallace, 1985).

The provisions most relevant to accounting in the Hong Kong Companies Ordinance are section 122, section 123, and the 10th Schedule. Sections 122 and 123 require every company to annually present a 'true and fair' profit and loss account and balance sheet fulfilling the detailed disclosure requirements of the 10th Schedule. The disclosure requirements set out in this schedule span over several items and sources of information including investments, liabilities, fixed assets, inventories, capital, the director's report and the profit or loss. As in the United Kingdom, licensed banks, insurance companies, and shipping companies are exempted from compliance with some disclosure requirements in the schedule. The HKSA actively

---

[1]See also An-Yeung (1980).

participates in discussions leading to amendments of the Hong Kong Companies Ordinance, particularly on those parts related to accounting. For example, in respect of the Companies (Amendment) Ordinance 1987, the HKSA was concerned about the shortened period of presentation of annual accounts by public companies from nine months to six months after the year end (HKSASN, 1987(a)). Besides the Companies Ordinance, the regulation of accounting in Hong Kong through the legal system is occasionally dealt with by other ordinances. The HKSA lists ten additional ordinances relevant to accounting covering the areas of banking, bankruptcy, commodity trading, estate duty, the inland revenue, insurance companies, securities, stamps, and trustees (HKSAN, 1988(a); HKSASN, 1985(b)).

Stock Exchange: The stock exchange is a secondary, weak source of accounting regulation. Before unification in 1986, there were four exchanges in Hong Kong and compliance with the listing rules of the exchanges was unsatisfactory until recently (Piper, 1986). There were few, if any, mechanisms to ensure compliance within any of the exchanges in the early years of the 1980s (Wallace, 1985). The stock exchanges were the main targets of regulation by the Securities Ordinance when it first became law in February 1974. The regulation of the securities industry in Hong Kong began with the establishment of the Securities Advisory Council in the early 1970s, something which was brought about by the Hong Kong stock market crash of that period. The main purpose of early Securities Ordinances was to require a minimum capital amount for brokers, and identify undercapitalised securities dealers. However, there were also many audit and accounting consequences, including requirements on bookkeeping, presentation of accounts, and timing of disclosure for securities dealers. The Ordinance also aimed at replacing the four existing exchanges by one unified stock exchange, which came into being in 1986 (McInnes, 1980). After unification, the government-supported stock exchange was strengthened to enforce its listing rules. However, the regulation of accounting by the stock exchange is still at an early stage. As with the amendment process in the case of the Companies Ordinance, the HKSA participates heavily in the process of formulating the listing rules (HKSAN, 1985).

The Hong Kong Society of Accountants: The HKSA, as the third source of regulation for accounting, is the body most directly involved with the accountancy profession in Hong Kong. As explained above, it works within the legal system and with the stock exchange, whose pronouncements form the backbone of its authority and support (HKSASN, 1985; Howard, 1987). The HKSA and its professional standards play a central role among the three spheres of accounting regulation in Hong Kong. As the direct regulator of the accountancy profession in Hong Kong, the HKSA is incorporated by the Professional Accountants Ordinance, and claims to be the only statutory licensing body of accountants in the colony. The Professional Accountants

Ordinance was originally promulgated in 1973, and has undergone two major amendments in 1977 and 1981, with further more minor amendments in other years.[2]

The basic purpose of the Ordinance is to maintain a register of professional accountants, and to issue practising certificates for public accountants by the HKSA. The trend in the amendments has been toward a tightening of requirements. As the only statutory body entrusted by the government to control public accountancy in Hong Kong (HKSAN, 1988(c)), the HKSA acts as the profession's disciplinary body, represents its members in discussions with Government, carries out an educational function by organizing post-qualification courses and represents the accountancy profession to members of the general public (Wallace, 1985). The HKSA is a protector of the profession as well as a regulator, and resists governmental interference or other external intervention such as from the stock exchange. Through continuously upgrading itself in the areas of professional examinations, post-qualification education, accounting, auditing, ethics and discipline, the HKSA aims to maintain its public esteem. The HKSA, among the three sources of regulation of accounting in Hong Kong, is therefore the most direct and significant regulator of the accounting profession.

Until 1973, when the Hong Kong Society of Accountants (HKSA) was founded, the public accountancy profession in Hong Kong was directly regulated by the government through the Authorised Auditors Board (HKSASN, 1983). Up to that time, accountants in Hong Kong could only become qualified through gaining membership of overseas professional bodies (HKSA, 1987), and public accountants authorised to audit the accounts of limited companies were listed in the Government Gazette every year (HKSAN, 1988(b)). Since establishment of the HKSA, auditors previously appointed by the Authorised Auditors Board have been entitled to call themselves "Public Accountants" while auditors registered by the HKSA have been distinguished as "Certified Public Accountants" (HKSAN, 1973).

Today, the accountancy profession in Hong Kong is growing rapidly. There are many professional firms in the city, and small firms are the basis of the profession (Wallace, 1985). Most Hong Kong professional firms have less than four partners. The 'big six' however, are the market leaders of the profession. As a self-regulating body, the HKSA is governed by its Council according to the Professional Accountants Ordinance and, in most years, practising members (particularly those from the 'big six') still have a significant influence on the Council. Partly because of a stable executive directorship as well as a stable Council membership in the HKSA since 1973,

---

[2]The current version of the Ordinance is mainly the 1977 edition plus the 1981 amendment, which includes the Ordinance itself and the professional accountants by-laws. According to Section 8 of the Ordinance, the HKSA has the authority to make by-laws for the Ordinance in its general meetings.

particularly in the 1980s, the HKSA has kept consistent strategies and working procedures throughout the period. However, it has grown rapidly, reflecting the importance of the accounting profession in Hong Kong's rapid economic growth[3].

Hong Kong Accounting Standards

As one of the earliest committees of the HKSA, formed in 1973 and firstly named as
the Professional Standards Committee, the Accounting Standards Committee (ASC) is
modelled on the British system to be responsible for the entire accounting standard
setting process in Hong Kong. The ASC is composed of practising accountants,
accountants in industry, and occasionally academics, without statutory restriction on
the proportion of the different kinds of members (HKSASN, 1987(b)). However, as in
the HKSA Council, practising accountants, particularly those from the 'big six' CPA
firms, usually take the lead in the ASC (Howard, 1987).

The working procedures of the ASC have remained unchanged over a number of
years and attempt to consider the views of all interested parties before standards are
issued in definitive form. Figure 1 exhibits the process by which the Accounting
Standards Committee issues Hong Kong accounting standards (Yuen, 1988). The accounting standard setting process in Hong Kong therefore involves a typical 'consultation process' (HKSA, 1987)[4].

Outside the ASC, all the three parties of preparers, users, and auditors of financial
statements are actors in the accounting standard setting process and submit their
views to the ASC during the exposure period (HKSA, 1981; HKSAN, 1987; 1986).
Thus the Hong Kong accounting standard setting process involves a sequence of
dynamics within the HKSA Accounting Standards Committee, between the HKSA
Accounting Standards Committee and the HKSA Council, and between the HKSA as
a whole and the general public.

The HKSA had issued several dozen ethical standards and guidelines, even more
auditing standards and guidelines, 15 accounting standards (i.e. the Hong Kong
Statements of Standard Accounting Practice or HKSSAPs) and seven accounting

---

[3]The annual total income of the HKSA in 1974 was HK$439,436, but the annual total income
today is over HK$10 million. HKSA membership statistics reflect the growth of the HKSA. In 1973,
the HKSA had only 566 members while in 1993 there were 7408 members. The size of the HKSA
student population in 1982 has grown more than three times from its size in 1981 (from 1964 to
7081). This was partly due to the adoption of a joint examination scheme in Hong Kong by the
HKSA and the United Kingdom's Association of Certified Accountants (ACCA) from January 1982.
[4]The consultation process sometimes leads to the shelving of proposed standards. For instance, a
proposed standard on 'segment reporting' was issued as a guideline rather than a standard because
the ASC believed that, after the due process of consultation, there appeared to be a lack of support
from the users of accounts reflected by negative comments on the exposure draft (HKSAN, 1984).

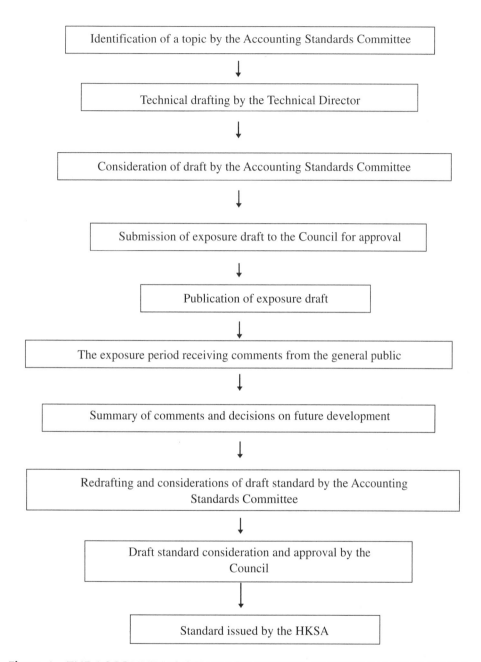

Figure 1   THE ACCOUNTING STANDARD SETTING PROCESS IN HONG KONG

guidelines. The 15 HKSSAPs are listed in Table 1. The Hong Kong accounting measurement and disclosure practices which are determined by these standards are described in the following section.

Table 1

LIST OF HONG KONG STATEMENTS OF STANDARD ACCOUNTING
PRACTICE AND THEIR EFFECTIVE DATES

Titles	Effective Dates
SSAP1 Disclosure of Accounting Policies	1 July 1975
SSAP2 Extraordinary Items and Prior Year Adjustments	1 January 1977
SSAP3 Stocks and Work In Progress	1 January 1977
SSAP4 superseded by SSAP15	1 January 1978
SSAP5 Earnings Per Share	1 January 1978
SSAP6 Depreciation Accounting	1 April 1978
SSAP7 Group Accounts	1 January 1982
SSAP8 Accounting for Contingencies	1 January 1983
SSAP9 Accounting for Post Balance Sheet Events	1 January 1983
SSAP10 Accounting for the Results of Associated Companies	1 January 1985
SSAP11 Foreign Currency Translation	1 January 1985
SSAP12 Accounting for Deferred Tax	1 January 1988
SSAP13 Accounting for Investment Properties	1 January 1989
SSAP14 Accounting for Leases and Hire Purchase Contract	1 January 1988
SSAP15 Cash Flow Statements	31 March 1992

VALUATION AND DISCLOSURE PRACTICES

As was mentioned in the introduction, the UK influence on accounting practices is very strong and the current Hong Kong financial accounting valuation and disclosure practices are virtually the same as those laid down in present UK standards. Financial statements of Hong Kong companies are normally prepared under the historical cost convention. There is no accounting standard requiring the effects of changing prices to be reflected in financial statements. However, the historical cost convention may be modified to state fixed assets at a professional or directors' valuation. HKSSAP 1 lists four fundamental accounting concepts that have to be followed in the preparation of financial statements and they are, going concern, accrual, consistency and prudence. The contents of published financial statements must also comply with the 10th-Schedule to the Companies Ordinance which details certain minimum disclosures. However, there is no prescribed format or choice of formats for financial statements under the Ordinance. HKSSAP2 requires that the results of discontinued operations, exceptional items and extraordinary items (very rare) be separately disclosed on the face of the profit and loss account. In addition, earnings per share should be disclosed on the face of the profit and loss account for both the current period and the corresponding prior period (HKSSAP 5). Cash flow statements are required under HKSSAP 15.

Property, plant and equipment are classified into two major categories: (a) depreciable assets (HKSSAP 6), and (b) investment properties (HKSSAP 13). Depreciable assets are defined as assets that: 'are expected to be used during more than one accounting period; have a limited useful life; and are held by a company for use in the production or supply of goods and services, for rental to others, or for administrative purposes'. In arriving at the value of depreciable assets, amortization, provision for depreciation or diminution in value of the assets must be considered. The revaluation of depreciable assets is allowed, but seldom occurs in practice. Land and buildings in Hong Kong are subject to special treatment. Almost all of the land in Hong Kong is leasehold. Where land is held and the relevant lease has an unexpired term of no less than 50 years (including the extensionable period to the year of 2047), it is not required to amortize the value of the land. Land held on leases with unexpired terms of less than 50 years should be amortized over the remaining period of the lease. Buildings are usually depreciated using the straight line method over the estimated useful life of 40 years or over the unexpired terms of the leases, if less than 40 years. Investment properties are normally stated at open market value and should not be depreciated except where the unexpired terms of the leases are 20 years or shorter.

Regarding the treatment of intangible assets, the Companies Ordinance requires that the written down amount of acquired goodwill, patents and trade marks be shown. Currently, there is no accounting standard, only an accounting guideline, dealing with goodwill. The common practice is to write off positive purchased goodwill to reserves at the time of acquisition or to amortize goodwill over its estimated useful life through the profit and loss account. Negative goodwill should be credited directly to reserves. For research and development costs, HKSSAP 16 requires research costs to be recognised as an expense in the period in which they are incurred, but allows capitalization of development costs in defined circumstances.

For current assets, the lower of cost and net realizable value (or market value) applies. The carrying amount of inventories must be determined separately or where impracticable, for groups of similar items. Methods such as FIFO and average cost are the most popular methods of inventories valuation, but LIFO is expressly not allowed.

Subsidiaries are defined in terms of majority shares and power and control of the composition of the board of directors. They are to be accounted for by the acquisition method, normally using full consolidation. Subsidiaries, however, can be excluded from consolidation on the grounds of dissimilar activities, immateriality, disproportionate costs and long delay, or because control is significantly impaired or held temporarily. The use of the merger method is not permitted under the

Companies Ordinance. Hong Kong companies mainly use the equity method for significant influence and interests in joint ventures in consolidated financial statements. Proportional consolidation is available as an option for non-corporate joint ventures. Significant influence is defined as an involvement in the financial and operating policy decisions of the investee company, which does not amount to control over those policies. The use of the acquisition method (or equity method) means that any goodwill arising on consolidation is separately identified and the appropriate accounting policy for purchased goodwill should be chosen.

Segmental reporting is relatively undeveloped in Hong Kong. There is currently no accounting standard, except for an accounting guideline, dealing with segmental reporting. The guideline merely requires directors to include in the directors' report: (a) the description of principal activities, and the turnover and contribution of each such activity to consolidated trading results; and (b) a geographical analysis of consolidated turnover and contribution for operations overseas which comprise more than 10 percent of the trading results of the group. The guideline, however, does not require the disclosure of segment assets and it is restricted to companies listed on the stock exchange.

The Companies Ordinance requires companies to disclose the basis of converting assets and liabilities expressed in foreign currencies. HKSSAP 11 requires that the closing rate method of translation be used for independent subsidiaries with exchange differences on translation recorded as a movement on reserves. The temporal method may be used only in certain specified circumstances where the foreign enterprise operates as a direct extension of the holding company. In that case, exchange differences on translation are treated as part of the result on ordinary activities before taxation (HKSA, 1984; 1985).

Accounting standard setters in Hong Kong have paid little attention to liabilities. For example, there has not been any accounting standard, guideline or exposure draft on the subject of pension costs, the restructuring and extinguishment of debt and new financial instruments. There are also no prescribed accounting standards for both current liabilities and long term liabilities. The general accounting treatment for these items is to include them in the balance sheet at face value so long as they represent obligations of the company. Regarding off-balance sheet financing, there has not been any specific attempt to emphasise the special features of such transactions, except that HKSSAP 14 aims to standardize the accounting treatment of leases by requiring that the substance of transactions (rather than form) be reflected in the financial statements. With respect to the accounting treatment of contingencies, it largely depends on the likelihood of outcome and the type of contingency being considered. Material contingent losses should be accrued in the financial statements where it is probable that a future event will confirm a loss that can be estimated with reasonable accuracy at the date on which the financial statements are approved by the board of directors. Possible contingent losses need to be disclosed unless the possibility of losses are remote. On the other hand, contingent gains should not be accrued in the financial statements. A contingent gain should be disclosed only if it is probable that the gain will be realised.

A summary of the contents of the HKSSAPs listed in Table 1 is contained in Table 2.

Table 2
THE 15 HONG KONG ACCOUNTING STANDARDS

HKSSAP1	Disclosure of (i) departures from four fundamental accounting concepts, (ii) accounting policies selected by the company, and (iii) departures from the selected accounting policies.
HKSSAP2	Extraordinary items (net of tax) are reported separately within the profit and loss account. A statement of retained profits/reserves disclosures any prior year adjustments (net of tax) with a restatement of the beginning balance of the retained profits/reserves.
HKSSAP3	Stocks and work-in-progress stated in lower of cost and net realisable value. Long-term contract work-in-progress stated in cost plus attributable profit minus foreseeable loss and progress payment received and receivable.
HKSSAP4	Statement of changes in financial position is required, but format or definition of funds are not specified. This standard is superseded by HKSSAP15.
HKSSAP5	Basic earnings per share and fully diluted earnings per share (subject to 5 percent level of materiality) for both current and corresponding previous years are reported in the profit and loss account. Basis of calculation on both numerator and denominator should be disclosed as well.
HKSSAP6	Depreciation method and estimates of useful life or residual value are not regulated. Detailed disclosure of selected depreciation policies are required. Deliberate discussion on depreciation or non-depreciation of land and buildings shows the unique importance of the real estate industry in Hong Kong. Also, the elaboration of the impact of the Sino-British Joint Declaration on the standard illustrates the international factor (in the case, the China factor) influencing on the accounting standards setting process.
HKSSAP7	Consolidation method is recommended to account for subsidiaries in group accounts. Detailed disclosure and equity method are applied to subsidiaries excluded from consolidation, for some approved reasons, in the group accounts.
HKSSAP8	Contingent loss, unless remote or immaterial in nature, should be accrued in the financial statements if its financial effect is estimable; should be disclosed in note if the effect is not estimable. Contingent gain unless remote or immaterial in nature should be disclosed in note.
HKSSAP9	Post-balance sheet adjusting events are accounted for in the financial statements, and post-balance sheet non-adjusting events are disclosed in note.
HKSSAP10	Equity method is recommended to account for associated companies in group

	accounts. Identification of associated companies is exercised by the criterion of 'significant influence' which is applied operationally by the guideline of 'holding more than 20 percent of equity shares of the investee company'.
HKSSAP11	For foreign transactions, the temporal method is recommended. For foreign investments, the closing rate/net investment method is recommend, though the temporal method is suggested for foreign subsidiaries serving as extensions of the parent company.
HKSSAP12	Deferred tax is required under the liability method on the basis of partial provision. Disclosures related to deferred tax can be provided in the profit and loss account and balance sheet or in footnotes.
HKSSAP13	Investment properties are not subject to depreciation unless their leases are expired in 20 years. Rather, investment properties of all listed companies and unlisted companies owning investment properties with book value over HK$50 million and in excess of 15 percent of the total assets value must be revalued every year by qualified valuers and every 5 years by external qualified valuers. Results of revaluations are moved in an investment property revaluation reserve account, but debit balances of the reserve account should be shown in the profit and loss account. Disclosures of details about investment properties are also required.
HKSSAP14	Operating leases and finance leases are differentiated, and different accounting treatments are applied to operating leases versus finance leases. Disclosures related to operating leases or finance leases are required, respectively.
HKSSAP15	This standard requires reporting entities which fall within its scope to prepare a cash flow statement as part of their financial statements setting out on a standard basis their cash generation and absorption for a period. This standard sets out the required structure of the cash flow statement and minimum level of disclosure.

AN OVERVIEW OF MANAGEMENT ACCOUNTING PRACTICES IN HONG KONG

Hong Kong is one of the most successful financial centres in the world, and many of its commercial activities are highly westernized. Against this background, it is natural to assume that management accounting skills should have reached international standard. However, it has only been since the beginning of the last decade that evidence on the nature of management accounting practices in Hong Kong has begun to be recorded. Two major surveys have been carried out, and these help to give a general picture of current practice. The first survey was reported in Liu (1986). This, among other things, described the typical functions of management accounting, the budgetary process and the profile of the management accountant in Hong Kong. The other survey was reported in Lynn (1989), and investigated the importance of various management accounting concepts and techniques with particular emphasis on the areas of budgeting, performance evaluation and pricing.

Liu (1986)[5] reported that, on average, about 6 percent of those employed in an accounting function are professionally qualified. Most of the accountants in the survey had completed post-secondary education and possessed recognized professional and academic qualifications. Post qualification working experience mainly fell within the range of five to 12 years, and most working experience had been obtained with business firms, rather than with professional firms. Senior executives preferred management accountants to hold a professional accounting qualification rather than an academic degree. Also, local qualifications are preferred to overseas ones. The ideal type of post-qualification experience was thought to be gained from local industrial and commercial firms and audit firm experience was considered to be of secondary importance. Two-thirds of the accountants surveyed were within the 30 to 39 year age range. About 45 percent claimed to earn a remuneration of HK$200 000 to HK$300 000 per annum. The average workload was reported as being around 48 hours per week and was regarded as heavy by most respondents. Most of the sampled companies had separately identifiable sections for the functions of financial accounting, controllership and treasurership, but not for management accounting. Nearly all companies had computerized some parts of the accounting function. Management accountants appeared to spend more time on administrative duties rather than on routine work. Most of their time was spent on annual report preparation, cash management, budgetary control and the provision of internal management information. Very little time was spent on providing external information.

This demographic information may give the impression that management accountants in Hong Kong are young and well paid. However, it is also necessary to possess practical qualifications and relevant experience. Management accountants generally have to be prepared to work long hours and take up other supplementary duties like those of financial accounting and administration.

---

[5]In Liu's (1986) study, 76 listed companies with the largest market capitalization were surveyed. Their industries included banking, hotels, industrial, textiles, merchandising, utilities. In addition, ten companies were further approached, and in their case subsidiaries or divisions with operations consisting of a wide range of activities were also included. For each sample company, two types of questionnaires were sent: one to the chief executive and one to the management accountant. The questionnaire addressed to the accountant was mainly used to seek his opinions on the use of management accounting information. That addressed to the chief executive was similar but simpler in content with emphasis on the company and management profile. For the 'accountant questionnaire', 35 responded, constituting a 41 percent response rate. For the 'executive questionnaire', 23 replied, equivalent to a 27 percent response.

Among the various management accounting techniques used, overhead apportionment was found to be most widely practised, followed by breakeven analysis and statistical analysis. Linear programming, probability estimates and computer modelling other than that for budgeting, were seldom used. Most accountants considered the income statement to be the most important financial report. Although nearly all companies prepared a cash budget, they placed a low value on cash forecasts.[6]

A number of the survey questions related to the use of budgets showed the importance of the techniques used in Hong Kong management accounting practices. The budget was usually broken down into departmental, revenue and expense headings, and product lines. Self-designed computer programs were used mainly to aid computations and to provide a database. Budget projections were based on historical costs, and less than a third of the companies used standard costs. The budgetary process seems to be well respected. Accounting staff are the most important participants in budget preparation and departmental managers in particular exert a large influence on the process. In the survey, senior management was described as giving a great deal of support to the budget, and it was discussed and approved by the main board in the majority of companies. Budget accuracy was generally believed to be high but there was differentiation among various items. Labour costs were the most easily predicted elements, followed by material costs and then by sales volume or level of output. The higher accuracy of the production budget may be due to it having fewer non-controllable costs. Most companies in the survey produced budget reports monthly, comparing the budget with actual performance. About two-thirds broke down the analysis into price and usage variances. However, only one-third based their comparisons on a flexible budget.

Budget information is therefore recognized as useful for performance evaluation and decision making, and opinions about its quality is favourable. However, many accountants think that improvement should still be made by more timely reporting. The general impression of the accountants is that the budget is essential in helping the companies to achieve their goals, and profit is regarded as the major yardstick for measuring the success of a company. Senior executives appear to hold similar attitudes toward the accounting function and the budgetary control system, as do accountants. Although in the survey they did not rate accounting to be as important as strategic development and marketing, they nevertheless considered management accountants as having the ability to exert a significant degree of influence on certain decision activities outside the areas of finance and MIS operations. The most notable of these activities were long-range plan-

---

[6]There has been controversy in the academic literature concerning the potential superiority of cash flow over profit in the supply of relevant information to management. Practices in Hong Kong suggest managers on the shop floor do not clearly see substantial advantages in cash flow as opposed to accrual accounting. It is, however, not known if the reasons for this are based upon the needs of rational decision making or upon something else — e.g. political pressures.

ning, discontinuing certain products and services and obtaining capital equipment. On the whole, Liu's 1986 study suggests that the management accounting function and the budgetary control systems of large Hong Kong companies have reached a degree of sophistication similar to those of the Western countries.[7]

In another large scale survey (Lynn, 1989)[8] it was found that responsibility aspects of the management of surveyed companies were mostly organized in the form of profit centres and cost centres. Revenue centres and investment centres were less important. This appeared to indicate that responsibility centres are allowed autonomy but they do not have jurisdiction over capital investment decisions. Evidence from this survey also showed that participatory budgets are prepared, mainly for the purposes of promoting a sense of responsibility. However, there was a need for improvement in budget preparation through the use of budget manuals, what-if analysis, standard costing, flexible budgets and articulation with long-range plans.

Hong Kong's accounting managers use a variety of capital budgeting techniques with no individual technique showing a commanding advantage. DCF is frequently used, followed by payback period, NPV, IRR, capital rationaling, project ranking and ARR. These findings seem to show more sophistication among Hong Kong users than their colleagues in some other East Asia countries, particularly in the preference for DCF techniques.

Hong Kong companies appear to be dominated by short-term considerations and have a tendency to quantify whenever possible. The two most common measures of performance were found to be return on investment and budget accomplishment. The rankings of other performance measures were: progressing towards a focus on more long range objectives; market share; qualitative factors; and residual income respectively.[9]

Lynn's 1989 study showed that much the same management accounting techniques are practised in Hong Kong as elsewhere. For example, variance analysis and cost allocation are used with high frequency. Breakeven analysis and marginal costing are also used to a lesser extent with statistical sampling, regression analysis and linear programming being less popular.

As far as pricing is concerned, market based pricing was voted the most popular method, probably reflecting the highly competitive environment in Hong Kong. Full, variable and target pricing received less support. With regard to transfer pricing, it was usually found to be set by top management and the major criterion adopted was market price followed by full costs, variable costs and negotiation, in that order.

---

[7]In particular, they are considered to assume an active and respectable role in promoting company performance. Management accountants are practice-oriented and it seems that they are not ready to implement academic theories before they are empirically demonstrated to be useful.

[8]The chief financial officers of 261 public companies (excluding those with foreign subsidiaries) were sent a questionnaire covering the areas of organisational structure, planning and control, management accounting techniques, and pricing. 58 or 22 percent of the companies responded.

[9]'Progressing towards long-range objectives' was rated only third after the other two.

Transfer prices set for the purposes of reducing taxes and tariffs were rare, presumably because most of the transfers were made within Hong Kong.

Further research findings by Lynn (1990), relating to foreign subsidiaries based in Hong Kong, found that 'comparison of budget with actual' and 'progress towards corporate objectives' were the two main performance yardsticks. Return on investment was not among the most preferred evaluation criteria. It may be an inappropriate measurement of performance in the context of the Hong Kong environment because many operations are carried out through subsidiary trading companies with relatively small investment bases and the measure might therefore produce unrealistically high rates of return. Furthermore, the practices of two of the most important countries in Hong Kong from a multinational perspective, Japan and the US, are possibly influential here. Japanese firms tend to concentrate on promoting profitability by increasing market share, and American firms have highly centralized transfer pricing policies in their home country. This suggests that a subsidiary's profit is not considered to be an appropriate indication of performance. Contrary to what was found in Lynn's 1989 study on local companies (which preferred short-term quantitative profitability measures for performance), attention seemed, in fact, to be paid to secondary evaluation criteria by large foreign manufacturers in Hong Kong (in particular, quality control, personnel relations, morale and production safety measures).

Apart from the general surveys just referred to, there are also several studies of management accounting practices on specific service industries. Liu (1990) studied the divisional performance measurement of four banks and found that frontline business divisions, such as deposits and loans, were mainly assessed by profit and business volume, while supporting divisions, such as accounting and EDP, are mainly assessed by cost efficiency and quality. There seems to be two problems connected with profit measurement. One is the difficulty of finding a fair basis for sharing common costs and revenues, the other is the lack of good computer systems capable of extracting data automatically from the financial accounting system for use by management accountants. Another problem is the effect of uncontrollable factors, especially those of the economic kind, which sometimes distort divisional performance. Managers are generally held responsible for most of their decisions and reward systems are highly geared to actual achievement although uncontrollables are recognized to a degree during assessment.

Liu and Ma (1991) examined the attitudes of two banks on the adoption of activity-based costing. Their findings showed that diversity of products seemed to be the main driving force for implementing activity-based cost systems. If a bank has a wide range of products and services, there is a case for a more accurate cost system so as to give realistic product and customer profitability reports. However, if the product range and indirect costs are small the need for such systems is much reduced. Furthermore, it was found that cost drivers and activities were firm specific and are difficult to identify. As elsewhere, it seems, the benefits of an activity-based cost system must be weighed against the costs of its implementation.

The performance indicators of an insurance company were studied by Liu *et al.* (1993). It was found that there is heavy reliance on financial measures, such as first year premiums and commissions, variance analysis of expenses, etc. The firm considered it difficult and costly to introduce quality measurement because of the intangibility and heterogeneity of the kinds of services rendered. There was also a lack of measurement of the attributes of innovation and flexibility. These difficulties and approaches mirror the similar problems of foreign companies and reflect the fact that large insurance companies in Hong Kong are mostly subsidiaries of overseas international companies and tend to follow the operational policies of their parents.

The research evidence indicates that management accounting practices in Hong Kong have reached a level of maturity and sophistication close to international standards. With a few exceptions, management accounting techniques and concepts are used to the same extent as in western countries. Performance measures are short-term and quantitatively oriented. Highly sophisticated statistical or operation research type techniques and models are seldom practised. This is similar to the findings in management accounting elsewhere and possibly reflects the fact that foreign controlled companies tend to follow the operational policies of their overseas parents.

CONCLUSION

As with the accounting development processes in many other countries, Hong Kong's accounting system has developed under the forces of local culture and international influences (Chan, 1988). To coordinate these forces and to establish the substance and reputation of Hong Kong's accounting profession, the HKSA employs a strategy of internationalisation of accounting standards. By integrating international accounting standards and those of other developed countries (e.g. the UK in particular) into Hong Kong's standards, a more advanced accounting technology has been transferred to Hong Kong. The international factor is particularly important in Hong Kong's accounting system. Consequently, the role of Hong Kong in the global economy and the involvement of multinational institutional investors in Hong Kong's capital market are the two variables which have the potential to shape Hong Kong's future accounting system. The study of these variables may therefore help to anticipate the future development of accounting in Hong Kong.

REFERENCES

Au-Yeung, P. (1983), 'Changes in company law introduced by the Companies (Amendment) Bill 1980', *Hong Kong Society of Accountants Students' Newsletter*, Vol. 4, No. 4, March, pp. 4–14.

Chan, A. (1988), 'The speculative accounting system in Hong Kong: Understanding Hong Kong's accounting reality', *Recent accounting and economic developments in the Far East,*

Center for International Education and Research in Accounting, University of Illinois at Urbana-Champaign, USA., pp. 197–218.

Hong Kong Society of Accountants (1981), *First long range plan report*, December.

HKSAN (Hong Kong Society of Accountants Newsletter), No. 1, 1973; No. 36, 1984; No. 40, 1985; No. 46, 1986; No. 52, 1987; No. 54, 1988(a); No. 56, 1988(b); No. 57, 1988(c).

HKSA (Hong Kong Society of Accountants) (1984), press release on 'Exposure draft on foreign currency translation', 12 June.

Hong Kong Society of Accountants (1985), press release on 'Standards on foreign currency translation and accounting results of associated companies', 18 February.

Hong Kong Society of Accountants (1987), *Second long range plan report*, October.

HKSASN (*Hong Kong Society of Accountants Students' Newsletter*), Vol. 4, No. 4, 1983; Vol. 7, No. 2, 1985(a); Vol. 7, No. 4; 1985(b); Vol. 9, No. 1, 1987(a); Vol. 9, No. 2, 1987(b).

Howard, L. (1987), 'Standards and their recognized authority', *Hong Kong Society of Accountants Newsletter*, No. 49, March, p. 22.

Kelly, S. (1983), *A study of environmental scanning in professional accounting organisations in Hong Kong*, unpublished M.B.A. Dissertation, University of Hong Kong.

Liu, K. (1986), 'Management accounting in Hong Kong: An economy wide survey of current practice' *Proceedings of the first South-East Asian university accounting teachers' conference*, Singapore, April, pp. 968–76.

Liu, K. (1990), 'The need for improvements in monitoring performance: Preliminary findings of a study of banks in Hong Kong' *Proceedings of the Northern Accounting Group annual conference of the British Accounting Association*, Leicester, England, September.

Liu, K., Fung, D. and A. Ng (1993), 'Performance measurement: The case study of a life insurance company in Hong Kong', *Proceedings of the fifth annual conference of accounting academics*, Hong Kong, April, pp. 313–22.

Liu, K. and A. Ma (1991), 'Activity-based costing in banks: A review of recent developments in Hong Kong', *Proceedings of the third annual conference of accounting academics*, Hong Kong, March, pp. 215–24.

Lynn, M. (1989), 'Management accounting maturity in Hong Kong: Evidence from publicly-listed companies' *Hong Kong journal of business management*, Vol. VII, pp. 49–70.

Lynn, M. (1990), 'Evaluation of foreign subsidiaries and their managers in Hong Kong' *Hong Kong journal of business management*, Vol. VIII, pp. 31–55.

McInnes, U. (1980), 'Audit consequences of the Securities Ordinance', *Hong Kong Society of Accountants newsletter*, No. 22, February, Appendix D.

Piper, A. (1986), 'Hong Kong's accounting law and regulations', *The Hong Kong manager*, April/May, pp. 30–42.

Wallace, P. (1985), 'The profession in Hong Kong', *Survey*, pp. 9–12.

Wallace, P. (1987), 'Introduction to Hong Kong company law', *Hong Kong Society of Accountants students' newsletter*, Vol. 9, No. 1, February, p. 6.

Yuen, S. (1988), *The institutional framework of accounting for Hong Kong*, Goodman Publisher, Hong Kong.

ACCOUNTING IN MALAYSIA & SINGAPORE: CULTURE'S LACK OF CONSEQUENCES?

A. MacGregor, M. Hossain and K. Yap[*]

BACKGROUND

Malaysia

Malaysia lies on the southern fringes of the South China Sea between latitudes 1° and 7° N and covers a land mass of approximately 330,000 sq. km. It consists of two main parts: western peninsular Malaysia which borders southern Thailand and the eastern states of Sarawak and Sabah in northern Borneo. Peninsular Malaysia has a spine of mountains running north-south with lowlands on each side. Eastern Malaysia rises from coastal lowlands to mountains in the interior along its border with Indonesia. Singapore island lies at the southernmost tip of the Malaysian peninsular and Brunei forms a coastal enclave of eastern Malaysia. The climate of both parts of Malaysia is equatorial — hot and humid throughout the year with evenly distributed rainfall. The western lowlands of the peninsular benefit from a placid climate whereas the lowlands of the east side of the peninsular and those of Sarawak and Sabah are affected by the north-east monsoon between October and March. Malaysia is rich in mineral deposits, including tin (especially alluvial deposits in the western lowlands) copper, coal, crude oil, bauxite and possibly uranium. The soil is of relatively good quality and tropical timber is abundant.

Malay peoples arrived in the areas which they now populate (Malaysia, Indonesia and the Philippines) in a series of migrations about four to five thousand years ago, displacing

---

*Respectively at the University of Otago, Massey University, The Malaysian Institute of Accountants.

earlier Melanesian populations. In the period 700 to 1300 AD, two powerful Hindu-Buddhist maritime empires, Srivijaya (based on the Straits of Malacca) and Majapahit (based on Java) dominated the Indonesia–Malaysia region. The modern history of Malaysia began with the establishment of a Muslim sultanate in Malacca in the early 15th Century which formed the basis of modern Malay institutions and customs. The Portuguese first established a European influence in the region by capturing Malacca in 1511 and were succeeded there by the Dutch in 1641. British influence was founded by the acquisition of the island of Penang and then Malacca in the late 1800s, shortly before a British trading colony was established in Singapore. These three possessions became known as the Straits Settlement and formed the basis of later British economic and political colonial rule in the area. Exploitation of tin and rubber throughout the period up to 1940 brought an influx of immigrant labour from southern China and the Indian subcontinent and was characterised by a period of relative political stability based upon an accommodation between local Malay rulers, a wealthy Chinese entrepreneurial class and British interests. In the aftermath of the World War II, a number of proposals for a unified Malaysian state led, against a background of communist insurgency, to the formation of an independent Malaya (i.e. peninsular Malaysia) in 1957. Sarawak and Sabah, together with Singapore, joined the 11 states of peninsular Malaya in the Malaysia Federation in 1963. Singapore left the Federation in 1965. The 1957 constitution, as subsequently amended, became the basis of the federal constitution of present day Malaysia. The British reinforced the position of the hereditary rulers of nine states and these offices survive today. These rulers form the Conference of Rulers who elect the King of Malaysia (Yang di-Pertuan Agong), a form of constitutional monarchy, for a five-year term. The parliament of Malaysia is bicameral, consisting of the Senate (Dewan Negara) and the House of Representatives (Dewan Rakyat). The federal Prime Minister holds effective executive power, although there are influential chief ministers in the states. The upper Senate consists of 70 members, 40 of whom are appointees of the monarch and 30 of whom represent the interest of the state. The lower House of Representatives, which is the main legislative body, consists of 180 members elected every five years. The federal structure is complex and dynamic. Changes in the constitution since 1957 have tended to limit the freedom of the judiciary (which is a separate branch of the constitution) and the powers of the monarchy. Ethnic Malays have enjoyed special privileges under the Constitution although this has been somewhat mitigated in recent years. The legal system is based upon English common law. The Federal (previously Supreme) Court has jurisdiction in disputes between the States and the Federal government. Malays presently make up about 55 percent of the population of 18 million, the Chinese 30 percent and ethnic Indians 10 percent. The Malays are mostly Muslims, the Chinese either Buddhists or Christians, and the Indians usually Hindu. The official language is Bahasa Malay with Mandarin, Tamil and English being widely used. English is taught as a second language in schools and is widely used in business. The density of the population is about 63 people per sq. km.

Malaysia's annual growth in GDP has often been in the region of 8 percent per annum in recent years, while population growth has been about 2.5 percent. GDP per capita is now well over US$3500 per annum. Agriculture, as in other developing countries, is *declining as a percentage of GDP but is important as an export earner (15 percent of exports) and still employs more than 20 percent of the working population (1993 figures). Palm oil, rubber, timber and cocoa are the principal agricultural crops. Mining contributes about 8 percent of GDP and petroleum and gas account for about 9 percent of export revenues. Manufacturing (e.g. electrical equipment, rubber products, timber products) has grown rapidly, producing 60 percent of Malaysia's export earnings, 30 percent of GDP and 24 percent of its employment by the early 1990s. The tertiary sector already accounts for just under 50 percent of GDP and tourism is now very important to the economy. Malaysia is heavily dependent on external trade (it has an export to GDP ratio of about 80 percent). In recent years, a surplus on the trade balance has been offset by the import of services to give a current account deficit of about 3 percent of GDP. Total overseas debt is around US$20 billion, and the country has foreign currency reserves of about US$27 billion. The main trading partners of Malaysia are Japan, the US, Singapore and the EC. Inflation, interest rates and unemployment have, on occasion, been high in the 1980s but are currently relatively low. Disparities in income distribution have been reduced in the 25 years following the introduction of the New Economic Policy. However large numbers of poor Malays still rely upon subsistence agriculture and one of the objectives of government policy is to further reduce levels of poverty among 'bumiputras'. Foreign trade initiatives through ASEAN and possibly APEC, will be important in protecting Malaysia's interests, as probably will be further movements in the direction of deregulation and the liberalisation of international trade. The unit of currency is the ringgit.*

Singapore

Singapore consists of one main island and about 50 small islets at latitude 1° 22′ N covering an area of 633 sq. km. The terrain is mostly low lying with a central plateau. Some land has been reclaimed from the sea. It has no significant natural resources apart from its deep water ports. The climate is equatorial, hot and humid with plentiful, evenly distributed rainfall.

Like its neighbours, Singapore was settled by Malays, although probably somewhat later, about 2000 years BC. The island was a port at the time of the Srivijaya and Majapahit maritime empires. It was destroyed by disputes between the Thais and the Javanese in the 14th Century and became a commercial backwater until the British East India Company developed the Straits Settlements as a part of its India–China trade route in the early 19th Century. During the period up to the beginning of World War II, when it was occupied by Japanese forces, Singapore grew in importance as the premier trading centre in the region and such was the scale of immigration from southern China that by the beginning of the 20th Century ethnic Chinese accounted for about three-quarters of the island's population. After a decade of left wing politics following 1945, Singapore gained internal independence from Britain in 1959, and by 1965 had joined and left the Malaysian Federation. The constitution of 1959 forms the basis of the present government of the Republic of Singapore. It has a President as the official head of state (elected by universal suffrage with limited executive functions since 1993) and a Prime Minister and Cabinet who exercise most executive functions. The legislature consists of a unicameral Parliament with

83 members elected at least once every five years. There are various provisions to reduce the possibility of ethnic groups being disadvantaged. The People's Action Party has dominated politics since 1959, never having been out of office. The legal system is based upon English common law. Chinese now make up about 75 percent of the total population of 2.8 million people, Malays 15 percent and Indians about 7 percent. With its small size, Singapore is one of the most densely populated countries in the world (almost 4,500 persons per sq. km). English and Mandarin are the main spoken languages. Malay and Tamil are also widely used.

Singapore's GDP was more than US$50 billion in 1993, and its growth rate per annum has averaged about 7 percent over the last ten years. Per capita, Singapore's GDP is the highest in Asia after Japan being approximately US$22 000 in 1994. Agriculture is insignificant as a contributor to GDP, with the manufacturing of high technology, high value added products, financial services and the entrepot trade being the most important sectors of the economy. Trade deficits are typically covered by the export of services and the receipt of foreign income to give current account surpluses (14 percent of GDP in 1993). The overall balance of payments is usually larger because of capital inflows. Total export values exceed GDP by a factor of about 1.5. Singapore's main trading partners are Japan, the US, Malaysia and the EU. Foreign debt is small. Multinationals provide more than 80 percent of the investment in manufacturing, with the US and Japan being the main source of funds. Singapore's economic prosperity began in the late 1960s when, following independence and the withdrawal of British military presence east of Suez, it was forced to adopt a combination of fiscal, monetary and direct policies designed to foster competition, guide producers towards export oriented growth, upgrade the infrastructure and exploit the country's position as a financial centre. Partly due to government action, the savings ratio is extremely high (more than 40 percent of GNP in 1993). The success of these policies and the benefit of a long period of stable government is also reflected in low unemployment, low to modest inflation and a gradually appreciating currency. The problems facing Singapore as an export dependent nation in the future are access to resources, protectionism in international trade and possibly the effects of an ageing population on economic growth. The unit of currency is the Singapore dollar.

R.J.W./A.C.M/M.H

INTRODUCTION

The purpose in this essay is to raise the question of whether culture does, or even can, make a difference to accounting in the context of accounting in Malaysia and Singapore. Is accounting a socio-technical artifact which transcends culture, or is it, as is more often suggested, a human process subject to cultural influences?

Certain human artifacts transcend culture. As a system, for example, the design of a car is governed by technological knowledge to such an extent that culture plays almost no part in its final form. To be sure, the hybrid car-motorbike, *the tuk tuk*, is unique to parts of Asia and the heavily ornate vehicles found in the Philippines are not found elsewhere. Nonetheless, the components of the system such as braking, steering, and engine are identifiable as such no matter from which culture they are viewed. People from extremely diverse cultures can, and do, maintain and drive vehicles from other cultures without additional training. That is, the differences between cars around the world are less remarkable than the similarities.

In a similar vein, it may be that the technological base of accounting is so strong that it too transcends culture. It is necessary to consider the nature of the accounting equation used, the measurement practices, the disclosure rules and the classifications employed to establish a variation. In itself, a variation does not denote a cultural influence. Establishing a cultural connection requires that the causal connections between cultural variables and accounting practices are specified and that the expected associations do indeed occur in the data.

In a reversal of the usual view of causation of accounting historians, Sombart (1919) argued that the development of accounting permits a mode of thinking which gives rise to capitalism and trade. This is a proactive role for accounting history rather than a reactive one. It is not necessary to go this far to believe that accounting is inextricably linked with commerce to such an extent that it is largely global economic and commercial realities which govern its development rather than particular cultural values.

Accounting in Malaysia and Singapore represents an interesting arena around which to discuss the influence of culture on accounting. The countries are geographically close and share a common recent colonial past of relatively short duration. Both countries have a Confucian influence from their Chinese cultures, but Malaysia is an Islamic country. From these cultural antecedents it should be possible, in the method popular in the field of international accounting, to specify in advance how these countries may differ from the western world (Confucian influence), how they may be similar to the rest of the British colonial world (Colonial influence) and finally how they may be expected to differ from one another (Islamic influence).

The next section contains a discussion of how the culture[1] of Malaysia and Singapore might affect the accounting in those countries. In the following two sections, the accounting structures and systems of both countries are described. The final section contains a discussion as to why it is that the accounting systems in these countries bear no relationship to the systems that might be expected solely on the basis of a cultural explanation.

---

[1] It is important to note that neither the notion of culture itself nor the methods employed to describe it are brought into question here. It may well be that Hofstede's IBM employees worldwide are representative of their cultures rather than being a somewhat select group of high achievers. It may even be that triangulating the results of a study of IBM employees with university students from the most selective universities in the same countries does indeed validate an instrument which taps general cultural values. These questions are left for others to study. Here it is proposed to concentrate on whether culture, so defined, will indeed affect accounting.

EXPLAINING ACCOUNTING VALUE DIFFERENCES BY REFERENCE TO CULTURAL FACTORS

In the introduction to this book the relationship between cultural values and accounting sub-cultural values, as proposed by Gray, were summarised. These relationships are repeated for convenience in Table 1 below.

Table 1
ACCOUNTING VALUES (GRAY)

Cultural Values (Hofstede)	Professionalism	Uniformity	Conservatism	Secrecy
Power Distance	–	+	?	+
Uncertainty	–	+	+	+
Avoidance				
Individualism	+	–	–	–
Masculinity	?	?	–	–

Source: Baydoun and Willett (1995)

Given the relationships in Table 1, it is possible to predict certain similarities and differences between Malaysia and Singapore from the culture value scores obtained by Hofstede. The relevant scores and ranks for Malaysia and Singapore are shown in Table 2.

Table 2[2]
CULTURAL SCORES & RANKS

Country	PDI SCORE	PDI RANK	IDV SCORE	IDV RANK	MAS SCORE	MAS RANK	UAI SCORE	UAI RANK	LTD SCORE	LTD RANK
Malaysia	104	1	26	36	50	25/26	36	46	n/a	n/a
Singapore	74	13	20	39/41	48	28	8	53	48	9

Source: Hofstede (1991)

Where there is a difference between the cultural score and rank (Table 2) for Malaysia and Singapore, accounting value differences between Malaysia and Singapore can be predicted using the relationships expected by Gray (Table 1). Where the

---

[2]Where PDI is power distance, IDV is individualism, MAS is masculinity, UAI is uncertainty avoidance and LTD is the Confucian long-term orientation.

difference between Malaysia and Singapore is slight (our judgment), then Singapore and Malaysia may be expected to hold the same accounting values. For example, there is a negative relationship between power distance and professionalism. That is, the more hierarchical a society, the less it would be expected that accountants would exercise professionalism. Because Malaysia is a more hierarchical society than Singapore, it is expected that Malaysia would incline less to professionalism than Singapore but more towards uniformity. These predictions are summarised in Table 3.

Table 3[3]
PREDICTED SIMILARITIES AND DIFFERENCES
ACCOUNTING VALUES (GRAY)

Cultural Values (Hofstede)	Score & Rank Differences	Professionalism	Uniformity	Conservatism	Secrecy
Power Distance	M>S	M<S	M>S	?	M>S
Uncertainty Avoidance	M>S	M<S	M>S	M>S	M>S
Individualism	M=S	M=S	M=S	M=S	M=S
Masculinity	M=S	M=S	M=S	M=S	M=S

In the case of the conservatism-power distance cell, because Malaysia scores differently from Singapore at the cultural level and Gray does not specify the relationship between power distance and conservatism, no prior belief is generated. In all other cases it is possible to specify the expected form of the relationship following Hofstede (1991) and Gray (1988). Clearly, where the Malaysian cultural score is judged to be the same as the Singapore score then, notwithstanding the direction of the cultural-accounting relationship, it follows that the accounting values would be expected to be similar in the two countries.

Before it can be decided whether these expectations are sustained, the development of accounting in Malaysia and Singapore will be considered in the next and subsequent sections.

ACCOUNTING IN MALAYSIA

In Malaysia, accounting is controlled by the Accountants Act 1967, which is administered by the Ministry of Finance. This Act created the Malaysian Institute of

---

[3]Where M is Malaysia and S is Singapore.

Accountants (MIA), which is responsible for licensing and registering the accountancy profession in Malaysia. In addition, Malaysia also has the Malaysian Association of Certified Public Accountants (MACPA) which was incorporated in 1958. This body is a self regulating professional body. The majority of members of the MACPA are also members of the MIA. Many members of the MIA are not members of the MACPA. In order to practice accountancy in Malaysia a person is required to be an MIA member at least.

Professional membership

The relationship between the MIA and the MACPA is a complex one. Both require a three year degree or equivalent for membership, both require relevant practical experience for membership. Nonetheless, the MACPA is closer to the model of an independent professional body seen in many developed countries than is the MIA. For example, in addition to providing professional recognition, the MACPA runs its own professional examinations and ethical pronouncements. However, the MIA does have plans to develop and implement its own examination system and does maintain its own by-laws on professional conduct and ethics.

The MACPA has about 2000 members. About 59 percent of the membership are either partners in, or employees of, accounting firms. The remainder work in industry, the public sector and financial institutions. The MIA has more than 8000 members. Of these, about 2200 work in accounting firms, with the remainder working in commerce, industry and so on.

Both the MACPA and the MIA have a continuing professional education (CPE) requirement. For the MACPA the requirement is 40 hours of CPE per annum, of which at least 20 must be in structured programmes. For the MIA, courses are awarded points and a registered accountant must complete a minimum of 40 structured points and 60 unstructured points per year. It is unclear how points are allocated to hours of course time.

Accounting regulation In Malaysia

Accounting practice in Malaysia is regulated by: (1) Companies Act 1965; (2) Accountancy profession; (3) Kuala Lumpur Stock Exchange.

Companies Act

Financial reporting in Malaysia is governed by the Companies Act 1965. The Companies Act 1965 requires companies to prepare annual audited financial reports in accordance with the Ninth Schedule of the act. The Ninth Schedule prescribes only minimal disclosure requirements for profit and loss account and balance sheets of companies. The *Companies Act* follows the British model in that it requires published financial statements to reflect a 'true and fair' view. But, as with the earlier British Act, no definition for 'true and fair' was provided in the Companies Act.

Accountancy profession

Generally Accepted Accounting Practices (GAAP) are given expression in accounting standards and technical bulletins issued by the MIA and MACPA. The MIA and MACPA undertake to review standards issued by the International Accounting Standards Committee and to adapt these to local conditions. In addition, the MIA and MACPA also issue Malaysian Accounting Standards (MASs) to include topics which are not covered within International Accounting Standards (IASs). Therefore, the generally accepted accounting standards in Malaysia comprise the 30 IASs adopted by the MIA and MACPA and the six MASs issued by the two bodies.

Moreover, the MIA and MACPA issue auditing standards. Accepted auditing standards in Malaysia are 24 International Auditing Guidelines (IAGs) issued by the International Auditing Practices Committee that have been approved for operation in Malaysia by the MIA and MACPA and one set of Malaysian Auditing Guidelines (MAGs) issued by the two bodies.

Generally, the Malaysian corporate annual report is made up of seven parts. These include:

(1) Directors' report: this gives information about corporate principal activities, dividend payments, directors' benefits, and subsequent events.
(2) Profit and loss account: this must include information on operating revenue, investment in associated companies, depreciation and amortization of fixed assets, intangibles and investments.
(3) Balance Sheet: this must contain information in accordance with the disclosure requirements of the Malaysian Companies Act 1965, and of the MIA and MACPA.
(4) Statement of changes in financial position: this shows a separate disclosure of sources and uses of funds.
(5) Accounts (footnote) disclosure: for example, significant accounting policies; details of authorised and issued capital; restrictions on distribution of reserves; category of depreciable fixed assets; amount of each main category of inventory; significant inter-company transactions and balances; nature and amount of contingent liabilities; amount of capital expenditure; nature and estimated financial effect of important events occurring after the balance date; investments showing separately those in government securities; amount received or receivable as progress payments; segment information relating to the turnover and profits and assets employed.

(6) Director's Statement: two directors, on behalf of all the others, must declare that the profit and loss account and balance sheet are 'true and fair' presentation of the corporate financial position (Price Waterhouse 1992).

(7) Auditor's report: the Companies Act of Malaysia stipulates that financial statements must be accompanied by the auditor's report and must give a true and fair view of the state of corporate affairs.

Kuala Lumpur Stock Exchange (KLSE)

The Kuala Lumpur Stock Exchange was established in 1960. Initially the trading used to take place in Kuala Lumpur as well as in Singapore. In 1973 the two exchanges were separated due to the secession of Singapore from Malaysia. In 1991 the International Finance Corporation (IFC) ranked the KLSE as the third largest emerging stock market in terms of business turnover after Taiwan and South Korea. The KLSE is mainly a self-regulatory body, but its several board members are nominated by the Ministry of Finance. Companies which wish to be quoted in KLSE must adhere to various accounting requirements set out both by the KLSE and the Malaysian Securities Commission (MSC). Before a company can obtain listing status, the KLSE requires the companies to lodge a complete set of annual reports for the last three years. These financial statements should disclose information considered to be relevant to potential investors, such as the level of turnover, the amount of investment and other revenues, directors' interest in the company, details of shareholders and the value of their equity, particulars of properties held including addresses, description, existing use, tenure of holdings and age of buildings, and an analysis of share ownership spread. In addition, the MSC requires that prospectuses issued by companies include an estimate of future earnings (Hossain *et al.*,1994). Aside from these specific listing requirements, the KLSE also requires companies to prepare annual audited financial reports in consistent with the Ninth Schedule to the Companies Act.

Management Accounting in Malaysia

Management accounting practice is very much influenced by UK and US practices. To date, Malaysia has not developed any separate standards for management accounting. Relatively little is known with regard to the management accounting practices in Malaysia. Northcott, Coy, and Poh (1994), Teoh and Lau (1989) and Isa (1994) carried out three separate surveys of management accounting practices in Malaysian firms. Northcott *et al.* (1994) and Teoh and Lau (1989) focused on capital budgeting strategies employed by Malaysian companies, while Isa (1994) focuses on activity based costing. The results of those surveys are presented below.

Capital budgets

Northcott, Coy, and Poh (1994) explored the extent to which theoretically recommended investment appraisal techniques are used in Malaysia and compared the Malaysian findings with those of New Zealand companies. This (e.g. questionnaire) was mailed to 180 companies listed on the Kuala Lumpur Stock Exchange (KLSE). Of these, 44 responses were received (a response rate of 25 percent, 44 out of 180 firms). The questionnaire consisted of three parts. These are:

(1) organisational background,
(2) overview of capital investment practice,
(3) choice of investment analysis techniques.

Concerning the objectives of capital investment decision making, 59 percent of the 44 companies indicated that capital investment played a most or very important role in their organisations. These respondents also considered that capital investment decisions were made to maximise return on equity, return on assets, return on sales, growth in sales, stability of earnings, and market value of ordinary shares. Northcott *et al.*, note that these findings are consistent with the results found in New Zealand.

With regard to the appraisal techniques, 98 percent (43 firms) claimed to use pay back period as a project evaluation method. All respondents (44 firms) indicated the use of more than one technique to appraise investment proposals. Of these, 98 percent (43 firms) indicated the use of net present value (NPV) and internal rate of return (IRR) at least "sometimes". Further, Northcott *et al.*, found that 98 percent (43 firms) of the sample Malaysian firms claimed to use weighted average cost of capital (WACC) for determining the investment hurdle rate. In contrast, only 30 percent New Zealand companies used WACC.

Northcott *et al.*, also asked whether Malaysian based firms undertake some sort of risk analysis in the capital budgeting process. Nearly 63 percent (28 firms) of Malaysian respondents indicated that they usually differentiate investment projects on the basis of risk, which is significantly higher than what they found in New Zealand companies (43 percent). Overall Northcott *et al.*, concluded that Malaysian companies rely more on sophisticated investment appraisal techniques than do those in New Zealand.

Comparison of capital budgeting practices between Malaysian firms and
foreign multinationals

Teoh and Lau (1989) compared the capital budgeting strategies employed by Malaysian companies with those of multinationals operating in Malaysia. A questionnaire was mailed to a randomly selected sample of Malaysian and foreign companies. The overall response rate was 23 percent. The major findings of their survey were as follows:

(1) The average annual capital expenditure by multinationals was four times greater than Malaysian companies. The amount of annual capital spending of the sample companies ranged from M$0.05 m to M$562 m.

(2) 95 percent respondents indicated they used at least two techniques to evaluate capital investment projects. The payback period was frequently cited by both Malaysian and foreign companies. In addition, the respondents indicated that they used discounted cash flow techniques (e.g., NPV and IRR), although not as extensively as payback period.

(3) the respondents also cited that they used various management science techniques (e.g., network, PERT, decision theory, computer simulation) as a further aid to the capital investment decision process. Foreign multinationals used a wider range of techniques than Malaysian firms. In general, Teoh and Lau (1989) found that foreign multinationals employed more sophisticated techniques than local firms.

Activity-based costing

Isa (1994) carried out a survey concerning the use of new management accounting techniques. Survey questionnaires were mailed to 300 companies. Completed responses were received from 67 companies, representing a response rate of 22 percent. She reported that traditional management accounting techniques were widely used in most Malaysian based firms. With regard to the allocation of overhead cost, she found that 43 percent Malaysian manufacturing companies used direct labour as overhead allocation base to measure product, while 20 percent respondents indicated machine hours, production volume, or direct materials as the frequently used cost drivers at their firm. Thirty-five percent indicated that they used multiple cost drivers, however almost every one of those respondents indicated direct labour as one of their cost drivers. This suggests that the use of activity based technique is not widespread.

In addition, Isa found in general there is reluctance on the part of Malaysian companies to use new management accounting techniques such as activity-based costing (ABC). She identified three reasons why traditional management accounting techniques continue to be used by Malaysian companies. These include: (i) lack of awareness of new techniques; (ii) lack of expertise to implement new techniques; and (iii) lack of top management support for change.

ACCOUNTING IN SINGAPORE

Understanding the nature of the structure and operation of accounting in Singapore is facilitated by understanding the way in which economic development is managed. The economy is, on the one hand, highly entrepreneurial and capitalistic, yet at the same time centrally controlled. Central planning is conducted under the auspices of such bodies as the Economic Development Board, The Singapore Institute of Standards and Industrial Research and the National Science and Technology Board. The mix of central planning and entrepreneurial activity is unusual by Western standards and yet, if judged against economic growth, must be regarded as a powerful combination.

Accounting in Singapore was, from its early days, quite naturally heavily influenced by developments in Britain. Significant development commenced in the early 19th Century after Stamford Raffles persuaded the British Government of India to allow him to develop a free trade area there. The first chamber of commerce was founded by Chinese merchants in 1837. Despite rising trade it was not until June 1963 that Singapore passed an act to enable its own national body of accountants; the Singapore Society of Accountants commenced operations in December of 1963. It is perhaps indicative of the declining British influence that this initiative was in response to a review by leading Australian accountants commissioned by the Singapore Government.

Accounting regulation in Singapore

Today, the accounting practices of corporate bodies operating in Singapore are regulated by: (1) Companies Act; (2) the Institute of Certified Public Accountants of Singapore (ICPAS); (3) the Public Accounting Board; (4) Singapore Stock Exchange. The influence of each of these bodies on corporate reporting practices are discussed below.

Companies Act

The Institute of Certified Public Accountants of Singapore (ICPAS) is the only professional body in Singapore. Prior to 1987 it was known as the Singapore Society of Accountants. The primary control on financial reporting in Singapore is the Companies Act, but other regulations are imposed by various bodies such as the Stock Exchange of Singapore and the Securities Industry Council. The Companies Act 1990 of Singapore requires every company to be responsible for the maintenance of books of accounts and other records. The Ninth Schedule of the Companies Act prescribes minimum statutory requirements which must be complied within the preparation of corporate financial reports (e.g., income statement and balance sheet). In keeping with earlier British acts it is a requirement that the accounts give a 'true and fair view'. The Ninth Schedule of the Companies Act requires the directors to disclose their interests and benefits in the company. This is to prevent any potential abuse of their position of power within the company (Meng *et al.*, 1994). The major requirements of the Ninth Schedule are listed below:

(1) The profit and loss account (or income statement) should include details of depreciation, investment income, gain and loss on sale of fixed assets, debt write-offs and provisions, directors' and auditors' fees, taxes paid and changes in reserves and provisions, and dividends paid for the year.

(2) The balance sheet must provide information relating to fixed and current assets, intangibles, share capital and reserves, current and non-current liabilities, contingent liabilities, and liabilities secured on assets of the company. Moreover, a detailed analysis of assets and liabilities, the basis of valuation and the basis of foreign currency translation must be disclosed in the corporate balance sheet.

In addition, the Companies Act requires all limited companies to appoint external auditors, who must be a member of the ICPAS. However, various amendments were enacted into the Ninth Schedule of the Companies Act in 1990 in order to bring it in line with the accounting standards adopted by the ACPAS. While the Ninth Schedule prescribes minimum disclosure requirements for income statements and balance sheets of companies, professional bodies such as the ICPAS play an important role in supplementing additional disclosures.

Relationship between Singapore and United Kingdom company law

Briston and Liang (1990) discussed the development of financial reporting in Singapore. They examined the impact the legislative influences on corporate reporting practices. They contended that prior to 1990, the companies legislation in Singapore was predominately influenced by India. While India in turn derived law from the UK and mainly from the British Joint Stock Companies Act 1844 and 1855. Therefore, according to this theory, until recently the Companies Act in Singapore was heavily influenced by British legislation through India. To document the British legislative influence on corporate reporting practices, Briston and Liang (1990) divided the constitutional history of Singapore into five stages:

(1) 1819 to 1823 — when Singapore was a dependency of British Bencoolen (now called Sumatra);
(2) 1823 to 1826 — when Singapore came under the direct control of the Government of India;
(3) 1826 to 1867 — when Singapore became part of The Straits Settlements (which included Penang and Malacca) and was under direct British-India rule from 1830 to 1867,
(4) 1867 to 1946 — the Straits Settlements came under direct colonial rule and,
(5) 1946 — when Singapore became a separate colony.

Thus financial reporting practices in Singapore followed trends found in British colonial territories and as such the companies law in Singapore drew its substance from UK Companies Acts.[4]

Institute of Certified Public Accountants of Singapore (ICPAS)

The accounting standards in Singapore are issued by the Accounting Standards Committee of the ICPA of Singapore under an arrangement with the Public Accountants Board who have primary responsibility for these matters. The process of standard setting in Singapore is quite simple. The committee does not write standards but modifies International Accounting Standards for local conditions where necessary. There is a consultative process which involves the Financial Reporting Standards Consultative Committee, the membership of which includes the chairmen of the top 100 companies. After the issue of a provisional accounting standard, there is public consultation which may involve further amendments to the International Accounting Standard before a final Statement of Accounting Standard (SAS) is issued. To date, the ICPAS has issued 26 SASs, three Provisional Statements of Accounting Standards, six Statements of Recommended Accounting Practice, 30 Statements of Auditing Guidelines and 19 Statements of Auditing Practice.

Entry to the ICPAS and for registration under the Public Accountants Board is by way of a three year degree and two years of practical experience after qualification. Accounting degrees are offered at the National University of Singapore. In addition, Nanyang Technological University offers an MBA degree in Accountancy. The first full-time accountancy programme in Singapore began in 1956. Joint accountancy courses by Nanyang University, and the University of Singapore were introduced in 1978. Today, the School of Accountancy is an integral part of the Nanyang Technological University.

The ICPAS has agreements with the Association of Certified Accountants and the Chartered Institute of Management Accountants in the UK for joint professional examinations which offer a non-degree route to membership. In addition, the ICPAS grants full membership to members of the major accounting bodies from America, Australia, Britain, Canada and New Zealand. By March 1994, the ICPAS had a membership of close to 7500. Under the 1987 Accountants Act, ICPAS is charged with the functions of advancing the study of accountancy, determining the qualifications of accountants and promoting the interests of the profession in Singapore.

---

[4]Some researchers have noted apparently significant differences between the Singapore and UK Companies Acts, for instance, Meng *et al.* (1994). However, many differences seem to be related to provisions introduced recently by the 1981 UK Companies Act which was heavily influenced by European law requirements.

Public Accounting Board (PAB)

In 1987, the PAB was created to control the financial reporting practices of Singaporean firms. The PAB is made up of representatives of the accounting profession appointed by the Minister of Finance. The PAB was specially created to act as a 'watchdog' body to oversee the registration of practising accountants. It is also charged with responsibility for determining the professional conduct and ethics of public accountants.

The Stock Exchange of Singapore (SES)

The SES is responsible for the surveillance of trading in the market and the activities of its members. The stock exchange has 26 local firms and seven international firms. Trading is governed by Security Industries Act. The SES requires listed companies to submit interim reports to the Exchange within three months after the end of the first six months of the financial year. In addition, the public listed companies are also required to submit preliminary financial statements not later than three months after the end of the financial year. The preliminary financial statements should include the details of sales turnover, or gross trading income during the preceding five years; trading prospects, particulars of directors, executives, a history of the company and a profit forecast.

The Singapore Stock Exchange (SES) issued a corporate policy statement in 1973 giving guidelines relating to corporate disclosure. This prescribed disclosure in a number of areas including the immediate public disclosure of material information by listed companies of their activities and the public clarification, rebuttal or confirmation of rumours and reports. It also prohibited insider trading.

Management Accounting

To date Singapore has developed no separate standards or guidelines on management accounting. Accountants in Singapore use management accounting concepts and techniques in multinational companies in such areas as corporate planning, tax management and information systems (Gosh *et al.*, 1987). In most Singapore-based companies, management accountants play an important role in the corporate planning area. Ghosh *et al.* (1987) surveyed 750 firms to compile information about management accounting techniques used by Singapore-based manufacturing and non-manufacturing firms. Areas covered included operating budgets, capital budgets, standard costing and performance measurement techniques (e.g., return on investment). The results of their survey and one by Kee (1989) are summarised below[5].

---

[5]The response rate of the Ghosh *et al.* (1987) survey was 23 percent (the survey questionnaire was mailed to 750 companies and 174 firms responded).

Operating budgets

Ghosh *et al.* (1987) found that operating budgets are used extensively as financial control technique in Singapore companies. Nearly 95 percent (165 out of 174 firms) of responding firms indicated that they used operating budgets as one of the major control mechanisms. Some of the respondents indicated that they compared the actual results with budgets, and used the comparison for performance evaluation of the managers.

Long-term planning

Most Singapore-based firms undertake some form of long-term planning. (68 percent or 118 out of 174 firms). Financial service companies (e.g. banking) used this approach more (over 80 percent) than those in other industries (e.g. manufacturing). The time frame used in preparing the long term plans varied across firms. Sixty-seven of the 118 firms used a time frame of less than three years, while 51 (out of 118) firms used a time span of more than three years in preparing long-term plans. In general, the results indicate that long range planning is used widely in assessing corporate strategies in Singapore companies.

Cash budgeting

Seventy five percent of the sampled firms (130 out of 174) used cash budgeting as a control device. This practice is less prevalent in the service industry. Only 50 percent of the banking and less than 50 percent of property sector companies indicated that they used cash budgeting techniques on a regular basis.

Break-even analysis

Break-even analysis is used extensively in Singapore companies, 55 percent of their companies used this technique for planning purposes. Of this number 25 percent used the technique regularly.

Standard Costing

Only 16 percent (28 out of 174) of the surveyed companies used standard costing techniques for control purposes fairly extensively, whilst another 32 percent (54 out of 174) of the companies used them partially. It was found that the use of standard costing technique was more extensive in manufacturing than in other industries. With regard to the use of variance reports the survey showed that approximately 39 percent of the companies responding prepared variance reports based on standard costing. A majority of the companies used the variance figures for control purposes.

Return on investment

With respect to performance measurement, it was found that the return on investment (ROI) technique is used widely in Singapore companies. Approximately 64 percent (110 out of 174 firms) indicated using it as a management control technique. Fifty of the 110 firms reported using gross investment as the base, while 48 firms used net investment as the base. The remainder employed other bases. Fourty-nine firms reported that ROI calculations were made on a divisional-departmentalised basis.

Capital budgeting

Most Singapore companies appear to prepare capital budgets for investment purposes. The companies tend to have formal submission requirements before major capital expenditures are authorised. A number of surveys have been undertaken to provide information on capital investment practices in Singapore e.g. Kee (1989)[6]. Almost two-thirds of Kee's respondents prepared longer-range capital budgets looking beyond two years. More than half (55 percent) had up-to-date capital budgeting manuals-written procedures. Nearly, 72 percent required formal screening and review of capital investment proposals, and 58 percent reviewed hurdle rates used for project evaluations regularly. In addition, it was found that firms in the industrial sector used more formal planning and administrative procedures than firms in consumer product sectors.

With respect to the evaluation procedures of capital investment projects, Kee (1989) found that a high percentage (82 percent) of sample firms required specific search and screening of alternatives. Almost all (92 percent) conducted formal evaluations before making investment decisions. With regard to evaluation techniques, it was found that payback was used by 69 percent of the sampled firms and was ranked as a major evaluation technique by the respondents. Kee also reported that net present value (NPV) technique was used by 51 percent of the respondent firms and was rated the most important evaluation technique by 26 percent respondents. The survey however, did not find much popularity for average accounting rate of return (AARR). This evaluation technique is employed by only 29 percent of sample firms and was ranked as an important method by only 18 percent of the respondents.

In addition, Kee (1989) investigated whether the choice of capital budgeting techniques varied with the nationality of firms operating in Singapore. The survey evidence revealed that a high percentage (79 percent) of Singapore-based North American firms used payback, but in conjunction with other techniques. The internal rate of return (IRR) was more popular with American firms as a primary method,

---

[6]In this case, Kee (1989) the survey questionnaires were mailed to 454 companies and the response rate was 17 percent.

accounting for 50 percent of the respondents. In contrast, the AARR was more popular among the Japanese firms. Nearly 42 percent of the Japanese respondents indicated that they used AARR as primary evaluation tool.

Overall, Kee (1989) found that:

(1) There is a trend towards greater reliance on NPV and IRR techniques although the payback method is still popular with Singapore based companies,

(2) The majority of firms require some sort of formal analysis of risk for capital investments,

(3) Most firms do not take inflation into account in their appraisal of capital investments; and

(4) Most firms have an established procedural framework with subsequent control of capital investment projects.

Comparison of management accounting practices between multinationals and locals

In another related survey, Ghosh and Yoong (1988) compared the multinational firms with local and regional firms with regard to the degree of sophistication attained in their management accounting practices. The sample consisted of 64 multinationals and 110 local or regional companies. With respect to the budgeting techniques, it was found that budgets were used widely in both classes of companies. The degree of the use of budgetary control techniques was reported to be higher in multinationals (97 percent of the firms) than in local firms (93 percent). In addition, multinationals were compared with local firms with regard to the use of other management accounting techniques (e.g., ROI, break-even analysis for profit forecasting, capital budgeting, transfer pricing). In general, it was found that management accounting practices in multinationals in Singapore tended to be more sophisticated than in other Singapore companies.

ACCURACY OF THE HOFSTEDE-GRAY MODEL

A comparison of the development and current state of accounting in Malaysia and Singapore show considerable similarities between the two countries. Amongst the similarities can be included: adherence to the 'true and fair' view; similar Companies Acts as the manner in which government bodies regulate the accounting profession; almost identical accounting standards; and similar professional membership recognition and requirements.

Indeed, because both countries have adopted International Accounting Standards without significant alteration, it is difficult to detect any significant differences in financial accounting practices and hence values. In a detailed analysis Iddamalgoda

(1994) shows that Malaysia follows international accounting standards very closely. It seems highly likely that a similar analysis of Singapore's standards would produce the same result. Given the argument that international accounting standards are heavily influenced by the USA, their wholesale adoption by Malaysia and Singapore is at variance with the idea that culture plays a significant role in determining accounting values and practices.

In addition, Nair and Frank (1980) located both Malaysia and Singapore in the same group of countries sharing similar accounting practices. Based on the 1975 Price Waterhouse survey of accounting practices, Nair and Frank derived the country groupings shown in Table 4 using factor analysis.

Table 4
NAIR AND FRANK COUNTRY GROUPS

Group I	Group II	Group III	Group IV
Belgium	Australia	Bahamas	Bermuda
Bolivia	Ethiopia	Germany	Canada
Brazil	Fiji	Japan	Jamaica
Chile	Kenya	Mexico	Netherlands
Colombia	Malaysia	Panama	Ireland (Republic)
France	New Zealand	Philippines	Rhodesia
Greece	Nigeria	USA	
Paraguay	Singapore	Venezuela	
Spain	South Africa		
Uruguay	Trinidad & Tobago		
Zaire			
	Group V	Group VI	Group VII
	Argentina	Denmark	Italy
	India	Norway	Switzerland
	Iran	Sweden	
	Pakistan		
	Peru		

Source: Nair and Frank (1980)

It follows that if accounting values give rise to accounting practices, and if accounting values are culturally derived, then the grouping of countries based on accounting practices will map to a grouping of countries based on cultural values. Unfortunately, for the purpose of making such a comparison, Hofstede's discussion of cultural values were presented in terms of bivariate plots of the variables. However, using the scores provided by Hofstede, it is possible to run a hierarchical cluster analysis to identify which countries are similar using his original four dimensions. These cluster groups are shown in Table 5 and include only countries that are common to both the Nair and Frank and the Hofstede studies. For this purpose, Hofstede's East Africa and West Africa are substituted for Nair and Frank's Kenya and Nigeria respectively.

Table 5
GROUPS FORMED FROM CLUSTER ANALYSIS
HOFSTEDE'S CULTURAL VALUES

Group 1	Group 2	Group 3	Group 4	Group 5
Argentina	Australia	Brazil	Denmark	Jamaica
Belgium	Canada	Chile	Netherlands	Singapore
France	Germany FR	Colombia	Norway	
Greece	Great Britain	East Africa	Sweden	
Spain	Ireland (Republic)	Iran		
Uruguay	Italy	Mexico		
	New Zealand	Pakistan	Group 6	Group 7
	South Africa	Panama	India	Japan
	Switzerland	Peru	Malaysia	
	USA	Venezuela	Philippines	
		West Africa		

Whilst there are undoubtedly some similarities between the two tables, there are also some significant differences. These differences, taken together with an absence of the predicted differences between Malaysian and Singaporean accounting values are sufficient, it appears, to question the role of culture in accounting in this instance. At the very least, these results suggest that culture plays only a limited part in determining accounting values.

Some cautionary remarks are also required about technical aspects of this approach to analysing the relationship between accounting and culture. Another feature of both factor analysis and cluster analysis when run on small data sets (such as these) is that additional cases both can and often do make quite marked differences to the results. For example, if the cluster analysis of the Hofstede value scores is re-run including all 50 companies instead of the 37 shown in Table 5, the groups change in some dramatic ways. Table 6 shows the results of the full cluster analysis.

Table 6

GROUPS FORMED FROM CLUSTER ANALYSIS
HOFSTEDE'S CULTURAL VALUES
ALL COUNTRIES

Group 1	Group 2	Group 5
Arab Countries	Australia	Belgium
Argentina	Austria	France
Brazil	Canada	
Chile	Germany FR	
Colombia	Great Britain	
East Africa	Ireland (Republic)	Group 6
Equador	Israel	Denmark
Greece	Italy	Finland
Guatemala	New Zealand	Netherlands
Indonesia	South Africa	Norway
Iran	Switzerland	Sweden
Mexico	USA	
Pakistan		
Panama		
Peru		
Portugal		
Salvador	Group 3	Group 7
South Korea	Costa Rica	Hong Kong
Spain		India
Taiwan		Jamaica
Thailand	Group 4	Malaysia
Turkey	Japan	Philippines
Uruguay		Singapore
Venezuela		
West Africa		
Yugoslavia		

Amongst the differences between Table 5 and Table 6 is a change of group membership for Malaysia and Singapore. In Table 5, Malaysia and Singapore appear in distinct groups, but with the larger number of countries included in the analysis in Table 6, their similarities become apparent. It is not known to what extent both Nair and Frank's factor analysis and this cluster analysis of Hofstede's data would change if all the countries in the world were included, but change they almost certainly would.

The major question here is: is this a problem with the theory or the data? There are concerns with both. For example, Gray and Radebaugh (1993) proposes different schemes for causality, and it is unclear under what circumstances each is appropriate (Gray and Radebaugh, 1993) offered Figure 1 as an explanation of environmental effects on accounting.

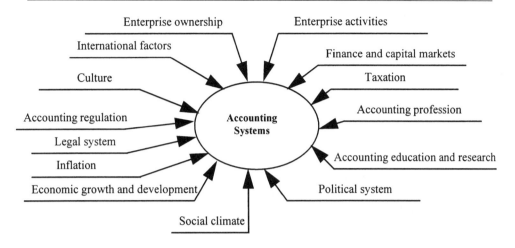

Source: Radebaugh and Gray (1993)

Figure 1: ENVIRONMENTAL INFLUENCES ON ACCOUNTING

Figure 1 suggests that a series of independent variables acts to influence accounting systems and (practices). This view of causality is extended and modified where Gray and Radebaugh show Figure 2.

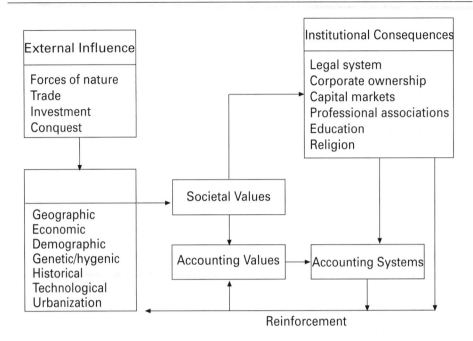

Source: Radebaugh and Gray (1993)

Figure 2: CULTURE, SOCIETAL VALUES, AND THE ACCOUNTING SUBCULTURE

When considering changes in values, this model is further altered to appear as shown in Figure 3.

There are two puzzling aspects to these changes. Firstly, accounting values move from being caused by societal values to be co-determining with them. Secondly, the figures show that the causes of accounting systems also appear to change. Although these changes are in part caused by shifting the level of analysis, they may also indicate that it is very difficult to study the culture-accounting link in isolation from other causal variables.

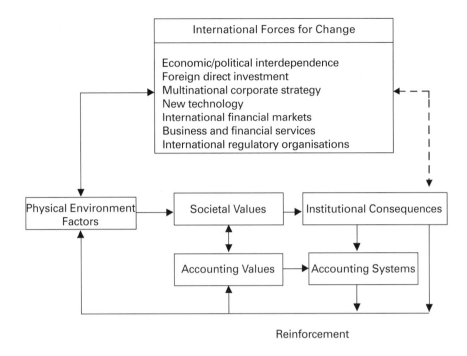

Source: Radebaugh and Gray (1993)

Figure 3: CHANGE AND THE DEVELOPMENT OF ACCOUNTING VALUES AND SYSTEMS INTERNATIONALLY

Fechner and Kilgore (1994) argue for a modification of the Gray and Radebough framework by proposing a model in which economic and cultural factors become moderating variables between accounting values and accounting practice as shown in Figure 4.

ECONOMIC FACTORS

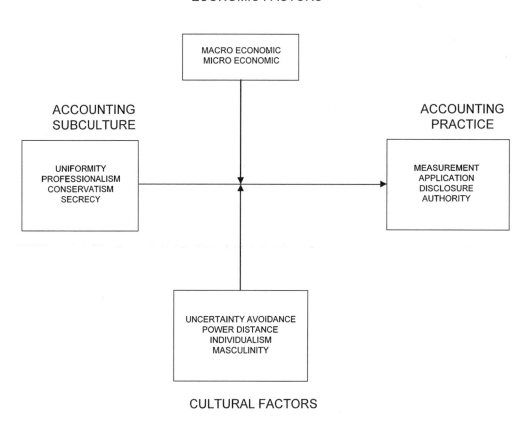

Source: Fechner and Kilgore (1994)

Figure 4: FECHNER AND KILGORE'S MODEL

The strength of this model is the clear role it gives to both economic and cultural variables. Its weakness is that the model is silent on those things that cause the accounting subculture values to be what they are. Furthermore, given the nature of the measurement of the variables in this model, it is difficult to see how it could be tested in any rigorous way.

CONCLUSION

It is not suggested here that culture is without consequences. Nevertheless, it is questionable whether culture influences accounting to the extent suggested in some of the literature. Other variables seem to play such an important role in the form and substance of accounting that even if culture does play a significant part, it is unlikely to be detected amongst the *noise* of the other variables.

There are undoubtedly some interesting patterns in accounting practices worldwide. The reason why a country selects one sub-set of practices rather than another are of importance. However, whether culture plays a part in these choices is unclear on the basis of the evidence presented to date. The examination of accounting in Malaysia and Singapore carried out here leads us to suggest that colonial history, the globalisation of the world economy and technology transfer have played a far more important role in forming accounting values and practices than has culture.

REFERENCES

Baydoun and Willett (1995), 'Cultural relevance of western accounting systems to developing countries', *Abacus,* Vol. 31, No. 1, March, pp. 67–92.

Briston, R.J. and F.S. Liang (1990), 'The evolution of corporate reporting in Singapore', *Research in Third World accounting*, Vol. 1, No. 1, pp. 263–77.

Economist (1990), *How to win in emerging stock markets,* The Economist Publications, London.

Euromoney (1990), *Asia Pacific investment guide*, Euromoney Publications, London.

Fechner, H.E. and A. Kilgore (1994), 'The influence of cultural factors on accounting practice', *The international journal of accounting*, Vol. 29, pp. 265–77.

Ghosh, B.C. and W.C. Yoong (1988), 'Management accounting in Singapore (II) — Comparing multinationals with local/regional companies'. *Singapore accountant*, January, pp. 7–9.

Ghosh, B.C., Yoong, W.C., and C.L. Hong (1987), 'Management accounting practices by manufacturing and non-manufacturing companies in Singapore (I)'. *Singapore accountant*, December, pp. 15–7.

Gray, S. (1988), 'Towards a theory of cultural influence on the development of accounting systems internationally', *Abacus*, Vol. 24, No. 1, pp. 1–15.

Gray, S.J. and L.H. Radebaugh (1993), *International accounting and multinational enterprises,* (3rd Edition), John Wiley & Sons Inc., New York.

Hofstede, G. (1991), *Cultures and organisations : Software of the mind*, McGraw Hill, London.

Hossain, M., Tan, L.M. and M.B. Adams (1994), 'Voluntary disclosure in an emerging capital market: Some empirical evidence from companies listed on Kuala Lumpur Stock Exchange', *The international journal of accounting*, Vol. 29, No. 4, pp. 334–51.

Iddamalgoda, R. (1994), *The legitimacy-effectiveness nexus of the IASC: An exploratory empirical investigation in five countries*, Unpublished PhD Thesis, University of Otago.

Isa, C.R. (1994), 'Activity based costing: An alternative costing system', *Akautan nasional* (Journal of the Malaysian Institute of Accountants), Vol. 5, No. 1, pp. 4–9.

Kee, C.K. (1989), 'A survey of capital investment practices in Singapore', *Singapore accountant*, November, pp. 10–18.

Kiam, O.S. (1988), 'New dimensions of accounting education: Malaysian accounting education at the crossroads', *The Malaysian accountants*, October–December, pp. 14–20.

Meng, T.T., Hoong, P.Y. and F.S. Liang (1994), 'Accounting education and practice: The Singapore experience', *The international journal of accounting*, Vol. 29, No. 2, pp. 161–83.

Nair, R.D. and W.G. Frank (1980), 'The impact of disclosure and measurement practices on international accounting classifications', *The accounting review*, Vol. LV, No. 3, July, pp. 426–50.

Northcott, D., Coy, D. and G.S. Poh (1994), 'Capital investment decision-making practice in Malaysian companies: A comparative study', *Proceedings of Asia-Pacific conference on accounting issues*, Taipei, Taiwan, November, pp. 20–3.

Price Waterhouse (1992), *Asia Pacific guide tax and investment*, Price Waterhouse.

Sombart, W. (1919), *Der Moderne Kapitalismus Vol. II,* (3rd Edition), Dunker and Humbolt, Munich and Leipzig.

Tay, J.S.W. (1994), 'Singapore', *Financial reporting in the West Pacific Rim*, in Cooke, T.E. and Parker, R.H. (eds.), Routledge Publications, London.

Teoh, H.P. and C.M. Lau (1989), 'A comparative study of capital investment strategies by domestic companies and foreign subsidiaries in Malaysia', *Proceedings of Asia-Pacific conference on international accounting issues*, Fresno, California, USA, October 11–13, pp. 143–46.

ACCOUNTING AND ITS ENVIRONMENT
IN NEW ZEALAND

*M.H.B. Perera and A.R. Rahman**

BACKGROUND

Situated in the South-West Pacific Ocean, New Zealand consists of two main islands between latitudes 46°36′ and 34°10′S, and covers an area of 270 500 sq. km. Geologically, the country is unstable with frequent earthquakes and some volcanic activity. Soils are reasonably fertile but with much variation, due to erosion in some instances. There are only limited commercially exploitable natural resources including gold, coal, natural gas and construction materials. Forests of indigenous and exotic species now cover about 28 percent of the surface area. The climate ranges more widely than what would be expected, given the oceanic position, from cool temperate along the coastal areas of the lower South Island, through quasi-continental and semi-arid in Central Otago, to the subtropical north of Auckland. The spectacular Alps of the South Island are a noticeable feature of the country's terrain and account for some of the country's unusual climatic features. New Zealand's total population is presently 3.4 million, of which about 80 percent are of European origin (predominantly British), 13 percent are of mixed Maori descent (indigenous people) and the rest consists mainly of Pacific Islanders and Asians.

The Maoris, whose language belongs to the Austronesian family group, are believed to have settled in New Zealand in a series of migrations from eastern Polynesia over the last millennium. In the early 19th Century, when the Europeans arrived in Australasia, the Maoris lived in tribal communities, used stone implements and practised horticulturalism.

*The authors are Professor and Associate Professor in the Accountancy Department at Massey University, N.Z.

New Zealand became a British colony in 1840 with the signing of the Treaty of Waitangi between the Maori and the British Crown. The treaty is recognised by the Maori as an affirmation of their rights, and occupies an important position in relation to much of the Government's activities at the present time. Intermarriages between the Maori and the European have led to a high degree of racial integration, and there is a growing recognition of the desirability, by both communities, to foster the elements of Maori culture as a way of promoting a distinctive New Zealand identity. The country became a fully independent nation within the British Commonwealth in 1947. It has a unitary, unicameral form of parliamentary government in the Westminster tradition and an independent judiciary. The law of New Zealand consists of several parts, i.e. the common law, statute law, regulations, by-laws and other forms of subordinate legislation. The common law is based on general rules developed by the judges in England when New Zealand was a British colony. A number of UK statutes are still in force in New Zealand. Many statutes empower the Governor-General to make regulations by Order-in-Council.

New Zealand's per capita GDP in 1992 was slighty more than US$12 000. Between 1980 and 1991, the economy had an average annual growth rate of about 1 percent per annum. During the period 1991–93, this figure rose to about 3 percent, and for the year ended 30 June 1994, it was 6 percent. The average annual rate of inflation between 1980–1991 was 10.3 percent, but is currently running at a lower level of less than 2 percent per annum. In 1991, 65 percent of the total Gross Domestic Product came from the service sector, 27 percent from industry and the balance from agriculture. Since 1970, the relative proportions of the GDP of both the agriculture and industry sectors have declined to their present levels from 12 percent and 33 percent, respectively, whereas that of services has increased from 55 percent. Nevertheless, farming and horticulture are major industries responsible for a high proportion of New Zealand's export earnings. These industries include sheep, cattle, deer and goat farming to produce meat, wool, dairy produce and hides. Dairy product exports alone provide about 20 percent of total merchandise trade receipts. New Zealand depends to a large extent on foreign investment for its capital requirements. In 1992, gross fixed capital formation was about 20 percent of GDP, compared to the OECD average of 21 percent and an East Asian average of about 33 percent. More than 50 percent of total foreign direct investment was from Australia, 23 percent from the UK, 8 percent from the US and 6 percent from Japan. There has been a nearly tenfold increase in the amount of portfolio investment in equities and bonds in the New Zealand market in recent years, from 4 percent at the end of 1986, to 39 percent at the end of 1992. The economy of New Zealand is heavily dependent on overseas trade. Between the First and Second World Wars, the UK remained the principal trading partner for New Zealand. Major economic shocks in the 1970s hastened New Zealand to reconsider its trade links. The most important problem was the inclusion of the UK into the EEC in 1973, which created market access problems for New Zealand into its historically most important agricultural export market. Another problem was the oil embargo in 1973 which dramatically increased transportation costs. Since then, attempts have been made to diversify New Zealand's overseas trade both in terms of markets and range of products. The currency devalued substantially in the first half of the last decade, reflecting the changing terms of trade but has recently begun to appreciate against the currencies of its major trading partners. Although the markets of Australia, the Euro-

pean Union and the US continue to account for a large proportion of New Zealand's trade, important trade links have been developed with a number of other countries in Asia, Latin America, the Middle East and Eastern Europe including Russia. Japan, Korea, Taiwan, China and Hong Kong together accounted for 26 percent of the total value of exports and 23 percent of total value of imports in 1991–92. The ASEAN countries are becoming an increasingly important market for New Zealand. The unit of currency is the New Zealand dollar.

M.H.B.P./A.R.R./R.J.W.

INTRODUCTION

This chapter describes aspects of accounting in New Zealand with particular emphasis on the latest developments in the economic, business, legal and regulatory environments. The next section explains the important changes that have taken place in the business and legal environment in recent years and a discussion on the nature of the accounting profession in New Zealand. The third section covers the structure and characteristics of New Zealand financial reporting, accounting regulation and the conceptual foundations of accounting and financial reporting. Section four deals with the development and features of management accounting.

THE BUSINESS AND LEGAL ENVIRONMENT AND THE ACCOUNTING PROFESSION

There have been a series of significant changes in New Zealand's business environment in recent years. Since 1984, the government has initiated a number of major reforms, i.e. significant across-the-board tariff reductions, a continued move away from import licensing (which disappeared completely in July 1992), the removal of restrictions on the operation of financial markets, and the reorganisation of state trading enterprises on a more competitive basis. These changes in the business environment have had a significant impact on the financial system, resulting in a rapid growth in money market activity, including that in the area of foreign exchange. The withdrawal of subsidies and import controls has left large areas of the domestic economy exposed to new levels of competition.

New Zealand has chosen to improve economic fundamentals rather than offer direct fiscal incentives to attract foreign investment. The Chief Executive Officer of the American food products company, Heinz, which acquired the New Zealand food producer, Watties, remarked that New Zealand's low inflation and interest rates, labour market conditions, tariff reforms, attractive transport costs and availability of low-cost raw materials were the reasons for Heinz's investment in New Zealand.

Improved export performance, stability of the dollar and the independence of the Reserve Bank in setting monetary policy to control inflation are also considered to be positive factors in this regard (Walker and Fisse, 1994).

Companies are the most usual form of business organisation in New Zealand. New Zealand has six companies with a market capitalisation exceeding $1 billion. The New Zealand Stock Exchange (NZSE) was established by the Shareholders Amendment Act of 1981. Since 1988, the NZSE has been restructured as a single national body run by a board with independent directors. The origins of the NZSE can be traced back to the gold boom period of the 1860s, when the first stock exchanges were formed where the gold fields were located. In 1872, the Auckland Sharebrokers Association was established to coordinate the activities of these exchanges. The Stock Exchange Association of New Zealand, which was established in 1915, was the forerunner to the present NZSE, which now operates under the authority of the Sharebrokers Act of 1908 as amended in 1981. The bulk of the stocks traded in the exchange today are company shares. Debentures are also traded, as are other loans to companies and government and semi-government stock. The exchange has a set of listing requirements and is responsible for the collection and promulgation of market information, and the operation and supervision of the trading system. An independent Market Surveillance Panel was established in 1989 to administer listing requirements. In 1991, the screen trading system was introduced. There has been a gradual decline in the numbers of both New Zealand and overseas companies listed on the NZSE. There were 137 New Zealand companies and 56 overseas companies listed with the exchange at the end of 1992, compared with 317 New Zealand and 82 overseas companies listed at the end of 1985. However, the NZSE now encourages more international investment in New Zealand than ever before (NZSE Annual Report, 1993).

The changes in the business environment since 1984 have made the New Zealand market highly competitive. This has necessitated certain legislative measures to prevent the market from being dominated by large companies and industries, and to protect the interests of consumers. These measures include the Law Commission Act of 1985, Commerce Act of 1986, Fair Trading Act of 1986, Securities Act of 1987 and Serious Fraud Office Act of 1990. The Law Commission was established by the Law Commission Act as an independent advisory body to undertake the systematic review, reform and development of New Zealand law. The Commerce Act aims to promote good competition in New Zealand markets and control restrictive trade practices and business acquisitions which lead to market dominance. It also provides for private remedies. The provisions of the Commerce Act are enforced by the Commerce Commission which was established under this act as a public enforcement agency. The Commerce Commission has investigative and administrative powers and also has responsibility for enforcing the Fair Trading Act. The Securities Commission was established under the Securities Act of 1987 to facilitate private capital investment in New Zealand, which it expected to achieve primarily by improving the efficiency and fairness of markets and enhancing public confidence in these markets. The Serious Fraud Office, which was set up under the Serious Fraud Office Act, is a specialist entity aimed at facilitating the detection, investigation and expeditious prosecution of serious fraud offenders.[1]

In recent years, a comprehensive review of New Zealand's company and securities law has been undertaken, covering the areas of companies legislation, securities legislation, financial reporting, takeovers, insider trading and insolvency. The primary aim of this review has been to achieve an acceptable balance between providing flexibility and encouragement for business and investment on one hand, and safeguards for the interests of shareholders and creditors on the other.

In the new competitive environment, there have been four pieces of important company legislation in 1993, i.e. the Companies Act, the Companies (Ancillary Provision) Act, the Takeovers Act and the Financial Reporting Act. The Companies Act aims at strengthening and simplifying company legislation in New Zealand. It:

(i)   reforms directors' duties, and for the first time includes them in the statute,
(ii)   abolishes the distinction between public and private companies,
(iii)   allows a company to be formed with one shareholder and one director,
(iv)   replaces the concept of 'par value shares' with that of 'no-par value shares', making the share premium account redundant,
(v)   allows a company to buy back its own shares,
(vi)   allows a company to have a Company Constitution instead of the Memorandum of Association and Articles of Association, and
(vii)   replaces the long standing capital maintenance test for paying out dividends with a two-pronged liquidity test and a balance sheet test.[2] The Companies (Ancillary Provisions) Act provides a three year transition period for existing companies to re-register under the new Companies Act. The Takeovers Act provides for the establishment of a Takeovers Panel for the purpose of recommending a takeovers code which is expected to encourage the efficient allocation of resources and competition for corporate control, assist in ensuring shareholders are treated fairly

---

[1]The Resource Management Act of 1991 and the Employment Contracts Act of 1991 can also be regarded as important developments in the legal environment in which business operates. The Resource Management Act aims to promote the sustainable management of natural and physical resources (including land and water use). The principles enunciated in the act are expected to be applied to management of all resources. The Employment Contracts Act of 1991, which replaced the Labour Relations Act of 1987, introduced a more flexible award system involving the direct negotiation of employment contracts between employers and employees, either individually or collectively. It removes union monopolies over such negotiations.

[2]The liquidity test requires a company to be able to pay its debts as they fall due, and the balance sheet test requires the value of the company's assets to be greater than the value of its liabilities, including contingent liabilities.

and promote the international competitiveness of New Zealand's capital markets. The Financial Reporting Act requires issuers of securities to the public to file audited financial statements with the Registrar of Companies. It has created an Accounting Standards Review Board to approve accounting standards. In preparing financial statements, public issuers are required to comply with accounting standards approved by the Board.

The accounting profession

The accounting profession in New Zealand is similar to that of any other Anglo-American country, and is organised on the basis of self-regulation. New Zealand has one national accounting body, the New Zealand Society of Accountants (NZSA), (soon to be known as the Institute of Chartered Accountants of New Zealand) compared, for example, to Australia, where there are two major professional bodies. There were four forerunners to the current professional accountancy body in New Zealand. These were the Incorporated Institute of Accountants of New Zealand, founded in 1894; the New Zealand Accountants' and Auditors' Association, founded in 1898; the New Zealand Society of Accountants, founded in 1908; and the New Zealand Institute of Cost Accountants, founded in 1944. The other three merged with the NZSA forming a single body in 1972 (Tower, 1992; Zeff, 1979). The NZSA is now an autonomous body which has been authorised by the New Zealand Society of Accountants Act of 1958 to control and regulate the practice of accountancy in New Zealand (Section 3 (4)(a)).

In 1993, the NZSA had a total membership of 19 645. In terms of occupational groups, 28 percent were commerce, industry and the services, 25 percent in public practice (principles and employees), 8 percent in public sector (local, central government, corporations), and 19 percent were overseas. New Zealand's accounting profession continues to be dominated by males who make up 80 percent of the total membership (NZSA, 1993a). In New Zealand, the involvement of universities in the education of future accountants goes back to the beginning of this century and over the years the NZSA has evolved into a full graduate entry system.[3]

During the last two years, the NZSA has undergone rapid change, particularly with regard to its structure and educational policy. These changes came about mainly as a result of the pressures exerted by its own members and some overseas account-

---

[3]For example, in 1911 the NZSA asked the then University of New Zealand to conduct examinations for the NZSA (Graham, 1960). In the 1960s and 1970s, a number of attempts were made to persuade members of the NZSA to agree to a system of graduate entry but without success. However, during the period 1972–1983 the proportion of new members who were graduates rose from 42 percent to 77 percent (Report to NZSA Education Committee, September 1983).

ing bodies as well as research findings.[4] In August 1994, the NZSA published a comprehensive document outlining a new structure and educational policy. Professional membership is now structured into three colleges recognising the distinctions among members in terms of qualifications and the extent of involvement in core accounting services.[5]

STRUCTURE OF NEW ZEALAND FINANCIAL ACCOUNTING AND ITS REGULATION

Accounting practices and rules in New Zealand have developed on a British pattern. Prior to 1946, there was no professional accounting promulgation. Reliance was placed mainly on professional judgement and the judgements and *dicta* of the judiciary. The underlying notion of preparing and presenting a financial statement was the true and fair view concept. The basis for the true and fair concept was the earlier English Companies Acts and later on the New Zealand Companies Act of 1933 (Tower, 1992; Zeff, 1979).

The period between 1946 and 1965 saw a gradual evolution of professional promulgations in Britain. In the same period, New Zealand experienced an almost verbatim adoption on the English Institutes' *Recommendations for Accounting Practice.* In the period that followed (1966–73), New Zealand-based standards were issued. However, the contents largely reflected overseas developments in Britain and the USA. Although the standards were given more weight than those given to the earlier recommendations, they were still not mandatory. The first mandatory standards were

---

[4]The international review report on the NZSA admissions policy (Lothian and Marrian, 1992) concluded that in order to ensure the future continued recognition of the NZSA qualifications internationally, the current admission requirements needed to be enhanced by including liberal study in the academic requirement, structuring practical experience through Approved Undertakings, and including Professional Accounting Schools and demonstration of professional competence as admission requirements.

[5]The three colleges are, the College of Chartered Accountants (CA), the College of Associate Chartered Accountants (ACA) and the College of Accounting Technicians (AT). Those seeking a career in public practice must attain the CA qualification. The admission requirements for the CA and ACA colleges which are expected to form the basis of high level accounting expertise have a common five year foundation including four years full-time tertiary study involving completion of an accountancy major degree programme and one year of general practical experience period with or without a mentor. A further two years of practical experience accompanied by further professional exams in the case of the CA qualification will then be required. (The AT qualification requires two years approved tertiary study and one year relevant practical experience with a supervisor/mentor (CA or ACA) of two years relevant practical experience while studying). The ATs are also required to attend an approved professional course and perform satisfactory. It is expected that the new admissions policy will provide the New Zealand accounting profession with the capacity to adapt to changing circumstances in performing its role in society in the future.

issued in 1974 (Tower, 1992). These standards were mandatory only for the members of the NZSA because the society had no authority over non-members and the standards did not have the backing of any institution of the state or the government directly. In this early stage of development, the standards did not have a conceptual basis. The need for having the standards was 'instinctive' (Zeff, 1979), i.e., the standards were prepared due to the demand for them to remove certain apparent abberations in a specific area of accounting at a particular point in time (Rahman, *et al.*, 1994).

In 1993, New Zealand standard setting entered a new age and era. The Financial Reporting Act of 1993 provided legislative support to the accounting standards, making such standards mandatory for all public issuers of securities and all companies except those specifically exempted by the act or any regulations enacted under the act. To complement the legal elevation of standards, the NZSA has produced a financial reporting framework to forge a conceptual basis for its standards. This new development has put New Zealand on equal footing with its Pacific rim neighbours, such as Australia, the USA and Canada, where similar processes have been set in motion. Under the current setting, the existing accounting standards of the NZSA are being revised to meet the new legal and conceptual parameters set by the Companies Act and the financial reporting framework, respectively.

New Zealand accounting practices and rules have continuously experienced influences from overseas institutions. These have been both *de jure* and *de facto*. The *de jure* influences came from the NZSA's involvement with other Anglo-American accounting bodies, the International Accounting Standards Committee (IASC), the International Federation of Accountants (IFAC), the Organisation of Economic Co-operation and Development (OECD) and the United Nations accounting programmes (Tower, 1992). The most dominant of these influences have been from the UK in the early phases of the standards development; the USA in the late 1980s and 1990s; the IASC since the inception of the IASC standard setting initiatives in the early 1970s; and, more recently, Australia because of the growing influence of the Closer Economic Relations (CER) agreement. Recent accounting standards indicate that a concerted effort is being made to align New Zealand standards with those of Australia and the IASC (see Appendix 1).

The *de facto* influences have mainly come from two sources: practising accountants and the multinational firms. The migration of people from Britain in the 19th Century saw the emergence of an economy and a business environment that was conducive to the adoption and development of accounting practices similar to that which existed in Britain. The direct migration of accountants from Britain and, later on, the creation of accounting bodies in a form and manner following that adopted in the UK, initiated an accounting profession that closely resembled its counterparts in Britain and other Anglo-American countries. The Anglo-American influences have been perpetuated through the presence and influence of multi-national firms of British origin, until around the 1970s; and of American and Austral-ian origin more recently. Overseas stock markets have also been instrumental in bringing outside influences to bear upon New Zealand accounting practices. The London stock exchange has traditionally been the source of finance for major New Zealand enterprises. Due to the current trend toward diversification in global capital markets, New Zealand firms have also ventured into the capital markets of the USA, Australia, Europe and Asia. Stock exchanges with their listing rules and accepted practices have been known to affect accounting practices of firms listed on them (Saudagaran and Biddle, 1992). Firms listed on overseas exchanges may bring in in-fluences of overseas practices in local conventions. This has been evident in the case of Telecom Ltd, whereby the firm after listing on the New York Stock Exchange used both the US and New Zealand accounting standards to report to the New Zealand market. Such changes in practice will be more frequent as listing on overseas stock markets increases. However, similar influences may be brought in through the direct investment of overseas investors into the New Zealand stock market. For instance, firms such as Cater Holt Harvey Ltd, are obliged to refer to FASB standards due to a large presence of US interests in its share capital.

New Zealand accounting standard setting has had its share of crises which in turn have provided an impetus for change. The controversy over equity accounting led to the creation of a standard on equity accounting in 1974. This standard was the first mandatory standard for which full compliance was expected from all the members of the NZSA (Tower, 1992). The inflationary influences of the early 1970s led to the creation of a current cost accounting standard. The indifference shown to this stand-ard by the government and the later non-compliance by preparers of annual reports gave the NZSA the first experience of the pitfalls of setting standards in controversial areas without the support of the major parties. In the late 1980s, the standard on investment properties (SSAP17) also suffered similar consequences for similar rea-sons. The standard was effective until the preparers withdrew their support for it, mainly due to the changed market conditions for investment properties. This typified the problem of enforcement without proper government support and added fuel to the argument that legislative backing was needed if accounting standards were to be viable instruments of accounting regulation.

The need for stronger accounting standards and greater disclosure regulation was also prompted by the 1987 stock market crash. The crash saw the demise of several large and many smaller firms listed on the New Zealand Stock Exchange. The inquir-ies eventuating from the aftermath suggested the need for a revision of the company regulatory regime. Proposals of several committees and institutions recommended greater statutory support for accounting standards and more disclosure on the part of the companies, especially those listed on the stock exchange. The result, the Financial Reporting Act and the revised Companies Act, were promulgated in 1993, beginning a new era of corporate financial reporting in New Zealand.

Financial accounting regulation

The main sources of accounting regulation in New Zealand are the companies legislation (Companies Act of 1993 and Financial Reporting Act of 1993), the Stock Exchange Listing Requirements and the Financial Reporting Standards. The legislative and stock exchange sources provide only for broad disclosure rules. The translation of these rules into detailed disclosure and measurement prescriptions are done through the Financial Reporting Standards. Due to the backing provided to these standards by the statute (Financial Reporting Act of 1993) and the requirement of the stock exchange that all listed companies follow such standards, the Financial Reporting Standards have emerged as the mainstay of financial reporting practices in New Zealand. As mentioned earlier, to provide conceptual rationale, the NZSA as the main formulator of accounting standards has recently adopted a conceptual framework. Future standards will be prepared under the aegis of this framework.

At the apex of the standard setting scheme in New Zealand, the Minister of Justice holds the responsibility for the formulation and enforcement of corporate law. The Minister appoints the members of the Securities Commission and the Accounting Standards Review Board (ASRB) and other constituent bodies of the scheme. The ASRB is a government-funded organisation consisting of four to seven members. The members must generally possess knowledge of, or have experience in, business, accounting, finance, economics, or law. It has no specified membership distribution criteria similar to its Australian counterpart. The New Zealand Accounting Standards Review Board (ASRB) plays a role similar to that of the pre-1988 Australian ASRB. It only reviews and approves standards for the purposes of the Financial Reporting Act of 1993. However, the board is also authorised to provide policy guidance with regards to financial reporting by companies and public issuers. The Board is required to liaise with the Australian Accounting Standards Board (AASB), with a view toward harmonising New Zealand and Australian financial reporting standards (Financial Reporting Act of 1993, Part III).

The Financial Reporting Standards Board (FRSB) is the financial reporting standard setting arm of the New Zealand Society of Accountants (NZSA). The Board and its constituent committees are responsible for the preparation of accounting standards that are submitted to the ASRB for approval. Although other bodies can submit standards for approval, the Financial Reporting Act of 1993 explicitly identifies the NZSA as a frequent source of standards (Section 24).

The Registrar of Companies is the watchdog for monitoring the compliance with statutes and regulations relating to companies, and the Securities Commission plays the role of monitoring compliance of corporate law by public issuers of securities as required by the Securities Act of 1978. Therefore, in the New Zealand environment, both the Registrar of Companies and the Securities Commission together play a role comparable to that of the Australian Securities Commission (ASC).

The primary obligation to ensure that accounting standards are being complied with lies with the auditors of financial statements. The auditor of a company, under the Financial Reporting Act of 1993, has specific obligations in respect to whether accounts or group accounts conform with approved accounting standards. Audit reports of non-exempt companies and public issuers of securities have to be filed with the Registrar of Companies along with the annual reports. In the event of noncompliance with approved accounting standards, the auditors are expected to issue qualified reports which, in turn, have to be sent to the ASRB and the Securities Commission by the Registrar of Companies.

The concept of presenting a true and fair view in financial reports seems to prevail in the statutory requirements. The Companies Act of 1993 and the Financial Reporting Act of 1993 prescribe the presentation of a 'true and fair view' in company financial statements. The recent attempt to formulate a financial reporting framework has sought to prescribe other concepts, the concepts of fair reflection and fair presentation of financial position, performance and cash flows. However, the NZSA concedes that these concepts are synonymous to the concept of true and fair view. Therefore, the latter still governs the preparation of financial accounting standards of the NZSA (NZSA, 1993b, Paragraph 5).

Comparatively, the New Zealand accounting regulatory structure is quite similar to that of other major Anglo-American countries (see Appendix 2). The differences between the regulatory systems of New Zealand and the other Anglo-American countries relate more to the degree of strength of the element of regulation rather than to underlying bases of regulation. For example, in regard to due process procedures, New Zealand does not have public hearings, whereas the US has public hearings; and both Australia and the US have a single regulatory authority that enforces regulations, whereas New Zealand has two bodies, the Registrar of Companies and the Securities Commission, each with undefined parameters to enforce regulations.

Statutory Requirement: The Companies Act of 1993 and the Financial Reporting Act of 1993 require the presentation of an annual report of a company or group of companies before the annual general meeting of a company. The Financial Reporting Act also extends the reporting requirements to public issuers of securities. Those who are not exempted by the Financial Reporting Act are expected to prepare a balance sheet and a profit and loss statement, and a cash flow statement where applicable, according to Generally Accepted Accounting Practice (GAAP).[6] Where necessary, the Act also requires the preparation of other statements under the Public Finance Act of 1989 and the Building Societies Act of 1965. GAAP is defined as the approved accounting standards that are applicable to an entity. If there are no approved accounting standards in an area, then the entity is expected to report according to the practices that have authoritative support of the accounting profession. If GAAP does not provide a true and fair view of financial position and performance, then entities are expected to provide additional information.

A company is exempt from reporting based on GAAP if its assets do not exceed NZ$450 000, it has a turnover of not more than NZ$1 000 000, it is not a public issuer, and it is not an overseas company (parent or subsidiary company). Exempt companies may prepare a balance sheet and profit and loss statement without any reference to GAAP. The disclosure requirements for these two statements for exempt companies are laid down in the Financial Reporting Order of 1994. The Financial Reporting Act includes tough penalties for noncompliance with its disclosure requirements. Fines of up to NZ$100 000 can be imposed on individual directors for not presenting the annual reports within the specified time limit or in accordance with the GAAP.

Stock Exchange Requirement: The New Zealand Stock Exchange Listing Requirements provide reporting requirements for listed companies in addition to the annual reporting requirements of the Companies and Financial Reporting Acts. These requirements are mainly in the form of disclosure schedules for preliminary and interim reporting. Interim reporting is on a half-yearly basis. The reporting schedules require balance sheet, profit and loss and cash flow information. The listing requirements explicitly require the use of accounting standards issued by the NZSA in preparing the necessary information.

Accounting Standards: A list of currently effective accounting standards is in Appendix 1. The practice of accounting in New Zealand in accordance with these standards is briefly discussed below.

Currently, the NZSA's conceptual framework is being used to revise all its existing standards before they are sent for review to the ASRB[7]. The conceptual framework,

---

[6] Where necessary, the Act also requires the preparation of other statements under the Public Finance Act of 1989 and the Building Societies Act of 1965.

[7] In December 1991, the Accounting Research and Standards Board (ARSB) of the New Zealand Society of Accountants (NZSA) proposed a financial reporting framework which contained seven exposure drafts. On that basis, the Financial Reporting Standards Board (FRSB), which replaced the ARSB, has recently issued a concepts statement, a differential reporting framework, an explanatory foreword for the financial reporting standards and two financial reporting standards aimed at providing disclosure guidance for general purpose reporting.

which is discussed further in the final section, proposes to provide some guidance for recognition and measurement of the various elements of financial reports. Based on these criteria, Financial Reporting Standard No. 2 (FRS-2) provides for the major accounting statements that a reporting entity should produce to fulfil the requirements of the Financial Reporting Act. These statements are: Statement of financial performance (profit and loss statement); Statement of movements in equity; Statement of financial position (balance sheet); Statement of cash flows; Statement of service performance (non-financial but quantitative statement for mainly public sector entities). Although FRS-2 requires the use of GAAP, certain entities qualify for exemptions, partially or fully, from some of the accounting standards under the Differential Reporting Framework (NZSA, 1994a) that accompanies the NZSA conceptual framework. Further details of what is to be disclosed in the above accounting statements are laid down in the standards dealing with specific accounting issues. Some of the important standards are discussed below.

Currently, the following standards deal with non-current asset accounting and reporting: SSAP[8]-3 *Depreciation of Fixed Assets*; SSAP-17 *Accounting Investment Properties* and *Properties Intended for Sale*; SSAP-28 *Accounting for Fixed Assets*. As indicated by the titles of the standards, the accounting profession in New Zealand has made a distinction between fixed assets and investment properties. The standardisation of accounting for fixed assets is a recent phenomenon in New Zealand, as SSAP-28 was issued only at the end of 1991. Earlier attempts to standardise the practice in this area were only with respect to (a) depreciation or disclosure (SSAP-9), and (b) investment properties. Attempts to standardise valuation practices and the treatment of valuations in the accounts have always encountered serious controversies.

Recent surveys (e.g. Wilson, 1992) show that most companies have been disclosing amounts for different types of fixed assets separately, a treatment suggested by SSAP-28. The most common types of fixed assets being disclosed are land, buildings, plant and equipment, motor vehicles and fixtures and fittings. There has been little disclosure of intangibles, such as goodwill, patents and trademarks. For land and buildings, disclosure of cost and valuation or combination thereof has been a common practice. For all other assets, especially plant and motor vehicles, the most common method of measurement has been cost. Companies tend to value their land and buildings every three years. Valuations are normally conducted by independent valuers who, in most cases, are members of the Institute of Valuers or the employees of the Government Valuer-General. The controversy associated with the treatment of revaluations in the accounts is reflected from Wilson's survey. It reveals that, prior to

---

[8]The acronym SSAP stands for Statement of Standard Accounting Practice. These are accounting standards produced by the NZSA. Once the SSAPs are approved by the ASRB, they become known as appropriately numbered Financial Reporting Standards (FRSs).

the imposition of SSAP-28, almost a third of the firms tended not to disclose their upward revaluations and almost half of the downward revaluing firms did not disclose their revaluations. However, this situation is rapidly changing under the SSAP-28 regime, where all such revaluations are required to be disclosed. Adhering to the SSAP-28 requirements, most companies seem to take upward revaluations to reserves and downward revaluations to the profit and loss statement. Although SSAP-3 requires disclosure of depreciation of different classes of assets separately, almost 90 percent of the companies disclose only a single amount representing the total depreciation for the year for all assets. A similar situation exists for accumulated depreciation. More than half of the companies disclosed the method of depreciation and the life of the assets.

The current version of SSAP-17 was issued in 1989 to replace the earlier version, which had to be withdrawn because of non-compliance by the preparers. The earlier version required disclosure of unrealised gains and losses on investment properties in the profit and loss statement. The current version allows for both disclosure in the profit and loss statement and direct transfer to revaluation reserve. The standard primarily applies to real estate properties which are 20 percent or less, occupied by the firm itself and similar properties that are intended for sale. Keenan (1992) indicated that almost all of the firms who disclosed that they had investment properties, disclosed those properties separately in the balance sheet. Only half of the disclosing firms mentioned their valuation methods, which in all cases were the net realisable value method. There was an almost even split between those who disclosed the unrealised value changes in the profit and loss statement and those who transferred them directly into reserves. Most firms contravened the requirements of the standard by disclosing properties intended for sale as non-current assets. A majority of firms failed to disclose the details of valuers and valuations, as required by the standard.

A large proportion of current assets of New Zealand firms listed on the stock exchange are inventories (Alley, 1992a). This area of accounting is governed by SSAP-4 'Accounting for Inventories'. The standard requires inventories to be valued at the lower of cost and net realisable value. Around 80 percent of the listed firms disclose inventories. In most cases, amounts were disclosed separately for different categories of inventories. First-in-first-out was the most favoured method of inventory costing. Last-in-first-out, being a method that was discouraged by the standard, was not at all in use. According to Speer, all firms listed on the stock exchange have accounts receivable and cash/bank as current assets. There also exists a vast variety of other current assets, such as bloodstock and livestock, reflecting the nature of industries in which New Zealand firms commonly operate. Short term deposits and advances were also quite commonly found current assets (Speer, 1992a). Disclosure of current assets is regulated by SSAP-4, 'Information to be Disclosed in Company Balance Sheets and Profit and Loss Accounts'.

Accounting for liabilities, including disclosure for contingencies, is covered by SSAP-9 and SSAP-15, 'Accounting for Contingencies'. According to Alley (1992b), most listed firms disclose a single amount for non-current liabilities in their balance sheets. However, a sizable minority also disclose a breakdown of different types of non-current liabilities. For current liabilities, once again, most listed firms showed one main head for current liabilities, with a large number of firms showing some significant liabilities, such as proposed dividends, provision for income tax and bank overdrafts separately. In a lot of cases, the balance sheet figures were broken up into their constituent parts in the notes to the accounts. Liabilities were generally listed in ascending order of liquidity, with the least liquid item coming first. The disclosure of contingencies has been gradually improving with almost 90 percent of the listed firms disclosing at least a quantified amount of their contingencies in 1990. However, the general nature of the contingencies was disclosed by only two-thirds of the reporting firms.

Disclosure requirements for equity items are also laid down in SSAP-9. The nature and extent of disclosure of equity items depend mainly on the types of equity a firm has (Speer, 1992b). This survey also showed a strong influence of companies legislation. Since the 1955 Companies Act required the disclosure of authorised capital and classes of capital, almost all of the listed companies disclosed these items. In most cases (90 percent of the companies), the number of shares issued and the amount of unpaid capital were also disclosed. However, with the removal of the need for having a par value for shares under the 1993 Companies Act, there will almost certainly be a shift away from the current form of reporting for capital items. Almost all listed firms having reserves disclose them under two broad headings: capital and revenue reserves. Within these two categories, retained profits, share premiums and asset revaluation reserves are the most common forms of reserves. However, disclosure of share premiums is an event of the past.

Business combination accounting in New Zealand is covered by two accounting standards: SSAP-8 Accounting for Business Combinations; SSAP-25 Accounting for Interests in Joint Ventures and Partnerships. Both of these standards apply to all forms of business entities including companies. SSAP-8 lays down the requirements for accounting by groups that have subsidiaries and/or associates. In the case of subsidiaries, the standard prescribes full consolidation using the purchase method. It does not disallow pooling for mergers where acquirer and acquiree firms are not identifiable. In the case of associates, the standard suggests the use of equity method of accounting. SSAP-25 prescribes the proportionate consolidation method for interests in joint ventures. For interests in partnerships, the standard suggests the use of SSAP-8, i.e., full consolidation where the partnership is controlled by the reporting entity and equity accounting where the partnership is significantly influenced by the reporting entity.

Neale (1992a) reported that in the period from 1988 to 1990, almost all firms that had subsidiaries followed SSAP-8 very closely. Subsidiaries were omitted only when the inclusion of the subsidiary's accounts in group accounts would provide misleading information. This is allowed by SSAP-8. The most common method of consolidating subsidiaries was the full consolidation method. For associates, the equity method was widely used. Joint ventures and partnerships between entities, especially corporate entities, are not common in New Zealand and no survey has been carried out since the enactment of SSAP-25. A pre-SSAP-25 survey of joint venture and partnership accounting practices shows that interests in such arrangements were accounted for using equity accounting (Neale' 1992b).

DEVELOPMENT AND FEATURES OF MANAGEMENT ACCOUNTING

Since 1984, the substantial programmes of economic reform and restructuring of the public sector enterprises by successive governments have had a major impact on manufacturing. A mix of macro- and micro-economic measures have liberalised the market for goods and investment in New Zealand and improved the international competitiveness of New Zealand businesses. Import duties and tariffs, and fiscal incentives for exports have been drastically cut. Rules regarding foreign ownership of local firms have been relaxed and new policies on full employment and economic diversification have been drawn to reduce costs of production and encourage development of new industries (New Zealand Yearbook, 1993; Hossain *et al.*, 1995). Manufacturing in New Zealand has undergone a quiet revolution in recent years in adapting to the modern manufacturing environment (Northcott *et al.*, 1990)[9].

In New Zealand, manufacturing is largely based on the primary sector which includes farming and forestry. The 1992 economic survey indicated that almost two-thirds of the sales and income of New Zealand manufacturing industries were associated with the primary sector. Because of the small size of the economy and the domination of the primary sector, small firms make up a significant proportion of the manufacturing sector. In 1991, companies employing less than 50 employees produced 85 percent of manufacturing output and represented 67 percent of the manufacturing workforce (New Zealand Yearbook, 1993).

The rest of this section explains the status of management accounting practices in New Zealand. The discussion covers awareness and adoption of manufacturing innovations (e.g., Just-In Time systems), product costing, transfer pricing, capital

---

[9]This survey focused on uptake of manufacturing innovations, capital budgeting, performance measures, product costing and short-term decision making. The survey covered 21 organisations and they were large by New Zealand standards. For instance, 18 of the 21 organisations were selected from a list of top 200 companies.

budgeting, performance measures, product life cycles and short-term decision making.

Management accounting practices

Adoption of Manufacturing Innovations: In a survey of management accounting practices in New Zealand manufacturing organisations, Northcott, *et al.* (1990) found a significant concern with quality manufacturing, for example, 76 percent of the companies had the operators assign their own quality control, half of the sample employed mistake-proofing machines and one-quarter had introduced computer-aided inspection. Although only half the sample professed to having adopted a full JIT approach to manufacturing, two-thirds had introduced frequent supplier deliveries and the use of standard containers. Nearly all of the respondents were attempting to achieve synchronised flow between stages of production. Furthermore, half had flexible manufacturing systems, and a third had some robotics. Nearly two-thirds of the sample were involved in materials requirements planning. The use of computerised support in manufacturing was patchy, with only one company professing to operate computer integrated manufacturing.

A study conducted by Upton (1993) on the use of Just-in-Time (JIT) systems in large New Zealand firms, in 1993 showed similar results. He found that JIT was used by only a third of 85 respondents, and a majority of this group started using JIT only within the last three years. His results also showed that there were some minor changes made to management accounting techniques to meet the needs of JIT. Very few differences existed between the accounting changes made by mature and non-mature JIT users providing sparse evidence of accounting lag in the implementation of JIT. Moreover, the JIT users displayed very little intention to comprehensively re-view their accounting systems. It also appeared that lack of superior performance by mature JIT users corresponded with the lack of accounting change. JIT users were focusing on aspects such as JIT purchasing, cell lay-out and Kanban systems. However, such endeavour was not widespread among JIT users. The main reason for a lack of initiative in the implementation of JIT and JIT associated techniques was the distances from customers and suppliers. This is in line with the findings in Ainikkal (1993)[10], where a similar reason was given by respondents for not maintaining zero inventory levels.

---

[10]This study involved a survey of 84 manufacturing companies (with sales turnover ranging from NZ$1.5 million to NZ$12 billion). Of the total sample, 50 percent was from the New Zealand top 200 listed companies and the balance was a random selection of smaller manufacturing companies. Data was collected through a questionnaire. The response rate was 48 percent.

In another survey of New Zealand companies, Corbett and Bayly (1991) found that JIT was mostly used by companies with repetitive operations producing batches of multiple products, assembly operations and continuous flow processes. It was found not to be suitable in its entirety for all manufacturing operations, especially where there is heavy reliance on overseas suppliers.

According to perceptions by manufacturers in the aforementioned two surveys, i.e., Upton (1993) and Corbett and Bayly (1991), the most significant problems in implementing JIT were unstable demand, diverse product lines or options, long supplier lead times, ignorance about JIT and a lack of top management support. Although Corbett and Bayly (1991) found resistance to change by the workforce as a reason for non-implementation of JIT, Upton (1993) did not find employee resistance to JIT implementation to be a major problem.

Robotics were hardly used by the companies surveyed in Ainikkal (1993). Computer-aided designs (CAD) and testing and inspection machines (T and IM) were the most commonly used tools. He points out that limited use of new manufacturing technologies in New Zealand may be due to low manufacturing capacity, the small local market and demand for industrial products overseas, the local labour market, government policies and the average small size of New Zealand companies.

In an earlier survey, it had been found that there was hardly any change in the cost structure of products over the last 10 years. Direct material remained, on average, as the major component of costs of products, followed by overhead costs (Ainikkal and Teoh, 1992).

Product Costing: Northcott, *et al.* (1990) found a preparedness among the interviewees to review the traditional absorption costing approaches and embrace ABC costing concepts, with a focus upon determining cost causality rather than on spreading indirect costs in the 'fairest' way.

This contrasts with another study (Norrish, 1992) which found that some of the management accounting topics taught in university courses, such as ABC and non-financial performance indicators, were not rated highly by management accountants in practice. This may be due to the differences in the nature of organisations covered in the two studies. While Northcott, *et al.* selected 21 large organisations, Norrish selected a random sample of all NZSA listed management accountants. It may be that most of the management accountants in Norrish's sample were in small organisations. This supports the view that large firms are more responsive to new ideas compared to small firms (Upton (1993) noted that large firms were more actively adopting JIT than small firms). This was also reflected in Ainikkal's (1993) survey results.

Ainikkal (1993) reported that the low level of technological change in the manufacturing sector seems to have resulted in the little change in management accounting techniques that have taken place. According to him, standard costing is favoured by a high percentage of firms, followed by full costing and marginal costing, which is the least used method of costing. Although many firms used labour as their sole basis for allocating overhead costs to products, more than 65 percent of the firms surveyed by Ainikkal (1993) used volume-related bases in allocating such costs. Low-tech organisations were more labour-dependent than high-tech industries for allocating their overheads. New management techniques, such as activity-based costing, life cycle costing, strategic management accounting and throughput costing are rarely found in practice. More than half of the firms surveyed by Ainikkal held inventory for three months or more. Very few firms (7.5 percent) adopted a policy of zero inventory. However, most firms did appear to manage to keep their inventories at minimum levels. The need for inventory was mainly attributable to the seasonal nature of the primary sector-based industries and the periodic importation of certain raw materials from overseas. Ainikkal and Teoh (1992) and Ainikkal (1993) reported that firms and their accountants, generally, showed little interest in changing to either new technologies, new management techniques or new accounting techniques. An overwhelming 80 percent of the respondents considered traditional management accounting techniques useful. Lack of awareness of new techniques, lack of top management support, lack of expertise and funds were among the other reasons given for not adopting new management accounting techniques. Both these studies included a mix of large and small firms.

However, Northcott, *et al.* (1990) believed that developments in theory and practice appeared to be pulling together in the area of product costing where dissatisfaction with traditional costing methods were producing a practical movement towards the ABC-type thinking.

Transfer Pricing: Alam and Hoque (1995)[11] reported that most companies surveyed used 'full cost' to establish a transfer price. The other methods used included market prices (18 percent), negotiated prices (11 percent) and variable cost based prices (10 percent).

They also found that 'divisional profitability' was the most important factor (72 percent) in determining the method of transfer pricing. Other factors which were considered very important included ease of understanding (64 percent), evaluation of managerial performance (59 percent), market stability (51 percent) and cost of administration (48 percent). Some transfer pricing method was used by 61 percent of the companies. These were large companies with multi-divisional structures and diverse products.

---

[11]They conducted a survey investigating the transfer pricing methods used by New Zealand companies and the factors that determine the choice of transfer pricing methods. The sample of companies surveyed included 120 of the top 200 New zealand companies.

Capital Budgeting: Northcott, *et al.* (1990) found that unsophisticated capital budgeting techniques were commonly used in practice, with payback as the most predominant. The other techniques used included accounting rate of return, internal rate of return and net present value, with NPV receiving the lowest ranking of all the methods. Some aspects of capital budgeting recommended in the literature, such as risk adjustment and post audit, appeared to be neglected. They concluded that there are differences between technically 'correct' capital budgeting techniques and the practice of capital budgeting in New Zealand manufacturing organisations.

Performance Measures: Northcott, *et al.* (1990) reported that traditional measures of performance (both financial and non-financial) were used in both automated and non-automated environments. They also found that the traditional measures of performance indicators such as sales/sales growth, net operating income (as a percent of sales), and gross margin gained high rankings; and the use of cash flows and inventory measures were high. Of the non-financial indicators, product quality, market share, customer service and labour productivity ranked highest.

Of the financial measures, cost of capital, residual income, contribution margin and return on equity/capital/total assets were perceived as being either counter-productive or of little value in an advanced technology environment.

It was found that there were organisational obstacles to bring about change in performance measurement systems, the most common being: higher priority given to the development of other systems, tradition, lack of understanding of options by decision makers, management emphasis on short-term performance and inappropriate performance measurement concepts. Other obstacles included management policies, the conservative nature of accounting and financial results, and the association of management compensation with short- rather than long-term performance measures. Further more, adaptation and improvement of performance measurement systems were considered less important than other, more pressing short-term management functions.

Product Life Cycle: Ainikkal and Teoh (1992) found that only 19 percent of the companies emphasised the mature stage as the focus for developing a strategy for their operations. The rest considered the development and growth stages as being of prime importance. Ainikkal and Teoh (1992) point out that 'Traditional management accounting techniques are designed mainly for the maturity stage of a product life cycle, which is characterised by a stable, mass-production environment. With increasing emphasis now being placed on the start-up and growth stages, traditional management accounting techniques lose much of their relevance.'

Short-term Decisions: Northcott, *et al.* (1990) report that short-term decision making techniques used included critical path analysis, simulation, regression and linear programming. The more conventional management accounting tools of cost-volume-profit analysis and economic order quantity models were used by 86 percent and 52 percent (respectively) of the organisations. They appear to believe that the organisations are moving towards greater use of theoretically correct short-term decision making techniques.

DISCUSSION AND CONCLUSIONS

As was mentioned earlier, the NZSA is currently developing its own conceptual framework. One of the central pieces of this framework, *The Statement of Concepts for General Purpose Financial Reporting* (NZSA, 1993b) is based largely on the IASC's framework (*IASC, 1989*). However, the IASC framework applies to those public sector and private sector entities that are regarded as commercial, industrial, or business reporting enterprises (para. 8), whereas the New Zealand framework, perhaps following the Australian example (SAC-1, paras 34–37), is designed to cover both public and private sector financial reporting requirements for all entities irrespective of whether they belong to commercial, industrial or business categories (NZSA, 1993b, para. 1.2). In fact, New Zealand's efforts to develop a conceptual framework contain a number of relatively progressive and even novel aspects. For example, with respect to the definition of the reporting entity, according to the NZSA (1993b), 'a reporting entity exists where it is reasonable to expect the existence of users dependent on general purpose financial reports for information which will be useful to them in terms of the objectives . . .' (para. 2.1). The application of the concept of reporting entity, as described above, will result in substantial changes to current practices in New Zealand. For example, some entities such as partnerships, trusts, government departments, and statutory authorities, which currently do not prepare general purpose financial reports, may fall within the definition of reporting entity. As a result, they may have to prepare such reports in accordance with Statements of Accounting Concepts and Accounting Standards. The application of the reporting entity concept will result in a government as a whole being identified as a reporting entity which therefore ought to prepare general purpose financial reports. In line with the reporting entity concept, the New Zealand government has taken the initiative in publishing crown financial statements since 1992.

Conceptual frameworks generally identify assets, liabilities and equity as the main elements of financial position statements, and revenues and expenses as the main elements of financial performance statements. The NZSA (1993b) has taken a further step in identifying non-financial elements included in financial reports, for example, those elements which are directed to service performance, i.e. inputs, outputs and outcomes.

In general, when discussing the conceptual issues underlying the definitions of the elements of financial statements, the NZSA (1993b) has adopted an asset and liability view as the basis. This means placing more emphasis on the balance sheet compared to the income statement. This approach, in common with many other Anglo-American countries in defining the elements of financial statements on a common basis, has helped to establish a clear linkage between the elements, as well as between the financial statements. For example, the concept of 'service potential' or 'future economic benefit' has been central to the definitions of assets, liabilities, equity, revenues and expenses (Petera and Rahman, 1995).

Certain types of complex financial instruments blur the distinction between equity and liability. Currently, New Zealand and Australia are trying to align their views on the issue of accounting for financial instruments. Not all aspects of the conceptual framework are as progressive, however. This is particularly so in the case of measurement issues. Conceptual frameworks often prescribe how things ought to be, and do not necessarily describe the way they are (e.g. FASB, 1976). However, the NZSA (1993b) simply describes the four measurement bases mentioned in IASC (1989, para. 100), i.e. historic cost, current cost, realisable (settlement) value, and present value (para. 9.2) without making any commitment. It might be argued that, the NZSA (1993b) has attempted to avoid the issue of measurement in financial reporting. The NZSA's position on the matter is clearly reflected in the statement that '. . . it is unlikely that any single measurement base can cater for every need or would be sufficiently reliable for financial reporting in all circumstances' (para. 9.10).

The conceptual framework may be seen as an attempt on the part of the accounting profession to respond to the fact that the environment in which accounting operates in New Zealand has undergone rapid change in recent years. A series of economic policy initiatives has been taken with a view to creating favourable conditions for investment. Increased economic activity in a highly competitive environment has exerted pressure on business firms to operate efficiently in order to be able to survive. The developments which have necessitated changes in the legal environment to safeguard the interests of consumers and investors, have also necessitated developments in thinking about the nature of accounting information.

The development of New Zealand's conceptual framework project throws into relief some of the particular ways in which changes in the environment may have influenced changes in financial and management accounting practices. In the area of accounting and financial reporting, major changes have taken place, particularly in regard to regulatory structure and standard setting. With the enactment of the Financial Reporting Act of 1993, the New Zealand accounting regulation entered into a new era of co-regulation where accounting standards of the NZSA have been given legal backing. Another important development is the formulation of a financial reporting framework to provide guidance for setting accounting standards. Accounting in New Zealand is also subjected to international influences such as the International Accounting Standards Committee. Currently, the accounting professions in Australia and New Zealand are working closely together in an attempt to harmonise accounting standards and practices under the Closer Economic Relations agreement between the two countries.

The accounting profession itself has been the subject of major reform. The New Zealand Society of Accountants will soon be known as the Institute of Chartered Accountants of New Zealand. The recently announced new admissions policy is aimed at ensuring that the prospective accountants will have a certain level of general intellectual capacity and a wide range of skills including communication, interpersonal, as well as technical skills. On the management accounting front, New Zealand is yet to experience major changes. The slow change to newer methods is primarily due to a slow change in management practices which, in turn, corresponds with the low level of technological change being experienced in the industrial domain. The reduction in the proportionate size of the manufacturing sector may further diminish the possibility of change in management accounting techniques. However, the low level of change is also attributable to the nature of manufacturing in New Zealand industries, which generally do not bear the same characteristics as their overseas counterparts.

REFERENCES

Ainikkal, J. and H. Teoh (1992), 'Overhead allocations and product life cycle emphasis — The New Zealand situation', *Accountants journal*, April, pp. 69–71.

Ainikkal, J. (1993), Exploring the New Zealand manufacturing environment, *Accountants journal*, July, pp. 28–31.

Alam, M. and Z. Hoque (1995), 'Transfer pricing in New Zealand', *Chartered accountants journal*, April, pp. 32–4.

Alley, C. (1992a), 'Accounting for inventories', *New Zealand company financial reporting: 1990*, Ryan J.B. (Ed), University of Auckland, New Zealand.

Alley, C. (1992b), 'Liabilities in New Zealand company financial reporting: 1990', Ryan J.B. (Ed), University of Auckland, New Zealand.

Corbett, L. and E. Bayly (1991), ' "It's simple and it's not easy!" The implementation of just-in-time in New Zealand manufacturing'. *A research report of the New Zealand manufacturing futures project*. Graduate School of Business and Government Management, Victoria University of Wellington.

Graham, A. (1960), *The First Fifty Years 1909–1959*, Wellington: NZSA.

Hossain, M., Perera, H., and A. Rahman (1995), 'Voluntary disclosure in the annual reports of New Zealand companies, *Journal of international financial management and accounting'*, Vol. 6, Iss. 1, pp. 69–87.

International Accounting Standards Committee (1989), *Comparability of financial statements,* IASC, London.

Keenan, M. (1992), 'Accounting for investment properties and properties intended for sale', *New Zealand company financial reporting: 1990*, Ryan J.B. (Ed), University of Auckland, New Zealand.

Lothian, N. and I. Marrian (1992), *New Zealand Society of Accountants international review of admissions policy*, June, NZSA, Wellington.

Neale, A. (1992a), 'Accounting for business combinations', *New Zealand company financial reporting: 1990*, Ryan J.B. (Ed), University of Auckland, New Zealand.

Neale, A. (1992b), 'Accounting for interests in joint ventures and partnerships', Ryan, J.B. (Ed). *New Zealand company financial reporting: 1990*, University of Auckland, New Zealand.

New Zealand Stock Exchange (1993), *Annual Report 1993*, NZSE, Wellington.

New Zealand Society of Accountants (1993a), *Annual Report 1993*, NZSA, Wellington.

New Zealand Society of Accountants (1993b), 'Statement of concepts for general purpose financial reporting', *New Zealand Accounting Standards*, NZSA, Wellington.

New Zealand Society of Accountants (1993c), 'Explanatory foreword to general purpose financial reporting', *New Zealand Accounting Standards*, NZSA, Wellington.

New Zealand Society of Accountants (1994a), 'Framework for differential reporting', *New Zealand accounting standards*, NZSA, Wellington.

New Zealand Society of Accountants (1994b), *Admissions policy*, March, NZSA, Wellington.

New Zealand Society of Accountants (1994c), 'Proposed Act and Rules of the Institute of Chartered Accountants of New Zealand', *New Zealand Yearbook-1993*. Department of Statistics, Wellington.

New Zealand Yearbook 1993, Wellington: Department of Statistics.

Norrish, B. (1992), *Management accounting: An analysis of the divergence between education and practice in New Zealand*, Unpublished Masters Research report, Massey University, Palmerston North.

Northcott, D., Kelly, M. and E. Schafer (1990), *Management accounting practices in some large New Zealand manufacturing organisations: An empirical study*, Unpublished research paper, Department of Accounting and Finance, University of Waikato, Hamilton.

Perera, H. and A. Rahman (1994), 'Conceptual foundation of accounting and financial reporting: Emerging commonality of purpose between Australia and New Zealand', *Pacific accounting review*, Vol. 7, Iss. L, pp. 1–23.

Rahman, A., Ng, L. and G. Tower (1994), 'Public choice and accounting standard setting in New Zealand: An exploratory study', *Abacus,* March, pp. 98–117.

Rahman, A., Perera, H. & S. Ganeshanandum (1994), 'Regional accounting harmonisation: A comparative study of the disclosure and measurement regulations of Australia and New Zealand', Accounting Association of Australia and New Zealand Annual Conference, Wollongong.

Rahman, A., Perera, H. and G. Tower (1994), 'Accounting harmonization between Australia and New Zealand: Towards a regulatory union', *The international journal of accounting,* Vol. 29, Iss. 3, pp. 316–33.

Ryan, J. (Ed) (1992), *New Zealand company financial reporting: 1990*, University of Auckland, New Zealand.

Saudagaran, S. and G. Biddle (1992), *Journal of international financial management and accounting,* Vol. 4 Iss. 2, pp. 106–48.

Speer, D. (1992a), 'Assets', *New Zealand company financial reporting: 1990*, Ryan J.B. (Ed), University of Auckland, New Zealand.

Speer, D. (1992b), 'Presentation of balance sheet', *New Zealand company financial reporting: 1990*, Ryan J.B. (Ed), University of Auckland, New Zealand.

Tower, G. (1992), *Accounting regulations an instrument of public accountability: A case study of New Zealand*, Unpublished Ph.D. Thesis, Massey University, Palmerston North, New Zealand.

Upton, D. (1993), *Just-in-time implementation and the impact of just-in-time on management accounting systems*, Unpublished Masters Research report, Massey University, Palmerston North.

Walker, G. and B. Fisse (1994), *Securities regulation in Australia and New Zealand*, Oxford University Press, Auckland.

Wilson, G. (1992), 'Depreciation of fixed assets, and measurement of fixed assets', in *New Zealand company financial reporting: 1990*, Ryan J.B. (Ed), University of Auckland, New Zealand.

Zeff, S. (1979), *Forging accounting principles in New Zealand*, Victoria University Press, Wellington.

APPENDIX 1
COMPARISON OF NEW ZEALAND, AUSTRALIAN AND IASC
ACCOUNTING PRONOUNCEMENTS
(ADAPTED FROM RAHMAN, PERERA & GANESHANANDUM, 1994)

New Zealand			Australia			IASC
SSAP No.(FRS)	New Zealand Standard/TPA	AAS No.	AASB No.	Australian Standard/TPA	IAS No.	International Standard
	Explanatory Foreword	AAG1		Foreword to Statements; Scope of Guidance Releases		Preface to Statements
	Statement of Concepts for General Purpose Financial Reporting	SAC 1–4		Conceptual Framework	18	Framework for the Preparation & Presentation of Financial Statements; Revenue
	Framework for Differential Reporting (Also Fin. Rep. Act)	SAC1	1025	Reporting Entity Concept; Application of Reporting Entity Concept (also Corporations Law)		
1 (FRS)	Accounting Policies	6	1001	Accounting Policies	1	Accounting Policies
2 (FRS)	Presentation of Financial Reports					
3	Depreciation	4	1021	Depreciation	4	Depreciation
4 (FRS)	Inventories	2	1019	Inventories	3	Inventories
5 (FRS)	Events after Balance Date	8	1002	Events after Balance Date	10	Contingencies & Events after Balance Date
6	Materiality	5		Materiality		
7 (FRS)	Ex-ord Items and Fundamental Errors	9		Exp. Carried Forward	8	Net Profit or Loss, Fundamental Errors & Changes in Acctg Policies
8	Business Combinations	18 24 21 14	1013 1015 1024 1016	Goodwill; Consolidations; Acquisition of Assets; Equity Accounting	27 28 22	Consolidated Financial Statements & Investment in Subsidiaries; Investment in Associates; Business Combinations

APPENDIX 1 (continued)

**COMPARISON OF NEW ZEALAND, AUSTRALIAN AND IASC
ACCOUNTING PRONOUNCEMENTS**

(ADAPTED FROM RAHMAN, PERERA & GANESHANANDUM, 1994)

New Zealand		Australia			IASC	
9	Balance Sheets and Profit and Loss Statements	1 5	1004 1018	P & L Disclosure of Revenue	5 13	Information to be Disclosed in Financial Statements Current Assets & Current Liabilities
10 (FRS)	SCF	12	1007 & 1026	SCF	7	SCF
11	Exp Carried Forward (Withdrawn, refer to Statements of Concepts)	9		Exp. Carried Forward		
12	Income Tax	3 AAG2 AAG4 AAG7 AAG8	1020	Income Tax Rate of Tax Tax Losses Dividend Imputation Capital Gains Tax	12	Income Tax
13	R & D	13	1011	R & D	9	R & D
14 (FRS)	Construction Contracts	11	1009	Construction Contracts	11	Construction Contracts
15	Contingencies				10	Contingencies & Events after Balance Date
16	Government Grants				20	Government Grants
17	Investment Properties				16 25	Property Plant & Equipment Investments
18	Leases	17 AAG3	1008	Leases Lessors and Lessees	17	Leases
19 (FRS)	GST					
20 (FRS)	Dividend Election Plan					

APPENDIX 1 (continued)

COMPARISON OF NEW ZEALAND, AUSTRALIAN AND IASC
ACCOUNTING PRONOUNCEMENTS
(ADAPTED FROM RAHMAN, PERERA & GANESHANANDUM, 1994)

	New Zealand			Australia		IASC
21	Foreign Currency	20	1012	Foreign Currency	21	Foreign Currency
22	Related Party	22	1017	Related Party	22	Related Party
23	Segments	16		Segments	14	Segments
24	Interim Statements					
25	JVs & Ptshps	19	1006	JVs	31	JVs
26	Defeasance of Debt	23	1014	Extinguishment of Debt		
27 (FRS)	Right of Set-off	23		Set-off of Debt		
28	Fixed Assets	10	1010	Revaluation of Non-Current Assets	16	Property Plant & Equipment
		21	1015	Acquisition of Assets		
29	Prospective Information					
30	Employee Share Ownership Plans.					Reporting Share Ownership Arrangements
31	Financial Instruments					
TPA1	Specified Pref Shares					
TPA4	EPS		1027	EPS		
TPA5	Live Stock					
TPA6	Extractive Industries	7	1022	Extractive Industries		
TPA7	Bloodstock					
SPSAC	Public Sector Concepts					
PSAS-1	Public Sector Accounting Policies	25	1023	Superannuation Plans	19	Retirement Benefit Costs

APPENDIX 1 (continued)
COMPARISON OF NEW ZEALAND, AUSTRALIAN AND IASC
ACCOUNTING PRONOUNCEMENTS
(ADAPTED FROM RAHMAN, PERERA & GANESHANANDUM, 1994)

New Zealand		Australia		IASC	
		26	General Insurance	26	Retirement Benefit Plans
		27	Local Governments		
		AAG5	Intangibles		
		AAG6	Fringe Benefit Tax		
		AAG9	Marketable Securities		
		AAG10	Monetary Assets and Liabilities		
		AAG11	Debt Restructuring		
		AAG12	Share Bay-backs		
	1025		Application of Reporting Concept Entity		
				14	Price Level Changes
				29	Reporting in Hyper-inflationary Economies
				23	Capitalisation of Borrowing Costs
				30	Financial Statements of Banks

SSAP = Statement of Standard Accounting Practice
FRS = Financial Reporting Statement
TPA = Technical Practising Aid
SPSAC = Statement of Public Sector Accounting Concepts
PSAS = Public Sector Accounting Standard

AAS = Australian Accounting Standard
AASB = Approved Accounting Standards of the Australian Accounting Standards Board
AAG = Accounting and Auditing Guideline
N.A. = Not available
IAS = International Accounting Standard

APPENDIX 2
ELEMENTS OF ACCOUNTING REGULATION:
A COMPARISON OF AUSTRALIA, NEW ZEALAND, UK, USA, AND IASC
(ADAPTED FROM RAHMAN, PERERA & TOWER, 1994)

Elements of Regulation	Australia	New Zealand	UK	USA	IASC
Structure: Policy Making	Ministerial Council Government Minister (Federal Attorney-General)	Parliament Government Minister (Minister of Justice)	FRC (25 members)	FAF	IASC Board & IFAC
Standard Setting	Government created independent body (AASB)	Government created independent body (ASRB)	FRC created ASB	FASB	IASC
Standard Formulation	Profession backed research body (AARF)	Profession backed research body (FRSB)	ASB	FASB	Steering Committee
Enforcement	Government body (ASC)	Government body (Registrar of Companies & Securities Commission)	Courts	Government body (SEC)	Member Countries, Member Professional Organisations, IOSCO, etc.
Regulated	Companies & public sector entities	Companies, public issuers & public sector entities	Companies	Listed Firms All companies	Constituents of above bodies
Beneficiaries	User of Financial Reports	User of Financial Report	User of Financial Reports	User of Financial Reports	User of Financial Reports
Concept of Reporting	True and Fair	True and Fair Present Fairly	True and Fair	Present Fairly	

APPENDIX 2 (continued)
ELEMENTS OF ACCOUNTING REGULATION:
A COMPARISON OF AUSTRALIA, NEW ZEALAND, UK, USA, AND IASC
(ADAPTED FROM RAHMAN, PERERA & TOWER, 1994)

Elements of Regulation	Australia	New Zealand	UK	USA	IASC
Mode of Regulation	Accounting Standards (backed by Corporations Law, Listing Requirements & Securities Legislation)	Accounting Standards (backed by Companies Act, Financial Reporting Act, Listing Requirements & Securities Legislation)	Accounting Standards (backed by Companies Act, Listing Requirements & Securities Legislation)	Accounting Standards (backed by SEC, Listing Requirements)	Accounting Standards (backed by regulatory systems of countries adopting the standards)
Process of Standard Setting	Exposure of EDs	Exposure of EDs	Exposure of EDs Urgent Issues Task Force	Exposure of EDs Public Hearing Consultative Committee (FASAC) Emerging Issues Task Force	Exposure of EDs
Mode of Enforcement	Legislative backing for standards	Legislative backing for standards	Review Panel(Power to require withdrawal & re-issue of statements)	SEC backing	Backing of the member bodies

ACCOUNTING PRACTICES IN
PAPUA NEW GUINEA

Fabian Pok[*]

BACKGROUND

Papua New Guinea (PNG) lies between latitudes 2°S and 12°S to the north of Australia and consists of the eastern half of the island of New Guinea (the western half of which consists of Indonesian Irian Jaya) together with a number of islands including the Bismarck archipelago and the island of Bougainville. The total land area is 462 840 sq. km. New Guinea is low-lying around the coastal region, with mangrove swamps and some mountain ranges in the interior. There are tropical rainforests, some deciduous forests and grassland areas inland. Some of the islands like Bougainville are mountainous. PNG has significant deposits of precious metals and copper as well as petroleum and natural gas. The climate is tropical maritime, hot and humid throughout the year in the lowland and cooler in the mountainous areas.

The indigenous people of PNG are mainly Melanesians, who mainly follow hunting and gathering practices and horticulture, all settled in New Guinea and the surrounding islands in prehistoric times. New Guinea was first claimed by Europeans (Spain) in the 16th Century but not colonised until the mid 19th Century. The British and Dutch East India companies claimed the eastern and western parts of the island respectively, and Germany annexed the north eastern part of the island in 1884. In 1906, the administration of the British element passed to Australia, which additionally took over the German

*Commerce Department, University of Papua New Guinea.

part in the aftermath of the First World War. In the Second World War, Japan invaded New Guinea and some of the islands. PNG reverted to Australian control after 1945 and became independent in 1975. The present unitary constitution dates from this time and provides for Westminster style of democracy with a governor-general acting on behalf of the official head of state — the British monarch. There is a unicameral national parliament of 109 members and the executive consists of a Prime Minister and other members of the National Executive Council, all appointed by the head of state from members of the legislature. The judicial system is based upon common law and the Supreme Court deals with matters of interpretation of the Constitution. About 95 percent of the native population are nominally Christians, but a belief in magic and pantheism is widespread. English is the official language but forms of pigin are spoken, i.e concoctions of local native languages and English. The present population of PNG is about 3.7 million people.

On the basis of this population estimate, PNG's per capita GDP was about US$700 in 1992. Some estimates of GNP per capita are higher, at about US$1000. GDP rapidly increased during the early 1990s from more sluggish growth rates of around 2 percent per annum in the previous decade. Agriculture is the most important sector of the economy, contributing about 25 percent of GDP and more than 70 percent of employment. The main non-commercial activity is subsistence agriculture, and the main commercial crops are coffee, cocoa and coconuts. Exports of timber are important for the economy, but there is a question of sustainability and they are expected to be eliminated by early in the next century. Manufacturing by contrast accounts for approximately 10 percent of GDP but employs less than 2 percent of the workforce. Products processed from foodstuffs, wood and metal are among the most important manufactures. Mining alone contributes 17 percent of GDP while employing only about 0.5 percent of the working population. The exploitation of mineral resources is one of the most important parts of the economy, contributing more than 30 percent of export earnings in recent years. Copper is the single most important element of mining extraction at the present time. Gold is also important, and gas and petroleum fields have recently begun to be developed. The service sector is large for an undeveloped economy, employing 17 percent of the workforce and producing 38 percent of measured GDP. The government usually runs a deficit funded by Australian aid. The current account is usually in deficit (about 20 percent of exports) and PNG's main trading partners are Australia, Japan, the US, Germany and South Korea. Total external debt in 1992 was about US$3736 m, about 90 percent of GDP. The annual rate of inflation averages about 5 percent. Despite migration to the urban areas, the extent of widespread subsistence agriculture means the impact on employment levels is reduced. The main feature of economic policy is the openness to foreign investment. Recent austerity measures introduced by the government have, however, included a wages freeze and a devaluation of the unit of currency. At the present time, ethnic unrest and crime appear to be the main hindrances to economic development in PNG. The unit of currency is the kina.

R.J.W.

INTRODUCTION

This chapter examines accounting practices in Papua New Guinea (PNG). In section one, the brief history of accountancy and the accounting professional bodies is explored. Section two discusses the adoption of accounting standards and contents of the balance sheets and income statements.

Current accounting practices were imported into PNG by colonial governments and multinational corporations. German and British companies operating in PNG thus transferred the accounting practices, systems of taxation and company law existing in their countries. They maintained the same accounting systems as their head offices so that consolidated financial statements could be easily constructed. On the whole, these organisations were not interested in the information needs of the people of PNG.

Hardman (1984) noted that during colonisation, the government and businesses in PNG relied on foreign accountants for the expertise required in foreign matters. Even today, most professional accounting firms and businesses rely on accountants trained overseas. The local accounting profession is in its infancy and there is a lack of qualified indigenous accountants.

PAPUA NEW GUINEA INSTITUTE OF ACCOUNTANTS (PNGIA)

The PNGIA was founded in 1974. It has no legislative backing but in effect governs the preparation of financial statements and conduct of accountants in PNG. In 1990 the PNGIA adopted extant international accounting standards (IASs) in their entirety. This action was prompted by increased multinational corporation activity in PNG due to the discovery of rich oil, gas and mineral deposits. Prior to this, little is known about the accounting standards and practices used by firms operating in PNG, although it seems highly likely, as was stated above, that each firm adopted the accounting standards and practices used by its parent companies overseas. Even after recent changes, the PNGIA has no legal powers to censure companies not following standards and practices adopted by the association. The best the association can do is to use its best endeavours to persuade members to use the standards and practices it has officially adopted.

Membership of PNGIA

The membership of the PNGIA is voluntary and therefore many accountants, especially expatriate accountants, choose not to be members. Pok (1992) noted that the membership of PNGIA consists of a very small percentage of the accountants working in this country. The PNGIA has a two-tier membership. All graduates from the two universities in PNG become affiliate members and affiliates who pass all PNGIA examinations become associates after three years of supervised, or five years unsupervised work experience.

PNGIA Examination

In 1979, the PNGIA decided to establish a professional examination system for students seeking full membership. Accounting graduates from the two universities in PNG (the University of PNG and the University of Technology) sit for the five examinations biannually. The first examination was taken in November 1982 (Gehde, 1982). The examination comprises five papers covering these topics: management accounting, financial accounting, auditing and professional practice, PNG company law, and PNG taxation law. Accountants who are members of other professional accounting bodies recognised by PNGIA are admitted to associate status without the necessity of sitting the examination.

Even though the examination system came into effect in 1982, so far only a few citizens of PNG have sat for and passed the examinations. There is no governing body to co-ordinate examinations and, therefore, multinational accounting firms in PNG take it in turn to organise the setting and marking of examination papers. When one firm is chosen, individuals within the firm are given the responsibility to co-ordinate the papers. The papers are reviewed by PNGIA Council members before students sit the examination.

Those Papua New Guineans who have passed all five papers and have three years of supervised practical experience can register as company auditors and liquidators. The registration of company auditors and liquidators is the responsibility of the Accountants Registration Board (ARB), a body sèt up by the government. Even though the professional examination and its qualification is not recognised internationally, in PNG it is now a widely accepted professional qualification (Onedo, 1994; Prossor, 1990).

ACCOUNTANTS REGISTRATION BOARD

In 1974, an Act of Parliament was passed to establish the Accountants Registration Board of Papua New Guinea (ARB or the Board). The main functions of the Board are to register qualified accountants, to determine qualifications for registration, to regulate the practice of accountancy in Papua New Guinea, and to investigate the activities of registered persons. The act requires that a person or member of a firm must be registered to be able to practise the profession of accountancy and to charge a fee.

To control the practice of accountancy, the Board is empowered to make rules. The Act mentions four specific areas, although the scope of the rules is not limited to these. These areas are:

(1) prescribing minimum qualifications for registration,
(2) prescribing standards to be adopted,
(3) recommending scales of fees, and
(4) setting out codes of professional ethics.

To date, the Board has only made rules relating to the prescribing of minimum qualifications for registration.

ACCOUNTING PRINCIPLES AND PRACTICES

Like many professional accounting bodies in developing countries, the PNGIA and the ARB have not formulated any generally accepted accounting principles. In practice, accounting principles tend to be those advocated by the international accounting firms represented in Papua New Guinea, who in turn are primarily influenced by accounting principles and practices followed in Australia. Much of the law relating to accounting matters will also seem familiar to those with a knowledge of UK company law.

The reason given by the PNGIA council for adopting IASs in 1990 was an increase in the complexity of business. Multinational corporations had in any case to comply with IASs so that this action seemed sensible and relatively costless in light of their dominance of the PNG economy. The PNGIA has also adopted certain accounting standards produced by professional accounting bodies in Australia. Recently, the association issued a standard on profit and loss statements (PNGIAS1), which was basically a reprint of the Australia Accounting Standards (AAS1). Thus the PNGIA is relying on international accounting standards supported by Australian Standards.

To date, the PNGIA and ARB have not prescribed any auditing standard to be followed by registered accountants. In practice, as with accounting standards, the accounting firms represented in Papua New Guinea have followed the auditing stand-ards of Australia.

FORM AND CONTENT OF FINANCIAL STATEMENTS

Financial statements prepared for distribution and reported upon by accounting firms normally conform to the reporting standards followed in Australia. They follow the usual Anglo-American style of presentation and contain a balance sheet, profit and loss statement (income statement), statement of retained earnings, notes to the accounts, and a statement of changes in financial position.

Income statement

The usual headings used in a statement of profit and loss (income statement) are those shown in Table 1.

Table 1
TYPICAL INCOME STATEMENT IN PAPUA NEW GUINEA

Operating profit before income tax	xxxx
Income tax expenses	xxxx
OPERATING PROFIT	xxxx
Extraordinary items (net of income tax)	xxxx
Unappropriated profits brought forward	xxxx
Appropriations:	
Dividends paid and/or proposed	
(interim and final)	xxxx
Transfers from or to reserves	xxxx
UNAPPROPRIATED PROFITS CARRIED FORWARD	xxxx

These are virtually identical with the elements found in Anglo-American income statements everywhere. All items of income and expense arising during the period, irrespective of whether they relate to ordinary business operations, prior periods or other events, are recorded through the income statement as a credit or charge to net profit. There is no statutory requirement to disclose turnover (sales and operating revenue) in a company's financial statements.

In determining operating profit, accounting principals are generally applied consistently from period to period. Significant accounting policies and methods are disclosed in notes to the financial statements. Expenses are matched with income, and the quantified effects of changes in accounting principles are disclosed as a note to the financial statements. Material, abnormal items or prior period adjustments relating to normal trading operations are included in operating profit, and details are disclosed separately as a note to the financial statements. Extraordinary profits and losses (net of income tax, if applicable) that arise from factors not in the normal business operations of the company are disclosed separately under the heading 'extraordinary items'. Examples are gains or losses arising from the disposal of a major section of a business, the disposal of an investment not acquired for resale and profits or losses attributable to a major currency realignment. The only permitted appropriations are dividends paid, or payable to shareholders or transfers to and from reserves (capital and revenue).

Balance sheet

Capital: The Companies Act provides the machinery under which companies are to be managed and administered. Some of the more important aspects of the legislation regarding a company's capital are as follows:-

1. A company is prohibited from dealing in its own shares and cannot hold shares in its own holding company.
2. Except as provided below, a company is prohibited from giving any financial assistance, directly or indirectly, in connection with the purchase by any person of shares in the company, and, where the company is a subsidiary, of shares in its holding company. This prohibition does not include the lending of money or the giving of a guarantee if the loan or guarantee is made in the normal course of the company's business on ordinary commercial terms. A company may provide financial assistance to employees (other than directors) *bona fide* in the employment of the company or a subsidiary to enable the purchase of fully paid shares in the company. Financial assistance may be given to trustees to hold shares by or for the benefit of employees of the company, including salaried directors.
3. A company can reduce its capital only with the consent of the Court.
4. No legislation authorises the issue of shares of no par value.

These provisions are very similar to UK company law provisions prior to recent changes there. A company may issue shares of various classes, e.g., ordinary shares (common stock) or preference shares (preferred stock). Details of share capital must be disclosed in the financial statements for each class of share. Where shares are issued at a premium, being the excess of the total issue price over their total par value, the premium must be recorded in a share premium account and disclosed as such under 'capital reserves' on the company's balance sheet. The premium can be applied only as provided for by company legislation.

Assets: Assets are valued in a variety of ways.

1. Marketable securities — The normal practice for valuing securities quoted on the official list of a stock exchange is at lower of cost or market value. Market value is generally considered to be the lowest of the last sale price, selling offer and bid offer. Where, at the date of the balance sheet, the market value of investments so calculated is lower than book value, the directors must consider whether a provision should be made for the diminution in value. Where the investments are held as current assets, a provision would usually be made. Where, however, the directors consider they have not decreased permanently below book value, a provision for diminution in value of investments need not be raised.

2. Inventories — Stock (inventory) is valued at the lower of cost or net realisable value, usually on an actual, average or FIFO basis. Cost is determined as the cost of purchase, plus costs of conversion, including direct labour and other production costs, ascertained in accordance with either the direct costing or absorption costing method. Production costs exclude expenses that relate to general administration, finance, marketing, selling, and distribution to customers. Livestock owned by agricultural producers receives special treatment. LIFO is not a permissible method for either accounting or tax purposes.

3. Real property — The valuation of real property will vary, depending on the circumstances in which the property is held. For example:
   a. Where land and buildings are held other than for resale, they are normally recorded at cost. The cost of buildings should be segregated from the cost of land, and the buildings depreciated over their estimated remaining life. Where there is an upward trend of property values, the increase in market value can be taken into account by revaluations of the properties, with the increment being taken direct to revaluation reserve.
   b. Where land and buildings are owned by property investment companies, they are sometimes regarded as being composite assets and are thus in the nature of 'investments'. A policy of not providing for depreciation has, until recently, been considered appropriate in such instances when it can be established that the current market value of the property investment is in excess of cost or where any decline in value below cost is considered not to be of a permanent nature.

4. Machinery and equipment — These assets, termed 'plant and equipment', are normally shown at cost less depreciation, or they may be included at a 'directors' or 'independent' valuation, which is usually in excess of cost. Depreciation is charged to trading profit on a consistent basis so that fixed assets are written off over their estimated useful lives. Factory buildings are not classified as plant and equipment for the purposes of accounting classification.

5. Depletion of natural resources — Often an important consideration in PNG financial statements, exploration and evaluation costs should be written off as a direct charge to income, unless such costs are expected to be recouped through successful development or sale of the area of interest, or activities have not yet reached a stage that permits a reasonable assessment of recoverable reserves. In the production phase, costs carried forward in the balance sheet are amortised on the basis of time or production output, the latter being the preferred basis.

6. Investment incentives — Such incentives are generally given in the form of tax benefits and are usually credited in the income statement as reduction of the income tax expense in the period in which the incentive is derived.

Consolidation

Consolidated financial statements are prepared incorporating the assets, liabilities and results of a parent company and its subsidiary companies, with all profits and losses on intercompany transactions being eliminated. Associated companies may be accounted for by using the equity accounting method or may be carried at cost, with only dividend income being brought to account.

Provisions and reserves

The term 'provision' is used to denote amounts set aside to meet:

1. Known liabilities, the amount of which cannot be determined with reasonable accuracy.
2. Diminutions in values of assets existing as at the date of the balance sheet, where the amounts involved cannot be determined with reasonable accuracy.

Amounts materially in excess of the provision required should be treated as a reserve, and increases in reserves are appropriations of profits rather than charges against profit. Again these provisions are very similar to those of the 1948 UK Companies Act.

There are two general categories of reserves: capital reserves and revenue reserves (including unappropriated profits). The expression 'capital reserves' should be used to describe reserves that, for statutory reasons or because of the provisions of the memorandum or articles of association (charter or bylaws) of a company, or for other legal reasons, are not free for distribution through the profit and loss account (income statement). A reserve shown as a capital reserve in one balance sheet may, owing to a change of circumstances, properly be transferred to a revenue reserve in a later period. A reserve that arises from a surplus on a revaluation of fixed assets is an example of a capital reserve. A further example of a capital reserve occurs when a company issues shares for which a premium is received in cash or in the form of other valuable consideration. The amount of that premium should be shown in the balance sheet as a 'share premium account' (or reserve). Revenue reserves are retentions of distributable profits available for general use in the business that have not been created in accordance with statutory requirements or in pursuance of any obligation or policy. The subdivision of such reserves under a variety of headings is unnecessary.

Income tax is provided by applying comprehensive tax-effect accounting (interperiod tax allocation accounting). Future tax benefits, on the other hand, should be carried forward in the balance sheet only where realisation of the benefit is 'assured beyond any reasonable doubt' or, in the case of losses for tax purposes, where realisation is 'virtually certain'. Adjustments to income tax provided in prior periods are included in income tax expense in the statement of profit and loss, and details are disclosed as a note to the financial statements.

Footnote disclosure

Accounting standards require a summary of accounting policies to be included in financial statements. Some disclosure requirements of company law are more conveniently dealt with by note rather than in the body of the accounts. Such items include:

1. The aggregate amount (or the estimated aggregate amount) and the particulars of capital expenditure contracted for, so far as no provision has been made for the amount of the expenditure.
2. Estimated maximum amount of contingent liabilities for which a company or group could become liable.

Again these items appear to derive originally from Schedule VIII to the 1948 UK Companies Act.

Other matters

Generally, financial statements for presentation to shareholders are prepared annually as at December 31, the financial year-end commonly adopted in Papua New Guinea, although other accounting periods may be adopted. The trend with subsidiaries of Australian companies has been toward June 30 year-ends.

The Companies Act does not give details of financial records required to be maintained. However, the Act does require that a company keep in the English language such accounting and other records as will sufficiently explain the transactions and financial position of the company and enable true and fair financial statements to be prepared. Such records must be kept at the registered office and in a manner to enable them to be conveniently and properly audited. A company is also required to keep certain other records, such as a register of shareholders, minute books, a register of charges, register of debenture holders, register of directors' shareholdings, and register of directors, managers and secretaries.

Auditors must be appointed by all companies except when all the shareholders of an exempt proprietary company agree not to do so at the annual general meeting. The auditor is required to report to the shareholders on every balance sheet and income statement laid before the company at general meetings. Balance sheets and income statements that meet the requirements of truth and fairness and contain the information required in the Companies Act must be laid before the company at a general meeting at least once every calendar year, together with a report signed on behalf of the directors with respect to the company's affairs. The balance sheet and profit and loss account must also be accompanied by a directors' statement and a secretary's declaration. The auditors' report, directors' report, directors' statement, and secretary's declaration must contain the information required by the Companies Act. A copy of the financial statements and of the various attachments must be sent to every shareholder at least once every calendar year.

CONCLUDING REMARKS

This chapter has focused on the history and development of financial accounting in PNG. The local accounting profession is in its infancy and has not developed its own accounting principles and standards. It has no legislative power although the ARB which has been given the power to develop or adopt accounting standards has in effect left this process in the hands of the accounting profession. The content of the income statement and balance sheets are virtually identical with the elements found in Anglo-American countries, especially Australia.

REFERENCES

Gehde, M. (1982), 'Professional examination in PNG', *Papua New Guinea journal of accounting*, July, pp. 28–33.

Hardman, J. (1984), 'Accounting in PNG', *The Australian accountant,* June, pp. 10–12.

Onedo, O. (1994), 'Accounting profession in Papua New Guinea', *Papua New Guinea journal of accounting*, December, pp. 25–38.

Pok, F. (1992), 'The history and development of accounting education in Papua New Guinea', *Accounting history*, Vol. 4, Iss. 1, pp. 25–40.

Prossor, B. (1990), 'Accounting professional examination, the way forward', *Papua New Guinea journal of accounting*, October, pp. 18–26.

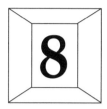

STRUCTURES AND FEATURES OF JAPANESE ACCOUNTING

*Akira Nishimura and Roger Willett**

BACKGROUND

Japan consists of four main islands and over 3000 others lying between latitudes 26°59′N and 45°31′N. Its terrain is mountainous with relatively narrow coastal strips of good agricultural land, about 14 percent of which is cultivated. Geologically, the Japanese archipelago is unstable, with many active volcanoes and geysers, and it is also subject to frequent earthquake activity. Sixty-seven percent of the land area is forested but otherwise the natural resource base is very limited. Climatically, Japan is monsoonal with wet summers and dry winters, but it experiences less extreme conditions than Korea and China on Mainland Asia at similar latitudes, due to the ameliorating effects of its maritime position.

The overwhelming majority of the population is Japanese, giving the country a homogeneous character unusual in a developed economy. Racially, like most of East and South East Asia, the Japanese are predominantly of mongoloid stock, the islands of Japan having been subjected to migration from the Asian continent over many thousands of years. The origins of the Japanese language are uncertain. It is very different to Chinese (despite superficial similarities to the Western eye) and is usually classed with the Altaic language family of Northern Asia, although it also possibly reflects some Austronesian influences from the South Pacific, particularly with respect to the vocabulary and the sound system.

*Faculty of Economics, Kyushu University, Japan; and Department of Accountancy, University of Otago, New Zealand, respectively. The authors are particularly grateful for the valuable comments of Professor T.E. Cooke, Exeter University, UK, on earlier drafts of this chapter.

It seems likely that the Japanese may have inherited some trading and seafaring traditions from South-east Asia as well as garden farming techniques from East Asia and pastoral traditions from the Steppe peoples. Modern analysis shows that the Neolithic Jomon culture (1000 BC to 300 BC) was proto-Japanese. The cultivation of rice probably spread from China during the subsequent Yayoi culture (300 BC to 300 AD). The first Japanese dynasty dates from 300 BC and during the 4th Century Japan formed a close connection with South Korea, leading to an increased cultural influence from China, particularly with respect to Confucianism and Buddhism. The emperors lost power in the 12th Century to the militarily powerful shogun and samurai warrior families although they continued in a nominal leadership role. The period up to the Meiji restoration of the powers of the Emperor in 1868 was marked by increasing isolation. Both Shinto and the specific structures of villages during the Samurai era contributed significantly to the collectivist patterns of Japanese culture. Specific village structures in the Samurai era as well as Shinto have contributed to shape a Japanese type of culture: collectivism. In 1274 and 1284, two Mongol invasions were successfully repelled early in the period but the country was henceforth frequently subjected to civil war. Trade with Europeans, primarily Catholic Portuguese, developed in the 16th Century, bringing the first influence of Christianity, but for the last 200 years up to 1853, during the Tokugawa period, Japan was effectively sealed off from the outside world. However, US and European states forced a trade treaty from Japan in 1854. After 1868, a deliberate policy of the assimilation of Western technology was pursued, firstly under a strongly hierarchical system with a powerful military independent of democratic control and latterly (since 1945) under a liberal democracy based on Western principles. Despite the differences in approach, both periods may be seen as a conscious attempt to preserve the integrity and identity of the Japanese way of life. The current constitution was established in 1946. The Emperor is the nominal Head of State without executive or legislative powers. The present Diet consists of a 512 seat house of representatives and a 252 seat upper council elected for four and six years respectively. The Prime Minister and Cabinet of Ministers form a Westminster type of executive while the judiciary consists of US style Supreme Court system with certain European characteristics (e.g. the six Codes, including the Commercial Code). The most important religion in Japan in terms of adherents is Shinto (90m). Buddhism in its various forms is also important. There are about 1 million Christians (mostly Catholics) and a smaller number of Muslims. Many Japanese are involved in more than one religion. The population is now over 124m (1991) and growing slowly, similarly to Western countries, at less than one half of one percent per annum. The population density is approximately 333 persons per sq. km. Tokyo, on the largest island of Honshu, is the capital city with a population of more than 8m people. Most Japanese today live in an urban environment.

Since the Meiji Restoration in 1868, the economic growth rate has been consistently high and averaged 4.1 percent in the period 1965–90. In 1994, GNP per capita was US$36 803 per person, the third highest in the world and greater than the per capita GNP of the United States. Japan, along with the US, is the economic leader of the Asia-Pacific region. Japan's economic success has been attributed to a variety of factors. Among these are relatively high domestic savings and investment rates, a work ethic and social values which foster a combination of competitive and collective action and a strong sense of *national identity. In addition, there have been favourable terms of trade in recent years and a structure of international relationships which allows the promotion of defensive domestic market policies while also providing relatively open access to competitors' markets. Agriculture now contributes only just more than 2 percent of GDP (1991), of which rice production is the largest single component. Japan is a world leader in paper production and, despite its own forestry resources, still imports most of its timber requirements. Manufacturing, in the form of ships, vehicles, synthetic fibre, electronics, paper and steel, makes up more than 27 percent of GDP. Almost half of the electronic equipment produced is exported. The service sector contributed about 60 percent of GDP in 1992 and continues to grow in importance as Japan develops as a financial centre. Japan's poor natural resources have required it to import its raw materials and export its manufactures. Its main trading partners are the US, China, Indonesia, Australia, Korea and Saudi Arabia (for imports) and Germany, the UK, Hong Kong, Singapore and Taiwan (for exports). The mark of Japan's economic success is its ability to maintain low rates of inflation and unemployment in periods of high growth and to consistently run substantial balance of trade surpluses. Despite recent political changes, there seems to be no reason to believe Japan's strong economic performance is about to end. Apart from the effect of an appreciating currency and current account surpluses on relationships with its main trading partners, Japan's main problems are likely to continue to be its access to natural resources (e.g. the possibility of worldwide restrictions on fishing practices) and an ageing population. The first two of these problems may be addressed in the future by negotiating long-term international arrangements with supplier countries (e.g. through APEC or ASEAN) and by changes in domestic policies relating to public expenditure. The unit of currency is the yen.*

INTRODUCTION

Japanese accounting has developed under the strong influence of European and American accounting practices since the Meiji Restoration of 1868[1]. Since that time, Western practices have coexisted with distinctive features embodying Japanese culture. Two of the most important of these are the integration of disclosure with conservatism in financial accounting and a proactive, preventative strategy combined with collectivism in management accounting (Nishimura, 1977; 1994).

---

[1]Fukuzawa, a pioneer of Meiji culture, translated a standard American bookkeeping textbook in 1873 (Bryant and Stratton, 1963; Previts and Merino, 1979). In the same year, the Ministry of Finance published *Ginko boki sheihou* ('*Detailed method of bank bookkeeping*') written by Shand, an Englishman, whom the ministry hired to modernise Japanese bank management practices. In April 1890, the Japanese Government first promulgated the Commercial Code, modelling it after Franco-German law. In June 1893, accounting requirements for joint stock companies were added. These accounting requirements came into force in 1899 (Fujita, 1966; Muller and Yoshida, 1968; Kurosawa, 1976; Dubois and Someya, 1977). Yoshida published an academic textbook on accounting in 1910 on the model of Hatfield's '*Modern Accounting*' (Aoki, 1976).

Japanese financial accounting was particularly heavily influenced by Germany before the Second World War. Close political and economic parallels between the two countries in the early part of the 20th Century led Japanese leaders to adopt a German style of commercial law (Nobes and Maeda, 1990; Evans *et al.*, 1988; and Muller and Yoshida, 1968) and, like the German financial accounting system, the Japanese system during that period was directly regulated by legislation (Aoki, 1976). After the end of the Second World War, under the impetus of the US occupation, the Japanese Government superimposed North American disclosure principles on the basically Germanic accounting system (Campbell, 1991). Procedures of rational and scientific management were also introduced from the West at this time (Kobayashi, 1976) and these have subsequently evolved into a specifically Japanese type of management style as a result of their integration with the principles of Japanese collectivism (Nishimura, 1994).

Japanese financial accounting has thus evolved from two heterogeneous types of accounting systems: one a mainly legislated accounting system, the other a system based on the principle of free voluntary disclosure[2]. However, free voluntary disclosure has been reliant on the power of authority (the US occupation or the government) rather than being the outcome of a balancing of the needs of users with the objectives of preparers. This state of affairs seems to be due to three main factors. One is the absence of any Japanese generally accepted principles of accounting similar to the US GAAP, the UK 'true and fair view' principle or even the German standard of 'orderly bookkeeping[3]. The other two are, respectively, the weakness of the influence of the accounting profession in Japan and the fact that the majority of the ordinary investing public are not usually closely involved in the management of Japanese firms. (Bloom and Naciri, 1989).

More recently, Japanese accounting has been affected by changing patterns of world trade and technological developments. The need to compete in international markets and to transfer Japanese accounting practices to their overseas affiliates has required consideration of questions of unification and harmonization in financial

---

[2]Under a legislated accounting system one might expect individual investors to benefit from the power of the state and the imposition of statutory regulations, particularly if their influence on measurement and reporting practices is weak. However, legislative accounting seems to have allowed Japanese companies to adopt conservative accounting practices, probably for the protection of creditors (Nobes and Maeda, 1990; Campbell, 1991; Iino and Inouye, 1984; AlHashim and Arpan, 1988). In contrast, under a free disclosure regime, market forces are more able to determine reporting practices, and individual investors and public accountants can observe, investigate and criticise apparently incompetent or inefficient management.

[3]Although *A statement of business accounting principles* provides that accounts should be prepared in accord with the principles of orderly bookkeeping, clearness of disclosure and consistency, these are not fundamental concepts which have been distilled from long-term Japanese accounting practices.

accounting and of the generalisability of Japanese management accounting techniques. The requirements of unification and harmonization appear presently to be strengthening the legislated element in Japanese financial accounting, continuing the traditional framework of disclosure (Arai, 1989). Unlike Germany where the legislator is 'absolved of the need to regulate all details' (Biener, 1986), in Japan it would seem that there is a perceived need for the preparation of the balance sheet and income statement to be regulated in detail.

The process of internationalization has also affected management accounting. Following the end of the Second World War, Japanese companies introduced many advanced systems from Western countries. Since then, they have created a specifically Japanese type of management accounting involving target costing and other accounting systems related to Just-In-Time (JIT) management (Nishimura, 1992; 1994; Foster and Horngren, 1993; Morgan and Weerakoon, 1989)[4]. Japanese management, influenced by US teaching, realised the integration of low cost and high quality, attracting international attention. Not only have Japanese companies transferred their style of management to their subsidiary companies and affiliates in foreign countries, but foreign companies have also started to introduce similar methods into their own management systems (Kharbanda and Stallworthy, 1991; Munday, 1991; Warner, 1992; Morgan, 1992; Gleave and Oliver, 1990; Marinaccio and Morris, 1991; Williams et al., 1991; Hariman, 1990; Ho, 1993; Morgan and Weerakoon, 1989). Japanese accounting therefore appears to be shifting from a formative period of assimilating foreign techniques to a period of harmonization and exportation of management technology. The current issues seem to be how to accommodate different accounting frameworks and avoid cultural friction (Whitley, 1991; Ueno and Wu, 1993; Rehder, 1989; Schein, 1987). Clearly it is important to clarify the fundamental structure and characteristics of Japanese accounting. The next section will describe, in view of its importance in this context, the nature of the relationship between ownership and management in Japanese companies. Section 3 describes the structure and characteristics of Japanese financial accounting and Section 4 examines the development and certain special features of Japanese management accounting and briefly discusses its influence on Asian accounting. The focus throughout will be on large Japanese motor and electronics companies. These companies represent the main force for growth and internationalization of the Japanese economy and it is they who have established close economic cooperation with, and transplanted the Japanese style of management in, Asia-Pacific countries.

---

[4]Readers interested in the general features of Japanese management accounting in comparison with the American system are referred to Bromwich (1989), Lee (1987), Shields et al. (1991), and Bailes and Assada (1991).

STRUCTURE OF FIRM OWNERSHIP AND MANAGEMENT

Generally speaking, Japanese companies have historically exhibited a lower ratio of shareholders' funds to total funds than do Western companies. According to Skully (1981), for example, Japanese companies obtained 17.5 percent of their funds from equity sources as opposed to 50 percent in the US companies (Skully, 1981).[5]

Table 1

STRUCTURE OF LIABILITIES AND CAPITAL IN LARGE
JAPANESE MOTOR AND ELECTRONICS COMPANIES (1992)
(EXPRESSED IN PERCENTAGES)

Company	Current liabilities	Fixed liabilities	Total Capital	Capital stock
Sony Corporation	29.3	22.7	48	11.7
Toshiba Corporation	50.1	21.2	28.7	7.6
Matsushita Electric In.	30.5	14.5	43.3	5
Hitachi Ltd.	44.1	18.7	37.2	6.9
Honda Motor Co.	35.9	15.3	48.8	5.8
Toyota Motor Corp.	25.3	10.7	64	4.2
Suzuki Motor Corp.	57.5	11.5	31	8.3
Daihatsu Motor Co.	62.1	11.5	26.4	6.3
Isuzu Motors Ltd.	61.1	33.2	5.4	4.8
Nissan Motor Co.	30.5	25.2	44.3	5.5

Source : The Ministry of Finance Publishing Office (1992), *Overall annual securities report 1992*, Tokyo.

As can be seen from Table 1, most motor and electronics companies in Japan have less than 10 percent of their activities funded by capital stock. Of the capital funding in these companies, an important component is provided by financial institutions, mainly banks and insurance companies, and inter-business credit (see Table 2).

Banks and financial institutions influence company decision making in a particularly Japanese way. As can also be seen from Table 2, the personal stake of directors in the equity of these large companies is minor. Although the participation of financial institutions in funding the Japanese companies shown in Table 2 is important, they usually do not second many representatives to the management boards of the

---

[5]This situation may be changing, however. By the end of 1980s the equity ratio of some Japanese firms had increased and in some cases was greater than their American counterparts (Ide, 1994).

Table 2

OWNERSHIP AND MANAGEMENT IN LARGE JAPANESE
MOTOR AND ELECTRONICS COMPANIES (1992)
(EXPRESSED IN PERCENTAGES)

Company	Holdings of top ten shareholders			Holdings of directors	Number of directors related to banks and governments
	Total	Financial institutions	Other		
Sony Corporation	28.46	23.08	5.38 (Reikei Co.)	1.11	7 (42)[*]
Toshiba Corp.	25.68	25.68	0.0	0.02	3 (41)
Matsushita Electric Industrial Co. Ltd.	27.00	23.59	3.41 (Matsushita Kousan Co.) Non-voting stocks	0.83	3 (36)
Hitachi Ltd.	24.06	21.62	2.44 (employee)	0.03	2 (37)
Honda Motor Co.	33.32	33.32	0.0	0.03	2 (36)
Toyota Motor Corporation	35.63	30.88	4.75 (Toyota Loom Manuf.)	0.81	1 (60)
Suzuki Motor Corporation	30.6	23.5	3.5 (GM) & 2.5 (Isuzu)	0.28	3 (34)
Daihatsu Motor Co. Ltd.	48.61	33.99	14.62 (Toyota)	0.18	0 (27)
Isuzu Motors Limited	56.03	18.53	37.5 (GM)	0.05	6 (40)
Nissan Motor Co.	33.53	33.53	0.0	0.08	4 (49)

[*] Number of total directors in each company is given in parentheses.
Source: Ministry of Finance Publishing Office (1992), *Overall annual securities reports 1992*, Tokyo.

latter. Usually, however, close personal relationships are developed in an informal 'coordination within the group' (*shachoukai*) rather than through the formal mechanism of the board of directors (Skully, 1981; Hudack and Orsini, 1992). Partly as a consequence of this, banks and insurance companies do not normally exert a strong, direct influence on the strategic decision making and the routine operating management of companies. However, they are likely to play a significant role in times of crisis. Thus ownership is separated from management in these companies only as long as business runs smoothly. As a result, top personnel can have a strong and stable position in management over a long period of time. If, however, a business starts running into difficulties and internal conflict arises, the banks in particular are likely to seek to intervene in its management. Unlike the typical Western response in these circumstances, though, banks and financial institutions often play an important role in joining forces in an all-out effort to rescue endangered firms in which they have an interest. As a result, the investing public have placed their trust in the firm's relationship with their banks rather than in the disclosure of information from the individual companies.

The Japanese pattern of ownership and the conservative accounting practices associated with it have led to an asymmetry of information between financial institutions and individual public investors (Hudack and Orsini, 1992). Also, a greater proportion of funds available for investment are channelled through the financial institutions than is the case in most Western countries. In the US and the UK, there are many diversified channels through which manufacturing companies can raise funds: individual investors, banks, institutional investors and so on. As a result, shareholders may exert influence in corporate governance. The open, diversified channels in the UK and the US are in definite contrast to the Japanese system of closed, simple channels (i.e. through the closed relationship between banks, firms, directors and auditors). Under these circumstances, the motor and electronics companies have tended to under-report their profits and assets and to adhere to conservative accounting policies on the basis that this policy best promotes long-term stable business management (Travers, 1975; Ohno *et al.*, 1975).

Owing to their strong connection with banks in Japan, the large motor and electronics companies have for a long time adopted a policy of stable growth and dividends. The Japanese Government has also supported the stable growth of large companies by giving special taxation reliefs under Corporation Tax Law[6]. Figure 1 shows the relationships between dividend per share, net income per share, and the ratio of dividend to after-tax profit in some of the large Japanese motor and electronics companies. Dividend per share tends to be stable over long periods of time with profit per share moving in the opposite direction to the ratio of dividend to after-tax

---

[6] The Japanese Government allows companies to adopt special depreciation and tax-exempt reserves in order to promote the import of advanced technology and the rationalization and internationalization of industry. Companies can depreciate one third of these facilities and machines in the first year if they are purchased for rationalization and research and development and, in the case of small-and medium-sized enterprises, where the expenditure is for structural improvement. Additionally, the following named reserves are tax-exempt: export development, research and development, and rationalization of equipment. With regard to the practice of conservative accounting policies related to depreciation and reserves, see Ohno *et al.* (1975) and Travers (1975).

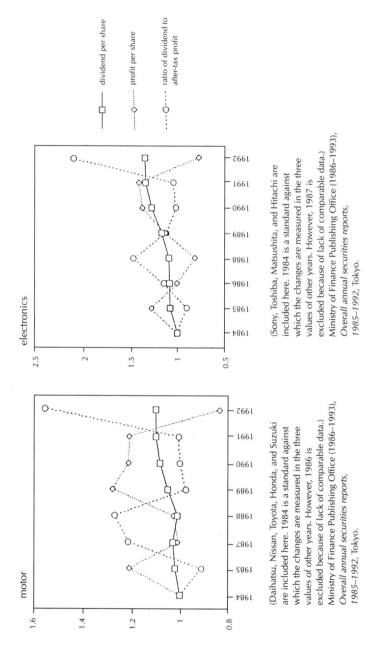

Figure 1 Relation between profit, dividend, and reserve in large motor and electronics companies

profit. It is clear that these companies have implemented a deliberate long term stable dividend policy. These practices have recently improved the ratio of capital stock and reserves to assets in Toyota, Mitsubishi, Honda, and Sony (Skully, 1981).

STRUCTURE AND CHARACTERISTICS OF JAPANESE FINANCIAL ACCOUNTING

Triple structure of accounting requirements

In Japan, accounting measurement requirements, as well as those relating to disclosure, are the subject of statutory regulations down to the minutest detail. The tendency to legislate and rely less on voluntary disclosure is encouraged, as it is in many Western countries, by the occasional scandal. This is illustrated by the legislative strengthening of disclosure and auditing regulations which took place after 1970 in the wake of Sanyo Special Steel Corporation in 1965 (Nakajima, 1973; Katsuyama, 1976)[7].

Financial accounting requirements take a threefold form in Japan: A Statement of Business Accounting Principles (SBAP), the Commercial Code (CC), and Corporation Tax Law (CTL)[8]. In addition, the Securities and Exchange Law (SEL) regulations are probably the most important single source of authority for listed companies. The SBAP is a quasi-legal regulation issued by the Business Accounting Deliberation Council representing the Ministry of Finance and applying to companies quoted on the Japanese stock exchange. The principles (which are described in more detail below) must be followed by all companies wishing to apply for or retain their listing and basically concern the preparation of financial statements and their audit under the SEL. The SBAP requirements are closer in spirit to the voluntary disclosure principles of the US and the UK and consist of seven general principles: truthfulness, an orderly system of bookkeeping, a distinction between capital transactions and income transactions, clearness of disclosure, consistency, conservatism, and uniformity (Hirota, 1981). On the other hand, the accounting requirements in the CC and the CTL are statutory regulations which every business enterprise, including sole traders

---

[7]In the amendment of 1974, the Commercial Code established a clause incorporating fair accounting conventions (*kousei naru kaikeikankou*) and made reference to the need to rely on these in interpreting the provisions of commercial bookkeeping under the law (Hirota, 1981; Fujita, 1986; 1991). Under this amendment, a big company whose capital stock is over 500 million yen or whose total liabilities are over 20 billion yen must have its financial statements audited by an inspector and a Certified Public Accountant. There are about 1.3 million stock companies in Japan. However, only about 1 000 are large firms.

[8]For a detailed explanation of Japanese accounting requirements, see: Cooke (1992); Hirota (1981); Japanese Institute of Certified Public Accountants (1987); Choi and Hiramatsu (1987) and Muller and Yoshida (1968).

and partnerships as well as joint stock companies, must obey in preparing their accounts[9]. The CC adopts a conservative position regarding the protection of creditors,
chiefly by placing restrictions on the payment of dividends[10]. The CTL has enacted
many special rules in its accounting requirements in an attempt to encourage the
modernization and internationalization of Japanese economy (e.g. special depreciation allowances, tax-exempted reserves and other special tax reliefs). Differences in
the requirements of the three sources of regulation necessitate listed companies producing as many as three different sets of financial statements: one for stock exchange
purposes and the potential investors; one for shareholders and creditors; and another
for the tax authorities. Also, many companies produce an English version that is simply a translation of the Japanese report.[11]

The CTL requires a company to prepare its accounts according to the statutory
regulations in the CC so that both laws have almost the same framework of accounting requirements. For tax purposes, companies consequently adjust the financial
statements approved in the general meeting of stockholders according to special
accounting requirements of the CTL. Prior to 1962, assets other than fixed assets such
as inventories and securities were valued at market prices and the balance sheet was
constructed on this basis. Fixed assets were valued at historical cost. In an amendment to the CC in 1962, the valuation principle for all assets was changed fundamentally from the market price method to historical cost. Every company was compelled
to depreciate fixed assets and the calculation of profit was changed from being based
on the difference between opening and closing balance sheet values to the method
of matching revenues against expenses (Dale, 1979; Iino and Inouye, 1984). After
the amendment of 1962, the fulcrum of accountability shifted somewhat from a creditor focus to one in which the needs of investors played a more important part. As a
result, gaps in the accounting requirements between the CC and the SBAP were
much diminished, and at the same time the accounting requirements of the SBAP
received an effective statutory basis. Differences between the two codes and their
reconciliation continue to be debated in academic circles from time to time[12].

---

[9]As in the US and the UK, the main differences in the legal accounting regulations applying to sole
traders, partnerships and joint stock companies relate to issues of the reporting and auditing of
information (Toda, 1984).

[10]A particularly conservative accounting principle with respect to dividends is embodied in the CC.
When the total of pre-operating expenses, research and development costs and experimental costs
exceeds the aggregate of statutory capital reserves and retained earnings, the excess must be deducted from income available for dividends. This is very important for restricting distributable
income.

[11]Nevertheless, financial statements are the foundation of the tax assessment, which is why tax has
an important impact on financial reporting.

[12]The debate over the interpretation of Clause 2, Article 32 concerning fair conventions and the
treatment of special reserves under Article 287–2 is an example. The latter was dealt with in a 1981
revision to the CC. The interpretation and treatment of the principle of consistency is also a matter
of argument (Arai, 1989).

Accounting practices according to the SBAP

To clarify the essential features of Japanese financial accounting, it is useful to consider the practices featuring in the 1993 report *'Yukashoken hokokusho soran'* (*'Overall annual securities reports'*) for the motor and electronics companies. The information is based mainly on securities reports submitted to the Ministry of Finance according to Article 24 in the SEL.

Securities: In almost all companies, the lower of cost or market is applied as the basis of the evaluation of short-term quoted securities[13]. Long-term quoted securities and unquoted securities are evaluated at cost, which is calculated by using a 'moving average method'. This is a conservative valuation policy intended to avoid showing any unrealized profit.

Inventories: With inventories, either the lower of cost or market, or the cost method is used. A number of different bases are used in the calculation of cost in the motor and electronics companies, examples being the LIFO method (Hitachi and Daihatsu), the recent purchase method (Matsushita, Honda, and Suzuki), the moving average method (Hitachi, Isuzu, and Toshiba), and the periodical average method (Honda, Nissan, Daihatsu and Suzuki).

   All the companies in Table 2 adopt standard costing systems which are used as the basis of their financial accounting systems. Cost variances are adjusted to actual cost at the end of each period according to tax law regulations. Nissan applies the order costing method to consignment products (e.g. the space shuttle) while other companies mainly use the process and class costing methods. Honda uses a process costing method for conversion cost based on direct actual costing.

Tangible and intangible fixed assets: In Japan the depreciation policies adopted by companies in their financial statements tend to follow the statutory useful life used for taxation purposes. In the case of tangible assets, nine of the ten companies shown in Table 2 employ the declining balance method with the only exception being Isuzu, which adopts the straight line method. Additionally, some companies, in pursuing the conservative strategy described earlier, occasionally shorten the legal useful lives of certain classes of machines and equipment by 20–30 percent (e.g. Toshiba, Matsushita, Suzuki, and Isuzu in 1993). In the case of intangible assets, all the companies depreciate on the straight line method using the useful lives prescribed by tax law. Almost all the companies charge research and development costs and expenses for issuing new shares directly to income in the period incurred. Only Honda amortizes the expenses of issuing new shares.

---

[13]The cost calculated by using a moving average method is compared with the market price on the closing day and the lower of cost or market is applied (Takeno, 1978).

Reserves: Reserves for guarantees relating to the after-care of motor vehicles and electronics goods, for promotion of sales, for loss from the repurchase of electronic computers and for deferred taxes are given a limited amount of taxation relief through the Special Taxation Measure Law (Nakajima and Suzuki, 1989). The first two special reserves are shown as current liabilities and the last two as fixed liabilities in the balance sheet.

Consolidated financial statements: There are two types of consolidated financial statements in Japan: statements based on the SEC of the US and those based upon the regulation of the SBAP. Some companies (e.g. Sony, Matsushita, Toshiba, Honda, and Hitachi) prepare their consolidated financial statements according to US GAAP and a Ministry of Finance regulation issued in 1976[14] allows such companies to substitute their US consolidated financial statements for ones complying with Japan's own accounting requirements. Other companies prepare their consolidated financial statements in accordance with the regulation of the SBAP (e.g. Suzuki, Isuzu, Daihatsu, Nissan, and Toyota).

The condition for consolidation is similar to the US and UK: a parent company, holding in substance more than half of the voting power in another company, must submit consolidated financial statements to the Ministry of Finance. There is no requirement for a consolidated cash flow statement similar to that required domestically from the parent company, which shows the actual and estimated cash flow from both operating and investment activities. Companies which belong to the SEC group prepare detailed consolidated cash flow statements and occasionally segment information disclosing sales, cost of sales, operating income by product categories and sales by geographical area. Among the SBAP group of companies, Daihatsu is exceptional in producing a consolidated cash flow statement. Other companies in this group give only segment information of sales by geographical area. Daihatsu gives only overseas sales. In the CC, there is no requirement concerning consolidated financial statements.

Also, similar to the practice in some other countries, Japanese regulations allow a parent company some scope for choice in the decision of whether to consolidate. According to a special exempting clause (Supplement 4: exclusion of minor subsidiary from consolidation) when the parent company has subsidiaries whose assets and

---

[14]Regulation regarding Terminology, Forms and Methods of Preparation of Consolidated Financial Statements and detailed instructions (Toda *et al.*, 1984). According to the former Regulation of Consolidated Financial Statements, unimportant subsidiaries whose assets, sales, and profit are less than 10 percent of those of the parent company could be excluded from consolidation. However, the amendment of the SEL in June 1993 abolishes the 10 percent rate. The JICPA prepares and releases practical guidelines on consolidated financial statements (Tezuka, 1993).

sales are so immaterial that their inclusion makes the consolidated financial statements misleading for judging the financial position and result of the group, it can exclude these subsidiaries from the consolidation (Hirota, 1981, JICPA, 1987(b); and McKinnon, 1984).

Auditing: In most of the above-mentioned companies, the audit report assumes a standardized form. The typical report specifies that certified public accountants have audited the balance sheet, income statement, statement of appropriation of profit, and the accompanying schedules according to the auditing standards[15]. Additionally, it must be specified in the report that certified public accountants in the audit corporation have no special interest in the audited company, as prescribed by Auditing Standards issued in 1956 (Toda, 1984). Cash flow statements[16] are not required to be audited. The SBAP only requires disclosure of cash flow statements in supplementary Schedules (Campbell, 1991).

Other: Three other specific matters are important in understanding the practice of Japanese financial reporting:

(i)   Rules regarding foreign currency items. The Business Accounting Deliberation Council (BADC) recommends that companies record yen amounts translated at the foreign exchange rate ruling when the transaction occurs. However, when the transaction involves futures contracts, it is valued at the relevant fixed amount. Exchange differences on short-term monetary items have to be disclosed in the income statement and the translation of foreign currency statements depends upon whether these are for a foreign branch or a foreign subsidiary (Cooke, 1994). Assets and liabilities in foreign currencies and the conversion rate used should be published as part of the disclosure of accounting policies in the financial statements.

(ii) The measurement rules in the CC require companies to explain the treatment of important leases fixed assets in footnotes to the financial statements. In June of 1993, the BADC promulgated a Statement of Accounting Standard relating to lease transactions according to which finance leases should be treated in the same way as an ordinary fixed asset purchase and sale while operating leases should be treated as an ordinary letting and hiring. Information about the latter is

---

[15]The following corporations should have their financial statements audited by a CPA or an audit corporation: 1. A corporation capitalized at 500 million yen or more; 2. A corporation with liabilities which aggregate 20 billion yen or more; 3. A corporation whose stock or debentures is listed on a stock exchange; 4. Corporations which plan to list their stocks on a stock exchange or publicly offer or sell them. (JICPA, 1987(c)).

[16]Readers interested in the development and problems of Japanese cash flow statements are referred to Someya (1964) and Campbell (1983).

divided into prepaid rentals due in more than one year and those due within one year after the balance sheet date.

(iii) The rule relating to interim financial statements issued in 1977 provides that interim financial statements should aim at providing relevant information to investors. 'Relevant information' means that it is useful for estimating management performance during the interim period (Arai and Kaneko, 1994).

Recent development of disclosure and auditing

Due to changes in domestic policy and the international situation, there have been a number of recent developments in financial disclosure and auditing in Japan. Domestically, in the wake of several scandals, the social responsibility of business enterprises and the adequacy of existing systems of disclosure and auditing have been called into question. Internationally, Japanese disclosure practices relating to affiliate and controlling interests have been criticized, particularly in North America.

The US/Japan Structural Impediments Initiative (SII) talks in 1990 recommended that Japan improve its disclosure of affiliates as follows:

(1) there should be extended disclosure of relevant transactions;
(2) consolidated financial statements should be treated as substantial, not supplementary documents;
(3) segment information should be given; and
(4) disclosure of sales by important customers should be made in individual financial statements. In compliance with these requests, an Ordinance of the Finance Ministry relating to the Disclosure of Enterprises was amended in December 1993, and the Securities and Exchange Commission promulgated the *Disclosure of Market Value of Marketable Securities, Futures Transactions, and Options* in order to extend disclosure of business enterprises trading on the securities exchanges. This regulation provides that companies disclose the risk of price fluctuations[17].

The SEL and its related ordinances and regulations were amended to improve the disclosure of business enterprises generally between June 1992 and March 1993. The main amendments consisted of the enlargement of the class of persons responsible for submitting annual securities reports, an extension of the securities concept, and improved disclosure in the annual securities reports and securities registration statements. The latter extends over dividend policy, management indices, and consolidated information (e.g. extent of consolidation and segment information). It is

---

[17]The implementation of the regulation to disclose the market value of debentures has been postponed for one year since it may prove difficult to calculate this objectively (Disclosure of Information on Market price, 1991).

worth noting that the SEC entrusts the Japanese Institute of Certified Public Accountants (JICPA) with the power to prepare and release practical guidelines related to the consolidated information.[18]

The CC was also amended in June 1993 to strengthen access of third parties to information and auditing practices. First, the amendment makes a lawsuit by representative shareholders easier to pursue in terms of cost[19], relaxes the requisite for shareholders' rights to pursue accounting records from 10 percent of outstanding stocks to 3 percent and enhances shareholders ability to audit the directors' management of a business. Additionally, it extends the auditors' period of employment from two years to three, guaranteeing their status more effectively. In large companies, 'more than three auditors' should be appointed in contrast to 'more than two' in the former CC. This better realises the original purpose of auditing among the objectives which was a presumption that at the least one auditor should not have an interest in the company. The code legally guarantees a committee of auditors with increased independence from directors (Tsuchiya, 1993).

The extent of Japanese financial disclosure and the quantity of information has increased year by year. The quality of information and its relevance to investors, customers, and citizens in comparison with internationally advanced standards of disclosure has become a subject of discussion for Japanese companies. There is a perceived need for the present disclosure and auditing systems, based on a close and political distribution of economic resources, to be shifted to a more visible and comparable one appropriate to an international, open market (Ide, 1994). Therefore, Japanese companies will need to make greater efforts to improve their disclosure and auditing practices as they become global enterprises. Although the recent amendments to the CC and the SEL is in the direction of increased disclosure of relevant

---

[18]Closed companies with more than 500 shareholders must submit their annual securities report to the SEC. Concerning the extension of the concept of securities, commercial papers and negotiable certificates of deposit issued by foreign companies, these are to be included in the securities classification and their issuers are to submit a securities report to the SEC. With regard to the disclosure of dividend policy, the use of internal reserves must be noted in the annual securities report. The segment information referred to earlier in the text must be shown as an explanatory note in the consolidated financial statements and audited by CPAs. Assets, depreciation, and capital expenditures by industrial type and segment must be disclosed beside sales and operating income. This is to be enforced by 1 April 1995. In addition, the SEC now requires companies to give segment information relating to sales and operating income by place, and foreign sales by area, to public investors. The former came into operation on 1 April 1994. The latter will come into operation on 1 April 1997.

[19] Previously such lawsuits had been treated the same as suits relating to property rights, the court costs of which are very expensive since they are calculated on the basis of claimed amounts. Now shareholder suits will be considered as claims of a non-property right type and their court costs will be restricted to only 8,200 Yen.

financial information, a strengthening of the social function of public accountants and the empowering of shareholders, it remains to be seen whether Japanese enterprises will be able to reorganize their closed affiliations and control systems and whether Japanese society will be able to improve its procedures of corporate governance.

To sum this section up, first, Japanese companies generally take a half-hearted attitude to voluntary disclosure, with most companies unwilling to publish more information than they are obliged to by legal requirements (see Cooke, 1991 (a)). Second, particularly with the important motor and electronics companies, there are two different standards of financial statements in one report — US GAAP and the local Japanese SBAP. Consequently it is sometimes more difficult than it perhaps should be for individual investors to analyse the financial position of their company. Third, Japanese asset valuation is conservative. This is a point which relates to the relevance of the information to the needs of the Japanese investor. Therefore, publicly available financial information in Japan could be criticised on grounds of secretiveness, consistency and relevance to the investor.

DEVELOPMENT AND FEATURES OF MANAGEMENT ACCOUNTING

Development of Japanese management accounting

The development of management accounting practices in Japan can, broadly speaking, be divided into two periods in the post Second World War era: the first up to the 1970s and the second, the period since. In the immediate post-war period, Japanese companies without access to developed domestic stock markets used foreign governmental and bank funds to reconstruct facilities damaged by the war and also to import advanced technologies. Foreign governments and foreign investors, especially banks, requested Japanese companies to both account for and plan for funds usage (Nishimura, 1992 and 1994), thus necessitating the extensive adoption of profit planning and budgetary control from the 1950s through to the 1960s. As a result, budgetary control developed more extensively in Japanese companies than either standard costing or direct costing.

Also during this initial period, Japanese companies established modern management organization and accounting control systems to accommodate the formation of modern joint-stock companies following the dissolution of the closed, pre-war pattern of family ownership *(zaibatsu)*. The financial statements of these 'cliques' had not previously been disclosed, and the US occupation imposed North American attitudes towards reporting in the process of replacing them. Simultaneously, also under US influence, modern statistical and accounting systems were established to manage the disrupted Japanese economy. To a greater or lesser degree, these factors influenced the development of budgetary control and internal control systems in Japan.

The Japanese Government was instrumental in establishing modern management accounting practices through the introduction of advanced planning and control systems from the US as part of the reconstruction of the economy and business management. The Ministry of International Trade and Industry (MITI) in Japan, especially, played a critical role in promoting the spread of modern management accounting from the 1950s to 1970s, publishing several important reports on modernization[20].

From the 1970s, while their American counterparts developed accounting for strategic decision-oriented management, managers in Japanese motor companies began to implement JIT in earnest (Nishimura, 1992; Kato, 1989). JIT was a response to a funds shortage and excess inventories brought about by the oil crisis of 1973. Linking up with the subcontractor system[21], JIT enabled a company to buy and produce just the amount of materials and parts it required for its finished products without the need to carry buffer stocks. The fundamental idea of this system is that a company begins production only when a customer issues an order (Hirano, 1990; Nishimura, 1992).

In the implementation of JIT, Japanese management exhibits two major characteristics. One is a strong control orientation which seeks collective and cooperative management at all levels in contrast to the decisive role typically played by senior management in North American organisations. The benefit of human resource management in the solution of problems is explicitly recognized. In particular, Japanese middle and lower managers play an important proactive role in anticipating problems before they occur. In this system, much depends upon the mutual trust between workers and managers, proper training, multiskilling of employees and a firm belief in the use of initiative to amend inappropriate plans. Essentially, everyone unites to ensure control of the operating process. The other characteristic is a focus on the longer term view. Quantitative models are not as important as is the case in North America. JIT depends on 'total quality control' in contrast to the 'economic quantity' which emphasizes short-term profit maximization. The combination of these two characteristics results in a production system based on the concept of zero inventory and zero defects and ultimately in an integrated management of low cost and high quality[22].

---

[20]These included: *The general principles of internal control in business enterprises* (July 1951); *Outlines of procedures related to execution of internal control* (February 1953); *Profit planning for implementation of business policy* (July 1956); *Profit planning in division* (August 1960); *Cost management* (December 1966); and *Future policy of business finance* (May 1972).

[21]More than 80 percent of small and medium sized enterprises in the motor and electric industries are dependent, as subcontractors, on parent companies (Small and Medium Enterprises Agency, 1980).

[22]The collectivist ethic in Japanese management may be traced to its origins in rice farming, a centralized state, religions (Confucianism, Buddhism, and Shinto), warrior traditions and other factors (Dunn, 1969).

Management accounting practices in motor and electronics machine companies

Target costing is closely related to JIT (Kato, 1989; Hiromoto, 1988; Lee, 1987; Yoshikawa *et al.*, 1989; Sakurai, 1990; Nishimura, 1994). Target costing consists of two processes: *genka kikaku* (cost design) and *genka kaizen* (continuous cost improvement). In the process of cost design, the target cost of a new product is estimated on the basis of a long-range profit plan, market price estimates, and consideration of the actual production environment. First, at the planning stage, the cost manager and design engineers develop the target cost on the basis of the structure of the new product under the responsibility of a *shukan* (a chief engineer) both to satisfy the needs of customers and with a view to penetrating competitive international markets. Second, at the implementation stage, the expected actual cost (i.e. the standard cost) is estimated from the viewpoint of value engineering[23]. Production departments and subcontractors try to achieve the target cost by improving production methods and adopting new materials and technology. Any variance between the target and the standard cost is thus minimised. Analysis of this variance has now become an important component of performance measurement in Japanese firms.

In the process of cost minimisation which takes place at the stage of mass production, the target cost is compared with the standard cost over a certain number of budgeted months (e.g. six months in Toyota), during which time improvements in efficiency may be obtained. Workers and managers in all departments at all levels are expected to suggest new cost and technological improvements on a daily basis in order to bring the standard cost close to the target cost (Tanaka, 1991; Monden, 1992).

Target costing plays an important role in JIT systems in motor companies. Interaction between cost accountants and design engineers, the relationship between low cost and high quality, the relationship between 'feedback' and 'feedforward'[24], and the processes of cost reduction in the design stage are unique features of JIT. Used effectively, they enable inventory levels and production defects to be brought close to zero.

The JIT system essentially consists of two subsystems: visible management and a new production system. Visible management, often called *kanban* in Japanese, relies partly on old Japanese culture (e.g. *miseshime*, the putting of an individual or group's failure on public display), and partly on advanced information systems. To implement the principle effectively in motor company workshops, *kanban* systems are

---

[23]A management technique which not only improves the usefulness of the product, but also reduces the cost in both design and production (Tamai *et al.*, 1978).

[24]A preparatory control system which indicates and organizes preventive activities before variances occur between plans and results. For more on this aspect of management, see Morgan (1992).

combined with computer-aided management systems and their essential joint function is to discover and remedy problems quickly.

The new production system consists of a strategy of small lots, zero inventories, multiskilling[25], short lead times, and a suitable arrangement of machines and a horizontal relationship between managers and workers (Hall *et al.*, 1991). The production system must be sufficiently flexible to solve the problems discovered in the process of visible management. In particular, the new 'pull production' method has contributed to the prevention of excess inventories and defects. Under this method, each stage of the production process should respond only to an explicit demand from a subsequent stage and should be able to rely on the immediately preceding stage of production for its input requirements. This contrasts to the traditional 'push production' method, in which the previous stage of a process produces output regardless of demand from its subsequent stage — often leading to superfluous inventories and the accumulation of defective parts (Hirano, 1990; Lee, 1987). Under the new regime quality is not necessarily traded off against cost (Daniel and Reitsperger, 1991).

Most large companies in the electronics industry have adopted a divisional organization and target costing strategy to attain the same aims of integration of low cost and high quality as the motor companies. Recently, divisional offices have been given increased control over research and development expenditure. Their role is to promote development (Tanaka, 1991). Each divisional organization is responsible for planning and controlling product design and target cost in cooperation with the head office. The principles of small group teamwork, total quality control, and zero defects are adopted to ensure realization of the budgeted profit.

Head offices adopt control systems of intra-company capital, credit, tax, interest flows and dividend flows in order to connect the divisional organizations into a unified whole. In the Canon company, for instance, divisional organizations can either use 'inner' funds or issue their shares in the stock markets. Each division pays 8 percent as intra-company interest and 4 percent as dividend, respectively, on borrowings and capital raised from the head office. General corporate expenses are assessed on divisions as 4 percent of sales and performance is evaluated on the basis of the profit figure, efficient usage of funds, the accomplishment level of budget, and the growth ratio. When a division organizes a new venture, the head office encourages its development by lowering the rate of intra-company interest, dividend, and the general corporate expenses percentage (Tanaka, 1991).

---

[25]Japanese companies use 'on the job-training' and the frequent redeployment of labour to enable employees to deal with various production processes. Multiskilling plays a role in reducing waiting time and increasing productivity (Marinaccio and Morris, 1991).

To summarise, the common features of Japanese management accounting in motor and electronics companies are the following. First, budgets are monitored by long or middle-term considerations. Budget management takes the concrete form of target costing. Second, cost management has a strong market orientation and shifts from a sole focus on 'reactive' cost reduction at the production stage to a more balanced 'proactive' focus on cost minimisation at the design and development stages. Cost minimisation at the design stage is then accompanied by continuous cost improvement at the production stage. Third, the fundamental objective of management is the integration of low cost and high quality and productivity. Fourth, large Japanese companies place importance on combining the principles of horizontal relationships between management and workers, small group teamwork, total quality control, and zero defects with advanced computer technology.

The impact of target costing on Asian management accounting

The Japanese principle of the integration of high quality and low cost is beginning to be perceived as being very important in Asia[26]. In particular, many companies in Asian countries have become interested in target costing as a way of increasing their competitive position in international markets.

Wang has argued that Taiwanese companies should adopt target costing in view of the increasing costs of labour and the rapid development of technology (Wang, 1984). Manufacturing firms in Korea have likewise expressed concern about quality control and cost design (Ho, 1992). Perhaps the most obvious benefits of adopting the target costing strategy, however, have been evident in China. The First Automobile Company adopted Toyota's management system of continuous improvement, high productivity and cost reduction in 1993. The Changchun Gear Wheel Factory, one of First Automobile's affiliates, raised production levels by 44 percent and labour productivity by 37 percent over the comparable period of the previous year (*People's Daily*, 29 May 1994). In China, as elsewhere in Asia, the popularisation and the implementation of target costing strategy has often been due to the transplanting of management practices through Japanese overseas affiliates.

However, the development of target costing in Asian countries has been significantly different from the situation prevailing in Japan in important respects. For example, the stage of *genka kaizen* has often been developed independently of the stage of *genka kikatu*. In Japanese motor affiliates in Thailand, for instance, the

---

[26]The highest quality of product may not however, always be the preferred option. The 'second best' may be preferred if it is associated with a lower price. Some Japanese companies have recently began to adopt strategies which explicitly consider the different levels of quality and cost appropriate to market conditions.

responsibility for cost design is usually in the hands of head office managers in Tokyo, while local factories usually just take charge of the continuous cost improvement stage of the process (Sigemi and Mizuno, 1987). This situation arises from the patterns of delegation of decision making in Japanese companies and is also presumably influenced by the cultural circumstances of the country of residence. Yamashita reports that in Thai-Japanese overseas affiliates, Japanese head offices and managers have strong powers in the areas of financial management and product development, while local managers tend to be only responsible for policies connected with sales, purchases, and personnel (Yamashita, 1993).

Japanese management is characterised as a cooperative and proactive one dedicated to prevention rather than cure, in which managers cooperate with workers to prevent failure from occurring. However, it may not always be possible or even appropriate to implement this approach in Asian factories, given the type of local conditions which often exist there. The prevention of defects is often impractical due to the lack of development of management controls and norms which do not necessarily favour the type of collective organisation common in Japan. High quality may instead be achieved through the use of cheap labour. If defective work is identified at some stage of the production process, it is simply returned to the previous stage and repaired — repeatedly if necessary. Such costly behaviour is possible only under conditions of cheap labour. Labour costs are so low in some Asian companies that they have succeeded in enhancing their shares of international markets with a high quality of output policy despite this highly inefficient method.

The success of a high quality strategy is therefore closely related to low salaries in Asian countries. As Dart's *et al's* (1990) survey shows, one of the major concerns of middle size enterprises in Singapore, Malaysia and Thailand is how to raise the motivation of employees. Thus it can be seen that continuous cost improvement, the Japanese training system, and the principle of the quality circle play an important role in the Asia-Pacific region but they do so in a rather different way and against a different background compared to that experienced in Japan. Japanese companies may in the future be forced to transfer more of the functions of research and development and strategic decision making to Asian countries because of the continuing appreciation of the Yen. As companies in East Asia seem to be eager to develop the system of target costing in order to strengthen their competitive positions in international markets, it is likely, therefore, that new types of target costing will continue to emerge.

CONCLUSION

Japanese accounting modelled itself on North American accounting systems after the Second World War. However, although Japanese and North American financial accounting systems continue to maintain a superficial resemblance, they have begun to diverge again in recent years, particularly in the case of the former with respect to the extent that state power is required to enforce disclosure. Accounting requirements in the Commercial Code hold an especially important position in the field of financial accounting. Japanese management also seems to be moving in a different direction from its North American counterpart with an emphasis on target costing, teamwork and the long-term view.

It is likely that at least some of these emerging differences are culturally based. A consequence of this is that the harmonisation of Japanese accounting with international standards may be more difficult than would at first appear, since the Anglo-Saxon countries which play a leading part in establishing international standards are more firmly wedded to the principles of voluntary disclosure and public auditing (Nakajima, 1976). The weakness of individual investors and public accountants makes it more difficult to control unfair practices in Japan. Nevertheless, international demands for greater amounts of fair disclosure are becoming stronger with the progress of advanced information technology and globalisation of the national economy (Walters, 1986). Japan has a significant role to play in promoting effective communication with other countries in view of her important position in the world economy. It could be argued, therefore, that large Japanese companies should aim to strengthen the true and fair disclosure of financial information and adjust the terminology, forms, and methods of their accounts in line with international standards in order to enhance comparability.

The long-term stable growth of the economy, stable dividend policies and the creative new developments in management accounting outlined in this chapter have all contributed to the success of long range business management in Japan. The new ideas developed by Japanese management are attracting international attention and foreign managers are eager to study and possibly use Japanese methods. In the transferring of Japanese management to other countries, however, Japanese companies should consider the possibility for conflict between the Japanese management style and the indigenous culture of transferee countries. This may become an important issue in the future in the internationalisation of the Japanese economy.

REFERENCES

AlHashim, D. and J. Arpan (1988), *International dimensions of accounting*, RWS-Kent, Boston, pp. 31–3.

Aoki, S. (1976), 'Japanese accounting after the Meiji era', *History of Japanese accounting development*, S. Aoki (ed), Doyukan, Tokyo, pp. 68–72.

Arai, K. and H. Kaneko (eds) (1994), *The compendium of accounting laws*.

Arai, K. (1989), *Formation and development of business accounting principles*, Chuo-keizaisha Co., Tokyo.

Bailes, C. and T. Assada (1991), 'Empirical differences between Japanese and American budget and American budget and performance evaluation systems', *The international journal of accounting*, Vol. 26, pp. 131–42.

Biener, H. (1986), 'Main approaches to standard-setting in German', *Harmonization of accounting standards,* OCDE, Paris, pp. 57–9.

Bloom, R. and M. Naciri (1989), 'Accounting standard setting and culture: A comparative analysis of the United States, Canada, England, West Germany, Australia, New Zealand, Sweden, Japan, and Switzerland, *The international journal of accounting,* Vol. 24, pp. 79–97.

Bromwich, M. (1989), *The revolution in management accounting?,* University of Sydney, Sydney.

Bryant, H. and H. Stratton (1963), *Counting house bookkeeping,* Ivison, Blackman, Taylor & C., New York.

Campbell, G. (1983), 'Current accounting practices in Japan', *The accountant's magazine,* August, pp. 303–5.

Campbell, G. (1991), 'Financial reporting in Japan', *Comparative international accounting,* Nobes, C. and R. Parker (eds), (Third Edition), Prentice Hall, Cambridge, pp. 234–51.

Choi, D.F. and K. Hiramatsu (ed) (1987), *Accounting and financial reporting in Japan,* Van Nostrand Reinhold (UK), Berkshire.

The Compendium of Accounting Law (Tokyo: Chuokeizaisha Co., 1994).

Cooke T. (1992), 'The impact of size, stock market listing and industry type on disclosure in the annual reports of Japanese listed corporations', *Accounting and business research,* Vol. 22, No. 87, pp. 229–37.

Cooke, T. (1991(a)), 'An assessment of voluntary disclosure in the annual reports of Japanese corporation', *The international journal of accounting,* Vol. 26, pp. 174–89.

Cooke, T. (1991(b)), 'The Impact of Accounting Principles on Profits: The US versus Japan, *Accounting and Business Research,* Vol. 23 No. 92, 1993, pp. 460–479.

Cooke, T. (1994), 'Japan' in *Financial reporting in the west Asia Pacific rim.*

Dale, B. (1979), 'Accounting in Japan', *The Australian accountant,* April, pp. 150–57.

Daniel, J. and W.D. Reitsperger (1991), 'Linking quality strategy with management control systems: Empirical evidence from Japanese industry', *Accounting organizations,* Vol. 16, No. 7, pp. 601–18.

Dart, J., Ng, I. and A. Saikar (1990), 'A comparative analysis of managerial practices among SME's from Malaysia, Singapore, and Thailand', *ASEAN economic bulletin,* Vol. 7 No. 1, July, pp. 85–95

Disclosure of Information on Market Price (1991), *Accounting View,* No. 183, October, pp. 11–6.

Dubois, A. and K. Someya (1977), 'Accounting development in Japan', *The accountant,* May 5, pp. 500–2.

Dunn, J. (1969), *Everyday life in traditional Japan,* Charles E. Tuttle, Tokyo, pp. 1–58.

Evans, G., E. Taylor, and O. Holzmann (1988), *International accounting and reporting,* Pws-Kent, Boston, pp. 41–2, 47.

Foster, G. and C. Horngren (1993), 'Cost accounting and cost management in a JIT environment', *Issues in strategic management accounting,* J. Ratnatunga (Ed), Harcourt Brace Jovanovich, Sydney, pp. 180–98.

Fujita, Y. (1966), 'The evolution of financial reporting in Japan', *The International journal of accounting,* Fall, pp. 49–73;

Fujita, Y. (1986), 'Accounting and reporting in Japan', *Harmonization of accounting standards,* OCDE, Paris, pp. 60–3;

Fujita, Y. (1991), *An analysis of development and nature of accounting principles in Japan,* Garland Publishing Inc. New York.

Gleave, S. and N. Oliver (1990), 'Human resources management in Japanese manufacturing companies in the UK: five case studies', *Journal of general management*, Vol. 16, No. 1 Autumn, pp. 54–68.

Hall, W., Johnson, T. and P. Turney (1991), *Measuring up: Charting pathways to manufacturing excellence,* Business One Irwin, Illinois, pp. 61–85.

Hariman, J. (1990), 'Influencing rather than informing: Japanese management accounting', *Management accounting,* March, pp. 44–6.

Hirano, H. (1990), *Practices of JIT production,* Nihhonkeizai Shinbun, Tokyo.

Hiromoto, T. (1988), 'Another hidden edge — Japanese management accounting', *Harvard business review,* July–August, pp. 22–6.

Hirota, J. (1981), *Handbook of Japanese accounting practice,* Chuo Keizaisha Co. Ltd., Tokyo.

Ho, S. (1993), 'Transplanting Japanese management techniques', *Long range planning,* Vol. 26, No. 4, pp. 81–9.

Ho, K. (1992), '*Present situation and problems of cost management systems; cost design in manufacturing firms* (unpublished), presented at a meeting of the General Meeting of Korean Accounting Institute, Spring.

Hudack, R., and L. Orsini (1992), 'A note of caution to users of Japanese financial reports: A demonstration of an enlarged exogenist approach', *The international journal of accountancy,* Vol. 27, p. 18.

Ide, M. (1994), *Japanese business finance and international competition,* Toyokeizaishinpo, Tokyo.

Iino, T. and R. Inouye (1984), 'Financial accounting and reporting in Japan', *International accounting,* P.H. Holzer (Ed), Harper & Row, New York, pp. 369–80.

Japanese Institute of Certified Public Accountants (1987a), *Corporate disclosure in Japan, overview,* JICPA, Tokyo.

Japanese Institute of Certified Public Accountants (1987b), *Corporate disclosure in Japan, accounting,* JICPA, July, Tokyo.

Japanese Institute of Certified Public Accountants (1987c), *CPA profession in Japan,* JICPA, July, Tokyo.

Kato, Y. (1989), 'Target costing support systems: Lessons from leading Japanese companies', *Management accounting research,* 1993, 4, pp. 33–47; *Development of Management Accounting Studies* (Tokyo: Zeimukeirikyoukai).

Katsuyama, S. (1976), 'Recent problems of the financial accounting system in Japan', *The international journal of accounting,* Fall, pp. 122–31.

Kharbanda, P. and E. A. Stallworthy (1991), 'Let's learn from Japan', *Management accounting,* March, pp. 26–8.

Kobayashi, Y. (1976), 'Development of budgetary control', *History of Japanese accounting development,* S. Aoki (ed), Doyukan, Tokyo, pp. 185–95.

Kurosawa, K. (1976), 'Formation of modern bookkeeping and accounting', *History of Japanese accounting development,* S. Aoki (ed), Doyukan, Tokyo, pp. 3–29.

Lee, Y. (1987), *Managerial accounting changes for the 1990s,* Addison-Wesley Publishing Co., Massachusetts.

Marinaccio, R. and J. Morris (1991), 'Work and production reorganization in a 'Japanized' company', *Journal of general management,* Vol. 17, No. 1, Autumn, pp. 56–69.

McKinnon, L. (1984), 'Application of Anglo-American principles of consolidation to corporate financial disclosure in Japan', *ABACUS,* Vol. 20, No. 1, pp. 16–33.

Monden, Y. (1992), *Cost management in motor enterprises,* Doubunkan, Tokyo.

Morgan, J. and P. Weerakoon (1989), 'Japanese management accounting: its contribution to the Japanese economic miracle', *Management accounting,* June, pp. 40–3.

Morgan, J. (1992), 'Feedforward control for competitive advantage: The Japanese approach', *Journal of general management*, Vol. 17, No. 4, Summer, pp. 41–52.

Muller, G. and H. Yoshida (1968), *Accounting practices in Japan*, University of Washington, Washington.

Munday, M. (1991), 'A case of Japanisation?' *Management accounting*, March, pp. 32–3.

Nakajima, N. and Y. Suzuki (1989), *Accounting practices in institutional and statutory accounting*, Chuo Keizaisha Co., Tokyo.

Nakajima, S. (1973), 'Economic growth and corporate financial reporting in Japan', *The international journal of accounting*, Fall, pp. 35–41.

Nakajima, S. (1976), 'Enactment of international accounting standards', *History of Japanese accounting development*, S. Aoki (Ed), Doyukan, Tokyo, pp. 231–5.

Nishimura, A. (1994), 'The recent development in Japanese management accounting and their impact on British and New Zealand companies', *Journal of political economics*, Kyushu University, Spring.

Nishimura, A. (1992), 'The development and future of management accounting in Japan and the USA', *Journal of political economics*, Kyushu University, September, pp. 109–20.

Nishimura, A. (1989), 'Development of study of management accounting', *Journal of political economics*, Kyushu University, October, p. 385.

Nishimura, A. (1977), *Study of financial disclosure*, Dobunkan, Tokyo.

Nobes, C. and S. Maeda (1990), 'Japanese accountants: Interpreters needed', *Accountancy*, September, pp. 82–4.

Ohno, K., Ichikawa, H. and A. Kodama (1975), 'Recent changes in accounting standards in Japan', *The international journal of accounting*, Fall, pp. 107–20.

Previts, J. and D. Merino (1979), *A history of accounting in America* (New York: A Ronald Press Publication).

Rehder, R. (1989), 'Japanese transplants: In search of a balanced and broader perspective', *Columbia journal of world business*, Winter, pp.17–27.

Sakurai, M. (1990), 'The influence of factory automation in management practice: A study of Japanese companies', *Measure for manufacture excellence*, S. R. Kaplan (Ed), pp. 48–53.

Schein, E. (1987), 'Does Japanese management style have a message for American managers?', *The art of managing human resources*, E. Schein (Ed), Oxford University Press, New York, pp. 209–27.

Shields, D., Chow, C., Kato, Y. and Y. Nakagawa (1991), 'Management accounting practices in the US and Japan', *Journal of international financial management and accounting*, Vol. 3, pp. 61–77.

Sigemi, Y., and J. Mizuno (1987), 'Structure of specialization and transfer of technology between Japanese overseas affiliates and local firms in Thailand', *Institute of Development of Economics*, Tokyo.

Small and Medium Enterprises Agency (1980), *The White Paper on small medium enterprises*, SMEA, Tokyo.

Skully, T. (1981), 'Japanese corporate structure: Some factors in its development', *The international journal of accounting*, Spring, pp. 67–98.

Someya, K. (1964), 'The use of funds statements in Japan', *The accounting review*, October, pp. 983–9.

Takeno, K. (1978), *Securities*, Chuo Keizaisha Co., Tokyo.

Tamai, M. (Ed) (1978), *Value analysis*, Moritake Publisher, Tokyo.

Tanaka, T. (1991), *Contemporary management accounting system*, Chuo Keizaisha Co. Ltd., Tokyo, pp. 29–122 and 189–208.

Tezuka, N. (1993), 'Recent development of disclosure system, *Accounting tax consulting*', No. 202, May, pp. 2–8.

Toda, S. (Ed) (1984), *Business and economic laws*, Sanseidou, Tokyo.

Travers, N. (1975), 'Financial reporting in the Japanese company', *Accountancy*, January, pp. 34–6.

Tsuchiya, T. (1993), 'Commentary on the outline of the Commercial Code amended on June of 1993', *Accounting tax consulting*, No. 205, August, pp. 2–8

Ueno, S. and F. Wu (1993), 'The comparative influence of culture on budget control practices in the United States and Japan', *The international journal of accounting*, Vol. 28, pp. 17–39.

Walters, E. (1986), Summary, OCDE, *Harmonization of accounting standards*, OCDE, Paris, pp. 17–9.

Wang, Y. (1984), 'Renovation of management accounting under new production conditions', *Monthly study of accounting*, Vol. 96, pp. 22–7.

Warner, M. (1992), 'How Japanese managers learn', *Journal of general management*, Vol. 17, No. 3, Spring, pp. 56–71.

Whitley, D. (1991), 'The social construction of business systems in East Asia', *Organization studies*, Vol. 12, No. 1, pp. 1–28.

Williams, A., Owen, B. and A. Emerson (1991), *The Nissan way, from conflict to commitment*, William Collins, Auckland.

Yamashita, M. (1993), 'The problems of management and accounting in Japanese overseas affiliates in Thailand', *Annual report of study for South-east Asia*, Vol. 35, pp. 25–38.

Yoshikawa, T., Innes, J. and F. Mitchell (1989), 'Japanese management accounting: A comparative survey', *Management accountant*, November, pp. 21–3.

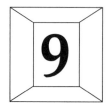

ACCOUNTING IN THE PHILIPPINES

*Joselito Diga**

BACKGROUND

The Philippine archipelago lies approximately 1000 km east of mainland South-east Asia above Borneo between latitudes 4°30′ and 21°20′N. It consists of two main islands, Luzon in the north, and Mindanao in the south, with 7000 smaller islands of the Visayas in between. The climate of the Philippines is maritime tropical, with a monsoon influence in the north. The land area of the islands, which is quite mountainous with relatively small areas of high quality arable land, is approximately 300 000 sq. km and contains a population of almost 68 million people, giving a density of about 230 persons per sq. km. Manila, the capital, is located in the relatively fertile plains of Luzon, which is home to most of the country's industry and the most densely populated part of the Philippines. The islands are quite well endowed with natural resources. Hardwood forests still cover over one third of the land area and the country is rich in deposits of coal, nickel, zinc, copper and cobalt.

The cultural history of the Philippines is rather different from that of other South-east Asian nations. The islands were populated by people of Malay origin from early times and were largely isolated from the Sino-Indian influences which affected much of the rest of the region. In particular, only a relatively small Islamic community had established itself among the Moro of the south by the time the Spanish colonised the islands. The Philippines was a Spanish colony from the 16th Century to 1898 when it was ceded to the United States of America after the Spanish-American War. Today, Filipino, based on Tagalog (a form of Malay), is the official 'native' language although English is widely

*Department of Commerce, Australian National University.

used, especially in commerce. Just under 95 percent of the population profess the Christian faith with most of the remaining 5 percent being Muslim. The Philippines became politically independent from the US in 1946 after three years of military occupation by the Japanese between 1942 and 1945. The present constitution came into effect in 1987 following a period of political instability. The Philippines is a democratic, capitalist republic in which a relatively powerful President is head of the executive. Legislative power is in the hands of a bicameral Congress consisting of a directly elected 24 member Sentate and a 200 member House of Representatives[1]. The judiciary is based on a Supreme Court system, with separate criminal and civil codes. Islamic courts have some jurisdiction in the southern autonomous provinces of Mindanao.

In 1996, the GDP was forecast at US$75 billion or about US$1,000 per capita. Although the Philippines has good natural resources and a potentially large domestic market, it is dependent upon imported oil for most of its energy needs. This and the lack of large areas of good agricultural land are probably the main natural constraints on the Philippines economy, to which agriculture is still an important contributor and employer despite the growing importance of refining, metal products and the manufacture of textiles, semiconductors and other electrical equipment. In the 1980s, the country's economic growth lagged behind much of Asia, due probably to inappropriate macroeconomic policies pursued during the Marcos years and, subsequently, to a combination of political uncertainty and natural catastrophes. These factors have lead to occasional high inflation (more than 50 percent in 1984, for instance), pronounced income distribution inequalities, widespread poverty (particularly in rural areas) and a lack of confidence among overseas creditors, resulting in a series of recurring economic crises necessitating rescheduling of loan repayments and drastic changes in domestic economic policy. The Aquino Administration inherited an economy with a history of trade and budget deficits, a heavy reliance on large, capital intensive firms, a neglected infrastructure and a substantial level of external debt (by 1990 this had reached US$24 billion). While these legacies may take time to overcome (e.g. witness the stoppages in production due to power cuts in Luzon in 1992), policies followed since 1986 have aimed at economic stabilisation and structural reform, focusing on opening up the economy. A policy of deregulation and privatisation, and economic growth which reached almost 6 percent in 1995, is currently being pursued. The Philippines' main economic potential lies with its largely literate and English proficient workforce, a significant number of whom possess managerial and technical skills. The current major trading partners of the Philippines are Japan, the US and the European Union. The Philippines is an active member of ASEAN and a participant in APEC dialogues. The unit of currency is the Philippine peso.

J.D/ R.J.W.

---

[1]The House of Represntatives is currently supplemented with up to 50 Presidential appointees. Senate members are elected for six years while House members are elected for three-year terms. The army has, in the past, been influential in politics.

INTRODUCTION

The Philippines membership of the economically dynamic South-east Asian region means that rapid changes are occurring in the economic, political and social environment in the country. These changes are being accompanied by moves toward greater integration into the world economy, a development laden with opportunities and risks. This chapter provides an overview of how accounting has progressed in relation to the environmental changes occurring in the Philippines. Its aim is to sketch the development and current state of accounting, as well as the likely direction of accounting changes in the future. The chapter is divided into four other sections. The next section deals with specific accounting legislation and the sources of standard setting in the Philippines. Sections three and four describe some specific areas of financial reporting and management accounting respectively while Section five analyses the influences which appear to have been instrumental in the development of general Philippine accounting practices.

ACCOUNTING LEGISLATION AND SOURCES OF ACCOUNTING STANDARDS

The civil law system in the Philippines is a blend of code and common law. The former was inherited from the Spanish while an Anglo-American common law system was imposed during the period between 1898 and 1946. Many Philippine statutes, including those governing commercial transactions, are patterned after US laws. The main sources of Philippine law now are the constitution, statutes passed by Congress, ordinances passed by local government units, rules and regulations based on statutes and accepted principles of international law.

With regard to financial accounting for business entities in the Philippines, two laws are particularly pertinent: the Corporation Code and the Revised Securities Act. The Corporation Code (*Batas Pambansa Blg.*68) enacted by legislature in 1980, is the primary corpus of law dealing with the formation and operation of corporations in the Philippines. This deals with the establishment of stock and non-stock corporations and includes provisions for special types of corporations such as those with the objects of education and religion. The Corporation Code was largely patterned after the old Corporation Law (Act No. 1459) enacted by the Philippine legislature in 1906 and based upon US corporate law (despite having a name which implies a European influence). The sourcing of finance through the issuance of corporate securities is governed by the Revised Securities Act (*Batas Pambansa Bld.*178) enacted in February 1982. This Act was patterned after the US Securities Act of 1933 and regulates: (a) the distribution of securities by requiring issuers to supply the public with adequate and reliable financial information and (b) the trading in securities, including the operation of securities markets.

Both the Corporation Code and the Revised Securities Act are administered and implemented by the Philippines Securities and Exchange Commission (PSEC). With regard to the Corporation Code, the PSEC prescribes the minimum reporting requirements for all corporations registered under the code[2]. Every such corporation is required to submit to the PSEC an annual report of its operations and a statement of its assets and liabilities covering the preceding accounting period, certified by an independent public accountant (Corporation Code, Sec 141). The PSEC may prescribe the form and contents of the financial statements submitted to it, although this has been limited to a general description of what should be included in the statements. The PSEC also implements and prescribes the reporting requirements for securities issued to the public under the Revised Securities Act. The provisions of the Corporation Code described above apply according to the legal form rather than the size of the entity. All corporations engaged in activities in the Philippines, whether for profit or not, must register with the PSEC. Moreover, under the Civil Code of the Philippines (Title IX, Book IV) partnerships with capital of P3000 or more, in money or property, must be notarised and registered with the PSEC. The provisions of the Revised Securities Act apply only to corporate entities that intend to raise capital through an equity offer to the public[3] or, having done so, intend to have their securities traded in an organised securities market such as the Philippines Stock Exchange. However, certain regulations issued by the PSEC apply only to entities of a certain size (SEC, 1993). For example, regulations concerning the submission of audited financial statements cover the following corporations: those with paid up capital of at least P50 000; those with more than 20 shareholders; those whose securities are offered for sale to the public; and branches of foreign corporations.

Financial reporting in the Philippines, especially its form, is influenced by direct legislative action in a number of specific instances. For example, financial accounting statements provide a basis for determining the amount of taxes due and for complying with requirements set by government regulatory bodies such as the PSEC. Usually, however, financial accounting standards are largely determined by the private sector, by powers delegated down through the political process, although these standards are normally supported by a number of government or quasi-government bodies. Both the PSEC and the Bureau of Internal Revenue (BIR), the body administering the income tax statutes, require most business entities to submit financial statements audited by recognised members of the Philippines Institute of Certified Public Accountants (PICPA) which reinforces the effectiveness of the standards.

---

[2]It is mandatory to register with the PSEC under the provisions of the Corporation Code prior to commencing business operations in the Philippines.

[3]An offer to sell securities to 20 persons or more is deemed to be a 'public offer'.

The Revised Accountancy Law decreed in 1975 by Presidential Decree No. 692 (PD 692) designated the Board of Accountancy (BOA) as the sole authority empowered to promulgate rules and set professional standards for PICPA members in the country, subject to approval by the Professional Regulations Commission (PRC). The body now most directly involved in initiating and developing standards is the Accounting Standards Council (ASC). These bodies are discussed below.

The PRC was created in 1973 by PD 223. Its primary function is to administer, implement and enforce the policies of the government regarding the regulation and licensing of various professions and occupations, (PD 223, Sec 5). Directly under the PRC are several Boards, including those in accountancy, engineering and medicine, which have responsibility for their particular professional areas. In general, the boards are charged with overseeing the practices of the professions in order that the adoption of measures enhancing the development and maintenance of high professional, ethical and technical standards are ensured (PD 223, Sec 6). Enactments of the boards have to be reviewed and formally approved by the PRC before they have the force of law.

The Board of Accountancy consists of seven members, all of whom are appointed by the President of the Philippines upon the recommendation of members of the profession. The primary objective of the Board is the supervision, control and regulation of the practice of accountancy in the Philippines (PD 692, Sec 2). Entry into the profession is contingent upon, among other requirements, passing the PICPA licensure examination administered by the board. Under PD 692, the 'practice of accountancy encompasses not only those in public accounting practice, but also those in government, commerce, industry and academia. A code of professional ethics with separate sections for these various categories was promulgated in 1978 with the assistance of the PICPA members and approved by PRC. The board is empowered to investigate alleged violations of the code of ethics as well as other rules promulgated by the board. In conjunction with the PRC, the Board approves all financial accounting standards issued by the ASC.

The PICPA was formed in 1929 and was recognised in 1975 by the PRC as the official body representing PICPA members in public practice, industry, government and education in the Philippines. Prior to the advent of the ASC, the PICPA was the main source of recommendations on accounting practices and auditing standards (first issued in 1949). It also issued rules of professional conduct for its members. The PICPA has been active on the international scene, sponsoring the first Far East Conference of Accountants in 1957 and the ninth Confederation of Asian and Pacific Accountants in 1979. It was also instrumental in organising the first forum of ASEAN accountants in 1976, which subsequently led to the formation of the ASEAN Federation of Accountants. The institute is a member of two international organisations involved in the harmonisation of accounting and auditing standards — the IASC and the IFAC.

The ASC was created in 1981[4] under the auspices of the PICPA to establish and improve generally accepted accounting principles (GAAPs) in the Philippines (Alindada, 1982). The council has eight members: four from PICPA; one each from three regulatory agencies, the SEC, the Central Bank, and the Board of Accountancy; and one member from the Financial Executives Institute of the Philippines (FINEX)[5]. The ASC issues Statements of Financial Accounting Standards (SFASs) and related. Interpretations which, when approved by the PRC, constitute GAAPs in the Philippines. So far, the ASC has released 22 SFASs, including one which deals specifically with the banking industry. Whenever appropriate, the ASC bases these standards on earlier pronouncements by the PICPA, the IASC, and the US Financial Accounting Standards Board (FASB).

The mechanism adopted by the ASC for setting up standards is similar to that adopted by the IASC and FASB. Initially, a task force prepares an exposure draft for a proposed accounting standard, and the draft is submitted for consideration. If approved by at least five of the eight council members, the exposure draft is distributed to PICPA members, FINEX members, and other interested persons and organisations in the business community for comment. The exposure period should be at least 60 days, unless a shorter period is approved by the ASC. Comments and suggestions received during the exposure period are then evaluated by the task force and the Council; necessary revisions are incorporated to the draft. If the revised draft is approved by at least five council members, it is issued as a standard. The standard is then submitted to the BOA and the PRC for endorsement and approval. Once approved, the standard becomes part of the law governing members of PICPAs in the country. The PSEC recognises that SFASs issued by the ASC and approved by the PRC constitute accepted accounting principles in the Philippines and should be used in preparing financial statements filed with the PSEC. In this regard, the PSEC has generally delegated the formulation of detailed rules on financial accounting valuation and disclosure to the ASC.

---

[4]The ASC was formed in response to a study made by the PICPA Committee on Accounting Research and Special Studies on the state of financial accounting standards and standard setting in the Philippines in 1979. The study revealed weaknesses regarding the recommendatory nature of standard setting at that time, lack of monitoring of compliance, lack of sufficient consultation outside the profession and a tendency to rely too heavily on US standards (Alindada, 1982).

[5]FINEX is a private organisation consisting mainly of persons involved in the finance, treasury and financial reporting functions of business enterprises (including some PICPA members). In general, membership of the FINEX is limited to those in middle and senior management positions in their respective organisations, such as accounting managers, controllers, vice presidents and chief executive officers.

FINANCIAL REPORTS AND STANDARDS

As might be expected from the foregoing, Philippines standards have been considerably affected by their relationship with their US counterparts. The ASC states in fact that, in establishing accounting standards, it will specifically take into account standards issued by bodies such as the IASC and the FASB. The financial statements, which form the basis of accounting information in the Philippines, consist of a balance sheet, a statement of income and retained earnings, and a statement of changes in financial position[6]. According to SFAS 1 ('Basic Concepts and Accounting Principles Underlying Financial Statements of Business Enterprises'), the basic purpose of financial statements is to provide useful information about the accounting entity[7] to owners and creditors in making economic decisions (sec C, para 1) and to present fairly the financial position, results of operations and other changes in financial position (sec C, para 3). Notes to the financial statements are also considered integral to the primary financial statements. The emphasis on fair presentation means that no standard or uniform format is prescribed for the financial statements. It is necessary, however, for these statements to conform to the measurement and disclosure standards prescribed by the ASC and other authoritative bodies (i.e. GAAP)[8].

Under the ASC's transitory provisions, Accounting Principles Bulletins (APBs) issued by the PICPA which have not yet been superseded by ASC pronouncements form part of the country's GAAP. At least five APBs have not been superseded thus far: Accounting for Income Taxes (No. 2); Accounting for Cost of Retirement Plans (No. 16); Interim Financial Reporting (No. 21); Accounting Responses to Changing Prices (No. 24); and Accounting for *Dacion en Pago* Arrangements (Special Bulletin,

---

[6]In July 1993, the ASC issued a standard that required companies to prepare a statement of cash flows in lieu of a statement of changes in financial position.

[7]Philippine business law does not specifically define the term, 'entities'. The following legal forms of businesses are recognised, however: (a) corporations; (b) partnerships; (c) joint ventures; (d) branches of foreign corporations, and (e) sole proprietorships. Of these forms, corporations and partnerships are treated as having a separate legal personality from their owners. Corporations may be partially or wholly owned by non-Filipinos, subject to restrictions on minimum local ownership for some businesses such as those in the retail trade, advertising, and natural resource exploitation and development. A stock corporation in the Philippines is very similar to that in the United States since the present Corporation Code was patterned after parallel US legislation. Ownership is divided into shares of stock, and owners liability is limited to the amount of their investment in the corporation. Corporate names are usually appended with 'inc' or 'incorporated' to designate their legal status.

[8]Some exceptions to this principle exist. Some government agencies, such as the monetary authorities (*Bangko Sentral ng Pilipinas*) for instance, prescribe formats and additional reports for certain entities under their jurisdiction. The PSEC has also issued 'Rules on the Form and Content of Financial Statements' (1975).

July 1981)[9]. These are what remain in force of 24 APBs and one special bulletin issued between 1970 and 1981.

The principal measurement basis in the Philippines is historical cost. This may be modified by the lower of historical cost or market value rule for certain assets such as inventories, marketable securities and investments. Upward revaluations based on replacement cost are also allowed for fixed assets, subject to the appraisal being made by an independent expert. The majority of the measurement conventions applicable to assets and liabilities, in general, are similar to those used in the United States or adopted by the IASC. For example, the full cost of inventories may be measured using any one of the recognised cost flow assumptions (specific identification, weighted average cost, FIFO, LIFO)[10]. LIFO is however not allowed for tax reporting purposes[11].

The upward revaluation of plant, property and equipment represents the only significant departure of Philippine GAAP from US GAAP in relation to valuation bases. The persistent and often double-digit inflation experienced by the Philippines in the early 1970s (as a result of the peso devaluation and the oil crisis) and in the early- to mid-1980s (because of the precarious balance of payments position) led to the belief that it was necessary to consider the impact of inflation on financial statements. For this reason the PICPA issued Special Bulletin No. 2 in November 1971 on the Revaluation of Fixed Assets. Revaluation was again dealt with in SFAS 12 issued by the ASC in 1985. In essence, the difference in accounting treatment from the US approach was based on a perception that the reporting environment, particularly in the persistence and magnitude of inflation, was significantly different between the two countries.

Following the emphasis on fair presentation, Philippine enterprises are not required to adopt tax rules for financial accounting purposes. As such, certain statutory adjustments may be thought necessary to reconcile accounting income to taxable income. Before 1995, no accounting standard was imposed on 'accounting for income tax'. In case of major differences between book and tax income, deferred tax accounting *may* be used, although the method is not mandatory. If deferred tax

---

[9]*Dacion en Pago* refers to a business practice in the Philippines which originated in the Spanish era of settling debt by the transfer of property to the creditor. Generally speaking, a gain or loss is recognised in the accounts based on the difference between the value of the non-cash payment and the amount of debt extinguished.

[10]Manufacturing or production overhead should be allocated to inventory on a rational and systematic basis (SFAS 4, para 5). General and administrative as well as selling expenses should be treated as period costs (Para 6).

[11]See below: The BIR recognises valuation at cost or market, whichever is the lower. However, it disallowed LIFO in 1985 under the National Internal Revenue Code Sections 144 and 145 which require taxation computations to clearly reflect income. LIFO may have been disallowed because it can lead to significantly reduced income figures in times of high inflation.

accounting is used, deferred taxes must be provided for all timing differences and computed using the tax rates in effect at the time the difference arose. The computation is usually simplified since neither tax loss carry forwards nor carry backs are allowed in the Philippines (BIR Regulations, 1992)[12]. In practice, Philippine companies which are subsidiaries of US corporations (e.g. Procter and Gamble, Caltex, IBM) will use the 'deferred tax method', following the existing accounting standards in the US formulated by the Financial Accounting Standards Board (FASB).

The deferral method referred to above is based upon the recommendations of extant APB No. 2, which is itself based upon US APB Opinion No. 11 (Accounting for Income Taxes). However, Philippine tax law generally requires that if the tax expense disclosed in the financial statements is not the same as the amount shown in the tax return, a reconciliation must be submitted with the return. Consequently, tax effects accounting tends not to be used in practice (SGV Group, 1984). Based upon the personal observation of the author, tax effect accounting is only used by local subsidiaries of US firms for the purpose of consolidating Philippine-derived income with their US parent companies. In this regard, while deferred tax is computed for internal reporting purposes (usually following whichever US FASB is under sway at the time), it is almost never reported for local filing purposes, such as for the BIR or PSEC statements[13]. In 1995, SFAS 23 came into effect. This standard required all companies to adopt deferred tax accounting, using the liability method and comprehensive basis of allocation.

A number of other matters pertaining to the presentation of the income statement should be noticed in passing. First, gross profit is shown as a separate item. Second, the general rule regarding depreciation is for all property to be depreciated on a rational and systematic basis over the life of the asset irrespective of the earnings of the enterprise (SFAS 6, para 12)[14]. Third, the effects of extraordinary items are

---

[12]The national government is the chief taxing authority. Tax legislation is enacted by the Philippine Congress and implemented by the Department of Finance. The BIR levies and collects direct income taxes from corporations and individuals, while the Bureau of Customs levies and collects four indirect taxes: customs and excise duties, VAT, a percentage tax applicable to some businesses and stamp duties. At the present time the income tax rate on domestic and foreign resident corporations is 35 percent while individuals suffer tax on a sliding scale between 0 percent and 35 percent. Corporations account and pay for tax on a quarterly basis.

[13]Most enterprises , however, adopt the prescribed tax reporting guidelines for expediency so long as such practices do not contravene prescribed accounting standards. For example, businesses usually use an allowable inventory valuation method (e.g., FIFO, moving average cost) or adopt depreciation rates prescribed by tax authorities for certain types of fixed assets. Tax laws tend to only indirectly have an affect on financial accounting by predisposing companies to adopt methods which satisfy both financial accounting and tax reporting requirements.

[14]SFAS 6 also provides guidelines regarding depreciation bases, estimated lives and depreciation methods. Acceptable methods include straight line, units of production, hours of use, sum of digits and reducing balance.

disclosed separately in the income statements. Guidelines for this treatment are provided in paras. 17–32, SFAS 13. Finally, all material accounting policies are required to be explained in the notes to the financial statements.

The Philippine Corporation Code recognises two types of consolidation accounting method for dealing with business combinations: the 'purchase' or 'acquisition' method and the 'pooling of interests' or 'merger' method. The former method should be used when the combination is in the nature of a takeover by one company of another, the latter when the two entities merge, neither one taking over the other. This follows US and similar Anglo-American practices[15]. Goodwill in general can only be recognised as a result of a purchase transaction and this rule applies to goodwill arising on consolidation. The amortisation of goodwill is treated similarly to other intangible assets, that is, it should be amortised over its estimated life but this may not exceed a 40-year period (SFAS 9). Until June 1991,when the provisions of SFAS 21 (Consolidation of Financial Statements) became effective, consolidated financial statements were not required except for financial institutions reporting to the Philippine monetary authorities[16]. Following PSEC regulations and the ASC's issuance of a standard on the matter, the following companies are now required to present consolidated financial statements:

(i)   Those where the total liabilities of any one entity in the group is more than P50 million (approx. US$1.7 million) or where total liabilities of the group are more than P150 million (approx. US$5 million) or;

(ii)   Those where the company is a financial intermediary, a company trading its securities on exchanges or in over-the-counter markets, or a company that issues commercial papers or other securities registered with the SEC under the Revised Securities Act. Existing standards also require that investments in associated companies be accounted for using the equity method if the parent company exercises significant influence over the investee company, where such investee company is not a subsidiary for consolidation purposes[17].

---

[15]Existing standards specify 12 conditions which must be satisfied before a transaction may be accounted for using the pooling of interests method. These can be classified into three categories based upon the following characteristics: (i) the attributes of the combining enterprises; (ii) the manner in which the interests are combined; and, (iii) the absence of planned transactions.

[16]The provisions of SFAS 21 have been incorporated in PSEC Regulations 'Covering Form and Content of Financial Statements Required to be Filed by Corporations whose Shares of Stock are Sold or Offered for Sale to the Public' (particularly, Article 5). They are effective ending on or after June 30, 1991.

[17]See Duque (1993). For financial reporting purposes, the terms 'subsidiary' and 'significant interest' are similar in meaning to those used in North America. In particular, the general condition for 'control' is ownership of a majority of the outstanding voting stock and significant interest occurs when ownership is between 20 and 50 percent (SFASs 10 and 20).

On a couple of other more minor matters concerning contingencies and retained reserves, it should be noted firstly that Philippine standards do not allow enterprises to record reserves for general contingencies. Loss contingencies may only be recorded as a charge to income if information available prior to the issuance of financial statements indicates that it is probable that an asset has been impaired or a liability had been incurred and the amount of the loss can be reasonably estimated. Gain contingencies are not allowed unless realisation is deemed virtually certain. Secondly, appropriations of retained earnings for any legitimate purpose are allowed although current period expenses should not be charged against retained earnings, but should be reflected in the income statement. When an appropriation is no longer required, it should be reversed directly to retained earnings.

The Philippines adopts a mandatory retirement benefits scheme for all private sector and government employees. Under this scheme, appropriate contributions from both employees and employers are remitted under designated government arrangements[18]. No special accounting treatment relates to this scheme except to account for the monthly accruals for employees' and employer's contributions. It is also common practice for companies to adopt private pension plans. For such plans, the existing pronouncement (PICPA APB No. 16) recommends that the normal pension costs and past service costs be determined on the basis of actuarial methods. The standard also requires that (a) past service cost be amortised over a 10 to 40 year period; (b) actuarial gains and losses, including realised investment gains and losses, be allocated over the current and future years; and (c) unamortised prior service costs be recognised in the balance sheet only if the pension plan imposes such prior cost as a legal liability.

Foreign currency transactions are generally translated at the exchange rate as of the transaction date. Exchange differences are generally treated as a gain or loss in the profit and loss statement. Two exceptions exist:

(1) exchange differences arising from depreciation of a currency that cannot be hedged for practical reasons and that affect liabilities directly related to the acquisition of assets from overseas may be capitalised as part of carrying amount of the related assets. The adjusted carrying amount of the asset should not exceed the lower of replacement cost and the amount recoverable from the use or sale of the asset;

(2) exchange differences from long-term monetary items may be deferred and recognised in the income of current and future periods on a rational and systematic basis over the remaining lives of the monetary items to which they relate (SFAS

---

[18]These arrangements are the Social Security System for private enterprises and the Government Service Insurance System for the public sector.

No. 8, paras 24–31). Financial statements of foreign operations are translated for consolidation purposes depending on the operational and financial relationships between the parent company and its foreign operations. Financial statements of entities *not* considered as integral to the parent's operations are translated using the current rate method and translation adjustments are reported as a separate component of stockholders equity (paras. 32–5). Financial statements of integral foreign operations are translated using the temporal method. Exchange differences arising from translation in the latter case are taken to income of the period, except when deferrals in the case of long-term monetary items and capitalisation in the case of unhedged liabilities related to asset purchases are allowed. The provisions of SFAS 8 are similar to the requirements of US FASB 52, 'Foreign currency translation'.

Finally, existing standards are silent or not very specific in defining the measurement guidelines for certain other types of transactions, including the treatment of leases, research and development and intangible assets. Philippine accounting standards have yet to address the issue of leases. At present, leasing is not a particularly popular form of financing in the Philippines, although a few finance companies do offer this facility. It appears that the major disincentive to the growth of lease financing is the high interest rates charged (in 1992, for example, rates went as high as 30 percent per annum). According to a survey made by a major Philippine accounting firm in 1984, the common or predominant practice is to capitalise leases when the agreement substantially transfers all the ownership, benefits and risks of the property to the lessee (SGV, 1984). Given the absence of pertinent local standards, it was noted that guidance on the criteria for accounting for leases was often sought from US FASB or IASC standards (AICPA, 1989).

Accounting for research and development costs is likewise not covered by a separate local accounting standard. SFAS 9 (Intangible Assets) mentions that research and development should not normally be treated as an intangible asset (Para 8). It also mentions that a separate ASC Statement will be issued on the matter. To date, however, no such standard has been issued. The predominant practice is to charge such costs to expenses, except in cases when deferral is justified (SGV, 1984). In this regard, specific guidance is again often sought from US or IASC standards. In the case of intangible assets generally, while a standard exists (SFAS 9), the standard does not address the specific valuation issues concerning such things as copyrights, brands, trademarks and franchises. Several reasons might account for such non-treatment. As regards valuation issues, their unresolved and controversial nature, particularly in the US from where the Philippines draws much guidance, possibly precludes the confident consideration of alternatives at this point. A full list of Philippine accounting pronouncements is contained in the appendix to this chapter.

MANAGEMENT ACCOUNTING

As with financial accounting, management accounting practices in the Philippines appear to be heavily influenced by US management accounting practices. While there is little available published data detailing the precise management accounting practices adopted by a majority of Philippine companies, the available evidence suggests the predominance of US practices.

First, the presence of US MNCs in the key industries would suggest the adoption of their parent's management accounting practices. Among the more prominent US MNCs operating in the country are Abbott Laboratories (pharmaceuticals), Caltex Philippines (petroleum refining and distribution), California Manufacturing (food processing), General Electric (consumer durables) and Procter and Gamble (consumables). US-based MNCs often occupy an important, if not dominant, position in their respective industries.

Second, the training and background of Filipino CPAs stresses US management accounting practices. The prescribed university management accounting curriculum covers concepts and techniques readily recognised as Western, which are reinforced by the use of textbooks authored by US academics (e.g., Copeland, Van Horne, Horngren and Foster, Shapiro). The 'management services' section of the Philippine CPA examinations also tests US-based material.

Case studies of several medium to large manufacturing firms conducted by the University of the Philippines have disclosed widespread use of formal procedures for budgeting, capital investment analysis and management of cash, receivables and inventory (Soriano, 1984; Saldana, 1985). Banks and other lending institutions routinely request fairly detailed financial forecasts, which suggests that most large companies prepare such reports for internal use as well. Based on the author's own experience, cost accounting records for medium to large manufacturing companies are fairly detailed and often employ standard costing procedures, particularly for critical manufacturing inputs.

It may also be noted that there are no separate Philippine management accounting standards as such. The Philippine Association of Management Accountants (PAMA), established in 1972, has recently been attempting to promote US management accounting standards, particularly those issued by the National Association of Accountants (NAA)[19]. This, of course, is not surprising since PAMA is an affiliated chapter of the US-based NAA (PAMA, 1993). Management accounting has not really been acknowledged as a separate profession in the Philippines. For example, there is no

---

[19]The PAMA consists mostly of CPAs working in commerce and industry.

designation of 'management accountant' in organisations, since the management accounting function is usually combined with the controllership function (Salgado, 1985). As such, the distinction between financial and management accounting is often blurred. In fact, the Revised Accountancy Law specifically acknowledges commerce and industry as a legitimate area of expertise for licensed CPAs.

INFLUENCES ON THE DEVELOPMENT OF PHILIPPINE ACCOUNTING

Several authors have discussed the importance of environmental factors on the development of a country's accounting system (e.g. Gray, 1988; Perera, 1989). The purpose here is to sketch the development and present status of Philippine accounting in relation to relevant environmental factors. The effect of these on the differences which exist between Philippine and US practices, and to some extent the way in which they may be expected to shape the future of accounting in the country, will then be discussed.

Various studies have clustered countries according to their accounting practices and environmental characteristics. In these, the Philippines is usually classified as part of the US-influenced group. In particular, empirical studies have pointed out the close association between accounting in the Philippines and in the United States. For example, the AICPA (1964, 1989) series on professional accounting in several countries and Enthoven (1975, 1977) point out a number of significant similarities. Several classification studies, some of which used statistical analysis, consistently group the Philippines with the US in terms of measurement and disclosure practices. Examples of these are AAA (1977), Da Costa *et al.* (1978), Frank (1979), Nair and Frank (1980), and Nobes (1984). As was seen in the last section, management accounting practices also seem to be most influenced by North American practices. In understanding the present state of accounting in the Philippines, therefore, it is useful to examine in a little more detail the historical involvement of the US in the development of the discipline in the Philippines.

The historical roots of the existing accounting profession in the Philippines was in the 1920s, an era when the United States was consolidating its colonial position. During this time, the profession was largely dominated by US and British practitioners who introduced ideas and practices prevalent in those countries to the Philippines[20]. The first legislation governing the practice of accountancy in the country was

---

[20]When the Philippines became an American colony, British accountants came to the country as employees and officers of various companies. A number of them left their employ to practise as accountants. Examples of British accounting firms of that era are Fleming and Williamson, 1902, and Henry Hunter Bayne & Co., 1906. Presumably, they brought with them current Anglo-accounting thought and practices.

enacted in 1923. In 1929, the Philippine Institute of Certified Public Accountants (PICPA) was formed as a voluntary organisation, patterned after the American Institute of Certified Public Accountants (AICPA). It was not altogether surprising, therefore, that the first president of the PICPA was an American, W.W. Larkin. Larkin was a senior partner in the US accounting firm of Clark & Larkin, which operated in the Philippines. He was one among a community of Americans who lived and worked in the Philippines. This period witnessed a significant increase in the number of US-owned business entities operating in the country. Larkin was a special case, however, since he was intimately involved in establishing the modern accounting profession in the Philippines. Larkin's influence may be gleaned in that he was one of those who instigated the then Philippine Legislature to pass Republic Act No. 3105, the Philippine Accountancy Law, which created the Board of Accountancy. Larkin sat as the first Chair of the Board and, incidentally, was awarded PICPA Certificate No. 1. He also served as president of the PICPA from its establishment in 1929 until 1934, and then again during the period 1936–37 (Santiago *et al.*, 1979).

As was seen earlier, financial accounting standards and practices in the Philippines are modelled largely after their US counterparts. The Philippines' conceptual framework for accounting, approved by the present standard setting body, the ASC, is based on the FASB's conceptual framework project (FASB, 1978) and most of the 23 accounting standards standards so far issued, are distillations of corresponding US pronouncements. Even in areas where the council has not issued any standards (lease accounting, for example) local preparers refer to appropriate US standards for 'guidance' despite the non-mandatory status of the latter. The position, with respect to management accounting, while less formally defined, is perhaps even more persuasive.

From a broader perspective, the US has had a profound and pervasive impact not only on the development of Philippine accounting, but more importantly, on the institutional and cultural characteristics of the country. The Philippine legal and political structure, for example, shares certain commonalities with its US counterparts. Many features of Philippine education originated from the system established by the Americans during the colonisation period. The Asian Institute of Management, for example, one of the most prominent schools for professional managers, was patterned after the Harvard Business School in the United States. In the case of accounting education, US accounting textbooks and US-trained academics facilitate the dissemination and acceptance of American accounting concepts and practices in the country.

Reinforcing such cultural bonds, the country's economy has, until very recently, been highly dependent on relationships with the US. For a significant period after Philippine political independence was achieved in 1946, US trade and investment has dominated the economic landscape and the private component of this still significant influence has been channelled through highly visible US-based multinational companies (MNCs)[21]. These enterprises brought with them their own management practices and concepts which, coupled with the Filipino's receptiveness to US ideas, have been assimilated into the local setting. Consequently, the prevalence of US accounting practices, both in the financial and management accounting spheres, reflects and is reinforced by the institutional and economic structures which derive from the colonial period[22].

Despite such similarities between US and Philippine accounting standards and institutions, differences between the two countries' underlying environment seem to have led to some of the conflicting financial accounting treatments mentioned earlier. The main environmental differences affecting accounting practices seem at least superficially to be economic, namely: high inflation, high interest rates, a relatively undeveloped capital market, the product nature of important industries and ownership patterns. It is not at all clear, however, what, if any effects these differences may have on management accounting practices.

The persistent double-digit inflation occurring in the Philippines during the 1980s led the ASC to allow the revaluation of fixed assets based on independent appraisals. This practice is not allowed in the US. The ASC opted to allow selective revaluation of fixed assets based on suitable price indices or on independent experts' appraisals. The issuance of an accounting standard on fixed assets represented a major departure from US standards. The standard maintained that the economic circumstances in the Philippines required recognising the impact of inflation on the accounts. For similar reasons (see above), the LIFO method of inventory valuation has rarely been practised in the Philippines. LIFO is an acceptable and popular method in the US.

As was suggested earlier, the growth of lease financing in the Philippines has been sluggish, possibly because of the high interest rate regime, particularly during the 1980s. If lower interest rates become the norm in the future (they are still averaging above 20 percent per annum in the early 1990s), it may be expected that leasing will become a more popular financing option for fixed asset acquisitions. However, the position regarding other 'off balance sheet' financing areas, such as contingent contracts and other recently developed financial instruments may not depend to the same extent on such short-term factors. These matters have not yet really figured

---

[21]There is, however, a paucity of research into the effects of MNCs on Philippines accounting practices.

[22]A study by Yoshihara in 1985 of the 250 largest Philippine industrial enterprises showed that 163 (65 percent) were locally-owned, while 87 (35 percent) were foreign owned. Of the local enterprises, half were owned by Chinese Filipinos (Migrant Chinese or Filipinos of Chinese ancestry). Of the foreign owned companies, 80 percent were US MNCs, while the rest were British, Japanese, Spanish, Anglo-Dutch and others. US MNCs are particularly visible in such industries as food, manufacturing, mining, petroleum refining, and the manufacture of consumer durables and pharmaceutical's. Of the six or seven foreign banks operating in the Philippines, Citibank (owned by New York based Citicorp) is by far the largest.

prominently in Philippines accounting. Several reasons might account for this, but possibly one major factor here is the relatively underdeveloped state of the capital market. The share market, for example, is still relatively undercapitalised at US$36 billion (June 1994). The private bond market is minuscule and alternative financing schemes such as options and futures are still germinal. Most substantial financing is done either through internally generated funds or through borrowings from financing institutions (which, incidentally, are owned by a select group of people) and there appears to be less incentive to engage in sophisticated financing arrangements to 'improve' the appearance of the balance sheet than might be the case in the US. Although if would be difficult to prove in an empirical study, it is generally perceived that significant business transactions owe less to strictly technical or economic considerations than to personal ones (e.g. is the person borrowing or guaranteeing the fund well-known in the community?).

Another factor which possibly contributes to the differences that exist in reporting practices compared to the US is the relative importance of the agricultural and extraction sectors of the economy. While significant growth has occurred in the country's manufacturing and services sector, agriculture still accounts for a significant portion of Philippines' output as well as being the primary employer. The Philippines is a traditional exporter of coconut, sugar, abaca and other agricultural products, as well as a significant producer of copper, gold, and other mineral resources. The 'proper' valuation of these products has therefore been an important accounting issue. Local standards allow these products to be stated at above cost (that is, at net realisable value), consistent with previous industry practices in the area[23].

As noted above, Philippine business is dominated by large multinational firms and closely held, family enterprises. The ownership structure therefore does not necessarily encourage widespread disclosure of internal business affairs. Thus, despite the existence of large corporate groups in the country, consolidated or group financial statements were not required (except for certain financial institutions subject to Central Bank regulations) until recently. In this regard, the PSEC provided the impetus for greater transparency and disclosure through accounting reports when it adopted new regulations concerning consolidated financial statements in the early 1990s. One of the reasons for the Philippines equity markets not expanding as rapidly as might otherwise have been expected could be the overall sluggishness of the economy and the reluctance of powerful families to relinquish controls over their companies. There

---

[23]SFAS 4 (Inventories) states that 'the primary basis of accounting for inventories is cost' (para. 4). In some cases, however, valuation above cost is allowed, particularly for agricultural, mineral, forest, and other products when the following three conditions are met: (i) the product units are interchangeable; (ii) the products are immediately marketable at quoted prices; and, (iii) appropriate approximate costs are difficult to obtain. When inventories are stated at selling prices, they should be reduced by the expected disposal costs (SFAS 4, para. 10).

are signs, however, that this may be changing and that greater pressure for transparency of corporate affairs will accompany increasing use of the share markets as a source of financing. The present state of affairs probably accounts for the reason why a number of specific disclosures which are mandatory in the US or in some other countries are not required in the Philippines. These include disclosures of earnings per share data, segment data, inflation adjusted statements (except for revalued fixed assets), employee and other social reports. Absence of disclosures in these areas may be attributed to the absence of demand for such information and reluctance of owners to disclose information thought to disadvantage the business in some way[24].

Finally, in summary of the little we know from the publicly available data which exists on the precise nature of the management accounting practices employed by Philippine corporations, it may be said that the indirect evidence suggests that US management accounting practices are predominant in the Philippines. First, the presence of US MNCs in key industries would suggest the adoption of their parent corporation's management accounting practices. Second, the only management accounting organisation in the country (PAMA) actively promotes US-based accounting standards. Third, CPAs usually also function as management accountants in organisations. Given the close link between Philippine and US financial accounting standards, as well as the educational emphasis on US-based management accounting practices, it is not unreasonable to expect US practices to be the norm in the Philippines. Much useful research is needed to describe and explain the origins and current practice of management accounting in the Philippines.

REFERENCES

Accounting Standards Council (1988), *Compilation of statements of financial accounting standards* Nos. 1–18, Manila, Philippines.
Accounting Standards Council (1988), *Preface to statements of financial accounting standards of the Accounting Standards Council*, Manila, Philippines.
Accounting Standards Council (1988), *SFAS No. 19 — Summary of generally accepted accounting principles for the banking industry*, ASC, Manila, Philippines.
Accounting Standards Council (1991), *SFAS No. 20 — Accounting for business combinations*, ASC, Manila, Philippines.
Accounting Standards Council (1991), *SFAS No. 21 — Summary of generally accepted accounting principles on the consolidation of financial statements*, ASC, Manila, Philippines.

---

[24]SFAS 7 (Contingencies and Subsequent Events) requires certain subsequent events to be disclosed in the financial statements. Examples of such events are sales of bonds or capital stock issues, purchases of businesses, settlements of litigation, loss of plant and inventories because of natural disasters and losses on receivables from conditions arising subsequent to the balance sheet date (paras. 21–2).

Accounting Standards Council (1992), *SFAS No. 22 — Statement of cash flows*, ASC, Manila, Philippines.

Accounting Standards Council (1994), *SFAS No. 23 — Accounting for income taxes*, ASC, Manila, Philippines.

Alindada, C. (1982), *The need for a structured standards-setting process*, Technical Paper No. 1, 36th PICPA Annual Convention, La Union, Philippines.

American Accounting Association (AAA) (1977), 'Report of the 1975–76 Committee on International Accounting Operations and Education', *The accounting review*, supplement, Vol. 52, pp. 65–132.

American Institute of Certified Public Accountants (1988), *The accounting profession in the Philippines*, AICPA, New York, USA.

American Institute of Certified Public Accountants (AICPA) (1964), *Professional accounting in 25 countries*. AICPA, New York.

American Institute of Certified Public Accountants (AICPA) (1989), *The accounting profession in the Philippines: Professional accounting in foreign countries series*, AICPA, New York.

Bureau of Internal Revenue (1992), *Compilation of revenue regulations*, Government Publishing, Manila, Philippines.

Central Bank of the Philippines (1990), *Regulatory accounting policies for banks and financial institutions*, CB Publications, Manila, Philippines.

Da Costa, R.C., Bourgeois, J.C. and W.M. Lawson (1978), 'Linkages in the international business community: Accounting evidence', *International journal of accounting*, Spring, pp. 92–102.

Duque, D. (1993), 'Consolidation of financial statements', *Accountants journal*, Vol. 42, No. 3, pp. 49–53.

Enthoven (1975), *Appraisal report: An evaluation of accountancy systems, developments and requirements in Asia*, University of North Carolina, North Carolina, USA.

Enthoven (1977), *Accountancy systems in Third World economies*, North Holland, Amsterdam.

Financial Accounting Standards Board (1978), *Statement of financial accounting concepts No. 1: Objectives of financial reporting by business enterprises*. Stamford, CT: FASB.

Frank, W.G. (1979), 'An empirical analysis of international accounting principles', *Journal of accounting research*, Autumn, pp. 593–605.

Gray, S.J. (1988), 'Towards a theory of cultural influences on the development of accounting systems internationally', *Abacus*, March, pp. 1–15.

Nair, R.D. and W.G. Frank (1980), 'The impact of disclosure and measurement practices on international accounting classifications', *The accounting review*, July, pp. 426–50.

Nobes, C.W. (1984), *International classification of financial reporting*, Croom Helm, Beckenham, UK.

Perera, H. (1989), 'Towards a framework to analyze the impact of culture on accounting', *International journal of accounting*, Vol. 24, pp. 42–56.

Philippine Association of Management Accountants (1993), *Currents — PAMA newsletter*, Vol. 17, No. 1, July–October.

Philippine Government (1975), *Presidential Decree No. 692 — The Revised Accountancy Law*, Government Publishing, Manila, Philippines.

Philippine Government (1980), *Corporation Code of the Philippines — Batas Pambansa Blg. 68*, Government Publishing Service, Manila, Philippines.

Philippine Government (1980), *National Internal Revenue Code*, Government Publishing, Manila, Philippines.

Philippine Government (1982), *The Revised Securities Act — Batas Pambansa Blg. 178*, AFA Publications, Manila, Philippines.

Philippine Institute of Certified Public Accountants (1967), *The public accounting profession in the Philippines*, PICPA, Manila, Philippines.

Philippine Institute of Certified Public Accountants (1978), *Accounting bulletin Nos. 21–24*, PICPA, Manila, Philippines.

Philippine Institute of Certified Public Accountants (1980), *Generally accepted accounting principles: A codification of accounting principles bulletins as of December 1977*, PICPA, Manila, Philippines.

PICPA Committee on Management Accounting (1981), 'An overview of management accounting', *Accountant's journal*, Vol. 31, No. 1, pp. 18–24.

Saldana, C. (1985), *Financial management in the Philippine setting*, AFA Publications, Manila, Philippines.

Salgado, C. (1985), 'Management accounting in the Philippines', *Accounting journal*, Vol. 35, No. 1, pp. 10–4.

Santiago R., Bravo P. and J. Gesmundo (1979), 'PICIPA's first five decades', *Accountants journal*, Vol. 29, No. 3–4, pp. 1–11.

Securities and Exchange Commission (1993), *SEC rules and regulations on form and content of financial statements*, Government Publishing, Manila, Philippines.

SGV Group (1984), *Comparative accounting practices in ASEAN*, SGV & Co., Manila, Philippines.

Soriano, E. (1984), *Business policy in an Asian context*, Sinagtala Publishing, Manila, Philippines.

Yoshihara, K. (1985), *Philippine industrialization: Foreign and domestic capital*, Oxford University Press, NY, USA.

Appendix
ACCOUNTING PRONOUNCEMENTS
ASC STATEMENTS OF FINANCIAL ACCOUNTING STANDARDS (SFASs)

No.	Title	ASC Approval Date
1.	Basic Concepts and Accounting Principles Underlying Financial Statements of Business Enterprises	Mar 1983
2.	Summary of Generally Accepted Accounting Principles on Cash	Mar 1983
3.	Summary of Generally Accepted Accounting Principles on Receivables	Mar 1983
4.	Summary of Generally Accepted Accounting Principles on Inventories	Mar 1983
5.	Summary of Generally Accepted Accounting Principles on Liabilities	Mar 1983
6.	Summary of Generally Accepted Accounting Principles on Property, Plant and Equipment (Carried at Historical Cost)	Sept 1983
7.	Contingencies and Subsequent Events	Sept 1983
8.	Accounting for the Effects of Changes in Foreign Exchange Rates	Dec 1983
9.	Summary of Generally Accepted Accounting Principles on Intangible Assets	Jan 1983
10.	Summary of Generally Accepted Accounting Principles on Investments	March 1983
11.	The Equity Method of Accounting for Investments in Common Stock	July 1984
12.	Revaluation of Property, Plant and Equipment Through Appraisal	July 1985
13.	Reporting the Effects of Disposal of a Segment of a Business and of Extraordinary Items and Prior Period Adjustments on the Results of Operations of an Enterprise.	Nov 1985
14.	Statement of Changes in Financial Position	May 1986
15.	Disclosure of Accounting Policies	May 1986
16.	Related Party Disclosures	May 1986
17.	Accounting Changes	Mar 1987
18.	Summary of Generally Accepted Accounting Principles on Stockholders' Equity	May 1987
19.	Summary of Generally Accepted Accounting Principles for the Banking Industry	Feb 1988
20.	Accounting for Business Combinations	Apr 1991
21.	Summary of Generally Accepted Accounting Principles on the Consolidation of Financial Statements	
22.	Statement of Cash Flows	July 1992
23.	Accounting for Income Taxes	Dec 1994

PICPA ACCOUNTING PRINCIPLES BULLETINS (APBs)

No.	Title
2	Accounting for Income Taxes (Chapter 14 in the PICPA Codification of APBs)
15	Earnings Per Share (Chapter 17 in the PICPA Codification of APBs)
16	Accounting for Cost of Retirement Plans (Chapter 18 in the PICPA Codification of APBs)
18	Information to be Disclosed in Financial Statements (Chapter 13 in the PICPA Codification of APBs)
21	Interim Financial Reporting
24	Accounting Responses to Changing Prices

PICPA SPECIAL BULLETIN

July 1981	Accounting for *Dacion En Pago* Arrangements

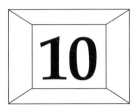

FINANCIAL AND MANAGEMENT ACCOUNTING PRACTICES IN THE REPUBLIC OF KOREA

Taesik Ahn[*]

BACKGROUND

The Republic of Korea (hereafter Korea) lies between latitudes 33°7′ and 38°30′N, south of a demilitarised zone of a depth of four kilometres between it and North Korea. Korea as a whole borders the south of the Manchurian region of modern China and the south-eastern region of Russia, forming a peninsula which protrudes into the East China Sea. The present boundaries of the country were basically established after the Second World War and modified by the presence of the demilitarised zone after the Korean War. Unlike much of insular South-east Asia, the Korean peninsula is relatively inactive geologically and earthquakes are rare. Most of the land is covered in pine forests and low-grade scrub in what was once an area of extensive hardwood forests decimated by over exploitation before 1945. The climate is continental rather than maritime, so wide variations in temperature between winter and summer are experienced. Natural resources are limited. Timber is not of high quality and, apart from some reserves such as graphite and anthracite coal, there are few mineral resources of economic significance. In particular the country has no oil resource.

*Ajou University, Republic of Korea. This research is supported by the Daewoo Foundation. The author is indebted to Eui-Hyong Kim and Ji-In Jang for their helpful comments. The Republic of Korea is referred to throughout this chapter as 'Korea'.

The Korean peninsula is believed to have been settled by Tungusic people after 3000 BC and its history is one of successive long-lived dynasties, particularly in the last thousand years. Foreign policy and culture generally were influenced by Korea's relations with China on the one side and Japan on the other — with occasional nomadic intrusions. Korea was a Japanese colony between 1910 (following the Russo-Japanese war) and 1945. The post-war political history of Korea is one based upon a close association with the US marked by frequent confrontation of the government with student and labour movements on issues relating both to economic and ideological matters. The Korean language, descended from the earliest settlers, belongs to the Ural-Altaic family, to which Japanese is related. The main religions of modern Korea are Mahayana Buddhism and Christianity. In 1985, approximately eight million Koreans professed to believe in each of these faiths, a large majority of the Christians being Protestants. The present constitution was formally established in 1987. The President as head of the executive, is elected by universal suffrage every five years and appoints the Prime Minister. The main executive body is the State Council consisting of both the President and the Prime Minister, and a number of other members appointed by them. The legislative body is the National Assembly consisting of approximately 300 members elected every four years. The judiciary consists of the Supreme Court, Appellate courts and provincial district courts and a legal system with German-derived elements. The land area of the Republic of Korea is 99 484 sq. km, and with a population of 43 m, this making it the sixth most densely populated country in the world in 1990. The population tends to be crowded into the areas of limited agricultural land. Seoul, the capital is situated in such an area and has a population of 11 million.

The Korean economy is one of the 'Tiger' economies of South-east and East Asia. Growth in GNP in the period 1982–91 averaged 9.9 percent per annum, including particularly high growth rates in manufacturing in some years (e.g. 18.8 percent in 1986). GNP stood at US$7466 per capita in 1993, and the level of net overseas debt was small, despite the occasional large trade and current account deficit. Unemployment is low (less than 2.8 percent in 1993), although inflation has often been quite high. Most of the post-war growth has taken place since 1963, when the first five-year plan was implemented. There have been seven five-year plans now, and in each one the planned growth rates were usually exceeded. Their economic success has been attributed to export-dominated growth policies, a plentiful supply of skilled and educated labour, and a willingness to accept modern technology. Only 12.3 percent of the workforce was employed in agriculture in 1993 compared with 63.1 percent in 1963, which indicates the extent of structural change. This sector is highly mechanized despite the high incidence of small owner occupied farms. Rice is the main crop, presently taking just less than two-thirds of the available agricultural land area. Manufacturing, construction and energy supply still account for about 35 percent of GDP. Electronics, textiles, and plywood are the main manufactures, and chemicals, steel, shipbuilding and motor vehicles are also important, each having been encouraged by explicit government policy measures in the past. The main problems facing the Korean economy are: its reliance on imported raw materials (all petroleum is imported, the timber for plywood manufacture is mostly imported, due to the poor quality of home supplies, and the electronics industry is becoming increasingly dependent upon imports from Japan); a continuing problem with labour disputes *and wage rises which threaten the country's international competitiveness; increasing protectionist sentiment in the US and Japan, Korea's major trading partners; and the appreciation of the local unit of currency, the won.*

T.A/R.J.W.

INTRODUCTION

The growth of the economy experienced by Korea in recent decades has accelerated the expansion and internationalisation of business enterprises, which in turn has induced the expansion of security markets. Consequently, both internal and external demands for accounting information and for its improved reliability have increased. Most of the recent developments in Korean accounting standards and related regulations have attempted to meet these new demands.

The Korean accounting environment, however, has some unique characteristics which impact negatively on current accounting practices. First, the ownership and management of most large corporations such as *the chaebols*[1] are concentrated in the hands of close knit families. Under these circumstances, accounting tends to be dominated by the objective of protecting the interests of the owner-managers and encouraging creative accounting practices. Objective reporting to outsiders is considered less important. This tradition has historically played a key role in decreasing the reliability and information content of financial statements in Korea.

A second factor influencing accounting practice is a long history of fund shortages. Fund acquisition is often considered to be one of the most critical factors for business survival and growth in Korea. Consequently, business performance has been largely determined by the amount of funds available and accountants' management reports have tended to become a periodic ritual lacking a close connection with managerial decision making.

The third major factor influencing accounting practice is the relative importance of tax regulations on accounting. Due to the concentrated ownership structure of major corporations, tax planning considerations relating to the interests of owner-managers often takes a priority in determining the accounting treatment of certain items which it would not have otherwise. Given the legal basis of tax law, this has the additional undesirable impact on accounting practice of distorting the basis of financial accounting and lowering the relative status of generally accepted accounting principles (Ahn, 1993).

---

[1] A *chaebol* can be defined as a business group consisting of large companies which are owned and managed by family members or relatives in many diversified business areas. Hyundai, for example, is largely owned and controlled by the Chung family.

The fourth and last important factor which should be mentioned is the political setting. Since 1945, the rapid development of the Korean economy has been based on a close and mutually beneficial relationship between large corporations and government (Steers *et al.*, 1989). The success of large corporations in particular have been dependent upon this close association. The importance and value of this well known relationship, however, is neither quantifiable nor even apparent from financial reports. This fact reduces the perceived usefulness of financial-statement-derived information to informed users and, consequently, the demand for accounting information.

Korean accounting practice has its origins in the *Sagae-Songdo-Chibubop* used in the Koryo Dynasty (Son, 1991). In 1903, however, Western accounting was first introduced by the Hansung Bank and traditional Korean bookkeeping practices were replaced by Western bookkeeping (Lee, 1993). Korean Corporate Accounting Principles (CAP) were first announced in 1958, heavily influenced by Japanese statements of Business Accounting Principles (Jang, 1993). The chief purpose of CAP was to standardise accounting practices. In 1974, however, Accounting Treatment Rules governing the accounting treatment to be adopted in the financial statements of companies listed on the Korean stock market were separately announced. These two sources of accounting standards were then integrated in 1981 to take the unified form on which the current Corporate Accounting Standards (CAS) are based. The CAS has been revised six times since 1981 to adapt it to the new trends of globalization of business activities and liberalization of capital markets. These recent revisions have been heavily affected by the GAAP of USA and International Accounting Standards (IAS). The 1990 revision to CAS included improvements in foreign currency accounting to facilitate the comparison of international business activities and additional disclosure to satisfy the information needs created by capital market expansion and diversification[2] (Jang, 1993).

The most recent revision took place in 1996, where emphasis was mainly placed on incorporating IAS into CAS so that the comparability of financial statements can be enhanced. Moreover, this revision implies a major shift in perspective from conservatism for creditors to information usefulness for investors (Choi, 1996).

Some examples of this revision include the market valuation of short-term investments, the adoption of deferred income tax method, and provision for alternative financial statement formats. This last revision significantly reduced the gap between IASs and Korean CAS.

The next section describes financial accounting regulation and is followed by a section outlining valuation principles. Section 4 discusses the financing of Korean firms and Section 5 looks in detail at management accounting practices.

---

[2]Disclosure of earning per share, footnote disclosure of accounts receivable discounted are such examples.

FINANCIAL ACCOUNTING REGULATIONS

Financial accounting regulations take the same triple form in Korea that they take in Japan: the CASs, the Commercial Law (CL) and Corporation Tax Law (CTL). Taken together, CASs can be characterized as a cookbook for the preparation of financial statements, the principal objective of which is to promote consistency and comparability between financial statements. Financial statements required under CASs include a balance sheet (BS), an income statement (IS), a statement of appropriation of retained earnings (SARE), and a cash flow statement.

In contrast to many Western countries, such as the US, Canada, and Australia, where the private sector is responsible for setting accounting standards, the Korean Securities and Exchange Commission KSEC representing the Ministry of Finance takes the main responsibility for standard setting in Korea. The Accounting Management Division (AMD) under the KSEC provides administrative and technical support to the standard setting processes. The Accounting System Advisory Committee, currently consisting of academicians, CPAs and business representatives, provides professional advice and largely determines the content of accounting standards (Lee *et al.*, 1993). Unlike the CL and CTL, a CAS is a quasi-legal regulation issued by the KSEC which applies to companies, subject to external audit under the External Audit Law (EAL)[3]. Nevertheless, other companies which are not subject to external audit are recommended to follow CAS in preparing the financial statements. Detailed descriptions of CAS are contained in the following section.

Unlike CASs, CL and CTL have a legal status and therefore have to be complied with in the preparation of accounts for all business entities. This affects financial reporting in various, fairly direct ways. CL, for example, is designed to protect creditors and is relatively conservative, placing certain restrictions on the payment of dividends. Similarly, CTL requires taxable income to be calculated by adjusting CAS income.

The main purpose of CASs is to provide 'useful' information for various users, i.e. information based upon accrual measurements which adheres to the principles of reliability, simplicity, full disclosure, consistency, materiality and conservatism (KSEC, 1990). The legal status of the other sources of accounting regulation, however, sometimes prevents financial accounting practices from following these precepts. Special depreciation, for example, has to be recorded in the financial statement for it to be recognised as a deductible item[4]. Another example is 'provisions for technology development': these should be recorded in financial statements as a liability for tax purposes in the case of companies not subject to external audit. There exist many

---

[3]Companies with an asset value of at least 6 billion Won (approximately US$7 500 000) are subject to external audit.
[4]Special depreciation is allowed in addition to CAS-based depreciation amount for items specified in the CTL.

other such instances, including bad debt expense estimation, foreign exchange loss treatment and the estimation of provisions for severance pay. Such items can be used as a means of accounting manipulation and income smoothing (Nam, 1992). Financial statements thus prepared for corporate tax purposes erode comparability both between companies and between periods (Korean Chamber of Commerce, 1993). The discrepancies between tax accounting and CAS are particularly significant and have to be resolved if the accounting basis of financial statements is to be improved and the possibility of conflicts with International Accounting Standards (IAS) is to be reduced.

VALUATION, CONSOLIDATION AND FOREIGN CURRENCY TRANSLATION

This section describes the detail of CASs with respect to the valuation of assets and liabilities which have to be followed by companies subject to external audit. According to the External Audit Law, the financial statements of companies subject to external audit have to be disclosed in a daily newspaper. The balance sheet format specified in the CAS has to be followed and the audit report takes a standardised form which specifies that certified public accountants have audited the financial statements in accordance with auditing standards (Samil, 1991). Additionally, CPAs must declare their independence from their clients.

Currently, audit engagements are based on a free choice contracting system whereby firms can choose auditors or audit firms freely although the mandatory appointment system is employed partially. This system is sometimes criticised for its negative impact on auditor independence. The audit fee tends to be determined by the asset size of a client company, which may impair the audit quality (Lee & Nam, 1994). Most of the large accounting firms in Korea have affiliations with the 'Big Six' Western firms, which helps to contribute to the internalisation of accounting practices.

Asset and liability valuation

Marketable Securities & Trade Accounts Receivable: Previously the lower of cost or market rule was applied in the valuation of marketable securities. Under the newly revised rules, however, market value on the balance sheet date is to be used for marketable security valuation. This implies that the unrealised difference between the market value and the carrying value is now to be recognised as a gain or loss in the period of amount.

Inventories: Inventories are valued at acquisition cost, which can be defined as the sum of the applicable expenditures incurred in bringing an article to its existing condition and location. These costs include the purchase price or manufacturing cost, transportation costs, insurance, and handling costs. It should be noted that financing costs incurred in a long-term manufacturing contract or in the construction of inventories such as machinery, ship, or buildings are to be added to the acquisition cost.

Although CAS lists six different methods for cost calculation (specific identification, FIFO, LIFO, moving average, weighted average, and retail), in a survey of 202 listed manufacturing companies, the weighted average method was found to be the dominant method, being adopted by 170 firms, with the FIFO method, adopted by 30 firms, in second place. Only two firms used LIFO (Lim,1991). The weighted average method may be preferred because of its simplicity. The lack of attraction in the latter method may be caused by the fact that LIFO is not permitted by the CTL. The lower of cost or market rule has to be used for the valuation of inventories where estimated net realisable value is used as a surrogate for market value. In case of quality deterioration, obsolescence and spoilage, the recorded value of the inventory is appropriately reduced.

Tangible Assets: As with most other assets, tangible fixed assets are valued at production cost or purchase cost plus related financing costs and incidental expenses of purchase. The straight line, declining balance, units of production or any other reasonable depreciation method is acceptable in charging depreciation under CAS. However, CTL, influenced in this respect by its Japanese counterpart, allows only the straight line and declining balance methods for the depreciation of tangible fixed assets and this limits the depreciation methods adopted in practice. Since CASs do not themselves specify useful lives for various assets, the CTL specifications are generally accepted by firms for determining the useful lives of their tangible fixed assets for accounting purposes. Taxation clearly plays a more significant role in determining accounting income in Korea than in some of the other countries of the Asia Pacific Rim. This fact is well illustrated by the 'special depreciation' charges, designed under the CTL to give tax benefits to certain companies, which were added to CASs in 1967 (Kim & Lee, 1993).

Intangible Assets and Deferred Charges: Intangible assets are valued at acquisition cost, net of amortization computed by the straight line or units of production methods. Capitalization of organization costs, new stock issue costs, debenture issue costs and research and development (R&D) costs are permitted, and costs so capitalized are valued net of amortization — based on a three or five year amortization schedule. In the case of R&D expenditure, a selective approach to capitalisation is taken, with ordinary R&D costs being expensed and disclosed as a selling and administrative expense item, while unusual R&D costs are capitalised and included with deferred charges.

Asset Revaluation: The Asset Revaluation Law (ARL) was adopted in 1958 when inflation was extremely high and has continued in force since then through to the present time. Revaluation of tangible fixed assets is permitted when the consumer price index rises above 25 percent per annum. CTL and CASs both recognise such asset value increases under the ARL and, in the latter case, this is a major exception to its normal historical cost principles. After revaluation asset values and the related depreciation charge are revised appropriately. Incremental values recognized by the ARL, however, are usually only significant for such limited purposes as the payment of revaluation tax, deferred loss compensation and capital transfers, particularly in supposedly preventing dividend payments out of unrealised profits. Despite the ARL's aim to maintain 'real' capital by rationalising the amount charged to depreciation, most incremental revaluation is associated with nondepreciable assets like land (Lee, 1993).

Despite the well-known theoretical arguments in favour of revaluing assets, in practice the discretionary nature of asset revaluation seriously reduces between-period and between-firm comparability. Subjective selectivity in assets revaluation also raises the question of unequal treatments among different classes of assets. During the first half of 1993, for instance, 27 listed firms filed asset revaluations producing gains of approximately $123 million per firm. The high incidence of revaluation may be due to a recent government announcement which indicated that asset revaluation may eventually be terminated (*Korean Economic Daily*, 31.3.1993).

Provisions and Reserves: Korean liability reserves include tax payment reserves, bonus reserves, and construction warranty reserves disclosed as current liabilities and retirement payment reserves, and special repair reserves disclosed as long term liabilities. CASs do not specify the detail of the calculation of warranty and special repair reserves, and consequently 'reasonable' estimates of such amounts, calculated under the rules of CAS, may not necessarily correspond to the prescriptions of CTL. Also with respect to provisions for severance pay, CASs and CTL define the amount to be expensed differently. Valuation reserves such as allowance for doubtful accounts, accumulated depreciation for fixed assets and valuation allowances for marketable securities are recorded as items deducted from the corresponding asset accounts. Finally, it should be noted that, as in the Japanese system, there are a number of statutory reserves defined by CAS. These include legal reserves (i.e. reserves receiving at least one-tenth of cash dividends until half of the level of the stockholders' equity account is reached) reserves for business rationalisation and reserves for the improvement of financial structure. Other voluntary reserves are reserves for business expansion, sinking funds, dividend equalisation and deficit recovery.

Consolidation practice

Accounting Rules for Consolidated Financial Statements (CFSs) were first introduced in the Accounting Treatment Rules for Listed Companies of 1974. Separate accounting standards for CFSs were established in 1984. On 27 June 1992 the accounting standards for CFSs were revised to redefine the basis of consolidation by adding a managerial control criterion. Due to (KSEC) Act 15, activated in 1992, the preparation, disclosure and external audit of CFSs became a legal requirement for controlling companies listed on the stock market. This requirement was later expanded to include all non-listed companies subject to an external audit (Samil, 1994).

Controlling companies prepare CFSs, including the same four major statements contained in the financial reports of individual companies listed earlier, and each is presented in conjunction with the figures for the preceding year for comparison purposes. The equity method of accounting for investments is not permitted in the case of the preparation of individual company financial statements although it is accepted for CFSs. While CFSs are considered to be the main financial statements in the US, they are considered as supporting the main, individual company financial statements in Korea. However, since the preparation and disclosure of CFSs is now a legal requirement it is expected that their relative status will become enhanced.

Both managerial control and voting control criterion are acceptable for defining the basis and scope of consolidation[5]. Despite the recent addition of the managerial control criterion, most of the detail of the consolidation standards resemble those of the US, which are based on the voting control criterion. The purchase method is dominant in consolidation accounting. Neither the pooling of interest method or proportioned consolidation method is acceptable (Chung, 1993). The current Korean standards may, in fact, fail to capture the financial status and operating performance of the *Chaebols* which make up such a large portion of Korean economy (Nam, 1992; Choi, 1993). According to current standards, the Hyundai group should prepare 11 different CFSs and the Samsung group should prepare 10, essentially because neither has distinguished controlling and subsidiary companies. However, internal fund transfers, mutual loan payment guarantee, internal transactions, and mutual personnel exchanges support the notion that member companies in each formally separate business group actually operate as one economic entity (Nam, 1993; Choi, 1993). Combined financial statements for business groups have been suggested as possibly being a more reasonable alternative approach to accounting measurement and disclosure under these circumstances (Nam, 1993).

Foreign currency translation accounting

The monetary/nonmonetary method is adopted by Korean CAS for foreign currency

---

[5](a) The voting control criterion applies when the controlling company owns more than 50 percent of the total outstanding capital stock of the other company; (b) The managerial control criterion applies, for example, when the sum of loan amount to its subsidiary, collateral to the subsidiary, and loan payment guaranteed by the controlling company exceeds 30 percent of its own equity.

translation. The current rate method, however, is allowed for the foreign currency translation of foreign subsidiaries and foreign branches. Acceptance of two different translation methods causes occasional confusion and may facilitate income smoothing.

Translation gains and losses arising from long-term foreign currency assets or liabilities are not to be recorded as deferred assets or liabilities but are to be included in determining net income for the period. Foreign currency translation gains and losses resulting from foreign branch and subsidiary operations are not deferred but are accumulated in a separate component of shareholders' equity called 'overseas business translation debit/credit'. These cumulative translation adjustments enter into the determination of net income only when the foreign investment is fully or partially sold or is liquidated by the parent.

FINANCING OF KOREAN FIRMS

Historically, the most critical constraint on the growth of Korean firms has been financing. Reliance is placed mainly on short-term financing. For example, the current ratio for manufacturing industry at the end of 1991 was 95 percent, indicating that a significant part of the acquisition of fixed assets must have been financed by the use of short-term funds[6]. Table 1 shows the financing patterns of manufacturing firms in Korea.

Table 1

Class					
METHOD OF FINANCING			(UNIT:%)		
Class	1988	1989	1990	1991	1992
Internal Funds	56.0	46.4	31.3	33.6	42.1
Accumulated Earning	21.3	18.2	7.1	9.8	10.2
Depreciation	28.7	24.1	21.0	19.8	27.5
Allowance	6.0	4.1	3.2	4.0	4.4
External Funds	44.0	53.6	68.7	66.4	57.9
Loan	9.6	27.6	5.4	3.8	4.9
Equity Increase	9.5	18.8	42.0	41.4	41.7
Others	24.8	7.2	21.3	21.2	11.3
Total	100.0	100.0	100.0	100.0	100.0

---

[6]The maturity period for corporate bonds, a major long-term financing device in Korea, is mostly three years, compared to a typical period of 10–30 years in developed countries.

Since the boom years of 1986–88, internal financing has been greatly reduced and represented less than 40 percent of total funds during the 1990–91 period. One of the most obvious features of Table 1 is the rapid growth in the importance of the equity method of external financing, although the relative proportion is subject to fluctuation over the period shown. During the year to 1992, only 4.9 percent out of the 57.9 percent of the total funding attributable to external financing was debt financed while 41.7 percent was equity financed[7].

A heavy reliance on direct financing, together with a concentrated ownership and management structure in firms, has probably reduced the management monitoring role of banks. The latter can be also attributed to the limited autonomy of banks caused by government interventions (Jinn, 1994; Yoo, 1993). Equity financing did not contribute to the reduction of financing cost, which is surprisingly high as may be observed from Table 2.

Table 2
RATIO OF FINANCING COST TO SALES   (UNIT: %)

Class	1988	1989	1990	1991	1992
Financing Costs to Sales	4.6	5.1	5.1	5.7	6.3

The most likely reason for the high financing cost is the relatively small portion of stockholders' equity compared to liabilities (Yoo, 1993). Table 2 shows financing costs as a percentage of sales. This steadily increases over the period shown. This data demonstrates the relatively weak financial structure of Korean corporations and the importance of financing for their competitiveness. Due to its critical importance, financing decisions and the securing of adequate funds for operating activities have been among the major problems facing Korean managers in recent years. This fact has contributed to a reduction in the perceived relative importance of accounting information for managerial decision making.

FEATURES OF KOREAN MANAGEMENT ACCOUNTING PRACTICES

Management accounting in Korea has developed with the growth of large corporations such as the *chaebols*. As with *chaebols*, Korean management accounting has a short history. The importance of financing for the survival and success of most corporations

---

[7]In case of Japan, equity financing takes only 4.8 percent out of 47.6 percent external financing (Yoo, 1993).

decreased the role of managerial accounting information for management decisions (Ahn, 1993). Moreover, the mandatory nature of financial accounting requirements has forced Korean firms to place more emphasis on financial accounting and tax data. These characteristics seem to have delayed the development of management accounting in Korea.

Ownership structure and management accounting

From the 1960s, successive Korean governments initiated a series of highly effective five year economic plans characterised by export-driven policies and focusing on the development of large business groups. The effect of this economic policy created the large scale industrial corporations known in Korea as *chaebols*. One survey of 434 listed companies showed that the largest stockholder on average owned 41.2 percent of the total outstanding shares (Lim, 1989). This ownership structure probably encourages the centralisation of decision making and enhances the position of the owner manager. The appearance of a divisional structure observed in some large corporations should not lead to the erroneous conclusion that decision making is actually delegated to any significant extent down to the division level. In a survey of 222 large companies, for example, Shin (1992) found that, of all respondents questioned, 79.9 percent expressed the view that owner managers have the final say on personnel matters concerning executives, 66.4 percent felt this to be the case where new investment decisions were concerned and 55.4 percent believed that the owner manager was similarly influential with regard to foreign investment decisions. This perception suggests that, to the extent that responsibility accounting exists within large Korean firms, it exists mostly in form rather than substance. As Jeon (1993) noted, although divisionalised organisation structure appears to be favored by large firms, decision making is actually quite centralised.

Partly due to the concentrated ownership structure and the centralised nature of decision making, the development of management accounting in Korea was not pursued until the 1970s. With the growing internationalisation of large corporations since the 1980s and the Government's liberalisation policy, however, Korean manufacturing firms have started to appreciate the importance of management accounting and the potential of new management tools, many of which are imported from Western countries. More recently, some firms have begun to adopt Japanese management techniques such as JIT and target costing. Although firms and academics have occasionally endeavored to develop and identify management practices unique to Korean corporations (Lee, 1992), they have not yet been widely adopted.

Survey results on Korean management accounting practice

Relatively little is known or documented concerning detailed management accounting practices used in Korea. Some parts of a survey carried out by Ahn & Lee (1994) to examine this gap in our knowledge are reproduced below. This survey investigated current management accounting practice in Korea through survey questionnaires sent to 250 electronics, electrical and machinery firms listed on the Korean Stock Market. 114 firms responded about various aspects of management accounting practices[8]. Items included in this survey were selected by reviewing the previous research on management accounting practices (Horngren *et al.* (1994) and Sakurai (1990)).

Organisation Structure & Decentralization: With respect to organisation structure, as can be observed from Table 3, 33.0 percent of the surveyed firms adopted divisional organisations, 35.7 percent functional organisations and 19.6 percent product-oriented organisations. The matrix form of organisation, one of the most flexible organisational types, accounted for only 4.5 percent of the firms in the sample. Interestingly, the more old fashioned functional structure still appears to be popular among high-tech manufacturing firms. There is some evidence, however, that more firms do now seem to be emphasising a greater flexibility in organisation structure and are converting their traditional hierarchical organisation structures to more team oriented ones (*Korea Economic Daily*, 23.4.1994).

Transfer pricing is typically adopted by divisionalised Korean firms in accounting for internal transactions. A cost-based price is the most popular option, although a between-divisions negotiated price and a head-office determined price are other alternatives sometimes used (Ahn & Lee, 1994). In the case of fund transfers to divisions, intra-company interest is applied, approximately within the range of 12 to 17 percent per annum. The financing function itself is usually controlled by head offices.

Table 3
ORGANISATION STRUCTURE

Class	Frequency	Percent
Product	22	19.6
Market	6	5.4
Function	40	35.7
Division*	37	33.0
Matrix	5	4.5
Others	2	1.8
Total	112	100%

*Product/market oriented group with embedded profit centre concept.

[8]See Ahn & Lee (1994) for more detailed information.

As was noted earlier, head offices also control divisions through personnel appointments, especially at higher levels. Thus, while the more routine sales and productions decisions are to a large extent delegated, the less routine financing, investment and employment decisions are mostly controlled directly by the head office. This supports the observation made above concerning the *de facto* high level of centralisation in Korean firms.

Product Pricing: It is interesting to note that 55 percent of the firms surveyed base their pricing policy on variable costs, while 45 percent use the absorption cost basis. In the case of homogenous products produced under favourable demand conditions, variable costing may be argued as working effectively as a pricing strategy. However, given the short life cycle and increasing variety of high-tech products, Korean accounting and pricing practices may have to become more sophisticated if they are to provide routine information relevant to the needs of decision makers concerned with the problem of covering overhead costs.

Table 4
BASIS FOR PRICING

Class	Frequency	Percent
Variable Cost	62	55.0
Absorption Cost	50	45.0
Others	3	2.6
Total	115	100%

Costing System Characteristics: With respect to the level of sophistication of Korean costing systems, the majority of respondent firms (64 percent) reported using a fairly specific product model or production lot costing approach, indicating a relatively sophisticated level of application. The product group costing approach was also popular. This is less sophisticated but less costly. If the variety of product models is low within the product group, the product group costing approach may satisfy the cost-benefit criterion of costing system design. The details are shown in Table 5.

Table 5
COSTING SYSTEM SOPHISTICATION

Level	Frequency	Percent
Production Lot	7	7.0
Product Model	57	57.0
Production Line	3	3.0
Product Group	28	28.0
Whole Factory	5	5.0
Total	100	100%

As can be seen from Table 6, the most usual cost centre chosen by respondent firms as the basis for allocating manufacturing overhead was the department (66 percent). A plantwide overhead rate was calculated by 20 percent of the firms in the sample. Despite the recommendation of machine hour as an appropriate allocation basis in an automated manufacturing environment (e.g. Horngren, *et al.*, 1994), individual machines seem to be only rarely adopted as a basis of allocation. This finding is consistent with Lee (1993) who also found that machines usually do not appear to be identified as a separate cost pool.

Table 6
OVERHEAD ALLOCATION RATE

Rate	Frequency	Percent
Plantwide	23	20.4
Departmental	74	65.5
Individual Machine	5	4.4
Others	10	9.7
Total	112	100%

When manufacturing overheads assume a significant portion of total product costs, the basis of cost allocation becomes an important issue for a number of well known reasons relating to the valuation of assets, performance measurement, pricing policy and organisational control. Recent manufacturing environment changes make this observation even more pertinent. As automation proceeds, it is commonly argued, direct labour hour becomes a less appropriate allocation basis (Cooper & Kaplan, 1988). As can be seen from Table 7, however, direct labour still seems to be the dominant allocation basis (used by 43 percent of respondent firms) despite the increasingly automated Korean manufacturing environment.

Table 7
OVERHEAD ALLOCATION BASIS

Allocation Basis	Frequency	Percent
Direct labour	43	43.4
Machine hour	6	6.1
Material	10	10.1
Product unit	12	12.1
Combination	25	25.3
Others	3	3.0
Total	99	100%

Whether this is due to theory being inadequate or to problems encountered in implementing other methods (such as the machine rate method, see Sakurai (1990)) is difficult to ascertain. However, it appears that increasing amounts of manufacturing overhead does not seem to be attracting the attention of management. Most of the resources and efforts are dedicated to cost management focus on direct material cost items (Ahn & Lee, 1994). This stands in contrast to the North American case where most resources are devoted to the control of direct labour items (Horngren, et al., 1994).

Cost Management: Standard costing traces direct costs to a cost object by using standard prices (or rates) and standard quantities of input. It focuses on variances of direct material costs and direct labour costs. As automation proceeds, manufacturing processes become more reliable so that direct material and direct labour variances become negligible (Hendricks, 1988). Moreover, short life cycles and a greater variety of products makes standard setting and updating very costly and difficult. Table 8 shows, however, that standard costing is still favoured by many of the surveyed firms (44.3 percent) as an important cost management tool. This may be because direct costs represent about 78.5 percent of the manufacturing costs of surveyed firms (Ahn & Lee, 1994). However, target costing is also gaining support as a major cost management tool (39.1 percent). This may imply that focus of cost management is beginning to shift from production to design.

Table 8
COST MANAGEMENT TECHNIQUES

Techniques	Frequency	Percent
Standard Costing	51	44.3
Target Costing/		
Cost planning	45	39.1
Budgetary System	19	16.5
Total	115	100%

A study by Yook (1992) reported that target costs are either set for total manufacturing costs (45 percent of the respondents of that study) or for direct manufacturing costs (35 percent). Most firms do not appear to subdivide cost targets into smaller items. Hence detailed cost targets for responsible individuals are rarely set, which reduces the probability of target cost achievement. Target costing in Korea seems to be at the early stage of development and currently lacks sophistication.

In Yook's survey (1992) of 350 large manufacturing, companies, actual costing was found to be the most popular cost management tool. Total quality control, cost planning, budgetary control and standard costing all followed actual costing in their importance for cost management[9]. It is not entirely clear how this fits in with the Ahn and Lee data referred to above. It may simply be an example of the financial accounting mentality being incorporated into management accounting practice. Nevertheless, leading firms do appear to recognise the importance of quality control. Samsung and other *chaebols* proclaim quality as their first objective to achieve and total quality management is the most favoured tool, the quality circle[10] being moderately used. JIT, however, is rarely used for quality control purposes (Ahn & Lee, 1994).

Capital Budgeting & Payback Period: Technological innovation has made investment decisions related to automated manufacturing riskier. The payback period method is thought to appear more attractive under these circumstances, because quick recovery of the invested amount is critical in a short product life cycle environment. Table 9 supports this view, listing the payback period method as being the primary capital budgeting technique used by the firms in the survey (31.5 percent). A study by Sakurai (1990) of Japanese companies showed similar results. Seventy-four percent of the surveyed firms reported using the payback technique. The internal rate of return (IRR) and accounting rate of return (ROR) were employed by 25.0 percent and 21.3 percent of the surveyed firms, respectively. Net present value (NPV) appears to be rarely used (5.6 percent).

Table 9
CAPITAL BUDGETING TECHNIQUES

Techniques	Frequency	Percent
Payback Period	34	31.5
IRR	27	25.0
NPV	6	5.6
Accounting ROR	23	21.3
Subjective Judgement	16	14.8
Others	2	1.9
Total	108	100%

As can be seen from Table 10, the average payback period employed by firms is

---

[9]Korean manufacturing firms selected 'quality management', 'purchasing management of materials', and 'improvement of defect ratio' as their most important problems to solve in the area of cost management. Japanese companies, however, chose 'purchasing management of raw materials', 'design rationalisation', and 'quality management' as critical tasks. It may be noted that design activity was not considered to be as important in Korea as it was in Japan.

[10]This is a group of volunteer employees who meet regularly to discuss their function and the problems they are encountering, to try to devise solutions to those problems, and to propose those solutions to their management (Aguilana & Chase, 1991).

an interesting indicator of firms' attitudes towards the investment decision horizon. Four or more years for the payback period is adopted by 50 percent of the firms surveyed, manifesting a relatively long-term perspective for most major Korean manufacturing companies. The centralisation of investment decisions to owners and managers may partly explain the reason of this long-term perspective. This result is comparable to that of another study which reported that 50 percent of Japanese companies use a payback period of four years or longer.

Table 10
PAYBACK PERIOD CUTOFF

Period	Frequency	Percent
1 year	1	0.9
2 year	15	13.2
3 year	41	36.0
4 year	9	7.9
5 year	24	21.1
more than 5	24	21.1
Total	114	100%

This was in contrast to US firms, of which only 12 percent used payback periods as long (NAA, 1988).

Performance Evaluation: Companies vary in choosing the key performance measure for divisions. Although return on capital employed (ROI) is one of the most popular measures in Western countries, Korean firms in the survey seem to prefer return on sales (ROS) in evaluating departments or divisions (45.6 percent of respondents). In addition to ROS, comparison of budget and actual results is another prevalent method used for division evaluations. The rare usage of ROI for division evaluation warrants an explanation. It may be due to investment decisions not being delegated to divisions, or possibly it may be due to the volatility of capital investment levels in high-tech companies making a reliable determination of a relevant capital figure for the denominator of the ratio difficult.

Table 11
KEY DIVISION PERFORMANCE MEASURE

Performance Measure	Frequency	Percent
ROI	5	4.9
ROS	47	45.6
Profit	9	8.7
Budget vs. Actual	31	30.1
Value Added	8	7.8
Others	2	1.9
Total	102	100%

The allocation of the corporate head office costs is a perennial problem in the performance evaluations of divisions. Most companies surveyed (59 percent) allocated head office costs to divisions. Some companies (13 percent), however, did not allocate head office expenses at all and 28 percent only allocated selected cost items. The typical allocation basis used for allocating head office expenses was sales volume although most managers are not satisfied with this method because of its lack of causality (Jeon, 1993).

Budgeting and Variance Analysis: It is difficult to draw fine distinctions between the various budget setting methods such as top-down, bottom-up or participative methods. The popularity of the participative method, however, is well evidenced by Table 12 with 48.7 percent of the firms sampled endorsing this approach. The bottom-up approach is rarely adopted. The top-down is still widely used (33.6 percent), again probably reflecting the centralised decision making nature of many Korean firms.

Table 12
BUDGET SETTING METHOD

Method	Frequency	Percent
Top-down	38	33.6
Bottom-up	18	15.9
Participative	55	48.7
Other	2	1.8
Total	113	100%

For strategic budget resource allocation, Zero-Based Budgeting was advocated by early researchers. Few firms, however, appear to have actually adopted the approach in practice. Budgeted amounts are usually set as objectives to be achieved. Although sometimes criticised for its lack of consideration of strategic matters, incremental budgeting is still practised by one-third of those large manufacturing firms sampled. Furthermore, variance analysis is the major control mechanism for budgetary control. A monthly variance analysis was employed by half of the companies surveyed and 30 percent of the firms performed variance analysis on a quarterly basis (Ahn & Lee, 1994).

Personnel Management: Traditionally, in Korean personnel management, seniority has been perceived to be of considerable importance in the evaluation process. The evidence of the survey reported here, however, appears to indicate that less emphasis is placed on the attribute of seniority than is usually believed. Although ranked second in Table 13, 'ability' seems to be being given more weight than is normally considered to be the case.

Table 13
CRITERIA USED FOR INDIVIDUAL APPRAISAL

Criterion	Frequency	Percent
Seniority	31	29.5
Personality Attributes	19	18.1
Performance	20	19.0
Ability	29	27.6
None	6	5.7
Total	105	100%

In some high-tech companies, 'star players' often gain rapid advancement. Even so, it may be surmised that seniority still plays an important role in determing who gets promoted in Korean firms (Steers *et al.*, 1989).

Employee evaluation is mostly an annual event[11]. The main types of incentives used are usually either based upon promotion or pecuniary incentives. Less than 10 percent of the total compensation, however, is incentive-based. It may be concluded, therefore, that performance evaluation is more closely linked with promotion than with monetary compensation.

CONCLUSION

The high concentration of ownership and management observed in Korean firms has facilitated centralised planning and coordination, the fast diffusion of top management initiatives, and a long term perspective being taken in planning capital investment projects. The negative side of the same attributes has, however, created an accounting environment where financial accounting and reporting is centred around owner managers and sophisticated management accounting practices are not always fully appreciated. Taken in conjunction with the legal status of corporation tax law, this has contributed to a distortion of the basis of Korean financial accounting and a diminution in the credibility of accounting information.

Nevertheless, with the enormous growth and internationalisation of the Korean stock market, potential investors and other domestic and foreign interested parties have begun to demand high quality accounting information and harmonisation with international accounting standards. Although recent revisions in corporate accounting standards have incorporated some of the changes necessary to accommodate

---

[11]54 percent of the surveyed firms performed employee evaluation annually and 34 percent performed a semi-annual evaluation (Ahn & Lee, 1994)

internationalised business activities, they still need to be further systematically coordinated with both tax law and company law in order to reduce current conflicts, to serve the original purpose of financial reporting and to support harmonisation with international accounting standards. Concentrated ownership structure and traditional shortages of funds have led to the development of sophisticated management accounting techniques being given low priority. Moreover, since connections with the government has been a major determinant of success or failure in the recent past, management accounting information and practices have been considered less important than they perhaps should have been and this has slowed down the development of management accounting practices in Korea.

Current Korean management accounting practices seems to be mainly derived from the financial accounting framework and is only slowly adapting to changes in the manufacturing environment. The survey results reported here show that actual costing, standard costing, and budgetary control are still the primary tools for cost management in many manufacturing firms. However, there is some evidence of change beginning to take place in management accounting practices. The focus of cost management seems to be shifting from the manufacturing stage to the design stage. A similar change may also be detected in personnel management, where ability is becoming a more important factor in promotion and the role of incentive based salaries is growing. Recent attempts have been made by some firms to integrate new management tools such as target costing into their management accounting systems although possibly these need to be 'Koreanised'. Accountants need to adopt strategic modes of thinking. The major barrier to overcome for managerial accountants in Korea is the old, traditional financial accounting mentality of *post facto* reporting based on financial performance measures.

REFERENCES

Ahn, T.S. (1993), 'Customer satisfaction accounting', *Korean accounting journal*, Vol. 1., pp. 115–35.

Ahn, T.S. and C.H. Lee (1994), 'Effect of manufacturing environment changes on cost management practices', *Korean accounting journal*.

Aquilana, N. and R. Chase (1991), *Fundamentals of operations management*, Irwin Bank of Korea, (1993), *Business financial statement analysis*, Bank of Korea.

Choi, C. (1993), 'Characteristics and consolidation scope of Korean chaebol companies', *Dong-Guk accounting journal*, Vol. 1, pp. 1–28.

Choi, B. (1996), 'Background and viewpoints on the revised Corporate Accounting Standards', *Korean CPA journal*, pp. 19–23.

Chung, J. (1993), *Advanced accounting*, Bakyongsa, Seoul.

Cooper, R. and R.S. Kaplan (1988), 'How cost accounting distorts product costs', *Management accounting*, April, pp. 20–7.

Hendricks, J.A. (1988), 'Applying cost accounting to factory automation', *Management accounting,* December, pp. 24–30.

Horngren, C.T., Foster, G. and S. Datar (1994), *Cost accounting: A managerial emphasis,* (7th ed), Prentice-Hall, New Jersey.

Jang, J. (1993), 'International harmonization of accounting standards in the Asia-Pacific region: A Korean perspective', *Towards international harmonization of accounting standards in the Asia-Pacific region,* Chung Ang University.

Jeon, J. (1993), 'Performance evaluation methods under divisional structure of corporations', Master's Thesis, Ajou University.

Jinn, T. (1994), 'Monitoring function of banks and future financing systems', *KNDIC journal,* Vol. 6, pp. 39–47.

Kim, S. and H. Lee (1993), *Practices and summary of corporate tax law,* Korean Tax Association.

Korean Chamber of Commerce (1993), *Rational adjustments between corporate accounting and tax accounting,* Korean Chamber of Commerce, Seoul.

KSEC (1990), 'Korean Securities & Exchange Commission', *Corporate Accounting Standards,* KSEC.

Lee, C. (1993), *Introduction to accounting,* Kyongmun-sa.

Lee, D., Jang, J. Na, I. and C. Lee (1993), 'New directions on the Korean corporate accounting standards setting process', Working Paper, Korean Accounting Association.

Lee, J. (1993), 'Restructuring of cost accounting systems based on factory automation', *Korean accounting review,* Vol. 16, pp. 123–46.

Lee, M. (1992), *Let's make Theory W,* Knowledge Industry, Seoul.

Lee, M. (1993), 'Problems and improvements in Korean corporate taxation systems', *Korean accounting journal,* Vol. 1, pp. 73–87.

Lee, Y. and S. Nam (1994), *Future tasks of Korean stock market for international competitiveness,* Korea Development Institute.

Lim, M. (1991), 'Inventory valuation methods of Korean manufacturing firms', Master's Thesis, Kyung Hee University.

Lim, W. (1989), *Ownership structure and protection of management rights of listed companies on the Korean stock market,* Korean Chamber of Commerce, Seoul.

NAA Tokyo Affiliate (1988), 'Management accounting in the advanced manufacturing surrounding: Comparative study on survey in Japan and U.S.A.'

Nam, S. (1992), 'How to increase the reliability of accounting information', *Sokang Harvard business review,* July–August, pp. 65–75.

Nam, S. (1993), 'Validity and expected benefits of combined financial statements for business group', *Korean accounting journal,* Vol. 1, pp. 41–61.

Sakurai, M. (1990), 'The Influence of factory automation on management accounting practices: A study of Japanese companies', *Measures for manufacturing excellence,* R.S. Kaplan (Ed), HBR Press, Boston, pp. 39–62.

Samil Accounting Corporation (1991), *Samil auditing theory,* Samil, Seoul.

Samil Accounting Corporation (1992), *Generally accepted accounting principles in Korea and the United States of America: A review and comparison,* Samil Accounting Corporation, Seoul.

Samil Accounting Corporation (1994), *Theory and practice of consolidated financial statements,* Samil Accounting Corporation, Seoul.

Shin, Y. (1992), *Korean management: Current status and prospects,* Bakyoungsa, Seoul.

Son, D. (1991), 'The recording and calculation system of Gaesung bookkeeping', *Korean accounting review,* Vol. 12, pp. 111–133.

Steers, R.M., Shin, Y.K. and G.R. Ungson (1989), *The chaebol*: *Korea's new industrial might*, Harper & Row, New York.

Yoo, H. (1993), 'Internationalisation and financial management of Korean corporations', *KNDIC journal*, Vol. 5, pp. 36–42.

Yook, K. (1992), 'An empirical study on the cost management systems of Korean manufacturing companies: With emphasis on target costing', *Korean accounting review*, Vol. 14, pp. 109–26.

FINANCIAL AND MANAGEMENT ACCOUNTING PRACTICES IN TAIWAN

*Frederick H. Wu, Jungpao Kang, Chih-Chung Yeh and Song-Horng Lin**

BACKGROUND

Taiwan is a group of one large and several smaller islands covering an area of approximately 36 000 sq. km and lying in the South China Sea 200 km off the coast of the Chinese mainland, north of the Philippines between latitudes 21°45′ and 25°38′N. The main island of Taiwan is mountainous, lies on the Pacific Ring of Fire and is subject to earthquakes. Forested areas cover about two-thirds of the land area and narrow alluvial plains in the west and small basins in the north are cultivated. The climate is maritime subtropical to tropical and is subject to the effect of the monsoon, with the north being wet in the milder period from October to March and the south being wet during the summer months between April and September. There are only minor deposits of natural resources such as coal, natural gas, limestone and marble.

The original inhabitants of Taiwan dating from more than 3000 years ago were Malayo-Polynesians. Apart from some small Chinese communities in the 14th Century, Chinese settlement did not occur on any scale until the period of Dutch colonisation between 1624 and 1661, partly out of the need for migrant labour and partly due to an exodus

*Professor, Department of Accounting, University of North Texas, Denton, Texas; Associate Professor, Department of Accounting, National Chengchi University, Taipei, Taiwan; Professor and lecturer, Department of Accounting, National Cheng Kung University, Tainan, Taiwan, respectively.

from southern China following the Manchu conquest of China. Between 1683 and 1895, when it was ceded to Japan following the Sino-Japanese War, Taiwan was a province of China and Chinese immigration increased substantially. Under Japanese rule, Taiwan was modernised, enjoying rapid economic growth and, after initially being a source of agricultural product for Japan, was industrialised as part of the war effort in the 1930s. Following the end of the Second World War, after Taiwan became the base of the Nationalist Kuomintang under Chiang Kai-shek in 1949, a complex mixture of legislative arrangements based upon Chinese, parliamentarian and presidential principles was implemented in a constitution originally designed to apply to the whole of China. The National Assembly is elected for a four-year term and convenes and acts only on constitutional matters and to elect and recall the President. The President is the head of state, elected for six years with wide executive powers. There are in addition five Yuans: An Executive Yuan headed by a premier who is appointed by the President but who is officially responsible to the Legislative Yuan (presently consisting of 161 elected members) which enacts legislation. There is also a Judicial Yuan (i.e. the judiciary which is of the Supreme Court type); an Examination Yuan responsible for supervising examinations for entry to public office; and a Control Yuan to oversee the work of the Executive Yuan. Until 1991 most members of the National Assembly, the main legislative body, was composed of members elected in 1948. The system was autocratic but provided a long period of stability in domestic affairs. The first fully democratic elections to the legislative assembly were held in late 1992 amid a certain amount of unrest and dissident activity and the present trend in domestic politics seems to be towards the 'Taiwanisation' of political power as the unity of the traditional Nationalist movement weakens. The political relationship with mainland China, which has dominated foreign policy since 1949, is still unresolved. The legal system is of the code law type. The majority of the population (84 percent) of about 21 million people is made up of Taiwanese (ethnic Chinese born in Taiwan) with mainland Chinese forming 14 percent and people of Malay origins only 2 percent of the population. The population density of 582 persons per sq. km is one of the highest in the world. The religious patterns reflect the population mix, with 94 percent being Buddhist, Confucian or Daoist, and four percent being Christian. Mandarin is the official language, but Taiwanese and certain other Chinese dialects (e.g. Hakka) are also spoken. Taipei, the capital, has a population of about 2 million people.

GDP in 1994 was US$216 billion or approximately US$11 315 per capita, growing in recent years at about 8 percent per annum. Taiwan's economic history in the 20th Century has been one of relative success, and under the post war Nationalist government, it was one of the first countries of the region to adopt export oriented growth policies in 1958. Agriculture, based on the small area of fertile soils, once the mainstay of the economy, had diminished to employing just over 12 percent of the population in 1992, while contributing about 3 percent of GDP. The main crops are rice, sugar cane, maize and sweet potatoes. Deforestation prevents the exploitation of timber resources. Manufacturing, where high technology processes are replacing traditional labour intensive industries, contributed about 30 percent of GDP and employment. The main manufactures are electronics, motor vehicles, plastic goods and textiles. The services sector contributed more than 56 percent to GDP in 1993. The Taiwanese economy's international competitiveness, which has caused exports to grow to more than US$97 billion *in 1993, is based upon low cost, high skilled labour and a high savings ratio (almost 30 percent of GNP) has enabled it to finance its economic expansion from domestic sources. A trade surplus, which covers a net import of services, typically gives a substantial surplus on current account. The level of foreign debt is small and foreign currency reserves were US$82 billion in 1992. These factors have combined with a low inflation rate, low unemployment and an appreciating currency to produce a strong economy. Taiwan's main trading partners are Japan, the US and Hong Kong. The government has intervened in the economy directly through the ownership of banks and other firms, as well as through the usual indirect channels of fiscal and monetary policy in the post war period, but may play a less important role in the future if privatisation continues. The unit of currency is the New Taiwan dollar.*

R.J.W.

INTRODUCTION

This chapter investigates the characteristics and related issues of financial accounting and management accounting in Taiwan. In the area of financial accounting, the development and current state of accounting standards are described in Section 2. In Section 3, the differences between Taiwanese and US GAAP are outlined, and in Section 4, auditing practices are described. Two major issues relating to the usefulness of current disclosure practices are analysed in Section 5, namely the lack of financial analyst expertise and the concentration of ownership in Taiwanese firms. On the subject of management accounting, after a brief reflection on the relevance of current techniques to the Taiwanese accounting environment in Section 6, current education and accounting practices are described in Sections 7 and 8 respectively. Section 9 concludes with some thoughts on possible future developments in financial and management accounting areas.

DEVELOPMENT OF TAIWANESE FINANCIAL ACCOUNTING STANDARDS

Prior to 1983, Taiwan GAAP were virtually non-existent and accounting standards were set by legislative regulation. Thus, at that time, tax laws, the commercial accounting law, governmental accounting regulations, auditing laws and US accounting textbooks formed the basis of accounting standards. In addition, any governmental unit that had jurisdiction over a private enterprise (e.g. the Ministry of Economic Affairs and Ministry of Finance) had the authority to impose its interpretation on any controversial accounting issues. Furthermore, many accounting alternatives were acceptable to the auditor. Under these conditions, the quality of financial statements was highly questionable.

The National Federation of Certified Public Accountants took over standard setting responsibilities in 1983. Later, in 1984, the Taiwanese Certified Public Accountants (CPA) established the Accounting Research and Development Foundation of the Republic of China (the Foundation), which has since been an independent standards-setting body. The objectives of the Foundation are to upgrade and promote Taiwan accounting and auditing standards, ensure continuing development of these standards, and assist industry in establishing a sound accounting system. The functions of the Foundation also include education and dissemination of information. Funded by donations, the Foundation comprises government officials, representatives from industry, academics, the Taiwan Securities and Exchange Commission (SEC) officials and practicing CPAs. The Foundation now has four committees, Financial Accounting Standards, Auditing Standards, Accounting Systems, and Education and Training, which relate to its various objectives. The Financial Accounting Standards Committee (FASC) is responsible for developing Taiwan accounting standards. FASC is similar to the FASB (Financial Accounting Standards Board) in the US. Every member of the FASC is working part-time. With the strong support of government agencies, including the Ministry of Finance through the SEC, the Ministry of Economic Affairs and of many local CPAs, accounting standards have been generally accepted and followed.

As of September 1995, the FASC has issued 24 pronouncements and 2 interpretations, and the Auditing Standards Committee has issued 27 statements of auditing standards. The Accounting Systems Committee has issued pronouncements on accounting systems such as those in the chemical, cement, banking and textile industries. Financial accounting standards and auditing statements are developed on the basis of US standards with reference to unique domestic characteristics. Only slight differences exist between Taiwan and US accounting standards. These are reviewed in the next section.

Current accounting standards

Financial accounting standards issued by the FASC constitute the GAAP in Taiwan. Prior to being issued, each Statement of Financial Accounting Standards is widely circulated for public comments, and FASC meetings are open to the public. This process is referred to as the *due process* of financial accounting standards. The purpose of the due process is mainly to incorporate unique Taiwanese characteristics. The FASC first selects an emerging issue. Then a specific task force is appointed to conduct related studies and prepare a draft, including feasible alternatives. An alternative is then selected as the exposure draft. The FASC finalises and issues the statement with an inclusion of public comments.[1] Finally, amendments and interpretations may follow, supplementing the original pronouncement.

A list of current titles of original pronouncements and interpretation is shown in Table 1.

Table 1
FINANCIAL ACCOUNTING STANDARDS

---

(1) Inventory of Generally Accepted Accounting Principles
(2) Accounting for Leases
(3) Capitalization of Interest Cost
(4) Statement of Changes in Financial Position (superseded by SFAS No. 17)
(5) Accounting for long-term Investment in Equity Securities
(6) Related-Party Disclosures
(7) Consolidated Financial Statements
(8) Accounting Changes and Prior Period Adjustments
(9) Contingencies and Subsequent Events
(10) Valuation and Presentation of Inventory
(11) Accounting of long-term Construction Contracts
(12) Accounting for Income Tax Credits
(13) Accounting by Debtors and Creditors for Troubled Debt Restricting
(14) Accounting for Foreign Currency Translation
(15) Disclosure of Accounting Policy
(16) Financial Forecasts Preparation Guidelines
(17) Statement of Cash Flows
(18) Accounting by Employers for Pensions
(19) Accounting by Development Stage Companies
(20) Reporting Segmental Financial Information
(21) Accounting by Issues and Holders of Convertible Bonds
(22) Accounting for Income Tax
(23) Interim Reporting
(24) Earnings Per Share

Financial Accounting Interpretations
(1) Revenue Recognition on Installment Sales
(2) Elimination Unrealized Intercompany Profit or Loss of Equity
     Security Investment Accounting Under the Equity Method

---

[1]A quorum of an FASC committee meeting must have over half of its members present, and any resolution for deliberating standard setting requires the consent of over two-thirds of members present.

Requirements of financial reporting for public firms

Securities Exchange Acts rather than accounting standards are the main legislative sources of financial reporting of public firms. All public firms are required to file quarterly, semi-annual, and annual financial reports which primarily consist of three-year comparative financial statements. When a firm goes public, either over-the-counter or on the Taiwan Stock Exchange, or a currently listed firm changes its capital, the firm must provide a prospectus which in addition to three-year comparative financial statements also contains financial forecasts. The format the financial forecasts uses is identical to those of comparative financial statements.

A listed firm must prepare a balance sheet, an income statement, a statement of changes in shareholders' equity, and a statement of cash flows, the formats and contents of which are all similar to those in the US. In addition, a firm must file supplementary schedules with the SEC. That is, each significant account presented in the balance sheet or income statement generally requires a supplementary schedule showing itemised contents. Significant receivables or payables must be reported separately. Information such as the market value of inventories, securities, or equity investments; the term of loans or borrowings; changes in long-term investments, fixed assets, capital surplus, and retained earnings must also be included in the supplementary schedules. The contents of mandated financial forecasts include a balance sheet, an income statement, and a statement of cash flows.

As in the US, consolidated financial statements are required when a publicly-held company has control over another company. Control is established if the investing company, either soley or with its subsidiaries, holds more than 50 percent of the investee's voting common stock. Unlike the US, however, consolidation is not required for companies in dissimilar activities such as manufacturing and banking. Also firms undergoing liquidation or reorganisation are not included in consolidated financial statements.[2]

DIFFERENCES BETWEEN US AND TAIWAN GAAP

Apart from the differences just mentioned, a general difference between the Taiwanese and the US GAAP is due to the uniqueness of the Taiwan environment in which tax laws and the Commercial Accounting Law dictate GAAP. In the past, tax accounting was virtually identical to financial accounting. Commercial Accounting Law[3] and tax

---

[2] Segment reporting requirements are exactly the same as in the US GAAP.
[3] The Commercial Accounting Law (the Law) promulgated in 1948 was brought into force in 1952 and amended in 1964, 1968, 1967, 1990, and 1995. The Law is not applicable to small partnerships or sole proprietors. The Law requires the accounting period to run from 1 January to 31 December. In addition, accrual accounting and double entry bookkeeping must be used.

law are also the main legislative sources for accounting treatment in non-public firms. A majority of Taiwanese enterprises are non-public, therefore the influences of tax laws and the Commercial Accounting Law on accounting practices are significant. Current accounting standards are consistent with accounting treatments regulated in this manner. Two major differences which exist between US and Taiwanese practices involve asset revaluations and the structure of stockholders' equity.

The practice of asset revaluation and the structure of stockholders' equity in Taiwan relate to tax incentives. When a firm revalues its assets, it can increase its deductible depreciation expense, even though this has an adverse effect on income statement.[4] Stockholders's equity comprises three parts, capital stock[5], capital surplus (paid-in capital), and retained earnings. The latter section consists of three items, i.e. gains on disposal of fixed assets[6], reserves for asset revaluations, and legal reserves. The gains on disposal of fixed assets and the reserves for asset revaluations are two items of appropriated retained earnings. Since all capital surplus items and retained earnings can be used for distributing dividends, mostly stock dividends, they are eventually transferred to the capital stock account.

All three items just mentioned have a legislative background. Accounting for gains on the disposal of fixed assets allows a firm to renew its fixed assets in line with provided tax incentives. Unlike the US, Taiwan GAAP retains the use of the ambiguous term 'reserve' in stockholders equity[7]. Furthermore, US GAAP does not have a concept equivalent to legal reserves which is more akin to a continental European concept[8]. The purpose of a legal reserve is to protect creditors by preventing distribution of capital to existing shareholders. Since more than 90 percent of dividend distributions in Taiwan are stock dividends rather than cash dividends, the effectiveness of the legal reserve requirement is very questionable.

---

[4]Taiwan GAAP permits assets to be recorded at cost or at cost plus appreciation deriving from asset revaluation pursuant to related government regulations. To reevaluate land, an amount equal to between 40 percent and 60 percent is charged to long-term debt as land value increment tax. The remainder of the appreciation is credited to a capital reserve account, *reserve for asset revaluation,* for use only to offset a deficit, or be transferred to capital.

[5] Taiwan Company Law stipulates that the par value of common stock must be $10 per share.

[6] In conformity with Taiwan GAAP, any gain on the disposal of property, plant and equipment must first be credited to non-operating income of income statement and then transferred to capital surplus in the applicable fiscal year.

[7]In order to avoid ambiguity, US GAAP does not employ the term 'reserve' (Dyckman, Dukes and Davies, 1992).

[8]Company Law requires a company to set aside 10 percent of its annual net income as a legal reserve until the accumulated reserve has reached an amount equal to the company's capital stock. This legal reserve may be used to offset a deficit, and when the reserve has reached 50 percent of the capital stock, up to 50 percent of it may be transferred to capital stock.

CURRENT AUDITING PRACTICES IN TAIWAN

Auditing in Taiwan consists of a financial audit and a tax audit.[9] The financial audit should accord with auditing standards, and the tax audit should accord with tax regulations. For tax purposes, specific documents or records are generally required as evidence of transactions, and certain limits are set on expenses such as entertainment and donations.

Pursuant to Company Law and the Securities Exchange Acts, a firm is required to provide audited financial statements when any one of the following conditions is met:

1. The firm is a public firm.[10]
2. The capital of a non-public firm exceeds NT$30 million.[11]
3. The bank loans of a non-public firm exceed NT$30 million.

As mentioned earlier, when a public firm changes its capital, it is required to prepare financial forecasts which must be reviewed by a CPA. The review of mandated forecasts concentrates on assessing whether their assumptions are reasonable.

In general, no significant difference exists between US and Taiwan auditing standards. Most US auditing standards have been adopted and promulgated as Taiwanese auditing standards, except where auditing procedures relate to special reports or disclosure requirements that are different from US. If no sources are available in Taiwan for resolving a particular auditing problem, the auditor usually refers to US auditing standards and literature. The standard auditor's report in Taiwan is identical to the pre-1988, two-paragraph, standard US short-form report. Reporting guidelines in Taiwan on the possible consequences of departing from the standard report, and on the type of report that will then be required, are also similar to those provided in US standards issued before 1988.

A list of current auditing standards as of September 1995 are shown in Table 2.

---

[9]If the tax returns of a firm are audited by a CPA, it can enjoy some tax advantages, for example 'blue filing'. Fewer examinations are made of blue filing companies by the Internal Revenue Service.

[10]Pursuant to the Securities Exchange Acts, if the capital of a firm exceeds NT$200 million, it is required to go public. A public firm may not be a listed company in the Taiwan Stock Exchange or in the over-the-counter market. To be listed in the TSE or OTC, the firm must go through a lengthy and rigorous procedure.

[11]In the case of a non-public firm, its audited financial statement are only used for bank loan purposes.

Table 2
AUDITING STANDARDS

(1) Basic Principles of Generally Accepted Auditing Standards
(2) Auditor's Report on Financial Statements
(3) Working Papers
(4) Audit Evidence
(5) Investigation and Evaluation of Internal Accounting Control
(6) Examination of Related-Party Transactions
(7) Representation Letter
(8) Confirmation
(9) Observation of Inventory Taking
(10) Audit Planning
(11) Review of Interim Financial Statements of Listed Companies
(12) Analytical Review Procedures
(13) Audit of Subsequent Events
(14) Fraud and Error
(15) Using the Work of Another Auditor
(16) Auditor's Consideration of an Entity's Ability to continue as a Going Concern
(17) Communication Between Successor and Predecessor Auditors
(18) Control of the Quality of Audit work
(19) Review of Financial Forecasts
(20) Using the Report of a Specialist
(21) First-Year Audit Engagements: Audit of Opening Balances
(22) Audit of Accounting Estimates
(23) Audit of Contingencies
(24) Materiality and Audit Risks
(25) Adoption of Internal Audit
(26) Audit Sampling

ISSUES CONCERNING THE CURRENT ACCOUNTING ENVIRONMENT

A major accounting issue in Taiwan, as elsewhere, relates to the usefulness of financial statements. Accounting standards may be reasonably comprehensive but, perhaps, not as useful as they could be. Thus the quality of financial statement information is questionable (Kang, 1995(a)). In Taiwan, this is argued to be due to a paucity of good financial information analysis and a high concentration of firm ownership. There are a number of reasons why this is so:

1. Investors lack experience in using financial statements and the proportion of institutional traders is small in comparison with uninformed investors.
2. Financial statements do not play a significant role in the loan market. Loan evaluations, for example, are often based upon pledges or mortgages and financial statements are used only for reference.
3. The financial analyst market is often neither competitive nor independent.

Consequently, the credibility of interpretations of financial statements is often questionable.
4. The subjectivity of estimates in financial statements which underlie the accrual basis of accounting may be exploited by management for reasons of self-interest.

Information intermediaries are among the key players assessing the usefulness of financial statements (Beaver, 1989). The Taiwanese accounting environment suffers a shortage of such intermediaries (Kang, 1994(a)) with the consequence that the Taiwan stock market contains a large proportion of uninformed investors, thereby increasing the negative effects of information asymmetry. This leads to inefficient resource allocation and a lower quality of financial statement information. Furthermore, the auditor has less incentive to provide a sound, professional opinion and more incentive to maintain only a minimum acceptable quality level (Kang 1995(a)). Thus additional and improved forms of information intermediary appear to be necessary.

What empirical evidence is available to support this viewpoint? Without intermediaries, financial reporting can become a tool for manipulating stock prices by informed investors. Studies (Kang, 1994(b)) have demonstrated that, prior to initial public offerings (IPO), firms have a strong incentive to manipulate earning numbers in order to meet the profitability requirement stipulated in the Securities Exchange Acts. Firms usually prepare overly optimistic mandated financial forecasts (Kang, 1995(b)). Real income manipulation is common among listed firms (Zen, 1995). Although abnormal returns surrounding financial reporting announcement dates are insignificant prior to announcement, significant abnormal returns can be detected surrounding voluntary management earning and sale forecasts in the public media (Zuo, 1994). No third-party verification is presently required for such voluntary management earnings and sale forecasts in the public media. Kang (1994(a)) proposed that an independent information credit rating agency might increase the credibility of financial statements. Ideally, information should be created by demand. However, this does not appear to work in Taiwan and the intervention of the SEC to attract a rating agency, like Moody, may be appropriate to help users rank the quality of financial statements.

The high concentration of ownership creates problems of adverse selection and moral hazard (Beaver, 1989). Evidence shows that more than 90 percent of listed firms in Taiwan are closely owned by a small number of families (Kang, 1995a). Although a high concentration of ownership can reduce agency costs (Jensen & Meckling, 1986), informed, large firm owners possess superior information compared to uninformed inventors. They also have a dominant market position. Thus outside, uninformed investors are placed at a disadvantage. Due to the structure of penalties, insider trading is not effectively controlled, and this enables the informed owner to make abnormal returns (Kang, 1995a). Furthermore, there is no incentive for the informed large firm owner to provide information.

On the positive side, the demands of capital-intensive industries for investment may mitigate the problem of high ownership concentration in the future. Relative to other Asian countries, Taiwan had lost the advantage of cheap labour and is shifting to developing more capital intensive products (e.g. the semiconductor). In order to reap economies of scale and make rapid, technological advancements, large amounts of capital are required. If traditional sources of finance are unable to meet this demand, they will be unable to dominate the corporate structure and thus, as the number of investors increase, so too will the pressure to adequately monitor financial statements. This should both reduce the negative effect of informational asymmetry between informed and uninformed investors and also decrease the potential for the manipulation of financial information. Continued economic development should therefore lead to improvements in the quality and usefulness of financial statements.

THE RELEVANCE OF MANAGEMENT ACCOUNTING TECHNIQUES IN TAIWAN

In 1984, Kaplan argued that managerial cost accounting techniques as described in the contemporary textbooks were mostly developed before 1925 and are no longer relevant to the current managerial environment. 'Old medicines will not cure new diseases', that is how Johnson and Kaplan (1984) described management accounting in their book, *Relevance Lost*. This book has led the accounting profession in the US to express concerns, and to begin a renewed effort to develop new managerial cost accounting techniques, which are relevant to an automated and computerised operational environment. Some new techniques are activity-based costing, target costing, life cycle costing, and quality-cost analysis. Thus the applicability of the old management cost accounting techniques to businesses in Taiwan is questionable in the context of today's economic environment.

With the rapid development and application of information technology, business firms in Taiwan are moving toward global, capital-intensive, automated, and computerised operations. Indeed, the present day business environment, internal and external, of Taiwanese firms is very similar to that of the US. Thus, the questions arise: Is the traditional management accounting as taught in colleges and universities still relevant today, and are the new management accounting techniques advocated by the US and other international educators relevant to business firms in Taiwan?

THE TEACHING OF MANAGEMENT ACCOUNTING

'Too much theory, too little practice', many practitioners in Taiwan complained. This complaint was heard in accounting journals and conferences. Management accounting textbooks, however, include both theory and applications. Cost accounting textbooks, in fact, often have more practical problems than theoretical discussions. The majority of management accounting textbooks used by colleges and universities in Taiwan are from the US. A few textbooks in Chinese are partially based on the US textbooks, and partially based on the needs of local business management. Perhaps due to the influence of the US, accounting educators have not taught management accounting to meet the needs of local business firms. Accounting students have learned many concepts and theories which have been developed in the US but which may not be relevant to Taiwanese business firms today.

It is evident that many educators and practitioners believe that a gap exists between applications in business and management accounting education in Taiwan. Professor Tsai of Central University (Tsai, 1995) pointed out that the current pedagogy in teaching management accounting is basically class lecturing supplemented by case discussion. The materials used for lectures are mainly borrowed from American textbooks and periodicals. Textbooks in Chinese are used in some cases. The relative importance of management accounting techniques, based on the answers to the question of how many instructors actually covered them in their class lectures, is shown in Table 3. Most of the topics in Table 3 were covered in class lectures except for a few topics such as productivity measurement (48.6 percent), decision tree (42.9 percent), planning and evaluation (34.3 percent) and network analysis (14.3 percent). These topics were not covered frequently because of the time limitations in the semester system; however, they were covered in production and operation management courses and operations research courses.

MANAGEMENT ACCOUNTING PRACTICES

Applications of management accounting techniques in Taiwan may be classified into four areas:

(1) traditional costing methods: batch costing, incremental costing, full costing, variable (direct) costing, and standard costing;
(2) techniques for planning, control, and decision making such as incremental cost analysis, cost behavior analysis, contribution margin analysis, cost-volume-profit analysis, operating budgeting, capital budgeting, responsibility accounting, efficiency and effectiveness measurements, and inter-company transfer pricing;
(3) quantitative techniques: inventory planning and control, learning model, linear programming, network analysis, regression analysis, and decision tree;
(4) techniques developed for new manufacturing environment: activity-based costing, target costing, production cycle costing, and productivity measurement and quality-cost analysis.

Table 3

THE RELATIVE IMPORTANCE OF MANAGEMENT
ACCOUNTING TECHNIQUES, BASED ON
THE RESPONSES OF ACCOUNTING PROFESSORS

Items	Management Accounting Techniques	Percent of responses	Ranking
1.	Cost-volume-profit analysis	98.6	1
2.	Contribution margin analysis	95.7	2
3.	Variable (direct) costing	95.7	2
4.	Incremental cost analysis	95.7	2
5.	Capital expenditure budgeting	94.3	5
6.	Cost behavioral analysis	92.9	6
7.	Responsibility accounting	92.9	6
8.	Transfer pricing	91.4	8
9.	Standard costing	91.4	8
10.	Operating budget	90.0	10
11.	Cost-benefit analysis	90.0	10
12.	Full costing	88.6	12
13.	Operational costing	87.1	13
14.	Inventory planning and control	84.3	14
15.	Batch costing system	81.4	15
16.	Learning curve	74.3	16
17.	Linear programming	67.1	17
18.	Quality cost analysis	64.3	18
19.	Target costing	58.6	19
20.	Product life cycle costing	52.9	20
21.	Productivity measurement	48.6	21
22.	Decision tree analysis	42.9	22
23.	Planning	34.3	23
24.	Network analysis	14.3	24

Source: Tsai, (1995)

Tsai (1995) conducted a survey of 459 manufacturing companies and 359 service companies in Taiwan for the purpose of understanding the current applications of management accounting in business organisations. The results are presented in Table 4.

One conspicuous fact disclosed by the survey is that service industries did not appear to apply management accounting techniques as widely as manufacturing companies, except operating budgeting and responsibility accounting. Three reasons may account for this situation. First, most management accounting techniques were originally developed from problems and issues arising in the manufacture of goods. Second, the rapid growth in service industries for the past decade outpaced the growth in developing management accounting techniques. Third, management accounting is quantitative in nature and harder to apply to the production of services, where the unit of measure is difficult to define.

Table 4

APPLICATIONS OF MANAGEMENT ACCOUNTING
TECHNIQUES IN BUSINESS FIRMS

Management Accounting Techniques	Manufacture Firms(N=459)		Service Firms (N=359)		Total (N=818)	
	Number	%	Number	%	Number	%
I. Traditional costing methods:						
1. Full costing	202	44.0 %	71	19.8 %	273	33.4 %
2. Batched costing	195	42.5	76	21.2	271	33.1
3. Direct (variable) costing	163	35.5	65	18.1	228	27.9
4. Standard costing	177	38.6	50	13.9	227	27.8
5. Processing costing	193	42.0	20	5.6	213	26.0
II. Planning, control, and decision making:						
1. Operating budget	378	82.4	303	84.4	681	83.3
2. Cost-effective measures	303	66.0	208	57.9	511	62.5
3. Capital budgeting	312	68.0	183	51.0	495	60.5
4. Responsibility accounting	241	52.5	190	52.9	431	52.7
5. Incremental cost analysis	275	59.9	109	30.4	384	46.9
6. Cost-volume-profit analysis	235	51.2	126	35.1	361	44.1
7. Contribution margin analysis	218	47.5	108	30.1	326	37.4
8. Cost behaviors analysis	206	44.9	99	27.6	305	37.3
9. Transfer pricing	190	41.4	82	22.8	272	33.3
III. Quantitative methods:						
1. Inventory control	351	76.5	126	35.1	477	58.3
2. Decision tree analysis	62	13.5	35	9.7	97	11.9
3. Network analysis	36	7.8	27	7.5	63	7.7
4. Regression analysis	42	9.2	18	5.0	60	7.3
5. Learning curve	47	10.2	10	2.8	57	7.0
6. Linear programming	37	8.1	12	3.3	49	6.0
IV. Techniques under current manufacturing environment:						
1. Productivity measures	227	49.5	79	22.0	306	37.4
2. Analysis of the cost of quality	114	24.8	25	7.0	139	17.0
3. Target costing	80	17.4	38	10.6	118	14.4
4. Activity costing	61	13.3	31	8.6	92	11.2
5. Product life-cycle costing	14	3.1	6	1.7	20	2.4

Source: Tsai (1995)

Based on an earlier survey, Tsai (1984) concluded that public companies used management accounting techniques more than private companies because public companies were better organised and controlled, with the adoption of many planning and control systems. If one compares the studies by Tsai (1995), Liao (1981) and Yan (1979), one discovers that applications of management accounting techniques today are much higher than the applications 10 years ago. Quantitative applications, however, have not made much inroad into service-oriented firms. A conclusion commonly found among all the studies is that operating budgets and capital expenditure budgets were widely adopted by business firms in Taiwan.

FURTHER ANALYSIS OF MAJOR MANAGEMENT ACCOUNTING TECHNIQUES

Table 5 is the summary of assessments by practitioners and educators of the applicability of management accounting techniques to business firms in Taiwan. The most applicable techniques were, in their ranking order, operating budget systems, incremental cost analysis, responsibility accounting, cost-volume-profit analysis, contribution margin analysis, and capital budgeting. The assessments reveal the fact that academicians more than practitioners tended to hold the view that management accounting techniques could be easily applied to business firms. Therein lies the gap between the theories and concepts preached by educators and the applications of theories and concepts by practitioners. The following conclusions may be derived from the data presented in Tables 4 and 5:

1. There was a difference between the academicians and the practitioners in their ranking of the applicability of management accounting techniques, albeit not a significant difference.
2. Product life cycle costing, which was derived from the recent manufacturing environment, was considered to have the least application to business firms by both practitioners and educators.
3. Those techniques which were ranked high, as indicated in Table 4, based on the number of adoptions by firms, were also ranked high, as indicated in Table 5, based on practitioners's perceptions of actual applications.
4. Many quantitative-oriented techniques such as linear programming, regression analysis, learning models, and network analysis were not adopted by firms as much as other less quantitative techniques.
5. Operating budgets and capital expenditure budgets which were viewed as most applicable management accounting techniques by both practitioners and educators, were actually adopted the most by business firms.

Five major management accounting techniques adopted by business firms in Taiwan are further explained below: operating budgets, standard costing systems, cost-volume-profit analysis, capital budgeting, and responsibility accounting.

Table 5

RANKING OF APPLICABILITY OF MANAGEMENT ACCOUNTING TECHNIQUES BY EDUCATORS AND PRACTITIONERS

Management Accounting Techniques	Practitioners		Educators		Total	
	Average	Ranking	Average	Ranking	Average	Ranking
1. Batched (Job) costing	3.58	9	3.93	10	3.62	9
2. Processing costing	3.34	16	3.89	12	3.43	15
3. Standard costing	3.50	11	4.00	7	3.58	10
4. Activity costing	3.01	19	3.28	20	3.08	19
5. Product life-cycle costing	2.21	25	2.85	25	2.40	25
6. Target costing	3.14	17	3.53	17	3.20	17
7. Full costing	3.45	12	3.85	13	3.50	13
8. Direct (variable) costing	3.44	13	3.89	11	3.51	12
9. Operating budgeting	3.79	1	4.29	2	3.84	1
10. Capital budgeting	3.67	5	4.12	5	3.72	6
11. Cost behavior analysis	3.35	14	4.11	6	3.46	14
12. Cost-volume-profit analysis	3.65	7	4.35	1	3.74	4
13. Contribution margin analysis	3.64	8	4.27	3	3.73	5
14. Incremental cost analysis	3.74	2	3.96	9	3.76	2
15. Responsibility accounting	3.70	3	4.13	4	3.75	3
16. Transfer pricing	3.34	15	3.73	14	3.40	16
17. Analysis of the cost of quality	3.05	18	3.42	18	3.12	18
18. Cost-effective measures	3.68	4	3.98	8	3.71	7
19. Productivity measures	3.52	10	3.55	16	3.52	11
20. Inventory control	3.66	6	3.59	15	3.65	8
21. Learning curve	2.91	23	2.92	23	2.64	24
22. Linear programming	2.45	24	3.19	21	2.66	23
23. Regression analysis	2.64	22	3.29	19	2.82	21
24. Decision tree analysis	2.87	20	2.97	22	2.89	20
25. Network analysis	2.65	21	2.85	24	2.68	22

Source: Tsai (1995)

Operating budgets

The application of operating budgets in Taiwan, based on surveys conducted by various researchers, are presented in Table 6 in chronological order. Samples for these surveys were mainly from manufacturing companies. The companies which practiced budgetary planning and control ranged from 76.2 percent in 1981 to 96.27 percent in 1986, out of all responding firms. Table 6 indicates clearly that operating budgeting is widely practised by business firms in Taiwan. The practice of operating budgeting may be discussed in terms of the following five aspects of the budgeting system:

(1) budget development,
(2) cost control,
(3) performance reports and communication,
(4) profit analysis, and
(5) administration of the budgetary control system.

Table 6
ADOPTION OF OPERATING BUDGETS BY BUSINESS FIRMS

Researchers	Year of Research	Sample Size	Data Collection	Type of firms Sampled	Adoption Rate
Chiu & Chang	1979	59	Questionnaire	Manufacturing	81.6 %
Yan, L. Y.	1979	87	Questionnaire	Manufacturing	89.0
Liao, S. L.	1981	140	Questionnaire	Manufacturing	76.2
Tseng, H.	1985	52	Questionnaire	Electric equip. (local & international firms)	87.0
Chen, J. Y.	1986	30	Questionnaire	Electronic	N/A
Lin, C. W.	1986	60	Questionnaire	Public firms	96.3
Chang, Z. L.	1992	112	Interview	Manufacturing	94.6
Tsai, W. S.	1995	818	Questionnaire	Manufacturing & service	83.3

Budget Development: Budgets have been widely practised by Taiwan business firms and are developed utilising the variable cost concept. Budgets developed from the variable cost concepts are generally referred to as flexible budgets. Budgets are finalised after a long series of discussions between department managers and the chief executive officer. The process of budget development begins at sales and production and follows with other functional budgets such as promotion and marketing budgets and general administration budgets, and ends with proforma financial statements and capital expenditure budgets.

Cost Control: In dealing with cost control in production, marketing, general administration, and research and development, a majority of companies classify costs into variable and fixed and the classification is accomplished mostly through account analysis and expert judgment. Regression analysis is rarely used.

Performance Reports and Communication: The majority of Taiwanese firms prepare performance reports with two major cost classifications, controllable and uncontrollable, for top-level managers. Most of the reports include the controllable portion only. Variances in the performance reports are communicated to the manager responsible for them and managers one level above the directly responsible manager. The investigation of variances is generally initiated from managers one level above the directly responsible manager, but in some cases it is initiated by the manager directly responsible.

Profit Analysis: Profit analysis in the form of income statement is also popular among Taiwanese firms in practising budgetary control. Usually, actual results such as gross profit, operating income, net income, earnings per share, and return on investment are compared to budgeted amounts.

Administration of the Budgetary Control: Most Taiwanese firms establish a budget committee to coordinate the development and implementation of the budgetary control system. Many companies with a budget committee administer budget development through a budget procedural manual and annual budget guidelines.

Standard cost systems

Empirical investigation was made of actual applications of standard costs in Taiwan. As indicated in Table 7, of those responding to the surveys, approximately 30 percent applied a standard cost system. For public companies, the adoption rate was 72 percent based on Lin's survey. To understand the practice of standard costs in Taiwan, the following two aspects of standard cost systems are discussed:

(1) Adoption of standard cost systems, and
(2) analysis and disposition of cost variances.

Adoption of Standard Cost Systems: The major reason for adopting a standard cost system in Taiwan was for performance evaluation. Other reasons included budget planning, cost control, pricing decision, and inventory evaluation. The reasons for firms rejecting the practice of using standard costs were the difficulty in establishing standards and high costs for practising a standard cost system (Yan, 1979). Standard

Table 7
SURVEYS OF ADOPTION OF STANDARD COST SYSTEMS

Researchers	Year of Research	Data Collection	Sample Size	Type of firms Sampled	Adoption Rate
Chiu & Chang	1979	Questionnaire	59	Manufacturing	56.0%
Yan, L. Y.	1979	Questionnaire	87	Manufacturing	29.0
Liao, S. L.	1981	Questionnaire	140	Manufacturing	20.7
Wu, K. J.	1984	Questionnaire	63	Manufacturing	32.0
Tseng, H.	1985	Questionnaire	52	Electric equip. (local & international firms)	42.0
Chen, J. Y.	1986	Questionnaire	30	Electronic	N/A
Lin, C. W.	1986	Questionnaire	60	Public firms	72.0
Yu, W. B.	1986	Questionnaire	59	General	20.3
Chang, Z. L.	1992	Interview	112	Manufacturing	31.2
Tsai, W. S.	1995	Questionnaire	818	Manufacturing & service	27.8

costs were based more on normal production volumes than on currently attainable volumes or ideal volumes. Also, standard costs were applied to production (direct materials, direct labour, and overhead) more than to non-production costs (marketing and general administration).

Analysis and Disposition of Cost Variances: Variance analysis focused on material costs (both price and quantity variances) according to the results of the surveys. To a lesser extent, variance analysis was applied to the overhead costs. The least used application of variance analysis in production was in respect of direct labour. The average frequency of variance analysis was once a month and variances were generally allocated to finished goods, work-in-process inventory and costs of goods sold on a proportional basis.

Cost-volume-profit analysis

Cost-volume-profit (CVP) analysis has been widely practised in Taiwan because of its simplicity in understanding and application. Both practitioners and academicians consider this technique to be of straightforward practical application. Table 8 reveals how much the CVP technique was adopted by firms in Taiwan for the period of 1979–95. Those companies with equity securities traded in the open market accounted for the greatest percentage of its application, as high as 95.1 percent based on Lin's survey (1986). Those manufacturing companies responding to the surveys steadily increased their applications of this technique from 41 percent in 1979 to 62.3 percent in 1992.

Table 8

SURVEYS OF ADOPTION OF COST-VOLUME-PROFIT ANALYSIS

Researchers	Year of Research	Sample Size	Data Collection	Type of firms Sampled	Adoption Rate
Chiu & Chang	1979	59	Questionnaire	Manufacturing	66.0 %
Yan, L. Y.	1979	87	Questionnaire	Manufacturing	41.0
Liao, S. L.	1981	140	Questionnaire	Manufacturing	46.2
Tseng, H.	1985	52	Questionnaire	Electric equip. (local & international firms)	74.0
Lin, C. W.	1986	60	Questionnaire	Public firms	95.1
Lin, M. J.	1990	56	Questionnaire	Public firms	67.9
Chang, Z. L.	1992	112	Interview	Manufacturing	62.3
Tsai, W. S.	1995	818	Questionnaire	Manufacturing & service	44.1

Why were some firms not utilising CVP analysis? Major reasons for firms' failure to apply CVP analysis were:

(1) lack of trained personnel,
(2) lack of resources in small-sized business firms, and
(3) lack of support by top management. The primary condition for using this technique is the classification of costs into variable and fixed costs. If a firm could not identify its costs as either variable or fixed, then CVP was not implementable.

What was the business decision most frequently made based on CVP analysis? The answer was commonly found to be the pricing decision. When firms in Taiwan attempt to set product prices, they estimate sales volumes, determine how much profit is to be allowed, and then the CVP relationship is used to derive a price. It was considered by many that the CVP technique made a significant contribution to the success of business firms in Taiwan.

Capital budgeting

Surveys of the practice of capital expenditure decisions by top management in Taiwan business firms are summarised in Table 9. The following discussion of the general practice of capital expenditure decision in Taiwan is classified into three major areas:

(1) capital expenditure evaluation,
(2) risk evaluation, and
(3) the process of capital budgeting.

Table 9
SURVEYS OF ADOPTION OF CAPITAL BUDGETING

Researchers	Year of Research	Sample Size	Data Collection	Type of firms Sampled	Adoption Rate
Chiu & Chang	1979	59	Questionnaire	Manufacturing	71.0 %
Yan, L. Y.	1979	87	Questionnaire	Manufacturing	41.0
Liao, S. L.	1981	14	Questionnaire	Manufacturing	49.2
Yeh, F. Y.	1984	65	Questionnaire	Manufacturing	45.6
Tseng, H.	1985	52	Questionnaire	Electric equip. (local & international firms)	77.0
She, S. Z.	1986	30	Questionnaire	Public firms manufacturing	52.0
Lin, C. W.	1986	102	Questionnaire	Public firms	93.4
Chen, J. Y.	1986	30	Questionnaire	Electronic	N/A
Hsu, T. Y.	1987	112	Questionnaire	Manufacturing	54.2
Wang, K. L.	1988	168	Questionnaire	Manufacturing	56.4
She, L. C.	1991	65	Questionnaire	Multi-national	48.3
Yang, J. C.	1991	89	Questionnaire	High-tech	52.6
Chang, Z. L.	1992	112	Interview	Manufacturing	54.5
Tsai, W. S.	1995	818	Questionnaire	Manufacturing & service firms	60.5

Capital Expenditure Evaluation: Capital expenditure, based on the projection of long-term cash inflows and outflows, is generally difficult to estimate. Thus capital expenditure decisions must be made with a high degree of subjective judgment and should be based upon a rational approach. In the Taiwan surveys, rational evaluation methods, commonly applied to capital expenditure decisions, were listed in the order of their popularity as follows:

(1) accounting rate of return,
(2) payback method,
(3) present value and
(4) internal rate of return.

The reasons for favouring the use of the accounting rate of return and payback method are, simply stated, practical. In the highly unstable political environment in many Asian countries, quick payback and high immediate returns are the way to deal with business risk. However, the net present value method and the internal rate of return method were also practised along with the two more popular ones, and may be used more and more as the political instability factor in Taiwan's economy plays a lesser role in determining the outcome of investment decisions. In the evaluation of capital expenditure projects, the adoption of a discount rate for discounting future cash flows is usually chosen to be the cost of the capital of the project or the firm's cost of capital. In addition, the income tax rate and the inflation rate might be considered by some firms in determining their discount rate. Table 9 indicates that more than 50 percent of the firms selected for surveys adopted at least one of the above four methods for evaluating capital expenditure projects.

Responsibility accounting system

To deal with the ever changing external environment, Taiwanese business enterprises like firms in other technologically advanced countries formulate an infrastructure in which responsibility centres are established with goals and plans. With different scopes of responsibility, responsibility centres may be classified into three types: cost centre, profit centre, and investment centre. Every type of responsibility centre pursues its established goals with a pre-determined plan, and the person in charge of a centre is responsible for the success or failure of the centre.

The practice of responsibility accounting in Taiwan is summarised in Table 10. The samples used for the studies, as indicated in Table 10, were mostly manufacturing companies, and data were collected from questionnaire surveys. Four aspects of responsibility accounting are presented below.

Table 10

SURVEYS OF ADOPTION OF RESPONSIBILITY ACCOUNTING SYSTEMS

Researchers	Year of Research	Sample Size	Data Collection	Type of firms Sampled	Adoption Rate
Chang, S. C.	1979	27	Questionnaire	General	30.0 %
Chiu & Chang	1979	59	Questionnaire	Manufacturing	45.7
Yan, L. Y.	1979	87	Questionnaire	Manufacturing	36.0
Liao, S. L.	1981	140	Questionnaire	Manufacturing	39.2
Tseng, H.	1985	52	Questionnaire	Electric equip. (local & international)	65.0
Lin, C. W.	1986	60	Questionnaire	Public firms	52.5
Yu, W. B.	1986	59	Questionnaire	General	52.5
Chang, Z. L.	1992	112	Interview	Manufacturing	42.9
Tsai, W. S.	1995	818	Questionnaire	Manufacturing & service	52.7

Adoption of Responsibility Centres: Although there is an increasing trend in practising responsibility centres by business firms in Taiwan, the concept is still not widely accepted. The main reason for not adopting and practising this concept, according to surveys, was the high cost of its implementation. High implementation costs might not be the real reason as it was also found that lack of expertise to implement the responsibility centre concept might have caused firms to be uncertain about the benefits to be derived from this practice. Table 10 indicates that a majority of firms in Taiwan had not practised responsibility accounting. According to the survey results (Yu, 1986; Chang, 1992; Tsai, 1995), firms in Taiwan practising responsibility accounting tended to use cost centres and profit centres more than investment centres.

Measurement of Responsibility Centres: Business enterprises in Taiwan measures performance in terms of net profit, although controllable profit by profit centres may be a better measure. Cost centres do not yield to the profit measure, and that explains the difficulty of adopting the cost centre concept by firms in Taiwan. Taiwanese firms have been practising centralised decision making and thus investment decisions have been vested with the board of the directors of the firm. This is the reason that management by investment centres has not been widely practised in Taiwanese firms. Based on the results of some surveys (Yu, 1986; Chang, 1992; Tsai, 1995), there were more financial measures of performance than non-financial measures. The commonly-adopted measures of cost-benefit are net income, contribution margins, controllable margins (the difference between revenues and controllable costs), and contributions by profit centres (controllable margin less direct or traceable fixed costs).

Cash Flow Management: Cash inflows and disbursements are, as a general practice in Taiwanese firms, managed centrally in the corporate headquarters. Even with a decentralised operational structure, business firms controlled cash management in the headquarters to achieve efficiency in the area of financial operation. This practice appears to weaken the authority of the responsibility centre managers and to defeat the purpose of responsibility centres.

Rewarding Systems: A reward system is essential for the success of implementing responsibility accounting. The study by Chang (1992) indicates that the companies using responsibility accounting would adopt a system to reward successful responsibility centres.

CONCLUSION

This chapter has provided some basic information on the financial and management accounting environment and practices in Taiwan. Basically, Taiwan accounting standards and practices are based upon US GAAP, but progress in the future is likely to be dominated by the increasing internationalisation of business. In particular, the following factors are likely to be influential in the development of Taiwanese accounting standards.

1. More foreign branches or subsidiaries will be established by Taiwan firms abroad and by foreigners in Taiwan.

2. International mergers and acquisitions and foreign currency exchange activities, e.g. hedging, risk, etc., will play more significant roles.
3. Taiwan may become established as an Asia-Pacific financial centre.
4. The interdependence between Mainland China and Taiwan is likely to become stronger.

Therefore, financial accounting issues are likely to become more sophisticated in the future. The harmonisation of accounting standards is an emerging issue in Taiwan. Current accounting procedures for handling consolidated financial statement and long-term investments require further improvements. Inter-company and inter-regional capital flows demand higher quality financial statements. Current accounting treatments for handling foreign currency exchanges and innovative derivative financial instruments are presently unable to fairly represent these complicated events. Improvements in accounting regulation are needed in all of these areas.

Likewise, management accounting is facing unprecedented challenges. Global competition, the rapid advancement of manufacturing technology, drastic swings in foreign exchange rates, total quality, right-sizing and just-in-time inventory — all of these demand more information to effectively control costs, determine product prices and provide value-added products or services to survive in a more competitive environment. Business firms in Taiwan have not, in general, maximised the benefits of management accounting. One reason for this is that the majority of firms in Taiwan are small-sized firms and owner-managers of these firms do not feel the need for sophisticated management accounting techniques to achieve proper control. Large companies are either monopolising the market or they are well protected by government regulations and, thus, they do not think that management accounting techniques are essential for their survival. Another reason for the failure to reap the benefits of good management accounting techniques is, unfortunately, the failure in teaching management accounting in colleges and universities. Colleges and universities taught management accounting based on textbooks written in the US and rarely attempted to modify the US materials to fit the needs of managers in Taiwan. No wonder, then, that business firms have been complaining that accounting students seemed to know a good deal of theory, but know nothing about applications.

Today, management accounting educators and practitioners in Taiwan must begin to work together to develop a set of techniques relevant to the needs of management in Taiwan. The following is an agenda for achieving this objective, pursued by both educators and professional organisations:

(1) Theoretical and practical management accounting education should be emphasised by increasing required semester credit hours at school and through the internship program.
(2) Graduate students should be encouraged to pursue research projects dealing with the practical problems of business firms.

(3) The interface between educators and practitioners should be promoted by holding seminars, round tables and panel discussions in which ideas about common concerns in management accounting practices can be discussed and exchanged.

This agenda addresses the problems faced by Taiwanese management accounting educators and may serve to direct researchers' attention to studying business problems and to produce relevant solutions.

REFERENCES

Anderson, H., Needles, Jr., B. and J. Caldwell (1989), *Managerial accounting,* Houghton Mifflin Company, Boston.

Beaver, W. (1989), *Financial reporting: An accounting revolution*, Prentice-Hall.

Chang, S. (1979), *A study of the performance evaluation of profit centres*, Graduate School of Business Administration, National Chengchi University, Taiwan, Unpublished Thesis (in Chinese).

Chang, Z. (1992), *The applications of management accounting for planning and control: An empirical study*, Graduate School of Accounting, Soo Chow University, Taiwan, Unpublished Thesis (in Chinese).

Chen, B. (1992), *A study of management accounting techniques in public enterprises*, Graduate School of Accounting, National Chengchi University, Taiwan, Unpublished Thesis (in Chinese).

Chen, C. (1980), *Management accounting*, Hwa-Tai Publishing Company, Taipei, Taiwan, (in Chinese).

Chen, J. (1986), *An empirical study of the functions of accounting information systems: electronic industries in Taiwan* (Taiwan, June), Unpublished Thesis (in Chinese).

Chiao, C. (1989), *Methods of assessment of business firms' goals, efficiency, and effectiveness: The case of Taiwanese large enterprises*, Graduate School of Business Administration, National Chiao Tung University, Taiwan, Unpublished Thesis (in Chinese).

Chiao, L. (1992), 'On improving the quality of accounting education', *Accounting research monthly*, Vol. 88, December, pp. 58–62, (in Chinese).

Dychman T.R., Dukes, R. F. and C.J. Davis (1992), *Intermediate accounting* (Revised edition), Irwin.

Hammer, L., Carter, W. and M. Usry (1994), *Cost accounting* (11th ed.), South-Western Co., Cincinnati, Ohio.

Holmstrom, B. (1979), 'Moral hazard and observability,' *Bell journal of economics*, Vol. 10, Spring, pp. 74–91.

Horngren, C., Foster, G. and S. Datar (1994), *Cost accounting – A managerial emphasis* (8th ed.), Prentice-Hall, Englewood Cliffs, N. J.

Hsu, T. (1987), *A study of the applications of capital budgeting by business firms,* Graduate School of Industrial Management, National Cheng Kung University, Taiwan, Unpublished Thesis (in Chinese).

Huang, J. (1990) and M. Wang, *Management accounting: Theory and practice,* Wu-Nan Publishing Company, (in Chinese).

Jensen, M.C., and W.H. Meckling (1986), 'Theory of the firm: Managerial behavior, agency costs and ownership structure,' *Journal of financial economics*, Vol. 3, October.

Johnson, H. and R. Kaplan (1984), *Relevance lost, the rise and fall of management accounting,* Harvard Business School Press, Boston, Massachusetts.

Kang, J. (1994a), 'Information intermediaries and public disclosure system', *Accounting research monthly,* September, Accounting Research and Development Foundation, Taipei.

Kang J. (1994b), 'Underpricing and the characteristics of initial public offerings', *Accounting research monthly,* November, Accounting Research and Development Foundation, Taipei.

Kang, J. (1995a), 'Theory of disclosure management', *Accounting research monthly,* Accounting Research and Development Foundation, Taipei.

Kang, J. (1995b), 'Mandatory financial forecasts and accounting regulation system', *Accounting research monthly,* August, Accounting Research and Development Foundation, Taipei.

Kaplan, R. (1984), 'The evolution of management accounting', *The accounting review,* LIX (3), July, pp. 390–418.

Li, C. (1989), 'The emerging trend of management accounting research', *Accounting research monthly,* Vol. 46, July, pp. 112–4, (in Chinese).

Li, F. (1993), *Contemporary management accounting* (7th ed.) Li, F. J. Publishing (in Chinese).

Liao, S. (1981), *A study of the functions of cost accounting in manufacturing companies,* Graduate School of Accounting, National Chengchi University, Taiwan, Unpublished Thesis (in Chinese).

Lin, C. (1984), *Management accounting,* Hua-Tai Publishing Company, (in Chinese).

Lin, C. (1986), *Accounting information systems to support decision making: An empirical study of public companies,* Graduate School of Business Administration, Tamkang University, Taiwan, Unpublished Thesis (in Chinese).

Lin, J. (1992), 'Issues and directions of the development of management accounting in Taiwan', *Management accounting,* Vol. 20, April, pp. 1–5, (in Chinese).

Lin, M. (1990), *A study of C-V-P applications in manufacturing industries,* Graduate School of Business Administration, National Chiao Tung University, Taiwan, Unpublished Thesis (in Chinese).

Lin, W. (1988), 'The newest direction of the development of management accounting', *Accounting research monthly,* Vol. 33, June, pp. 58–63, (in Chinese).

National Association of Accountants (1981), 'MAP committee promulgates definition of management accounting', *Management accounting,* January, pp. 58–9.

Pohr, J. (1932), 'Budgetary control and standard cost in industrial accounting', *The accounting review,* March, p. 31.

She, L. (1991), *A study of factors underlying capital expenditure decisions in multi-national companies,* Graduate School of Accounting, Soo Chow University, Taiwan, Unpublished Thesis (in Chinese).

She, S. (1986), *A study of capital expenditure decision and evaluation,* Taiwan, June, Unpublished Thesis (in Chinese).

Tsai, M. (1984), *A study of applications of management accounting in public companies,* Graduate School of Business Administration, Chinese Culture University, Taiwan, Unpublished Thesis (in Chinese).

Tsai, W. (1995), *An investigative study of management accounting education and practice in Taiwan* (A report to National Science Council, Taiwan, March), Unpublished Thesis (in Chinese).

Tseng, H. (1985), *Analysis of the effectiveness of accounting information usage: A empirical study of Taiwanese and foreign companies in the electric instruments industries,* Graduate School of Accounting, National Chengchi University, Unpublished Thesis (in Chinese).

Tu, R. (1989), 'Analysis of the differences between theory and practice', *Accounting research monthly,* Vol. 48, September, pp. 50–1, (in Chinese).

Wang, K. (1988), *A study of manufacturing companies' capital budgeting practice and effectiveness in Taiwan,* Graduate School of Business Administration, National Sun Yat-Sen University, Taiwan, Unpublished Thesis (in Chinese).

Wang, Y. (1992), 'The developments and changes in management accounting', *Accounting research monthly,* Vol. 77, February, pp. 43–7, (in Chinese).

Wang, Y. (1993), 'Renovation of management accounting for manufacturing industries', *Accounting research monthly,* Vol. 96, August, pp. 25–7, (in Chinese).

Yan, L. (1979), *A study of applications of accounting information to managerial decisions in Taiwan,* Graduate School of Business Administration, National Chengchi University, Taiwan, Unpublished Thesis (in Chinese).

Yeh, F. (1984), *Risk analysis of capital expenditures,* Graduate School of Accounting, Soo Chow University, Taiwan, Unpublished Thesis (in Chinese).

Yong, J. (1991), *Evaluation of investment risk of multi-national high-tech companies in Taiwan,* Graduate School of Accounting, National Chengchi University, Taiwan, Unpublished Thesis (in Chinese).

Yong, L. (1983), *The behavioral assumptions of management accounting practice in Taiwan,* Graduate School of Accounting, National Chengchi University, Taiwan, Unpublished Thesis (in Chinese).

Yu, W. (1986), *A study of theory and practice of responsibility accounting,* Graduate School of Business Administration, National Sun Yat-Sen University, Taiwan.

Zen, K. (1995), *The relationship between operating performance and earnings management,* Unpublished thesis, National Chengchi University.

Zuo, R.P. (1994), *Media disclosure management: The characteristics of timeliness relating to financial accounting information,* Unpublished thesis, National Chengchi University.

ACCOUNTING REGULATION AND PRACTICE IN THAILAND

*Mahmud Hossain and Mike Adams**

BACKGROUND

Thailand lies in mainland South-east Asia between latitudes 6° and 20°N, bordering Cambodia and Loas to the east, Myanmar to the north and west, and Malaysia to the south. It consists of a long isthmus stretching towards Malaysia, mountain ranges on the Myanmar border, the Korat plateau bordering Loas and a fertile river valley in the extensive central plains around the Chao Phraya which runs into the Gulf of Siam. The isthmus region is tropical, hot and humid throughout the year. The main central parts of the country are subject to the influence of the monsoon, being wet and warm between May and September, and dry and cool between November and March. The eastern mountains have a rain shadow effect on the central plains but these are irrigated by water from the Chao Phraya. The Korat plateau is semi-arid. The most important resource at the present time is the fertility of the central plain. Timber resources, once substantial, have been reduced by deforestation. There are a number of relatively minor mineral deposits, and in recent years significant reserves of natural gas and phosphate have been discovered. Small reserves of oil have also been found.

The area of what is now modern Thailand was peopled in late prehistory by Mon Khmers from western China, possibly displacing earlier Austronesian populations and later becoming Hinduised. The Thais, who about 2000 years ago had established the

*The authors are from Massey University, New Zealand, and Glasgow University, UK, respectively.

kingdom of Nan Chao in the Yunnan province of China, expanded southward, assimilating the Mons from the 9th Century. By the 13th Century, Nan Chao had fallen to the Mongols and the Thais established their homeland in the valley of the Chao Phraya. Here, Indian culture was assimilated via the Mon Khmers and Thai miltary influence extended to its neighbours in Cambodia, Mayanmar and Malaysia. Although never a colony of a European power, Thailand's history has been considerably affected by European colonial policy. After an early flirtation with Portugal and France, a period of deliberate isolation ended with the destruction of the nation's capital, Ayudhya, by the Burmese. The capital was moved to Bangkok in 1782 and for the colonial period in South-east Asia, Thailand fell mainly within the British sphere of influence, avoiding colonial status partly through the need for a buffer between British and French interests and partly through the political abilities of successive Thai monarchs. During the period up to the late 1930s, Bangkok grew into an important trading centre benefiting from the rice trade. A bureaucracy developed which extended control over the remoter areas of Thailand and led to the development of an educated elite who were instrumental in the bloodless coup that ended the monarchy in 1932. Most indigenous Thais were still rural peasants, with the Chinese, many of whom had migrated in the 19th Century, forming the basis of the working and entrepreneurial classes. In the lead up to the Second World War, Thailand aligned itself with the Japanese and, as a result of this, suffered less privations than some other areas of the region. In the aftermath of the war, the government through to 1972 was pro-US and authoritarian, the post-war democratic constitution having been abrogated in 1952. Thailand became an important focus of US military strategy in the Vietnam War. The resulting development in infrastructure and the capitalist economic policies it encouraged (through US investment) had the effect of bringing about great social changes, particularly through the movement of the rural peasantry to Bangkok. During the years after the Vietnam War, the country switched between experiments in democratic processes and autocracy. The 1991 Constitution provides for the democratic institutions of a constitutional monarchy with a bicameral legislature consisting of an appointed Senate of 270 members (with power of veto only) and an elected House of Representatives of 360 members. Executive power resides with the Prime Minister and his Cabinet. The judicial system is based upon a combination of code and common law elements. The present population of more than 58 million (a density of about 114 per sq. km), consists mainly of ethnic Thais with between one and two million Muslims, mostly Malays in the southern regions, and small numbers of other indigenous groups. Most ethnic Chinese (possibly 20 percent of the population) have adopted Thai citizenship. Theravada Buddhism is the main religion, with small representations of Christianity, Confucianism and Islam in the south. Apart from Thai, English is spoken as a second language by the educated elite.

In the last ten years, Thailand has been one of the fastest growing economies in the world. GDP growth has been between 7 and 9 percent per annum since 1986. GDP in 1992 was approximately US$ 110 billion or just under US$ 2000 per capita. Although still a mainly agricultural economy, with two-thirds of the working population being employed in this sector, only 11 percent of GDP was attributable to agriculture in 1993, the main products being rice, sugar cane, fish and rubber. Nevertheless, agriculture is an *important export earner, providing almost 30 percent of export earnings in 1991 (Thailand is the world's leading exporter of rice). Timber now has to be imported due to a ban on commercial logging due to deforestation. Manufactures of textiles, electronic equipment and other items make up the bulk of the remaining exports and contribute about 30 percent to GDP. Natural gas production is sufficient to meet 30 percent of domestic demand, but petroleum finds have so far been small. About 50 percent of GDP in 1992 was attributable to the service sectors and tourism is the chief source of foreign currency. The need to import machinery and consumer goods usually leads to a balance of trade and current account deficit. This was, for a time, financed by overseas loans so that overseas debt in 1990 amounted to more than US$ 26 billion but recent budget surpluses have reduced the debt to GDP ratio. Since 1986, considerable funds have been invested in Thailand by Japan, Hong Kong, Taiwan, Singapore, the US and the EU. Thailand's main trading partners are Japan, the US, Singapore, the EU and other nations of the Asian Pacific region. Apart from reducing overseas debt levels further, the main problems facing the Thai economy are preserving access to raw materials for its manufacturing industries, competing against newly emerging low-cost neighbours in its region and developing its infrastructure, the backward state of which is likely to discourage foreign investment. Another non-economic factor is the effect of rapid development on culture and the environment which the Thai authorities have shown by several policy pronouncements to be of concern to them. The unit of currency is the baht.*

R.J.W.

INTRODUCTION

In this chapter, the developments in Thailand's regulatory environment are outlined, and the important role played by accounting in the burgeoning Thai economy examined. In particular, the development of accounting regulation, formulation of accounting-based stock exchange rules, the increasing influence of professional accounting standards, and the prospects for management accounting are considered. It is contended that Thailand's rapid economic growth is likely to further the demand for generally accepted accounting practice (GAAP), and the acquisition of new skills among accountancy practitioners. The important part played by United States (US) investment in the country, and the preference of Thai authorities for US-type accounting practices also suggests that future progress is likely to continue to be based on the US model.

ACCOUNTING REGULATION IN THAILAND

Accounting regulation and practice in Thailand does not have a long history like that of countries such as the UK and the US (Priebjrivat, 1992). Prior to the 1960s, accounting in Thailand was largely a simple bookkeeping function performed for the internal use of managers and to satisfy the purposes of taxation legislation. However, this state-of-affairs is changing as a result of recent economic growth and industrial development (Tay, 1994). Presently, accounting practices of corporate bodies are controlled by:

(1) regulations introduced by government ministries;
(2) guidelines of the Securities' Exchange of Thailand (SET), and associated securities legislation; and
(3) the accounting standards of the Institute of Certified Accountants and Auditors of Thailand (ICAAT), and international accountancy bodies. The impact of each of these three institutions on corporate accounting in Thailand is examined further below.

Ministerial regulation

Thailand's Ministry of Commerce requires all corporations and registered partnerships to establish and maintain proper accounting records, and to have their annual financial statements audited by certified (i.e., licensed) auditors. In 1976, the Ministry of Commerce issued Regulation No. 2 (BE 2519), which prescribes formats and minimum disclosures for the profit and loss account and balance sheet, but does not cover the treatment of accounting items. This regulation seeks to standardise the financial reporting practices of Thailand-based companies, and thereby promote the confidence of investors, particularly those from overseas.

Thailand's taxation legislation also requires consistency between financial and tax reporting if any allowances are to be claimed back from the inland revenue department. Thus, as with some European countries, such as France and Germany, taxation regulations can have an important influence on the financial reporting practices of Thai businesses. Indeed, Tay (1994) writes that many aspects of Thai law ' . . . appears to have been influenced by Franco-Germanic practices, with the result that the accounts produced, especially by non-quoted companies, are sometimes of more use for tax purposes than for financial analysis' (p. 204). Moreover, like many developing countries, Thailand's public sector has traditionally been financed mainly from the revenues of indirect taxes and customs duties, which require relatively unsophisticated national taxation accounting systems (Holzer & Tremblay, 1973). More recently, the emerging importance of direct taxation in the funding of the activities of the Thai public sector has led not only to better tax accounting within organisations, but also to improved inland revenue service accounting systems. In addition, increasing numbers of qualified accountants have been employed to manage the national tax accounting systems.

In 1978, the Thai Government passed the Public Companies Act (BE 2521) in order to facilitate growth of the domestic stock market. There is considerable overlap between the 1978 Act and Ministerial Regulation No. 2, particularly with regard to the form and content of the published annual financial statements, and the requirement for them to be subject to audit each year. The 1978 Act requires that the annual reports of Thai public companies include information pertaining to their ownership of subsidiaries and private companies, the value of directors' shareholdings, and details of contracts between the company and its directors (Tay, 1994). The 1978 Act also prescribes that companies use at least 5 percent of annual earnings to create a non-distributable reserve, until that reserve constitutes 25 percent of the nominal value registered capital. Furthermore, under the 1978 Act, companies must file a copy of their audited annual report with Thailand's Registrar of Companies within one month of the annual general meeting.

Securities Exchange of Thailand (SET)

The development of the capital market in Thailand began with the establishment of the Bangkok Stock Exchange (BSE) in 1962. The BSE was the first organised stock exchange in Thailand, and initially there was very little share trading on the market. In 1969, the Thai Government — with the assistance of US Securities and Exchange Commission (SEC) — reorganised the BSE, and five years later passed the Securities Exchange of Thailand Act (1974). This Act established a new regulatory body — the Securities Exchange of Thailand (SET) — which had the primary objective of mobilising domestic and international capital in order to finance industrial development and national economic growth. The SET commenced operations in April 1975 by trading in the shares of 14 public companies. By June 1994, the volume of trade had grown to include trading in the shares of 408 listed companies from all sectors of the economy, including 16 in banking, 38 in finance and securities, 21 in insurance, 13 in commerce, 40 in the agribusiness, 27 in building and furnishing materials, among many others. By September 1991, market capitalisation on the Thai stock exchange amounted to approximately US$32 billions (Kulick and Wilson, 1992).

Moreover, foreign investment has played an important role in the rapid growth of SET. Prior to 1986, investment in SET by foreign investors was small and accounted for roughly 8 percent of total turnover of the market (*Economist*, 1990). The main restrictions faced by foreign investors were the various statutory limitations placed on foreign ownership by the alien business laws. For example, under these laws, foreign ownership in corporate equities was restricted generally to a maximum of 49 percent of issued share capital. However, such limit varies depending on the type of industry within which the entity operates. For instance, in the case of bank and finance companies, foreign ownership was limited to 25 percent of issued share capital. Recently, statutory restrictions on foreign ownership have been relaxed in order to attract foreign investment in Thailand. Indeed, like indigenous companies, overseas-controlled corporations are eligible to apply for, and to receive, generous subsidies and tax incentives from (Tay 1994). Despite these initiatives, the Thai Government does not currently plan to develop the country as an offshore financial centre, like Hong Kong and Singapore (Kulick & Wilson, 1992).

Like every major international stock market, the SET is governed by a set of rules and regulations designed to make the market fair and open to all investors. The SET's regulations are modelled on the US model, and in particular the recommendations of Professor Sidney M. Robbins, a former chief economist of the US SEC, who was appointed by the Thai Government in the early 1970s to make proposals as to the development of the Thai stock market. Indeed, the 1973 Robbins Report provided the basis for the Securities Exchange of Thailand Act (1974), and its administration under Thailand's Ministry of Finance (MOF). The Robbins Report also recommended the establishment of the Securities Exchange Commission of Thailand (SECT) to oversee the regulation of the stock market, and to promote the development of improved corporate disclosure requirements. Together with the SET, the SECT has assumed responsibility for developing the domestic stock market, and seeks to prevent unfair trade practices, such as insider trading. Indeed, provisions to provide greater investor protection exist under both SET rules and the Securities Exchange of Thailand Act (1974). Nonetheless, despite such rules, regulations and good intentions, some commentators (e.g., Priebjrivat, 1992) contend that the enforcement of provisions against perpetrators of insider trading, and other abuses, has been somewhat lax in practice. Companies which seek quotation on the SET are also required to provide information with regard to the operations of the company, namely its profitability, capitalisation, growth and prospects, so that outside investors are able to make better informed judgements. The financial reporting requirements of the SET undoubtedly have led to the increasing importance of accounting in the Thai economy (Tay, 1994). Specifically, the SET requires its corporate members to make quarterly and annual financial statements and disclose certain accounting information as follows:

(i) *Quarterly returns:* these must be audited by a certified auditor within 45 days from the end of each quarter, and typically such returns include income statements and balance sheets for the most recent quarter and the equivalent calendar quarter of the previous year.

(ii) *Annual reports:* these must also be audited by a certified auditor and submitted to the SET within four months from the end of the accounting period. The SET requires that the annual report contains two consecutive years' financial information prepared in accordance with the requirements of Ministerial Regulation No. 2, the Public Companies Act (1978), and accounting standards promulgated by the Institute of Certified Accountants and Auditors of Thailand (ICAAT). In cases where standards do not exist, the SET requires that companies follow the practices of the International Accounting Standards Committee (IASC) and the US Financial

Accounting Standards Board (FASB). Under SET rules, the notes to financial statements must also disclose other information, such as collateral for loans, restrictions imposed by debt covenants, and other company obligations affecting shareholders' benefits. The annual reports prepared by SET members should also incorporate a report from the chairperson of the company, including details of business activities and key financial results for the year.

In addition to the above requirements, a publicly-listed (or SET-authorised) company is required to file separate annual returns to the SET within three months from the end of the financial year. This information should include:

(i) *General information*: for example, company name, address, amounts of listed or authorised securities; description of business and results.
(ii) *Segmental disclosures*: for example, subsidiary and associated company activities, value of shareholdings in subsidiaries; percentage of voting rights held in subsidiary and associated companies.
(iii) *Details of corporate shareholders*: for example, their number and distribution; principal shareholders, and the value and number of executive share ownership schemes.
(iv) *Particulars of executive officers and directors*: for example, names, date of employment, business experience, and their interest in transactions in which the company is also a party.

Accounting standards

Generally, the accounting principles and practices of the IASC and US FASB are widely recognised in Thailand. Strictly speaking, however, it is the accounting methods and disclosure requirements prescribed by Thai law, plus the promulgations of ICAAT, which constitute Thai GAAP. Corporate compliance with Thai accounting standards is monitored by the Ministry of Commerce and reinforced by ministry regulations. Since the early 1980s, the ICAAT has issued the 16 statements on Thai accounting principles and practice shown in Table 1. These are based largely on the promulgations of the IASC. Additionally, there are 31 authoritative audit guidelines in place modelled on US auditing practices, and the ICAAT is developing more of these in order to improve the standard of corporate audits in Thailand (Akathaporn *et al.*, 1993; Tay, 1994).

THAILAND'S ACCOUNTANCY PROFESSION

The ICAAT was established in 1948 as an independent professional body, and as at the end of 1994 it had approximately 900 members. The present structure of the

Table 1

STATEMENTS ON THAI ACCOUNTING PRINCIPLES

1. Basic Assumptions on Accounting.
2. Accounting Policies.
3. Extra-ordinary Items.
4. Accounting Changes.
5. Earnings per share.
6. Revenue Recognition.
7. Leasing-Lessor Arrangements.
8. Long-Term Contract.
9. Accounting for Land, Buildings and Equipments.
10. Depreciation.
11. Bad Debts and Allowance for Bad Debts.
12. Marketable Securities.
13. Disclosure for Related Companies.
14. Research and Development Costs.
15. Interest Capitalization.
16. Current Assets and Current Liabilities.

ICAAT comprises an executive board, plus six sub-committees with responsibilities for financial accounting, auditing, taxation, ethics, management accounting, and professional education and development. The accounting and auditing sub-committees are the largest, with 18 members representing public practice, academia and the government sector. The financial accounting sub-committee is responsible for researching emergent accounting issues, developing new accounting standards, and issuing exposure drafts to members and others, prior to approval by the board of the ICAAT. Following the approval of an accounting standard, the Board of Supervision of Auditing Practices (BSAP) is responsible for monitoring whether ICAAT members comply with extant accounting promulgations. Thus, the accounting standard-setting process in Thailand mirrors closely that of the US, UK, and other Western countries.

Whilst the ICAAT was formed in 1948, the auditing profession was not formally recognised by the Thai Government until 1962. Thailand's Auditor Act (1962) was passed in order to establish and regulate standards for the academic qualifications and experience requirements of public certified auditors. The 1962 Act also formally established the BSAP whose 15 members control and monitor Thailand's auditing profession. The monitoring function performed by the BSAP mainly entails:

(1) setting and marking licensing examinations for auditors twice a year; and

(2) monitoring the annual reports prepared by all publicly-listed companies operating in Thailand for compliance with GAAP. To be eligible to sit the licensing examination, candidates must hold a Bachelors Degree in Accounting, be a Thai national of least 20 years of age, and have a minimum of 2000 hours relevant auditing/accounting experience. In this regard, Thai arrangements for licensing

auditors is similar to the US system for qualifying Certified Practising Accountants (CPAs). Holders of a Thai auditing licence are expected to abide by the ICAAT's Code of Ethics (1968) (which is based on the US Code of Professional Conduct), audit at least five companies per annum, and attend continuing professional courses offered by the ICAAT. Certified auditors in Thailand also have to apply for the renewal of their licences every five years. Some accounting education is available at the secondary school level in Thailand (Holzer and Tremblay, 1973). However, the majority of Thai accountancy students normally follow a four-year university degree or diploma at a technical college. The first accountancy programme at a tertiary establishment in Thailand was launched in 1938 at the University of Thammasat. In 1993, there were 30 universities and technical colleges offering accountancy programmes, with some universities offering doctoral programmes. Many Thai accounting academics have studied in the US, and indeed, some Thai universities (e.g., Chulalongkorn University) have long-established collaborative programmes with prestigious US business schools (Akathaporn et al., 1993).

In their study, Akathaporn et al. (1993) explore perceived underlying problems facing accounting education and practice. A survey of accounting educators and practising accountants in Thailand was conducted to compile the necessary information and to make recommendations for improvement. Survey questionnaires was mailed to 437 accountants, comprising 78 accounting academics, 120 government accountants and 239 accountants from the corporate sector. Of these, 285 questionnaires were returned, representing an overall response rate of 65 percent. The survey evidence identified three groups of factors which respondents felt to have obstructed the development of accounting education and practice in Thailand, namely: (a) educational factors; (b) professional factors; (c) other factors.

Educational factors

With regard to educational factors, Akathaporn et al's 1993 survey suggests that:

(i)   the existing accounting curriculum is perceived to be irrelevant;
(ii) there is an acute shortage of qualified accounting instructors; and
(iii) there is a lack of suitable accounting textbooks, particularly printed in the Thai language. Concerning the accounting curriculum, the respondents indicated that the content of present accounting programmes are not maintained in a manner which keeps pace with the rapidly changing business environment, and that overall, accounting education falls considerably short of the current and future needs of the Thai economy. Furthermore, the survey evidence reports that there is an insufficient number of accounting textbooks written in the Thai language, and that this is a major problem as the level of English proficiency of most Thai students is generally low.

Professional factors

Akathaporn *et al.* (1993) also cite that there has been a traditional lack of public recognition and respect for accountants in Thai society. They suggest that a major reason for this is that most businesses in Thailand are characterised by a large number of small and medium-sized family-owned firms where there is a strong degree of owner-management control. Senior executives, middle mangers, and owners of these businesses find accounting difficult to both understand and to apply effectively to the needs of their businesses. Thai business people often consider accounting information to be necessary only for computing taxation liabilities, and for completing and filing tax returns, and other statutory accounts. Akathaporn *et al*'s survey also found that because accounting standards issued by the ICAAT do not have statutory backing, there is little incentive for many companies to comply with accounting standards. Respondents also indicated that because the ICAAT is perceived to be inactive in professional activities, it does not have the respect and the support of many people from the accounting profession, academia and the business community in Thailand. Moreover, some respondents expressed concerns with regard to other issues, such as the perceived irrelevance of accounting and auditing standards, insufficient education and training facilities and the lack of accountability of the ICAAT to its membership.

A lack of sufficient number of accounting publications is perceived to be a major problem. The survey indicated that, overall, the Thai accounting community is not well informed about new accounting issues and developments in practice. Furthermore, the ICAAT's Accountants Journal does not have a wide circulation, thus limiting the scope for debate, interaction and exchange of ideas among accountants.

Other factors

Akathaporn *et al.* (1993) report that the lack of government support for accounting and the accountancy profession is the most significant issue which has obstructed the development of accounting education and practice in Thailand. They argue that future progress in accounting education and practice is likely to be achieved only as a result of greater government support, particularly with regard to statutory backing for accounting standards. Another problem cited was the negative influence of social and cultural factors on the accounting profession. Compared with other professional groups, such as lawyers and doctors, the accounting profession is not held in high esteem by Thai society. The key factors contributing to this widely-held public perception include: the low usage by Thai managers of accounting information in the making of business decisions; the generally unsophisticated nature of accounting systems in Thai companies; and the perceived lack of professionalism and ethical behaviour of some accountants and auditors. The underlying influence of the local cultural tradition in the development of accounting and accounting information systems is well-documented in the academic literature. For instance, Baydoun and

Willett (1995) suggest ' . . . cultural differences may lead to many specific differences in the requirements of users of accounting information . . .' (p. 84). For example, in Thailand the philosophy of Buddhist religion, rather than economic rationalism, frequently influences why and how people make decisions.

MANAGEMENT ACCOUNTING IN THAILAND

The importance of management accounting in helping managers to better plan and to control their organisations becomes evident particularly in the early stages of a country's economic development (Holzer and Tremblay, 1973). To date, Thailand has not developed separate standards or guidelines on management accounting, and thus the quality of management accounting, and the expertise of management accountants, in Thailand varies greatly between entities. As mentioned previously, this situation probably reflects the fact that most indigenous businesses are small or medium-sized family-owned enterprises, in which accounting information has not been traditionally perceived as being important to effective management decision making. As a consequence, in the majority of indigenous Thai-owned companies, formal management accounting practices simply do not exist. Furthermore, in many indigenous companies, even financial accounting systems are likely to be poorly developed (Tay, 1994). This situation could reflect the lack of suitably trained managers and accounting staff (Holzer and Tremblay, 1973). Some researchers (e.g., Perera, 1989) argue further that Western-type accounting systems have little relevance to developing countries because indigenous cultures frequently perceive uses for accounting information which are fundamentally different from those of developed countries. As stated previously, in Thailand, business decisions are often made in the best interests of the family or the Buddhist religion, rather than purely economic reasons. However, it is likely that users of accounting information in developed and developing societies will also have a growing number of information requirements in common, particularly as finance and trade become more internationalised (Baydoun and Willett, 1995).

However, three important factors appear to underscore the emerging importance of management accounting in Thailand. First, the recent growth in the size of Thai-owned companies, the increasing incidence of joint ventures, and the establishment of large multinational enterprises in the country, is leading to more interest among Thailand's business community in management accounting issues so that they can better manage business growth. Second, the raising of capital through the Thai stock exchange and overseas underpins recent corporate growth. The functioning of such markets requires information about the underlying corporate structures and its prospects, which necessitates improvements in management accounting information systems, as well as systems for taxation and financial reporting. Third, it is becoming increasingly apparent among some politicians and sections of the Thai accounting community that the performance of the government sector has to be measured in a more tangible (i.e., profit-orientated) way than has hitherto been the case. Like in the corporate sector, the demand for better accounting and more transparent record-keeping has led to considerable interest in cost management techniques, such as costing, budgeting and performance measurement, and to developing the skills of management accountants.

Bailes (1990) carried out a survey of management accounting practices in the Thai corporate sector. In general, his results suggest that subsidiaries of foreign companies are relatively more developed in using advanced management accounting techniques compared with Thai-owned firms of equivalent size. His survey focused particularly on the nature of the budgeting systems employed in Thailand-based companies, and he compares these results with those reported in a similar study carried out by Asada *et al* (1989) on US and Japanese management accounting practice. In Bailes' (1990) study, a survey questionnaire was mailed to the company controller or accounting manager of each of the 500 largest companies operating in Thailand. Completed questionnaires were returned by 98 companies, representing a response rate of 20 percent. The major findings obtained from Bailes' (1990) survey are as follows.

Type of budgets used

The survey evidence indicated that only two-thirds of Thai companies use a master budget, compared with 93 percent of Japanese companies and 91 percent of US companies cited by Asada *et al* (1989). Bailes (1990) attributed this phenomenon to the relatively underdeveloped nature of the Thai economy compared with Japan and the US. As pointed out previously, such a finding could also reflect the proportionately low numbers of qualified management accounting staff in the Thai corporate sector, and the lack of managers adequately trained in cost management techniques (Holzer and Tremblay, 1973; Perera, 1989; Tay, 1994).

Logistics of budget preparation

Bailes' (1990) survey reported that the average number of days spent in preparing the annual budget was 49 days, which is much lower than for Japanese and American companies. This situation could reflect a lesser degree of thoroughness in budget preparation in Thai companies, due to several factors, such as a simpler budgetary process, less resources and commitment devoted to budgeting, and low numbers of professionally qualified accountants compared with Japanese and US companies. Interestingly, Thai firms held four meetings on average to discuss the budget, which was the same as in US companies which have more complex budgetary procedures, and twice as many as that held by managers in Japanese companies. This finding could reflect the trait of Thai culture which involves managers in considerably more protracted discussions and deliberations in business matters compared with their counterparts in Western companies (Kulick and Wilson, 1992).

Management participation in budgeting

In addition, subjects responding to Bailes' (1990) survey were asked to assess the extent of managerial participation in the budgetary process. The results suggest that the majority of Thai managers have some involvement in the formal discussions of the budget committee more than 50 percent of the time, which was roughly comparable to those managers of Japanese companies, but considerably less than in US companies. This finding therefore suggests that there could be scope for educating corporate management further in budgets and budgetary control, and involving them to a greater extent in the budgetary process than has hitherto been the case.

CONCLUSION AND FUTURE PROSPECTS

Thailand has experienced rapid economic growth and industrial development over the last two decades or so. Accounting regulation has played, and continues to perform, an important role in managing economic activity and facilitating the flow of capital investment in the Thai economy. Both the development of accounting regulation and the education and training of Thailand's accountancy profession has been influenced greatly by Western (particularly US) practices. It is expected that accounting and accountants will play an increasingly important role in the future management and development of Thailand's economy. In particular, developments in the application and use of Western-type management accounting practices, such as budgeting and performance measurement, are likely to figure prominently in future management activities both in the public and private sectors. Despite the scope for improvement in regulation and accounting practice, the state of development of accounting in Thailand is reported to be more advanced than in some other developing countries (Holzer and Tremblay, 1973). This situation is attributed largely to Thailand's rapid economic growth, and the influence which Western capital and enterprise has played, and will continue to play, in that development.

The reason why Thailand has developed Franco-German practices in some respects, such as taxation law, and Anglo-American approaches in issues of accounting measurement and disclosure is an interesting empirical question which arises from this and other reviews of accounting in Thailand. It is plausible that since Thailand was not colonised by European powers in the 19th Century in the same way as some other countries of the region, such as Malaysia and Vietnam, it was able to choose practices which match more closely its cultural, social and economic requirements. It is also plausible that choice of legal and accounting structures could reflect the

Hofstede-Gray schema that the nature of accounting practices reflect cultural determinants in the local environment. For example, Baydoun and Willett (1995) cite that French accounting systems are associated with high uniformity and low professionalism, while Anglo-American accounting systems reflect the reverse. Thus, locally uniform systems of indirect taxation could have led Thai authorities to adopt the Franco-Germanic style of tax law, whereas accounting issues requiring professional judgement, such as that exercised with regard to the form and content of financial statements, may have suggested that Anglo-American practices were more appropriate. The application of theoretical frameworks of the sort described above to the form and development of accounting in Thailand could thus offer researchers a fruitful basis for future empirical research.

REFERENCES

Akathaporn, P., Novin, A.M. and M.J. Abdolmohammadi (1993), 'Accounting education and practice in Thailand: Perceived problems and effectiveness of enhancement strategies', *The international journal of accounting*, Vol. 28, No. 3, pp. 259–72.

Asada, T., Bailes, J.C. and M. Amano (1989), 'Empirical differences between Japanese and American budget and performance evaluation systems', Working Paper, Oregon State University, USA.

Bailes, J.C. (1990), 'Budget preparation and goals in Thailand', Paper presented at the Second Asian-Pacific Conference on International Accounting Issues, October 10–3, Vancouver, BC., Canada.

Baydoun, N. and R. Willett (1995), 'Cultural relevance of Western accounting systems to developing countries', *Abacus*, Vol. 31, No. 1, pp. 67–92.

Economist (1990), *How to win in emerging stock markets*, The Economist Publications, London.

Euromoney (1990), *Asia Pacific Investment Guide*, Euromoney Publications, London.

Holzer, H.P. and D. Tremblay (1973), 'Accounting and economic development: The case of Thailand and Tunisia', *The international journal of accounting*, Vol. 9, No. 1, pp. 67–80.

Kulick, E. and R. Wilson (1992), *Thailand's turn: Profile of a new dragon*, Macmillan Press, London.

Perera, M.H.B. (1989), 'Accounting in developing countries: A case for localised uniformity', *British accounting review*, Vol. 21, No. 2. pp. 141–58.

Priebjrivat, A. (1992), *Corporate disclosure: A case of the securities exchange of Thailand*, Unpublished doctoral thesis, Stern School of Business, New York University, NY, USA.

Tay, J.S.W. (1994), 'Thailand', *Financial reporting in the west Pacific Rim*, Cooke, T.E. and R.H. Parker, (eds.), Routledge Publications, London.

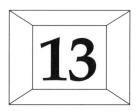

ACCOUNTING IN INDONESIA

Joselito Diga and Hadori Yunus[*]

BACKGROUND

Indonesia is an archipelago of about 13 600 islands to the south of mainland Asia, north of Australia, covering an area of nearly two million sq. km. The main islands, straddling the equator between 5°55'N and 11°S and stretching over 4800 km from west to east, are Java, Sumatra, Bali, Kalimantan, Sulawesi, Irian Jaya, the Moluccas and Timor. The capital Jakarta is situated in Java. High mountains skirt the southern edge of Sumatra, Java, the northern region of Kalimantan, Sulawesi and Irian Jaya. Elsewhere, much of the lowland areas are swampy or acidic, although there are important fertile, alluvial plains in places such as Java and Bali, based upon volcanic deposits. The climate of Indonesia is maritime tropical, hot and with plentiful rainfall evenly distributed throughout the year, with a few exceptions. Indonesia possesses extensive reserves of coal, oil, natural gas and timber. There are also usable reserves of nickel, bauxite, gold and copper and other minerals.

Indonesia was populated in prehistory by Melanesians who were pushed towards the eastern areas by Malayo Polynesian peoples about 5000 years ago. These two groups still form the dominant racial stock of Indonesia today. The underlying cultural patterns of Indonesia have been significantly affected by those of the Indian subcontinent. The Hindu empire of Srivijaya, based in Sumatra, Malaya and Majapahit in Java, controlled most of the Indonesian archipelago until the 15th Century. By 1450, Hindu and Buddhist ideologies had been displaced as the official forms of worship by Islam, although there is some fusion of these faiths with older animistic belief systems. These turned into a variety of

*Department of Commerce, Australian National University, Canberra, Australia; and Department of Accounting, Gadjah Mada University, Indonesia respectively.

forms which contributed to giving Indonesian society an appearance of great cultural diversity. Indonesia was a Protestant Dutch colony from the 16th Century until 1941, and became independent following the withdrawal of Japanese troops in 1945. The present constitutional policy of Pancasila (consensus, tolerance and unity) provides for a political system in which the President, as head of the executive, exercises considerable influence over the legislature. A periodically elected unicameral House of Representatives of 500 members (supplemented with Presidential appointees) is the official legislative body — while the People's Assembly (Majelis Permusyawaratan Rakyat) meets every five years to appoint the President and Vice-President as well as formulate official policy. The army holds a special place in the Indonesian constitution. The legal system is based upon Roman-Dutch law. The Criminal Law is codified, applying equally to all, but application of the Civil Law depends upon membership of one of three groups: Muslim, European and Alien Orientals (a classification which owes something to the Dutch colonial influence). The judicial system gives wide powers to the Shari'a courts over Muslims in civil matters, although Muslims have the right to elect to be dealt with by the secular courts. Today, apart from indigenous Indonesians there are about three million ethnic Chinese living in the country. Nearly 90 percent of the entire population are Muslims, with the remaining 10 percent being predominantly Christian. The main language is a form of Malay referred to as Bahasa Indonesia, although at least 25 languages (including Javanese) are spoken in the islands. English is a commonly spoken foreign language. Indonesia today has a population of around 195 million people — a density of approximately 98 persons per sq. km, although the bulk of the population is found in Java.

The Indonesian economy is of a capitalist type but with a significant element of central planning. From 1980–91, the estimated GDP per head rose 5.5 percent annually, accelerating to around seven percent per year from 1992–95, while the population increased at an annual average rate of 1.8 percent. Since 1969, under the 'New Order' of President Surharto, a series of rolling five-year plans (Repelita) succeeded in achieving relatively high and stable economic growth rates with a current account deficit (arising from the import of services) being financed by foreign aid and long-term investment. The main characteristic of the policies followed was to diversify agriculture, mining and manufactured products, to reduce dependence on oil and gas export revenues and, in particular, to expand production in labour intensive industries. This has been achieved against the backdrop of the deregulation of the financial sectors of the economy and tight monetary policies which have on occasion seen interest rates rise to more than 30 percent. Due to massive amounts of investment in infrastructure, the level of publicly guaranteed overseas debt has increased considerably since the 1960s (US$60 billion in 1991), and its control through greater domestic, private investment will presumably be required in the future to maintain the impetus of the last two decades. The changing structure of the Indonesian economy is reflected in the fact that manufacturing became the largest sector in terms of GDP, which was ahead of agriculture for the first time in 1991. Nevertheless, the agricultural sector still employs more than half of the working population, which to some extent reflects deliberate policy. In recent years, Indonesia has become self sufficient in rice production, having once been the world's largest importer of rice. Despite the success of economic policy, however, considerable inequalities in the distribution of *wealth remain, an issue which needs to be addressed in the coming years. Indonesia's main trading partners are Japan, the US, the EU and Singapore. Indonesia continues to play an important role in international affairs. The country is currently the leader of the group of Non-Aligned Countries. It is one of the founding members of the Association of South-east Asian Nations (ASEAN), where it continues to influence diplomatic developments in South-east Asia. In 1994, Indonesia also hosted the Asia Pacific Economic Cooperation (APEC) forum of 22 Asia-Pacific countries whose central aim is to liberalise trade and investment in the region. The unit of currency is the rupiah.*

J.D./R.J.W.

INTRODUCTION

This chapter discusses the development and current features of Indonesia's financial accounting and management accounting systems. This first section considers the historical and educational basis of the modern accounting profession in Indonesia. The second section describes the growth of the accountancy profession, and the third section examines the regulatory framework for financial reporting. Indonesian accounting standards are discussed in the fourth section. The fifth section describes aspects of management accounting in Indonesia.

Accounting education

The elements of double-entry bookkeeping were introduced into Indonesia in the 17th Century by the Dutch. The East Indies Company was established by the Dutch as the principal vehicle for commercial activities during the colonial mercantile era. Its presence had a significant and persistent impact on the means of doing business in Indonesia.

Colonial economic activities rapidly accelerated during the 19th and early 20th Centuries. As a result, the demand for trained accountants and bookkeepers increased. During this period, there was an influx of Dutch and British accountants into the colony recruited to help administer the vast estates, mills and industrial enterprises in the colony. For a short period (1912–14), the Batavia (now Jakarta) branch of the Amsterdam Stock Exchange operated to cater to the financing and investing needs of Dutch nationals. This was followed by the establishment of stock exchange agencies in important trading posts such as Semarang (Central Java) and Surabaya (East Java), where most of the Dutch plantations, estates and mills were located (Yunus, 1990).

The interruption of Dutch colonial rule by Japan's military occupation of Indonesia from 1942–45 succeeded in providing opportunities for local accountants to hold important positions in the Ministry of Finance that were previously held by Dutch nationals. The post-independence era of the 1950s saw the resumption of commercial activities wherein Dutch accounting practices were widely in use. Moreover, training of accountants at the tertiary level was still based on the Dutch accounting system. However, the nationalisation of Dutch-owned enterprises and the expulsion of Dutch nationals in 1958 resulted in a shortage of technical, including accounting, expertise.

It was a combination of Indonesian nationalist sentiment (directed mostly against the Dutch) and the presence of US educational institutions that encouraged alternatives to be sought to the well-entrenched Dutch financial accounting and reporting system. The seeds of this change were planted through active links between Indonesian and American universities established through Ford Foundation grants in the 1950s. Further impetus was provided when the government sent Indonesian nationals overseas, particularly to American universities, for tertiary education following the Dutch exodus. A particularly influential academic work during this early period was Suhadji Hadibroto's doctoral thesis, *A comparative study of American and Dutch accountancy and their impact on the profession in Indonesia*. The study strongly advocated the 'pragmatic approach', prevalent in the US, which was perceived to be more appropriate for the Indonesian environment.

The introduction of US accounting thought and practices, however, blended well with the still widespread use of Dutch accounting methods, particularly in government agencies. During the 1950s and 1960s, most practising accountants were still trained under the Dutch system. During the period from 1960 to 1975, however, an increasing number of tertiary institutions, including the government-based State College of Accountants (STAN), began to shift their accountancy programmes from the Dutch to the US system. This shift culminated in 1975 in the directive issued by the Ministry of Education and Commerce, mandating that accounting education in Indonesia must from that time be modelled solely on the US system. The government was still largely concerned with the shortage of qualified accountants. It was perceived that the US accounting educational system afforded a more flexible and effective way of increasing the number of qualified accountants in the country.

THE ACCOUNTANCY PROFESSION

The birth of the modern Indonesian accounting profession was ushered in by the passage of Law No. 34 of 1954 which restricted the use of the designation '*Akuntan*' (Accountant) to persons holding a 'doktorandus' (Drs) degree from a recognised tertiary academic institution. The Drs degree, which was equivalent to North American and UK masters degree, was obtained by completing a university '*sarjana*' course first offered by the University of Indonesia in 1952. The *Accountancy Law* was important in that it paved the way for Indonesian nationals to aspire to a professional qualification without the need to obtain training from overseas, as had been the case during the Dutch colonial period.

The duly recognised professional accountancy body, *Ikatan Akuntan Indonesia* (Indonesian Accounting Institute or IAI), was founded in 1957 by the first batch of graduates of the University of Indonesia accounting course. The first chairman of the IAI was Professor Soemardjo Tjitrosidojo, a Dutch-trained academic. They were joined by six other local accountants who qualified under the Accountancy Law. The IAI's objectives, among other things, are to promote the status of the accounting profession, support the national development of Indonesia, and upgrade the skills and competence of the IAI's (Yunus, 1990).

The change in the Indonesian Government's economic policies under President Suharto augured a much more significant role for professional accountants. The liberalization of the economic environment for both domestic and foreign enterprises led to an increased demand for services of professional accountants. In 1967, the first partnership between a local and international firm was established. Santoso Harsokusumo joined with Arthur Young under Indonesian Accounting Law. The government permitted this arrangement on condition that the new firm assisted the training of Indonesian accountants and the development of the Indonesian accounting profession. The following year the Philippine firm, SyCip, Gorres and Velayo established a partnership with Utomo. Despite the subsequent passage of Ministry of Finance Decree No. 76/1971, which restricted the terms and conditions of joint partnerships, six other major international accounting firms established correspondent firms with Indonesian accountants between 1971 and 1975.

The accountancy profession has become an important force in the Indonesian business community. As of 1992, there were an estimated 11 500 accredited accountants in Indonesia (Price Waterhouse, 1992) and the increase in demand for accounting-related services in the country is drawing more students into the discipline. There is fierce competition for qualified accountants in the private sector because nearly half are employed by the government service. In fact, until the 1990s, all accounting graduates were required to serve for at least three years in government service.

Although the IAI is not a designated licensing body of accountants in Indonesia, the organisation has been, and continues to be, involved in an important role in the development of Indonesia's financial accounting framework. The IAI originally co-ordinated with the Money and Capital Market Team[1] to develop the Indonesian corporate securities market. The IAI's task was to assist in developing an appropriate set of financial reporting and auditing guidelines that would enhance confidence in

---

[1]Following the advice of the World Bank, the Indonesian Ministry of Finance created the Money and Capital Market Team, a government advisory body, on 6 January 1970. The objective of this body is to study and recommend procedures for reinvigorating the Indonesian money and capital markets.

the fledgling capital markets. In December 1973, the IAI adopted three sets of standards dealing with general Indonesian accounting principles (*Prinsip Akuntansi Indonesia*); auditing standards *(Norma Pemeriksaan Akuntan)*; and a code of ethics (*Kode Etik Akuntan Indonesia*). The IAI established committees to oversee the implementation and development of these standards. Importantly, the Directorate General of Taxation, the *Bapepam* (Capital Market Executive Board) and the IAI agreed that the Tax Department would accept audited financial statements of companies as a basis for tax assessment, subject to certain guidelines (Siddik and Jensen, 1980).

The IAI is also closely involved in shaping the future development of Indonesia's financial reporting. The Indonesian Accountancy Development Foundation (*Yayasan Pengembangan Ilmu Akuntansi Indonesia*) was established in 1974, under the auspices of the IAI. The objective of this foundation is to orient the development of the accounting profession towards the needs of private businesses and the Indonesian community in general. It provides training programmes and research related to the Indonesian accounting system.

Finally, the IAI works with overseas accountancy bodies to ensure that the local profession keeps abreast of international developments. The IAI is represented in the ASEAN Federation of Accountants, the Confederation of Asian-Pacific Accountants, and the International Federation of Accountants. It is also a member of the International Accounting Standards Committee. In its September 1994 National Congress, the IAI endorsed the use of International Accounting Standards (IAS) promulgated by the International Accounting Standards Committee (IASC) as a basis for domestic financial accounting standards. IAI specifically adopted 21 IAS which have since been approved for use by publicly-listed companies in 1995.

REGULATORY FRAMEWORK

The commercial regulatory framework in Indonesia blends two elements. First, certain laws have been carried over from the Dutch colonial era. Dutch laws were influenced by French Napoleonic Codes in the 19th Century. Their legal policy in Indonesia may be described as 'dualistic', because Dutch laws were applied to Westerners, but not to locals who were governed by various *Adat Rechts* (traditional laws). This has resulted in legal pluralism in the present Indonesian legal system. Another important set of Indonesian laws were passed by the governments of President Sukarno and President Suharto in the post-Independence period. In contrast to some other countries, laws affecting commercial activities are formulated through Presidential decrees and regulations issued by pertinent government agencies. In general, the legal framework affecting present financial accounting practices includes the companies and investment laws, income tax laws and securities market regulation. More details of these are given below.

Financial reporting requirements are set by government agencies responsible for regulating specific sectors and industries. The agencies concerned with aspects of financial reporting in Indonesia include:

(i) *Bank Indonesia.* Apart from administering the country's monetary policies, the Indonesian central bank prescribes financial reporting requirements for all banks and non-bank financial institutions operating in Indonesia.

(ii) *Pertamina.* This state petroleum agency is responsible for regulating all aspects of the oil and gas industry in Indonesia, including exploration, production and distribution. Pertamina also administers all production sharing contracts involving joint ventures with foreign companies. The financial reporting requirements for the industry are prescribed by Pertamina.

(iii) *Ministry of Finance.* This ministry administers the Accountancy Law and is involved in overseeing activities of the Directorate General of Taxation and the securities market regulator, *Bapepam.*

(iv) *Directorate General of Taxation.* This agency is responsible for administering tax laws. It prescribes the books of accounts and financial statements required of all corporate taxpayers.

(v) *Bapepam. Bapepam* acts as the overall securities regulator of the corporate securities market in Indonesia. Together with the privately-operated Jakarta Stock Exchange and Surabaya Stock Exchange, *Bapepam* specifies the reporting requirements of domestic companies that intend to raise finance through a public issuance of its securities.

Companies and investment laws

A new companies law, referred to as the Limited Company Law *(Undang Undang Perseroan Terbatas),* was introduced in March 1995. The new law requires that limited companies maintain adequate financial and other records and provide financial statements, particularly a balance sheet and income statement, to shareholders. The new companies law is scheduled to take effect in March 1996, with the government expected to form a new agency charged with implementing provisions of the new law.

Prior to the new companies law, the Indonesian regulatory framework specified only broad requirements pertaining to financial reporting. The Indonesian Commercial Code of 1848, which was patterned on the early Dutch Commercial Code (*Wetboek van Koophandel*), specifies in broad terms the record-keeping requirements for business entities which are still in force until the new law takes effect. It requires that anyone carrying on a business must keep records that would allow the rights and obligations of the person to be determined at any time. The Commercial Code, however, does not specify the accounting records or detailed procedures through which these provisions are to be carried out. Every Indonesian company is also required to prepare a balance sheet within six months of the fiscal year end; however, there is no requirement to file that balance sheet or have it audited.

Separate legislation has been passed allowing the formation of limited liability companies known as *Perseroan Terbatas* or PT's. Foreign joint venture companies, known as PMAs (*Permodalan Modal Asing*) are also allowed under the *Foreign Investment Law* of 1967. Government regulations require all PMAs to undergo an audit by a government recognised auditor and to submit financial statements to the Foreign Investment Co-ordinating Board (BKPM). In contrast, domestic companies are obliged to undergo an audit only under certain circumstances, such as if required by government agencies (e.g. Bank Indonesia) or if they receive a loan from a government bank of over Rupiah 75 million (about US$34 000).

Income taxation

Indonesia underwent a significant reform of its direct tax system with the promulgation of several new statutes in 1983, particularly the *General tax provisions and procedures Law No. 6*, the *Income tax Law No. 7*, and the *Value-added tax Law No. 8*.

Indonesian income tax laws are administered by the Director General of Taxes, except for taxation of the oil and gas industry which is primarily administered by the State Audit Authority (BPKP). Tax regulations require Indonesian businesses to maintain and preserve detailed accounting records in Bahasa Indonesia for at least ten years. Records in English may be kept by foreign enterprises upon approval by the tax authorities.

Tax returns must be accompanied by audited financial statements, which consist at least of a balance sheet and income statement, and selected additional supporting schedules. For tax purposes, the corporation's profit must be determined in accordance with Indonesian GAAP prepared under the accrual method of income determination.

Tax regulations specify certain guidelines which affect Indonesian corporations' choice of accounting policies. Among the most important regulations are the following:

1. Inter-company transactions are subject to scrutiny by the Director General of Taxes who has the authority to redetermine income and expenses relating to related-party transactions (Law No. 7 of 1983, Art. 18).
2. Inventories must be valued on the basis of fully absorbed, historical costs, using either FIFO or average cost methods. A valuation method must be used consistently, unless prior approval is obtained to change the method.
3. A tax-free revaluation of property and equipment is not allowed unless expressly approved through a special decree of the Minister of Finance. Such decrees have been issued, following government-sanctioned devaluations of the Indonesian rupiah in 1971, 1979 and 1986. For accounting purposes, companies may record

such revaluations without being taxed on the revalued amounts since the profit is deemed unrealised. Depreciation charges for tax purposes, however, must be based on the original cost (or on an earlier authorised revaluation). Revaluations not authorised by government decree must be noted in the auditor's report.

4. Exchange gains and losses arising from official devaluations of the rupiah are taxable and deductible when realised. Gains and losses for translation of foreign currency assets and liabilities at year-end are recognised for tax purposes, even if unrealised, if the method is applied consistently. Foreign currency loans, however, must be registered with Bank Indonesia (Indonesia's central bank) in order for exchange losses to be tax deductible.

5. Indonesian tax laws classify property and equipment into four categories for depreciation purposes. Depreciation allowances of between 5 percent and 50 percent per annum are allowed using the declining-balance method, except for buildings which are depreciated on a straight-line basis. Similar rules apply to the amortisation of intangible assets (e.g., rights to land use), depending on the estimated life of the asset. The pre-operational costs of business may be capitalised and amortised at a rate of 50 percent per annum (declining-balance method).[2]

6. Leasing activities are only allowed for machinery and equipment. All lease payments are tax deductible, whether they pertain to operating or finance-type leases. Also, depreciation charges are tax deductible for finance-type leases.

7. Provisions for doubtful debts are generally not deductible, except when the debt is proven to be uncollectible. State-owned and private banks, however, may claim the increase in reserve for doubtful debts, as specified by the tax authorities.

Securities market regulation

Under the Indonesian legal system, laws governing the securities markets are promulgated not by a legislative assembly but through executive authorities such as the President and the Minister of Finance. The existing *Capital Market Law* was promulgated in 1952 (Law No. 5) shortly after Indonesia's independence to regulate trading in the Batavia (now Jakarta) stock market. The 1950s, however, were a turbulent period in Indonesia's history and the stock exchange was virtually shut down in 1958, following the nationalisation of Dutch-owned companies.

In the early 1970s, plans were made to re-establish the short-term money and long-term capital markets. Several organisations, including the IAI, were involved in setting up the regulatory foundation for the subsequent operation of the capital markets. These plans culminated in Presidential Decree No. 52 of 1976, which created two bodies. First was the Capital Market Executive Agency (*Badan Pelaksana Pasar*

---

[2]Cursory evidence suggests that Indonesian companies follow tax guidelines in computing their depreciation for financial reporting purposes.

Modal, or *Bapepam*), whose role is to supervise the operations and development of Indonesia's corporate securities markets. The second was PT (*Persero*) *Danareksa*, a national investment trust company, whose responsibility is to hold in trust securities investments intended for eventual distribution to indigenous Indonesians.

Bapepam has been and continues to be highly influential in determining financial accounting regulations in Indonesia. Prior to the privatisation of the Jakarta Stock Exchange (JSE) in 1990, *Bapepam* also managed the country's largest stock exchange. It promulgated the listing and reporting requirements for all firms raising finance through the stock exchange. At present, *Bapepam* exercises overall supervision over securities markets activities and promulgates policies for the regulation of securities transactions.

As part of the regulatory framework over corporate securities activities, *Bapepam* has issued a circular, *Directives Regarding the Form & Content of Financial Statements of Indonesian Listed Companies.* This circular, patterned after the US Securities and Exchange Commission's Regulation S-X, mandates the format and disclosures of financial information of all companies listed on the JSE. The regulations require that financial statements be prepared in accordance with generally accepted accounting principles (GAAP) in Indonesia (promulgated by the IAI) and in conformity with *Bapepam* regulations (Enclosure VIII, *Bapepam* Circular SE-24/PM/1987). In addition, all financial statements submitted to *Bapepam* must be audited by a recognised public accountant or state accountant.

At the time of writing, a new capital markets law to replace the extant 1952 law is under consideration. It is expected that the new law will clarify the supervisory and investigative powers of *Bapepam.* The new law also aims to streamline the bureaucratic process involved in going public so that medium and even small-sized companies are given the chance to raise capital in the stock markets. Finally, in regard to financial reporting of publicly-listed companies, *Bapepam* has officially supported the accounting profession's shift towards using International Accounting Standards promulgated by the IASC. The new accounting standards take effect for financial years ending in 1995.

The Jakarta Stock Exchange

The Jakarta Stock Exchange (JSE) is one of two privately-operated corporate securities exchanges in Indonesia. It is by far the largest and most active stock exchange in the country. Following a series of government-led reforms in the late 1980s, the JSE has become one of the fastest growing and most attractive emerging markets in the world. From a market capitalisation of a mere US$72 million at the end of 1988, the JSE has grown to a market of about US$50 billion at the end of 1994 (an almost 700-fold increase in only six years). At present, there are more than 200 domestic companies listed on the JSE.

These developments have encouraged the development of Indonesia's financial reporting system. The JSE influences financial reporting practices of member companies by specifying listing requirements and periodic corporate disclosures. The listing requirements of the JSE are as follows:

(i)   a registration statement as a public company declared effective by *Bapepam* for a public offering;
(ii)   financial statements audited by a Public Accountant registered with *Bapepam*, with an unqualified audit opinion for the most recent fiscal year;
(iii)   a minimum of one million shares to be listed;
(iv)   a minimum of 200 shareholders, whether individual or institutional, with each shareholder having a minimum of one trading unit (one lot or 500 shares);
(v)   the company must have been founded and in operation for a minimum of three years;
(vi)   the company has made operational income and net profit for the two most recent fiscal years;
(vii)   minimum total assets of Rupiah 20 billion; minimum stockholders equity of Rupiah 7.5 billion, and minimum paid up capital of Rupiah two billion;
(viii) Companies having gone public must have a minimum capitalisation value of fully paid shares of Rupiah four billion and public companies a minimum paid up capital of Rupiah two billion.

The periodic corporate disclosures include:

(i)   Financial statements consisting of an annual report audited by an accountant registered with *Bapepam*, to be submitted not later than 120 days from the date of fiscal year-end; A mid-year report which need not be audited but which must be submitted not later than 60 days after the fiscal mid-year; an audited report which must be submitted within 90 days of the fiscal mid-year; Financial statements submitted accompanied by an unqualified audit opinion no later than 120 days from the fiscal mid-year; and quarterly reports submitted no later than 60 days from the end of each fiscal quarter.
(ii) Any relevant information prescribed by *Bapepam* which may affect the value of the security or the investment decision. Such information includes mergers, acquisitions, consolidations, stock splits, stock dividends, changes in management, replacement of the public accountant, replacement of trustees, legal claims, and other important information possibly affecting share prices on the exchange.

ACCOUNTING STANDARD-SETTING

The process of setting accounting standards in Indonesia combines elements of private sector and government policy formulation. The statutory basis for maintaining accounting records is the Indonesian Commercial Code and, when it takes effect, the new Limited Company Law. Also, relevant Presidential Decrees and guidelines issued by executive agencies are considered part of the regulatory framework governing financial reporting in Indonesia. The Ministry of Finance, in particular, plays a prominent role in overseeing government policies concerning financial reporting by privately-owned companies.

In general, the government has been content with allowing the private sector, particularly the Indonesian Institute of Accountants (IAI), to specify detailed accounting rules for businesses. The first set of accounting standards was formulated in 1973, as part of the measures designed to re-invigorate the Indonesian capital markets. The Indonesian Accounting Principles (*Prinsip Akuntansi Indonesia*) prepared by the IAI became the cornerstone of generally accepted accounting principles in Indonesia. Prompted by accelerated economic reform and deregulation in the 1980s, the IAI significantly revised Indonesian accounting principles with a new set of standards in 1984. Another important shift occurred in September 1994 when the IAI National Congress endorsed the use of IAS as a basis for domestic financial reporting. The detailed accounting pronouncements have been renamed Financial Accounting Standards and are expected to take effect in 1995.

The formulation of the revised set of accounting principles was straightforward. First, the IAI's board of directors commissioned the Committee on Accounting Principles (a sub-group of the IAI) to prepare a draft set of accounting standards. The draft was then circulated amongst IAI members, relevant government agencies, business representatives and other interested users. Following a period of exposure, the draft was revised to incorporate any changes warranted by the comments received. The revised draft was then endorsed by the Committee on Accounting Principles to the IAI board of directors and, when approved became part of the rules governing members of the IAI.[3] Aside from the set of basic accounting principles, the IAI has from time to time issued statements of accounting standards on particular topics of relevance to accounting practitioners in Indonesia.

While the accounting principles and standards of the IAI are not sanctioned by law, government agencies have generally supported the implementation of these standards by Indonesian companies. *Bapepam* and JSE generally require listed companies to undergo an independent audit to ensure that financial statements conform to Indonesian accounting principles. The Directorate General of Taxation and the Bank Indonesia also require that companies under their jurisdiction use Indonesian accounting standards. These factors generally encourage a high degree of compliance with the accounting standards prescribed by the IAI. As mentioned previously, in 1994 *Bapepam* concurred with the IAI move towards adopting IAS. This development is consistent with the general trend among ASEAN accounting professions, specifically in Malaysia, Singapore and Thailand, of directly supporting IAS for

---

[3]Virtually all government-registered public accountants are also members of the IAI.

domestic use. Finally, a provision in the new Limited Company Law requires the government to specifically concur with the recommendations of the IAI regarding new accounting standards before such standards become effective.

Summary of GAAP

The adoption of IAS for domestic financial reporting has changed significantly the content and structure of Indonesian accounting requirements. The most significant shift was towards the adoption of 'Financial Accounting Standards' (FAS) to replace the old Indonesian Accounting Principles (PAI), which were last revised in 1984. The new accounting standards were taken directly from 21 IAS (Table 1). In addition, the IASC's 'Framework for the preparation and presentation of financial statements' was wholly adopted.

Table 1
IAS ADOPTED AS INDONESIAN FINANCIAL ACCOUNTING STANDARDS

IAS 1   – Disclosure of Accounting Policies
IAS 3   – Depreciation Accounting
IAS 7   – Cash Flow Statements
IAS 8   – Net Profit or Loss for the Period, Fundamental Errors and Changes in Accounting
            Policies
IAS 9   – Research and Development Costs
IAS 10 – Contingencies and Events After the Balance Sheet Date
IAS 11 – Construction Contracts
IAS 13 – Presentation of Current Assets and Current Liabilities
IAS 14 – Reporting Financial Information by Segment
IAS 15 – Information Reflecting the Effects of Changing Prices
IAS 16 – Property, Plant and Equipment
IAS 17 – Accounting for Leases
IAS 18 – Revenue
IAS 21 – The Effects of Changes in Foreign Exchange Rates
IAS 22 – Business Combinations
IAS 24 – Related Party Disclosures
IAS 25 – Accounting for Investments
IAS 27 – Consolidated Financial Statements and Accounting for Investments in Subsidiaries
IAS 28 – Accounting for Investments in Associations
IAS 30 – Disclosures in the Financial Statements of Banks and Similar Financial Institutions
IAS 31 – Financial Reporting of Interests in Joint Ventures

The transition to IAS represents a slight shift away from US-based accounting standards, although the requirements are still firmly Anglo-US in content. In contrast to the most recent FAS, both the 1973 and 1984 versions of the PAI were based on US accounting pronouncements. The 1973 principles was patterned after *Accounting Research Study No. 7*, 'Inventory of Generally Accepted Accounting Principles for Business Enterprises', published by the AICPA. The 1984 accounting standards, while drawing upon the earlier PAI, also used concepts and methods formulated by the US Financial Accounting Standards Board (FASB). Accounting statements promulgated after 1984 by the IAI usually drew upon US FASB or IASC standards as a basis for specifying domestic accounting standards. For example, Indonesian accounting principle Statement No. 1 (*Accounting for Transactions in and Translation of Foreign Exchange*) adopts concepts and methods from the FASB's SFAS No. 52 and IASC's Statement No. 21.

The influence of Dutch accounting concepts on Indonesian accounting principles has diminished significantly following the pervasive adoption of US accounting concepts and principles. On a practical and theoretical level, however, with one significant exception there does not appear to be much conflict between US and Dutch accounting principles. The main exception is current cost accounting. The Dutch emphasis on accounting principles reflecting 'sound business practice' led to the acceptability of current replacement cost as a valuation method. In contrast, the historical cost method as in the US is now the preferred valuation basis in Indonesia. The revaluation of property and equipment is also discouraged, except in the circumstances outlined ealier.

Some of the salient features of general accounting principles, which follow Anglo American practice in the main, include the following:

Purpose of Financial Accounting: The general purpose of financial accounting is to provide financial information regarding a company that will be useful in making economic decisions by a variety of users, particularly investors, employees, lenders, suppliers, customers, governments and their agencies and the general public. (Framework for the Preparation and Presentation of Financial Statements, FPPFS). Financial information must include those relating to a company's assets, liabilities and capital, its profit-generating potential and its financing and investing activities. In order to be useful, accounting information must meet four qualitative characteristics, namely understandability, relevance, reliability and comparability (FPPFS, pars. 24–42).

Basic Financial Statements: Basic financial statements include the balance sheet, profit and loss statement and retained earnings, cash flow statements and notes to the financial statements. Comparative financial statements covering at least two years are recommended. Financial statements must also be prepared on an annual basis, except for publicly listed companies, which must also submit semiannual financial statements.

Income Determination and Presentation: In general, profit is determined using the accrual method. Revenue is recognised when it is realised, which generally means that the sale has been made or the service rendered. Several exceptions to revenue recognition are allowed: (1) point of production; (2) percentage of completion; (3) time of payment. Specific Financial Accounting Standards provide guidelines on the use of exceptions to the accrual basis of revenue recognition. Expenses, as far as practicable, are matched against the related revenues. Separate disclosures are made for the following items in the income statement: sales, cost of goods sold, operating expenses, other income and expenses, extraordinary items, effect of changes in accounting policies, and income tax. Earnings per share data are now required disclosures for publicly-listed companies.

Treatment of Tax Differences: Indonesia did not adopt IAS recommendations on accounting for income taxes (IAS 12). At present, companies may choose to calculate income tax based on the accounting profit or the taxable profit, using the appropriate tax rate. If the income tax is calculated based on the accounting profit, any book and tax difference is recorded as a 'deferred income tax' charge or credit and allocated to the income tax liability in future years (PAI Art. 9.1).

Contingencies: A provision for contingent losses must be recorded if these are likely to occur and the amount of the loss can be estimated. Contingent gains are not recorded but should be disclosed in the notes to the financial statements. The provisions under the new FAS are consistent with the recommendations under PAI Art. 12.

Asset Valuation and Disclosures: Assets are grouped into the following classes and presented in order of liquidity: current assets, long-term investment, fixed assets, intangible assets and other assets. With regard to current assets, marketable securities are stated at the lower of acquisition cost or market value. Debtors are shown at their gross amount less any provision for estimated uncollectibles. Stocks or inventories are stated at the lower of cost or market value. Cost may be determined using FIFO, LIFO, weighted average, or moving average method. However, since January 1, 1984, tax authorities have not allowed companies to use LIFO as a basis for stock valuation for tax purposes (similar to UK practice and in contrast to US practice). Long-term investments are stated at cost. However, if the company exerts a significant influence over the investee, then the equity method is required. Indonesian FAS based on IAS 27 (Accounting for Investments in Subsidiaries) and IAS 28 (Accounting for Investments in Associations) provide specific guidelines for determining what constitutes control or influence over other companies. Significant influence is defined by the '20 percent or more of voting power' rule. Property and equipment (fixed assets) are generally stated at historical cost. Except for land, asset values must be amortised over the estimated useful life of the assets. Allowable depreciation methods include the straight-line, declining balance or unit of production methods. Depreciation rates may also be composite, group or by individual classes of assets. Indonesian tax law provides some guidelines regarding depreciation (discussed above). Intangible assets, including goodwill, must be recorded at acquisition cost. All such assets must be amortised systematically over the life of the particular asset. For goodwill, Indonesian FAS based on IAS 22 do not set a particular period for amortisation, except that the amount should be amortised to income on a systematic basis over its useful life.

Treatment of Liabilities: Financial statements must distinguish between current liabilities, long-term liabilities and other liabilities. All known and existing liabilities must be provided for, even if the amount cannot be exactly fixed. They are generally stated in the amount required to settle each liability. As mentioned earlier, contingent liabilities must be recorded when certain conditions are met.

Accounting for Capital or Owners' Equity: The value and quantity of share capital, subscribed capital and paid in capital must be presented for each type of share. Share capital is recorded at its par or nominal value. Amounts in excess of par are recorded as a share premium (*agio*) and forms part of the 'Additional paid in capital'. Treasury or reacquired shares that have been issued may be accounted for using the cost method or the par value method. In no instance must profit or loss be recognised for treasury share transactions. Retained earnings must be presented separately from share capital. Separate disclosures are made for unappropriated retained earnings and earnings earmarked for particular purposes, such as for plant expansion. Quasi-reorganisations in order to reduce or eliminate a deficit is allowed. Finally, in case of revalutions of fixed assets, a revaluation surplus is presented as a separate item between 'additional paid in capital' and 'retained earnings'.

Statutory Reserves: Legal reserves to protect creditors similar to those seen in German and French reporting are not required. Dividends, however, may only generally be issued from unappropriated retained earnings. Indirectly, therefore, the disclosure of separate items in stockholders' equity provides notice that certain capital accounts must legally be maintained.

Accounting for Mergers and Acquisitions: The appropriate accounting method for business combinations and mergers is determined by observing the economic significance rather than the legal form of the transaction (FAS based on IAS 22). The pooling of interests method is generally used when the majority of shareholders of an acquired company retain a controlling interest in the continuing business. Otherwise, the merger should be accounted for using the purchase method. Goodwill recognised from a purchase of another entity may be amortised by the purchasing company for tax purposes.

Consolidated Financial Statements: Consolidated financial statements are now mandatory for publicly-listed companies under Indonesian FAS (based on IAS 27). In general, consolidation is required if the company owns, directly or indirectly through subsidiaries, more than 50 percent of voting power of a company. In certain circumstances, however, control is presumed to exist even if less than half of the voting power is owned (defined in IAS 27). Investments in non-consolidated subsidiaries may be accounted for using the cost or equity method, depending on the degree of control exercised by the investor company (IAS 28). Consolidation is irrelevant for tax purposes.

Additional Required Disclosures: Publicly listed companies are also required to disclose additional information in the notes to the accounts.[4] Apart from general accounting principles, the IAI periodically releases statements of accounting standards on particular topics of importance. These have included such matters as accounting for transactions in, and translation of, foreign currency; accounting for interest during periods of construction (this provides for capitalisation of interest expense incurred during asset construction under certain conditions); accounting for leases; and an accounting standard for the oil and gas industry. The last mentioned sets out accounting procedures in line with the accounting regulatory guidelines promulgated by Pertamina (the state-owned oil and gas company) for oil and gas companies operating under production-sharing contracts with the government.[5]

Recent developments in Indonesian accounting standards indicate a decisive shift towards IAS. The adoption of IAS, which is consistent with a continuing trend toward an Anglo-US character for Indonesian accounting away from European forms, also represents a standardisation of many accounting treatments which have so far been optional for publicly listed companies. The adoption of IAS is also reflective of the tremendous growth of the Indonesian capital markets in recent years, and of the internationalisation of a growing number of Indonesian companies that now seek listing in the US and UK stock markets.

---

[4]These include a summary of significant accounting principles; details of changes in the application of accounting procedures; assets used for guarantees or as liens; explanation of the company's pension policy; restrictions in using retained earnings for dividends; commitments and contingent liabilities; significant lease commitments; profit sharing plans; option rights for company directors and officers to purchase shares; certain post-balance sheet date events; earnings per share.

[5]Several studies and exposure drafts are also currently being considered in the following areas. (1) Accounting for related party transactions; (2) Financial statement primary debt which is subordinated by differences in deferred foreign exchange; (3) Accounting for fixed assets revaluations; (4) Disclosure of changes in financial position; (5) Accounting for discontinued operations and extraordinary items; (6) Accounting for expenses of share issues; (7) Revision of accounting statement; and (8) Accounting for cooperative institutions.

MANAGEMENT ACCOUNTING

Management accounting in Indonesia has followed a different pattern of evolution compared to the development of financial accounting. Historically, financial accounting and reporting practices, influenced by the old Dutch systems, had taken shape long before the Indonesian Independence Declaration. Now, decades later, they have changed significantly following the adoption of US accounting systems. The development of management accounting came about at the same time US systems were starting to penetrate accounting education in Indonesia. This influence was particularly noticeable in the large companies which expanded rapidly with the issuance of the Foreign Investment Law in 1967 and Domestic Investment Law in 1968, shortly after foreign investors and multinational corporation (MNCs) were first allowed to operate in Indonesia.

There is little available published data and research about management accounting practice in Indonesia. However it can be reasonably assumed that cost and management accounting principles and techniques have been applied in most large and medium sizes companies. Accountants working within these organisations graduate from local universities and higher education institutions and typically apply management accounting techniques borrowed from the US. This influence is transmitted through the curriculum syllabus and text books of the higher education system, which is largely based upon US practice and theory.

In line with the relatively late development of management accounting practice in Indonesia, there are no separate management accounting standards and in particular no recommendation or pronouncements have been issued by the Indonesian Institute of Accountants.

The Institute did not begin to develop a specialist division in the management accounting area until 1986, when the Fifth National Congress decided for the first time to form a section to develop management accounting as a distinct profession. After almost ten years since the establishment of the Management Accountant's Section within the Institute, however, there seems to be little interest in developing the section's activities. This situation prompted the Institute, in its recent Seventh National Congress in Bandung to reorganise the Management Accountant's Section into the Management Accountant's 'Compartment' in order to encourage management accountants in large organisations to more actively contribute to the enhancement of the profession of management accounting.

Based on the authors' own experiences, most medium to large size companies, especially publicly-listed companies and MNCs, have their own distinctive management accounting systems. Most of these maintain cost accounting records in considerable detail, especially in manufacturing firms. Some apply pre-determined cost or standard cost systems in order to better control their production activities. More specifically, most applications of management accounting in practice are designed to produce production cost information to measure inventories in the balance sheet and cost of goods sold in the income statement. For this purpose, most data is based on the full costing method. It is very uncommon to find the use of data for decision making based upon direct or variable costing in practice. Even those companies which use computerised accounting systems tend not to use computers as an integrated tool for applying management accounting techniques (such as budgetary control systems, short- and long-range planning, special decision making support systems and corporate planning).

In most government owned companies, there are separate budgetary systems and accounting information systems. As in the private sector, there is little or no integration between budgeting and accounting, and so there is no use of integrated accounting systems as a tool for decision making. Existing systems are primarily for supervision, fulfilling an accountability function rather than controlling business activities and serving a management decision making function. The reason for this may be the absence of a strong management science background among accountants performing managerial roles. Management accounting practices in Indonesia are thus likely to develop in line with management and business practices and the general accounting environment itself. These are likely to be determined by outside authorities, or economic and political factors. This is especially true for government owned companies or subsidiary firms within large holding companies.

Another factor which is likely to influence the development of management accounting techniques is the cultural environment. The conservative characteristics and paternalistic culture of most Indonesians, for example, probably makes it difficult to easily or independently make an important or strategic decision. Other culturally related aspects of the environment are implicit in the establishment of laws and regulations which set down the responsibility of management and directors of the company and are stated in the company law or commercial code. The traditions of a management audit process to measure the performance efficiency of company management and management social responsibility do not yet exist, however. Even as the new Limited Company Law takes effect in 1996, there are still few regulations linked to the measurement of management efficiency and responsibility. Such laws and regulations are needed to spur the development and sound practice of management accounting. In an era of growing internationalisation of accounting practices, of course, Indonesia cannot stand apart from the influence of the globalisation, of business practice and management. An increasingly competitive environment makes it imperative that improved management accounting principles and techniques should be followed. Thus the prospects for the development of management accounting in Indonesia are good if the accounting profession can respond in a timely fashion to rapidly changing environmental conditions.

CONCLUSION

The development and current features of Indonesia's financial and management accounting systems reflect a variety of international influences. The basic framework for widespread commercial activities was established during the Dutch colonial era, although the country's political independence has seen a gradual but decisive shift towards Anglo-US accounting standards and practices. As in other ASEAN countries, Indonesia now directly supports the use of IAS as a basis for domestic financial reporting purposes. The growing importance of accessing international capital markets reinforces the perceived advantages of adopting IAS. In this regard, it is expected that the future development of Indonesia's financial and management accounting systems will be linked closely to accounting developments in the US, UK and the IASC. The growth of the Indonesian economy is also expected to strengthen and expand the role of the Indonesian accounting profession in setting and implementing accounting standards in the country.

The effect of indigenous culture is quite subtle and not readily evident in Indonesian accounting requirements, which reflect an international flavour. Nonetheless, culture is expected to play a pervasive role in the actual operation and implementation of accounting rules and procedures, particularly at the level of management. Much research needs to be done to uncover specific, but subtle, effects of culture on the various roles of accounting in Indonesian organisations. It is particularly desirable that such research contribute to improving the effectiveness and efficiency of Indonesian organisations, which are such important components of Indonesia's modernising economy.

REFERENCES

Abdoclkadir, K. and H. Yunus (1994), 'Developments in Indonesian accountancy', *Conference proceedings —7th international conference on accounting education*, Jakarta, Indonesia.

Badan Pelaksana Pasar Modal (*Bapepam*) (1986), *The Indonesian capital market fact book*, Bapepam, Jakarta.

Badan Pelaksana Pasar Modal (*Bapepam*) (1989), *Circular SE-24/PM/1987 — Directives regarding the form and content of financial statements of Indonesian listed companies*, Jakarta.

Briston, R.J. (1990), 'The evolution of accounting in developing countries: Indonesia and the Solomon Islands as case studies for regional development', *Research in Third World accounting*, Vol. 1. pp. 195–216.

Hadibroto, S. (1962), 'A comparative study of American and Dutch accountancy and their impact on the profession in Indonesia', *unpublished PhD dissertation*, Lembaga Pencrbit Fakultas Ekonomi, Universitas Indonesia, Jakarta.

Ikatan Akuntan Indonesia (IAI) (1989), *Indonesian accounting principles — Unofficial English translation*, Jakarta.

Jakarta Stock Exchange (1993), *Fact Book 1993*, Jakarta Stock Exchange, Jakarta.

Price Waterhouse (1992), *Doing business in Indonesia*, Price Waterhouse, Jakarta.

Samidjo, *Pengantar hukum Indonesia (Introduction to Indonesian law)*. CV Arminco, Bandung.

Siddik, A. and H. Jensen (1980), The evolution of accounting in Indonesia, Academy of Accounting Historians, Working Paper No. 46.

Sukoharsono, E.G. and M.J.R. Gaffikin (1993), 'The genesis of accounting in Indonesia: The Dutch colonialism', *Indonesian journal of accounting and business society,* Vol. 1, No. 1, pp. 4–26.

Yunus, H. (1990), *History of accounting in developing nations: The case of Indonesia.* Tim Koordinasi Pengembangan Akuntansi, Jakarta.

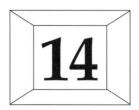

ASPECTS OF FINANCIAL AND MANAGEMENT ACCOUNTING IN MACAU

Desmond Yuen and Anita Wong*

BACKGROUND

Macau comprises an area of about 20 sq. km formed of a Chinese mainland peninsula on the west side of the Guangzhou river estuary and two small adjacent islands to the south about 64 km from Hong Kong between latitudes 22°10' to 22°15'N. Physically, Macau consists of low granite hills and the peninsula has a level coastal plain formed from reclaimed land. It has a subtropical climate, hot and humid in May to September and cooler and drier between October and April. There are few natural resources.

The Portuguese established a trading post on the Macau peninsular in 1537. It did not become a Portuguese territory, however, but remained a province of China until 1887 following the establishment of the colony of Hong Kong by the British in 1842. Macau was not occupied by the Japanese in the Second World War and became an overseas province of Portugal with direct representation in Lisbon until 1976. In that year, by the passing of the Organic Law, Macau gained political autonomy as a special territory of Portugal. The constitution thus established is still in effect. It provides for executive authority to be vested in a Governor responsible to the President of Portugal. Legislative power (including finance) is in the hands of a Legislative Assembly consisting of 16 elected members and seven members appointed by the Governor for a four-year term. In the elections of 1984 Chinese residents were allowed to vote, and by deliberate policy ethnic Chinese Macanese dominated the legislature for the first time. In 1988, it was formally agreed between China and Portugal that Macau would become a special administrative region of the People's Republic of China, similar to the position of Hong Kong after 1997,

*Faculty of Business Administration, Department of Accounting, Macau University.

in 1999. Macau's defence and foreign policy will be determined by China, but otherwise Macau will enjoy considerable autonomy, particularly over economic and social policy. The Basic Law drafted by China envisages a continuation of the form of the present Legislative Assembly (subject to some expansion) with a majority of elected members. The Chief Executive will be nominated and selected by a local electoral college of 300 local representatives. The judiciary is based on a code law system, and after 1999 will follow the Chinese 'Basic Law'. The density of the population is very high (more than 20 000 people per sq. km) and most people live on the peninsula where the city of Macau is situated. Between one quarter and one-third of the population of slightly more than 350 000 people are Portuguese citizens, almost all of ethnic Chinese origin. Portuguese is the official language of administration, but more people speak Cantonese and English. Confucianism, Doaism, Buddhism and Roman Catholicism are the most widely followed religions.

Macau's GDP in 1993 was about US$5 billion or US$15 000 per capita with an annual growth rate in recent years of between 8 and 9 percent. Competition from Hong Kong and the silting up of Macau's harbour prevented its growth as a major commercial centre in the late 19th and early 20th Centuries. Gambling activities which became associated with the territory at that time are still a significant component of the now important tourist industry. This produces nearly 40 percent of GDP and employs 12 percent of the workforce. Manufacturing has traditionally been based upon textiles but recently diversification into the production of plastics, toy-making and electronics has taken place. Construction activity has increased, with public expenditure on infrastructure projects such as the new airport and a highway to the PRC and also with new hotels and casinos financed by Japanese, Taiwanese and US capital. Attempts have been made recently to promote Macau as a centre for international finance and offshore banking. There is no foreign exchange control. The balance of trade was in deficit in the three years to 1993 after a long period of surpluses. Usually the government runs a surplus on its budget and the total public expenditure was 4 percent of GDP in 1993. Macau's main trading partners are the PRC, the US, Hong Kong, the EU and Japan. There has been little unemployment in the last ten years, but price inflation has been of the order of about 7 percent per annum. The local currency is linked to the Hong Kong dollar. For the first 50 years following its return to China, the province of Macau will retain its own customs barriers, will be exempt from government taxes and be permitted to retain its capitalist system. Its current outstanding economic problems relating to land shortages, shortages of skilled labour, energy and water supply will presumably be alleviated when this occurs. The unit of currency is the pataca.

R.J.W.

INTRODUCTION

Accounting is a relatively new profession in Macau. There is no formal organization granting professional qualifications. However, the qualification of Certified Public Accountant is granted by the government to persons having at least ten years professional practice in the field of accounting. Award of the qualification may also be given at the discretion of the government to any person who possesses appropriate commercial experience. Until about ten years ago, most professional accountants were imported from other countries, especially the UK, the US and Canada. In 1983, the government began to implement standard accounting practices in a new law, the *Decreto-Lei No. 34/83/M*. A new body, the Macau Society of Certified Public Accountants (MSCPA) is currently being established in order to place accounting qualifications in Macau on a uniform basis. Sources at the MSCPA suggest that it plans to cooperate with other overseas professional bodies such as the Chartered Association of Certified Accountants and the Chartered Institute of Management Accountants from the UK and the Canadian Management Accountants and Canadian General Accountants in establishing appropriate examination arrangements. The MSCPA does not have its own local professional examinations and does not have the authority as yet to provide its own professional qualification.

The following section details Macau's accounting legislation and standards. Section 3 covers more details of asset and liability definition, while Section 4 describes the local taxation system. Section 5 provides an outline of some management accounting practices in Macau, and the final section briefly reflects upon present influences and possible future developments in the country.

ACCOUNTING LEGISLATION AND STANDARDS[1]

Portuguese and Macau accounting legislation (Plano oficia de contabilidabe)

Macau accounting standards have evolved from Portuguese standards. The current accounting standards were adopted on 1 January, 1984. The government of Macau, under *Decreto-Lei No. 34/83/M*, designed an accounting standard based on the local economic environment enabling all business sectors to follow a uniform accounting system for both internal and external reporting. *Under Lei No. 21/78/M*, the taxation law, it is compulsory for all companies to prepare a standard form of financial statement, including a balance sheet and income statement.

The preparation of these statements applies to all types of business in Macau, except in two cases. Sole traders with no more than four persons in a manufacturing company, and sole traders with fewer than three persons in a commercial or trading company, do not need to prepare reports. Although there is a standard format for the preparation of financial statements, the Macau Government permits subjective estimation in the computation of operation income and in the valuation of assets. However, it requires companies to state clearly the reason for the subjective estimation and the method of valuation.

---

[1] See Macau Government (1983).

Main accounting categories and the Uniform Accounts Code (The Macau Legislation, Decreto-Lei No. 34/83/M, 1994.)

Accounting standards identify ten main categories of accounts. According to the Uniform Account Code, the first digit of the Code must bear the same number as the account category, e.g. the currency accounting category is '1', and the cash account code within this category is '11'. All companies in Macau have to follow this uniform system of numbering accounts when preparing the financial statements.

Standard formats for the construction of balance sheets and income statements stem directly from the accounting categories. Accounts categories 1 to 5 relate to balance sheet items (see Table 1). Accounts categories 6 and 7, together with beginning and ending inventory balances, summarise information about the companies' operational results (i.e. its profit or loss). Overall results are identified in category 8. Category 8 also includes other sources of income, including extraordinary income together with accumulated operating income from prior years. The tax authority in Macau uses category 8 to estimate the taxable income of companies. Sometimes a detailed explanation is required, including a list of the elements in the calculation. Categories 9 and 0 are reserved for internal uses, including costing, financial analysis and the preparation of other reports. There is no standard format for management reports.

Table 1
STANDARD ACCOUNTING CODE AND THE ACCOUNTING
CATEGORIES

Balance sheet items	1. currency
	2. trading account, account receivable and account payable
	3. inventory
	4. capital asset
	5. equity, provision account, and the accumulated profit and loss.
Operation result	6. cost relates to the company's operations
	7. revenue relates to the company's operation
	8. result (profit or loss)
Other accounting subject	9. cost accounting
	10. others (internal reports)

The standard format of the financial statements and accounting subjects codes in Macau

The Balance Sheet Format: The balance sheet is divided into three sections: assets, liabilities and the net value of the equity. The first section consists of assets, while liabilities and equity are shown together in the second and third sections of the balance sheet. The listing of the assets is made according to the accounts liquidity, the more liquid assets being listed first. Liabilities should be listed according to their payment priority and equities according to their history. The balance sheet figures comes directly from the general ledger. Table 2 describes the standard format of the balance sheet and the relevant accounting codes.

Table 2
SUMMARY OF BALANCE SHEET FORMAT

General ledger Account subject code			Total
		Assets	
11	1.	Cash	x
12/13/14	2.	Bank account	x
21	3.	Account receivable	x
32 to 37	4.	Inventory	x
41/42/43	5.	Other assets (including fixed assets)	x
	6.	Prepaid account	x
27	7.	Total assets value	x
		Liabilities	
22 to 26	8.	Account payable	x
22 to 26	9.	Unearned revenue	x
	10.	Total Liabilities	x
		Equity	
51/52/53	11.	Capital	x
58/88	12.	Retained Earnings	x
	13.	Total liabilities and equity	x

Other Important Balance Sheet Rules: The accounting rules governing the calculation of the assets stipulate how Macau companies may amortise their asset values. Depreciation and replacement value details are listed in the asset section of the balance sheet. Accounting standards allow the setting up of two kinds of provision funds: provisions for bad debts and similar provisions to reduce the value of the asset; and provisions regarding future payment obligations such as those for unearned revenues which are posted to the liabilities section of the balance sheet. Finally, liabilities are divided into two kinds — short-term liabilities being those with maturity dates shorter than one year; and others which are referred to as long-to-medium term liabilities.

Standard Income Statement Format: It is compulsory for companies in Macau to prepare income summary reports under the tax rules. Table 3 presents the standard format of the statement, together with the standard accounting code that applies to the statement.

Table 3
STANDARD FORMAT OF THE OPERATING INCOME STATEMENT

Accounting code				Accounting code			
32/67/37	6.	Opening inventory	x	71	1	sales	x
31/61	7.	Purchase	x	72	2	service fee	x
32/36/37	8.	Close inventory	x	33/34/35	3	inventory	
				74 to 78	4	adjustment	x
61	9.	Inventory cost	x x	82/38	5	other	
						income	x
62	10.	Subcontracting	x			total	x
						income (B)	
63	11.	Supplies and services rendered by third parties	x				
64	12.	Tax	x				
65	13.	Salary and wages expense	x				
66/67		Other expense and liabilities	x				
		Total cost (A)	x				
		Profit (loss)	x				

Footnotes are attached to disclose additional information. There are no rigid rules governing the detailed information disclosure and this thus depends on company policy. The following must, however, be disclosed:

(i)   *Outside relationships*: In the case of a multinational company, it is necessary to show the value of 'local' assets as a percentage of the total assets of the whole company. In addition, if there is some foreign equity investment or participation involved, the total amount should be disclosed in a footnote. The company should also show information concerning any foreign investment, including its overseas asset value, the total value of foreign purchases (including inventory and fixed assets) and the amount of direct sales to overseas markets.

(ii)   *Particulars about associated companies and major shareholdings including*: (a) The associated company's short, medium and long term liabilities; short, medium and long term receivables; financial assets, inventory and fixed assets values and sales should be disclosed in footnotes.[2] and (b) the total personal liabilities of major shareholders or partners, together with the benefits that they can obtain from the company. Major shareholders are those whose investment is not less than 10 percent of the company's capital.

(iii) *Other information*: allocation of costs such as the managing director's entertainment expenses, wages and salaries of staff or any other personnel expenses; other liabilities which are not stated in the company's financial statement; supplementary obligations, including mortgages, down-payments and deposits received from third parties; the amount of inventory not kept in the company (e.g. in-transit, consignment or in the hands of third parties etc); withdrawals of capital; tangible assets, including those that are still work-in-progress; bad debts.

(iv) *Estimation methods*: e.g. the inventory valuation methods and if it is different from the previous year.

Other accounting standard and methods

In the case of current assets which are denominated in foreign currencies, it is necessary to state in a footnote whether the value obtained via the rate of exchange on the date of settlement is lower than on the acquisition day. In the case of liabilities which are denominated in foreign currencies, it is necessary to calculate the estimated values using rates of exchange on the obligation date. If the exchange value on the settlement date is greater than previously estimated, a provision should be set up based upon the settlement date exchange value — but only if this is lower. Otherwise no adjustment is necessary.

The estimation of inventory value must be based on one of the following methods: acquisition cost; production cost; acquisition cost (production cost) or market value, whichever is lower; some other standard may be accepted, if sufficient support can be given. Any one of the weighted average method, FIFO, LIFO and standard cost can be used. The total inventory handling expense and the warehouse expense are considered to be part of the acquisition cost. The estimated market value of inventories is subject to an upper and lower limit. The upper limit is the current selling price less the normal profit margin while the lower limit is the cost. The difference between acquisition cost (or the production cost) and an estimated market value of the inventory is also disclosed.

Acquisition costs of financial assets must be kept on record. If the acquisition price is greater than the market price, a provision must be made to reflect the possible loss. If there is any gain on such assets, however, acquisition cost is used. The value

---

[2] A company is an associate if the investing company owns 10 to 25 percent of the associate's total equity.

of tangible assets should be estimated in accordance with invoice prices and any other expenses necessary to produce the assets. If a company produces its own assets, the cost of the purchased material should be capitalised. The value of intangible assets is also based on acquisition costs.

DEFINITION OF ASSETS AND LIABILITIES AND THE RULES FOR VALUATION (*DECRETO-LEI NO. 4/90/M*)

Definition of assets

According to the *Regime Fiscal Das R integracoes E Amortizacoes Do Activo Imobilzado*, assets should be presented in the balance sheet in two broad categories: fixed and current, or tangible and intangible assets. Fixed assets are those which are intended for use on a continuing basis for a company's business operations over more than one year and will not be converted into cash under the normal business activities of the company. Other assets are reclassified as current assets.

Definition of liabilities

Liabilities are divided into two categories, the long-term and short-term. Long-term loans are those which do not have to be repaid within the accounting period. Under *Lei No. 21/28/M*, maturities of more than one year are said to be long-term liabilities. As time passes and the time for repayment of the long-term loans approaches, these loans are classified as current liabilities. Current liabilities are those which normally have to be paid off within one year (as defined in Macau accounting legislation).

Amortization and the valuation rule of assets

Depreciation expense is the allocation of the cost of an asset over its economic life. It is a measure of the asset's wearing out, regardless of whether this arises from use, passage of time, or obsolescence through technology and market changes. The value of fixed assets and accumulated depreciation are based on the following: (a) the price of purchasing the assets together with the additional costs necessary to make the asset operational but excluding the interest if purchased on credit; (b) the direct and indirect material cost of the assets; (c) other costs e.g. the cost of assuming the assets are in good condition. If the value of the asset is unknown, it is necessary to estimate the value for accounting purposes. For tax purposes, if the *Plano Oficial de Contabilidabe* believes that amortization of the depreciation expense is much more than the actual expense, the company will be notified and required to correct the estimation.[3]

In the case of the purchase of second-hand assets, estimation is based on the asset's remaining economic life. Depreciation is based on the acquisition cost, however. If repairs are greater than 10 percent of an asset's book value, the cost can be classified as 'extraordinary' repairs. Effectively, this means that the repair is taken as extending the economic life of the asset and is a part of its value.

Rules of computation of the amortization

Two approaches to calculating depreciation are in use in Macau. One is the maximum allowable rate, the other a lower rate of half the maximum level. The maximum rates are shown in Table 4. At the end of its useful life an asset may still have production capacity. However, any resulting value cannot be treated as depreciable and is not an allowable expense for tax purposes except under certain conditions accepted by the *Direccao dos Servicos de Financas*. If a company does not know the value of its land, the cost of the land is taken to be 20 percent of the total asset value of the company.

Special rules for valuation assets.

There are a number of special rules relating to the valuation of assets which should be noted. If the cost of fixed assets is less than Ptc2000, the depreciation can be fully written off in the year of purchase. However, if these assets are part of other larger fixed assets, the cost should be added to the cost of the latter and depreciation should be calculated on the total amount. Should extraordinary factors cause fixed assets to decrease in value, the company is obliged to identify those factors in footnotes to the accounts. Legal expenses are normally included as part of the value of fixed assets although the value of land excludes any associated legal expenses. Finally, if a company leases fixed assets which need repair, a depreciation allowance will be granted to the company.

---

[3] Under the *Decreto-Lei No. 4/90/M*, rules regarding valuation by replacement cost have only been issued as guidelines and there is no need to disclose replacement cost in the financial statement. Fixed assets such as land and buildings are permitted to be revalued if they have appreciated in value.

Table 4
THE HIGHEST RATES FOR COMPUTING OF THE DEPRECIATION EXPENSE AND THE ESTIMATION OF THE ECONOMIC LIFE FOR AN ASSET IN MACAU:

First group — Buildings and other architectures	rate (%)	useful life
1.1 Living, business and administration building	2%	50
1.2 Industrial building including garage; warehouse; oil station; and parts of architecture of general fixture of car park, hotel and the same kind	4%	25
1.3 Light architectures including fibre; wood; zinc; etc	20%	5
1.4 Metallic reservoir for liquid, fuel	10%	10
1.5 Metallic and mortar-made pier	14.29%	7
1.6 Other building and architectures	8.33%	12

Second group — Fixtures and Fittings		
2.1 Central heating and cool air conditioned system (including refrigerator)	14.29%	7
2.2 Production and distribution system of electric and gas	10%	10
2.3 Water gathering and water distribution system	10%	10
2.4 Fix extinguish (sprinkler and security system)	10%	10
2.5 Radio broadcast and wireless television system	14.29%	70
2.6 Central communication, radiophone and radiotelegraph	10%	10
2.7 Telecommunication steel and underground cable	5%	20
2.8 Elevator, lift	10%	10
2.9 Others	10%	10

Third group — Transportation		
3.1 Aeroplane	12.51%	8
3.2 Ship (any kind of ship)	10%	10
3.3 Light vehicle (including car and van) and motorbike	20%	5
3.4 Heavy vehicle (including bus and lorry)	16.66%	6
3.5 Trailer, Folk style crane, automatic loading vehicles	14.29%	7
3.6 Non-automatic vehicles	25%	4
3.7 Unidentified other transportation or loading cargo vehicles	14.29%	7

Fourth group — Furniture, Comfortable Fittings and Decoration		
4.1 Office furniture	20%	5
4.2 Furniture of hotel, restaurant and of the same kind of business	20%	5
4.3 House furniture	16.66%	6
4.4 Carpets and the same kind	33.33%	3
4.5 Decorating articles (excluding work of art)	33.33%	3
4.6 Other unidentified object	16.66%	6

Table 4 (continued)

Fifth group — Office Equipment	rate (%)	useful life
5.1 Computer, minicomputer and file processing machine	25%	4
5.2 Other office fitting equipment (including copy, fax machine etc)	20%	5

Sixth group — Fixtures and Machines	rate (%)	useful life
6.1 Non-electronic fixture and machine	14.29%	7
6.2 Electronic fixture and machine	20%	5
6.3 Moving hand crane, crane, pulling machine and other related road construction machine	16.66%	6

Seventh group — Instruments, Tools and Utensils	rate (%)	useful life
7.1 Central warm and cool air conditioned system, refrigerator, ventilator that is not in the second group.	20%	5
7.2 Audio-visual equipment, laboratory instrument, electronic instrument and precision instrument, measuring and control equipment	25%	4
7.3 Table utensils and kitchen utensils	50%	2
7.4 Tools and special function utensils	33.33%	3

Eighth group — Other Elements	rate (%)	useful life
8.1 Film, music tape and cassette tape	25%	4
8.2 Metallic cargo container used in transportation	12.5%	8
8.3 Transportation container and other packages	33.33%	3
8.4 Computerized program	33.33%	3
8.5 Mould, character block and coin mould	33.33%	3
8.6 Fire distinguished and safety utensils	33.33%	3
8.7 Clothed, towel, china and glass container	50%	2

Ninth group — Intangible Assets and Deferred Expenditures	rate (%)	useful life
9.1 Beginning deferred expenditure (including preliminary expense, marketing survey, investigate and advertising expense and other beginning expenditure)	33.33%	3
9.2 Not the beginning deferred expenditure (including in capital, change in law position of enterprise, issue of debenture, market investigation, advertising campaign, group change or improvement investigation, fiscal liabilities caused by acquiring or producing the assets, even if not used in the accounting period).	33.33%	3
9.3 Decorating of the building project and deferred maintenance	33.33%	3
9.4 Trademark	10%	10
9.5 Transfer, patents, license, and other authority	*	

Table 4 (continued)

Tenth group — Not Included In The Last Group Assets

10.1	Tax payer should state the appropriate depreciation rate and reason that the *Direaccao dos Servios de Financas* accept.

* rate is decided according to the actual condition approved by *Direccao dos Servios de Financas*

TAXATION AND THE FORM OF COMPANIES

Taxation

The tax system of Macau has evolved from the Portuguese tax system. All commercial and industrial activities which are conducted in Macau are taxable in accordance with the tax rules. The tax rate in Macau is relatively low compared to other Southeast Asian countries and the tax system is one of the simplest in the world. The major public revenue comes from the Complementary Tax and the tax revenues which are collected from the gambling industry.

There are both direct and indirect taxes. Direct taxes include an Industrial Tax (*Contribuicao Industrial*), the Complementary Tax (*Imposto Complementar*), a Professional Tax (*Imposto Profissional*), an Urban Property Tax (*Contribuicao Predial Urbana*), and a Gift and Inheritance Tax (*Sisa*). The indirect taxes include a Tourism Tax, Stamp Duties, a Consumption Tax, revenue from Certificates of Origin (a kind of export tax) and other miscellaneous revenues.

When accounting for companies, it is important to be aware of both the Professional Tax and the Complementary Tax.

Professional Tax: 'Salary' or 'income' tax has been renamed as the 'Professional' tax. The tax authorities require companies to withhold tax on employees' net chargeable income tax every month and remit it directly to the authorities. Thus, employees suffer tax by deduction at source. All revenues, whether in monetary form or otherwise, derived directly from work, are subject to tax. There are two groups of taxpayers, Group 1 and 2 respectively. Group 1 includes those employed by companies in Macau. Group 1 taxpayers pay their Professional Tax at rates on a sliding scale between 10 percent starting at Ptc70 000 per annum and 15 percent on income over Ptc210 000 per annum. The Group 2 taxpayers are those providing professional and technical activities or who are self-employed. In this case, Professional Tax is calculated according to government determined fixed rates for different professions. Examples of this group of taxpayers are auditors, civil engineers, chemists and surgeons. If the amount of the Professional Tax calculated from these fixed rates is less than the amount obtainable by using the tax rates for the Group 1 taxpayers, Group 2 taxpayers are required to pay the greater amount.[4]

The Complementary Tax: 'Profits' tax has been renamed as the 'Complementary' tax. The taxpayers of Complementary tax are divided into two groups, Group A and B respectively. Group A taxpayers consists of persons or companies who are required to have a standard accounting system, capital of not less than Ptc1 000 000 and who have paid profits tax for the last three years averaging Ptc500 000 or more. The financial statements of this group must be audited by a recognized Macau auditor or accountant. Group A taxpayers compute their tax based upon rates beginning at 2 percent on income over Ptc20 000 and rising to 30 percent on income over Ptc300 000. All other companies are classified as Group B. Group B taxpayers are required to report their financial situation to the government individually and they are taxed based on their self-estimated profits. However, the self estimated taxable profit must be vetted by the Finance Department. The tax rate varies by industries and is determined on a case by case basis (Hui and Noronha, 1991).

Forms of companies

There are four types of commercial company in Macau.

Private Limited Company (Sociedade Por Quotas): In this type of company, the liability of each shareholder is limited to the amount that it contributed. There is, however, an important additional liability. If some of the shareholders fail to pay the full amount of the shares and the company experiences financial problems, the other shareholders may be required to contribute the unsettled amount of equity. Each shareholder may hold different amounts of shares in the companies. The transfer of shares is made by public deed through notary in Macau. If the shares are transferred to outsiders, it requires permission of two-thirds of the company's shareholders.

Public Limited Company: This is a joint stock company (*sociedade anonima*). Members are liable only for the payment of their shares. The company can raise capital from the public by issuing shares. Each share has the same value. They are freely

---

[4] Certain groups are exempted from Professional tax: 1. Civil servants; 2. Servants of public administration utility; 3. Missionaries; 4. Personnel working for foreign or international organizations which have contracts with the Portuguese Government or the territory of Macau; 5. Ambassadors; 6. Apprentices and workers over 60 years of age without permanent jobs.

transferable privately or publicly. The corporation needs ten or more initial stockholders and each of these must pay for a proportionate share of the total stock amount. Currently, the minimum capital for corporations is Ptc30 000 000. The stockholder's general meeting is held once a year. Although Macau law covers Public Limited companies and other public companies, the absence of a stock market in Macau means that many large companies base themselves in areas such as Hong Kong. The Macau Government requires foreign public limited companies which have headquarters in Macau to provide a translation of the corporation's registration certificate in Portuguese.

General Partnership: In general partnerships (*sociedade em nome colectivo*) all members are personally liable for the company's debts. Other distinctive characteristics of this type of organisation are: all partners are managers of the company; decisions are made on the principle of 'one man, one vote' and do not depend on the amount of capital contributed by each partner; the transfer of a partnership interest to outsiders or any changes concerning the partnership agreement must be approved unanimously.

Limited Partnership: In limited partnerships (*sociedade em comadita*) there are two types of partners; those with and those without limited liability. It requires two or more persons to set up the limited partnership, at least one of whom must be the general partner. The capital required is not less than Ptc10 000. The liability of each limited partner is limited to the amount that they contribute to the partnership. This type of company combines the characteristics of general partnerships with public limited companies. Only the general partner of the partnership can be involved in the company's daily operation. Limited partners only contribute capital and take no part in the management of the company. The transfer of shares is made by public deed through a notary in Macau. As in the case of the general partnership, if the shares are transferred to outsiders, it requires the consent of the other partners.

Procedure of forming companies

Certain criteria must be met in order to form a company in Macau. The first basic requirement is that there is a minimum number of parties. At least two persons are needed to form a company. However, a public limited company requires at least ten persons. Persons means legal persons, not only individuals e.g. a company can be a shareholder of another company. A second requirement relates to the legal capacity of the parties. Minors cannot enter a company contract without the written permission of their parents. Husband and wives can, however, be shareholders of the same company. Third, permission must be given to the company name by the commercial registry. The registrar can reject the name if it is identical or similar to another company's name which has already been registered, or if the name offends the public morals and will be publicly unacceptable. Fourth, a company cannot conduct an illegal activity. Economic activities can only be exercised by persons who are appointed by the majority of the shareholders. In the banking and insurance sectors, permission must be obtained from the Governor prior to the incorporation of a company. There are additional restrictions and requirements for these sectors e.g. banks must be public limited companies with a minimum share capital of Ptc30 000 000. Fifth, companies should keep a document that specifies the powers of the management and of the shareholders. This is the basic instrument for the constitution or incorporation of the company. It is equivalent, in common law legal systems, to the memorandum and articles of association combined.

MANAGEMENT ACCOUNTING

Accounting standards in Macau, the *Piano Oficia de Contabilidabe,* set the main accounting categories, the uniform accounts code and the standards for financial statements. Categories 9 and 0 are reserved for a company's internal use, including the costing, financial analysis and the preparation of other reports. However, there is no standard format for these costing and management reports. In fact, very little information about management accounting practices in Macau is publicly available. Some details of the characteristics of management accounting systems were obtained by the authors through informal interviews conducted in various industries in Macau and these are reported in this section. As mentioned above, Macau's revenue mainly comes from tourism, gambling, and the manufacturing sectors. Consequently, special emphasis was given to the hotel and the manufacturing industries. In addition, two of the biggest public utility companies were also included in the study. The basic approach to management accounting in Macau is consistent with that described in texts such as Kaplan and Atkinson (1986).

Hotel management accounting

Managers from ten five star hotels were interviewed. It was found that most of the senior accounting posts were held by expatriates who had received their accounting training in their countries of origin, or in the country where the headquarters of the hotel was situated. There was no department solely responsible for management accounting. Preparing management accounting reports is part of the duties of financial accounting departments which perform the cost control functions of management responsibility centres. In fact, different departments also performed their own budgeting and make their own investment decisions. Although casinos are located within the hotels, the latter do not own the former and receive only rent from the casino. Consequently, the casinos' management and its accounts are separate from the hotel's management and general accounts.

Budgeting and the Internal Control System: Budgets were prepared from the bottom up i.e. the department heads or managers were involved in setting-up their own departmental budgets. Department managers were also members of budget committees. Such committees are required for the overall coordination of the budget and to ensure that the final budget packages are realistic and workable. The formal preparation of the budget is the function of the accounting departments. The hotel's financial controller gathered all the information and consolidated it into a final budget for submission to the general manager for approval. Department heads revised the budgets monthly. Each month, budgets for the remaining months of the year were revised to adjust for any changes in circumstances. One of the main purposes of the budget is to outline in advance the revenues expected to be generated and the cost involved in achieving these revenues to later compare these to actual results. During the hotel's general meeting, the department heads were required to explain such variances to the general manager. Typically, variances were broken down into price and quantity variance for the management reports. It was found that some department heads have problems in setting attainable goals. This was specially true for the sales departments. Sales managers set targets higher and higher every year because their performance evaluation to top management was based upon sales performance. Several of those interviewed noted that Macau's shortage of skilled labour made it difficult to recruit a sufficient number of well-trained employees to cope with increased sales volume.

Food and Beverage Outlets: One of the largest revenue sources for hotels in Macau is from food and beverage outlets. In order to have good internal control, all the hotels surveyed had introduced computer systems into their accounting departments. Having served a customer, waiters entered orders directly into the computer so that the information was instantaneously available in the kitchen or bar, the cash register and the accounting department, giving prompt delivery to customers and cashing of money received. At the end of each week, the cash register's total amount was reconciled with the amounts recorded in the accounting department. Some of the hotels' accounting departments produced management analysis of this data in the form of average cheque, average cheque by time of day and the seat turnover. Ledger control in the food and beverage activities was evidently being deemed to be essential in preventing possible loss from employee fraud.

Accounts Receivable and Cash Management: The management of accounts receivable and accounts payable is already one of the most important functions of management accounting in the hotel trade. The ageing report was carried out periodically, once a month usually, uncollectable overdue accounts receivable were removed from the accounts receivable ledger. Accounts were settled in most currencies. Management accounting reports were required to show if there was any exchange profit or loss. At the end of each month, the management department prepared a bank reconciliation and the bank furnished a statement showing daily deposits, the amount of each cheque paid and other items added to or subtracted from the bank balance. Paid cheques accompanied the bank statement. This management control system effectively provided a review of the hotels bookkeeping records.

Management Accounting in the Public Utilities Institutes: Two public utilities institutes, *Electricity-Companhia De Electricidade De Macau* (CEM), and *Telecom Companhia De Telecom De Macau* (CTM) employ a large portion of the population of Macau and are two of the Macau's largest and most profitable organizations (CEM, 1994; CTM, 1994). Senior personnel in the accounting department are sent to Portugal to receive both financial and management accounting training.

Government Involvement in Management Accounting Practice in CEM and CTM: In 1981, with the support of the Macau Government, CEM reconstructed its organization structure in the form shown in Figure 1, to enhance its efficiency and provide a high quality electricity service.

The company has an exclusive concession to produce, import, export, transport, distribute and sell electricity in the territory of Macau under a Concession Contract signed by the Macau Government and CEM in 1985. The concession period is valid for 25 years and subject to certain conditions contained in Concession Contract. In 1987, the Macau Government reduced its shareholding to only 8 percent, making the largest shareholders a Chinese-French company and a Chinese-Portuguese company, each with 45 percent share of capital. The remaining 2 percent is in the hands of minority shareholders. CEM is controlled by the Administrative council and its members are appointed by the shareholders.

In 1985 Telecom changed from a government-owned to a privately owned operation. The Macau Government retained only 1 percent of its shares. CTM committed a great deal of its investment and manpower resources to improving the quality of its services. Some management decisions, however, such as setting the tariff price are determined by the Macau Government. CTM is committed to implementing a price reduction plan. The first phase was implemented at the beginning of 1995, and the second phase has yet to be implemented. The government can use its administrative authority to force CTM to reduce its telephone tariff. At its 1995 annual general meeting, CTM announced a 1994 profit in excess of Ptc200 million, an increase of 12 percent over the previous year. Total sales revenues in 1994 were Ptc1000 million, giving a profit rate of 20 percent. This is the highest profit rate among the public utilities.

Scheme of Control: Management accounting in CEM is handled by the internal auditing and the budgeting and control departments. Internal auditing is responsible for the internal check of the bookkeeping records and reports any irregular events which appear in departmental records. The management accounting department falls

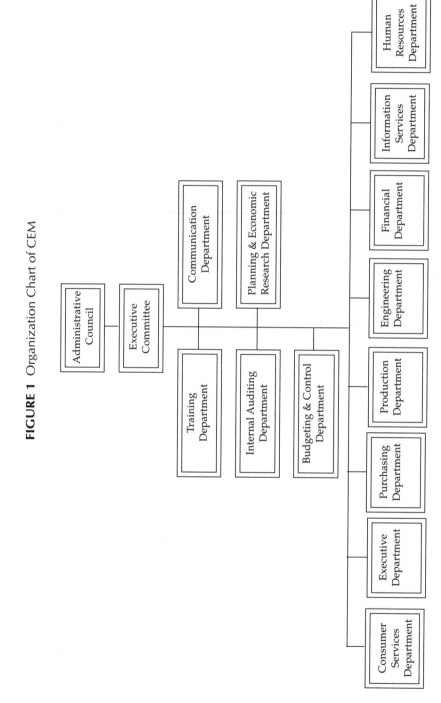

FIGURE 1 Organization Chart of CEM

under the heading of financial activities, which is one of the seven core activities of its organisation. As was noted above, some management and accounting decisions in CEM and CTM are determined by a 'Scheme of Control Agreement' with the government. The agreement regulates the permitted rate of return to shareholders of the company. If the profits of either company exceed a predetermined rate, the companies have to transfer the excess amount to a development provision account which may only be used to improve the electricity or telecom facilities respectively. In addition, the companies must set aside some of the excess profits to provide for tariff stabilization (i.e. to smooth price movements). The companies are permitted to revalue tangible fixed assets in accordance with these provisions. The revaluation surplus must be allocated to the shareholder's fund, provision for development and provision for tariff stabilization and cannot be distributed to shareholders. Macau's complementary tax is 15.75 percent on profits before provisions are made under the Scheme of Control. The amount of spending on capital projects which are deemed to be in the interest of the economic development of Macau are deducted from assessable income in equal annual instalments over three years.

Budgeting and Internal Control: The departments of both CEM and CTM are responsibility centres. They have autonomy and managers run the departments with minimal control from top management, including staffing and budgeting. They set their own departmental budgets. Department managers are also the members of the finance committees. Such committees are responsible for the overall co-ordination of budgets and for ensuring that the budget is implemented. The formal preparation of the budget is the function of the budgeting and control department in CEM and the management accounting department in CTM. The main duty of the head of Budgeting in CEM and the head of management accounting at CTM is to prepare a final budget and submit it to the Executive Committee for approval. The heads also approve and allocate resources to each department every three months, prepare the management accounting reports, and perform variance analysis of actual results from budget.

Accounts Receivables Management: The largest source of revenue for the two companies is from the customer paying tariff bills. The collection of accounts receivables is one of the most difficult tasks for the accounts or finance department at both CTM and CEM. In a recent attempt to reduce administration costs, a proposal for a joint payment collection service for customers of CTM, CEM together with SAAM (the water authorities in Macau) has been formulated which permits using a single payment system for electricity, water supply and telephone services.

The manufacturing sector management accounting

Bill of Material: There are about 3000 factories in Macau employing 50 percent of Macau's labour force. Most of the factories are small in size, employing less than 100 workers. Formal management accounting practices are not common. Accounting departments handle the bookkeeping records, including receivable and payable accounts. They prefer more highly qualified accounting personnel[5]. Simple management accounting analysis is sometimes conducted by the heads of departments and the directors of the factories. Controlling the bill of material (BOM) by using variance analysis is the most important task. The BOM can highlight price variances for each individual component of products by showing the difference between the standard and actual cost. The BOM is also used to ascertain whether suppliers are charging reasonable prices.

Relocation costs: Recently, some manufacturers have shifted production to nearby Chinese cities in order to reduce production costs and transportation costs. The calculation of costs is therefore important. The definition of relocation costs by the manufacturer in Macau is simply the cost of transferring production to China. If the total production cost, including the transfer of imported material and skilled labour, together with Chinese local supplies of material and labour is higher than manufacturing in Macau, then transfer to China will not be considered. Sometimes, particularly if the product is export-oriented, the transportation cost of the products from China back to Macau (in order to obtain the advantages of quotas from the EEC or US) will be included in the calculation. On the other hand, if the products are intended for the Chinese market, the decision of setting up the production centre in China is based upon the labour costs and availability of production materials in China versus Macau. The motivation for transfer is therefore based upon strict rational economic criteria rather than on social, political or other grounds.

CONCLUDING REMARKS

Portuguese practice, as would be expected, affects the form of Macau accounting. Accounting standards are mostly derived from Portugal. The Macau Government translates accounting statements into Chinese because most businesses in Macau are owned by ethnic Chinese. Some of the 'translations' are very confusing, however, which makes it difficult to assess the impact of standardised rules on the *practice* of accounting. Whatever the case, the principles underlying current accounting standards

---

[5] Including persons with level three qualifications of the London Chamber of Commerces' bookkeeping exams.

are expected to remain essentially unchanged during the 50-year period after the reversion of Macau back to China in 1999. In contrast, management accounting and other financial management practices are very much affected by UK and US practice. This is at least partly due to the training of accounting personnel which has, in the past, taken place mostly overseas. It would appear therefore, at least superficially, that Chinese culture has little affect on attitudes towards accounting in Macau.

This may change in the future given the ethnic Chinese character of the population. Macau now provides more opportunities for local accounting training. Macau University provides basic training for all aspects of accounting and finance and international audit firms have begun operating in Macau. Since 1990, the latter have also provided various types of professional training for local people. Hopefully, the MSCPA will cooperate with professional firms and the Macau Government to provide a more uniform professional qualification and develop Macau's own professional examination system.

REFERENCES

CEM (1994), *CEM Yearbook*, Companhia de electricity de Macau, SARL.
CTM (1994), *CTM Yearbook, Companhia de telecommunicacoes de Macau,* SARL.
Hui, B.Y and C. Noronha (1991), *Macau tax and economy*, Macau Management Association.
Kaplan, R.S. and A.A. Atkinson (1986), *Advanced management accounting*, Prentice-Hall.
Macau Government (1983), 'Accounting standards', Assenado em 13 de Junho de 1983, Publique-se, O Govemador Vasco de Almeide e Costa.

ACCOUNTING SYSTEMS IN CAMBODIA

Dyna Seng[*]

BACKGROUND

The Kingdom of Cambodia lies in the south-western Indochinese peninsula in South-east Asia and covers an area of 181 916 sq. km. It is bordered by Thailand and Laos to the north, by Vietnam to the east and by the Gulf of Thailand to the south. Geographically, Cambodia is dominated by large central lowland covering about three-fourths of the total land area and by the Mekong river and several of its branches, which flow southward through the eastern part of the country. The central lowland surrounds the lake Tonle Sap. The river system, the Mekong river and lake Tonle Sap, flood much of the central lowland during the rainy season. The Mekong river drains most of Cambodia and flows for about 505 km averaging about two km in width throughout its course through the country. Each year, its floodwaters deposit a layer of fertile soil over the countryside, which enriches the land. The climate is tropical and humid. The wet season is from May to October and the dry season is from November to April. The temperature is generally between 20°C and 36°C, and the annual average in Phnom Penh, the capital of Cambodia, is 27°C.

The majority of the population in Cambodia belong to the Mon-Khmer ethnic group. The people of Cambodia are called Cambodian or Khmer. The Khmers were established in the present area of Cambodia by the end of prehistoric times. A non-Khmer state of Funan based upon sea trade had strong ties with Indian and Sumatra and some diplomatic and cultural links also existed with China between 200 and 500 AD. Around 800

*Accountancy Department, University of Otago, New Zealand.

AD after several hundreds of years of contention between northern and southern king-dom (the Chenla period), the powerful state of Angkor was established in northern Cam-bodia and had an important influence on surrounding countries, especially Vietnam and Thailand. By 1300 AD, Angkor had diminished in authority and, until the French colonial period, Cambodia existed as a succession of small, weak states dominated by Vietnam and Thailand. Cambodia became a French protectorate in 1863 and was incorporated into French Indo-China (i.e., Vietnam, Laos and Cambodia). The French protectorate pre-vented Cambodia from being divided between Vietnam and Thailand. Some modernisa-tion of the infrastructure took place, notably in the form of roads and railways. Between 1940–45 the Japanese took military control of Cambodia but left much of the formal administration in French hands. Independence was obtained on 9 November 1953. In 1955, King Sihanouk, who had been crowned in 1941 and then aged 18, abdicated in favour of his father and became the leader of a new political party as Prince Sihanouk. In 1970, Sihanouk was deposed by a right-wing coup, led by the then Prime Minister, Lt-Gen. Lon Nol. In 1975, after a period of turmoil the Khmer Rouge (Communist Khmer) gained control of Phnom Penh. The country was subjected to a programme of radical social change immediately after the Khmer Rouge's assumption of power. The towns were largely evacuated, and their inhabitants put to work in rural areas. Many of hun-dreds of thousands died as a result. In 1979, Phnom Penh was captured by invading Vietnamese-led forces, and the People's Republic of Kampuchea, a communist state, proclaimed. Under international pressure and military resistance from a variety of sources, Vietnam withdrew its forces from the country in 1989. Following a period of difficulty, a Peace Agreement was brokered by the UN and signed in 1991. In 1993, about 90 percent of the electorate participated in UN administrated elections to the Constituent Assembly, which were contested by 20 political parties. Under its present constitution, Cambodia is a constitutional monarchy. The monarch, Prince Sihanouk, is the Head of State, selected by a Throne Council from among three descendants of the royal lines. Legislative power is vested in the 120-member National Assembly, which is elected for a term of five years by universal adult suffrage. Executive power is held by the Cabinet, headed by the Prime Minister, who is appointed by the King, at the recommendation of the chairman of the National Assembly, from among the representatives of the winning party. The legal framework and professional arrangements have been strongly influenced by France. The principal religion of Cambodia is Theravada Buddhism. An estimated nine-tenths of the population are Buddhists. The national language of Cambodia is Khmer, but other lan-guages such as Vietnamese, Chinese, French and English are also used. The population, in 1991, was estimated at about 8.8 m with a density of 50 per sq. km, making it one of the most thinly populated countries in South-east Asia. Phnom Penh had an estimated population of 900 000 in 1991.

The economy of Cambodia is based on agriculture and related industries. Cambodia is a relatively economically undeveloped country. The civil war during the past two decades has largely prevented the kind of advances seen in other South-east Asian countries. Agriculture employs three-fourths of the workforce and is dominated by subsistence farm-ing. Rice is the chief staple food. The main kinds of natural resources are timber, gem-stones, some iron ore, manganese, phosphates and hydropower potential. Industry accounted for about 12 percent of Gross Domestic Product (GDP) in 1992. The main

kinds of manufacturing are handicrafts, rice milling, sugar, liquor, beer, tyres, pharma-
ceutical products, textiles, cement and soap. The Royal Government of Cambodia an-
nounced that it was to encourage the establishment of agro-industrial enterprises (sugar
and vegetable oil refineries and factories producing paper pulp) and promote the produc-
tion of fertilizers, petroleum and heavy construction and mechanical equipment. Energy
is derived mainly from timber. In the early 1990s, a thermo-electric power plant was
under development, and a diesel-electric power station was being restored. Over the past
decade Cambodia has been coming to terms with the destruction of its economic base
by war and political upheaval. It remains one of the world's poorest countries, with an
estimated annual income per head of between US$200 and US$210 at the beginning of
1993. GDP expanded by 13.5 percent in 1991 and by 6–8 percent in 1992. In 1993,
output declined dramatically in the second quarter of the year, probably due to a lack of
confidence in the political situation, but is expected to grow at an average annual rate
of about 3 percent per annum. Cambodia's main problems are a lack of skilled
labour and a poor infrastructure. In the first six months of 1991, there was a trade deficit
of US$159.4 m and consumer prices almost doubled in 1992. The inflation rate was
50 percent in the first half of 1990. In 1986, Cambodia's gross long-term debt was
US$622 m, of which 61 percent was owed to the USSR and other members of the now
defunct Council for Mutual Economic Assistance, and 38 percent to members of the
Organisation for Economic Co-operation and Development. The major trading partners
in 1991 were Singapore, Thailand, Vietnam, Japan, and Hong Kong. Cambodia's major
imports are fuel, agricultural materials, construction materials and consumer goods, while
its major exports are rubber and timber. The unit of currency is the new riel.

DS/R.J.W.

INTRODUCTION

Accounting systems are designed to measure and report the economic activities of
entities over a period of time. However, the objectives of accounting tend to differ
somewhat between capitalist and socialist countries. In capitalist countries, accounting
information is used by both external and internal users for their decision making. In
socialist countries, accounting information is used mainly by the central government
for economic planning and control (Lebow & Tondkar, 1986). Obviously, the need for
accounting information varies from country to country, depending upon the relative
congruence or divergence between the public policies or national philosophies which
guide its methodology (Berry, 1982). Cambodia is a developing country and as such
the same considerations with regard to accounting apply to it as they do to other
developing countries (see Enthoven, 1991).

   While accounting in developed countries has undergone a long evolutionary
process, the history of accounting in Cambodia is very short. The French Unified
Accounting System (UAS) was adopted by Cambodia after it gained independence
from France in 1953. This system was abandoned in 1975 but re-established in 1993.

During most of the intervening years, the Vietnamese socialist system of accounting was used in its place. Cambodia has thus experienced both capitalist and socialist forms of accounting in recent years and this makes it more difficult to assess the present situation regarding the state of accounting and also to speculate confidently on the future shape of Cambodian accounting[1]. Nevertheless, an understanding of the recent historical development of accounting in Cambodia is necessary in any attempt to rationalise present practices and the next section provides more detail on this matter. In Section 3 the structure of ownership of Cambodian businesses is briefly described and its implications for accounting noted. Section 4 provides more detail on standard setting and present accounting practices. It also reflects upon the way in which certain specific important items in financial statements are treated or may be expected to be treated in the future. Section 5 contains some concluding remarks.

HISTORICAL DEVELOPMENT OF ACCOUNTING IN CAMBODIA

During the period of the French Protectorate and until April 1975, Cambodia adopted the French accounting system. The Cambodian accounting system during that period, like the French accounting system itself, was dominated by legal considerations (Most, 1971)[2]. The core of financial accounting and reporting in Cambodia was the national accounting code that applied to the keeping of accounts and their presentation. As in France, the national accounting code or chart of accounts was published under the title *Plan Comptable General*. The contents of the *Plan*, adapted from France, resemble an accounting manual, with a chart of accounts, instructions and guidelines for its application, and a model balance sheet and profit and loss account. The Plan was applied in all state agencies of an industrial or commercial type and in both privately owned and publicly owned firms.

The effects of the *Plan Comptable General* on financial accounting and reporting have been deeply pervasive. There would hardly be a practising Cambodian accountant whose professional training was not based on the *Plan*. As a result, it appears that the intellectual conditioning of accountants in Cambodia is more akin to the training of a lawyer, with its emphasis on the specifics of written law, rather than to the more judgemental and decision-oriented training of accountants in the English-speaking world. However, the *Plan* facilitates interpersonal and inter-enterprise communication between accountants and users.

---

[1] It is very difficult to obtain reliable information on the state of financial accounting practice in Cambodia at the present time and much of the material contained in this chapter has been obtained through personal communication with members of Cambodian Government.

[2] During the period of colonial rule by the French, educators and native higher ranking officials often received their education in France.

Between April 1975 and December 1978, Cambodia was ruled by the Communist regime led by Pol Pot. During that time there was no currency and no financial accounting system in use in the country. There was, in fact, no school or any form of education at all. Part of the doctrine of the Khmer Rouge was derived from the Marxist theory of value. The emphasis of such a system was on accounting for physical quantities. The accounting system was based upon an extreme form of a command economy. No importance was attributed to the monetary value of wealth and thus to the establishment of market prices by demand and supply. Consequently there was no place for the kind of financial accounting systems used in Western countries during the Pol Pot period.

When Vietnam took control of Cambodia in December 1978, Cambodia adopted the Vietnamese accounting system (which was mainly based on the Soviet Union's accounting system and is described in the chapter on Accounting in Vietnam). The Vietnamese left in 1989 but use of their system continued until the middle of 1993. The Vietnamese accounting system during that period consisted of a set of standardised accounts defined for the enterprise by the central government. All firms, either in industrial or commercial sectors, followed standardised accounting rules and procedures. The enterprise accountant, therefore, was given almost no decision making responsibilities. Standardisation of this type enabled the aggregation of data at regional and national levels and hence accounting data from one group of industries could easily be added to the information compiled by other industries. This uniformity was an important element in the central planning and control within the Cambodian economy. However, there were problems associated with this system. For example, because prices and output quotas for most goods were set by the government as part of its management of the national economy, it could manipulate the profits of an enterprise. Moreover, prices set by governments do not usually respond sufficiently quickly to changes in market conditions. As a result, the Vietnamese form of accounting system failed to measure and report information concerning the economic efficiency of enterprises. Another problem relating to the Vietnamese system was that enterprise managers did not have enough incentive to produce consistently high quality goods since there were guaranteed markets for their goods. These factors together have left a legacy of poor quality, inefficiently produced goods showing graphically the economic consequences that inappropriately designed accounting systems can have on a society.

Cambodia readopted the French style UAS in 1993. French accounting text books have been translated for teaching purposes and the French *Plan Comptable General* in a modified form became effective on 1 January 1994[3]. This is essentially the same

---

[3]Such is the level of secrecy surrounding these matters that it has not been possible to ascertain the extent of modifications to the French system. In the absence of evidence to the contrary it would appear modifications are minimal.

approach as is taken with respect to the law in general: the Cambodian Government uses French law as a starting point and implements its provisions after making appropriate changes or revisions. In the future, it is hoped that international aid may alleviate the lack of resources which is responsible for this approach to law making. An example of current aid of this type is a four-year business program sponsored by Georgetown University of the USA in the Accounting and Finance Department of the Institute of Economics in Phnom Penh. This program seeks to emphasise the training of specific skills such as accounting, management, quantitative analysis and marketing. It is especially important to provide this type of education in Cambodia because business skills are in short supply and is likely to continue to be so for a number of years[4].

STRUCTURE OF OWNERSHIP

Generally speaking, the typical firm is family owned in Cambodia. There is presently no clear distinction between sole trader, partnership, and company organisations like that which exists in western countries, although this may change with new companies legislation which is currently being debated. Usually, therefore, there is no separation between management and ownership as the family unit both runs and manages the business. In smaller businesses there is a lack of extensive bookkeeping records. This may be due to the fact that little trade is conducted through credit, as well as that most of the trading firms are family owned and operated. This, of course, hampers the development of the Cambodian accounting profession.

Businesses are not presently required to prepare annual financial statements and file them with the tax authorities, and there are few companies in the industrial and service sector in Cambodia. Foreign companies usually use the procedures of their home countries in accounting for their Cambodian subsidiaries. Subsidiaries' records are also typically kept in the language of the country of origin of the holding company, with minimum financial recording taking place in Khmer. The government is now planning to require foreign companies operating in Cambodia to prepare their financial statements using Khmer language versions as well as their language of origin for tax purposes.

The situation in Cambodia at present is characterised by weakness and under-development in the financial sector. The absence of extensive commercial banking facilities is retarding the growth of economic affairs. Partly because of the absence of

---

[4]See Tan (1974). The appendix contains an illustrative curriculum of a four-year business program in a Cambodian university.

such facilities, credits are furnished, in the majority of cases, by individual dealers and lenders at a very high rate of interest, usually with no written contract. Capital thus tend to be self-funded or borrowed from relatives or friends. Banks may lend up to 30 percent of the market value of building which is used as security. The term of loans is usually short, for a maximum of three months with the possibility of renewal. Interest charged is typically high (e.g. currently over 1.5 percent per month)[5]. There is no organised capital market in the form of a stock exchange.

ACCOUNTING PRACTICES

Toward the end of 1993 accounting in Cambodia changed from a simple cash receipts and disbursements system to the use of an accrual-based system. This change is presumably attributable to the more open government economic policies now being pursued toward the outside world and to social and political developments. For example, English as well as French is now being taught in schools and universities, whereas during the Vietnamese occupation Vietnamese and Russian were taught alongside French as foreign languages.

The state of standard setting and sources of legislation

There is no statement of accounting standards and no professional accounting body. However a new, separate professional institution called the *Compagnie Nationale des Commissaires aux Comptes (CNCC)* is in the process of being formed. It is intended that this body will set accounting standards so that foreign companies will have to conform to those standards when preparing financial statements. It should, however, be noted that there is also no system of accounting standards in France comparable to those of the International Accounting Standards Committee, the UK Accounting Standards Board or the US Financial Accounting Standards Board (Standish, 1991). Consequently, the development of Cambodian accounting will not necessarily be accompanied by the establishment of the type of regulatory framework which seems to be developing in some other South-east Asian countries such as Malaysia and the Philippines.

Before 1975, Cambodia followed a Companies Act promulgated in 1965 which was mainly based on French companies law. This legislation is currently being used as a model for a new Companies Act.

---

[5]This information was obtained verbally from sources within large Cambodian financial institutions.

Valuation of assets

The valuation rules used for non-monetary assets in Cambodia are as follows. Fixed assets are valued at cost and depreciation is charged using the straight line method and applying standard rates for differing structures. For example, depreciation is computed at the rate of between 2 percent and 5 percent per annum for different types of construction materials, while plant, machinery, and furniture are depreciated at the rate of 10 percent per annum. These practices probably reflect the influence of the French and Soviet accounting principles, for both stress uniformity and consistency, though not necessarily for the same reasons. In the case of inventories, the basic rule is the lower of cost and market. Prior to 1994, stock was always valued at the weighted average cost of acquisition or production. Since the beginning of 1994, the value of inventories can be measured on a first-in first-out basis or weighted average cost. Where the market value rule is applied, a provision is expensed and the stock is carried forward at written down value, as is done in comparable situations under the Anglo-American system of accounting.

Profit and loss account

The profit and loss account may be prepared, at the option of an enterprise, either in a two-column format with costs on the left-hand side and revenues on the right-hand side, or in a single column, narrative form. The *Plan* requires cost classification on the basis of the nature or type of expenditure rather than on the basis of function or purpose, which is the method commonly adopted under the Anglo-American approach. This reflects the objective of the state that cost classification be homogeneous between enterprises and across industries in order to enhance the usefulness of economic statistics and inter-firm comparisons and for the purpose of price regulation (Standish, 1991).

Taxation

Accounting for taxation is affected by a number of matters peculiar to Cambodia. The tax structure of most developing countries is characterised by a heavy dependence on indirect taxes and custom duties, and Cambodia is no exception to this pattern. This is in part due to the absence of sound accounting practices. Without reliable accounting data, the national administration of an income tax becomes a difficult, if not impossible, task. Cambodia is mainly a cash economy in which few contracts are signed, few records are kept and there is little systematic recording of workers' incomes. This lack of information makes it difficult to form reliable estimates of tax liability. Direct taxation requires not only satisfactory accounting at the enterprise level but also a qualified staff of accountants for the collection and administration of tax revenues (Holzer & Tremblay, 1973).

Three main types of taxes are levied on businesses in Cambodia at the present time. These are a 'patent' tax, a sales tax and a profits tax. The patent tax is similar in form to what would be described as a sales tax in Anglo-American accounting terminology. It is levied on the production of goods or services with liability being based on last year's sales. The Cambodian 'sales' tax on the other hand is also a turnover tax levied on gross receipts from the sale of goods or services and from exports and imports. The sales tax is not usually levied on very small businesses due to difficulties in collecting the tax, but the patent tax is levied on such firms, although, in practice, liabilities are often determined by negotiation with collectors on the spot. The 'profit' tax, as the name suggests, is calculated on the profits made by businesses. However, as with the case of the patent tax, it is generally not possible to assess liability accurately for the reasons given above[6].

It is intended to introduce income taxation on personal incomes. The Finance Ministry recently stated that the proposed tax bands will be levied at 5 percent on monthly salaries of between US$300 and US$400, 15 percent on salaries between US$400–US$4000, 20 percent on US$4000–US$8000 and 30 percent on salaries over US$8000 (*Phnom Penh Post*, 17–30 June 1994). The lower income level appears to be around the annual salary level of government employees. It seems, however, quite likely that there will be significant assessment and collection problems since the majority of taxpayers are not required to file income tax returns. It is not altogether clear as to how the new tax system will affect businesses in general and accounting in particular. However, the net effect of higher personal income and corporate profits taxes will probably be to increase the relative tax burden on those companies conducting their affairs in accordance with the spirit of the new legislation, i.e. high profile companies such as multinational companies (MNCs) which are important to the future economic growth of the country. Given the current state of the Cambodian economy, there is a danger that the new tax regime might provide greater incentives towards corruption. Furthermore, the new taxes will probably not encourage inefficient and dishonest companies to reform. Reform, however, is essential if Cambodia wishes to grow economically, for it must support the development of competitive businesses and encourage farmers who are unproductive by modern

---

[6]The patent tax is paid once at the beginning of each year and is levied at a rate of between 0.5 percent and 1 percent on last year's sales. The sales tax is paid monthly at the end of each month and is levied between 1 percent and 2 percent. It is intended that companies will be required to pay an upfront monthly 0.5 percent tax based on profit forecasts (*Phnom Penh Post*, 8–21 April 1994). The profit tax ranges between 8 percent and 40 percent. Corporate profits tax is currently 20 percent. In addition to these direct taxes, Cambodian businesses have to pay a daily space levy of between 100 riels (5 cents) and 200 riels (10 cents) and customs duties on imported goods. Seventy percent of the government's revenue currently comes from custom duties (*Asia Alert*, February 1995). Like the sales and patent taxes, the space levy is often determined by negotiation. The space levy is small relative to the other taxes.

standards of agriculture to join the urban economy (*Phnom Penh Post*, April 22–May 5, 1994).

Consolidation accounting

Cambodia has adopted the French method of consolidation accounting. In France, consolidation accounting was introduced as a result of the adoption of the EEC Seventh Directive and is now compulsory for economically defined groups except for those falling below a specified size limit (Pham, 1988). Previously, and this was reflected in Cambodia's accounting system prior to 1975, the focus had been on the ability of individual companies to discharge their obligations to third parties and the state. However, due to the need to obtain finance on international capital markets, it is understood[7] that groups resident in Cambodia are or will be permitted to adopt certain accounting principles that depart from previously accepted French accounting standards and are comparable to Anglo-American standards.

Majority control through equity is the defining criteria for consolidation. Aggregation of accounts is line by line carried through after eliminating intra-group transactions. In the case of enterprises owned by partners or a limited number of shareholders (such as joint ventures) the proportion of equity owned determines the fractional amount to be consolidated in the case of each individual account. The equity method is used in the case of non-controlling equity investments of at least 20 percent. Here the proportion of equity in capital, accumulated reserves and retained income applicable to these interests is reported as such in the investing party's consolidated accounts.

Auditors

Prior to 1994, government inspectors audited the accounts of state enterprises on an irregular basis. Inspectors were then under the control of the Ministry of Justice and prior to that they were under the control of the Ministry of Finance. Once the new Cambodian CNCC equivalent of its French counterpart has been formed, inspectors will be under its control. There are also controllers under the supervision of the Inspectors. These hold less senior qualifications[8]. Auditors are required to certify whether the financial statements conform with legal requirements (*regularite*) and that the application of accepted valuation rules has been carried out in good faith (*sincerite*). Generally speaking, however, external and internal auditing and related auditing professional organisations are not well developed in Cambodia at the present time.

---

[7]This opinion is based upon communications with staff of the Institute of Economics, Phnom Penh.
[8]In France the auditor is also controlled through the French Compagnie Nationale des Commissaires aux Comptes.

Management accounting

Partly due to recent historical events and, in particular, the effect of a command economy over the preceding decade and a half, management accounting as a professional designation is as yet a relatively unimportant element in the accounting system of Cambodia. The entrepreneurial and managerial classes frequently have inadequate training in sound management accounting techniques to enable them to develop satisfactory levels of skill in efficient planning, decision making and control. As a consequence, cost records tend to be poorly maintained and based upon *ad hoc* cost and allocation procedures. Unlike financial accounting, where there is at least some chance that the appropriate professional skills will be learnt on the job, with management accounting techniques, unless the more advanced approaches to scientific management are taught in tertiary institutions, it is likely that the relevant higher, professional management accounting skills will not be learnt at all.

The major problem in management accounting, then, is education. However, steps are now being taken to address this issue. Management accounting has begun to be taught at the Phnom Penh Institute of Economics. This, of course, pushes the problem of skill shortages back one further step: teachers are not highly qualified and their pay is poor by international standards. In addition, for want of competent teachers and appropriate pedagogical means, the problem is exacerbated. Teaching aids such as textbooks, labs, projectors, etc. all increasingly essential in the promotion of scientific management, are deficient. Furthermore, few publications are available. However, it is to be hoped that greater opportunities to travel abroad and the organisation of local conferences will help to alleviate this problem in the future. An issue which periodically crops up, and which relates to some extent to the use of the accounting system model, is the choice of French or English as the medium of communication. Students sometimes complain that English would be more useful as an international language but, to date, this viewpoint has not received support from either politicians or the bureaucracy, many of whom tend to have been educated in France. Most students and officials still tend to go to France to continue their study although examples of top politicians being educated in countries like Australia are now more common. The predominant non-indigenous language used in commercial transactions in South-east Asia today is English. Thus it may be that the Anglo-American system of education may be more relevant to the needs of the new generation of Cambodians.

Nevertheless, as things stand today, the main influence on management accounting thinking is likely to be dominated by French thinking in the short term. However, although the cultural background and present education and training systems in Cambodia points toward French influences, the management accounting practices adopted by new large organisations setting up businesses in Cambodia are likely to become more influential in the longer term future. Table 1 gives some details of newly established firms in Cambodia in the early part of 1995.

Table 1
INVESTMENT PROJECTS APPROVED SINCE THE PROMULGATION OF
INVESTMENT LAW, AUGUST 4, 1994

No.	Company name	Country	Activity
1.	Asia Pacific Breweries Ltd	Singapore	Brewery
2.	Kudong Corporation	Cambodia/Korea	Garment
3.	Panorama Industrial Co Ltd	USA	Garment
4.	Prominent Wing Group	Hong Kong	Garment
5.	Wing Hung International Co Ltd	Hong Kong	Garment
6.	CWT/Sihanoukville Port	Singapore	Dry port
7.	Raffles International	Singapore	Tourism (royal/grand hotels)
8.	FACB	Malaysia	Royal sports and turf
9.	Indosat	Indonesia	Telecom
10.	Leader Universal Holdings Berhad	Malaysia	Power cables
11.	Cambodian Mankok Garment Factory Co Ltd	China	Garment
12.	Wing Group Cambodia-Development Invt. Co Ltd	Australia/Cambodia	Cigarette
13.	Cooper and Lybrand Indochina Pte Ltd	Singapore	Auditing, accounting tax advisory
14.	Brasseries BGI Cambodge	France	Service
15.	Kamsa Tobacco Corporation	Cambodia/HK	Beer brewery and soft drink
16.	Cambodia Blue Bird International Garment Co Ltd	China	Tobacco and cigarettes
17.	Leader Universal Holdings Berhad	Malaysia	Garment
18.	Angkor Development Co	Taiwan	Energy
19.	Advance Resources Pte Ltd	Cambodia/Malaysia	Agriculture
20.	Royal Housing (Cambodia) Co Ltd	Canada	Palm oil plantation
			Construction system
			Manufacturing plant

Source: *The Cambodia Times*, January 15–21, 1995.

As can be seen, there are relatively few new firms which are directly owned by French organisations. Most, in fact, appear to come from Malaysia and elsewhere in the South-east Asia region. This makes it most likely that Anglo-American and possibly Japanese styles of management and management accounting will become more influential on practices in Cambodia in the future.

CONCLUSION

The need for reliable and fuller accounting information will become more important as industrial development of the Cambodian economy takes place. It is an indispensable tool of management and its absence may be a serious handicap to the growth of indigenous enterprises. It seems most likely in this context that Cambodia will follow the same practices as those of its more powerful economic neighbours in the Asia-Pacific region.

The history of accounting systems in Cambodia is very short. Cambodia was under a French protectorate for 91 years and accounting developed under the strong influence of French culture until April 1975. Under the Communist regime led by Pol Pot between April 1975 and December 1978 Cambodia had no accounting system whatsoever and there was no currency in use during that time. Latterly, between 1979 and 1993, Vietnamese practices were influential and recently Cambodia has reverted to a French system though with more Anglo-American influences. Against this background of change, accounting in Cambodia is now faced with a series of technical, educational and operational problems. The function of accounting and auditing in all sectors of the economy is not yet well developed. Furthermore, it is not clear to what extent the importance of the development of accounting for Cambodia's economic development is recognised.

REFERENCES

Berry, M. (1982), 'The accounting function in socialist economies', *The international journal of accounting*, Vol. 8, No. 1, pp. 185–98.

Enthoven, A. (1991), 'Accounting in developing countries', *Comparative international accounting*, C. Nobes and R. Parker (Eds), (3rd edition), Prentice-Hall, pp. 254–80.

Holzer, H. and D. Tremblay (1973), 'Accounting and economic development: The cases of Thailand and Tunisia', *The international journal of accounting*, Vol. 9, No. 1, pp. 67–80.

Hooper, F.H. and W. Yust (Eds) (1994), *Britannica book of the year*, Encyclopaedia Britannica, Inc., Chicago.

Lebow, M. and R. Tondkar (1986), 'Accounting in the Soviet Union', *The international journal of accounting*, Vol. 22, No. 1, pp. 61–79.

Most, K. (1971), 'The French accounting experiment', *The international journal of accounting*, Vol. 7, No. 1, pp.15–27.

Pham, D. (1988), 'France and The Seventh Directive', *International group accounting*, Gray, S.J. and A.G. Coenenberg (Eds), Croom Helm, pp. 76–94.

Scheid, J.C. and P. Walton (1992), 'France', *European accounting guide*, Alexander, D. and S. Archer (Eds), Academic Press.

Standish, P. (1991) 'Financial reporting in France', *Comparative international accounting*, C. Nobes and R. Parker (Eds), (3rd edition), Prentice-Hall, pp. 159–93.

Tan, K.H. (1974), *Role of the universities in development planning: The Khmer Republic case*, Regional Institute of Higher Education and Development, Singapore.

Appendix
CURRICULUM FOR FOUR YEAR CAMBODIAN BUSINESS PROGRAMME

Year 1: Introductory year
   The goal in the first year is to expose the student to the many different functional skill areas of business.

First Semester		Second Semester	
Introduction to Management	45	Management II	45
Economics I	45	Economics II	45
Accounting I	45	Accounting II	45
Marketing I	45	Marketing II	45
English for Business	90	English for Business	90
Total contact Hours	270	Total Contact Hours	270

Year 2: Second year students will continue studies in the core curriculum subjects of Accounting, Management, Quantitative Analysis and Marketing and add to the knowledge gained during the first two semesters.

First Semester		Second Semester	
Business Policy and Procedures I	45	Business Policy and Procedure II	45
Money and Banking	45	Taxation	45
Managerial Accounting	45	Cost Accounting	45
Business Statistics	45	Market Research	45
English	90	English	90
Total Contact Hours	270	Total Contact Hours	270

Year 3: In the third year students are required to select an area of specialization. The choice will be either Manufacturing and Marketing or Accounting and Finance.

First Semester
Core Courses

Organizational Behaviour	45
Personnel Management/Labour Relations	45
Fundamentals of Corporate Finance	45
Business English	45
	180

CURRICULUM FOR FOUR YEAR CAMBODIAN BUSINESS PROGRAMME
(continued)

Specialized Courses

Manufacturing and Marketing		Accounting and Finance	
Production Management	45	Financial Management	45
Marketing Management	45	International Trade	45
Total Contact Hours	270	Total Contract Hours	270

Second Semester
Core Courses

Organizational Behaviour II	45
Human Relations	45
Business Law	45
Business English	45
	180

Specialized Courses

Manufacturing and Marketing		Accounting and Finance	
Manufacturing Technology	45	Financial Institutions	45
Individual R&D project on		Individual R&D project of	
Manufacturing and Marketing	45	Financial/Accounting subject	45
Total Contact Hours	270	Total Contact Hours	270

Year 4: Fourth year students will be expected to spend a significant portion of their time doing individual research and expanding their knowledge base.

First Semester
Core Courses

Business Ethics	45
Cambodian National Economic Policy	45
Cambodian Industry and Trade	45
Cambodian Agribusiness	45
	180

Specialized Courses

Manufacturing and Marketing		Accounting and Finance	
Inventory Management and Logistics	45	Investment Management	45
Advertising	45	Principles of Auditing	45
Total Contact Hours	270	Total Contact Hours	270

CURRICULUM FOR FOUR YEAR CAMBODIAN BUSINESS PROGRAMME
(continued)

Second Semester
Core Courses

Research Methodology	45
R&D of Business Plans	90
Seminars	90
	225

Specialized Courses

Manufacturing and Marketing		Finance and Accounting	
Capital Budgeting and Investment	45	Topics in Corporate Finance	45
Total Hours	270	Total Hours	270

Note: These are comprehensive final examinations. Successful completion of the above programme of study entitles the student to the degree of Bachelor of Science in Business Administration.

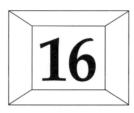

ACCOUNTING STANDARDS AND PRACTICES IN CHINA

Ge Jiashu, Z. Jun Lin, Liu Feng[*]

BACKGROUND

The Peoples Republic of China covers over 9.5 m sq. km between latitudes 18°30′ and 53°N and is the third largest country in the world after Russia and Canada. It borders many countries including Russia and India. Its eastern seaboard is 14 000 km in length and there are 5000 islands, mostly small, but including the larger island of Hainan. Physically, China is divided into vast ranges of mountains, plateaus and basins in the west, and fertile richer valleys and plains in a band of land to the east. The climate is dominated by the effect of the monsoon, giving dry, cold winters and wet, warm summers. The size of China and its terrain mean there are large temperature and rainfall differences, ranging from cold and dry in the north west to sub-tropical in the south east. The east is forested while the west is grassland and desert. Much forest is presently in commercially inaccessible areas (e.g. the Mongolian plateau). Furthermore, apart from the fertile eastern deltas, much of China's land area is unsuitable for agriculture, with only about 10 percent classified as arable and a further 28 percent as pasture. Even here, long-term soil erosion means that 40 percent of the presently cultivated area is of poor quality. Nevertheless, China is relatively resource rich. It possesses large deposits of coal and oil and there are also economically important deposits of tungsten, aluminium, tin, mercury, manganese, salt and graphite.

*Respectively Professor, Xiamen University, China; Associate Professor, University of Lethbridge, Canada; Associate Professor, Xiamen University, China.

The distinctive characteristics of Chinese culture appears to have originated in prehistory. People of Mongoloid race were present in north China in the middle Palaeolithic era and by the time of the bronze age Shang Dynasty (2500 to 1100 BC) a definitely Chinese culture had emerged centred on the Yellow river area (Henan Province). The following Chou Dynasty (1100–221 BC) saw the development of Confucianism and Doaism. The Han Dynasty (206 BC–221 AD) consolidated control over most of what is now the heartland of modern China and created a bureaucracy to run its empire. Buddhism spread in the aftermath of the fall of the Han Empire, the latter being reunited and extended under a new bureaucracy of considerable sophistication by the Tang Dynasty (618 – 907). Much that is associated with being Chinese — race, language, religion, attitude and organisation — was thus established over two thousand years ago. A succession of later dynasties fought, sometimes lost to (but nevertheless absorbed), barbarian cultures before Western imperialism began to seriously impact upon the structures of Chinese society in the 19th Century. The last Qing emperor was deposed in 1911. The period up to 1937 was marked by civil war between nationalist and communist forces. Between 1937–1945 events were dominated by resistance to, and later liberation from, the Japanese and it was during this time that the Chinese Communist Party (CCP) established itself politically throughout China. The communists defeated the nationalists in a short period of civil war (1945–48) and the People's Republic of China was founded on 1 October 1949. The present socialist constitution dates from 1982 and is defined over a unitary state of 22 provinces, five autonomous regions (including Tibet) and three municipalities (including Beijing). Officially, the National Peoples Congress (NPC), consisting of approximately 3000 deputies and its smaller standing committee, is the main legislative body selected for a five-year term. The NPC chooses the President (the official Head of State) and the ministers of the chief executive body, the state council, including the Premier. The Judiciary consists of a Supreme Peoples Court (which is responsible to the NPC under the constitution), Local Peoples Court and various special courts. The CCP, while having no formal authority, exercises effective control through possession of all important positions of state. The Chinese language is a member of the Sino-Tibetan family. A variety of Chinese dialects are spoken, of which Mandarin is the official language of discourse. A number of other minority languages from other family groups are spoken by between 30 and 40 m people, the most important being the Turkic and Mongolian tongues of the Altaic family. Apart from Confucianism and Daoism, Buddhism has more than 180 m followers. There are also quite large Islamic communities in the north-west of China (about 20 m) and at least nine million adherents of Christianity. Ninety percent of China's present population of almost 1.3 b lives in 15 percent of the country's land area in the east. Urban areas are particularly densely populated. Shanghai, for example, has a population density of 2242 persons per sq. km while the large western province of Qinghai has only six persons per sq. km.

According to World Bank statistics, in 1992 China's GNP was US$442 346 m (US$380 per capita) having grown by an average of 8 percent per annum in the period 1985– 1992. A draconian birth control policy helped to maintain a relatively low official population growth rate of 1.5 percent per annum over the decade to 1992. Agriculture, the principal crops of which are rice, cotton, tobacco, tea, sweet potatoes, wheat and maize, accounts for about one quarter of GDP (including forestry) and employs three-fifths of *the workforce. About half the agricultural land area is irrigated. China also possesses some of the largest numbers of animal livestock in the world. Industry accounts for about two-fifths of GDP, one-sixth of the workforce and has been growing annually at over 20 percent per annum in recent years. China is the world's largest producer of coal, cotton and cement. Small cottage industries are still important: of eight million industrial enterprises 100 000 are state owned and over six million are individually owned. Two and a half million are classified as being in heavy industry. In the post-war period, enterprises have had the role of welfare agencies as well as production units but this may change with current reforms. The service sector currently accounts for only 15 percent of the workforce. Energy needs are met mainly from coal and oil and, despite considerable potential for development, hydro electric power presently supplies only 4.5 percent of the country's energy. China has been in a foreign trade surplus in most recent years but seems to experience deficits as soon as tight controls are relaxed (e.g. 1985). The major component of imports are machinery, transport and chemicals, while exports are chiefly manufactures and agricultural products. Attitudes towards foreign investment has changed considerably since the 1970s and China's external debt had increased to US$69 320 m in 1992, almost three times as high as the level in 1987. Most foreign investment comes from Hong Kong and Macau. The currency has devalued several times in recent years partly because of deliberate policy and partly due to economic forces. Inflation which averaged 7.5 percent in the period 1985–90 was recorded at 15 percent in 1993. Since 1949 primary and secondary education has had a relatively high participation rate (86 percent in 1989) but free higher education was abolished in 1985. This latter policy change in education and some of the problems with inflation, the exchange rate and the level of foreign debt reflect China's recent attempts to reform its economy. The new policies are attempting to combat a number of problems including corruption, unproductive economic units and the underemployment associated with socialist central planning methods. However the remedies lead to new problems which then also have to be addressed: e.g. bankrupt firms, unemployment, loss of control of secondary credit sources, disparities in regional income, inequalities between economic groups and the need to negotiate trade policies with international trading parties. Policy changes and reversals in recent years in response to these problems reflect a trial and error approach to new structures and methods adopted by a socialist economy in transition. The unit of currency is the yuan.*

R.J.W.

INTRODUCTION

The development of Chinese accounting since 1949 and the birth of the so-called 'New China,' can be roughly divided into two major phases, demarcated by the promulgation of *The Accounting Standards for Business Enterprises* (ASFBE) in 1992[1]. The ASFBE has brought about substantial changes in Chinese accounting.

---

[1]Ministry of Finance, China, 1992.

After the foundation of the People's Republic of China in 1949, a highly central-ized command economy was built. Under this system, the state held the ownership, the right of use, and the distribution of all means of production and carried out rigid economic planning and control from the highest level to the grassroots. The state-owned enterprises simply played the role of production units carrying out the state's economic plans. Government authorities provided all capital and current funds for enterprises' operations and collected all their profits. Business managements had very little power in operational decision making. Under such a system, the basic accounting objective was to directly serve the economic planning and control func-tions of the government. Business accounting, for a long period, was limited to book-keeping and followed fairly strict government regulations on the maintenance of capital, allowance for expenditures, product costing, and income calculation and distribution[2].

China began ambitious economic reforms in the late 1970s, with the goal of shift-ing from the command economy to a market-oriented economy (called a 'Socialist market economy' in China). The economic and administrative relationships between state and enterprises have been progressively adjusted, aimed at exposing the state-owned enterprises to market mechanisms and risks, and promoting their productivity and efficiency. Accordingly, accounting for business enterprises has been undergo-ing a process of continuous adaption to accommodate the changing needs derived from the process of economic reforms (Lin, 1989). In particular, the emergence of new business ownership patterns, such as foreign-capital affiliated businesses and stock companies, etc., has expanded the user groups and information needs of enter-prise accounting beyond that of the government authorities. Furthermore, with the opening up of the Chinese economy, there has come about an increasing amount of accounting internationalization in China in recent years. These changes have brought Chinese accounting to a new phase of development in the early 1990s.

This chapter delineates the recent progress in Chinese accounting. The discussion focuses primarily on financial accounting, including the sources of legislative re-quirements, the evolution of Chinese accounting standards, the significant account-ing principles adopted by the ASFBE and the current practices for some significant transactions. Management accounting remains in a developing stage in China and is discussed briefly with an introduction to China's management accounting research and certain comments concerning Chinese-style management accounting.

---

[2]Readers who are interested in the old Chinese accounting systems under a centralized command economy may refer to *Accounting and Auditing in the People's Republic of China*, a research study jointly published by Shanghai University of Finance and Economics, China, and The Centre for International Accounting Development, University of Texas, USA (see Lou and Enthoven, 1987). Lou, E. and A.J.H. Enthoven (1987) *Accounting and Auditing in the Peoples's Republic of China*, Coopers & Lybrand Foundation, 1987.

SOURCES OF LEGISLATIVE REQUIREMENTS ON ACCOUNTING

Accounting practices in China are highly regulated. There are two kinds of accounting regulations in effect, one deriving from business legislation, the other from government administrative regulations.

China's National People's Congress (NPC) promulgated *The Accounting Law of The People's Republic of China* in 1981, which was amended in 1993. *The Accounting Law* sets forth the highest level of legislative requirements on accounting work in the country. It legalizes the basic accounting objectives, the statutory responsibility of accountants, the legal authority of accounting standards and regulations, and the fundamental accounting principles and procedures to be followed in organizing accounting work. For example, *The Accounting Law* stipulates that accountants in various entities have the obligations of: 1) supervising firms' economic and financial transactions in terms of the related legislation and regulations; 2) safeguarding the state's properties and interests in business entities; and 3) ensuring the authenticity and adequacy of the books and accounting information disclosed. In addition, the law delegates authority for setting national accounting regulations and standards to the Ministry of Finance. Other central ministerial authorities may also be able to stipulate certain industry-specific accounting regulations, but they must obtain the consent of the Ministry of Finance in advance.

As accounting serves mainly as a tool to facilitate the state's administration of business activities and to safeguard the state's interests, other business legislation has also laid down some requirements on accounting measurement and financial disclosure. *The Corporation Law of the People's Republic of China* (1993) contains specific provisions on account-keeping for all corporations and *The Regulation on Securities Exchanges* (1992) and its *Supplementary Guidelines for Information Disclosure* (both issued by the State Council of China) specify the types and manner of accounting information to be released by the publicly-listed corporations in the country.

The Taxation Law of The People's Republic of China (The Taxation Law) contains certain provisions on accounting measurement and reporting. The state's taxation policies have a dominant influence on business financing and accounting since the Taxation Law mandates that enterprises must comply with the financing and accounting regulations promulgated by government finance and taxation authorities, including the requirements for the scope and criteria of business expenditure and financing, product costing, and profit allocation[3]. Accounting records must be in

---

[3]Chinese financial accounting standards directly incorporate the provisions in tax laws that give specifications on enterprises' accounting and reporting. In addition, government authority has stipulated very specific guidelines or rules on enterprises' financing transactions. For instance, the State Ministry of Finance issued *The General Rules for Business Financing* (GRFBF) and 13 industrial financing regulations in 1992. These financing regulations provide very detailed requirements for business enterprises' financing activities and income (profit) determination and allocation. They also serve as a framework for the new ASFBE pronounced in the same year. Thus, the taxation laws and government regulations for business financing play a dominant role in the formulation of Chinese accounting standards.

conformity with tax laws and other statutory rules on business financing. Usually accounting income is not allowed to depart from taxable income.

The Chinese government has also enacted legislation to accommodate the special needs of various kinds of businesses with foreign affiliations. Among them are the *Law of the People's Republic of China for Enterprises with Foreign Investments* (1992)[4] and the *Income Tax Act for Enterprises with Foreign Investments* (1992) which include specific accounting provisions and reporting requirements for all kinds of business entities with foreign investments, such as joint ventures with Chinese and foreign investments, business corporations or associations with Chinese and foreign partners, and branches or subsidiaries of foreign corporations operating in China.

Although there exist a variety of sources of legislation governing business accounting and financial reporting, most are consistent with each other and are primarily aiming at serving the state's economic interests. Originally, a few provisions in the legislation for businesses with foreign capital were somewhat different from that for the state-owned enterprises which resulted in certain differences in accounting treatment and reporting practice. Most of these differences were eliminated with the implementation of the new national accounting standards on July 1 1993 (Ge and Lin, 1993).

DEVELOPMENT OF FINANCIAL ACCOUNTING STANDARDS

Besides legislative requirements, Chinese accounting practices are guided by government accounting regulations and authoritative accounting standards. Before 1992, the main body of accounting regulations was contained in a number of Uniform Accounting Systems (UASs) established by the Ministry of Finance and other ministerial authorities[5].

To facilitate the central government's economic planning and control function, accounting regulations were originally promulgated for different types of ownership and industry separately. However, *The Uniform Accounting System for State-owned Manufacturing Industrial Enterprises* has an overriding influence on other sets of industry-specified UASs. Usually, each set of UASs contains the standardized Chart of Accounts and Format of Financial Statements applicable to the particular industry.

---

[4]The law is to replace *The Law of the People's Republic of China for Joint Ventures with Chinese and Foreign Investments* originally enacted in 1980, in order to expand applicability to other kinds of businesses with foreign investments, such as sole foreign capital companies.

[5]The UASs are a series of accounting regulations for different industries and types of business ownership. The Ministry of Finance has stipulated some of the leading UASs, while other ministerial authorities in the central government have issued the remainder. There were over 100 specific accounting regulations in existence before 1992.

New forms of business ownership and operating patterns have emerged in China resulting from economic restructuring since the late 1970s. As the UASs, originally designated primarily for the state-owned enterprises, became difficult to apply, certain new accounting regulations were promulgated. In particular, *The Accounting Regulation for Joint Ventures with Chinese and Foreign Investments* (ARFJV) was introduced in 1985. The ARFJV, differing significantly from the UASs, adopted internationally accepted accounting principles to the maximum extent possible under China' socialist economy (Lefebvre and Lin, 1990). The ARFJV was replaced by *The Accounting Regulation for Enterprises with Foreign Investments* (ARFFIE) in 1992, in an effort to expand its applicability to all kinds of business entities with foreign investments in China. These two regulations have made a direct contribution to the improvement of Chinese accounting in recent years. It has also promoted the advance of accounting internationalization in China (Fang and Tang, 1991).

Another new set of accounting regulations, applicable to enterprises experimenting with the share capital system (stock companies), was also introduced in 1992. Technically, the new regulation is fairly similar to the ARFFIE (or the former ARFJV) and resembles prevailing practice in North America. Significantly, this new accounting regulation has officially extended the application of the internationally accepted accounting principles to state-owned enterprises which have been converted into stock companies.

In the early 1980s, as a result of the dramatic changes in China's economic and business administrative systems, it became evident that a redesign of the accounting regulations for state-owned enterprises was necessary. After more than ten years of study and preparation, The Ministry of Finance decided to replace the UASs with a set of authoritative accounting standards similar to International Accounting Standards (IASs) and the GAAP of western countries. In late 1992, the ASFBE (referred to in the Introduction) was released. This aimed to harmonize accounting regulations across all industries and types of business ownership in the country. The new standards became effective on July 1, 1993.

The ASFBE specifies the fundamental accounting principles and general guidelines for accounting practice. It has incorporated most of the internationally accepted accounting principles, modelled after the IASs[6]. At the same time the Ministry of Finance has also issued 13 new industrial accounting regulations (called 'Industrial Accounting Systems' in Chinese) as a supplement to facilitate the

---

[6]However, there exist certain differences between the ASFBE, the IASs and North American GAAP. The major ones relates to the application of valuation principles and allowance or provisions. See the following sections for more detailed discussion.

implementation of the ASFBE by various industries[7]. At present, the ASFBE and these 13 Industrial Accounting Systems serve as authoritative accounting standards in China.

The Chinese Government is contemplating further improvements in accounting standards. It has been decided that a set of transaction-based accounting standards (resembling North American GAAP) will replace the existing industrial-based accounting standards. With financial support from the World Bank and technical assistance from Arthur Anderson & Co., a Special Task Force on Accounting Standards under the Ministry of Finance is working on the preparation of a series of specific accounting standards. About thirty specific accounting standards for the most common accounting transactions (including inventories, fixed assets, the cost of borrowing, income tax, pension plans, business combinations, etc.) are expected to be issued over the two year period 1995–96. The new accounting standards will further narrow the gap between Chinese accounting practices and those prevailing in North America (Lin *et al.*, 1993).

NATURE OF VALUATION RULES FOR ASSETS AND LIABILITIES

The concepts of 'going-concern' and 'accrual basis' are the foundation of valuation rules in China. Historical cost (called 'actual cost' in China) is the mandatory measurement attribute for valuation of assets and liabilities. However, this accounting principle is applied more rigidly in Chinese accounting in comparison to North American practices. For example, the ASFBE states that enterprises should not adjust their book valuations even though market prices have changed substantially, except in the cases specified and approved by government authorities. In most circumstances, the actual cost is the only attribute measured for assets and liabilities in Chinese accounting.

Exceptions to the actual cost valuation rule must meet the rigid specifications set out by government authorities. According to *The Tentative Regulation for Valuations of State-Owned Properties*, promulgated in 1991 by The State Council of China,

---

[7]The State Ministry of Finance stipulated 13 specific industrial accounting regulations in late 1992, to replace those existing accounting issued by other central ministerial authorities, or to accommodate the emerging new industrial sectors resulting from the economic reforms. The new accounting systems include those covering the following industries: *Accounting System for Industrial Manufacturing Enterprises, Accounting System for Commerce and Trade Enterprises, Accounting System for Transportation Enterprises, Accounting System for Nonbanking Financial Institutions, Accounting System for Tourist and Service Enterprises, Accounting System for Capital Construction Enterprises, Accounting System for Real Estate and Land Development Enterprises, Accounting System for Aviation and Space Astronautic industries, Accounting System for Broadcasting and Television Enterprises,* and *Accounting System for Enterprises Operating Abroad, etc.*

state-owned enterprises must conduct a revaluation of their assets and liabilities when they are going to be sold, merged, combined or converted into stock companies or other forms of business involving a different ownership structure. Different measurement attributes other than actual cost, such as the present value of future income, replacement cost, current market value, and liquidation value, may be allowed for this purpose. In practice, the first two alternatives are those most commonly used in a revaluation. A revaluation is usually conducted by an external appraiser and the restated values must be approved by the State's administrative authorities.

Prevailing Chinese measurement principles and valuation practices reveal that accounting is assumed to function with the purpose of safeguarding the State's properties or financial interests in business enterprises. This obligation has remained unchanged with the implementation of the new accounting systems in 1993. It has been suggested that the purpose of government's prohibition of the use of measurements other than actual cost in the normal course of business is to protect the State's interests, or to ensure the state's taxation revenues (Lou, 1992). The revaluation of assets, for example, is allowed only under very limited conditions. Such practices are subject to further restrictions such as the prescription on the writing-down of the book value of the State-Owned enterprises, in order to prevent the loss of State properties and other interests in businesses[8].

SIGNIFICANT FINANCIAL ACCOUNTING PRINCIPLES

In addition to the valuation of assets and liabilities, other significant financial accounting principles or practices under the ASFBE in China are summarised below.

Depreciation: All fixed assets should be depreciated by systematic methods, based on the total years of expected lifetime or the total output or production capacity of the asset. Usually, the Ministry of Finance specifies the depreciation period, rates and specific methods for major categories of assets. Business entities may choose from among these depending upon the industry involved.

According to the ASFBE of 1992, accelerated depreciation may now be applied under certain circumstances. However, advance approval of the government's finance or taxation authorities is needed. In current practice, accelerated depreciation methods are rarely used.

---

[8]For instance, the government's regulation on revaluation stipulates that the downward revaluation of the properties or assets in state-owned enterprises is not permitted. The revaluation must be submitted to, and approved by the State Administration Bureau of State-Owned Properties.

Intangibles and Goodwill: Externally-generated intangible assets are usually re-cognized, examples of those being franchises, industrial know-how, trademark, copyright, land usage fees, etc. Intangibles are valued on the basis of transaction costs or expenses, and reported separately on the balance sheet. They should be amortized over periods regulated by government finance departments. The amortization period should not be less than ten years if no regulated amortization period is available. In practice, most intangibles are amortized over a ten-year period while business set-up expenses are usually amortized over five years.

Goodwill is included in intangible assets, but no specific statutory procedures for goodwill accounting currently exist. However, the ASFBE requires that goodwill, like other intangible assets, must be amortized over a period equal to its estimated useful life. Again if the useful life can not be determined, the amortization period should not be shorter than ten years.

Foreign Currency Translation: According to the ASFBE, business enterprises must use Chinese currency (RMB ¥) as the recording currency. However, foreign currency may be chosen as the recording currency if it is the functional currency in operation[9]. Otherwise transactions denominated in foreign currencies should be translated into Chinese currency based on the official exchange rates on transaction dates. No matter which currency is used as the recording currency, the closing balances of all foreign currency items must be translated into Chinese currency utilizing the exchange rates ruling on the balance sheet date. Exchange gains and losses resulting from the translation should be included in current income accounts as a component of the financing expenses. When the amount of translation gains and losses is large, it may be amortized within a period of one to five years if such a course of action is previously agreed with the government finance and taxation authorities.

Allowance and Reserves: Before 1993, allowances and reserves were not permitted in Chinese accounting practices. The only exception was for State trading companies called 'State Commodity Circulation Enterprises'. However, these companies were only permitted to record allowances for inventories suffering a reduction in realisable value[10].

---

[9] 'Functional currency' is defined as the currency by which an entity conducts its main operation. For example, if a joint venture's business transactions (importation of materials and sales of products) occur mainly in Hong Kong, then, HK$, as the functional currency, can be used as its record-ing currency.

[10] For reasons of obsolescence or changes in market conditions, certain commodities may some-times only be sold at a large discount. State-owned trading companies in this position frequently have to reduce the prices of such inventories.

However, the ASFBE (1992) has incorporated the principle of 'prudence' into its basic framework and it is now permitted for enterprises to record allowance for bad debts. Again, however, the application of this practice is very restrictive. Advance approval of the government finance and taxation authorities is required and the amount of the allowance for bad debts is not to exceed 3 percent of the total sales in the period.

In the case of corporations, certain kinds of reserves are required before net income can be distributed. According to *The Corporation Law* of 1993, all corporations must set aside 10 percent of their net income (after income tax) as 'statutory earnings reserves', another 5 to 10 percent as 'statutory reserves for employees welfare', and any other reserves determined by the board of directors. A company may only stop appropriation to the statutory earnings reserves when the reserve's balance exceeds 50 percent of its total registered capital.

Consolidation: The ASFBE of 1992 and other legislation stipulates that consolidated financial statements must be provided if a company maintains a majority interest (more than 50 percent) in another company, except for those circumstances in which consolidation is deemed inappropriate. When a subsidiary has not been included in the consolidated financial statements, that fact and the reasons for it should be disclosed. In addition, when a subsidiary is omitted from consolidation, the group reports should include the separate financial statements of the subsidiary to show: a) details of the holding company's interest; b) the nature and amount of any transactions with that subsidiary and c) shares and amounts due to or from the subsidiary. When a subsidiary is excluded from the consolidation on the grounds of lack of effective control, it should be incorporated in the group accounts under the equity method of accounting.

ILLUSTRATION OF CHINESE FINANCIAL STATEMENTS

Although there are some differences in accounting practices for different industries and types of business ownership, the formats of financial statements for all business entities in China are highly uniform because they are specified in detail by the authoritative accounting standards and regulations. The following formats for financial statements are recommended by *The Accounting System for Manufacturing Industrial Enterprises* promulgated by the Ministry of Finance in 1992. They are adopted by most industrial enterprises and corporations in the country.

Table 1 is the standardized format of the Balance Sheet. Evidently, it is fairly similar to that used in North America. All items are listed in order of decreasing liquidity. As mentioned earlier, actual (historical) cost is the only measurement attribute allowed for assets and liabilities. For example, inventories are reported by the actual costs or acquisition costs. The lower of cost or market could not be used even if market prices have fallen substantially.

Table 1
ILLUSTRATIVE FORMAT OF BALANCE SHEET (Note 1)

Assets	Liabilities & owners' equities
Current assets	Liabilities
Cash	Notes Payable
Short-Term Investment	Accounts Payable
Notes Receivable	Wages Payable
Accounts Receivable	Welfare Funds Payable
(–) Allowance for Bad Debts	Taxes Payable
Net Accounts Receivable	Accrued Expenses
Inventory	Current Liabilities
Prepaid Expenses	Long-Term Loans
Current Assets	Bonds Payable
	Long-Term Accounts Payable
Long assets	Other Long-Term Liabilities
	Long-Term Liabilities
Long-Term Investments	
Equipments & Plant	Owners' equity
(–) Accumulated Depreciation	
Net Equip. & Plant	Capital
Intangible Assets	Capital Reserves (Note 2)
Deferrals	Statutory Reserves
Other Assets	Undistributed Earnings (Note 3)
Long Term Assets	Owners' Equity
Total assets	Total liabilities & owners' equity

Notes:
1. Extracted from *The Accounting System for the Manufacturing Industrial Enterprises* of 1992. Minor revisions are made for simplification purpose.
2. The terminology of 'Capital Reserves' is a literal translation. The item consists of: (1) Paid-in Surplus; (2) Appreciation from assets revaluation; and (3) Capital derived from donations.
3. This item plus the 'Statutory earnings reserves' would be equal to the 'Retained earnings' figure in North American income statements.

The owners' equity section of the balance sheet includes four sections. The two sections relating to assets are quite similar to their counterparts in North American balance sheets. A third section deals with liabilities while the fourth consists of equity reserves, the statutory earning reserves and employees welfare reserves. Only assets of a value corresponding to the level shown in part 4, undistributed earnings, may be distributed directly to owners.

It is worthy of mention that employee welfare reserves, accrued as a certain percentage of the total amounts of employees' salaries, are designated to fund employees' benefits, such as housing subsidies, medical treatment, bonuses, etc. Although

Table 2
ILLUSTRATIVE INCOME STATEMENT

1. Sales Revenues			xxxxxx
less:	Costs of Goods Sold	xxxxx	
	Sales Expenses	xxxx	
	Business Taxes	xxxx	(xxxxxx)
2. Sales Profits			xxxxx
plus:	Profits From Other Operations	xxx	
less:	Administrative Expenses	(xxx)	
	Interest Expenses	(xxx)	xxx
3. Operating Income			xxxxx
plus:	Income from Investments	xxx	
	Gains from Extraordinary Items	xx	
less:	Losses from Extraordinary Items	(xx)	xxx
4. Total Income (Net profits or losses)			xxxxx

these reserves are reported as a component of owners' equity, they may not be distributed to the owners of the firm. The usage of employees welfare reserves must follow the strict expenditure guidelines and criteria stipulated by government authorities. Thus, the reserves are more like a liability to employees than to the usual western notion of a reserve. Recently, the inconsistency of this item with the owner' equity has evoked debate in Chinese academic circles (Liu and Carroll, 1993).

In Chinese accounting, the income statement usually excludes information about income distribution, which is reported in a separate statement of income distribution. The income statement itself is supposed to be a comprehensive measure of profits or losses realized in a period. The statement should therefore include all items relating to income, including extraordinary items. Unlike the income statement of North America, income taxes are not regarded as an expense of the enterprise, but rather as a distribution of income from the business entity[11] to the state. Consequently income taxes are reported in the statement of income distribution, rather than the income statement.

---

[11]According to the new government regulations, income (profit) is distributed to government as income taxes, while the after-tax income (profit) is left for the enterprises to use for expansion and growth, employee bonuses, or other welfare or benefits.

Besides the balance sheet and income statement mentioned above, a statement of changes of financial position (SCFP) is required by current accounting regulations. In practice, the statement has been prepared as a source and application of funds statement. However, the most recent accounting standards have encouraged enterprises to issue cash flow statement (CFS). The CFS will probably replace the SCFP as a result of China's effort to further harmonize its accounting practices with internationally accepted accounting principles.

MANAGEMENT ACCOUNTING IN CHINA

It was only in the late 1970s that the concept of 'management accounting' was introduced by a few leading accounting academicians in China. Since then, research in management accounting has gained momentum, particularly in academic circles. However, the practical implementation of management accounting is relatively weak. In this section, the progress of studies on management accounting in China will be discussed, followed by a brief elaboration of the practical procedures employed in Chinese management accounting.

Management accounting research and education

Although some sort of management accounting techniques have been in use in Chinese accounting since the 1950s, 'management accounting' was an unknown subject to most Chinese accountants up to the late 1970s (Yu 1980; Bai 1988). The reasons of the long-time ignorance of management accounting in China were twofold. First, political concerns have prevented Chinese accountants from learning about accounting developments in the West. Under the former Soviet-style political and economic systems, the benefits of Western accounting (including management accounting) were denied for ideological reasons. Second, in the highly centralized command economy, the role of business accounting was mainly restricted to a bookkeeping function serving the state's planning objectives and the supervision of enterprises' financial transactions. The lack of decision making power by business managers within the command economy generated little demand for the study and implementation of management-oriented accounting techniques.

As a result of China's new policy of 'Opening to the Outside World' in the late 1970s, Chinese accountants began the study of the Western accounting. The relatively new area of management accounting attracted much attention. A few pioneering academicians made great efforts to systematically translate or introduce the western management accounting literature (Cheng and Ding, 1983; Yu, 1988). Forums and symposia were held, and foreign specialists were invited to give lectures on the subject. However, efforts during the period from the late 1970s to the early

1980s were limited to the introduction of the basic principles of Western management accounting. The concepts involved were rather superficial in nature (Bai, 1988).

More recently, management accounting principles have been studied in greater depth to determine which appear to be suitable to China's situation, which should be modified or adapted, and how such modifications should be made. Academic discussions and practical experiments were both part of this process. Frequently, a comparison of China's own experience with those of Western countries can be made. Many academicians and practitioners have contended that some management accounting techniques, such as standard costing, budgeting control, variance analysis, responsibility accounting, and performance evaluation, etc., have long been used in China. Substantial efforts have been devoted to generalize or theorize on the existence of a specifically Chinese version of management accounting (Tang, 1984; Yang, 1985; Ding and Yang, 1985; Yu, 1988). The majority of Chinese accountants, however, believe that the management accounting experience of the West is relevant and useful and that it should be incorporated into Chinese accounting (Yu, 1981; 1988). Possibilities for the integration of Chinese and Western experience has been explored in some large enterprises (Yu, 1991).

Alongside the progress of economic reforms, business enterprises have gained considerable autonomy in making operating decisions. The demand for decision-oriented accounting information has thus grown considerably since the late 1980s. Consequently, the education and training of management accounting has begun to be emphasized. Many textbooks on the subject of management accounting have been published by Chinese authors. Furthermore, management accounting has become a required course in most of the accounting education programs throughout the country. Research interest of this subject remains high and numerous papers in this field are published each year (Liu and Carroll ,1993).

Management accounting practices

Compared to the rapid development of research and education, progress in the practical application of management accounting is relatively slow. Although many advanced western techniques have been explored in theory, they are as yet rarely employed in the real world. To date, management accounting in most business enterprises remains in traditional Chinese form.

Functional Structure: In most enterprises, in contrast to practice in North America, the management accounting function is not separated from financial accounting. Both functions are usually carried out by accountants in a single unit called the 'Financing and Accounting Division' under the supervision of a Chief Accountant. Frequently, the same team of accounting staff will perform the work of both financial and management accounting. In fact, the financial accounting is a dominant function while management accounting is a secondary function in most enterprises[12].

Planning and Budgeting: Budgeting is a management accounting area that most Chinese accountants can appreciate in a practical context. Under a highly centralized command economy, planning or budgeting is performed at various levels. However, the focus of budgeting is on working capital or short-term decisions and the cash budget is the key component. Most enterprises have to prepare a budget of cash receipts and payments on a monthly basis, and, in some cases, for intervals of just ten days. Since a shortage of cash will cause immediate operational difficulties, most managers demonstrate a great deal of interest in this budget and control process.

Relatively speaking, capital budgeting and long-term decisions receive less attention in a command economy. As government is the main provider of capital for most enterprises, business managers have little motivation to control expenditure in this area. At present, only stock companies and foreign-capital-affiliated entities have emphasized capital budgeting. Technically, for most long-term decisions, the most commonly used budgeting tool is payback-period analysis. More sophisticated techniques, such as net present value (NPV) analysis, are rarely used.

Departmentalized and decentralized control of current funds: For a long time, many enterprises have adopted a decentralised system of working capital management by allocating the total amount of current funds to various functional departments and to various lower levels within the departments. Managers in each department or subunit are often responsible for the maintenance of the closing balances or budgeted returns of the funds relating to their operating activities. Apparently, this procedure is similar to cost centre or profit centre accounting in North America.

Internal Business Accounting System (IBAS): The IBAS was originally developed by a large steel enterprise in northern China in the early 1960s. Its primary purpose is similar to responsibility accounting and performance evaluation in western management accounting. That is, it is designed to promote production efficiency and effectiveness by enhancing the accountability of internal departments and divisions. Under this system each department or division is treated as a relatively independent production unit which should account for its contribution to the enterprise-wide profit margin. Production flows (both materials and services) among various departments or divisions are accounted for based on budgets and standard costs. Each department

---

[12]In many cases, the management accounting function is limited to the procedures of preparing budgets and financial analysis. Management accounting is usually treated as a supplementary tool of financial accounting.

and division is evaluated and rewarded according to its actual contribution to the fulfilment of predetermined financial and operational targets.

This procedure has been adopted by many industries and enterprises since the early 1980s. Innovation or improvements to the technique have been incorporated, however. For example, the 'internal enterprise banking system' was added to the IBAS in some large enterprises in the late 1980s. Under this system the internal transfer of materials, parts or semi-products and services is accounted for based on either full cost or market price equivalents. 'Internal monetary notes' are used for both accounting and control purposes. Each department or division determines its production costs and profit margins accordingly. This approach has been proved to be very effective in enhancing the profitability of the enterprise as a whole.

Standard Costing and Variance Analysis: Standard costing is used by many large enterprises in the valuation of purchased inventory or in product costing. However, emphasis is usually placed on the simplification of record keeping, rather than the control dimension[13]. Inventories are recorded using pre-determined standard costs or expenditures quoted during the period. Differences between standard costs and actual costs are determined by physical inventory procedures at the end of the period, and the book records are adjusted accordingly. The volume of recording work during the period could be reduced although some academicians and practitioners have recently advocated the significance of this procedure as a control mechanism, but the practical achievements remain less than satisfactory.

CONCLUSION

Chinese accounting has undergone dramatic changes in recent years. The motives for change are derived from market-oriented economic reforms. As the Chinese economy moves toward integration with world markets, accounting internationalization in China becomes inevitable. Following the introduction and implementation of new accounting systems in 1993, accounting practices in China have become similar to their counterparts in western countries and in North America in particular.

---

[13]Certain environmental factors make it difficult to emphasise control aspects. For instance, the supply of raw material and sales of products have long been controlled by the state authorities. Although this has changed considerably in the course of the economic reforms, there remain enormous uncertainties and risks in purchasing and sales activities owing to severe shortage in the supply of raw materials in the market. Many enterprises have to purchase inventories, whenever they are available, as a buffer against uncertainty and market risks. This tactic has nullified the practicability of inventory control in most circumstances.

Nevertheless, considerable gaps between Chinese accounting and western practices remain. These stem from differences in the legal, social and economic context within which each operates. Even with the dramatic changes of recent years, the former highly centralized administrative systems still have a pervading and persistent influence on business accounting. Since the state remains as the main owner or capital provider of most business enterprises, business accounting is required to assume the obligation of safeguarding the State's properties and financial interests. Thus, Chinese financial accounting remains subordinate to a series of statutory requirements in terms of the State's financial and taxation policies. This leads to the considerable differences in the orientation of Chinese accounting as compared to the North American practice.

Chinese accounting is highly regulated and continuing efforts are being made to improve national accounting regulations. The most recent efforts have been aimed at:

1) replacement of industry specific accounting regulations with a uniform set of national accounting standards; and

2) the adoption of internationally accepted accounting principles to narrow the differences between Chinese accounting and the rest of the world, particularly North American practice. It is expected that the issuance and implementation of new accounting standards will significantly increase the understandability and comparability of Chinese accounting information, with respect to the GAAP of North America and other western countries.

Chinese accountants have been, since the late 1970s, exposed to the development of western management accounting. This subject is a relatively new topic in Chinese accounting research. Many western management accounting principles have been researched and efforts are being made to introduce some into practice. Currently, research efforts have shifted from a systematic importation of western methods to comparison and generalization of the specifically Chinese experience of management accounting. This viewpoint is also being incorporated into the accounting education program in the country.

However, the practical application of management accounting is far behind the achievements in research. Except for some Chinese-style management accounting techniques, most western management accounting techniques have yet to be applied in practice. With increasing demands for a management decision-oriented accounting information system, resulting from China's move towards a market economy, it is anticipated that management accounting will play a much more significant role in business management in the country than has previously been the case.

REFERENCES

Bai, Z.L. (1988), 'Accounting in the People's Republic of China — contemporary situations and issues', *Recent accounting and economic developments in the Far East,* Centre for International Education and Research in Accounting, University of Illinois, pp. 27–50.

Cheng, S. and P. Ding (1983), 'On the development of accounting theory — based on mathematics and political economics', *Jiangxi accounting* (in Chinese), No. 1.

Ding, P. and J. Yang (1985), 'Topics requiring further research in implementing the Western management accounting', *Shanghai accounting* (in Chinese), No. 3.

Fang, Z.L. and Y.W. Tang (1991), 'Recent accounting development in China: An increased internationalization', *The international journal of accounting,* Vol. 26, No. 1, pp. 88–103.

Ge, Jiashu (1992), 'How to use international experience for reference in the development of China's accounting standards', *Accounting research* (in Chinese), No. 2.

—, and Z. Jun Lin (1993), 'Economic reforms and accounting internationalization in the People's Republic of China', *Journal of international accounting, auditing & taxation,* Vol. 2, No. 2, pp. 129–43.

Lefebvre, C. and L.Q. Lin (1990), 'Internationalization of financial accounting standards in the People's Republic of China', *The international journal of accounting,* Vol. 24, No. 4, pp. 170–83.

Lin, Zhijun (1989), 'A survey of current accounting development in China', *Advances in international accounting,* Vol. 2, pp. 99–110.

—, Qu, X. and Chen Feng (1993), 'Improving accounting regulations in China: Towards internationally accepted accounting principles', *Conference Proceeding,* ACME III/ICMM VI *Joint international conference on transfer technology and comparative management,* Los Angeles, USA.

Liu, F. and R. Carroll (1993), 'Accounting research in China', *Accounting research* (in Chinese) No. 5.

Lou, E. and A.J.H. Enthoven (1987), *Accounting and Auditing in the Peoples's Republic of China,* Coopers & Lybrand Foundation.

—, (1992), 'A comparative study of Sino-foreign accounting standards', *Accounting research* (in Chinese), No. 2.

Tang T. (1984), 'On the establishment of management accounting with Chinese characteristics', *Finance and accounting* (in Chinese), No. 2.

Yang, J.W. (1985), 'Several issues needed to be resolved before the establishment of management accounting with Chinese characteristics', *Finance and accounting of Guangdong* (in Chinese), No. 3.

Yu X. (1980), 'On the scientific nature of accounting from the perspective of development', *Journal of issues on Chinese economy* (in Chinese), No. 5.

—, (1981), 'On the main features of modern management accounting and its absorbability and implacability in China', *Journal of issues on Chinese economy* (in Chinese), No. 1.

—, (1988), 'The general character of Chinese and US management accounting and an analysis of the new Chinese management accounting style', *Recent accounting and economic developments in the Far east,* Centre for International Education and Research in Accounting, University of Illinois, USA, pp. 51–64.

—, (1991), 'A brief introduction to international management accounting', *Fujian accounting,* (in Chinese), No. 1, pp. 1–11.

ACCOUNTING SYSTEMS IN THE DEMOCRATIC PEOPLE'S REPUBLIC OF KOREA

Sang-Moon Choi[*]

BACKGROUND

North Korea stretches roughly half way down the relatively mountainous 600 miles of the Korean peninsula between latitudes 37°59′ and 43°1′N. Its northern land border is formed with the Manchurian area of mainland China while its southern border is formed with the demilitarised zone north of the Republic of Korea. It is bounded on its western side by the Yellow Sea and on its eastern side by the Sea of Japan. Unlike Japan, the area is not prone to earthquakes and volcanic activity. North Korea's climate is monsoonal with dry, cold winters and warm, wet summers. The average temperatures in the middle lowland areas are −8°C in January and 24°C in July. The country receives about 90 cm of rainfall annually. Quite inaccessible densely forested interior mountainous regions stretch down from China through the centre of the country, flanked on each side by coastal lowlands. The eastern lowlands are narrow and discontinuous. The western lowlands contain most of the useable agricultural land, population and the capital, Pyongyang. North Korea is rich in mineral resources including coal, iron, tungsten, manganese, zinc, copper, lead, gold and uranium. There is no known deposit of oil, however. Almost three-quarters of the land is covered by forest, mostly conifers and birch. Although some minor deforestation has occurred a replanting programme is in process.

---

*Professor, College of Business, Pusan National University, Korea.

The Korean peninsula has been settled for well over a millennia by people speaking Korean (a language which has similarities with Japanese), and is relatively homogenous racially (see also the background notes to chapter 10). Culturally Korea has been influenced by China, particularly through Confucianism and the traditions of Chinese bureaucracy. Buddhism and Christianity have also been important at certain times in the past but neither are particularly important overt belief systems in present day North Korea. Ch'ongogyo, a 19th Century Korean combination of Confucian, Buddhist and Christian teachings, is tolerated by the State for certain purposes. In 1945, at the end of the Second World War, troops from the US and Russia occupied the country and disagreements led to the Korean War (1950–53), at the end of which the peninsula was divided at the 38th parallel into North and South. The North, lead by the Korean Workers Party (KWP), has since pursued socialist economic policies, while the South has followed capitalist principles. The socialist model of the command economy used in the North was borrowed from Russia and has followed, under the direction of Kim Il Sung, a policy of Chuch'e ('self reliance'). The current political structure is based upon the constitution formulated in 1972. The main legislative assembly is a unicameral Supreme People's Assembly of 687 members (1990) who are elected by universal suffrage every four years. Power is in the hands of the Communist Party's Politburo appointed from elected members of the Central Committee who exercise control over the Administrative Council, the executive arm of the constitution. The Presidency, the head of state, is currently held by Kim Jong Il, the son of the recently deceased Kim Il Sung, and is a position of considerable central power. The judiciary is composed of judges of the Central Court elected by the People's Assembly for a period of three years and a number of lesser provincial, city and county courts. The legal system is based upon a mixture of communist theory, German civil law and some Japanese influences. The population is presently about 22 million, with a density of approximately 200 per sq. km, growing at about 1.5 percent per annum. The urbanisation rate is about 70 percent.

As part of the Japanese empire between 1910 and 1945, the North was industrialised more rapidly than the South and by 1945 almost two-thirds of Korea's heavy industry was located there. Since then, government economic policies, constrained by a perpetual shortage of labour, have been determined through a series of long term plans ranging from three to seven years in length, the most recently completed plan having run over the period 1987–93. These plans have been dominated by the principle of Chuch'e and a Stalinist emphasis on the needs of heavy industry. Socialism in the form of the state ownership of the means of production and the collectivisation of agriculture was achieved by 1958. Initial success in raising output after the Korean War had been followed by growing problems of shortages in energy supply, food and equipment and shortfalls in meeting output targets. In the 1970s, a policy of importing technology from the West was followed. Since 1984, a limited relaxation of controls over foreign enterprises and over peasant markets selling surplus produce at free market prices has been apparent. The latest policy pronouncements point to the development of special economic zones similar to those being used by China, and to a greater emphasis on consumer goods, food

production, light industry and foreign trade. Foreign trade is presently small by compari-
son with most other countries and North Korea still remains one of the world's most
secretive, inaccessible and highly centralised, planned economies. North Korea's GNP
was estimated at just under US$22 billion or about US$1000 per capita in 1990. Agricul-
ture is dominated by collectives and state farms. The most important crops are paddy rice
and maize. Grain has had to be imported in recent years to meet domestic demand and
intensive use of chemical fertilizers has led to land degradation and water pollution.
There are ambitious irrigation and land reclamation projects in progress designed to in-
crease the area of land available to grow rice. Despite its forestry reserves timber has had
to be imported from the CIS. The main source of protein is seafood and other fish. The
most important manufactured products are iron and steel, machinery, chemical fertilizers
and fibres, cement and textiles. The mining of raw materials is an important sector of the
economy. Hydro-electric power, based upon the mountainous hinterland and originally
developed by the Japanese, has recently declined in importance compared to thermal
stations (due to difficulties of transmission, drought and capital costs) and in 1991 pro-
vided less than half of the electricity output of the country. Exports consist of surplus
production and goods required to fund imports of machinery and raw materials. Unfa-
vourable trade balances, especially in the period of importation of Western technology,
led to large levels of overseas debt (estimated at US$10 300 m in 1993) and problems
with Western creditors. An important source of overseas currency now consists of the
remittances of Korean expatriates living in Japan. The major trading partners are currently
China, Japan and Russia. Trade with South Korea is small but may increase in the future.
The unit of currency is the won.

R.J.W.

INTRODUCTION

The structure of accounting systems, the range of accounting functions, the
management of accounting data, and the roles of accountants are all influenced by
the form of economic systems. To understand the accounting system of North Korea,
therefore, it is necessary to understand the accounting systems in socialist economies
in general, and then to understand the economic and enterprise management systems
of North Korea, which are the basis of its accounting system. This chapter outlines
some basic facts about the socialist accounting system of North Korea. The sections of
this chapter are quite wide ranging, covering some aspects of socialist economies in
general; the economic system of North Korea, in particular; the forms of bookkeeping
used; the role of the national budget; accounting policies of ordinary enterprises and
joint management enterprises; the valuation of assets; cost accounting; accounting
reports; the accounting inspection (audit); and accounting education.

ACCOUNTING SYSTEM OF SOCIALIST ECONOMIES AND THE ENTERPRISE MANAGEMENT SYSTEM OF NORTH KOREA

Accounting system of socialist economies

In socialist command economies, central government makes overall plans for all enterprises as a part of an exercise in state planning. These plans are then followed by individual enterprises. The ownership of enterprises resides in the State and a common accounting system governs all firms. The accounting entity is the basic unit of the national economy. Central government uses the accounting system as a means of control and the focus of accounting, as in capitalist economies, is to safeguard the assets of enterprises, verify whether the assets have been used for predetermined purposes, and provide a summary report of enterprises' activities to the proprietors, i.e. central government.

A common accounting system governing all enterprises requires the standardized management of accounting data, and it is thus necessary for the state to maintain a chart of accounts, a standard form of accounting report, and standardised rules for processing accounting data. Accounting procedures are then executed according to legal stipulation. The standardization process simplifies the skills required for accounting and accountants are to some extent reduced to the role of ciphers.

Development of enterprise management systems in North Korea

In the course of constructing a socialist economy, the economic and enterprise management systems of North Korea have changed several times. Although North Korea has been influenced by the USSR and China, it has also sought to develop an enterprise management system fitting its own objectives. The historical development of the enterprise management system of North Korea will now be briefly described.

Immediately after 1945, North Korea nationalized the major means of production. A centralized economic system was established, upon which the management of state enterprises was based. In November 1946 the North Korea Provisional People's Committee promulgated the 'Management Law of State Enterprises' subjecting the management system to centralized planning, direction, command and control. By the end of the 1950s, the initial phase of reconstruction was giving way to the need for greater output and efficiency of the state industrial sector. This led to the development of the *Dae An* work system in 1960 as a new, improved theory and practice of economic management.

Under the *Dae An* system, industrial enterprises are run by Factory Party Committees rather than by individual managers. The committee consists of about thirty managers, engineering staff and workers from whom a smaller executive board form the day-to-day decision making body (Jeffries, 1993). This system is designed to promote party ideology. The business system of *Dae An*, along with the similar but more strongly one-man management system of the *'Chung San Ri'* method in agriculture, has been the basis of North Korea's management since the 1960s and is a part of the larger policy objective of self-sufficiency.

Adverse conditions, mainly due to the decrease of economic aid from other socialist nations and the deficiency of operating capacity in equipment management, led North Korea to seek Western funds and technology in 1984. Despite difficulties in generating trade on the same scale as South Korea, this policy represents something of a withdrawal from the earlier policy of complete self-sufficiency. It has taken place beside a reversal of some of the large scale amalgamation of earlier years and along with legislation encouraging joint ventures with foreigners. In 1985, for example, North Korea enacted a series of subsidiary laws and regulations such as the *Detailed Enforcement Regulations of the Joint Management Law*, the *Income Tax Law for Foreigners and its Detailed Enforcement* and the *Income Tax Law for Equity Joint Ventures and its Detailed Enforcement*. It remains to be seen whether North Korea will follow the path of China further in this respect.

THE ACCOUNTING NORMS OF NORTH KOREA AND THE FORM OF BOOKKEEPING

Accounting rules of North Korea

In North Korea as elsewhere, accounting can be a powerful tool in tracing the performance of economic plans and the exercising of control over enterprises. It is therefore a key mechanism by which the state carries out its economic policy. As stated above, accounting rules generally have the force of law in North Korea.

The *Regulations on Fixed Assets Management*, the *Regulations on Self-supporting Systems of the State Enterprises*, and the *Standard Form* are among the standardized accounting rules that have been legally stipulated to date (BKLR, 1994). Accounting regulations that deliver a basic but overall structure of North Korea's standardized accounting rules are the *Accounting Regulations of North Korea* and the *Detailed Regulations on the Financial Bookkeeping Calculation of Equity Joint Ventures* (KDI, 1994; BKLR 1994).

Accounting regulations typify the standardized accounting rules of North Korea and are universally applied to enterprises and government administration alike. Announced by the North Korea Provisional People's Committee on 12 August 1946, the *Accounting Regulations of North Korea* (Park, 1994) may be viewed as a statement of the most basic, primary accounting rules applicable to all enterprises. These were based on the third clause of the *Provision on the Constitution of North Korea Provisional People's Committee* (Kim, 1994), which laid out the basis for nationalizing the means of production. The *Detailed Regulations on the Financial Bookkeeping Calculation of Equity Joint Ventures* is the most recently established, detailed enforcement regulation on accounting. It was enacted under clause 30 of the Equity Joint Ventures Law, and, unlike the accounting rules applicable to enterprises under the enterprise management system of North Korea, it applies only to foreign investment firms.

The form of bookkeeping

Bookkeeping is standardized throughout the nation by the uniform, methodological directives of the Central Statistics Bureau and the Department of Treasury in the State Planning Committee. Together with statistics and business calculations these lay the foundation for the data collection system of the socialist, command economy. Depending upon its field of application, bookkeeping in North Korea is divided into enterprise bookkeeping, institution bookkeeping, and household bookkeeping. Enterprise bookkeeping applies to businesses, institution bookkeeping to government agencies and household bookkeeping to civil households, respectively. Enterprise bookkeeping can be further subdivided into industrial, agriculture and commercial bookkeeping, depending upon the type of industry where the enterprise operates. Institution bookkeeping can similarly be divided into budgeting and banking institution bookkeeping (Han, 1993). At the time of the formation of co-operatives in agriculture a type of single entry bookkeeping was used. However, all enterprises and institutions of North Korea nowadays use double entry bookkeeping. As in the West, bookkeeping by double entry is a system which connects assets with their sources of funds.

Forms of bookkeeping are further divided into the four types: (a) journalising table (b) journalising diary (c) diary ledger and (d) journalising ledger. They are distinguished simply on the basis of how the documents, diaries, journals and ledger are combined in the process of operating the system (Choi, 1994). Since 1958, the journalising diary-type of bookkeeping has been used in enterprise accounting. This form of bookkeeping has the advantage that the entries are simple, the information produced is useful, and the entries are carried out in an ordinary, sequential process, not concentrated toward the end of a month.

The journalising diary type of bookkeeping is similar to the methods familiar to Western accountants. The general procedure for implementing the method is as follows. When a transaction occurs, it is journalised. If the transaction affects more than one set of accounts it is entered in the journalising diary. Either every day or every five days, the amounts entered in the journalising table are summed and entered in the accounts ledger[1]. Periodically, either every ten days or otherwise at the end of each month, a table of total transaction amounts and a table of accounts balances for each title are prepared to check that calculations have been made accurately. At the end of each month or quarter, a statement of financial position is prepared.

THE ACCOUNTING SYSTEM OF NORTH KOREA AND THE ROLE OF THE NATIONAL BUDGET

The role of national budget

The budgets of enterprises in the socialist economy are a part of the national budget, which central government uses as a means of controlling enterprises. In North Korea, the national budget is estimated to have been around 90 percent of total GNP in recent years. The national budget under the accounting system of North Korea plays an important function of allocation as well as of control.

The national budget is prepared by the Department of State Affairs and is submitted to the People's Conference, which examines, debates and adopts it in the form of a law. Through the Department of Treasury, quarterly plans are supervised and executed *via* local administrative committees. Judging from the fact that budgets thus prepared have never been altered since the establishment of the socialist government in North Korea, it appears that the role played by the Department of Treasury is extremely significant in carrying through policy. The Department of Treasury also carries out the business of quarterly and annual closing of the accounts, at the same time assuming the obligation of reporting their contents to the People's Committee.[2] The national budget consists of the central and local budgets. The central budget is formed at the national level and is used for the functioning of central authorities. The

---

[1]The principle of double entry followed in transferring data to the ledger is that accounts are classified into asset accounts and fund sources accounts. In asset accounts, a transaction increase in assets is entered on the debtor side, a decrease on the creditor side, the balance always being on the debtor side. In fund sources accounts, transactions increasing a fund source are entered on the creditor side, a decrease in the debtor side, with the balance always being shown on the creditor side. Naturally the beginning-of-period balance, the amount of changes in the accounts ledger, and the end-of-period amounts on the debtor and the creditor side must all agree. These principles seem in accord with those used in the West.

[2]The fiscal year in North Korea is from January 1 to December 31.

targets of the central budget include large-scale state enterprises, nationwide institutions, social-cultural bodies, institutions for social security, jurisdiction, prosecution, justice, and rail-road transportation (whose business has special characteristics).

Although North Korea maintains an extremely centralized, planned economic system, attention is also given to the development of local budgetary systems. The purpose of the local budgetary systems appears to be to reduce the burden on the central budgeting process and to improve efficiency in economic management by enhancing the consciousness of local administrative units. The local budget is formed and used for certain necessary expenses of local administrative units and prepared and executed by local administration under the unified directives of central authorities. The focus of the local budgeting process is small-scale institutions, enterprises and lower level social-cultural institutions. The main sources of revenue in these budgets are transaction revenues of the target institutions, the profits of cooperatives, service fees, subsidies from the central budget, repayment costs of fixed asset, local maintenance funds and sales revenue of national properties. The main expenses include the construction costs of local industry, rural accounting costs, administration costs of the local civic area and other costs relating to education, cultural matters, health management, and the management of local institutions, etc.

Accounts of the national budget

Budget revenue now consists of what is known as the 'accounting revenue of socialism'[3]. This comes from three main sources:

(i)   transaction revenues,
(ii)   profits of state enterprises, and
(iii)   profits of cooperatives.

Transaction revenue is the value added earned from the sales of consumption goods produced by state enterprises or cooperatives and sold to consumers by adding a certain fraction of the wholesale price to the price of the consumption goods to provide enterprise net income[4]. The prices of all commodities are essentially set by the State (Park, 1994). State enterprises and production cooperatives have the obligation of delivering the physical amounts on which these values are based to the state. The profits of state enterprises are net earnings less the retained earnings determined by the state. The latter are sometimes interpreted as a form of corporate income tax by Western analysts. However, they are not viewed as a tax in North Korea,

---

[3]Three other earlier revenue headings, taxes, aid and 'other' had all been dropped from analysis by 1974.

[4]The wholesale price is itself determined by adding a margin to the average production cost, which includes wages, intermediate expenses, depreciation and social insurance costs.

but rather considered as the surplus value created by state enterprises which belongs to the state as the owner of the enterprises. Cooperatives also have to pay a share of their profits to the state in return for their share of the means of production. These amounts are levied on quarterly closing accounts for the production cooperatives and convenience cooperatives and on a certain ratio of sales revenue for fisheries co-operatives. The profits of cooperatives are the most important source of local budget revenues.

Government expenditure is divided into the following major categories:

(i)   economic expenses for the people,
(ii) policy expenses for social culture,
(iii) expenses for national defence, and
(iv) expenses for national management.

The first of these, economic expenses for the people, is similar in nature to expenses for economic development. It includes expenditures on basic construction investment, on fixed capital for productive purposes, the supply of current working capital, business expenses for the people's economy, and the supply of large reconstruction funds. The category, 'business expenses for people's economy', includes items such as expenses for science and technology, expenses for city management, expenses for local business, expenses for overseas business, and expenses for maintenance and repairs. None of these items can be appropriated for other purposes.

Policy expenses for social culture include expenses of education, culture, health, and social security. This is similar to the classification of social development expenditure by the IMF. However, it also includes expenses for training government staff and propaganda. Expenses for national defense includes expenditure on the development of the defence industry, basic investment on fortifications of the whole country, training of members of the military staff, modernisation of the army, and general military. Finally the expenses of national management includes such things as travel expenses, expenses in the maintenance of buildings, and expenditure on equipment used to maintain state-run institutions. Also included are the expenditures of management on social and cultural polices for the people's economy.

ACCOUNTING POLICY FOR ENTERPRISES AND EQUITY JOINT VENTURES

Enterprises

An enterprise is an economic unit that independently organizes and processes its business, covering its expenses with revenues earned by producing goods and services. The concept of the enterprise is equivalent to that of firm in the market economy, the major difference being that ownership is in the hands of the state. The consequence of this is that the purpose of the financial reports of enterprises is to report their business performance and financial condition to the state. State enterprises were first established when the major industries were nationalized in August, 1946. Co-operatives enterprises were established with the organization of production partnerships by handicraftsmen. The means of production are now almost entirely in the hands of the state. However, there have been recent policy moves which may indicate a softening of attitude towards foreign ownership of joint ventures and the promotion of zones of free trade.

Organization of enterprises and the position of accountants

The management of industry in North Korea is very formally defined, by comparison with the West, and is divided into functional areas of planning, facilities management, materials management, labour management, production management, financial management, and rear management[5]. This classification applies not only to factories and enterprises which are main targets of industry management, but also to the organization of agriculture and construction. The basic unit of management in industry is the factory. The management and operation of factories is effected by a dual structure of a manager and a 'secretary on duty'. The former is in charge of practical man-agement matters while the latter is a political appointee designated by the party. Under the manager of the factory, and of particular significance in the management structure, are the first agent, business vice-manager and administration vice-manager. The first agent is in charge of the business plan, technology preparation and the direction of production process. The business vice-manager is responsible for materials supply, product management and transportation while the administration vice-manager normally takes charge of the accounting function. Factories are supposed to be self-supporting and it is thus necessary for the accounting department to work out the budgets necessary for achieving the production target, organise ways of raising funds for various expenditures, and to settle accounts.

Elements of expenditure and income

These are typically similar to those found in Western accounting e.g. production costs, administrative overheads and the like. However, there are some distinct elements which would not seem so familiar in the capitalist system, such as living expenses for workers, repayment costs and depreciation charges for fixed assets, costs of cultural activities and penalties for mismanagement. In fact, most of these have their counterparts in Western accounting, e.g.: wages; head office charges for fixed assets; entertainment etc. The net income of enterprises is sometimes called 'enterprise profit'

---

[5]'Rear management' is a 'catch all' category referring to the management of all the other functions except those mentioned specifically i.e. planning, facilities management etc.

and partly distributed to the state budget as the 'centralized net income' and partly retained as the 'enterprise fund'. Payments to the state are split between state and local funds. In contrast, a large part of the net income of co-operatives is distributed to their own funds (e.g. the culture and welfare fund) and only a small portion is paid to the state.

The Equity Joint Ventures is a limited company jointly funded and managed by North Korea and foreign investors. It is similar to an equity-partnership whereby the net operating income and the residual value at liquidation are shared according to the ratio of initial investments. The closing accounts of the Equity Joint Ventures follow the principles determined by the Department of Treasury whereby net income is found by subtracting from annual total income all costs (including selling and administrative costs) incurred in producing the revenue.[6]

THE VALUATION OF ASSETS

Current assets and fixed assets

The concept of current and fixed assets used in North Korea is virtually identical to that used in market economies and it includes similar categories of items such as raw materials, fuel, purchased and half-finished goods in the case of current assets and purchased, durable production and administrative facilities, in the case of fixed assets. For the sake of practical convenience, current assets include tools which, although used in the production process several times, are lowly priced and relatively quickly worn out. However, the basic distinction between capitalist and socialist economies remains: the state *owns* the assets, enterprises simply *use* them.

Depreciation of fixed assets

Under the North Korean system, depreciation cost is a reserved monetary fund designed to compensate the state and to provide a sinking fund for the value of fixed assets shifted to products through wearing out in the production process. Depreciation is added to the production cost and is recouped through sales revenue. Depreciation is thus viewed, at least partly, as a way of securing a replacement. The total depreciation charge is estimated as follows:

Total depreciation charge = initial price + total amount of repairs – remaining value + withdrawal cost.

---

[6]Details of categories of costs, assets and sources of funds under which these calculations are made can be obtained from Choi (1994).

The annual depreciation charge is then computed as 'total depreciation cost/ estimated life of the asset'. Both the cost and estimated life of fixed assets follows the *Provisions for fixed assets management* (BKLR, 1992). The straight line depreciation method is in general use in domestic enterprises, although depreciation methods such as the 'constant percentage of declining balance method' are sometimes regarded as a way of increasing the production price and hence of providing a basis for greater labour exploitation. In the case of joint management enterprises, however, the depreciation method is a matter of contract between the parties involved.

Valuation principles

The valuation of a fixed asset is based either upon the full initial price, residual initial price, full restoration price, or the residual restoration price.[7] Fixed assets are registered in the fixed asset chart at the amount valued and are reflected in the same way in the financial condition table. Revaluation may take place if changes in reproduction conditions occur. Nationwide revaluations of fixed assets were carried out in 1957, 1960, 1964 and 1979. Current assets are valued by reference to their actual purchase price or production cost while imported goods are valued by translating import prices to domestic monetary prices[8].

COST ACCOUNTING

Cost is a monetary expression of the material and labour charges that have been incurred in the production and sales of a product. As mentioned earlier the items included as costs under the various headings of the accounting system are similar to those used in capitalist economies. In particular the same distinctions are made between direct and indirect costs; fixed and variable costs; production and selling costs (Han, 1993; Kim, 1994).

Cost accounting in North Korea is an integral part of the overall accounting system and is classified into 'planned' versus 'performance' cost accounting. Planned and performance cost accounting are equivalent to 'budget' and 'actual' cost accounting

---

[7]The initial price of a fixed asset is the price based on the condition of constructing or reproducing the asset at the time it was received. The restoration price is the price evaluated after considering variations in labour expenses following changes in reproduction conditions. The full price of a fixed asset is the price not counting the deterioration of its function due to physical wear and tear, while the residual price counts such deterioration.

[8]Domestic monetary prices are equal to import prices multiplied by the *official* exchange rate. The official rate is determined politically irrespective of rates prevailing on currency markets.

respectively in market economies. Variances from standards are identified when actual costs determined in the manner described earlier are compared to the predetermined costs set by the State. Cost accounting processes involve the identification of cost elements, from which are deducted the values of work in progress whereby total cost is calculated. Unit costs per product (or job) are obtained by dividing total costs by the number of products (or jobs) produced.

Cost accounting processes differ according to the characteristics of the technical processes and the production organization in which the costs arise. Methods of cost accounting are classified into either the 'step' or the 'non-step' method. The step method involves calculating enterprise costs based upon the identification of expenditures along the sequential steps of the production processes. It is applicable to the metalwork, mechanical products, chemical, and textile industries. The non-step method derives direct costs without calculating stepwise cost expenditures, and is applied in the electric industry. Cost accounting involves initial costing at the work site, departmental cost accounting, and then accounting at the financial management office. The general principle is for each product to be costed at full cost, i.e. including elements of overhead costs and depreciation.

ACCOUNTING REPORTS

The North Korean system of the closing of financial accounts is a process of numerically determining, investigating, and discussing the performance of the financial plan and the financial condition of an enterprise on the basis of regular bookkeeping data. The closing reports of ordinary enterprises are comprehensive financial documents of the fund composition and financial results of an enterprise for a fiscal period, and are comparable to financial statements in a market economy such as Republic of Korea. The reports consist of a statement of financial condition, a statement of performance of financial plans and a statement of financial bookkeeping closing analysis.[9] The Appendix to this chapter contains a summary chart of accounts for equity joint ventures. Accounting reports in North Korea have been heavily influenced by those of Russia and the People's Republic of China. The latter's influence is expected to become more pronounced in the near future.

---

[9]The financial statements of a Equity Joint Ventures include a statement of financial condition, a statement of cost accounting, a statement of income and distribution, a statement of profit and loss, a statement of administrative expenses and a statement of depreciation for fixed assets. These therefore differ from those of an ordinary enterprise both in kind and in content. This reflects socialist theory to some extent.

Statement of financial condition

Representing the overall financial position of an enterprise, the statement of financial condition, the equivalent of the balance sheet in a market economy, is of prime importance. The report possesses socialist features in a number of respects. It is a fundamental document which shows the financial condition of an enterprise by contrasting managerial assets to sources of funds. The report used to be called the 'governmental balance sheet'. The assets and corresponding fund sources as of the beginning and end of the fiscal period are presented in parallel form and the report can be prepared either on a monthly, quarterly, semi-annual or annual basis. The assets on the left hand side and fund sources on the right hand side are classified in groups, including fixed assets and the corresponding fixed funds, current assets and the corresponding current funds, monetary assets, and retained income. The statement of financial condition, used as a means of practical direction and control, is a major tool of an enterprise. It does not only allow a comprehensive analysis of fund uses and the results of financial activities but also enables the establishment of corrective measures for improving managerial activities.

Statement of financial bookkeeping closing analysis

The statement of financial bookkeeping closing analysis is a counterpart of the income statement in the market economy. It is another basic document which shows the specific features of the execution of financial plans and the results of financial activities. It discloses a variety of enterprise financial activities including production, sales, execution of cost plans, execution of a profit plans, distribution of profits, the governmental budget payment schedule, the collection and distribution of funds for labour remuneration, the accumulation and appreciation of enterprise funds and changes to fixed assets.

Statement of financial plan accomplishment

This statement is a comprehensive document of the execution of financial plans and is prepared on a quarterly basis. It shows the accomplishment of financial plans with respect to the production, construction, works, sales income, costs, profits, governmental budget payment, living expenses, fixed assets, current funds, and maintenance funds, etc. Enterprises must prepare financial bookkeeping closing statements in compliance with the directions of the Department of Treasury on a monthly, quarterly and annual basis. The statements carry the signatures of the responsible personnel of the enterprise as well as the financial inspector (i.e. auditor). The enterprise should analyse the financial condition and prepare measures for improvement of the enterprise's operation.

ACCOUNTING INSPECTION

The accounting inspection of North Korea corresponds to the accounting audit in the market economy. Central government performs this function for local administrative organs and for enterprises however, as opposed to the external audit carried out by professionals (e.g. CPA) in capitalist societies. Inspections of administrative bodies and enterprises basically follow the same principles, subject to minor practical differences. Inspections of Equity Joint Ventures comply with the *Detailed Rules for Joint Ventures Act*, 1992.

Accounting verification for administrative bodies

The function of this procedure is to guarantee the rational operation of the national finances by inspecting the financial conditions of the auditee body, to ascertain if the appropriate financial rules have been properly observed and if the nation's assets have been properly safeguarded. The inspection is carried out by the Department of Treasury and the People's Committee of local governmental units. It takes the form of either 'documentary' inspection or a 'spot' inspection.

Documentary inspections are performed periodically *via* document surveys, whereas spot inspections are carried out by inspectors sent by central government at least once a year. Each auditee body has to submit monthly and quarterly statements of financial condition along with relevant documentary evidence to the inspection authority. In a spot inspection, books, documentary evidence and property are physically verified. On completion of the spot inspection, the inspectors prepare evaluation reports and the prescriptions indicated in the report have to be followed up and reported upon within due time limits.

The accounting inspection for enterprises

The function of the accounting inspection of state enterprises is similar to that for administrative bodies. The process involves examining the status of the financial rules and financial accounting of the enterprises and is performed at least once a year. The accounting inspection for state enterprises is carried out as a spot inspection in principle. However, when deemed necessary, the authority can demand submission of accounting documents necessary for a documentary inspection. The accounting inspection usually covers the overall financial activities of the state enterprises but is sometimes limited to segmental aspects. Again the Department of Treasury usually takes charge of the accounting inspection. If necessary, however, the Department of Finance of the Peoples Committee of Provisional Government can delegate authority to the accounting inspection sector of an enterprise to carry out the inspection informally. On completion of the spot inspection, the inspector in charge compiles an evaluation report, the prescriptions of which must be observed by the state enterprise.

ACCOUNTING EDUCATION, QUALIFICATION EXAMS, AND RESEARCH ACTIVITIES

Accounting schools are run for the purpose of training personnel for the financial or accounting activities of the state enterprises. The curriculum typically consists of political science, economics, tax theory, budgeting theory, finance, accounting, cost accounting, statistics and business administration. The Department of Treasury is in charge of the administration of the schools.

Accounting staff are classified as either: financial clerical workers; statistical clerical workers; senior accountants; treasurers; and advanced accountants. In order to qualify as legitimate accounting staff, one of the following routes must be taken: passing qualification tests specified by regulation; graduation from either a junior college or a university majoring in finance or accounting (in which case exemption is given from qualification exams); graduation from training centres acknowledged by the finance and accounting function qualifications screening committee; or qualification by the screening committees' authority.

Those who have graduated from a professional training centre, officially acknowledged by the finance and accounting qualifications screening committee with a training period extending over more than three months, are automatically given the title of Accountant. Those who have achieved a recognised qualification in a finance or accounting function in other countries maybe given the title of Accountant by the screening committee's authority without having to take any further formal qualification tests. Graduates from technical junior college with a finance or accounting major are given the title of Senior Accountant without further tests. Graduates from colleges or universities majoring in finance and accounting such as Pyongyang College of Commerce, or Pyongyang Peoples' Institute of Economics are given the title of Treasurer. The title of Advanced Accountant is endowed by a judging committee after being recommended either by ministers, bureau directors, the president or dean of a university or college, the president of a bank, the chairman of the central committee of the North Korean Consumers' Cooperative Association, chief executives of a political party or other social organizations, the president of the Association of Management Calculation Research or a member of the judging committee.

The Association of Management Calculation Research, under the control of the Department of Treasury, aims to develop and disseminate advanced theories in the field of management accounting as well as to contribute to the economic reconstruction of North Korea by aggregating all necessary theories and techniques in this field. Some of the major fields of the activities of the association include research and education with respect to the advancement of management computational theories, practical techniques, the publication of periodicals and books to help disseminate knowledge, the sponsoring of symposiums and technical contests, assisting the activities of the finance and accounting qualifications screening committee and other related matters necessary for the development of management accounting.

CONCLUDING REMARKS

The foundation of enterprise accounting in North Korea is as a channel for processing and reporting enterprises activities in accordance with the standardized accounting rules determined by the central authority. The fundamental characteristics of the North Korean accounting system include the following: asset accounts are not distinguished from expenses and a distinction is not made between capital liabilities and revenues in the same manner as in the West. Bookkeeping is performed only in the form of sources *versus* the uses of funds. The arrangement of accounts in accounting reports follows the most-fixed-first basis, so that accounts are presented in reverse order to their liquidity. China used to display similar characteristics in its accounting system for national enterprises prior to 1993. Since 1993, however, China has witnessed a dramatic change in its reporting systems, moving much closer to International Accounting Standards. North Korea also amended its stipulations for foreign investments in 1992 and through the Joint Venture Act of 1994. Assuming the Far Eastern political situation continues to develop as it currently appears to be doing, the accounting system in North Korea is expected to follow a similar course of change as in China in the near future.

REFERENCES

BKLR (1992) Board of Korea Legislation Research, *Equity joint ventures law system of North Korea*, The Board of Korea Legislation Research, Seoul.

BKLR (1994) Board of Korea Legislation Research, *Foreigner investment law system of North Korea*, The Board of Korea Legislation Research, Seoul.

Choi, S.M. (1994), 'The equity joint ventures accounting system in North Korea', *North Korea and unification research theses No. 1*, The Board of National Unification, Seoul.

Han, I.G. (1993), 'Accounting system of North Korea', *Accounting*, No. 29, Korea Institute of Certified Public Accountants, Seoul.

Jeffries, I. (1993), *Socialist economies and the transition to the market — A guide*, Routledge.

Kim, T.I. (1993), *The management and operation system of state enterprises*, The Board of National Unification Research, Seoul.

Kim, B.H. (1994), 'Research on accounting system of North Korea', *North Korea and unification research theses No. 1*, The Board of National Unification, Seoul.

KDI (1994) Korea Development Institute, *The economic tendency of North Korea*, Korea Development Institute, Seoul.

KTPC (1994) Korea Trade Promotion Corporation, *The practice of North Korea investment*, Korea Trade Promotion Corporation, Seoul.

Park, J. (1994), *The present condition and transition of finance of North Korea*, Korea Development Institute, Seoul.

Appendix
CHART OF ACCOUNTS OF THE EQUITY JOINT VENTURES

No	Accounts	No	Accounts No A's	B's	Accounts Assets	Attribute Sources
1	Fixed assets	01	10	20	■	
	1. buildings		11	21		
	2. structures		12	22		
	3. electrical equipment		13	23		
	4. faculties		14	24		
	5. tools		15	25		
	6. packing materials		16	26		
	7. fixture		17	27		
	8. technical records and books		18	27		
2	Facilities and fixtures	20			■	
3	Raw materials	21			■	
4	Subsidiary materials	22			■	
5	Fuel	24			■	
6	Container and package materials	25			■	
7	Small tools and fixtures	26			■	
8	Spare parts	27			■	
9	Labour protection materials	29			■	
10	Materials for management	30			■	
11	Goods net arrived net	34			■	
12	Materials for processing	35			■	
13	Expense for purchasing materials	37			■	
14	Basic production cost	52			■	
15	Half-finished goods	53			■	
16	Cost of construction and assembly	54			■	
17	Office expenses	57			■	
18	Company management cost	68			■	
19	Business cost carried forward	71			■	
20	Finished goods	76			■	
21	Goods sent	77			■	
22	Difference between price and cost	80				■
23	Sales expense	86			■	
24	Cash	96			■	
25	Bank deposits	97			■	
26	Other monetary assets	105			■	
27	Paid wages	106				■
28	Prepayment of travel expenses	107			■	
29	Acquisition from materials	108			■	
	transaction	124			■	
30	Other acquisitions	125				■
31	Payment for materials transactions	126				■
32	Other payment	136				

CHART OF ACCOUNTS OF THE EQUITY JOINT VENTURES (continued)

No	Accounts	No	Accounts No A's	B's	Accounts Attribute Assets	Sources
33	Settlement for material budget	137				■
	1) income tax		1			
	2) profit of enterprises		2			
	3) others		3			
34	Social insurance institutions settlement	138				■
35	Internal settlement	146			■	■
36	Distribution of profits	148			■	
	1) income tax		1			
	2) reserve fund		2			
	3) other funds		3			
	4) profit		4			
37	Registered fund	152				■
38	Depreciation of fixed assets	153				■
39	Equity joint ventures	154				■
	1) reserve fund					
	2) other fund					
	i) extension of production and technique development fund		1			
	ii) prize fund		2			
	iii) cultural and welfare fund		3			
40	Bank loan	171				■
41	Profit and loss	176				■
	1) sales profit		1			
	2) other profit		2			
42	Indemnity (revenue) of properties insurance	177				■
43	Interest profit and loss	178			■	■

The columns 'A' and 'B' contain third and fourth digit numbers reflecting, possibly, the location or function of the items accounted for (e.g. 'A' could represent factory items and 'B' administrative items). The solid square symbol represents the classification of each account as an asset or a source of funds.

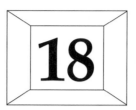

SYSTEMS OF ACCOUNTING
IN VIETNAM

*Laurent Aleonard**

BACKGROUND

Vietnam lies between latitudes 8°4' and 23°15' North bordering China to the North and Laos and Cambodia to the West. It has a coastline facing onto the South China Sea. There are two large, fertile delta areas: in the plains of the Songkoi (Red River) in the northern region of Tonkin which contains Hanoi, and the Mekong in the old southern region of Cochin China which contains Ho Chi Minh City (Saigon). The Mekong is by far the larger of the two deltas, covering three times the area of the Songkoi. In between the two deltas lies the narrow coastal strip of Annam backed by the mountainous and heavily forested Chaine Annamitique. The deltas are fertile, supporting wet rice agriculture and there are substantial hardwood timber reserves in the Central highlands. Vietnam has a number of important mineral reserves including anthracite, phosphate, tin and zinc. Oil is produced off-shore and there are also reserves of natural gas. Hydro-electric power generation is being developed but the main source of electricity is from thermal power stations. The climate of Vietnam is tropical monsoon with a wet season between May and September. The north of the country, however, has a cooler season in January and February. The total land area is 330 341 sq. km with a population of approximately 66 m, giving an average density of 200 persons per sq. km.

The northern part of Vietnam may have been settled by the ancestors of the modern Vietnamese from what is now southern China as early as the third millennium BC and

*Professor associé au Groupe ESC Reim's, France.

there is some evidence of a distinctive bronze age civilisation by 1000 BC. People speaking the definitely non-Chinese Vietnamese language became subjects of the Han Empire in 112 BC and remained as such for the next one thousand years until regaining their independence in 938 AD but without apparently losing their ethnic identity. The capital of this new, centralised Vietnamese state was in or near what is now Hanoi and over the next 900 years it expanded its territory against Cambodia and the Hinduised state of Champa further south. The latter had disappeared by the time the French colonised the area in the late 19th Century. Hanoi and Saigon became the effective twin capitals of French Indo-China (i.e. Vietnam, Cambodia and Laos) until the Second World War and during this period the Vietnamese adopted a romanised script. The Japanese took military control of the region during the war but left the Vichy French officials in nominal, administrative charge until close to the end of the war. By 1945 the communist Viet Minh had emerged as the strongest political force for independence and their campaign against the French, who had been reinstated by the Allies following the Japanese surrender, led to the division of the country into North and South by the Geneva Agreement of 1954. This partition lasted until the fall of Saigon in 1975 to the Viet Minh, two years after the withdrawal of American troops from South Vietnam. The constitution has changed three times since then. The present constitution, signed in 1992, maintains a socialist state with the Communist party organisation (General Secretary, Politburo, Central Committee, Party committees and Party Congress) existing in parallel with the apparatus of government. The latter consists of a 395 member National Assembly, which is the legislative body, a President as head of state, an executive consisting of a Prime Minister and a number of Ministries and the Judiciary headed by the Supreme People's Court. Elections for most offices and positions (which are by secret ballot) take place at five-yearly intervals. The important role of the Communist Party can be seen by the fact that of the 603 people standing for seats in the National Assembly in 1992, only two were non-Party candidates and neither of those were elected. All the members of the government are Party members at present and Vietnam is not therefore a pluralist society. Nevertheless the 1992 Constitution, while being socialist, enshrines a number of important individual rights which indicate a tolerance of capitalist principles including the right to use state land on a long term basis and to transfer and inherit such land. Individuals are permitted to own businesses and legal property cannot be nationalised. Furthermore, although the press is subject to supervision by the Ministry of Information and Culture, religious freedom is guaranteed. The main religions in Vietnam today are Mayahana Buddhism and Confucianism and in addition about six million people follow the Roman Catholic faith. One of the most positive benefits of socialist policy in recent years has been the national education system at primary and, to a lesser extent, at secondary school level. Although only 1.5 percent of the population currently go on to tertiary education, Vietnam has a high literacy rate compared to other Asian countries (88 percent). Much of the population resides in the delta areas and in parts of the Songkoi plains the population density reaches 1500 persons per sq. km. Ethnic Vietnamese make up about 87 percent of the present population.

Vietnam's GDP appears to have grown by slightly more than five percent per annum during the period 1978–90 while the yearly growth in population was probably between two percent and three percent. In 1993 GNP per head was estimated at US$170. Agricul-

ture is by far the most important sector, employing more than 70 percent of the workforce. In recent years there has been an expansion of dry crop produce (groundnuts, tobacco, rubber, tea and coffee) and seafoods are also important, constituting about 12 percent of total exports. Forestry and mineral resources make the primary sector an important export earner. Manufacturing, discouraged during the French colonial period, now makes up an estimated 25 percent of GNP, contributes 48 percent of exports and employs 11 percent of the labour force. Present policy is to move from heavy to light industrial products. Vietnam's main trading partners were Russia and China up to the late 1980s but these have been rapidly replaced by Asian countries (particularly Singapore and Japan) in the 1990s, which now take 70 percent of Vietnam's exports and 60 percent of her imports. Recent years have seen trade deficits, dramatic falls in the international value of the currency (the Dong) and some years of very high inflation (e.g. 800 percent in 1988). However, the promotion of exports of tropical foods and consumer goods together with a limitation on imports led to Vietnam's first trade surplus in 1991. The external debt burden in 1991 was variously estimated to be between 50 percent and 100 percent of GDP in 1991. Nevertheless the earnings of the country have grown rapidly in 1993 and 1994 and this has successfully attracted quite large amounts of foreign investment from European and Asian countries despite a partial US embargo resulting from issues remaining unsettled from the war years. Vietnam has a number of problems to overcome including: the need to avoid drastic policy changes; a dependence on overseas technology to exploit its natural resources; an inadequate transport system; social and environmental difficulties associated with unemployment (as the economy restructures and the size of the army is reduced); and deforestation and soil erosion. However, Vietnam's geographical position relative to the trade routes of the Asia-Pacific region, its natural resources and educated workforce promise well for the future, given a period of stable government and consistent market-economic policies. This perception is underscored by the recent admission of Vietnam into ASEAN.

R.J.W.

INTRODUCTION

There are two major difficulties in studying the Vietnamese accounting system at the present time. One problem is the accessibility of data. The Vietnamese accounting literature is scarce, mainly limited to regulatory and technical texts and a few accounting manuals, which as far as it is possible to judge are compilations of foreign pedagogical works. Most of these documents have not yet been translated or summarized otherwise than for use by foreign investors or within the framework of economic and cultural missions. They are thus not yet readily accessible for the purpose of academic research. Another problem is that Vietnam is currently undergoing a period of economic transition which, though favourable to the evolution of ideas, makes it difficult to distinguish superficial events from underlying patterns. In particular the Vietnamese legal system is currently undergoing a complete transformation and since accounting regulation comes in at the end of this process, it is necessary to reply upon anecdotal evidence concerning the perceptions of participants and upon direct observation.

Nevertheless the transformation of Vietnam into a market economy offers the research worker the opportunity to explore more deeply the issue of 'accounting neutrality'. In this context previous research has revealed four criteria differentiating between accounting mores in the planned economy and various forms of accounting pluralism in the market economy, namely: material pluralism in valuation methods; formal pluralism in the representation of transactions and transformation flows linked to activities of the firm; legal pluralism in the scope of accounting laws; and social pluralism in the identification of the users of accounting information (Richard, 1980).

Another issue examined in this chapter is the role of external influences on the evolution of accounting in Vietnam. Like many Eastern European countries, Vietnam is in need of training programmes in most of the disciplines relating to company management. Western management techniques are imported through international projects of cooperation and through business contracts between Vietnamese and foreign companies.[1] The transfer of techniques involves the interests of countries which are Vietnam's trading partners, since it may result in a choice between the French and Anglo-American approaches to accounting (Aumiphin, 1993). However this probably oversimplifies matters. When the embargo on exchanges with the USA is lifted, the trends which are in evidence in Hanoi, the still very Francophone political capital, will not necessarily be the same as those observed in the Americanised economic capital of Saigon.

In this paper, the same criteria as that which prevailed in the previously cited works above will be used. This is that product (revenue) accounting and cost accounting constitute *'the core of accountancy and the critical point of accounting systems'* (Richard, 1980). However, methodological constraints direct attention to trying to understand the factors that explain the development of the accounting system and to assess the stakes of the main players. Thus, the question is asked: how will the transition to a market economy modify Vietnam's existing accounting system? Broadly speaking the factors which determine the answer to this question can be grouped into two categories: internal and external transition factors. The first corresponds to the social, regulatory and legal mechanisms that are required in a market economy: legislative machinery, regulation and the creation of new sources of finance for firms. The second relates to matters such as commercial and economic cooperation, management training, and business practice — matters which are likely to be influenced by external interests (e.g. the projects of foreign investors).

---

[1]'Identifying priority investment projects', *The Saigon Times* 13 May 1993. 'Vietnam: les premiers pas des écoles de gestion', *Les Echos* 4 May 1993.

The development of the remainder of this chapter is based upon this classification. The next section describes the main characteristics of the Vietnamese accounting system currently in use and, by analogy with the Soviet system which has inspired it, identifies the critical points for its development in a market economy. Section 3 describes the accounting system in the non-state sector and Section 4 deals with the legal and regulatory mechanisms which seem to be required in Vietnam's progress towards a market economy. In Section 5, external zones of influence will be discussed, taking as the focus of interest the special (but very significant) case of joint venture companies. This will be illustrated with the results from a short field study carried out in Hanoi. Finally some conclusions will be drawn on the effect of these various influences on the teaching of accounting and financial management in Vietnam.

THE VIETNAMESE ACCOUNTING SYSTEM

The existing Vietnamese accounting system rests on a body of regulatory texts applicable to Vietnamese firms, supplemented by specific provisions relative to companies with foreign capital. Local Vietnamese firms are governed by a regulation on public accountancy issued in May 1988 and a ruling on accounting and statistics issued in October of the same year. Provisions relating to companies with foreign capital appear in the Law on Investments originally promulgated in December 1987[2] and in an instruction issued by the Ministry of Finance in October 1989, laying down accounting principles applicable to joint ventures.

The Vietnamese accounting system can be divided into two main parts: *the Unified Accounting Plan* applicable to state owned companies and an accounting system applicable to non-state production and trading companies, under the scope of which fall companies with foreign capital. Each part is regulated by a series of texts, neither of which have force of law, but both of which impose administrative obligations.

The Unified Accounting Plan

The Unified Accounting Plan (UAP) has not yet been translated into either French or English. Regulations defining the plan (additional to those mentioned above) include accounting regulations applicable to state companies issued in April 1988, the UAP issued in December 1989 and rules governing the accounting of public industrial

---

[2]The Law on Investments was subsequently amended in June 1990 and February 1991.

firms issued in April 1990. The following discussion is based on the UAP regulations of which several French translations are underway. The UAP is similar to the old Soviet system of accounting and displays two of its main characteristics:

(i)   it integrates the accounts of the firm with those of the state and
(ii) it includes elements of general accounting, cost accounting and budgeting. However, unlike the Western approach, the function of the latter is to determine production costs (Meyer, 1992).

Accounting is conceived of as a tool to control the realization of the national economic plan at the firm level. This is based on a revised view of the firm and of what is known as 'economic accounting'.[3] The basic idea is that the firm has a legal status, it has funds which constitute the physical and technical base of its activities and it carries out its activities according to the objectives imposed by the plan, compliance with these being mandatory. However the firm, in accordance with the profitability constraints imposed on it, must be self-financed, any residual profit being shared with the State.[4] The purpose of the balance sheet in this system is to form the basis of the settlement of accounts at the end of the financial year. Accounting thinking in Vietnam possesses the same two characteristics as in the Soviet Union, the absence of an autonomous accounting theory and osmosis between accounting and economic science. This is witnessed by the existence of common regulations on accounting and statistics.[5] These adaptions mainly concern cost accounting.

As with the Soviet accounting system (Meyer, 1990) the UAP comes in the form of a list of accounts. This divides into nine main categories of accounts, three of which (classes 2, 3 and 4) relate to 'cost accounting'.[6] More precisely the classes are as follows: Class 1, *Tai san co dinh* — Fixed assets; Class 2, *Du tru san xuat* — Stocks intended for production (raw materials, supplies and other stocks); Class 3, *Chi phi* — Production costs or expenditures (these are direct and indirect costs chargeable to

[3]As Meyer (1992) points out, this has resulted in a distortion of accounting practice, the aim being to prove the realization of the objectives of the plan rather than to provide a true picture of the economic and financial situation of the firm.
[4]Making a profit notably supposes that prices are fixed according to production costs, something which price deregulation in Vietnam has invalidated.
[5]Resorting to analogies with the Soviet accounting system to study its Vietnamese counterpart is inevitable pending an accurate review of the history of the conditions in which the latter was introduced. In addition to the exhaustive translation of texts dating back to 1988, we would need to reconstitute the decision process and the role played by the Soviet accounting profession and to interview the authors of the plan. The Ministry of Finance is currently working on sector-based adaptations to the plan.
[6]'Cost accounting' in the Soviet model refers to all customer and sub-accounts of 'Synthetic' accounts (per product, customer or supplier, expressed in currency or physical units) which appear in the accounting plan. This terminology does not correspond to that of the French accounting plan. The list subdivides into two digit synthetic accounts and three digit analytical sub-accounts.

goods, grouped together into principal and auxiliary sections); Class 4, *Thieu thu va ket qua* — products intended for sale (these are stocks of finished goods); Class 5, V*on bang tien* — Cash available or monetary means (these express the financial links between the company and state economic organs); Class 6, *Thanh toan* — Accounts payable; Class 7, *Thu nhap* — Miscellaneous earnings or financial results (these express the different modes of profit distribution); Class 8, *nguon von* — Capital funds and reserves; Class 9, *Nguon von tin dung* — Debts and financial credits (these cover all the short or long term modes of financing such as loans and debts, bank credit etc.)

The application of accounting rules is standardised whereas the presentation of financial statements is not (although a standard presentation has been proposed). Companies are under no obligation to publish financial statements other than for the use of the Ministry of Finance. The latter exercises fiscal control through the intermediary of its financial inspectors whose role is to check the calculation of taxable profit declared by the company leader.[7]

Very precise cost calculation standards have been defined in the choice of the work units, account transfers and the methods of cost allocation. This follows from a conception of cost control as a guarantee against the dilapidation of the socialist ownership of the means of production. Production cost is calculated at the different stages of production before fixing an overall production cost. These aspects of the UAP have caused it to be criticised for its complexity and lack of flexibility. The problem is that cost accounting does not, under the Soviet approach, sufficiently take into account the specificities of the firm. This is presumably the reason why we are currently witnessing a new sector-based differentiation of the Vietnamese accounting system.

The classification of funds into production and distribution in accordance with Marxist-Leninist theory results in an interpretation of the notion of assets which is different to that used in the West. Thus, for example, the UAP reckons on depreciation costs to recompense the State for the assets it has made available to the firm.[8] Furthermore, all acquisitions, losses and transfer are transferred to statutory funds, i.e. those which measure the contribution from the State budget. The cost of renewal (depreciation) is effectively withdrawn from the bank and not just posted as it would

---

[7]The management control function, as conceived in the West, is often confused with that of the financial inspector of the Ministry of Finance. The idea that the internal economic management of the firm can be carried out by a player other than the chief executive or the accountant, or that it can be checked from the inside, for other than purely fiscal or cost price related motives, is not yet very widespread.

[8]These assets only include corporeal assets excluding land. It will be noticed further on that this point proves especially problematic when it comes to calculating the Vietnamese contribution to capital in the creation of joint ventures.

be in the West. Withdrawals made by the Ministry can be redistributed according to the needs of other State units (Meyer, 1992).

Vietnamese accounting is heavily influenced by the need to provide information for taxation. Taxable income is calculated on the basis of turnover, after deducting what are considered to be 'reasonable' operating expenditures. Table 1 illustrates the typical calculation.

Table 1
TAXABLE INCOME

Turnover		Proceeds of sales
	+	Proceeds of sub-contracting for third parties
	+	Proceeds of provision of services
	+	Commissions on sales
	+	Inserts of financial operations
	+	Profits from economic cooperation (Note 1)
'Reasonable'	−	Depreciation of fixed assets used for production
expenditures	−	Heavy repair expenditures
	−	Purchase of raw materials & energy
	−	Salaries & Wages (Note 2)
	−	Administration expenses
	−	Financial interest on loans from the State
	−	Expenses linked to the consumption of products & services
	−	Amounts reserved for social insurance funds
	−	Commercial costs
	−	Insurance costs
	−	Import/export taxes, taxes on turnover
	−	Training expenditure within the limits of budget (Note *)
	=	Taxable results

Notes:
1. This usually concerns firms operating with a foreign partner, as in case of a joint venture for example.
2. Excluding the Chief Executive's salary in the case of private firms.

Expenditures considered as 'exceptional' in relation to operations are not included in the calculation of taxable profit. Examples include such items as: losses due to activity cessation, defective production, damage caused by individuals, fines, bonuses, investment amounts, expenses 'financed by other sources of capital' and expenses which 'do not conform to State rules'.[9] The Ministry of Finance has expressed

---

[9]The last two items in this list are perplexing. Their nature and origin need to be examined more closely but the last most likely refers to contraband activities on the Black Market.

its intention to make accounting and tax regulations conform to international norms. As in the Soviet system, the Vietnamese system contains elements which are closer to cash flow than to accruals principles. Recognition rules are based on the delivery or provision of service and taxable profit in particular is calculated as the difference between expenditures and receipts (rather than between income and expenses). This practice can be explained by transaction patterns between firms. These are often informal and do not systematically result in an accounting document being drawn up (an invoice on delivery, for example). Furthermore most expenses are paid in cash, in local as well as in foreign currencies. Means of payment such as credit transfers, bills, and cheques are not yet commonly used in Vietnam (Aumiphin, 1993). This makes it possible to subordinate accounting rules and financial information to opportunist objectives.[10] The development of the Vietnamese accounting system may modify the current emphasis of the UAP on tax control in favour of more economic objectives such as the more efficient internal management of firms. At the present time the publication of financial statements outside the Ministry of Finance seems to be uncommon.

THE ACCOUNTING SYSTEM IN THE NON-STATE SECTOR

The non-state sector accounting system is constituted from several sources, the most important being the accounting systems of individual and private commercial firms, co-operatives, and collective economic establishments; a regulation governing accounting systems for the commercial sector dated April 1990; and a state decree on accounting systems for production and trading activities, dated December 1990.

A detailed plan of an accounting system applicable to non-state firms has recently been implemented by a decision of the Ministry of Finance, dated December 1994. The system applies to private and public firms carrying out industrial or farming activities. Like the UAP it includes 9 classes of accounts: Class 1: Transferable assets — money in cash or at bank (in Vietnamese currency, foreign currencies or other valuables: gold, precious stones, etc), securities, raw materials, supplies, wares; Class 2: Fixed assets — corporeal and incorporeal; Class 3: Payable debts — short, medium and long term loans, taxes, social debts; Class 4: Owner capital — operating capital, reserves; Class 5: Receipts — sales minus bad debts; Class 6: Production expenditure and commercial expenditure — purchases (of raw materials, supplies), salaries, production costs, commercial costs; Class 7: Receipts from other activities

---

[10]As an example, take the seemingly frequent practice consisting of recording depreciation costs beyond the accounting depreciation period (three or five years) by taking into account the difference between the conventional and technical life span of equipment (a car for example is used for an average of ten years).

— financial proceeds and exceptional proceeds; Class 8: Expenditure linked to other activities — financial charges and exceptional charges and Class 9: Income statement.

This system draws its inspiration from the French *Plan Comptable General*, borrowing its presentation of assets and debts. The system has been adapted to the new Articles of Association instituted by the *Law on Individual Companies* and the *Law on Limited Liability Companies* dated December 1990. The former law applies to small individual companies, whose owners are personally liable for their firms' debts. It lays down the principles of private enterprise. The latter law institutes two new legal structures: companies by share (CBS) and limited liability companies (LLC). The provisions of this law are similar to those of French company law concerning the creation of the firm, its administration, increases in capital, and the cessation of its activities. Vietnam now recognises the principle of the perpetual life of firms and of the autonomy of operating without regard to government or administrative tutelage.[11] Where partners are involved they exercise a right of ownership over the capital of the company, and receive dividends and suffer losses proportionally to their investments.

In the case of CBS's, capital is divided into registered shares, at least 20 percent of which has to be subscribed by the founders. Such companies may issue shares or bonds under certain conditions. Also they must have two controllers elected at the AGM. The law specifies that at least one of these must have some accounting expertise. The law also has direct consequences for the accounting systems of non-state firms. Fixed assets are grouped with the firm's own assets and consequently, these can now include financial and incorporeal as well as corporeal fixed assets. Furthermore the autonomy of the firm with respect to the allocation of its profits is recognised. The number of third parties involved in the internal management of the firm have multiplied and the more widespread publication of financial statements is envisaged. The new law also introduces the concept of a Vietnamese financial market.

The main effect of the law on Limited Companies has been to disclose the firms set-up as joint ventures in the Vietnamese economic and legal environment. It is likely that from now on such companies will adopt either the CBS or LLC form to benefit from more liberal provisions than those foreseen in the 1987 Law on Foreign Investments. The main provisions of this law, as they are applicable to firms with foreign capital, will be briefly outlined with a view to detecting their implication for the development of the Vietnamese accounting system.

The Law on Investments allows three different types of organisation.

(i)   *The business cooperative*: This takes the form of a contract between a Vietnamese party and a foreign party aiming to carry out a common production activity,

---

[11]Except for applications concerning company creation authorizations that have to be referred to the Popular Committee of the relevant town or province.

without setting up a formal company structure. Commercial contracts for simple supplies or exchanges of goods or services are excluded from this category;

(ii) *The 100 percent foreign firm*: This must be created in limited liability company form and enjoys Vietnamese legal status. The law says little about its operation and administration; and

(iii) *The joint venture*: This corresponds to the joint creation of a limited liability company by the Vietnamese party and the foreign party, the partners being liable to the limit of their contribution to the registered capital. The last is by far the most popular form of enterprise, which suggests it is likely that the rules governing and operating it will be further developed in the future.

The joint venture is a legal person under Vietnamese law, entitled to keep its accounts either according to the Vietnamese accounting system or to a foreign model. The law defines three notions of capital:

(i) *Global capital* which groups together all the capital destined to finance the firms permanent means of operating (lands, buildings, materials and equipments), including loans;

(ii) *Legal capital* which refers to the capital that the partners commit themselves to contribute, and thus excludes loans. This must amount to at least 30 percent of the global capital and the foreign contribution cannot be less than 30 percent of the legal capital; and

(iii) *Registered capital* which in principle is equivalent to the legal capital.

The Vietnamese Government is most attentive to the equal distribution of the profits between parties involved. It is particularly keen to avoid the Vietnamese side being remunerated only to the level of its effective contribution to the global capital, when this contribution is small. This factor is important for accounting if the nature of the contributions are considered. Those from the foreign side tend to be in the form of foreign currencies, corporeal assets (factories, buildings, materials, tooling) and incorporeal assets (partners, know-how licences). The contributions of the Vietnamese side may be of a financial nature (usually in Vietnamese currency) but often come in the form of natural resources (raw materials), elements of corporeal assets or user rights to lands or waterways. Such contributions are measured on the basis of prices in international markets although the date of valuation (date of contract or date of effective contribution) is typically not mentioned. This raises delicate arbitration problems when negotiating a joint venture contract[12] and also causes difficulties in the

---

[12]In this respect, it may be noted that the State Committee in charge of cooperation and investments, an interdepartmental body under the Council of Ministers, exerts a power of control on the value investments; It can in particular require a revaluation of contributions. La législation de la vie des affaires au Vietnam, November, 1992.

accounting valuation of the firm's assets, especially those contributed by the Vietnamese side. The management autonomy of joint ventures is clearly defined in the same way as it is in the Law on Companies and private firms or firms with foreign capital now form accounting entities in their own right.

So far the discussion has focused mainly on the regulatory and legislative environment which, in the absence of any conceptual framework and accounting laws, defines the form of Vietnamese accounting. Attention will now be turned to an examination of the options with which the Vietnamese accounting system is currently confronted, looking specifically at the main internal and external factors that are likely to be influential.

THE CULTURAL, LEGAL AND REGULATORY ADJUSTMENTS REQUIRED FOR THE CREATION OF MARKET ECONOMY

Substituting a market economy for a planned, centralised economy requires the revision of Vietnamese accounting theory. Soviet theorists reject most of the common notions of capitalist accounting such as personification theory, the theory of exchange or the theory of the balance of assets and liabilities (Richard, 1980). Consequently a revision has two prerequisites: the calling into question of the foundations of the Soviet model and the collaboration of business, industrialists, administrators and academics.

The Vietnamese accounting profession, trained mostly in the USSR or GDR, appears to be isolated linguistically, geographically and theoretically. What new accounting thinking there is has been initiated by non-specialists, whose access to foreign literature, exchanges with delegations of foreign experts and consultancy activities with private Vietnamese firms have made them aware of the issues involved in the changing accounting and financial information environment. The process of change thus raises the question of the balance between the different participants in the debate on the revision of Vietnamese accounting.

The debate has crystallised around the issue of the transition to a market economy. As mentioned by Meyer (1992) this point has been raised by Russian theorists:

> "Why is it necessary to revise the accounting plan? Among essential determining causes we will mention: the transition towards a market economy, the arrival of firms which are no longer State firms and effective involvement in international relations.[13]"

Vietnam presents all three of these causes. But it remains to determine whether revision will be carried out by means of adjustment and adaption or whether there

---

[13]L.Z. Schnejdman, Commentaries on the accounting plan, quoted in Meyer (1992).

will be a radical break up with, at stake, the alternatives of the French *Plan Comptable General* and Anglo-American accountancy.

The East German case[14] is possibly relevant in this context. Here the factors found to be important were: the upholding of collectivisation of the means of production in certain key sectors' of the economy; the grouping of firms into sector unions which protect them from the over pressing supervision of ministries; economic reform allowing for sufficient management autonomy; and more equity in the distribution of profits between the firm and the State. It is not yet certain that the Vietnamese accounting system will need to undergo a revolution, as long as economic liberalisation does not involve calling into question the very foundations of the socio-economic environment.

In the next two sub-sections two related matters will be discussed. Firstly, the likely pattern of revision to existing accounting practices will be considered. Secondly, the sources from which these revisions are likely to be drawn will be discussed.

The revision of the accounting plan

The transition towards a market economy translates into the introduction of trading relations, the free circulation of the currency, and accession to the private ownership of production goods. Consequently, the revisions of the accounting plan must focus on accounts pertaining to the retention of current assets in the firm; credit and borrowing operations with banks and other private persons; and a redefinition of the assets which constitute the wealth of the firm. The modifications introduced by the Soviets between their 1985 and 1991 accounting plans will be used as a basic model for the changes which are likely to take place in Vietnam (Meyer, 1992).

The first stage of accounting reform consists in formalising and clarifying basic principles. Many of these will probably remain intact. For example, there is the obligation for any firm, state or private, to keep full accounts. Others which will remain will presumably include the obligation of regularity in the keeping of accounts; the principle of the true image; the obligation to settle accounts with a minimum frequency; and the principle of the continuity of operating (in particular, the value the assets does not correspond to the liquidation value). However, two fundamental reforms which it seems likely will be required are the principle of the exclusiveness of the accounting year and the principle of caution. Both result from a new conception of the firm (state or private) as an accounting unit responsible for its management and having to provide information to third parties on the financial performance of its activities. The independence of the accounting year and the corollary principle of

---

[14]See Richard (1980).

accrual accounting in the Anglo-American sense, require the transfer from cash based accounting to income and expenses based accounting. This evolution will result in a change in the nature of depreciation accounts and the creation of provision and deferred and accrued accounts. Furthermore, it implies the systematic use of accounting recording for any entry or movement on an account, and thus to an in-depth reform of business practice.[15] As for the principle of caution, it is the conse-quence of the application of the mechanisms of a market economy. These introduce economic decisions into the firm, and makes it responsible for the management of risk. It may be anticipated that Vietnam will follow the pattern taken by the Soviet system of 1991 which systematised depreciation recording and provisions for bad debts and recommended the valuation of stocks at probable sales price.

Meyer (1992) underlined to what extent the application of market economy prin-ciples upset the theoretical conceptions and mentalities of the Soviet accounting profession. It was evidently not possible to achieve complete transformation in the former Soviet Union. In the case of the principle of the independence of accounting years, receivables and charges due were not systematically recorded even after the reforms. Moreover, in order to avoid generating too radical a disruption, a project to adopt international accounting norms and an accounting plan similar to the French *Plan Comptable General* (PCG) had to be abandoned. Similar resistance may be expected to new ideas in Vietnam and will be reinforced by the informal nature of trading practices and the traditional Vietnamese mistrust of transactions recorded through book entries.

Possible sources of revised accounting practices

Based upon what happened to the old Soviet accounting system, it would seem that the transition to a market economy naturally led the Russian accounting profession to adopt the French model. This evolution may be taking place in Vietnam, where the French accounting profession led a number of successive missions in 1991 and 1992. Moreover, the PCG was translated into Vietnamese in 1989 at the request of the Ministry of Finance.

In addition to the historic, cultural, economic and financial ties (Aumiphin, 1981) that link Vietnam to France (the French language is still very influential in govern-ment and university circles in Hanoi), legal logic argues in favour of the French ac-counting plan. The need to reinforce business legislation and to control commercial transactions is a priority. Not only does this affect the state sector but also, and more

---

[15]In the medium term this will probably only affect certain key sectors of the Vietnamese economy, notably tourism and certain trading activities. Payment by credit card has appeared in some of the big hotels in Saigon and Hanoi. The Vietcombank introduced three types of credit cards for use by private individuals and firms in July 1993 (Sources: The Saigon Times, 1 July 1993).

particularly, private firms. The law inevitably play a strongly regulatory role with regard to entrepreneurs in a competitive environment distinguished by the existence of a contraband economy. Legislation with these characteristics is currently well under way. Among the texts in preparation are a Civil Code, a Code of Civil Procedure, a text relative to the civil status of foreign residents in Vietnam, a Code of Commerce, a law on insurance, and a law on Tribunals of Commerce.[16] This legislative machinery is strongly influenced by French law, thus making the PCG appear as a complementary mechanism. The PCG offers the advantage of instituting very accurate accounting norms, both at the levels of the use of accounting information and of the presentation of financial statements. It constitutes an instrument of regulation that is all the more necessary, since available accounting competencies are scarce and the effort involved is training professionals in the transition phase of the socio-economic environment requires a clear framework.

However, this evolutionary option seems to be meeting some resistance, a fact which arises from conflicts of interest between different ministries. One of the most important causes of this is the North-South differentiation in the Vietnamese economy. The unification of North and South Vietnam in 1975 was founded on the principle of economic complementarity. This was translated into a division of labour between the North which concentrated on the heavy industries and the agricultural South which was heavily financed by foreign investments. The result of this has been a latent rivalry between the political capital Hanoi and Ho Chi Minh, the economic capital (heavily influenced by the American presence in the 1960s and 1970s).

Against this background a considerable influence is exerted by Saigon business circles on the strategic importance of international cooperation projects and on Hanoi's decisions. Ernst & Young, one of the 'big six' accounting firms, now operates in Ho Chi Minh. It has developed privileged relations not only with the Ministry of Finance but also with UNO consultants and it engages in intensive teaching and training activity in the fields of accounting and the development of the market economy.[17] The influence of Anglo-American accounting is all the more significant in the south of Vietnam in that it crystallises the debate around the creation of the financial markets that are necessary for the diversification of company sources of financing.

As far as the accounting system is concerned, the conditions underlying the creation of a Vietnamese financial market are not neutral. Depending upon whether preference is granted to Vietnamese investors (local or expatriates) or to foreign investors (as is currently the case), not only will the factors of influence be different but so also

---

[16]La législation de la vie des affaires au Vietnam, November, 1992.
[17]'Ernst & Young: the first auditing company in Vietnam', Vietnam Economic News, Vol. 3, No. 18, 30 April 1993.

will be the needs. The alternatives appear to be either a system developed from within according to the French model, oriented towards the valuation of assets and the preservation of the capital of the firm; or a system remodelled to cater for the needs of the suppliers of foreign capital[18]. This very oversimplified presentation of the alternatives between the PCG and Anglo-American approach to accounting suggests two alternatives in the future development of Vietnamese accounting. As the example of Russia showed, there is strong probability of a natural evolution towards the French plan, for both cultural and economic reasons, something which is reinforced by the location of political and academic power in Hanoi. However, the need to diversify the sources of financing of the economy, especially in the south of the country, reinforces the likelihood of the growing importance of foreign capital and thus of an Anglo-American influence in Vietnamese accounting. In the next section the manner in which this influence exerts itself in practice in joint venture firms will be discussed.

THE MANAGEMENT AND CONTROL OF JOINT VENTURES IN VIETNAM

"With the development of relations with foreign countries and that of joint-ventures, accounting becomes the basis of international talks." (Meyer, 1990).

De facto, the Law on Investments foresees special provisions relative to the accounting system of firms with foreign capital. As pointed out previously, the latter are free to adopt the accounting system of their choice providing it conforms to international rules and usage (without any reference to any specific authority, such as the FASB) and is agreed beforehand with the Vietnamese Ministry of Finance.

Accounting regulations applicable to joint ventures

The accounting system of the joint venture must be described in the investment application file presented to the Vietnamese state committee in charge of investments and appears in the contract drawn up between the Vietnamese and foreign parties. The file must specifically provide the following information: the reference accounting plan or system (Vietnamese or foreign); the language[19], units of measure, and currency

---

[18]In this context the impending lifting of the American embargo leads one to predict a growing influence of the Anglo-American accounting system.

[19]In principle accounting entries have to be made in Vietnamese, but they may also be made in another 'commonly used international language' with the agreement of the Ministry of Finance. In the same way, the accounting units of measure have to be the same as those used in Vietnam. The currency unit is the Vietnamese dong. However, dispensation may again be authorised.

units used; overall accounting documentary evidence; the list of accounts; the different accounting documents (account, books, ledgers); and the financial statements which are to be drawn up annually (balance sheet, income statement, annual report)[20].

It is possible for joint ventures to change their accounting system with the authorization of the Ministry of Finance. The accounting year usually corresponds to the calendar year, from Jan. 1 to Dec. 31, although different closing dates may be adopted with special dispensation. Financial statements have to be filed in with the State Committee in charge of cooperation, and with the revenue department of the Ministry of Finance. Finally, joint ventures may choose their depreciation method, straight line or accelerated (depreciation rates are fixed according to the nature of the assets). The accounting principles and rules applicable to joint ventures, as far as is able to be discerned, follow the directions described above concerning the revision of the Vietnamese accounting system. They stress the liability not only of the firm's chief executive but also of its head accountant. The former is accountable to the Ministry of Finance for the bookkeeping and the law initiates an evolution in business practice by imposing the obligation to keep documentary accounting evidence for all operations. The firm's accounting is controlled once a year by a body appointed by the Ministry of Finance. However, the nature of this auditing body does not appear to be defined as yet.

The fact joint ventures enjoy the freedom to choose their accounting system makes this type of firm a useful place in which to conduct field observations of the developments in Vietnamese accounting. The choice of the accounting system is negotiated and reflects the relative contributions of each partner in the registered capital. These choices indicate the trends that are likely to appear in the medium term. The use of one accounting system rather than another in firms with foreign capital will undoubtedly exert an influence on Vietnamese executives, on the accounting profession and in academic circles. Some preliminary observations in this regard are made below on the basis of a survey on the management control of joint ventures.

The accounting practices of a sample of four companies

Four firms set up either as joint ventures, or on the basis of a licensing contract with a foreign company, form the basis of the following observations. These were a cement factory, a television set manufacturer, a hotel and a food processing company. The main characteristics of this sample are summarised in the following table.

---

[20]It seems however, though it has not been possible to check this information, that a quarterly accounting report may also have to be drawn up. (*La législation de la vie des affaires au Vietnam*, November, 1992).

Table 2
CHARACTERISTICS OF FIRMS STUDIED

	Cement factory	TV set manufacturer	Hotel	Food processing firm
Type of partnership	Joint venture	Licence concession	Joint venture	Joint venture
Nationality of foreign partnership	French	Japanese	French	Singapore
Turnover	US$52 Million (*forecast*)	US$4.4 Million (1991)	US$7 Million (1992)	US$126 000 (*forecast*)
Payroll	300 employees	345 employees	270 employees	125 employees
Foreign partner contribution	Partners, technology, 70% of registered capital	Technology, electronic components	Technology, 43% of registered capital	60% of registered capital (Note 1)
Vietnamese partner contribution	Factory, 30% of registered capital	Factory (*no disclosure of registered capital repartition*)	57% of registered capital (*other contributions not disclosed*)	40% of registered capital (Note 2)
Language used for management	Vietnamese and French	Vietnamese	Vietnamese, French and English	English
Profit sharing protocol	Proportional to contribution	*Not disclosed*	Proportional to contribution	Proportional to contribution
Management and control system	Budget control, cost accounting	Budget control (no cost accounting or internal control)	Budget control, planning system, internal control, monthly reporting, cost accounting	Cost accounting
Accounting system used	French accounting plan	Accounting plan close to PCG 82	French accounting plan	Anglo-American accounting

Notes:
1. The registered capital of joint venture amounts to US$1 m; the total amount of assets is US$2.4 m (US$1.9 m of fixed assets). Foreign partners contributions include initial capital in US$, technology and equipment.
2. The Vietnamese side's contribution includes initial capital (in Vietnamese Dongs), and ownership rights in land and buildings.

These examples stress the importance of management technology transfers from the foreign partner to the Vietnamese side, with the exception of the television set manufacturer whose management system remains traditional and separate from that of its Japanese partner. The transfers materialise under different forms, from the adoption of cost accounting to the presence of foreign resident managers (as in the case of the hotel). They all have one common point: the adoption of the accounting system of the foreign partner. In this respect, the case of the Franco-Vietnamese cement factory is particularly interesting, with its implementation of a separate provisional cost accounting.

The existence of technology transfers in the field of management reinforces the idea that joint venture accounting will prove a key factor in the evolution of Vietnamese accounting. Under these conditions, one may attempt to anticipate this evolution by assessing the share of the different countries that are representative of the different accounting models in international investment projects in Vietnam. In 1992 these were as shown in Table 3.

Table 3
INTERNATIONAL INVESTMENT PROJECTS IN VIETNAM

Country	Overall amount of investments (forecasts in $US millions)	Number of projects recorded
AUSTRALIA	2,650	23
TAIWAN	1,565	70
HONG KONG	681	90
FRANCE	460	29
JAPAN	443	29
GREAT BRITAIN	434	12
THE NETHERLANDS	388	7
FORMER USSR	316	43
SOUTH KOREA	215	17
CANADA	160	10

Source: *Saigon Times*, 1 July 1993.

This table only gives an indication of trends, since it groups together several types of projects (for instance joint ventures, and the aid programmes of international organisations such as the World Bank and UNO) whose influence on the management systems of Vietnamese firms is not always comparable. Nevertheless, all of them call into question Vietnam's traditional methodological infrastructures, i.e. the statistical system, economic accounting and company accounting (Nguyen, 1992).[21]

Taking into consideration the cooperation and exchange relations which Vietnam is keen to promote, the dilemma with which the Vietnamese accounting system is confronted is revealed. As was indicated in Table 2, the introduction of new accounting technologies involves major interests in the teaching of accountancy and company management. This matter will be discussed in the last, concluding section.

CONCLUSION

The transition towards a market economy which Vietnam is currently undertaking has led to technology transfers of a particular nature which affect the management orientation of firms. These transfers, originally very informal, have tended to become more significant within the framework of commercial contracts and investment projects with foreign partners[22]. Furthermore they have gained a growing share of economic and cultural exchange programmes. Thus, of the 95 million French Francs budgeted for co-operation between France and Vietnam, 20 million were to be devoted to economic training, customs regulation, and finance (*Les Echos*, 4 July 1993). One may assume that these transfers will influence, at least indirectly, the orientation given to the Vietnamese legislative and regulatory framework which is currently being developed. They contribute to the demarcation of economic, commercial and cultural zones of influence which many countries exporting to Vietnam appear to appreciate. The nature of local management training is becoming increasingly competitive if we are to judge from the growing number of schools and training centres which are opening up in Hanoi and Ho Chi Minh City.

---

[21]This table needs to be complemented with the North American investments in preparation pending the lifting of the US embargo, which both sides have long been waiting for. In 1993, 160 US firms (including Bank of America and Citybank) had obtained from the Treasury Department a licence authorising them to explore the Vietnamese market. The number of missions of American experts and industrialists to Hanoi and Ho Chi Minh is growing, encouraged by the Vietnamese authorities who emphasise their concern not to see Vietnam monopolised by some investing countries; (source: Time, 2 August 1993).

[22]A recent article (The Saigon Times, 13 May 1993) underlines the attention the Vietnamese and foreign investors give to the transfer of management methods and techniques. Such transfers have become an element of negotiation in business practice.

Beyond the diversity of techniques and methodological approaches that it is giving rise to, this competition will sooner or later raise the question of the coherence and standardisation of practices and of regulations that will gain momentum from them. The stakes are particularly crucial for company accounting and financial management, which constitutes one of the basic factors in the transition to a market economy. As Meyer (1990) noted in the effects of the 1985 economic reforms on the management of State firms in the former Soviet Union, the use of accounting is felt when companies start developing possibilities for autonomous action.

This autonomy was recognised by the Vietnamese state in the laws on individual companies and limited companies published in December 1990. It already applies in joint ventures, where most of the time it has resulted in the adoption of the foreign partner's accounting system. In the long run, the absence of accounting standardisation is likely to lead to confusion in the economic and financial valuation of firms and to slow down future investment decisions. At the same time, the growing heterogeneity of practice makes statistical evaluation difficult, even if one restricts oneself to the national accounting system[23]. So far, the teaching of accounting has mainly focused on enacting laws and principles, outside of any explicitly stated conceptual framework. The very few accounting and management manuals available are not conducive to theoretical reasoning. It is to be feared that compilations hastily translated from the Anglo-American literature will only add further to the confusion. Hopefully it will be possible to avoid reproducing in teaching and training what appears to be happening in practice: the juxtaposition of disparate techniques and rules drawn from French, Anglo-American and even Japanese methods.

Teaching must rest on a clear and shared understanding of the objectives assigned to the system of accounting and the financial management of firms. The recent laws on companies obviously contribute to this but are insufficient. Presumably we can expect a harmonisation of the principles applicable to State firms, private firms, and firms with foreign capital which currently come under three different legislations. Also to be expected is a renewal and diffusion of theoretical thinking on the objectives and uses of company accounting and management. The development of a specifically Vietnamese referenced framework is probably a necessary intermediate stage in this process. Only at this stage will it be possible to undertake real transfers of technology in the field of management within the context of tenders launched at the initiative of the Vietnamese administration.

This discussion of accounting and management techniques for the use of Vietnamese firms underlines the need to clarify and adapt the theoretical foundations of the accounting and management techniques exported to Vietnam, so that they may

---

[23]For instance, it seems that not all joint ventures simultaneously keep their accounting in accordance with the Vietnamese unified accounting plan.

serve as instruments of training and judgment. This suggests that concerted and complementary action should be taken by exporting institutions such as professional bodies and organisations dealing with accounting practices. It is probably with this in mind that the French profession developed a company accounting system, based closely on the *Plan Comptable General*, conceived of as a theoretical and practical aid to accounting normalisation. Its promoters consider its three objectives to be 'clarifying accounting language, offering accounting mechanisms, and providing a base for training in-depth accounting techniques' (Delesalle and Gehard 1991). The same principles are applied to studies at the Franco-Vietnamese Centre in Hanoi, which has a double vocation: the training of future company executives (especially for joint ventures) and of teachers who will develop practical and theoretical training programmes. Complementary professional and academic approaches may well prove to be the key to the renewal of the Vietnamese accounting system and cost accounting. Their contribution could be theoretical and not only strictly technical or normative. This would perhaps lead to a redefinition of Vietnamese accounting within a wider and less opportunistic perspective than that which would develop if the only alternatives open to Vietnam were a choice between the French *Plan Comptable General* and the Anglo-American system.

REFERENCES

Aumiphin, J. (1981), *La présence financiere et économique Française en Indochine*: 1859–1939, Doctorate of Law, institute du Paix et du Développement, Nice, Sophia-Antipolis.

Aumiphin, J. (1993), *Comptabilité au Vietnam: de la finalité à la normalisation, Bulletin du CFG*, No. 1, B1, July.

Delesalle, E. and G. Gelard (1991), 'Exporter la comptabilité: le systéme comptable d'entreprise', *Revue Française de Comptabilité*, No. B223, May, pp. 75–91.

Luu, T. (1992), *Les conditions de création d'un marché financier au Vietnam*, Research paper, DIGEM-Vitnam, EAP, Paris, unpublished working paper.

Meyer, M. (1990), 'Introduction à la comptabilité d'entreprise en Union Soviétiqe', *Revue Française de comptabilité*, No. B211, April, pp. 93–9.

Meyer, M. (1992), *La comptabilité de l'entreprise russe, L'Harmattan*, Paris.

Nguyen, V. (1992), '*Qelques spécificités dans la gestion de projets internationaux de développement au Vietnam*', Research paper, DIGEM-Vitnam, EAP, Paris, unpublished.

Richard, J. (1980), *Comptabilité et systémes économiques: URSS et RDA*, Doctorate, University of Paris I Panthéon-Sorbonne.

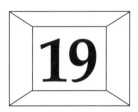

REFLECTIONS ON THE RELATIONSHIP BETWEEN CULTURE AND ACCOUNTING PRACTICES IN THE ASIA-PACIFIC REGION

Roger Willett, Akira Nishimura and Nabil Baydoun[*]

INTRODUCTION

The introductory chapter to this book discussed the 'environmental hypothesis' in the accounting literature, i.e. the belief that the environment may have a significant influence on the form taken by accounting practices in different countries. Several aspects of the general accounting environment were discussed, namely physical, cultural, political and economic. At some risk of prejudging the matter, the order of the following chapters dealing with each country in the region was structured to reflect what appeared from these to be the dominant effect on overt accounting practices: the effects of colonial and neo-colonial political influences.

The justification for this statement will be discussed below. From the similarities in accounting practices exhibited by the countries of the same group and differences compared to countries in other groups, it would appear that environmental factors, broadly defined, do have an effect on such things as the form of regulation and the general approach toward the production of financial statements. What it is intended

*Professor of Accountancy, University of Otago, New Zealand; Professor of Management Accounting, Kyushu University, Japan; and Professor of Accounting, Northern Territory University, Australia; respectively.

to do here in the concluding chapter is examine the more specific 'cultural hypo-thesis', i.e. the belief that cultural factors affect accounting practices. With a few exceptions (e.g. the chapter on Malaysia and Singapore); the relationship of culture to accounting technology has been left implicit in the discussion contained in most of the essays in this book. Indeed, it may be that, on close examination of this matter, one is led to conclude that there is no discernible impact of culture on accounting practice.

However this issue, which is the subject of some debate in the accounting litera-ture at the present time (e.g. see Baydoun and Willett, 1995) should at least be aired since the evidence needed to arrive at even that negative conclusion would amount to progress beyond what is currently known. To encourage a critical examination of this issue in the context of the practices described in this book, therefore, some aspects of these practices will be reviewed, some key concepts in the study of culture outlined and a framework suggested within which evidence for and against the cul-tural hypothesis might be usefully marshalled in future research. The possibility of a significant converse relationship of the impact of accounting technology *on* culture will also be analysed. Finally the prospects for harmonisation in the Asia-Pacific region will be briefly discussed.

SIMILARITIES AND DIFFERENCES IN ACCOUNTING SYSTEMS

When one considers the details of the accounting systems which have been described in the preceding chapters of this book, one is struck, at least at the superficial level, more by the similarities rather than the differences between the accounting practices of the countries of the region. Most of the accounting systems have been described as variants of the Anglo-American, European and Soviet[1] type or some hybrid of these. These are the accounting technologies which have been imported into the region 'off the shelf'. The adoption of these systems by the countries of the region, based upon the descriptions given in earlier chapters and following the order of the chapters, is shown at the top of Table 1.

These accounting systems are similar in a number of broad ways. They are heavily based upon the analysis of transactions cost data, classified into assets, liabilities, expenses and revenues, in a double entry bookkeeping system. North Korea, for example, with its Soviet-style system uses exactly the same basic rules of debit and credit with interpretations of 'assets' and 'sources of funds' which are instantly recog-nisable by a Western accountant. Profit is calculated as some function of the differ-ence between revenues and expenses after eliminating stocks and work in progress (i.e. the 'cost of sales' adjustment). All the systems include a depreciation adjustment

---

[1]That is an accounting system based upon that of the old USSR.

Table 1
ACCOUNTING SYSTEMS IN THE ASIA-PACIFIC REGION

	Australia	Malaysia	Singapore	Hong Kong	New Zealand	Papua New Guinea	Japan	Philippines	South Korea	Taiwan	Thailand	Indonesia	Macau	Cambodia	China	North Korea	Vietnam
Type of accounting system	UK	UK	UK	UK	UK	UK	US/German	US	US	US	US	Dutch/US	Portuguese	French	Soviet/US	Soviet	Soviet/French
Professionalism	H	L	H	H	H	NA	H	L	L	L	L	L	NA	NA	NA	NA	NA
Conservatism	L	H	L	L	L	NA	H	H	H	H	H	H	NA	NA	NA	NA	NA
Uniformity	L	H	L	L	L	NA	H	H	H	H	H	H	NA	NA	NA	NA	NA
Secrecy	L	H	L	L	L	NA	L	H	H	H	H	H	NA	NA	NA	NA	NA
Power distance	L	H	H	H	L	NA	H	H	L	H	H	H	NA	NA	NA	NA	NA
Uncertainty avoidance	L	L	L	L	L	NA	H	L	H	H	L	L	NA	NA	NA	NA	NA
Individualism	H	L	L	L	H	NA	L		L	L	L	L	NA	NA	NA	NA	NA
Masculinity	H	H	L	H	H	NA	H	H	L	L	L	L	NA	NA	NA	NA	NA
Confucianism	L	NA	H	H	L	NA	H	L	H	H	H	NA	NA	NA	H	NA	NA
Specific factors Colonial history	British	British	British	British	British	British	-	Spanish/US	Japan	-	-	Dutch	Portuguese	French	-	Japan	French

Notes: NA: Not available
Figures are based on Hofstede (1991) and Eddie (1991).

against profit. The reports, required to be given to users, always include a balance sheet and profit and loss account (or their equivalents). Even in instances where more significant, basic, structural differences can be observed, such as the use of cash measurements in the Cambodian economy, the stated intention of the authorities is to move towards 'improvements' by adopting the procedures of one of the major accounting technologies listed above (in the case of the Cambodian system, this is the French UAS). So the basic data, the way in which it is processed and the reports required to be given to users are all very similar.

The countries of the region differ mainly in the way they have adjusted some of the less structurally important aspects of these accounting systems. The most obvious differences can be classified under the headings: the use of objective rather than subjective data (e.g. actual transactions costs rather than current values); the type of calculations used as estimates (e.g. LIFO versus FIFO, lower of cost and market etc.); the parties to whom access to information is granted; the quantity of information disclosed; the degree of standardisation in reports; the extent to which delegated powers are given to the parties involved in determining accounting rules; and the identity of the parties given delegated powers, if any. These headings are partially related in an overlapping way to Gray's four accounting dimensions. The first two are related to Conservatism, the third, fourth and seventh to Secrecy, the fourth and fifth to Uniformity and the fifth, sixth and seventh to Professionalism. It is debatable, however, if these observable differences have anything to do with deep cultural values.

Market values of various sorts are used to alter asset values to a greater or lesser extent in the countries of the region, usually, but not necessarily in accord with the practices of the 'parent' country from which the accounting system was originally imported. China, North Korea and Vietnam occasionally re-value assets wholesale in accordance with government regulations while the western style economies follow less systematic rules. On the whole, though, these differences seem to be quite small and derivative (in the sense that they are usually closely related to imported practices) with changes of policy usually being prompted by the impact of the immediate economic environment (e.g. inflation rates). Some countries permit or insist on revaluations to a greater or lesser extent (e.g. the Philippines and South Korea) and some, particularly in countries with socialist economies where statistical and bureaucratic considerations are paramount, disallow certain types of provision accounting or require adherence to specific methods in the calculation of depreciation. Cost and not economic value is the usual basis of measurement everywhere. Calculation rules like lower of cost and market and estimation procedures such as FIFO also seem to be mainly derivative or a response to recent economic conditions. Thus North Korea and the socialist countries generally appear to stick more strictly to cost while most countries, particularly those following Anglo-American practices, use the lower of cost and market rule. There are also minor differences between countries in other areas, for example Japan allows LIFO valuations of inventories but this method of estimating cost has, since 1984, been forbidden in Indonesia. However, nowhere within the region, it would seem, are any innovative measurement rules used which are significantly different from those used in western accounting systems.

The parties to whom access to information is granted varies to a greater extent. Leaving aside multinational companies (MNCs) the reporting practices of which are largely determined by transnational factors, the groups to which information is reported are more restricted in socialist countries. Comparison of the practices of these and the other countries of the region in this respect indicates that access to information is a function of the political framework and of whether the system is oriented towards government objectives (including Brunei as well as the socialist states) or is otherwise credit or capital market based (see Nobes, 1995). The same forces presumably explain the quantity of information produced which in most cases is inversely related to access although the quantity of information given to enfranchised users in each country is difficult to assess at any level of detail from the data available. The accounting system of North Korea produces a welter of detailed information for the managers of the command economy while the countries of Singapore, Australia and New Zealand provide much more aggregated information to a wider variety of users.

The accounting systems of the countries of the UK and US groups are probably the least standardised. In particular, Hong Kong and Singapore both follow relatively *laissez fairre* practices which may also be an effect of their trading position. On the other hand, the countries following socialist and continental European traditions are more highly standardised. Powers are delegated to a greater extent and the professional status of accountants is highest in those countries with US and UK systems and lowest in the socialist countries. In the former status is achieved through specialised financial knowledge while in the latter the lack of status is probably due to the lack of a market to sell that expertise as well as a general theoretical view which traditionally has been disinclined to place a high social value on the provision of financial services.

The question which then arises is: Do cultural factors appear to have any significant relationship with these observable characteristics? MacGregor *et al.* argued, using Hofstede-Gray analysis in chapter 5, that they did not. However the cultural hypothesis needs to be examined in a regional, not just a country-specific context. One simple way to test the hypothesis would be to see if Hofstede's cultural values predict accounting values in the region in accordance with the relationships shown in Table 2 of the first chapter.

Hofestede's scores for cultural values classified into 'high' and 'low' categories are shown in Table 1 for the countries where they are available together with estimates of scores for Gray's accounting values classified on a similar basis[2]. The measures shown

---

[2]Countries are shown as 'high' if they had scores for the relevant variable greater than the average score and 'low' otherwise.

are taken from Hofstede (1991) and Eddie (1991). The latter are subjective estimates based upon the method suggested by Nobes (1984). Two things may be noted about the values shown in the Table. Firstly, there is quite a strong pattern for the accounting values which follows the colonial effect used to order the countries and secondly Hofstede's first four values predict the accounting value scores about 67 percent of the time, a statistically significant result at the 5 percent level[3]. Indeed if Eddie's (1991) sources for Japan are replaced by those suggested in Radebaugh and Gray (1993) the apparent relationship between cultural influences and Gray's values become even stronger.

It would, however, be *blasé* to take this analysis at face value as a straightforward confirmation of Gray's hypothesis. The measures attributed to Gray's variables are, after all, subjective and there must be some suspicion that they may unconsciously prejudge the very relationship they are designed to test. Furthermore, there appears to be a strong connection between the colonial influences already noted as being a significant factor explaining accounting practices and Gray's accounting values. Consequently it becomes unclear as to which of the two effects is more important in the region. Some insight on this issue may be provided by observing what happens in those cases where the Hofstede-Gray model breaks down, namely Hong Kong and Singapore. Here the neo-colonial influence predominates and one consequently suspects that the apparent confirmation of the Hofstede-Gray theory suggested by the data in Table 1 is in reality more likely to be little more than a consistency brought about by an *association* between the cultural and accounting variables due to an underlying cause. In fact it may even be evidence of an acculturation effect of colonisation and more specifically of an implicit effect of the importation of an accounting mind-set *on* cultural values.

Management accounting practices

The contributions to this book show that our state of knowledge and the development of our theoretical understanding of the practice of management accounting in the Asia-Pacific region lags behind financial accounting. The most detailed descriptions and analysis come from those countries where western customs are firmly implanted (e.g. Australia and New Zealand). Furthermore, most of the systematic research findings which have been reported in other countries of the region, such as the PRC, South Korea and Taiwan, are based on examining the extent of the use of western practices. Japan is the major exception to this with a distinctive style of management and what appear to be emerging new approaches to accounting analysis in the form

---

[3]If each prediction is treated as a single trial in a sequence of Bernoulli experiments.

of concepts such as target costing. With this exception, however, the picture revealed largely gives a similar appearance to that found in the case of financial accounting: of a uniformity of management accounting practices throughout the region. The problem here, of course, is that only relatively little empirical research and, to an even greater extent, relatively little theoretical analysis has been carried out specifically in the region. Very little work seems to have been done, for example, to analyse the relationship between styles of management, organisational forms and accounting methodology outside of the Japanese experience.

It is quite possible that this lack of information about management and management accounting practices may mask significant differences in approach compared to western practices. Most of the more systematic data collected about management accounting practices comes from large firms and, often, from multinational companies. Virtually nothing appears to be known about the decision making practices of small, indigenous firms in the countries of the region. This probably biases our perceptions of what is happening in practice and the need for research into management practices in smaller firms in the region is certainly something which needs to be addressed. Nevertheless it is possible to reflect on the information available, in the context of cultural factors, in the same manner as was done with financial accounting practices.

The uses of management accounting reports, aspects of control, internal forms of accountability and agent-principal contracting arrangements are presumably all susceptible to the influences of culture. For example, the horizontal two-way management system which seems to be naturally adopted in Japanese organisations and the need to communicate as teams and between teams of different disciplines may call for reports of a different nature compared with those designed for traditional western reporting purposes. Unfortunately, the *resumés* of studies carried out in Australia, China, Hong Kong, New Zealand and South Korea provide little, systematic documented evidence on internal disclosure practices.

Target costing seems to be the most significantly different management practice in the region. The main characteristics of target costing are shown in Table 2 with an assessment of how the characteristics of Japanese management practices differ from those typically found in the West.

The style of management in Japan is relatively proactive compared to the more reactive or passive approach taken by Western firms and the organisational form of Japanese firms is characterised by a horizontal structure of control in which a two-way flow of information is encouraged (Marinaccio and Morris, 1991). The Japanese approach to control is for managers to co-operate with workers to solve problems

Table 2

CONTRAST BETWEEN JAPANESE AND WESTERN
APPROACHES TO MANAGEMENT ACCOUNTING

Management organisation characteristics	Japanese practices	Western practices
Management Style	Proactive	Reactive
Form	Horizontal, two-way	Vertical, one-way
Objectives	Zero inventory and defects	Rational inventory and defects
Information Systems	Feedforward	Feedback
Accounting Systems	Target costing:	Standard costing:
	Design and continuous improvement of standards	Explanation of variances from standards

affecting the entire production cycle together. The collective responsibility which results from this process plays an important part in establishing close and effective teamwork (Kharabanda and Stallworthy, 1991). This stands in contrast to the vertical, personalised, structure of control with a one-way flow of information typically found in western companies. Top management prepares a goal based upon a statistic such as return on capital employed. Division managers then make local budgets based upon this overall plan and these are implemented at shop floor level. Apart from some consultation in budget preparation, the emphasis is on decision making at the higher levels of management with a one-way command structure as opposed to the interactive and consultative approach taken by Japanese management.

Another significant difference in the Japanese approach to management is the tactic of setting ideal rather than rational objectives. This is illustrated in the goals of zero inventory levels and zero defects in quality control. The rational western view-point is embodied in the presumption of a trade-off between high quality and low cost which finds expression in the policies of economic order quantities and accept-able levels of defects. The aim of target costing is not simply to determine costs by working backwards from the price necessary to provide a certain share of a potential market. It is also designed to fulfil the requirements of JIT and zero defects in produc-tion and is a part of the overall, inter-departmental, integrated approach to the deci-sion making processes adopted in Japanese firms.

The information and control systems which run in tandem to facilitate these goals and policies have been described as 'feedforward' rather than the 'feedback' systems which characterise the western approach to these matters. The feedback approach, with the periphery reporting back to the core and being issued instructions, has evolved to serve the vertical one-way form of organisation described above. The feedfoward system based upon the *Kanban* principle and computer aided management has evolved with the objective of foreseeing and preventing problems before they occur (Morgan, 1992).

Target costing thus is an accounting process which reflects the characteristics of Japanese management. Its key elements of price based, cost design and continuous improvement through cross functional co-operation embodies the principles of proactive management style, the horizontal two-way form of management organisation, the search for 'perfect', minimum cost output and the need for foresight and prevention. In comparison to western methods of standard costing, target costing may be characterised as a process which focuses on a rigorous analysis of the variance between the target cost and the standard cost at the design and planning stage of production. If successful, in conjunction with much tighter control and the other aspects of management described above, this eliminates the difference between the standard and actual costs in production.

These characteristics of the Japanese approach to management accounting and also possibly a putative eastern form of approach to management generally seem to boil down to four main attitudes: being proactive, preventative and cautious; the desire for collective and efficient organisation; the need for two-way channels of communication; and a striving towards perfection rather than a rationally satisfactory result. How do these characteristics tie in to Japan's cultural values as measured by Hofstede's cultural value survey? According to Hofstede, Japan ranks towards the higher end of the Power Distance scale, the lower half of the Individualism scale, high on Uncertainty Avoidance and first on Masculinity. It scores highly on the Confucianism scale. This seems consistent with attitudes evident in the organisational practices described above and with one's general impressions of Japanese society. An acceptance of and respect for authority associated with moderate to high values for Power Distance and Confucianism would promote the effective running of business. Lower values for Individualism encourage behaviour appropriate to the achievement of collective goals and a two-way consultative process. High Uncertainty Avoidance would lead to the cautious, proactive and preventative approach while high Masculinity would be consistent with the determined, single minded and systematic seeking after absolute standards (Hofstede, 1991).

These *ex post* rationalisations of certain traits of Japanese management accounting practices by reference to underlying cultural values should, perhaps, not be taken too seriously. There are many intervening effects which more precisely explain the nature of Japanese accounting (e.g. the training systems imported from the West after 1945 (Nishimura, 1992; 1994). However it remains that deeper cultural factors do at least in some instances seem to impinge upon certain behavioural aspects of management accounting practice. Moreover culture also seems, albeit in sometimes quite remote ways, to allow certain practices imported from outside to establish themselves and evolve more readily than others. This, again, is a matter of the effect of acculturation referred to above in the context of financial accounting practices.

Culture's consequences for accounting or accounting's consequences for culture?

From the foregoing analysis of financial reporting and management accounting practices in the countries of the Asia-Pacific region it appears that the effect of culture is not very much in evidence, if at all, on the most observable aspects of practice *viz.*, in the identity, the type and format of financial statements and the basic methods of data collection. However certain *behavioural* aspects of accounting seem to have the potential to be influenced by cultural factors. Thus the double entry bookkeeping system and the form and content of financial reports might be relatively culturally impervious, but the way accounting standards are negotiated, the views which are considered to be important in this process and the perceived purpose for which accounting information is most useful, might not.

This observation, if it is valid, has many implications for future research but three stand out as being especially significant in the context of the Asia-Pacific region. Firstly, there is a broad continuum in the region between what might be called the 'Hindu' and Confucian mind set. Interspersed along this continuum is the western European, rationalist outlook. The potential effect of these cultural differences on the adoption of accounting practices would make an interesting study. However it may be that the positivistic approach to acquiring knowledge, which is currently the most popular approach in this area of the accounting literature and is exemplified by Hofstede and his followers, is not the most appropriate methodology to adopt to investigate such an issue. Secondly, even if cultural factors do affect accounting practices it is not clear over what length of time they might be expected to act. It may for instance be that a relatively long period of isolated cultural equilibrium is needed for cultural factors to impact on accounting practices (such as the periods of time which allowed the European accounting systems to acquire distinctive characteristics). Consequently it may make more sense to look for quite small specific changes to accounting practices over longer periods of time than has so far been attempted in order to test the cultural hypothesis. Thirdly, and possibly most importantly, as has been alluded to on several previous occasions it may be that a more significant relationship between culture and accounting is in the converse direction to that usually postulated in the accounting literature. That is, perhaps the most interesting and clearest examples of the relationship lie in the effect that the importation of accounting technology has *on* cultural values.

These questions cannot be answered here, but they raise clear research issues which may eventually provide some interesting answers to the kind of debate currently taking place in the international accounting literature. To carry such research through more thoroughly, however, two things are required: firstly it is necessary to consider more precisely what are the essential cultural elements in the accounting environment and what are appropriate techniques for investigating them; and secondly it is necessary to consider in detail what is meant by accounting practices and, more specifically, by an 'accounting technology'. The next two sections will discuss these matters and the processes of acculturation in turn with a view to providing an improved conceptual basis from which the aforementioned research issues can begin to be more effectively explored.

CONCEPTS OF CULTURE AND THEIR RELEVANCE TO ACCOUNTING RESEARCH

The current importance of the Hofstede framework in the international accounting literature make it a natural starting point in a discussion of the elements of culture. Culture in Hofstede's sense of the term and its relationship to other constructs such as the environment and social institutions etc. can be seen from Figure 1. Hofstede's framework is contained within the inner box. The manner in which the three constructs, environment, culture and institutions relate to each other and the part played by a fourth concept, the *modal personality*, in the chain of cause and effect in which they all coexist and drive the processes of social adaptation is important in understanding how the relationship between culture and accounting might be investigated.

Starting at the left of Figure 1 it is generally supposed that the environment influences the form culture takes (e.g. Triandis, 1972). There are too many factors affecting both constructs and too much variability to suppose that it might be possible to predict the form a culture might take based simply upon a detailed knowledge of the environment. Nevertheless it is often possible after the event to 'explain' certain traits of culture as a plausible outcome of environmental factors. Hofstede's (1991) book contains plenty of such examples. In accounting one can think of plausible explanations of how the environment may fairly directly affect the accounting method. In agricultural ventures for instance the natural harvest cycle may impose a corresponding accounting period and possibly a preference for the current cost valuation of inventories so as to relate performance measurement to the same harvest cycle. The longer and much more tenuous indirect links which may exist between environment and accounting systems *via* the intermediaries of culture and social institutions are more difficult to discern and sometimes quite tenuous. For example, the monsoonal climate and physical terrain of certain parts of South-east and East Asia make it suitable for garden farming and wet rice agriculture. The irrigation projects which then make agricultural effort more effective encourages large scale organisation. Education in the skills appropriate to such endeavour and the political systems most conducive to its development permit, even though they do not necessarily promote, the

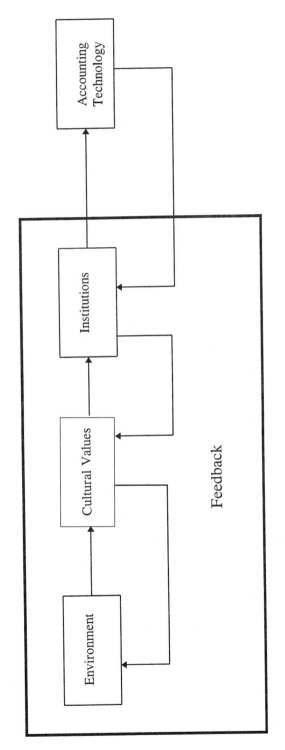

Figure 1 Hofstedes view of the relationship between culture and institutions.

growth of large scale bureaucracy. Finally the demands of bureaucracy leads to a system of accounting that is highly detailed and uniform and intensely conservative and secret — very much like the socialist system of accounting in China.

Such theorising is an illustration of how easily plausible links between environment, culture, institution and accounting systems can be constructed. In fact, the pattern of the background information that introduced each chapter of this book was motivated by the possibility of such connections: the environment, including its cultural elements, *permits* certain developments in accounting systems although it does not *determine* them. However, given the complexity of the connections between cultural factors and accounting practices it once again raises the question of whether it is appropriate or sensible to attempt to study the relationship in the positivistic manner often assumed to be demanded in the application of Hofstede's framework (White, 1949, 1975; Sahlins, 1960).

Looking now at the second box in Figure 1, Hofstede's definition of culture given earlier is actually just one among many which can be found in the literature on psychology, anthropology, sociology and other cognate disciplines (e.g. see Kroeber and Kluckohn, 1952). If culture is restricted to human societies then it is closely connected with language. For present purposes it is probably sufficient to regard the culture of a particular human group as *the system of beliefs of the group as expressed in the language of that group.* Expressed beliefs either take the form of factual or ethical propositions and it is evident that these may possibly affect accounting practices. If a questionnaire survey were to reveal, for instance, the expressed belief of members of a particular group that the payment of interest was wrong and should be prohibited, it might be expected that this could affect the content of the financial statements in that interest payments and all items leading to interest payments such as debentures would disappear from financial statements.

Language itself may, in either superficial or deeper ways, affect concept formation and the development of technologies such as accounting and data processing (Postman, 1966). Description and meaning are both susceptible to translation. In these and other respects language may influence the exact form and interpretation of accounting information. Furthermore language boundaries are often related to racial groupings, a fact which makes language useful data to the extent that physical or genetic traits may contribute to an understanding of existing cultural traits. This is particularly useful in the complex South-east Asian region. The possibilities for linguistic analysis in this area seem promising (see Belkaoui, 1995).

As to how research may be undertaken to investigate 'accounting culture' in a more general sense, belief systems may be revealed to the researcher through the perceptions and actions of the persons studied. The extent to which the two are consistent is a source of considerable interest in cultural research generally (Bochner, 1986). Perceptions and attitudes are typically investigated by questionnaire surveys in the accounting literature. Hofstede's (1980) study referred to previously, for example, used the IBM database which is founded on a survey conducted by the company to measure the attitudes and work values of its employees. Interviews and case studies are also standard methods of enquiry. Other possible avenues of investigation are the critical analysis of textual material and other artifacts of a culture (as in physical anthropology) and both perceptions and actions may be examined by physical observation and an analysis of the historical record (Kaplan and Manners, 1972; Harris, 1968).

In a specifically accounting context, Chow *et al.* (1994) conducted four experiments with samples of final semester Japanese and American MBA students to examine preferences for specific management controls at the interface between the organisations and the external labour market. Harrison used questionnaires to examine the impact of culture and personality on the relation between reliance on accounting performance measures in the evaluative style of superiors and work related attitudes of subordinates (Harrison, 1992). Surveys were also used by Pratt and Beaulieu (1992), Strange (1992) and Frucot and Sheraton (1991) to examine culture — accounting issues. Rentsch (1990) used interview and questionnaires to examine the relationship between people's membership of social-interaction groups and the meanings they attach to organisational events and a similar approach was used by Suzuki (1988) to investigate the problems facing Japanese students studying MBA in the US. Using a case study approach Robey and Rodriquez-Diaz (1989) described the attempt of an MNC to implement an automated accounting system in two of its subsidiaries situated in Latin America. A similar approach was also used by Soeters and Schreuder (1988) to examine the interaction between national and organisational cultures in accounting firms. Further removed from positivist tendencies, a number of studies have traced the historical development of accounting technology, sometimes with special reference to cultural factors (Willmott *et al.*, 1992). The value of Hofstede's framework in this context lies in its role as a structure within which to appreciate the linkages between a variety of research endeavours such as these which would otherwise appear piecemeal. It is unlikely, however, that the subtleties of belief systems and their impact on accounting will be revealed by simply counting responses to specific questions and observing certain actions. The need for a more critical approach to accounting issues is nowhere, perhaps, more apparent than in this particular area.

Turning now to the third box in Figure 1, the impact of culture on institutions is discussed in Hofstede (1991). In accounting the most significant institutions of concern are professional accounting firms, professional organisations, those departments of government under whose jurisdiction comes the responsibility for financial reporting and the running of state enterprises and those parts of a large organisation which pertain to the functions of management accounting. All of these areas have been researched, often extensively, but not usually from a cultural perspective. Individual professional firms and government departments are relatively difficult to investigate from the inside. The nature of administration in the PRC, for example, does not lend itself easily to study by external researchers and studies of professional associations in a European and developing world context usually emphasise the exercise of power. Although a number of studies of a descriptive nature have been carried out recently in the Asia-Pacific area, more analytically based investigations of the behavioural effects of accounting systems, while common in the West (e.g. Gul *et al.*, 1993; Otley, 1980) are so far uncommon in Asia.

Institutions are the social channels through which cultural traits are transmitted to accounting systems. It is important therefore in the analysis of accounting practice to understand how beliefs implemented by culture (e.g. kinship structures, correct forms of behaviour etc.) may affect the structure of organisations and the relationships between members of organisations. This might lead to a better appreciation of why a particular form of financial reporting or management control exists or, perhaps, what these should be in order to best accomplish a cultural objective. The target costing developed by some Japanese firms, for example, is in part a direct response to economic circumstances (i.e. of the need to minimise costs in the competitive world economy of the 1970s). However the rapidity and single-mindedness of the response, its innovative and unique nature and even the perception of what is it and what it does, appear to have a particularly Japanese flavour. The relative paucity of knowledge about management accounting techniques in the Asia-Pacific region suggests that more resources should be devoted to organisational research in firms of the region. The same comment applies to professional and governmental organisations. For instance, it would be interesting to know more precisely what real, as opposed to apparent, reasons lie behind the adoption of international accounting standards by some of the countries of the region.

Leaving aside for the moment the matter of exactly what an accounting technology is (this will be discussed in the first part of the next section) the remaining element in Figure 1 which requires some comment is concept of the *modal personality*. This concept which is discussed by Singer (1961) seems to be worthwhile resurrecting as a theoretical construct in the context of present emphasis in accounting research on interpreting cultural values through survey data. While the institution is the complex social structure of interest in the cultural study of accounting and the individual response to a specific questionnaire item is the atom of enquiry, the modal personality is the basic unit of theoretical and empirical analysis. Researchers have little choice in examining a system of beliefs but to observe and record the behaviour and attitudes of individuals as their basic datum. Individuals transmit their beliefs to each other and to the researcher through language and this, interpreted by the researcher, becomes an important part of the record of the culture of the group to which the individuals belong. It is possible to see in this fact why an examination of the cultural impact on accounting practices is inherently complex. Although it might be possible to roughly describe the 'typical' Japanese or 'typical' Australian, anything more than a cursory acquaintance with individuals soon reveals considerable variability in behaviour and attitude[4]. The modal personality is thus a long list of highly variable attitude and behaviour patterns which are usually not independent of one another. To explain how this average collection of attributes comes about through the interaction of many individuals in different environmental and institutional contexts over long periods of time and how they may be reflected in the specific practice of accounting in the present day is therefore a task to which considerable care and attention to detail must be given.

In this respect research in the theory of personality and the effect of changes in the cultural environment on the accounting personality would seem to be called for. This is necessary to complement historical and critical studies of cultural change and also the behavioural study of organisations referred to above. It is also relevant to issues related to the process of cultural evolution but which have not yet been dealt with systematically in the accounting literature, namely the issue of acculturation through the imposition of accounting technology. This matter will be discussed below after a more precise characterisation of an 'accounting technology' has been given. What is an accounting technology is often not clearly defined. It has been argued elsewhere that the failure to consider exactly what constitutes an accounting technology has lead to an inefficient focusing on issues in the study of the cultural impact on accounting (Baydoun and Willett, 1995). The basis of this argument is reviewed in the next section.

ACCOUNTING TECHNOLOGY

Apart from Japan, Australia and New Zealand most of the economies of the Asia-Pacific region were classed as less developed Asian and Asian-Colonial (for Hong Kong and Singapore) by Hofstede (1980). There is a substantial literature which questions the relevance of accounting systems which originally evolved in Western Europe and North America ('western accounting systems') to the needs of developing countries (e.g. Briston, 1978; Samuels and Oliga, 1982; Wallace, 1990; Hove, 1986). Since this question is clearly pertinent to the context of the present work the findings of such analysis should be of interest. However the analysis is typically vague in both the definition of the problem and in the statement of its recommendations.

---

[4]This last remark should remind us of the dangers of ethnocentrism, a bias introduced in cultural analysis by the object of study being interpreted by an investigator from a different culture (Triandis, 1972). Cultural anthropologists refer to the different approaches to this problem as the *emic* (the study of a culture from within) and the *etic* (the study from without, (Berry, 1980)). Studies of the latter type tend to be characterised by a more objective, 'scientific' methodological approach while the former tend to be more subjective and impressionistic although there seems to be no logical reason why this should be the case (see Harris, 1968).

A major difficulty lies in the lack of a precise idea of exactly what parts of an accounting system fail the test of relevance, what 'relevance' entails and, sometimes, even what an accounting system is exactly. The theory proposed by Baydoun and Willett (1995) concerning what an accounting system is and how culture factors affect the different elements of it, may be summarised as shown in Figure 2[5].

The smaller box contains what will be referred to as the *technology of accounting*, that is the processes developed by a society for taking accounting measurements, making calculations based upon those measurements and disclosing those calculations to users. The larger box contains the elements of the *accounting environment*, users, preparers, their decision models and actions and the regulatory framework. The diagram in the figure has been drawn so that the most physically determined aspects of accounting technology and the accounting environment are shown towards the bottom of the Figure while the most socially determined aspects, such as the rules for proper disclosure, appear towards the top. The implication suggested by the triangular shape drawn under the heading 'Effect of culture' is that *a priori*, by definition, culture will affect those parts of the accounting environment mostly determined by social factors to a greater degree than it will affect those parts mostly determined by physical factors. For example, the measurement of physical input–output relationships in the production of commodities is little, if at all, affected by culture. More susceptible are the management structures of firms. A motor vehicle needs four wheels in Japan just as much as it does in Australia. However, the structures of management in Australian firms tend to be more individualist and hierarchical emphasising functional relationships and management by objectives, whereas in Japan the emphasis is on group strength, a free form of command, human relationships and management by consensus (Fukuda, 1988).

This pattern of physical *versus* social components and their different relationship with matters cultural is repeated in the analysis of accounting technology. Those parts towards the bottom of the Figure, the *measurement* aspects of accounting, are more closely related to purely physical considerations than are the parts towards the top of the Figure, the *disclosure* aspects of accounting. It is extremely important to appreciate the significance of the distinction between measurement and disclosure processes in accounting. Failure to consider these processes separately when attempting to formulate theories about accounting systems in relation to other variables (such as culture) leads to the confused analysis of several entirely different processes as if they constituted a single problem. The process of accounting measurement involves collecting evidence of transaction costs (through invoices and other documents) and

---

[5]In its explicit reference to the accounting *environment* generally rather than just to accounting *technology* this representation is a slight extension and clarification of the theory described in Baydoun and Willett (1995).

Effect of Culture

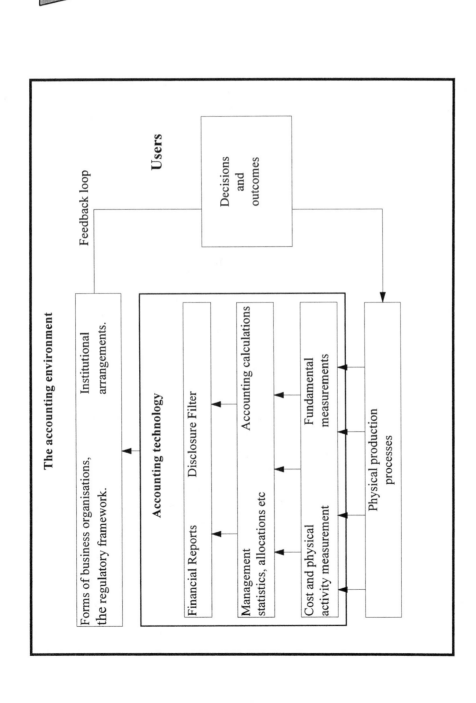

Source: Adapted from Baydoun and Willett (1995)

Figure 2 The accounting environment.

relating these by a rough statistical method called 'matching' based upon physical production relationships[6]. This data is used to derive calculations like the earnings figure which have statistical properties which are likewise relatively impervious to cultural factors. The process of disclosure on the other hand depends upon certain channels of communication. Such channels are very definitely functions of cultural variables. Disclosure is affected to a much greater degree than is the process of measurement by considerations of the rights and powers of users to obtain information, the duties of preparers to provide information and a host of complex issues relating to the institutional arrangements of the society in which accounting disclosure takes place. Thus while the choice of accounting measurement system may in the first instance be to some extent socially determined and while the particular forms of derived calculations made for specific purposes may also be affected by cultural variables, disclosure practices, which are determined by a large number of social factors, are much more likely to be influenced by cultural elements since the character of the rights, obligations and powers relating to information disclosure varies in many systematic ways across cultural boundaries.

The significance of this analysis for the issue at hand is that our knowledge as accountants of our own technology should inform us to look for the effects of culture more in some parts of accounting practice than in others. Specifically it should be expected to find more evidence of the effect of culture at the disclosure end of the accounting process, to a lesser extent in the way accounting numbers (especially performance measures) are calculated and possible not very much, if at all, in the way the basic data relating to transactions costs and economic activities is gathered, classified and recorded. In the context of the relatively uncharted territory of developing countries in general and the Asia-Pacific region in particular, clues about where to start looking for the effects of culture and how to assess the relevance of an accounting system to society's needs is especially important because of the paucity of evidence. It is apparent that nearly all accounting practices have been imported from outside the region, mostly within the last century. As the effects of culture (if they do exist) may possibly make themselves felt only over relatively long periods of time it will probably be difficult, either through a positivist examination of actual practices or through a more informal, critical, normative type of study of a wider range of subject matter, to discover instances which will lead to a definitive finding on this issue — like finding a needle in a haystack, in fact. This analysis and that of the preceding sections suggests therefore that, at least initially, evidence of the effects of culture on accounting practices in the Asia-Pacific region should be sought, by whatever method is chosen for the purpose, in the behavioural areas of the accounting regulatory framework, aspects of management control in firms and, as regards accounting technology itself, in the processes relating to the *disclosure* of financial

---

[6]See Willett (1991) and the literature cited therein for a fuller description of this 'transactions' theory of accounting. Most 'economic' theories of accounting measurement typically fail to distinguish the measurement and disclosure issues referred to in the text.

information. One should only, however, expect to find differences in the area of measurement practices on rare occasions.

Reflections on cultural evolution and acculturation

The overall picture obtained from the discussion of the similarities and differences in accounting systems in the Asia-Pacific region is reasonably consistent with the theory of the differential impact of cultural factors on accounting practice just outlined. The basic techniques of the measurement and classification of transaction costs into expenses, revenues, assets and liabilities and the manner in which the resulting information is presented in balance sheets, income statements and, sometimes, cash flow statements seems to be relatively unaffected by cultural boundaries. However there are many small differences in the information disclosed in financial statements in different countries.

Analysis of the overt characteristics of the accounting systems of the countries of the region in terms of the cultural variables suggested by Gray as was seen earlier leaves considerable room for doubt even if it appears to point in the direction of cultural factors being at work. Furthermore, other, broader viewpoints like the one mentioned at the end of Section 2 do not appear to reveal a more conclusive role for culture in determining accounting practices. On the basis of the historical record, if cultural variables do influence accounting practice, one would expect to observe broad differences in accounting practices corresponding to the triadic grouping: the Confucian societies — China, Hong Kong, Macau, Singapore, Taiwan, Japan, the Koreas and Vietnam; the Hinduised societies of the remainder of insular and peninsular South-east Asia[7]; and the European settler societies, Australia and New Zealand. However, on the surface at least, this classification seems to shed no further light in terms of explaining overt accounting practices in the region than does the Hofstede-Gray approach. Indeed, as has been emphasised throughout, if it was desired only to predict which type of accounting system one would find in a particular country, one would not have to look very much farther than a few key political and economic variables. Colonial history, political ideology and the economic and political power of the US in the region statistically 'explain' most of the variation in the

---

[7]The basis of this classification and the historical justification for the theory of the Hinduisation (i.e. assimilation of culture from the Indian subcontinent) of South-east Asia is described in Hall (1981) and Williams (1976). There is actually some recent empirical evidence that this theory does reflect, some characteristics of accounting systems in the Asia-Pacific region (Secord and Su, 1994). Generally speaking the influence of Indian culture decreases with the increase in geographical distance from India. Vietnam is considered to be Sinic rather than Hinduised and the small state of Singapore is predominantly a Chinese enclave for recent historical reasons. The extent to which the Philippines can be considered to be either Hinduised or Sinicised is questionable. Its physical position places it on the periphery of both the Indian and Chinese spheres of influence and it was probably the best example of an insular, indigenous Malayo-Polynesian culture in South-east Asia prior to the period of European colonisation.

choice of accounting technology. The colonial factor is overwhelmingly important. If there was no formal European colonisation (e.g. as in Japan, Thailand, China and Korea) then US practices become very influential. The style of accounting technology adopted, in fact, appears to be a function of the dominant political force at the time of its initial assimilation.

What, then, is the cultural context of the similarities and differences in accounting practices? This brings us back to the topic of cultural diffusion and cultural colonialism or 'acculturation'. In the case of cultural evolution it has been argued that, in order to trace the effect of culture on accounting practice, it is necessary to look closely at the marginal differences in accounting practice, especially in areas of disclosure where change has taken place over quite long periods of time. The problem with a theory of this type, however, is that even the complete absence of evidence concerning marginal changes in disclosure practices would not necessarily disconfirm the theory. It is a theory of *long run* effects and, at the present time, it is not known how 'long' the long run is i.e. it is not known how long it is necessary to have to wait to witness the effect of culture on accounting technology. Hence, since culture is itself a variable that is evolving, it may be that the cultural parameters which an accounting technology may be required to satisfy, have in fact already moved on before the technology has had the opportunity to catch up. Thus a cultural equilibrium may never be reached, making the job of attempting to identify the effect of cultural values on an accounting system virtually impossible to successfully complete.

Consequently it may well turn out that a more interesting and worthwhile research question which accountants should be addressing is not so much the effect of culture on accounting technology but the effects on cultural values of the importation of western accounting systems. It is reasonably clear from this study and others of similar groups of countries (e.g. Cooke and Parker, 1994) that acculturation and not cultural evolution is probably the single most important factor determining the patterns of accounting and disclosure in developing countries *in the short term*. Consequently while the previous discussion of the appropriate strategy to adopt in searching for evidence of the evolution of accounting practice still holds insofar as long term patterns are concerned, it is of some interest also to consider how evidence of acculturation due to the adoption of western accounting technology might be observed over a shorter time scale.

Analysing the processes of acculturation involves emphasising different methods of investigation and a different conception of the role of accounting technology compared to those which are relevant to the analysis of cultural evolution. Rather than concentrating on the extent to which belief structures may lead to the transformation of accounting technology, the effect of accounting technology in moulding belief structures must be emphasised. Key concepts in this respect are those of 'power', 'social control', the dehumanisation of workplace relationships and, more generally, the secularising influence of economic rationalism on fundamental cultural values[8]. Accounting technology may in fact be seen as one of the basic instruments of the economic rationalist. Once the quantities in financial statements are accepted as the legitimate basis for determining social choice, accounting acquires a pseudo-scientific status as the final, objective arbiter between conflicting viewpoints on many matters which have important social, cultural and environmental, as well as economic, consequences. For example, a key idea in the context of accounting's role regarding economic rationalism is profit maximisation. Used as a criteria for determining the flow of investment funds, especially by MNCs in conjunction with the liberalisation of world trade, the application of this principle appears to have brought considerable material benefits to Asia and South-east Asia in recent years. However it has sometimes brought environmental disaster (e.g. the Bopal incident in India) and its possibly subtle and far reaching effects on individual belief systems has yet to be seriously researched. In order to appreciate how such issues might be investigated in accounting it is worthwhile reflecting on the differences between modern, western cultural values and those possessed by societies in our region at the time western influences were first felt.

The characteristics of modern western societies are that they are highly complex entities with very specialised functions and differentiation of structure. Their values are secular, individualistic and most would claim to be democratic. Personal relationships in these societies are based upon formal contracting relationships, often expressed in terms of monetary debt, property relationships involving the concept of ownership, identification of one's loyalties with the state and a hierarchy related to measures of wealth or income. In contrast the societies of the Asia-Pacific region were pre-modern at the beginning of the colonial era. Their values were and still are to a greater extent than in the west, based upon religion, affiliation to the family or tribe and the non-exclusive use rather than exclusive ownership of society's resources. Furthermore formal debt relationships expressed in monetary terms are much less important than in modern western societies. Many of these traits are similar to those found in pre-modern western society. However in the case of the west, capitalism evolved gradually over a period of several hundred years whereas developing countries had the full weight of capitalist doctrine thrust upon them overnight, so to speak.

This raises the interesting question of what effect did the adoption of the principles of economic rationalism and, more particularly, the principles of cost accounting have on personal attitudes, the structure of family relationships, pre-existing organisational forms and, indeed, the myths and symbols of the societies of the region? These matters have not been addressed explicitly in any of the chapters of this book

[8]This is the reason for the remark made in the introductory chapter of this book that this type of research falls into the category (iii) literature of the literature review.

but there is some evidence that they constitute more than just academic issues. The assimilation and adaptation of western economic rationalism by the Confucian societies is perhaps one of the most interesting topics for future study in the Asia-Pacific region[9].

Given the apparent Chinese proficiency with respect to the study of commercial subjects and mathematics and the way in which Chinese culture generally seems to have embraced the principles of economic rationalism it may be that some cultures have a greater capacity to accommodate and use accounting technology than others. Japan and the Koreas also seem to share this trait. Perhaps long held Confucianist traditions, the requirements of a secular bureaucracy and the importance of large, stable organisations to the economy are significant factors in understanding the impact of western accounting systems on cultures of the Asia-Pacific region. In this respect a historically based, cultural classification of the countries of the Asia-Pacific region on a Confucianist-European-Hinduised continuum of the kind mentioned above might prove to be more significant in studying the effects of accounting technology on culture than it appears to be in the study of its converse, the effects of culture on accounting technology.

PROSPECTS FOR HARMONISATION

Finally, in concluding this discussion of the cultural hypothesis in the context of accounting in the Asia-Pacific region, it seems appropriate to consider briefly the prospects for harmonisation. By the above account the prospects for standardisation seem strong. Countries of the region seem to be importing western accounting techniques wholesale without paying very much attention to cultural sensitivities. However, this is not what is meant by harmonisation (Nobes, 1984). It is, in fact, noticeable that some of the arguments put forward in the harmonisation debate run contrary to the approach being adopted in practice by countries of this region. Perera (1989) and others have argued that the goal of comprehensive harmonisation is unrealistic and that regional harmonisation, recognising the cultural needs of local areas, is a more practical objective. The almost unseemly haste with which some of the countries of the Asia-Pacific region are rushing to adopt either international accounting standards (e.g. Malaysia) or those of specific Western countries (e.g. China and Cambodia) do not appear to reflect this viewpoint.

The question arises, therefore, as to whether this tendency is what it appears to be? Is it evidence that harmonisation and perhaps even standardisation of accounting practices of the region towards internationally recognised norms are inevitable and

---

[9]For a general discussion of the viewpoint that the environment itself is culturally determined see Steward (1977).

likely to be rapid or is it possibly a sensible take-over of a technology which will later evolve to accommodate the demands of local users? It seems likely that both of these outcomes are possible. The pressures of globalised business relationships and the influence and power of multinational companies are likely to lead to pressures for accounting standards which can be applied with equal authority in different parts of the world. These standards are probably appropriate for large organisations dealing in the international sphere. In China, Vietnam and to a lesser extent in North Korea, the importation of western standards mainly affects foreign enterprises, although it may be expected that this will inevitably influence other types of firm over time through the processes of education and training.

It is also possible that the technology imported from Western countries will be modified with time to accommodate local circumstances. As was explained above, however, the period in which such adaptions take place may be such that it not be possible to observe the effects of evolution for some considerable time. If evolution does take place rapidly enough to be reliably determined, the current process of the wholesale importation of accounting practices is likely to be followed by a period in which certain aspects of accounting technology will be adjusted by the countries of the region. In this respect the theory outlined here suggests that the adapted elements are more likely to be disclosure practices and, to a lesser extent, the specific calculations appearing in financial statements. In that case it is predicted that the initial period of standardisation will continue until all the countries of the region have assimilated sufficient measurement and disclosure practices among their larger internationally oriented firms to satisfy the requirements of global capital markets. After that, these practices are likely to permeate downwards to smaller local organisations and, in the process, be subjected to indigenous cultural influences, particularly as regards disclosure issues.

There appears to be no particularly significant reason why countries of the region might depart from the transaction cost basis of accounting toward cash flow, market value accounting or other more fundamentally different forms such as order-based accounting measurement. It remains to be seen whether new indicators, different from the traditional earnings indicators, may be developed to fulfil any distinct, specific needs of local users. Perhaps it is more likely that all the regions of the world will move toward a more globally homogenous society, at least with respect to economic relationships, as the wealth produced by world capitalism (Wallerstein, 1979) alters the worldwide distribution of economic power. If this is the case then cultural factors may lose even the tenuous effect on accounting practices which has sometimes been supposed. Possibly, therefore, the most significant question for the countries of the Asia-Pacific region is not if and how measurement or disclosure practices may evolve chasing a constantly changing cultural equilibrium, or how harmonious should they be with practices elsewhere, but rather what profound effects are likely to be seen on the cultural values of the region from the adoption of western account-ing techniques which embody the philosophies of economic rationalism and which are so different from the traditional eastern outlook. Whichever research approach is adopted to examine these issues, it seems clear that more critical, historical and evaluative studies will be required if the issues of the cultural impact on accounting practice are to be examined without trivialising the subject matter.

REFERENCES

Baydoun, N. and R. Willet (1995), 'Cultural relevance of Western accounting systems to developing countries', *Abacus*, March, pp. 67–91.

Belkaoui, A. (1995), *The linguistic shaping of accounting*, Quorum Books.

Berry, J. (1980), 'Introduction to methodology', *Handbook of cross-culture psychology methodology*, Volume 2, Treandis, H. and J. Berry (Eds), Allyn and Bacon.

Bochner, S. (1986), 'Unobtrusive methods in cross-cultural experimentation', *Handbook of cross-cultural psychology: Methodology*, Volume 2, Triandis, H.C. and Berry, J.W. (Eds).

Briston, R.J. (1978), 'The evolution of accounting in developing countries', *International journal of accounting education and research*, Fall.

Chow, C.W., Y. Kato and M.D. Shields (1994), 'National culture and the preference for management controls; An explanatory study of the firm-labor market interface', *Accounting, organisations and society*, Vol. 19, May–July, pp. 381–400.

Cooke, T. and R. Parker (1994), *Financial reporting in the West Asia-Pacific Rim*, Routledge.

Eddie, I.A. (1991), 'Asia-Pacific cultural values and accounting systems', *Asia-Pacific international management forum*, Vol. 16, No. 3, pp. 22–30.

Frucot, V. and W.T. Sheraton (1991), 'Budgetary participation, locus of control, and Mexican managerial performance and job satisfaction', *Accounting review*, Vol. 66, January, pp. 80–99.

Fukuda, K.J. (1988), *Japanese-style management transferred: The experience of East Asia*, Routledge, London.

Gul, A.F., W. Glen and A.R. Huang (1993), 'The effects of environmental uncertainty, computer usage, and management accounting systems on small business', *The journal of small business finance*, Vol. 2, Iss. 3, pp. 251–71.

Hall, D. (1981), *A history of South-east Asia*, (4th Ed), MacMillan.

Harris, M. (1968), *The rise of anthropological theory*, Harper and Ross.

Harrison, G.L. (1992), 'The cross-cultural generalizationability of the relation between participation, budget emphasis and job related attitudes', *Accounting, organisation and society*, Vol. 17, January, pp. 319–39.

Hofstede, G. (1980), *Cultures consequences*, McGraw-Hill.

Hofstede, G. (1991), *Cultures and organisations: Software of the mind*, McGraw-Hill.

Hove, M.R. (1986), 'Accounting practice in developing countries: Colonialism's legacy of inappropriate technologies', *International journal of accounting*, Fall, pp. 81–100.

Kaplan, D. and R.A. Manners (1972), *Culture theory*, Prentice-Hall.

Kharabanda, O. and E. Stallworthy (1991), 'Lets learn from Japan', *Management accounting*, March, pp. 26–33.

Kroeber, A. and C. Kluckohn (1952), *A critical review of concepts and definitions*, Reabody Museum, Vol. 47, Cambridge Mass.

Marinaccio, R. and J. Morris (1991), 'Work and production reorganisation in a "Japanesed" company', *Journal of general management*, Vol. 17, No. 1, Autumn, pp. 56–69.

Morgan, M.J. (1992), 'Feedforward control for competitive advantage: The Japanese approach', *Journal of general management*, Summer, pp. 41–52.

Nishimura, A. (1992), 'The development and future of management accounting in Japan and the USA: A comparison of management philosophies', *The journal of political economy*, Vol. 57, August, pp. 109–20.

Nishimura, A. (1994), 'The recent developments in Japanese management accounting and their impact on British and New Zealand companies', *The journal of political economy*, March, pp. 325–45.

Nobes, C. (1984), *International classification of financial reporting*, Croom Helm.

Nobes, C. (1995), 'Corporate financing and its effects on European accounting differences', Unpublished working paper, University of Reading.

Otley, D.T. (1980), 'The contingency theory of management accounting: Achievement and prognosis', *Accounting, organisations, and society*, pp. 413–28.

Perera, M.H.B. (1989), 'Towards a framework to analyse the impact of culture on accounting', *International journal of accounting*, Vol. 24, pp. 42–56.

Postman, N. (1966), *Language and reality*, Holt Rinehart and Winston.

Pratt, J. and P. Beaulieu (1992), 'Organisation culture in public accounting, size, technology, rank, and functional area', *Accounting, organisation and society*, Vol. 17, No. 7, October, pp. 664–84.

Radebaugh, L. and S. Gray (1993), *International accounting and multinational enterprises*, Wiley.

Rentsch, J.R. (1990), 'Climate and culture: Interaction and qualitative differences in organisation meanings', *Journal of applied psychology*, Vol. 75, December, pp. 668–81.

Robey and Rodriquex-Diaz (1989), 'The organizational and cultural context of systems implementation: Case experience from Latin America', *Information and management*, Vol. 17, Iss. 4, Nov, pp. 229–39.

Sahlins, M.D. (1960), 'Evolution: Specific and general', *Evolution and culture*, Sahlins, M.D. and E.R. Service (Eds), University of Michigan Press.

Samuels, J.M. and J.C. Oliga (1982), 'Accounting standards in developing countries', *The international journal of accounting*, Fall, pp. 69–88.

Secord, P. and Xijia Su (1994), 'An empirical analysis of culture and accounting models in Asia', *Asian review of accounting*, Vol. 2, No. 1, March.

Singer, M. (1961), 'A survey of culture and personality theory and research', *Studying personality cross-culturally*, Harper and Row.

Soeters and Schreuder (1988), 'The interaction between national and organizational culture in accounting firms', *Accounting organisations and society*, Vol. 13, pp. 75–85.

Steward, J.H. (1977), *Evolution and ecology: Essays on serial transformation*, Steward, I.C. and R.F. Murphy (Eds), University of Illinois Press.

Strange, N. (1992), 'German management accounting', *Management accounting*, Vol. 70, October, p. 46.

Suzuki, N. (1988), 'Master-minding the thrust abroad: An American education for the Japanese', *Management decision*, Vol. 26.

Triandis, C.H. (1972), *The analysis of subjective culture*, John Wiley & Sons, Inc.

Wallace, O. (1990), 'Accounting in developing countries: A review of the literature', *Research in Third World accounting*, Vol. 1, pp. 3–54.

Wallerstein, I. (1979), *The capitalist world economy: Essays*, Cambridge University Press.

White, L.A. (1949), *The science of culture, a study of man and civilisation*, Farrar, Straus.

White, L.A. (1975), *The concept of cultural systems: A key to understanding tribes and nations*, Columbia University Press.

Willett, R.J. (1991), 'Transactions theory, derived accounting measurement and stochastic processes', *Abacus*, September, pp. 117–34.

Williams, L.E. (1976), *South-east Asia — A history*, Oxford University Press.

Willmott, *et al.* (1992), 'Regulation of accountancy and accountants: A comparative analysis of accounting for research and development in four advanced capitalist countries', *Accounting, auditing & accountability journal*, Vol. 5, pp. 32–56.